A COMPANION TO

SANSKRIT LITERATURE

A COMPANION TO
SANSKRIT LITERATURE

Spanning a period of over three thousand years, containing brief accounts of authors, works, characters, technical terms, geographical names, myths, legends and several appendices

SURES CHANDRA BANERJI

MOTILAL BANARSIDASS
Delhi Varanasi Patna
Bangalore Madras

First Edition: Delhi, 1971
Second Edition: Delhi, 1989

MOTILAL BANARSIDASS
Bungalow Road, Jawahar Nagar, Delhi 110 007
Branches
Chowk, Varanasi 221 001
Ashok Rajpath, Patna 800 004
24 Race Course Road, Bangalore 560 001
120 Royapettah High Road, Mylapore, Madras 600 004

ISBN: 81-208-0063-x

PRINTED IN INDIA
BY JAINENDRA PRAKASH JAIN AT SHRI JAINENDRA PRESS, A-45 NARAINA INDUSTRIAL AREA, PHASE I, NEW DELHI 110028 AND PUBLISHED BY NARENDRA PRAKASH JAIN FOR MOTILAL BANARSIDASS, DELHI 110007.

To

ŚRĪMATĪ RAMALĀ DEVĪ

the author's Lifelong Companion,
this COMPANION
is dedicated as an humble token of love and
admiration for her indefatigable help in
making the publication of this book a
fait accompli.

PREFACE TO THE SECOND EDITION

It is heartening to note that the first edition has been exhausted, and there is still demand for the book.

In this edition, we have added the following new appendices: Science in Sanskrit, Music, Dance and Dramaturgy, Military Organisation and Art of Warfare in Ancient India. The information under Authors and Works has been brought up to date, as far as practicable. Under Technical Terms Astronomy and Astrology have been included.

January, 1989 S.C. BANERJI

PREFACE TO THE FIRST EDITION

In course of his studies in Sanskrit literature and research relating to various aspects of it, the author of the present work often felt the need of a vade mecum containing brief accounts of authors and works, information about the principal characters of Sanskrit plays, poems and prose works, the meaning of certain technical terms in common use, the common geographical names and the notable myths and legends.

In studying a particular branch of Sanskrit Literature, one comes across the names of authors and titles of works relating to other branches. Moreover, the reader is often confronted with technical terms some of which are not always explained adequately, if at all, in the standard Sanskrit lexicons. For example, a student of Alaṃkāra literature stumbles upon philosophical and grammatical jargon. While perusing Smṛti digests and commentaries on Prācīna Smṛti, one finds references to various works on Jyotiṣa, Tantra and Purāṇa. In going through commentaries on poetical works and dramas, the reader meets with the names of authors and works in respect of lexical literature, erotics, music etc. Histories of Sanskrit Literature abound in references to works and authors relating to various aspects of this literature. Thus, the curious reader feels, at every step, the necessity of consulting a reference book enlightening him, within a brief compass, on the various authors, their dates and personal history, and the contents of different works as well as the meaning of the technical terms. It is not possible for a student of Sanskrit literature, while studying a particular branch of this literature, to consult histories of the various other branches, e.g., Philosophy, Tantra, Smṛti, Purāṇa and so on. Nor is it practicable for him to keep, ready at hand, dictionaries explaining the technical terms relating to diverse subjects. Sanskrit literature abounds in the names of places, rivers, mountains etc. It is, therefore, necessary to have some idea of their location, extent and present names. References to various myths and legends are frequently met with, particularly in the poems, prose works and dramas.

The author of the present work has been actuated by a desire to remove these difficulties of the reader, which he, as a lover of Sanskrit literature, has felt very keenly. The author's desire for preparing such a work gained a strong impetus from such works relating to English literature as the *Oxford Companion to English Literature* by Harvey and the *Reader's Handbook* by Brewer. The question that posed itself to the author's mind was this—if so many reference books of the above kinds should be written on English literature why should there be none relating to Sanskrit literature?

There have been some attempts to produce reference books of certain types relating to Sanskrit Literature. There are, for example, dictionaries of philosophical and grammatical terms. The monumental *Vedic Index* is indispensable to scholars studying the Veda. Dowson's *Classical Dictionary of Hindu Mythology*, V. Fausböll's *Indian Mythology* are very useful works for the student of mythology and religion. Macdonell's *Vedic Mythology* is a valuable work of reference. Garrett's *Classical Dictionary of India* is of a miscellaneous character, and deals with a good deal of matter relating to the Indian manners and customs. The excellent book, entitled *L' Inde Classique*, by Renou and Filliozat, is a sort of general survey of the Indian literature and culture; it is not confined to Sanskrit Literature alone nor has it the same scope as the present work. Moreover, being in French it is accessible only to a limited number of readers. Excepting Dowson's book, none of the above works supplies the aforesaid needs that prompted the author to take up the present work. Dowson, however, gives accounts of only a few of the authors and works, but hardly explains any of the technical terms used in any branch of Sanskrit literature. Moreover, even after the latest edition of Dowson's book many new facts about authors, works and geographical information have come to light. Besides, newer editions of works have been printed and some Sanskrit books have been edited or translated for the first time.

The great problem that confronts the writer of such a book as this is the one of selection. Sanskrit literature is vast in extent and varied in content. It is hardly possible for one single person to prepare a register of all of the authors and works of this literature which developed through a period of nearly four thousand years. Consequently, a selection has to be made. No two persons, however, can agree as to which of the authors and works should be included. For our present purpose, we have tried to make the collection in such a manner that no important author of work, belonging to any of the branches of Sanskrit literature, is omitted.

In adding accounts of the authors and works, care has been taken to ensure that no important fact is left out. The needs of the general reader, rather than that of the specialist, have always been kept in view. Attempts have been made to make the information as precise as possible: prolixity has been carefully avoided. In describing the merits of authors and works, objectivity has been our aim and personal predilection or bias has been eschewed. Important bibliographical information has been laid down under the authors and works, wherever possible. In noting the editions of different works, the recent ones have been generally preferred unless the older ones have some special importance. Particular care has been taken to mention the noteworthy translations of works into foreign languages. Along with works have been dealt with those Sanskrit inscriptions which throw considerable light on various aspects, especially chronological problems, relating to Sanskrit literature. In certain special cases, works in manuscript form have been incorporated. Such noteworthy works as are known only from literary references, and have important bearing on the history of Sanskrit literature have also been included.

The treatment of myths and legends is fairly exhaustive in Dowson's work referred to above. So, in the present work, we have touched upon only the most noteworthy myths and legends. Under each entry has been given only such information as will suit the needs of the general reader.

So far as geographical names are concerned, these have been dealt with exhaustively in such works as the *Ancient Geography of India* by Cunningham, *Geographical Dictionary of Ancient and Medieval India* by N.L. De, *Historical Geography of Ancient India* by B.C. Law and *Studies in the Geography of Ancient and Medieval India by* D.C. Sircar. Hence, in the present work, only the prominent names, commonly found in Sanskrit literature, have been mentioned. Bare information as to location, extent and importance has been given under each name and the identification with the corresponding modern names, wherever possible, has been stated.

As regards characters, we have selected the important ones from the standard poems, prose works and dramas. So far as prose works are concerned, we have utilised only those of Daṇḍin, Subandhu and Bāṇabhaṭṭa. In regard to poetical works, we have taken into consideration the Mahākāvyas of Kālidāsa as well as of Aśvaghoṣa, Bhāravi and Māgha. Kālidāsa's *Meghadūta* has also been consulted for this purpose. Of the poems of the age of decadence only the *Naiṣadha-carita* has been utilised. Coming to the dramas, besides those of Aśvaghoṣa, Bhāsa and Kālidāsa we have taken into account the following:

Mṛcchakaṭika, *Mudrārākṣasa*, *Mālatīmādhava*, *Uttararāmacarita*, *Priyadarśikā*, *Ratnāvalī* and *Nāgānanda*.

The problem of selection is formidable in the case of techincal terms. For our present purpose, the technical terms have been culled from the branches of Sanskrit literature, indicated in the beginning of Part IV of this work. As the number of such terms is legion, we have selected only those which are of comparatively common occurrence and interesting to the general reader.

A few words are necessary about the matters dealt with in the appendices. The chronology of the Sanskrit works and their authors presents a perplexing problem to scholars. The dates are mostly conjectural and are often based on the relative chronological positions of the authors. Yet, in the tottering chronological structure there are a few sure planks. It has, therefore, been deemed necessary to note, in an appendix, the broad and well-known dates which have a close bearing on the history of Sanskrit literature.

Foreigners, interested in Indian literature, may naturally have a curiosity about the beginnings of the study of the Sanskrit language and literature in the West. So, an appendix has been devoted to the names of the foreign scholars with respective dates and works, who played important roles in introducing Sanskrit language and literature to the countries of the West.

With a view to dispelling the widespread, albeit erroneous, impression that Sanskrit literature contains ideas far removed from practical life, of the 'brooding' East and as such, has only a limited appeal, an appendix has been devoted to the influence of this literature on the literatures of the world. The other appendices will speak for themselves.

In a work like this, one must take the help of earlier writers. The author takes this opportunity to express his heartfelt gratitude to all of them; their works have been mentioned in appropriate places of the work as well as in the Bibliography appended at the end.

The author must express his gratitude to Dr. R.C. Majumdar, Dr. S.K. Chatterji and Dr. R.C. Hazra for their many kind words of encouragement and suggestions. Sincere thanks are due to Principal H.B. Sarkar of Kharagpur College, West Bengal, for valuable information about the influence of Sanskrit in the Far East. Sri Sibdas Chaudhuri, Librarian, Asiatic Society, Calcutta, has laid the author under obligation by suggesting the names of useful books and promptly supplying them from the Library of the Society. The author has profited by discussion with Dr. J.N. Banerji (alas, now dead), formerly of Calcutta University, and with Prof. S.K. Saraswati of Benares Hindu University.

While conventional transliteration has been followed in the names of Sanskrit authors and works, it has not always been adhered to in the names of authors of modern books and editors and translators of Sanskrit texts.

This work has been written on a novel plan. In a pioneer venture like this, lapses are likely. All suggestions for its improvement will, therefore, be gratefully received. The author will consider his labours, spread over for several years, amply rewarded if the book be of some use to those who are interested in the various aspects of Indology as revealed in the vast and ancient Sanskrit literature.

Despite all care, some errors of print have crept into the book; this is sincerely regretted.

The matters, which escaped our notice while writing the work and those which came to light after it had been put to print, have been incorporated in the Addenda. In this portion, at first the page of this work and the location of the addition have been indicated and then the additional matter has been written.

March, 1971 S.C. Banerji

ABBREVIATIONS

ABORI	*Annals of Bhandarkar Oriental Research Institute*, Poona
AGGW	*Abhandlungen der königl*. Gesellschaft der Wissenschaften zu Göttingen, philol.—histor. Klase
AIOC	All-India Oriental Conference
AKM	*Abhandlungen für die Kunde des Morgenlandes, herausg von der Deutschen Morgenländischen Gesellschaft*
AR	Archiv für Religionsgeschichte
ASS	Ānandāśrama Sanskrit Series, Poona
BIB. BUDDH.	Bibliotheca Buddhica, Leningrad
BIB. IND.	Bibliotheca Indica, Calcutta
BenSS	Benares Sanskrit Series
BORI	Bhandarkar Oriental Research Institute, Poona
BSOS / BSOAS	*Bulletin of the School of Oriental and African Studies*, London
BSS	Bombay Sanskrit Series
CSS	Chowkhamba Sanskrit Series, Benares
GOS	Gaekwad's Oriental Series, Baroda
GSAI	*Giornale della Societa Asiatica Italiana*
HOS	Harvard Oriental Series
IA	*Indian Antiquary*
IHQ	*Indian Historical Quarterly*, Calcutta
IJHS	*Indian Jour. of History of Science*
IL	*Indian Linguistics*
IT	*Indian Thought*, Allahabad
JA	*Journal Asiatique*
JAOS	*Journal of American Oriental Society*
JAS	*Journal of Asiatic Society*, Calcutta
JBORS	*Journal of Bihar and Orissa Research Society*
JBRAS	*Journal of the Bombay Branch of the Royal Asiatic Society*
JOIB	*Journal of Oriental Institute*, Baroda
JOR	*Journal of Oriental Research*, Madras
JRAS	*Journal of Royal Asiatic Society*

JRASB	*Journal of the Royal Asiatic Society of Bengal*, Calcutta
KSTS	Kashmir Series of Texts and Studies
MBH	*Mahābhārata*
NIA	*New Indian Antiquary*
NSP	Nirṇayasāgara Press, Bombay
RAM	*Rāmāyaṇa*
SBE	Sacred Books of the East, Oxford
SBH	Sacred Books of the Hindus, Allahabad
SBJ	Sacred Books of the Jainas (Arrah)
TSS	Trivandrum Sanskrit Series
VIZSS	Vizianagram Sanskrit Series
WZKM	*Wiener Zeitschrift fur die Kunde des Morgenlandes*
ZDMG	*Zeitschrift der Deutschen Morgenlandischen Gesellschaft*
ZII	*Zeitschrift fur Indologie und Iranistik, herausg, von der Deutschen Morgenlandischen Gesellschaft*

CONTENTS

INTRODUCTION

The present work bears the title '*A Companion to Sanskrit Literature.*' It is, therefore, necessary to acquaint the general reader with the scope and extent of Sanskrit literature. All that we can do here is to give a broad survey of this literature, from the earliest times, in its varied aspects.

The Aryans, who settled at first in the north-west of India and then migrated to other parts of the country, have happily left written records in the *Ṛgveda* which is indeed the oldest available work of the Indo-Europeans. From this Veda we learn that the Vedic people were agricultural and pastoral. They used to believe in many gods which were mostly personifications, with anthropomorphic traits, of natural phenomena. The *Ṛgveda* introduces us to an advanced stage of civilization which, as a scholar aptly puts, has dawn but no twilight. No author or compiler of the Veda is known. It consists of hymns supposed to have been revealed to certain Ṛṣis (seers). This Veda has earlier and later strata. It is difficult, if not impossible, to determine the age of this ancient work. With regard to the question of its age, scholars differ not by centuries but by millenniums. While some would assign it to 6000 B.C., others would bring it down to about 1200 B.C.

There are three other Vedas, viz. *Yajurveda*, *Atharvaveda*, and *Sāmaveda*. The *Yajurveda* deals with sacrifices. The *Atharvaveda* reflects real popular belief by dealing with magic, witchcraft, sorcery and various spells used for healing diseases, causing harm to enemies etc. The *Sāmaveda* contains matters to be sung at the time of sacrifices.

Towards the end of the Vedic period, ritualism developed to a great extent. As a result, treatises in prose were written on theology and the procedure of sacrifices. These were called *Brāhmaṇas*.

Included in the Brāhmaṇas were what were called Āraṇyakas (forest-texts) which were partly ritualistic and partly speculative.

The concluding portions of the Āraṇyakas were the Upaniṣads or esoteric texts dealing with questions like Ultimate Reality, individual soul, universal soul, the *summum bonum* of existence etc.

As accessories to the Vedas originated the Vedāṅgas. Some of these are ritualistic while the others are exegetical. The Kalpasūtras, comprising Śrauta-sūtras, Gṛhya-sūtras, Dharma-sūtras and Śulva-sūtras, are ritualistic Vedāṅgas. The Śrauta-sūtras deal with details of Vedic rites and rituals. The Gṛhya-sūtras dwell chiefly on the rites and sacraments for the householder. The Dharma-sūtras lay down civil and religious law. The Śulva-sūtras, dealing with the dimensions of sacrificial altars, are the earliest works on geometry.

The exegetical Vedāṅgas are Śikṣā (phonetics), Vyākaraṇa (grammar), Nirukta (etymology), Chandas (metrics) and Jyotiṣa (astronomy). These are necessary for correctly reading and interpreting the Vedas.

The epics, *Rāmāyaṇa* and *Mahābhārata*, constitute a large bulk of Sanskrit literature. The nucleus of these works is very ancient, and used to be sung from place to place till at last the stories were written down. But, the extant epics do not represent their original forms; the present forms are the result of additions and alterations through ages. Portions were interpolated into them in later times. The age of the epics poses a baffling problem to scholars. Winternitz is of the opinion that if the *Mahābhārata* had its final form about the fourth century A.D., the *Rāmāyaṇa* received its present shape a century or two earlier. Around the original nucleus of the epic stories diverse myths and legends and various matters have gathered in course of centuries; this is more striking in the case of the *Mahābhārata*.

The Purāṇas are an important branch of Sanskrit literature. They are broadly divided into two classes, viz. Major and Minor. Each of these classes is traditionally known to comprise eighteen works. The minor Purāṇas are called Upapurāṇas. The authorship of Purāṇic works is attributed to the legendary Vyāsa. As a matter of fact, these are not unified works written by particular authors at particular periods. These assumed the present forms through centuries. These are sectarian works dealing with a diversity of matters, besides the traditional five topics of Creation, Re-creation, Genealogies of gods and sages, Manu-periods of time and Genealogies of kings. These works are valuable for the student of Indian sociology and religion. They also contain useful information about the early political history of India. The age of the Purāṇas is difficult to determine. They, however, appear to have been composed in the period between the fifth century B.C. and the sixth century A.D.

The Tantras are a class of works dealing partly with philosophy and partly with occultism. They deal with mystical charms and spells, diagrams, initiation etc. There are both Brahmanical and Buddhistic Tantras. The early Tantras appear to have originated about the fifth or sixth century A.D.

There is a large number of philosophical works in Sanskrit. Germs of philosophy existed in the Vedas. In course of time, philosophical ideas were developed and systematized in the form of Sūtras. Six different orthodox philosophical systems exist. These are Mīmāṃsā, Vedānta, Nyāya, Vaiśeṣika, Sāṃkhya and Yoga. The terse philosophical Sūtras were elaborately commented upon. These comments, in their turn, were commented upon with a view to making them more intelligible, and compendiums came to be composed. Thus a vast philosophical literature grew up through centuries. In this connexion, we should add that, in medieval India, particularly in Mithilā and Bengal, schools of Navya-Nyāya (neologic) developed. These schools introduced a new methodology, and indulged in hair-splitting niceties of academic discussion relating chiefly to epistemology.

Besides the orthodox systems of philosophy noted above, we have also the heterodox schools of the Buddhists, the Jainas and of the materialist Cārvāka. They have developed their own views after raising their voice of protest against the Brahmanical ideas rooted in the Vedas.

What is known as Classical Sanskrit Literature originated about the fourth century B.C. when Pāṇini, the great grammarian, stereotyped the language by means of rigid rules. In the Vedic times, the language had an unfettered growth, being rich in inflexional forms. But, Classical Sanskrit began to grow within the fixed framework prepared by Pāṇini. The most outstanding figure in Classical Sanskrit Literature is Kālidāsa. In the pre-Kālidāsa period, prose, poetry and drama were cultivated. But, early works of these classes appear to have been lost. Of the pre-Kālidāsa works, we have the dramas of Aśvaghoṣa and Bhāsa and the poetical works of the former. No prose Kāvya of the pre-Kālidāsa age has come down to us. Of Kālidāsa we have three dramas, two Mahākāvyas and a lyric poem. Nearly a score of other poetical works are attributed to Kālidāsa. While most of these are definitely works of inferior poets, the authorship of a few is doubtful. The poetical works and plays, written in the post-Kālidāsa age, are very large in number. Kālidāsa's age is a subject of great controversy among scholars. While some assign him to the first century B.C., others would bring him down to the fifth century A.D. Most modern scholars believe that he flourished about the fifth century under the Guptas.

About the ninth or tenth century A.D. the age of decadence of Sanskrit literature set in. The poems, prose works and dramas produced in this age, lack originality and betray the authors' anxiety to show off their literary skill.

Quite a number of works in Sanskrit have been written on Civil and Religious law, these works being classed as Smṛti or Dharmaśāstra. There are over twenty versified works belonging to *Prācīna Smṛti.* Based on these were the Smṛti digests of which several schools are distinguished according to variations in local customs and differences of interpretation. Besides these digests, belonging to Neo-Smṛti (Navya Smṛti), we have authoritative commentaries on *Prācīna Smṛti*, particularly on the works of Manu and Yājñavalkya.

India also produced a good number of works on technical and scientific subjects. Of such subjects, mention may be made of politics and statecraft, grammar, poetics, prosody, lexicography, dramaturgy, erotics, pornography, etc. as the important ones. It is interesting to add that even the art of theft attracted the attention of Indian writers. They have made it clear that in writing treatises on the art of thieving it is not their object to teach it to people but to warn them against the nefarious tactics of thieves.

Other technical and scientific subjects on which treatises

have been written in Sanskrit are medicine, astronomy, astrology, mathematics and botany. Allied with medicine is chemistry. Architecture and sculpture have claimed the serious attention of several scholars.

Indian economy having been pre-eminently agricultural, it is natural to expect that agriculture should form the subject-matter of some works. Unfortunately, we do not know of any work other than the *Kṛṣi-parāśara* or *Kṛṣi-saṃgraha* devoted exclusively to various agricultural operations.

India has been a land of kings and queens through the ages. Naturally, therefore, horses and elephants have been inextricably bound up with Indian life. They were used not only for military purposes but also for hunting excursions and joy-rides. Hence the necessity was felt for treatises dealing with the manner of their acquisition, training, maintenance and their treatment in diseases. We have at present some works on Gaja-śāstra and Aśva-śāstra.

Among the fine arts, music and painting were extensively cultivated chiefly under the encouraging patronage of kings. The *Kāmasūtra* speaks of sixty-four *Kalās* (arts). Of these, music has claimed a good number of works. Some works either wholly or partly deal with other arts.

There are some works dealing with miscellaneous matters. Of these, interesting are those dealing with the art of letter-writing and of examining jewels.

It is interesting to note that Sanskrit literature was not limited to the confines of India. This literature and the culture enshrined in it spread to remote lands in the Far East, e.g. Cambodia, Malaya, Sumatra, Borneo, Java, Bali and the Philippine islands. Such nearer neighbours of India as Tibet and Burma were deeply influenced by this literature. In some of the above places, treatises were composed in Sanskrit and Sanskrit inscriptions were freely written. Even China and Japan betray the influence of Sanskrit literature. Persia and Arabia in the Middle East show their early acquaintance with Sanskrit literature. That this literature was cultivated in Central Asia is amply borne out by the finds of manuscripts of important works in that region. From very early times the West has been acquainted with this literature through translations. The Greeks were probably the earliest European people to influence, or to be influenced by, this literature particularly in the fields of astronomy, medicine and mathematics. German philosophers like Goethe, Schopenhauer, Humboldt etc. became admirers of Indian literature and philosophy. It is the British conquest of India that gave the European scholars the great impetus to study Sanskrit language and Sanskrit literature in its various branches; it should, however, be stated that the western scholars began to take interest in Sanskrit in the wake of the European penetration into India.

It may not be out of place here to add a few words about the Sanskrit language. Ordinarily, the language in which the Brahmanical literature, from the Veda downwards, was composed, is called Sanskrit. But, scholars would call it Old Indo-Aryan. The Vedic language shows the vigour of a living language refusing to move within the narrow grooves set by grammar. It is more multiform than what is designated as classical Sanskrit, and its vocabulary, in some cases at least, differs considerably from that of its descendant. The Vedic language also differs from the classical language in certain phonological phenomena and syntax. It was Pāṇini (c. 5th or 4th century B.C.) who stereotyped the language with the rigorous fetters of grammatical rules and thus laid the foundation of classical Sanskrit.

Through the natural process of evolution the Old Indo-Aryan language passed to a stage which is called Middle Indo-Aryan comprising Pāli, the various regional Prākrits and local dialects.

A further stage of evolution of the language is represented by the modern or new Indo-Aryan languages of the different parts of India.

PART I

AUTHORS

ABHINANDA : At least two authors of this name are known; one is the author of the *Kādambarī-kathā-sāra*, and son of Jayanta Bhaṭṭa (9th century), author of the *Nyāyamañjarī*. Appears to have been a Kashmirian. The other Abhinanda, usually styled as Gauḍa, is son of Śatānanda and author of the *Rāma-carita*. Śatānanda's son seems to have been a protege of Devapāla, the Pāla king of Bengal in the 9th century A.D. Some of the Sanskrit anthologies cite verses attributed to Abhinanda, which cannot be traced in the above works. Gauḍa Abhinanda appears to have composed also the Laghu-yogavāśiṣṭha, an epitome of the well-known *Yogavāsiṣṭha*.

[For a discussion on the identity of Abhinanda, see *Padyāvalī*, ed. S. K. De, pp. 182-84. Also see *New Indian Antiquary*, II; V. Raghavan in *ABORI*, xvi, and in *S.K. De Memorial Vol.*]

ABHINAVAGUPTA : A great Kashmirian, famous in poetics, dramaturgy and the Śaiva philosophy of Kashmir. His celebrated commentaries on the *Dhvanyāloka* and the *Nāṭya-śāstra* are respectively the *Kāvyāloka-locana* (popularly known as *Locana*) and the *Abhinava-bhāratī*. In the *Locana* he refers to a commentary by himself on Bhaṭṭa Tauta's *Kāvya-kautuka*. At least forty-one works of Abhinava are known. Of his Tāntric philosophical works the following have been published hitherto :—

Tantrāloka, Paramārtha-sāra, Tantra-sāra, Mālinīvijayavārtika, Parātriṃśikā-vivṛti, Bodha-pañcadaśikā, Tantra-vaṭa-dhānikā, Īśvara-pratyabhijñā-vimarśinī.

Also published is Abhinava's *Bhagavadgītārtha-saṃgraha*. V. Raghavan thinks that he wrote also the works *Paryanta-pañcāśikā* and *Rahasya-pañcadaśikā* (*Journal of Oriental Research*, Madras, XIV, 1940). In his *Parātriṃśikā-vivaraṇa*, he tells us that he was son of the Kashmirian Cukhala, grandson of Varāhagupta and brother of Manorathagupta. He can be assigned to a period between the last quarter of the tenth century and the first quarter of the eleventh. His interpretation, called *Abhivyakti-vāda*, of Bharata's well-known dictum on *Rasa* was very popular and profoundly influenced later writers.

[For an exhaustive account of the life and works of Abhinavagupta, see K.C. Pandey, *Abhinavagupta, A Historical and Philosophical Study*, Benares, 1963, 2nd Ed.. Also see R. Gnoli, *Aesthetic Experience According to Abhinavagupta*, 2nd ed., 1968; J.L. Manon and M.L. Patwardhan, *Śāntarasa and Abhinavagupta's Philosophy of Aesthetics*, Poona, 1969; L. Silburn, *Hymnes de Abhinavagupta* (Traduity and commentes), Paris, 1970; V. Raghavan, *Abhinavagupta and his works*, Varanasi, 1980.]

ĀḌHAYARĀJA : Mentioned in an introductory verse (18) of the *Harṣa-carita*. Pischel first identified him with Harṣavardhana (See Pischel in *N.K.G.W.*, Göttingen, 1901).

AHOBALA : Author of the important work on music called *Saṅgīta-pārijāta*. Flourished in the 17th century. Refers to the *Rājataraṅgiṇī* and the *Rāgavibodha*, and defends the view of Rāmāmātya.

AKALAṄKA : A famous Jaina philosopher believed to have flourished between 720 and 780 A.D. The following works on logic are known to have been written hy him :—

(1) *Laghīyastraya*, (2) *Nyāyaviniścaya*, (3) *Pramāṇa-saṃgraha*, (4) *Siddhiviniścaya*, (5) *Rājavārtika*, (6) *Aṣṭaśatī*

On the first four works, the author himself wrote short commentaries. The last two are commentaries on Vācaka Umāsvāti's *Tattvārthasūtra* and Samantabhadra's *Āptamīmāṃsā* respectively. Akalaṅka criticized Dharmakīrti's philosophy.

AKṢAPĀDA : The true Nyāya philosophy is ascribed to Akṣapāda (c. 150 A.D.). Sometimes identified with Gotama or Gautama (q.v.)

ALAKA : Another name of Alaṭa (q.v.)

ALAṬA : Author of a small portion of the *Kāvya-prakāśa* left incomplete by Mammaṭa. Son of Rājānaka Jayānaka, and author of the *Viṣamapadoddyota* commentary on Ratnākara's *Haravijaya*. Also called Alaka or Allata, and appears to have been a Kashmirian.

ALLARĀJA : Author of the *Rasaratna-pradīpikā*. Supposed to have flourished in the thirteenth century A.D.

ALLATA : Another name of Alaṭa (q.v.).

AMARASIṂHA : Author of the celebrated lexicon, entitled *Nāmaliṅgānuśāsana*, popularly called *Amara-kośa*. Supposed to have flourished in the fourth century A.D., Amara was a Buddhist. Tradition makes him one of the nine distinguished men (*nava-ratna*) of the court of Vikramāditya.

[For a discussion on the age of Amara, see *Nāmaliṅgānuśāsana*, ed. H.D. Sarma and N.G. Sardesai (Introduction), Poona, 1941 and Intro. to the ed. pub. by Adyar Library, Madras, 1971.]

AMARU (or AMARUKA) : Author of the *Amaru-śataka*. Supposed to have flourished some time between the 7th and the 8th century A.D. Mentioned by Ānandavardhana, the rhetorician, and verses from Amaru's work are quoted by Vāmana, also a rhetorician. The legend goes that the soul of Śaṃkarācārya entered into the dead body of king Amaruka. Then Amaruka composed his poem.

ĀNANDAGIRI : A pupil of Śaṃkara, and author of the *Śaṃkara-vijaya*, *Nyāya-nirṇaya* and *Tarka-saṃgraha*. Also called Ānandajñāna.

ĀṆANDARĀYAMAKHI : A Brahmin who lived in Tanjore in South India in the first half of the seventeenth century. A playwright well-versed in Āyurveda. His drama is entitled *Jīvānanda*.

ĀNANDATĪRTHA : See Madhva.

ĀNANDAVARDHANA : According to the *Rāja-taraṅgiṇī* (v. 34), he adorned the court of Avantivarman (855-84 A.D.), king of Kashmir. The *Dhvanyāloka*, a celebrated work on poetics, is generally attributed to him. Some scholars think that he wrote the *Vṛtti* portion of the above work, while the *Kārikā* portion was composed by another writer, usually referred to as Dhvanikāra. Ānandavardhana appears to have been son of one Nonopādhyāya. To Ānandavardhana is attributed also the devotional poem called *Devī-śataka*. The Prākrit poem, *Viṣamabāṇalīlā*, and the Sanskrit *Arjuna-carita* are ascribed to Ānandavardhana by his commentators. He himself refers to his work, entitled *Dharmottama*, a commentary on the *Pramāṇa-viniścaya* of Dharmakīrti. He, for the first time, succeeded in establishing that *Dhvani* or suggested sense is the soul of poetry.

[See R. Mukherji, *Ānandavardhana's Literary Theories*.]

AṄGIRAS : One of the twenty traditional writers of original Smṛti. An *Aṅgiras-smṛti* and a *Bṛhad-aṅgiras-smṛti* exist. References are found to a *Madhyama-aṅgiras*. Date uncertain.

ANIRUDDHA BHAṬṬA : A famous Smṛti writer of Bengal. Vallālasena, king of Bengal in the 12th century, mentions Aniruddha as his Guru. Author of the Smṛti digests called *Hāralatā* and *Pitṛdayitā* (also called *Karmopadeśinīpaddhati*). A *Cāturmāsya-paddhati* also is supposed to have been written by him.

ANNAṂ BHAṬṬA : Author of the well-known *Tarka-saṃgraha* and its commentary called *Dīpikā*. He was an Andhra scholar of South India, and flourished in the later part of the 17th century. He wrote also a commentary, called *Mitākṣarā* on the *Aṣṭādhyāyī* as well as the *Uddyotana*, comm. on Kaiyaṭa's *Pradīpa*.

ANUBHŪTISVARŪPĀCĀRYA : An ascetic of the 12th century A. D., supposed to be the author of the Vārtikasūtras in the *Sārasvata-vyākaraṇa*.

ĀPADEVA : Author of the *Mīmāṃsā-nyāya-prakāśa*, popularly called *Āpadevī*, a guide-book for the *Pūrva-mīmāṃsā* philosophy. Some information about him is found in the *Smṛti-kaustubha* of his son, Anantadeva. We learn that he came of a family of Marāṭhā Brahmins well-known for learning and religious devotion. The great-grandfather of Āpadeva was Ekanātha who should perhaps be distinguished from the poet-saint Ekanātha (d. 1609). Āpadeva's grand-father was also called Āpadeva and father Anantadeva. Our Āpadeva probably flourished in the early part of the 17th century. He was a follower of the Bhāṭṭa school of Mīmāṃsā.

[For identification of Āpadeva, see P. K. Gode in *F. W. Thomas Pres. Vol.*, Bombay, 1939.]

APARĀDITYA : Another name of Aparārka (q.v.).

APARĀRKA : Also called Aparāditya, he appears from his work to have been a Śilahāra king born in the family of Jīmūtavāhana of the Vidyādhara race. Author of a huge commentary called *Aparārka-yājñavalkīya-dharmaśāstra-nibandha*, popularly known as *Aparārka*, on the *Yājñavlkya-smṛti*. Probably flourished in the first half of the 12th century.

ĀPASTAMBA : One of the twenty traditional writers of original Smṛti. Author of a Gṛhya-sūtra, a Dharma-sūtra and Pitṛmedha-sūtra. The school of Āpastamba is supposed to have originated in south India. The *Āpastamba-dharma-sūtra* is assigned by P.V. Kane to some period between 600-300 B.C.

ĀPIŚALI : An ancient grammarian, mentioned by Pāṇini (iv. 3.98) and his commentators like Patañjali, Helārāja and others.

APPAYYA DĪKṢITA : Also called Apya or Appa, Appayya should be distinguished from Appayya, son of a brother of this Appayya and author of an *Alaṃkāra-tilaka*. Appayya Dīkṣita appears to have flourished in the third and fourth quarters of the 16th century. Author of three works on poetics, called *Kuvalayānanda*, *Citra-mīmāṃsā* and *Vṛttivārtika*. Besides these, he wrote also the *Lakṣaṇa-ratnāvali*, a work on dramaturgy.

[See A.L. Gangopadhyaya, *Contribution of Appaya Dīkṣita to Indian Poetics*, Calcutta 1971 : H. Rameshan *Appaya Dīkṣita* ; R.R. Mukherji, *Contribution of Appayya Dīkṣita to India Poetics*.]

ĀRYABHAṬA : There are two writers of this name. Āryabhaṭa I was an astronomer and author of the *Āryabhaṭīya*, the *Daśagītikā-sūtra*, the *Āryāṣṭaśata*, *Kālakriyā* and the *Gola*. He appears to have written also the *Sūryasiddhānta-prakāśa*, a commentary on the *Sūryasiddhānta*. Born at Kusumapura (Pāṭaliputra) in 476 A.D., he, for the first time, dealt with mathematics in relation to astronomy. He declared that the earth is spherical and rotates on its axis. He used letters of the alphabet to indicate numerals. Āryabhaṭa II, known to Alberuni, wrote the *Āryasiddhānta* which is assigned to c. 950 A.D. An astronomical work, called *Mahāsiddhānta*, is attributed to an Āryabhaṭa.

[See B. Datta, Two Āryabhaṭas of Alberuni, *Bulletin of Calcutta Mathematical Society*, 1926; Āryabhaṭa, the author of the Gaṇita, *Ibid*, 1927; S. Prakash, *Founders of Sciences in Ancient India*, New Delhi, 1965, Chap. X. Also see P. C. Sen Gupta's paper 'Āryabhaṭa, the father of Indian Epicyclic Astronomy' in *Jour. of Deptt. of Letters*, Calcutta University, Vol. XVIII.]

ĀRYADEVA : Also called Deva, he was known as Kāṇadeva (the one-eyed Deva) and Nīlanetra (the blue-eyed one). From Hiuen Tsang and I-Tsing we learn some facts about his life. Āryadeva is said to have been a pupil of Nāgārjuna who appointed him as his successor. Āryadeva's biography was translated into Chinese by Kumārajīva (c. 405 A.D.). He lived probably towards the end of the second century A.D. and the beginning of the third. Besides the *Catuḥśataka*, the *Hastavāla-prakaraṇa* or *Muṣṭi-prakaraṇa* is attributed to him. Two short treatises, ascribed to Āryadeva, are translated by Bodhiruci in the Chinese *Tripiṭaka*. The work, called *Cittaviśuddhiprakaraṇa*, is sometimes attributed to him.

ĀRYAŚŪRA : Author of the *Jātaka-mālā*. Supposed to have flourished in the third or fourth century A.D. The Chinese traveller I-Tsing mentions the *Jātaka-mālā*, and the frescoes of Ajantā bear out the existence of the text at the time.

ASAṄGA : Asaṅga, more properly Vasubandhu Asaṅga, was a brother of Vasubandhu and a famous Buddhist philosopher probably of the fourth (or acc. to some, fifth) century A.D. He contributed to the Vijñānavāda school of Buddhist philosophy by his works called *Yogācāra-bhūmiśāstra* and

Mahāyāna-sūtrālamkāra. He appears to have been born to a Brāhmaṇa in Puruṣapura (Peshawar), and was originally an adherent of the Sarvāstivāda school.

[See G. Tucci, Buddhist Logic before Diṅnāga, *Journal of Royal Asiatic Society*, 1929; *Doctrines of Maitreya(nātha) and Asaṅga*, Calcutta University, 1930.]

AŚVAGHOṢA : Author of the poetical works called *Buddhacarita*, *Saundarananda* and *Gaṇḍī-stotra-gāthā*. Also wrote the drama entitled *Śāriputra-*(or, *Śāradvati-putra*)*-prakaraṇa*. Supposed to have been a contemporary of Kaniṣka (c. 1st cent. A.D.). Son of a Brahmin, he embraced Buddhism, and is known to have belonged to the Sarvāstivāda school.

[For a legendary biography of Aśvaghoṣa, see W. Wassiljew, *Der Buddhismus*, St. Petersburg, 1860. B.C. Law's *Aśvaghoṣa* (Asiatic Soc. Monograph, Calcutta, 1946) is a noteworthy study. P. C. Bagchi, The Rāṣṭrapāla-nāṭaka of Aśvaghoṣa, *Sardesai Comm. Vol.*, Bombay, 1938, may be consulted. Also see Y. S. Hakeda, Buddhist Hybrid Sanskrit Words in Aśvaghoṣa'a Kāvyas, *JAOS*, Vol. 82, No. 2, 1962; A. Gawronski, *Aśvaghoṣa*, Ossolineum, 1966 (Polish trs. of extracts from *Buddhacarita and Saundarananda*); B. Bhattacharya, *Aśvaghoṣa*, 1976; S.K. Datta, *Aśvaghoṣa as a Poet and a Dramatist* 1979.]

ĀŚVALĀYANA : Supposed to have been a pupil of Śaunaka (q.v.), he probably flourished in the 4th century B.C. or earlier. Author of the *Āśvalāyana-gṛhyasūtra* and *Āśvalāyana-śrauta-sūtra*.

ATRI : One of the twenty traditional writers of original Smṛti. An *Ātreya-dharmaśāstra* exists. Besides, there are several works styled *Atri-smṛti* or *Atri-saṃhitā*. Two works called respectively *Vṛddhātreya-saṃhitā* and *Laghu-atri* are also known. Being mentioned in the *Manu-smṛti* (III. 16), Atri appears to be older than that work.

BĀDARĀYAṆA : The accredited author of the *Brahma-sūtra*, also called *Vedānta*, *Uttara-mīmāṃsā* or *Śārīrakamīmāṃsā*. A tradition identifies Bādarāyaṇa with Vyāsa. Some scholars place him some time between 500 and 200 B.C., while others suggest 200 A.D. as the lower terminus of Bādarāyaṇa's date. Acc. to Jacobi, his Sūtra was composed between 200 and 450 A.D.

[See under Vyāsa *infra.*]

BALADEVA : Author of the *Govinda-bhāṣya* and the *Prameya-ratnāvalī* among others. Born in Orissa in the eighteenth century A.D. His works exercised considerable influence on Bengal Vaiṣṇavism.

[See S.K. De, *Early History of Vaiṣṇava Faith and Movement in Bengal*, Calcutta, 1961.]

BĀLAKṚṢṆA TRIPĀṬHIN : Author of the *Praśasti-kāśikā*. Supposed to have flourished between 1600 and 1675 A.D.

BĀLAMBHAṬṬA : Bālambhaṭṭa or Bālakṛṣṇa Pāyaguṇḍa, son of Vaidyanātha and Lakṣmī, was a south Indian. According to some, he was the same as Vaidyanātha Pāyaguṇḍe. Probably flourished between 1730 and 1820 A.D. He wrote, *inter alia*, the *Bālambhaṭṭi*, a well-known commentary on the *Mitākṣarā* of Vijñāneśvara. He also wrote commentaries on some grammatical works, e.g. *Śabdakaustubha*, *Śabdaratna*, *Śabdenduśekhara*, etc. Some scholars think that the author of the grammatical works was a different person. A comparatively modern scholar of the same name and an inhabitant of Tanjore wrote the small grammatical work called *Bālabodhinī*, and *Bālarañjanī*.

BALARĀMA PAÑCĀNANA : Author of the sectarian grammar, called *Prabodha-prakāśa*. A *Dhātu-prakāśa* is also attributed to him. He was probably a Brahmin. We do not know anything about his time or native place.

BALLĀLASENA : See Vallālasena.

BĀṆABHAṬṬA : Author of the prose works, called *Kādambarī* and *Harṣacarita*. A devotional lyric, entitled *Caṇḍīśataka*, is also attributed to him. From the autobiographical account contained in the introductory portions of the *Kādambarī* and the *Harṣacarita* we have some information about his personal history. Bāṇabhaṭṭa was son of Citrabhānu and Rājyadevī.

His patron was king Harṣavardhana (606-647 A.D.) of Thaneswar.

[For a summary of all questions regarding Bāṇabhaṭṭa and his works, as also for a full bibliography, see A.A. Maria Sharpe, *Bāṇa's Kādambarī* (Diss. No. V. De Vlaamsche), Leuven, 1937. Also see S.V. Diksit, *Bāṇabhaṭṭa—his life and literature*, Belgaum (Bombay), 1963, and N. Sharma, *Bāṇabhaṭṭa, a literary study*, Delhi, 1968. For geography in his works, see D.K. Kanjilal in *IHQ*, XXXIV, p. 123. Also see P.V. Sharma, Botanical Observations of Bāṇabhaṭṭa, *Raghavan Felicitations Vol.*, Delhi, 1975, and K. Krishnamoorthy, *Bāṇabhaṭṭa*, Delhi, 1976.]

BĀṆEŚVARA VIDYĀLAṂKĀRA : A descendant of Śobhākara, he flourished in the district of Hughly in West Bengal in the 17th-18th century. Besides having been one of the compilers of the *Vivādārṇava-setu*, he wrote also the Campūkāvya, called *Citra-campū*, the Mahākāvya, *Rahasyāmṛta*, the drama named *Candrābhiṣeka* and several stotras.

BAUDHĀYANA : Well-known as author of the *Baudhāyana-kalpa-sūtra* comprising *Śrauta*, *Gṛhya* and *Dharma-sūtras* and *Śulva-sūtras* of Baudhāyana. The Dharma-sūtra is assigned by P.V. Kane to some time between 500 and 200 B.C. A *Pitṛmedha-sūtra* of this author is also known.

BHALLAṬA : Author of the *Bhallaṭa-śataka*. Stated, in the *Rājataraṅgiṇī* (v.204), to have flourished under the Kashmirian king Śaṃkaravarman (883—902 A.D.).

BHĀMAHA : Author of the *Kāvyālaṃkāra*, a famous work on poetics. One of the earliest writers on poetics and supposed to have been a Kashmirian, Bhāmaha probably flourished between the close of the seventh century and beginning of the eighth. Earliest exponent of the Alaṃkāra school which appears to have been founded earlier, he emphasized Alaṃkāra as the essential element of poetry.

[See G. Tucci, *Bhāmaha and Diṅnāga*, Bombay, 1930.]

Another Bhāmaha appears to have been a writer on metrics and rhetoric; he probably belonged to the 15th cent. A.D.

BHARATA : Supposed author of the earliest extant work on dramaturgy, called *Nāṭya-śāstra*. Date controversial. Probably flourished earlier than the fourth or fifth century A.D. Sometimes referred to as Ādi-Bharata. Bharata appears to have propounded, for the first time, the theory of *Rasa* in connexion with drama. A work on music, called *Gītālaṃkāra*, is also attributed to Bharata.

[For life, works and question of identity, see S.K. De, *History of Sanskrit Poetics*, 1960.]

BHĀRATĪTĪRTHA : Joint author of the *Pañcadaśī* (q.v.).

[See T.M.P. Mahadevan, *Philosophy of Advaita with special ref. to Bhāratītīrtha Vidyāraṇya*.]

BHĀRAVI : Author of the Mahākāvya entitled *Kirātārjunīya*. Mentioned in the Aihole inscription of 634 A.D. which, therefore, is the lower limit of his date. Appears to have influenced Māgha, a later poet.

[For the alleged relation of Bhāravi and Daṇḍin, see S.K. De in *IHQ*, I, 1925, III, 1927; G.H Sastri in *IHQ*, III.]

BHARTṚHARI : Author of the lyric poems entitled *Nītiśataka*, *Vairāgya-śataka* and *Śṛṅgāra-śataka*. A *Puruṣārthopadeśa* is also attributed to him. Identified by some with Bhartṛhari, author of the grammatico-philosophical work called *Vākyapadīya*. The Chinese traveller I-Tsing testifies to the death of the grammarian Bhartṛhari around 651 A.D. Bhaṭṭi, author of the *Rāvaṇavadha*, popularly known as *Bhaṭṭi-kāvya*, is identified by some scholars with the author of the *Vākyapadīya*. The grammarian Bhartṛhari is supposed to have written also the *Mahābhāṣya-dīpikā*, a commentary on the *Mahābhāṣya*.

[For the three *Śatakas*, together with comm. of R. Budhendra and Eng. trs., see A.V. Gopalachariar, *Bhartṛhari's Nīti, Śṛṅgāra* and *Vairāgya Śataka* etc. The three poems translated by B. Stoler Miller. Also see D.D. Kosambi, *Śatakatrayādi-subhāṣita-saṃgraha*, Bombay, 1948. The *Mahābhāṣya-dīpikā* has been edited by K.V. Abhyankar and V.P. Limaye, *ABORI*, Vols. XLIII, XLIV, XLV. It has been edited also by V. Svaminathan, under the title *Mahābhāṣya-ṭīkā*, Varanasi, 1965. Both editions based on an incomplete MS.

For *Vākyapadīya*, see infra. See J. Filliozat, à propos de la religion de Bhartṛhari, *Silver Jub. Vol. of Z.K. Kenkyusyo Kyoto University*, Kyoto, 1954; C.K. Raja, I. Tsing and Bhartṛhari's Vākyapadīya, *S.K. Aiyangar Comm. Vol.*, Madras, 1936, S. Ram, Bhartṛhari's date, G. Jha. Res. Institute, Allahabad. Also see Intro. to *Puruṣārthopadeśa*, ed. K.V. Sarma, Hoshiarpur.]

BHARTṚMEṆṬHA : See Meṇṭha.

BHĀSA : A dramatist mentioned, inter alia, by Kālidāsa, Bāṇabhaṭṭa and Rājaśekhara. The existence of Bhāsa's works was unknown till the early years of the present century. About 1910-11 A.D. one Gaṇapati Śāstrī discovered, at Trivandrum in south India, a bundle of manuscripts containing the following dramas :—

1. Madhyama-vyāyoga.
2. Pañcarātra.
3. Dūtavākya.
4. Dūtaghaṭotkaca.
5. Karṇabhāra.
6. Ūrubhaṅga.
7. Bāla-carita.
8. Pratimā-nāṭaka.
9. Abhiṣeka.
10. Svapnavāsavadatta.
11. Pratijñā-yaugandharāyaṇa.
12. Avimāraka.
13. Cārudatta.

Śāstrī published these dramas between 1912 and 1915. He put forward arguments to prove that these works were the lost dramas of Bhāsa. Since then a keen controversy has been raging among scholars as to the real authorship of these dramas. Scholars like Pārānjape, Keith and Thomas agree with Śāstrī, while Kane, Barnett, Raddi and Pisharodi oppose this view. Sukthankar and Winternitz, however, think that the evidences available hitherto do not prove anything conclusively about the authorship of Bhāsa so that the problem should remain open.

Of the above dramas, the *Svapna-vāsavadatta* is by far the

most well-known. Bhāsa's date is still uncertain. Different scholars place him in different periods from the fifth century B.C. to the eleventh century A.D. Since Kālidāsa refers to him, he cannot be later than the fifth century A.D.

[For exhaustive accounts about Bhāsa, his works and the Bhāsa problem, see A.D. Pusalker, *Bhāsa, a study*, Lahore, 1937. All the Bhāsa dramas edited by T. Gaṇapati Śāstrī in Trivandrum Sanskrit Series, 1912-15 and by C. R. Devadhar in *Bhāsa-nāṭaka-cakra*, Poona, 1937. The plays trs. into English by Woolner and Sarup, Oxford University Press, 1930-31. Some of the individual dramas have been separately edited and translated.]

BHĀSARVAJÑA : Probably a Kashmirian of the ninth century A.D. Author of the *Nyāya-sāra*, a tract on logic.

[See S.C. Banerjee *Cultural Heritage af Kashmir*, Calcutta, 1965, pp. 121-22].

BHĀSKARA : Author of the *Bhāskara-bhāṣya*, a commentary on the *Brahmasūtra*, he flourished probably in the ninth century. For his views, see under *Bhāskara-bhāṣya*.

A Bhāskarācārya, born c. 1036 Śaka (=1114 A.D.), was a noted mathematician and astronomer. Son of Maheśa Daivajña or Maheśvara, he is said to have been born in village Vijjala in Deccan. Of the various works written by him the most well-known are the *Siddhānta-śiromaṇi* and the *Līlāvatī*. His other works are as follows :—

Bījagaṇita, *Bījopanaya*, *Karṇakutūhala* (also called *Grahāgama-kutūhala*), *Brahmatulya*, *Brahmasiddhāntatulya*, *Brahmatulya-siddhānta*.

A Bhāskara (born c. 600 A.D.) appears to have composed the *Āryabhaṭīya-sūtra-bhāṣya* or *Āryabhaṭīya-tantra-bhāṣya*, the *Mahā-*(or, *Bṛhat-*)*-bhāskarīya*, a treatise on astronomy in eight chapters, and the *Laghubhāskarīya*, an abridged version of the *Mahābhāskarīya*.

[See B. Datta, The Two Bhāskaras, *IHQ*, VI 1930.]

BHAṬṬA ĀHLĀDAKA : Author of the *Delārāma-kathāsāra* and probably a Kashmirian.

BHAṬṬA BHĪMA : Another name of Bhaumaka.

BHAṬṬA LOLLAṬA : Probably a Kasnmirian of the 9th century, he is famous for the interpretation of Bharata's *Rasasūtra*. His interpretation is known as *Utpatti-vāda*.

BHAṬṬANĀYAKA : There are literary references to his work on poetics, called *Hṛdaya-darpaṇa*, which is lost. From later writers, particularly from Abhinavagupta, we learn that his interpretation of the famous *Rasa-sūtra* of Bharata is known as *Bhukti-vāda*. Generally assigned to the end of the 9th century and beginning of the 10th. Perhaps identical with Bhaṭṭa Nāyaka mentioned by Kalhaṇa as having flourished in the reign of Śaṃkaravarman, son and successor of Avantivarman of Kashmir.

BHAṬṬANĀRĀYAṆA : Author of the drama entitled *Veṇi-saṃhāra*. Supposed to have flourished between the eighth and ninth century A.D. A tradition of doubtful historical veracity makes him one of the five Brāhmaṇas brought from Kanauj by king Ādiśūra of Bengal.

A Bhaṭṭanārāyaṇa is supposed to have written an introduction to the *Daśakumāra-carita*.

BHAṬṬĀRAHARICANDRA : Mentioned in an introductory verse (12) of Bāṇa's *Harṣa-carita* as author of a prose Kāvya. He is said to have composed a romance called *Mālatī*. Being mentioned by Bāṇa he may be assigned to the 5th or 6th century A.D. Perhaps this poet is praised in verse 2130 of the *Sadukti-karṇāmṛta*. He may be identical with Haricandra who is quoted in the above anthology. Verses of Haricandra are quoted in other anthologies too.

BHAṬṬA TAUTA : Abhinavagupta pays tributes to him as his teacher. Tauta appears to have written a work on poetics, called *Kāvya-kautuka* which is now lost.

BHAṬṬI : Author of the Mahākāvya entitled *Rāvaṇa-vadha*, popularly called *Bhaṭṭi-kāvya*. Supposed by some to be identical with Bhartṛhari, author of the *Vākyapadīya*. The lower terminus of his date is placed about the middle of the sixth century A.D.

[On Bhaṭṭi's relation to Bhāmaha in the treatment of poetic figures, see S.K. De, *Sanskrit Poetics*, I.]

BHAṬṬOJI DĪKṢITA : Author of the *Siddhānta-kaumudī*. Bhaṭṭoji's chief contribution is the arrangement of Pāṇini's rules under different topics, e.g. *Kāraka*, *Samāsa* etc. He has also commented upon the *Sūtras*. He wrote also the *Śabda-kaustubha* commentary on Pāṇini's grammar. He himself wrote a commentary, called *Bālamanoramā* and *Prauḍha-manoramā* on the *Siddhānta-kaumudī*. The *Vaiyākaraṇa-siddhānta-kārikā* is also attributed to him. A South Indian, Bhaṭṭoji used to live at Varanasi where he built up a school of grammarians. Bhaṭṭoji Dīkṣita was son of Lakṣmīdhara, brother of Raṅgoji Dīkṣita, father of Bhānu Dīkṣita (variously called Vīreśvara Dīkṣita or Rāmāśrama) and pupil of Śeṣa Kṛṣṇa. To Bhaṭṭoji is attributed also the astronomical work, called *Tithinirṇaya*. Some assign Bhaṭṭoji Dīkṣita to a period between c. 1575 and 1625 A.D. Others place him between c. 1570 and 1635 A.D. Yet others place his life and literary activity between 1547 and 1633 A.D. Besides the above works, some thirty more, including a *Vedabhāṣya-sāra*, are attributed to Bhaṭṭoji Dīkṣita.

[For a discussion on the date of Bhaṭṭoji, see P.K. Gode in *Studies in Indian Literary History*, Vol. II, pp. 65-74. For a list of Bhaṭṭoji's works, see *Ibid*, p. 75. Also see S. Bali, *Bhaṭṭoji Dīkṣita, his contribution to Sanskrit Grammar.*]

BHAṬṬOTPALA : Well-known as a commentator on the works of Varāhamihira, the name of his commentary on the *Bṛhat-saṃhitā* being *Bṛhatsaṃhitā-vivṛti*. Appears to have flourished in the later half of the 10th century A.D. He himself wrote the astrological work called *Horāśāstra*. His works are of historical importance, because he cites passages from lost works. A Bhaṭṭotpala, who was later than 1099 A.D., appears to have composed the *Bhāsvatī-ṭīkā* on Sadānanda's astronomical work called *Bhāsvatī*.

BHAUMA : Same as Bhaumaka (below).

BHAUMAKA : Author of the Mahākāvya called *Rāvaṇārjunīya*. Also called Bhaṭṭa Bhīma, Bhūma or Bhauma, he appears to have flourished earlier than the 11th century. Some scholars think that the poet is quoted in the *Kāśikā* (q.v.) commentary on the *Aṣṭādhyāyī*.

BHAVABHŪTI : Author of the dramas entitled *Uttara-rāma-carita*, *Mahāvīra-carita* and *Mālati-mādhava*. From the autobiographical account contained in his works we learn that he was born in a Brahmin family of Kāśyapagotra in Padmapura situated probably in Vidarbha. Grandson of Bhaṭṭagopāla, Bhavabhūti was son of Nīlakaṇṭha, and Jātukarṇī. He had the title of Śrīkaṇṭha, and is mentioned in the *Rājatarṅgiṇī* as a court-poet of King Yaśovarman of Kanauj (c. A.D. 725-753).

[On Bhavabhūti's scholarship, see Keith in *JRAS*, 1914, Peterson in *JBRAS*, xviii, 1891. For appreciation of his poetic merits, see A. Kumaratatacarya, *Bhavabhūti-bhāratī*, Madras; T.S. Rao, *Bhavabhūti and his masterly genius*, Poona; A. Barooah, *Bhavabhūti, his place in Sanskrit Literature*, Calcutta. Also see R.D. Karmarkar, *Bhavabhūti*, Dharwar (India), 1963; R.G. Harshe, *Observation Sur La Vie et. l'OEuvre de Bhavabhūti*; S.V. Dixit, *Bhavabhūti : his life and literature*; V.V. Mirashi, *Bhavabhūti*; J.B. Khanna, *Observations on the Life and Works of Bhavabhūti* (Eng. trs. of Harṣa's works), 1974; V. Gera, *Mind and Art of Bhavabhūti*. V.A.R. Sastri's Bhavabhūti and Mīmāṃsā, in *A. Chettiar Comm. Vol.*, Annamalainagar, 1914 and Raghavan's Bhavabhūti and Arthaśāstra in New Indology, *Fetschrift W. Ruben*, Berlin 1970, may be consulted; P.B. Acharya, *Tragi-comedies of Shakespeare, Kālidāsa and Bhavabhūti*, New Delhi, 1978.]

BHAVADEVA BHAṬṬA : A famous pre-Raghunandana Smṛti writer of Bengal. He describes himself, in his works, as Bālavalabhībhujaṅga. He was minister for peace and war to king Harivarmadeva, and an inhabitant of the village Siddhala in the tract of Bengal known as Rāḍha. Date controversial. Appears to have flourished some time between 800 and 1100 A.D. His works are the *Karmānuṣṭhāna paddhati* (also called *Daśakarma-paddhati*, *Saṃskāra-paddhati* or *Chandoga-paddhati*), *Prāyaścitta-prakaraṇa* (or, *-nirūpaṇa*), *Sambandha-viveka* and *Śava-sūtakāśauca-prakaraṇa*.

BHĀVA MIŚRA : Author of the Āyurvedic compilation called *Bhāvaprakāśa*. Son of Laṭakana, he was court-physician of

Emperor Akbar in Delhi. Besides the above work, he wrote also the works called *Harītakyādi-nighaṇṭu*, *Guṇaratnamālā and Tāntrika-cikitsā.*

BHELĀCĀRYA : Supposed author of the *Bhela-saṃhitā* (q.v.).

BHIKṢU GOVINDA : Author of the medical work called *Rasahṛdaya* (q.v.).

BHOJA : Mentioned also as Bhoja-rāja, he was king of Dhārā, son and successor of Sindhurāja and nephew of Muñjavākpatirāja. Flourished in the first half of the 11th century A.D. His *Sarasvatī-kaṇṭhābharaṇa* deals with poetics and *Śṛṅgāra-prakāśa* with poetics and dramaturgy. His other published works are as follows, dealing with the subjects mentioned against each :— *Samarāṅgaṇa-sūtra-dhāra*—chiefly architecture and iconography; *Yukti-kalpataru*—statecraft, politics, building of cities, testing of jewels and characteristics of books etc.; *Tattva-prakāśa*—religio-philosophical topics; *Rāja-mārtaṇḍa*—commentary on the Yoga-sūtra; *Cārucaryā*—on personal hygiene.

The poem *Govindavilāsa* is supposed to be a work of Bhoja. The *Rāmāyāṇa-campū* is ascribed to him. He is also supposed to be the author of the grammatical work called *Sarasvatī-kaṇṭhābharaṇa.*

[For an account of Bhoja, see Intro. to the ed. of the *Śṛṅgāra-prakāśa* by V. Raghavan. Also see V. Raghavan's Inaugural Address to Seminar on Contribution of Bhoja to different Indological studies, 1970, Deptt. of Sanskrit, Vikram University, Ujjain; R.C. Hazra, Is the *Yukti-kalpataru* a work of Bhoja ?, *P.K. Gode Comm. Vol.*, Poona, 1960. On Bhoja's authorship of the *Govindavilāsa*, see B.L. Rajpurohit, *Summaries of Papers, A.I.O.C.*, 1974.

BILHAṆA : Famous Kashmirian poet. Born at Koṇamukha (=village Khunmoh) near Pravarapura, son of Jyeṣṭhakalaśa and Nāgadevī. He appears to have travelled widely, his itinerary having included Mathurā, Vṛndāvana, Kanauj, Prayāga, Benares, Ḍāhala (Bundelkhand) and Gujarat. He finally settled in the court of Kalyāṇa where he composed the *Vikramāṅkadeva-carita* in honour of his patron, the

Cālukya king Vikramāditya VI Tribhuvanamalla (1076-1127 A.D.) who conferred on him the title 'Vidyāpati'. It is believed that he had to leave that territory on an order of confiscation of his property from the king whose displeasure he had incurred. Besides the above work, he composed also the well-known erotic lyric called *Caura-pañcāśikā* or *Caura* (*Caurī*) *-surata-pañcāśikā*. Many stanzas of Bilhaṇa have been quoted in the anthologies.

BILVAMAṄGALA : See Līlāśuka.

BODHĀYANA : A poet to whom is attributed the play called *Bhagavadajjuka*. Probably flourished some time between the beginning of the Christian era and the 4th century A.D.

BOPADEVA : See Vopadeva.

BRAHMADEVA GAṆAKA : Son of Śrīcandra, alias Candradeva of Mathurā, Brahmadeva appears to have flourished in the latter half of the 11th century.

BRAHMAGUPTA : A famous writer on astronomy and astrology. Son of Jiṣṇu, he was born in 598 A.D. Author of the *Brāhma-siddhānta* (628 A.D.) or *Sphuṭa-siddhānta* and the *Khaṇḍakhādyaka*, he did not recognize the diurnal motion of the earth. Some scholars think that he based his *Brāhma-siddhānta* on the *Brahma-siddhānta* portion of the *Viṣṇudharmottara-purāṇa*. From the testimony of Alberuni we learn that he was a native of Bhillamāla near Multan. He appears to have lived in the court of a Chāpa King Vyagramukha. [See S. Prakash, *A Critical Study of Brahmagupta and his works*.]

BRAHMATRA VAIDYANĀTHA : Author of the drama, *Bhairava-vilāsa*.

BṚHASPATI : One of the twenty traditional writers of original Smṛti. The well-known commentators and digest-makers quote extensively from Bṛhaspati's work which has not yet been recovered. A short versified Smṛti of Bṛhaspati exists. A Dharmasūtra also of Bṛhaspati appears to have been written. From the *Arthaśāstra* of Kauṭilya Bṛhaspati appears to have founded a school of politics and statecraft. The extant *Bārhaspatya Arthaśāstra* seems to be a later work. A

Bṛhaspati is supposed to have been the founder of the school of philosophy called after the name of his pupil, Cārvāka.

BṚHASPATI RĀYAMUKUṬA : See Rāyamukuṭa.

BUDHASVĀMIN : Author of the *Bṛhatkathā-śloka-saṃgraha*, the Nepalese version of the *Bṛhatkathā*. Date unknown, but supposed to have belonged to the 8th or 9th century A.D. Acc. to Lacôte, the author must have lived about the 5th or 6th century A.D.

CAKRAPĀṆIDATTA : Son of Nārāyaṇa, an official of the Gauḍa king Nayapāla (11th century A.D.) and pupil of Naradatta, Cakrapāṇi belonged to Lodhravalī Kulīna family which, according to tradition, used to live in the district of Birbhum in West Bengal. His *magnum opus* is the *Cikitsā-sāra-saṃgraha*, or *Cikitsā-saṃgraha*, an original work on Āyurveda. His other works on this science are the *Śabda-candrikā*, *Dravya-guṇa-saṃgraha*, *Cikitsā-sāra* or *Gūḍhavākya-bodhaka*, *Sarva-sāra-saṃgraha* and commentaries on the works of Caraka and Suśruta, the commentaries being called respectively *Āyurveda-dīpikā* or *Caraka-tātparya-dīpikā* and *Bhānumatī*.

CĀṆAKYA : See Kauṭilya. To Cāṇakya are attributed the works called *Cāṇakya-sūtra* and *Cāṇakya-rājanīti-śāstra*. A Cāṇakya is credited with writings on medicine; he is known to Arabic writers as Śānaq.

[See, Sternbach, *The Spreading of Cāṇakya's Aphorism over Greater India*, Calcutta, 1969.

For Cāṇakya as a writer on medicine, see C. Zachariae, *WZKM*, xxviii. 206 f.]

CAṆḌEŚVARA : One of the great Smṛti writers of Mithilā. Son of Vīreśvara, he was, like his father and grandfather, a minister; he was a minister of king Harisiṃhadeva of Tirhut in the early years of the 14th century. The *Smṛti-ratnākara* or *Ratnākara*, his magnum opus, is divided into seven sections, viz. *Kṛtya*, *Dāna*, *Vyavahāra*, *Śuddhi*, *Pūjā*, *Vivāda* and *Gṛhastha*. His other works are: *Kṛtya-cintāmaṇi*, *Rājanīti-ratnākara*, *Dāna-vākyāvalī*, *Śiva-vākyāvalī* and *Śaiva-*

mānasollāsa. He exercised considerable influence on the later writers not only of Mithilā but also of Bengal.

CANDRADEVA : See Rudradeva.

CANDRAGOMIN : Probably a Bengali Buddhist scholar of the 7th century A.D. or of an even earlier date. Author of the celebrated *Cāndra-vyākaraṇa*. Also credited with the authorship of the following works:—

Lokānanda, a drama.

Nyāya-siddhyāloka, a work on Nyāya philosophy.

Ārya-tārādevī-stotra-muktikā-mālā, a number of hymns.

A Candrācārya is mentioned in the *Vākyapadīya* (q.v.), II. 489.

To the author of this name are ascribed the Tāntric works called *Siṃhanāda-sādhana*, *Mahākāruṇika-stotra*, *Rakṣācakra* and *Abhicāra-karma*. The *Mahākāruṇika-stotra*, the epistle called *Śiṣyalekha-dharma-kāvya* and the hymn *Manoharakalpa* are also ascribed to Candragomin.

CARAKA : Author or compiler of the oldest work on Āyurveda called *Caraka-saṃhitā* which in its present form appears to have been recast by Dṛḍhabala. Tradition makes him physician of Kaniṣka (1st or 2nd century A.D.), the Kuṣāṇa King.

CĀRVĀKA : Believed to be the founder or greatest exponent of the materialistic philosophy called after his name. Supposed to be a pupil of Bṛhaspati. According to this school of philosophy, pleasure is the highest goal of life, it does not recognize Vedic authority, denies the existence of soul and other world and refuses to accept all means of knowledge excepting perception. No work of this school exists, but its views are refuted by certain orthodox schools of philosophy.

[See D. Chaṭṭopādhyāya : *Lokāyata*, New Delhi, 1959.]

CINTĀMAṆI BHAṬṬA : Supposed to have been responsible for the Ornatior recension of *Śuka-saptati*. Probably flourished in the 13th century A.D.

CITSUKHĀCĀRYA : An advocate of Advaita Vedānta. His

works are the *Advaita-pradīpikā* and the *Tattva-pradīpikā*. He is well known as a commentator on Śaṃkara's comm. on the *Brahmasūtra*. He commented also on Śrīharṣa's *Khaṇḍanakhaṇḍakhādya*. Appears to have flourished in the 12th century A.D.

[See V.A. Sharma, *Citsukha's Contribution to Advaita*, Mysore, 1974.]

DAKṢA : One of the twenty traditional writers of original *Smṛti*. Author of a *Dakṣa-smṛti*. Date unknown, but earlier than Yājñavalkya who mentions him (I. 4).

DĀKṢĪPUTRA : See Pāṇini.

ḌALLAṆA (Ḍalbaṇa or Ḍalhaṇa) : A famous commentator on the *Suśruta-saṃhitā*, the name of his commentary being *Nibandha-saṃgraha*. Son of Bharupāla, and a Brahmin inhabitant of the place, called Aṅkola, he is supposed by some to have flourished in the 13th century A.D., while others think that he was either earlier than or contemporaneous with Cakrapāṇi (11th century).

DĀMODARA : Also called Catura Dāmodara and son of Lakṣmīdhara, he was one of the connoisseurs of music at the court of Emperor Jahangir or Shah Jahan in the 17th century. Author of the *Saṃgīta-darpaṇa*, a well-known work on music. He is supposed by some to have been a descendant of Catura Kallinātha, a famous commentator on Śārṅgadeva's *Saṃgīta-ratnākara*.

DĀMODARAGUPTA : Author of the *Kuṭṭanī-mata*, the celebrated pornographical work. Mentioned by Kalhaṇa as a poet and minister of king Jayāpīḍa of Kashmir (779-813 A.D.)

DĀMODARA MIŚRA : A redactor of the *Mahānāṭaka* (q.v.).

DAṆḌIN : One of the earliest writers on poetics, the name of his work being *Kāvyādarśa*. Supposed to have flourished in the first half of the eighth century A.D. The prose romance, entitled *Daśakumāra-carita*, is also generally believed to have been written by him. Some scholars think that the work called *Avantisundarī-kathā* is also by Daṇḍin, and constitutes the lost earlier portion of the *Daśakumāra-carita*.

[See S.V. Dixit, *Daṇḍin : His Life and Literature.* Also see D.K. Gupta, *A Critical Study of Daṇḍin and his Works*, Delhi, 1970; *Society and Culture in the time of Daṇḍin*, 1972; R. Mukherji, *Daṇḍin*'s *Literary Theories*; M. Singh, *Subandhu and Daṇḍin*, New Delhi, 1979.]

DATTILA : Author of the *Dattila*, a well-known work on music. Mentioned in the *Nāṭya-śāstra* as one of the immediate disciples of Bharata (probably earlier than 4th or 5th century A.D.). According to a tradition, he was son of Mataṅga.

DEVA : See Āryadeva.

DEVADATTA : Author of a version of the *Śuka-saptati*. To a Devadatta is ascribed the *Dhātu-ratnamālā* (q.v.), a work on medical science.

DEVANANDIN : Otherwise known as Pūjyapāda, he was the author of the *Jainendra-vyākaraṇa*. He probably flourished in the later part of the fifth century A.D.

DEVAṆṆA BHAṬṬA: Also called Devaṇa Bhaṭṭa, Devānanda, Devendra, Devagaṇa or Devaṇācārya, he is described as son of Keśavāditya Bhaṭṭa. A South Indian, Devaṇṇa exercised great influence in southern India. Probably flourished in the second half of the 12th century or the first half of the 13th. His *Smṛti-candrikā* is a well-known Smṛti digest. There is a work on music and dancing called *Saṃgīta-muktāvalī* by the same author.

DHANAÑJAYA : Author of the well-known work on dramaturgy, called *Daśa-rūpaka*. He describes himself as son of Viṣṇu. Appears to have enjoyed the patronage of Muñja, the Paramāra king of Mālava, who reigned in the last quarter of the 10th century A.D. Some identify him with Dhanika, author of the *Avaloka* commentary (q.v.), while others think that the two were brothers. A Dhanañjaya, perhaps called Śrutakīrti, a Digambara Jaina who wrote between 1123 and 1140 A.D., is the author of a Mahākāvya called *Rāghava-pāṇḍavīya* (q.v.).

DHANAPĀLA : Author of the prose Kāvya entitled *Tilaka-*

mañjarī. He was a Śvetāmbara Jaina and son of Sarvadeva. He wrote his work under Muñja Vākpatirāja of Dhārā in about 970 A.D.

DHANIKA : Son of Viṣṇu and minister of Utpaladeva (Muñja). Author of the well-known commentary called *Avaloka*, on the *Daśarūpaka* of Dhanañjaya. From the *Avaloka* we learn that he wrote also a treatise, entitled *Kāvya-nirṇaya*. Some scholars hold that he was a brother of Dhanañjaya (q.v.), while others think that Dhanika was identical with Dhanañjaya.

DHARMADĀSA SŪRI : Author of the *Vidagdha-mukha-maṇḍana*, a work on enigmatology and *Citra-kāvya*. He appears to have been a Jaina ascetic who flourished earlier than the last quarter of the 13th century. Acc. to some, he worked in South India, under Yādava king Kṛṣṇa who ascended the throne in 1247 A.D.
[See L. Sternbach in *Indologica Tauriniensa*, *I*, para 17; V. Raghavan in *P.K. Gode Comm. Vol.* 3. 224.]

DHARMAKĪRTI: A Buddhist logician of the seventh century. Author of the well-known *Nyāya-bindu* and *Pramāṇa-vārtika*. A *Pramāṇa-viniścaya* (Chap. I ed. and trs. T. Vetter, Wien, 1966) exists in Tibetan, the original Sanskrit text being lost.
[See N.J. Shah, *Akalaṅka's Criticism of Dharmakīrti's Philosophy—a study*, Ahmedabad, 1966.]

DHARMARĀJA: Author of the *Vedānta-paribhāṣā*, a well-known manual of the Vedānta according to the school of Śaṃkara. Flourished in the 16th century and was a disciple of Veṅkaṭanātha.

DHĪRANĀGA : An inhabitant of Arālapura, Bhadanta Dhīranāga was author of the drama called *Kundamālā*. Flourished earlier than the fifth century A.D. Some of the verses of this writer, quoted in the *Subhāṣitāvali* and the *Sadukti-karṇāmṛta*, are not traceable in the *Kundamālā*.

DHOYĪ : Also called Dhoī or Dhoyika. Author of *Pavana-dūta*, and a court-poet of Lakṣmaṇasena (12th-13th century), king of Bengal. The poet was a Brāhmaṇa, acc. to some, a Vaidya acc. to others, while yet others think that he belonged to the weaver class. Verses of Dhoyī not traceable in the *Pavana-dūta*, have been quoted in the anthologies entitled *Sadukti-karṇāmṛta*, *Subhāṣita-muktāvalī* and *Śārṅgadhara paddhati*.

ḌHUṆḌUKANĀTHA : Author of the Āyurvedic treatise called *Rasendracintāmaṇi*. He is supposed to have flourished in the 15th century.

DHVANIKĀRA : The supposed author, as distinguished from Ānandavardhana the Vṛttikāra, of the *Kārikā* portion of the famous work on poetics called *Dhvanyāloka*. The name of Dhvanikāra is considered by some to be Sahṛdaya. [See S.K. De, *Sanskrit Poetics*, I.]

DIṄNĀGA : Chief of the early Buddhist logicians. Probably lived before 400 A.D. and wrote the *Pramāṇa-samuccaya*, the *Nyāyapraveśa*, and other texts most of which are preserved only in translations. In verse 14 of the *Meghadūta* some commentators find a covert reference to this Diṅnāga as a hostile critic. The work, entitled *Prajñā-pāramitā-piṇḍārtha*, epitomizing in 58 verses the *Aṣṭasāhasrikā-prajñāpāramitā*, is also attributed to Diṅnāga. I-Tsing ascribes eight other philosophical works to him.

[See G. Tucci, *Bhāmaha and Diṅnāga*, Bombay, 1930; E. Frauwallner, Dignāga und anderes, *Festchrift Winternitz*, Leipzig, 1933; M. Hattori, *Diṅnāga on Perception*, Cambridge; H.N. Randle, *Fragments from Diṅnāga*; S. Mookerjee, *Buddhist Philosophy of Universal Flux*.]

DṚḌHABALA : Son of Kapilabala, he was a Kashmirian of the 8th or 9th century A.D. Some would place him in the 7th cent. A.D. He revised the *Caraka-saṃhitā*, and added several chapters to it. The extant *Caraka-saṃhitā* is the result of revision and addition by him.

DURGASIṂHA : Author of the well-known commentary, called *Vṛtti* or *Kātantra-vṛtti* on the *Kātantra* or *Kalāpa-vyākaraṇa*. He himself wrote a Ṭīkā on the Vṛtti. A *Paribhāṣā-vṛtti* is also attributed to him. He probably flourished in the eighth century. It is doubtful whether this Durgasiṃha was identical with Durgācārya, commentator on the *Nirukta.* Acc. to a tradition, Amarasiṃha was merely a title of Durgasiṃha who was really the compiler of the *Amarakośa.*

GADĀDHARA : Several scholars of this name are known. Of them, two are very famous. One was a logician of Bengal, who brobably flourished in the first decade of the 17th century. He commented on the *Tattva-cintāmaṇi* of Gaṅgeśa, the *Āloka* of Pakṣadhara Miśra and on several works of Raghunātha Śiromaṇi as well as on the *Kusumāñjali* of Udayana. Besides, he wrote many works known as Vāda-granthas, e.g. *Śakti-vāda*, *Mukti-vāda* etc.

Of the many Smṛti writers of this name, the most well-known is Gadādhara, son of Nīlāmbara, who flourished probably in the second half of the 15th century and wrote the works entitled *Kāla-sāra*, *Ācāra-sāra* *Vrata-sāra* and *Śuddhisāra.*

GAṄGĀDĀSA : Author of the *Chandomañjarī*, a celebrated work on prosody. He describes himself as son of Vaidya Gopāladāsa and Santoṣā and author of the *Acyuta-carita*, *Kaṃsāri-śataka* (*Gopāla-śataka*) and *Dineśa-śataka.* Mentions Jayadeva who flourished towards the close of the 12th century. Some think that he was a Bengali while, acc. to others, he belonged to Orissa.

[See P.K. Gode, *IHQ*, 1939, Vol. xv, pp. 512-22.]

GAṄGĀDEVĪ : Author of the *Madhurā-vijaya.* Wife of Kampana or Kamparāya, son of Rukka I (c. 1343-79 A.D.) of Vijayanagara.

GAṄGEŚOPĀDHYĀYA : Author of the *Tattva-cintāmaṇi*, a famous work on Nyāya philosophy. This work served as the firm foundation of the Bengal and Mithilā schools of Navya-Nyāya. Date uncertain. Appears to have flourished in Mithilā some time between the middle of the 13th century and the first quarter of the 14th.

[See J. Mohanty (tr.), *Gaṅgeśa's theory of truth*, Santiniketan, 1966; G. Sastri, *Maṅgalavāda* by Gaṅgeśa, Calcutta.]

GAUḌAPĀDA : A famous philosopher who was Śaṅkarācārya's teacher's teacher. Acc. to some, he flourished in Bengal in the beginning of the eighth century A.D. or the end of the 7th. Others think that he lived in the 6th century. Author of the *Gauḍapāda-kārikā*, a commentary on the *Māṇḍūkya Upaniṣad*, as also of the *Uttara-gitā* and a commentary on the *Sāṅkhya-kārikā of Īśvarakṛṣṇa*. *Śrīvidyāratnasūtra*, a Tantric work, is attributed to him. Some think that the author of the *Gauḍapāda-kārikā* is different from that of the commentary on the Sāṃkhya system. Gauḍapāda is the earliest systematic exponent of the Advaita Vedānta. He was familiar with Buddhist doctrines which he accepted insofar as they were not in conflict with his own Advaita-vāda.

[See T.M.P. Mahadevan, *Gauḍapāda—a Study in Early Advaita*, Madras, 1960.]

A Gauḍapāda, supposed to be different from the author of the *Gauḍapāda-kārikā*, was author of the *Gauḍapāda-bhāṣya*, an abridgment of the *Māṭhara-vṛtti* (q.v.).

[See V. Bhattacharya, Gauḍapāda, *Winternitz Memo. No.* (ed. N.N. Law), Calcutta, 1938, and the *Āgamaśāstra of Gauḍapāda*, ed., trs. and annotated by the same scholar, Calcutta, 1943.]

GAUTAMA : One of the twenty traditional writers on original Smṛti. A *Gautama-dharmasūtra* exists. Date uncertain. The work probably originated some time between the 4th century and 2nd century B.C. A *Pitṛmedhasūtra* and a *Śrāddhakalpa* are also attributed to Gautama. A Gautama or Gotama (c. 500 B.C.) is supposed to have founded the Nyāya philosophy by his *Nyāya-sūtra*.

[See *Gautama : The Nyāya Philosophy*, Delhi, 1978.]

GHAṬAKARPARA : Traditionally one of the Nine Jewels in the court of Vikramāditya. The *Ghaṭakarpara-kāvya*, a lyric poem, is ascribed to him. For the significance of the name, see remarks under *Ghaṭakarpara-kāvya*.

[See S. L. Katre, The Ghaṭakarpara Problem, *Vikrama Vol.*, Ujjain, 1948.]

GOBHILA : Author of the well-known *Gobhila-gṛhya-sūtra* and a *Gobhila-smṛti*.

GONARDĪYA : Appears to have been an authoritative grammarian. Several times mentioned in the *Mahābhāṣya* (e.g. on Pāṇini I. 1.21, 29; VII. 6. 101). Some scholars think that it was the name assumed by Patañjali himself who belonged to the place called Gonarda.

GOṆIKĀPUTRA : An ancient grammarian mentioned by Patañjali in his *Mahābhāṣya.* Nāgeśa identifies him with Patañjali himself. (Vide *Uddyota* on *Mahābhāṣya-pradīpa* on Pāṇini I. 4.51.)

GOPĀLA BHAṬṬA : A prominent figure in the history of Bengal Vaiṣṇavism. He is stated to have been son of Veṅkaṭa Bhaṭṭa, a South Indian Brahmin. A follower of Caitanya, the greatest exponent of Bengal Vaiṣṇavism, Gopāla was one of the six Gosvāmins of Vṛndāvana. The *Haribhakti-vilāsa*, the most authoritative work on the social and religious practices of the Vaiṣṇavas of Bengal, is ascribed by some to him. The *Satkriyāsāra-dīpikā*, dealing with sacraments, is also attributed by some scholars to this writer. [On his life and authorship of the *Haribhakti-vilāsa*, see S. K. De, *Early History of the Vaiṣṇava Faith and Movement in Bengal*, Calcutta, 1961.]

GOPĀLAKṚṢṆA BHAṬṬA : Belonging to the thirteenth century, he was the author of the Āyurvedic treatise called *Rasendrasāra-saṃgraha.*

GOTAMA : Also called Gautama, he is supposed to have flourished in the 6th century B.C. To him is ascribed the *Nyāya-sūtra*, the earliest treatise on Nyāya philosophy.

GOVARDHANA : Author of the lyric poem entitled *Āryā-saptaśatī.* Son of Nīlāmbara Somayājin, brother of Balabhadra and teacher of one Udayana. Enjoyed the patronage of king Lakṣmaṇasena of Bengal (c. 1185-1205 A.D.). Mentioned by Jayadeva in the *Gīta-govinda.* Acc. to Jayadeva, none can match Govardhana in erotic compositions. Some scholars hold that Govardhana's patron was Pravarasena, author of the *Setubandhakāvyam.*

[For an account of the author, see Pischel in *Holfdichter des Lakṣmaṇasena*, Göttingen, 1893. Also see P.K. Das Gupta, Poet

Govardhanācārya and his association with king Lakṣmaṇasena, *Summaries of Papers*, *AIOC*, 1974.]

GOVINDADĀSA : Author of the Āyurvedic work called *Bhaiṣajya-ratnāvalī*. He flourished probably towards the end of the sixteenth century.

GOVINDĀNANDA : A well-known figure in the Smṛti literature of Bengal. From his autobiographical account we learn that he was son of Gaṇapatibhaṭṭa, a resident of Bāgḍī (= old Vyāghrataṭī) in Medinīpura in West Bengal. Had the title Kavikaṅkaṇācārāya. Appears to have flourished a little earlier than Raghunandana. His works are : *Dānakriyā-kaumudī*, *Śuddhi-kaumudī*, *Śrāddhakriyākaumudī*, *Varṣakriyā-kaumudī* and *Kriyā-kaumudī*. Besides these, he wrote three commentaries—the *Tattvārtha-kaumudī* on Śūlapāṇi's *Prāyaścitta-viveka*, the *Artha-kaumudī* on Śrīnivāsa's *Śuddhi-dīpikā* and a commentary on the *Śrāddha-viveka* of Śūlapāṇi. His date has been fixed as 1510-1550 A.D.

[See B. Bhattacharya, The Bengal Nibandhakāra Govindānanda ...his date, *Pro. AIOC*, 1966.]

GOVINDARĀJA : From his works we learn that son of Bhaṭṭa Mādhava and grandson of Nārāyaṇa, he lived on the Ganges. Believed to have flourished in the later half of the 11th century A.D. Author of a celebrated commentary on the *Manu-smṛti*, and also of the *Smṛti-mañjarī*. A *Sahagamana-vidhi* is also attributed to him.

GUṆACANDRA : Joint author of the *Nāṭya-darpaṇa* (q.v.), he was a pupil of Jaina Hemacandra and perhaps flourished between 1100 and 1175 A.D.

GUṆĀḌHYA : Author of the lost *Bṛhat-kathā* (q.v.). According to one tradition, Guṇāḍhya was born at Pratiṣṭhāna and became a favourite of king Sātavāhana. It is said that having lost a wager with Sarvavarman, author of the *Kātantra* grammar, Guṇāḍhya abjured the use of Sanskrit, retired to the Vindhya hills and wrote the *Bṛhat-kathā* in Paiśācī Prākrit. Another tradition makes him a resident of Mathurā enjoying the patronage of king Madana of Ujjayinī. It says that he wrote in Paiśācī on the advice of sage Pulastya. Guṇāḍhya appears to have flourished about 4th century A.D.

[See S.N. Prasad, *Studies in Guṇāḍhya*, Varanasi, 1977.]

HALĀYUDHA : A well-known writer in the history of the Smṛti digests of Bengal. From the account given in his work he appears to have been a Dharmādhyakṣa (Chief Judge) and son of Dhanañjaya. From his mention of Lakṣmaṇasena, Halāyudha appears to have been a contemporary of that king (c. 1185-1205 A.D.). The title of his only work, discovered hitherto, is *Brāhmaṇa-sarvasva* or *Karmopadeśinī*. Raghunandana, in his *Ekādaśī-tattva* and *Śuddhi-tattva*, attributes a *Saṃvatsara-pradīpa* to Halāyudha whose identity with the author of the *Brāhmaṇa-sarvasva* is not admitted by some scholars. The works entitled *Dvija-nayana* and *Śrāddha-paddhati-ṭīkā* are associated with a Halāyudha whose identity with the present writer is not beyond doubt. [For a full account, see introduction to ed. of *Brāhmaṇa-sarvasva* by D. Bhattacharya and the same scholar's paper 'A Pre-Sāyaṇa Vedic Commentator of Bengal', *Our Heritage*, Vol. I, pt. II. Also see D. C. Bhattacharya and R.C. Hazra in *IHQ* XXI.]

Another Halāyudha is the author of the *Kavirahasya* (q.v.) and the lexicon called *Abhidhāna-ratnamālā*, and appears to have flourished in the 10th century A.D.

HARADATTA : Author of the *Padamañjarī*, a valuable commentary on the *Kāśikā*. Probably a native of the Tamil region, he was son of Padma-(or, Rudra) kumāra, younger brother of Agnikumāra and pupil of Aparājita. One Haradatta, who probably flourished some time between 1100 and 1300 A.D. and was perhaps different from the author of the *Pada-mañjarī*, is the author of the *Ujjvalā* commentary on the *Āpastamba-dharmasūtra* and the *Mitākṣarā* commentary on the *Gautama-dharmasūtra*. The author of the *Pada-mañjarī* appears to have flourished in the later half of the eleventh century.

[See D.K. Kharwandikar, Date of Haradatta, *Summaries of Papers, AIOC*; 1974.]

HARIBHADRA : Belonging to the 8th century (10th cent. acc. to some), he wrote the following works on philosophy, particularly on Jaina Philosophy : *Ṣaḍdarśana-samuccaya*, *Lokatattva-nirṇaya*, *Yoga-dṛṣṭi-samuccaya*, *Yoga-bindu* and *Dharma-bindu*. *The Abhisamayālaṃkārāloka*, a commentary on the *Abhisamayālaṃkāra-kārikā*, is attributed to him (Ed. G. Tucci, Baroda, 1932).

A Haribhadra, supposed by some to be identical with Haricandra, is the author of the *Jīvandhara-campū*.

HARICANDRA : Author of the *Jīvandhara-campū*. Probably flourished after 900 A.D. May or may not be identical with Haricandra, author of the *Dharmaśarmābhyudaya*. This Haricandra appears to have belonged to the Digambara sect. He was son of Ārdradeva and Rādhā and brother of Lakṣmaṇa of the Kāyastha Sanomaka family. He had the title of Sarasvatīputra. He is mentioned by Rājaśekhara in his *Karpūramañjarī*.

A Bhaṭṭāra Haricandra is mentioned in Bāṇabhaṭṭa's *Harṣacarita* (Intro. verse 12) as famed for a prose work.

A 'verse of Haricandra occurs in Vallabhadeva's *Subhāṣitāvalī* (No. 161). Among great poets, a Haricandra is mentioned in the *Sadukti-karṇāmṛta* (No. 2130).

[For date of the Jaina Haricandra, see V. Raghavan in *Jour. of Gaṅgānāth Jhā Res. Inst.*, xxvi, Pt. 4]

HARINĀTHA : Probably a Smṛti writer of Mithilā. Supposed to have flourished in the first half of the 14th century A.D. Author of an authoritative Smṛti digest called *Smṛti-sāra* or *Smṛti-sāra-samuccaya*.

HARIṢEṆA : Author of the Allahabad Stone Pillar Inscription (c. 350 A.D.) in honour of the Gupta king Samudragupta. This inscription provides a positive instance of the cultivation of refined Kāvya style in that remote age.

HĀRĪTA : One of the twenty traditional writers on original Smṛti. There appear to have been two authoritative writers of this name : one was author of a Dharmasūtra and the other of a metrical Smṛti on legal matters. Verses of Hārīta appear to have been widely known long before the 6th century A.D. Hārīta, the jurist, appears to have flourished some time between 400 and 700 AD.

[See R.C. Hazra, Did Hārīta know Tantras, *IHQ*, June and Sep., 1960.]

HARṢA : To be distinguished from Śrīharṣa (q.v.). The dramas, *Ratnāvalī, Priyadarśikā and Nāgānanda*, are attributed to Harṣa. Some identify him with King Harṣavardhana of Thaneswar, who ruled from 606 to 646 or 647 A.D.]

[See D. Devahuti, *Harsha, a political study*, Oxford, 1970; 2nd ed., Delhi, 1983.]

HASTIPAKA : See Meṇṭha.

HEMACANDRA : Originally named Cāṅgadeva, he was son of Caciga and Pahinī. Born at Dhunduka or Dhandhukā (in Ahmedabad), he became a Jaina monk (1088-1172 A.D.) and wrote the grammatico-historical poem *Kumāra-pāla-carita* or *Dvyāśraya-kāvya*, partly in Sanskrit and partly in Prākrit, in honour of Kumārapāla, the Caulukya king of Anhilvāḍ. Author also of the philosophical work *Pramāṇa-mīmāṃsā* and of the grammatical work called *Siddhahema-candrābhidhasvopajña-śabdānuśāsana*, popularly known as *Śabdānuśāsana*. He wrote also the *Kāvyānuśāsana*, a work on poetics and the *Abhidhānacintāmaṇi*. His Jaina work, *Triṣaṣṭi-śalākā-puruṣa-carita* is well-known. On his grammar he himself has written two glosses called *Laghuvṛtti* and *Bṛhad-vṛtti* and the commentary known as *Bṛhan-nyāsa*.

[See G. Bühler, *Über das Leben des Jaina-Mönches Hemacandra*, Wien, 1889 (Trs. into Eng. by M. Patel in the Singhi Jaina Series, 1936); H. Jacobi in *Encyclo. of Religion and Ethics*, VI. On the author's works on various subjects, see S.K. De, *Sanskrit Poetics*, I; S. K. Belvalkar, *Systems of Sanskrit Grammar*, Poona, 1915; Th. Zachariae, *Ind. Woer-terbücher*, Strassburg, 1897.]

HEMĀDRI : A great figure in the Smṛti literature of South India. From the account given by himself we learn that he was son of Kāmadeva and grandson of Vāsudeva. He describes himself as being in charge of the imperial records of Mahādeva (1260-71), the Yādava king of Devagiri (=modern Daulatabad), and also as being his minister. His encyclopaedic Smṛti digest is entitled *Caturvargacintāmaṇi* divided into sections called *Vrata*, *Dāna*, *Śrāddha*, *Kāla*, etc. A *Śrāddha-kalpa* is also attributed to him.

To a Hemādri is attributed the commentary, *Raghuvaṃśa-darpaṇa* on the *Raghuvaṃśa* of Kālidāsa.

HEMAVIJAYAGAṆI : Author of the book of tales, called *Kathā-ratnākara*. He flourished about the 17th century and was a Jaina.

INDRA : Name of a great grammarian who is perhaps referred to by Pāṇini by the word *Prācām*. Believed to have been the founder of the Aindra school of grammar.

ĪŚVARADATTA : Author of the play called *Dhūrta-viṭa-saṃvāda*. The lower limit of the date of the work is fixed by Hemacandra's quotation and reference in the *Kāvyānuśāsana* at the end of the 11th and begining of the 12th century.

ĪŚVARAKṚṢṆA : Author of the *Sāṃkhya-kārikā*. Sometimes identified with Vindhyavāsin. Earlier than Vasubandhu who is assigned to the 4th century A.D. Īśvarakṛṣṇa, identified by Svapneśvara in his *Kaumudī-prabhā* with Kālidāsa, appears to have been atheistic.

[On Īśvarakṛṣṇa and his work, see S.K. Belvalkar in *Bhandarkar Comm. Vol.*, Poona, 1917 and Keith in *The Sāṃkhya System*, 1924 (2nd ed.).]

JAGADĪŚA TARKĀLAṄKĀRA : A prominent figure in the Bengal school of Navya-Nyāya. Flourished at Navadvīpa most probably towards the middle of the sixteenth century. Son of Yādava Tarakavāgīśa and great grandson of Sanātana Miśra, father-in-law of Caitanya, Jagadīśa wrote a number of original works and commentaries. Of his original works, the most famous is the *Śabda-śakti-prakāśikā*. His commentary on the *Tattva-cintāmaṇi* of Gaṅgeśa is called *Mayūkha*. Besides, he commented on the *Dīdhiti* of Raghunātha Śiromaṇi. The *Tarkāmṛta* also is ascribed to him.

[For an account of his life and works, see D. C. Bhattacharya, *Vāṅgālir Sārasvat Avadān*, Vol. I.]

JAGADĪŚVARA : Author of the *Hāsyārṇava* (q.v.).

JAGANNĀTHA : Author of the *Rasa-gaṅgādhara*, a celebrated work on poetics. He describes himself as son of Peru Bhaṭṭa and Lakṣmī. Pupil of Kṛṣṇaśeṣa, he was a South Indian Brahmin, and appears to have received the title of Paṇḍitarāja from Shah Jahān (1628-58 A.D.), Emperor of Delhi. After criticising the views of the earlier writers he defines poetry as a linguistic composition which brings a charming idea into expression. Jagannātha's *Citramīmāṃsā* is another work on poetics. His other works include the erotico-didactic poem *Bhāminī-vilāsa*, the eulogistic works called *Āsapha-vilāsa*, *Jagadābharaṇa* and *Prāṇābharaṇa*, the last three being eulogies respectively of Āsaf Khān, brother of Nūr Jahān, queen of Emperor Jahāngīr, king Jagatsiṃha of Udaipur and king Prāṇanārāyaṇa of Kāmarūpa. For other poetical works of Jagannātha, see S.K. De : *Sanskrit Poetics* (2nd ed.), I, p. 233, f.n. 1. His *Manoramā-kuca-mardinī* is a grammatical work directed against Bhaṭṭoji Dīkṣita's commentary, called *Prauḍha-manoramā*, on the *Siddhānta-kaumudī*.

[For a list of his works, See L.R. Vaidya's ed. of *Bhāminī-vilāsa* (Intro.) Bombay, 1887. Also see *Paṇḍitarāja-kāvya-saṃgraha*, ed. A. Sarma, Hyderabad, 1598.]
See R.Mukherji, *Jagannātha*'s *Literary Theories*.

A Jagannātha wrote the *Varṇakramalakṣaṇa*, a commentary on the *Ṛk-prātiśākhya*.

The *Sāra-pradīpikā*, a commentary on the *Sārasvata-vyākaraṇa*, was written by one Jagannātha.

Jagannātha Tarkapañcānana, son of Rudra Tarkavāgīśa of Bengal, compiled the huge Smṛti digest called *Vivāda-bhaṅgārṇava* in 1773 A.D.

JAIMINI : Supposed author of the *Mīmāṃsā-sūtra* for which the earliest period assigned is the 4th century B.C.

[See Jaimini as the advocate of women's right, *Summaries of Papers*, *AIOC*, 1969, p. 387.]

JALHAṆA : Compiler of the anthology entitled *Subhāṣita-muktāvalī* or *Sūkti-muktāvalī* (1257 A.D.). Son of Lakṣmīdhara, he flourished in the reign of the Yādava king Kṛṣṇa who came to the throne in 1247 A.D. From the *Rājataraṅgiṇi* (viii. 621f) he appears to have written the poem *Somapāla-vilāsa* which is an account of his patron Somapāla. Another person of the same name composed the poem called *Mugdhopadeśa* (q.v.).

JAMBHALADATTA : Author of a version of the *Vetālapañcaviṃśati*. The date and personal history of the author are unknown.

JAYADATTA SŪRI : Son of Vijayadatta and a Mahāsāmanta, he flourished probably later than the 15th century. Author of the huge *Aśva-vaidyaka* which appears to be a digest of various works dealing with the diseases of horses and their treatment.

JAYADEVA : Author of the *Gītagovinda*, a well-known lyric poem. One of the court-poets of Lakṣmaṇasena, the last Hindu ruler of Bengal (c. 1185-1205 A.D.). Son of Bhojadeva and Rāmādevī (or, Vāmādevī or Rādhādevī) and an inhabitant of Kenduvilva which is identified by some with the village called Kendulī on the river Ajaya in the district of Birbhum, West Bengal. Mithilā and Orissa also claim Jayadeva.

This Jayadeva appears to be different from Jayadeva, author of the drama *Prasanna-rāghava*, Jayadeva, author of the Kāvya called *Śṛṅgāra-mādhavīya-campū*, Jayadeva, author of the *Chandas-sūtra* as well as from Jayadeva, author of the *Rati-mañjarī*. Some scholars identify the author of the *Gītagovinda* with Jayadeva, author of the rhetorical work *Candrāloka*, but there are cogent arguments against the identity. Many stanzas of Jayadeva, quoted in the anthologies, are not traceable in the *Gīta-govinda*.

A Jayadeva appears to have been the author of a small grammatical work called *Iṣṭatantra-vyākaraṇa*. A Jayadeva, also called Pakṣadhara Miśra, was a famous Neo-logician of Mithilā.

[On life and wor of Jayadeva and various connected problems see S. K. De, *Early History of Vaiṣṇava Faith and Movement in Bengal*, Calcutta 1961. Also see S. K. Chatterji, Jayadeva kavi, *A. S. Dhruva Memo. Vol.*, III, Ahmedabad, 1944-46. For Jayadeva, the writer on Prosody, see P. K. Gode, Studies in Indian Literary History, I, p. 138 ff. See P. K. Das Gupta, *Jayadeva and some of his contemporaries*, Calcutta, 1982.]

JAYĀDITYA : Co-author of the *Kāśikāvṛtti*, a celebrated commentary on the *Aṣṭādhyāyī*. May be identical with Jayāditya of Kashmir who, according to I-Tsing, died about 660 A.D.

JAYADRATHA : Author of the *Haracarita-cintāmaṇi* (q.v.) and a Kashmirian as is indicated by his titles Rājānaka and Mahāmāheśvara. May have been a brother of Jayaratha, commentator on Abhinavagupta's *Tantrāloka* and Ruyyaka's *Alaṃkāra-sarvasva*. Flourished in the first quarter of the 13th century under Rājadeva of Kashmir.

JAYANTA BHAṬṬA : Father of Abhinanda (q.v.), Jayanta appears to have flourished in Kashmir in the 9th century. Author of the well-known *Nyāya-mañjari* and the play called *Āgamoḍambara*.

JĀYASENĀPATI : Author of the *Nṛtta-ratnāvali* on dance. He was commander of elephant-forces under Gaṇapatideva, the Kākatīya ruler of Varangal.

JHALAKIKARA, V. Compiler of the *Nyāya-kośa*.

JIMŪTAVĀHANA : A noted pre-Raghunandana Smṛti writer of Bengal. In his works he is described as *Pāribhadrīya* which, perhaps, refers to a section of the Brahmins of Bengal. Date uncertain, but appears to have flourished after the 11th century, according to some, after the 13th century, according to others. His works are the *Kālaviveka*, *Vyavahāramātṛkā* and *Dāya-bhāga*. The first and the last work appear to have been parts of a larger treatise called *Dharmaratna*. His *Dāya-bhāga* was, through centuries, of paramount authority in Bengal in the matters relating to inheritance and succession.

JINENDRABUDDHI : A Buddhist and author of the *Kāśikāvivaraṇapañjikā* or *Nyāsa* (c. 700 A.D.), a well-known commentary on the *Kāśikā-vṛtti* which is a celebrated commentary on the *Aṣṭādhyāyī*. Believed to have flourished in the 8th century. Some scholars identify him, not on adequate grounds, with Pūjyapāda Devanandin, author of the *Jainendra-vyākaraṇa*.

JĪVA GOSVĀMIN : A prominent figure in the history of Bengal Vaiṣṇavism. Son of Anupama, brother of Rūpa Gosvāmin and Sanātana Gosvāmin, he finally settled in Vṛndāvana where he was one of the six venerable Gosvāmins. Date not known with certainty. His fame was established in the 16th-17th century. A versatile scholar, Jīva was a prolific writer. His works on different subjects are as follows :—

(a) Vaiṣṇava Philosophy.
  (i) The six Saṃdarbhas, viz. *Tattva*, *Bhagavat*, *Paramātma*, *Kṛṣṇa*, *Bhakti* and *Prīti*.
  (ii) *Sarva-saṃvādinī*.

(b) Vaiṣṇava theology.
  Commentaries on the *Gopālatāpanī-upaniṣad* and several other works relating to Vaiṣṇava theology. A commentary, called *Krama-saṃdarbha* on the *Bhāgavata-purāṇa* and an abridgement of Sanātana's *Vaiṣṇava-toṣaṇī* commentary on the tenth chapter of the *Bhāgavata*.

(c) Vaiṣṇava Kāvyas.
  (i) *Gopāla-campū*.
  (ii) *Saṃkalpa-kalpa-druma*.
  (iii) *Mādhava-mahotsava*.
  (iv) *Gopāla-birudāvalī*.

(d) Rasa-śāstra.
  (i) *Rasāmṛta-śeṣa*.
  (ii) Commentary, called *Durgama-saṃgamanī*, on Rūpa Gosvāmin's *Bhakti-rasāmṛta-sindhu*.
  (iii) Commentary, called *Locana-rocanī*, on Rūpa's *Ujjvala-nīlamaṇi*.

(e) Vaiṣṇava Ritualism.
  Kṛṣṇārcā-dīpikā.

(f) Grammar.
  (i) *Harināmāmṛta-vyākaraṇa*.
  (ii) *Dhātusūtra-mālikā*.

[For a full account of the life and works of the author, see S. K. De, *Early History of the Vaiṣṇava Faith and Movement in Bengal*, Calcutta, 1961. Also see U. Bhattacharji, The Philosophy of Jīva Gosvāmin, *K. B. Pathak Comm. Vol.*, Poona, 1934; J. N. Sinha, *Jiva Gosvāmin's Religion of Devotion and Love*, Benares].

JÑĀNENDRA SARASVATĪ : Author of the famous *Tattvabodhinī* commentary on Bhaṭṭoji's *Siddhānta-kaumudī*. He was a pupil of Vāmanendra Sarasvatī, and probably flourished in the first half of the eighteenth century.

JONARĀJA : A Kashmirian writer. He wrote the *Dvitīya-rājataraṅgiṇī* as a continuation of the *Rājataraṅgiṇī* which was left incomplete due to Kalhaṇa's death. His patron was Sultan Zain-ul-Abidin (14th c. A.D.). Jonarāja's work ends abruptly due to his death in 1459 A.D.

[See S. Das, Jonarāja and Dvitīya Rājataraṅgiṇī, *Summaries of Papers, AIOC*, 1974.]

JUMARANANDIN : The most famous writer of the Jaumara school of grammar. Sometimes wrongly regarded as the founder of this school. Probably flourished in the 14th century A.D. and revised the *Saṃkṣipta-sāra* (q.v.) and the comm. *Rasavatī* on it.

JYOTIRĪŚVARA : Author of the drama entitled *Dhūrta-samāgama*. Surnamed Kaviśekharācārya, he was son of Dhaneśvara and grandson of Rāmeśvara and belonged to the family of Dhīreśvara. He wrote under the Vijayanagara king Narasiṃha (1487-1507 A.D.). According to some MSS, he was son of Dhīrasiṃha and his patron was Harasiṃha identified, not on very good grounds, with Harisiṃha of Simraon (1324 A.D.). To Jyotirīśvara are attributed also the works on erotics called *Pañcasāyaka* and *Raṅgaśekhara*.

KAIYAṬA : Probably a Kashmirian, he was son of Jaiyaṭa, surnamed Upādhyāya, and disciple of Maheśvara. A tradition makes him a younger brother of Mammaṭa. He must have flourished earlier than c. 1300 A.D. Some scholars place him in the 11th cent. A.D. Author of the *Pradipa*, a celebrated commentary on the *Mahābhāṣya*.

[See *Mahābhāṣya*, Vol. VII. pub. by D.E. Society, Poona; V. Raghavan in *Ṛtam*, *K.A.S. Iyer Fel. vol.*, Lucknow, Dates of Helārājā and Kaiyaṭa.]

KALHAṆA : Author of the well-known historical poem entitled *Rājataraṅgiṇī*. He was son of Campaka who was a minister of king Harṣa of Kashmir (1089-1101 A.D.). He mentions Jayasiṃha (1127-59 A.D.) as the reigning sovereign.

[Ref : S.C. Banerji, *Cultural Heritage of Kashmir*, Calcutta, 1965.]

KĀLIDĀSA : The greatest poet and dramatist in Sanskrit literature. Author of the Mahākāvyas called *Raghuvaṃśa*, *Kumāra-sambhava*, the lyric poem entitled *Meghadūta* and the dramas *Abhijñāna-śākuntala*, *Vikramorvaśīya* and *Mālavikāgni-mitra*. Cantos ix to the end of the *Kumārasambhava* are supposed by some to be later interpolations. The lyric poem *Ṛtu-saṃhāra* is attributed by some scholars, without convincing reasons, to Kālidāsa. Nearly a score of other Kāvyas are traditionally attributed to Kālidāsa. The well-known among them are the *Nalodaya*, the *Puṣpabāṇavilāsa* and the *Śṛṅgāra-tilaka*. Many later poets assumed the name of Kālidāsa, e.g. Abhinava-Kālidāsa, Ākbarīya Kālidāsa etc. The versified work on prosody, called *Śrutabodha*, is also attributed to Kālidāsa.

The date of Kālidāsa, the master-poet, is controversial. While some place him in the first century B.C., others bring him down to the fifth century A.D. Most modern scholars assign him to the Gupta period. The lower terminus of his date is fixed by the mention of his name in the Aihole Inscription of 634 A.D.

Tradition makes him a court-poet of Vikramāditya. The earliest of the several kings bearing this epithet ruled about the first century B.C. Candragupta II, the Gupta king, was also styled Vikramāditya. According to a legend, Kālidāsa was an arrant fool in his early age, and acquired prodigious learning and poetic skill through the grace of Goddess Kālī whom he had propitiated by severe penance. Nothing definite is known about his native place. Daśapura in Malwa, Ujjayinī, Kashmir, Vidarbha and Ceylon are some of the places that claim his birth.

[The following are some of the noteworthy studies relating to his life and works :—

ACHARYA, P.B. : *Tragicomedies of Shakespeare, Kālidāsa and Bhavabhūti*, New Delhi, 1978.

AGRAWAL, V. S. : Art Evidence in Kālidāsa, *JUPHS*, xxii.

———: Kālidāsa and Sanskrit Buddhist Literature, *JUPHS*, xxiii.

AIYAR, T. K. R. : *A Concordance of Kālidāsa's Poems*, ed. V. Raghavan, Madras, 1952.

ALTEKAR, M. D.: Aesthetics of Kālidāsa, *Vikrama Volume*, Ujjain, 1948.

APTE, M. V. : The Flora in Kālidāsa's Literature, *ABORI*, xxxii.

AUROBINDO : See, Srī Aurobindo.

BANDYOPADHYAYA, P. : Vedicism in Kālidāsa, *Proc. of AIOC*, 1966.

BANERJI, S. C. : *Kālidāsa-kośa*, Benares, 1968.

———: *Kālidāsa Apocrypha* (To be published).

BASU, H : Kālidāsa and Fine Arts, *Summaries of Papers, AIOC*, 1969, p. 376. *Kālidāsa Apocrypha* (in Press), Chowkhamba, Benares.

BHANDARKAR, D. R. : Solecisms of Śaṃkarācārya and Kālidāsa, *IA*, XLI, 1912.

BHANDER, C. S. J. *Imagery of Kālidāsa.*

BHATT, G. K. : *Appointment with Kālidāsa*, Ahmedabad, 1982.

BHATTACHARYA, M. : *The Birth-place of Kālidāsa*, 1938.

BHATTACHARYA, S. P. : Kālidāsa and the Harivaṃśa, *JOIB*, VII.

BHAU DAJI : *Essay on Kālidāsa.*

BHAVE, S. S. : *Kālidāsa : National Poet of India.*

CHAKLADAR, H. C. : *The Geography of Kālidāsa.*

CHAKRAVARTI, S. K. : Epistles in Kālidāsa—a Study, *Summaries of Papers, AIOC,* Silver Jubilee Session, 1969, p. 82.

CHANDRASEKHARAN, T. : The Birds and Beasts of Kālidāsa, *C. K. Raja Pres. Volume,* Madras, 1941.

CHATTERJI, A. C. : Kālidāsa—his Poetry and Mind.

CHATTOPADHYAY, K. C. : *Date of Kālidāsa.*

———: *Studies in Kālidāsa*

CHAUDHURI, T. P. : Linguistic aberrations in Kālidāsa's writings. *Jour. of Bihar Res. Soc.,* xxxvi, pts. 3-4, Patna, 1951.

COLLINS, M. : *Geographical Data of the Raghuvaṃśa, etc.*

DASS, K. : The Kitchen and Bar of Kālidāsa, *Summaries of Papers, AIOC,* 1914.

DEB, B. : The Flora in Kālidāsa's Literature, *ABORI,* xxxvi.

DIKSITAR, V. R. R. : Religion of Kālidāsa, *C. K. Raja Pres. Volume,* Madras, 1941.

DVIVEDI, C. : *Kālidāsa and Shakespeare,* Kashi, 1923.

———, M. R. C. : Dhvani in Kālidāsa, *Summaries of Papers, AIOC,* 1977.

EMANEAU, M. B. : Kālidāsa's Śakuntalā and the Mahābhārata, *JAOS,* Vol. 82, No. 1, 1962.

FOULKES, T. : *Kālidāsa Variants,* 4 Vols.

GAWRONSKI, A. : *The Digvijaya of Kālidāsa,* Krakau, 1914-15.

GHOSH, S. N. : *Kālidāsa, an estimate of his literary merit.*

GODE, P. K. : A Psychological Study of Kālidāsa's Upamās, *Proc. of the First Oriental Conference,* 1919.

GOPALAM, V. : *Studies in Kālidāsa,* Visakhapatnam (Andhra), 1976.

GOSWAMI, S. : *Philosophy of Kālidāsa.*

GRUNWEDEL, A. : die Tibetische ubersetzung von Kālidāsa's Meghadūta, A. *Bezzenberger Comm. Vol.* Göttingen, 1921.

GURNER, C. W. : Personification of night as woman in Kālidāsa, *D. R. Bhandarkar Volume,* Calcutta, 1940.

——— : Kālidāsa's use of the Incarnation theme, *B. C. Law Volume,* Pt. I, Calcutta, 1945.

HARICHAND, P. : *Kālidāsa Et L' Art Poetique De L'inde*, Paris, 1917.

HARRIS : *An Investigation into some of Kālidāsa's views*, Evans Ville, Indiana, 1884.

HILLEBRANDT, A. : *Kālidāsa*, Breslau, 1921.

HOERNLE, A. F. R.: Kālidāsa and Kāmandaki, *IA*, XLI, 1912.

HUTH,G : *Die Zeit des Kālidāsa*, Berlin, 1890.

IYER, T. L. V. : The Musical Element in Kālidāsa, *Jour. of Oriental Research*, Madras, IV.

JANA, N. C. : *Vaiṣṇav Kavitāy Kālidāser Uttarādhikār*, Calcutta (in Bengali).

JHALA, G. C. : *Kālidāsa—a study*, 1949.

KALLA, L. : *The Birth-place of Kālidāsa*, Delhi, 1926.

KARMARKAR, R. D. : *Kālidāsa*, Dharwar, 1960.

KIBE, M. V. : Further Light on the date of Kālidāsa, *Siddha-bharati* (S. Varma Vol.), II. Hoshiarpur, 1950.

KRISHNAMOORTHY, K. : *Kālidāsa*, New York.

LAHA, S. C. : *Kālidāser Pākhī* (Birds in Kālidāsa's works. In Bengali), Calcutta.

LAW, B. C. : *Geographical Aspect of Kālidāsa's Works*, 1976.

LELE, V. R. : Heroines of Kālidāsa, *Summaries of Papers, AIOC*, 1974.

LEUMANN, E. : Das Geschlecht der Raghufiurstnder Anfang Von Kalidasa epischer Diehtung. *Festschrift E. Windisch*, Leipzig, 1914.

LIEBICH, B. : *Das Datum Des Candragomin's und Kālidāsa's*, Breslau, 1903.

——— : *das datum des Kalidasa*, Festgabe Delbruck, Strass-burg, 1912-13.

MAINKAR, T. G. : *Kālidāsa : His Art and Thought.*

MAIJADHAR, M. : *Kālidāsa and Shakespeare*, 1969.

MANSINHA, M. : *Kālidāsa and Shakespeare*, Delhi, 1968.

MAZUMDAR, N. G. : Home of Kalidasa, *Indian Antiquary*, XLVII.

MAJUMDAR, G. N. : Kālidāsa and Music, *ABORI*, vii.

MAJUMDAR, N. : Vātsyāyana and Kālidāsa, *IA*, XLVII.

MIRASHI, V. V. : A new theory about the home of Kālidāsa, *ABORI*, XLVII, 1961.

——— : Kālidāsa as seen in his works, *Vikrama Volume*, Ujjain, 1948.

——— : and N. R. NAVLEKAR : *Kālidāsa: Date, Life and Works*, Bombay, 1969.

MISHRA, M. : *Metres of Kālidāsa*, 1977.

MISRA, V. N. : The Mango-blossom imagery in Kālidāsa, *JAOS*, Vol. 82, No. 1, 1962.

NARANG, S. P. : *Kālidāsa Bibliography*, New Delhi, 1976.

NAYAR, V. U. K. : Kālidāsa's discovery of India, *Nehru Felicitation Volume*, Calcutta, 1949.

PATEL, G. V. : Gītā and Kālidāsa, *Summaries of Papers*, *AIOC*, 1974.

PATHAK : On the date of Kālidāsa, *JBRAS*, XIX, 1895.

——— : Kālidāsa and the Hūṇas of the Oxus Valley, *IA*, XLI, 1912.

PILLAI, K. C. : *Similes of Kālidāsa*, Santiniketan, 1945.

PILLAI, P. K. N. : *Kālidāsa* (an assessment by Ānandavardhana), 1974.

RAGHAVAN, V. : Kālidāsa, the Kālikāpurāṇa and Māgha, *Woolner Comm. Vol.*, Lahore, 1940.

——— : Bibliography of Translations of Kālidāsa's Works, *Indian Literature*, XI, 1968.

——— : Women Characters in Kālidāsa's Dramas, *Annals of Oriental Research*, Madras, IV, II, 1940.

——— : Vālmīki and Kālidāsa, *K. V. R. Aiyangar Comm. Vol.*, Madras, 1940.

——— : Kālidāsa and Smṛtis, *Jour. of Bombay Branch of Royal Asiatic Soc.*, New Series, XXIX. ii. 1954.

——— : Kālidāsa's Kuntaleśvara-dautya, *B. C. Law Volume*, II, Poona, 1946.

——— : *Mahākavi Śrī Kālidāsa-subhāṣitam*, Madras, 1940.

——— : *Love in the poems and plays of Kālidāsa*, Bangalore, 1955.

RAMANUJAMUNI, S. K. : *Padāvalī of Meghasandeśa and Kuntaleśvara-dautya of Kālidāsa*, Triplicane, 1939.

RAMANUJAṢVAMI, P. V. : Kālidāsa and Śūdraka, *Gopālakrishnamacharya Comm. Vol.*, Madras, 1942.

RAMASWAMY, K. S. : *Kālidāsa*, pts. 1, 2.

RAO, K. V. V. : Social consciousness of Kālidāsa as reflected in his dramatic compositions, *Summaries of Papers*, 5th World Skt. Con., Varanasi, 1981.

RAO, U. V. : Daiva and Puruṣakāra in Kālidāsa, *C.K. Raja Pres. Vol.*, Madras, 1941.

RUBEN, W. : *Kālidāsa : The Human Meaning of his Works.*

——— : Vālmīki and Kālidāsa, *JOIB*, VI.

RYLAND, C. A. : The plant Karṇikāra in Kālidāsa's Works, *Indian Culture*, Vol. XV (*B. M. Barua Comm. Vol.*), Calcutta, 1949.

SABNIS, S. A. : *Kālidāsa—his style and his times*, Bombay.

SANYAL, K. K. : *Kālidāsa, a study*, Calcutta, 1981.

SARKAR, S. C. : Kālidāsa, and his contemporaries in a Tibetan Reference, *Jour. of Ganganath Jha Research Institute*, I.

SARMA, D. : *An Interpretative Study of Kālidāsa*, Benares, 1968.

SARMA, P. P. : Kālidāsa: his scientific interpretations of certain physical phenomena, *K. B. Pathak Comm. Vol.*, Poona, 1934.

SASTRI, C. R. N. : Ancient Indian Life as depicted in the works of Kālidāsa, *Vikrama Vol.*, Ujjain, 1948.

SASTRI, K. A. N. AND RAO, S. R. : Kālidāsa's quest after the cultured mind, *S. K. Belvalkar Felicitation Vol.*, Benares, 1957.

SCHARPE, A. : *Kālidāsa-Lexicon*, Brugge (België).

[The first volume of this book is designed to contain the texts of Kālidāsa's works, and the second volume is to contain a word-index, with lexicon, to these works. Of vol. I, the following parts have been published :—

Part I (Containing text of the *Abhijñāna-śākuntala*), 1954.
Part II (Texts of the *Mālavikāgnimitra* and the *Vikramorvaśīya*), 1956.
Part III (Texts of the *Kumāra-sambhava*, the *Meghadūta*, the *Ṛtu-saṃhāra* and uncertain verses).
Part IV (Text of the *Raghuvaṃśa*) reported to be in press.
Vol. II reported to be under preparation.]

SEHGAL, S. R. : Vedicism in Kālidāsa, *Summaries of Papers, AIOC*, 1974.

SEN, N. M. : An astronomical basis for fixing the age of Kālidāsa, *JAS*, Bengal, 18.1.

SEN, P. C. : *Bhāratātmā Kavi Kālidāsa* (in Bengali), Calcutta.

SEN GUPTA, P. C. : Astronomical Time-indication in Kālidāsa, *Jour. of Royal Asiatic Soc. of Bengal*, XI.

SHAH, H. A. : Kauṭilya and Kālidāsa, *Quarterly Jour. of Mythic. Soc.*, IX.

SHARMA, D. : *An Interpretative Study of Kālidāsa.*

SHARMA, Y. : *Kālidāsa* (Amar Chitra Kathā).

SHASTRI, H. C. : *Kālidāsa* (Alaṃkāraśāstra), in French, 1917.

SHASTRI, H. P. : Kālidāsa, his home, *IA*, XLVII.

SHASTRI, N. S. : The three Kālidāsas, *Pro. of Oriental Conference*, XV.

SHIVARAMAMURTHI : *Epigraphical echoes of Kālidāsa.*

——— : *Numismatic Parallels of Kālidāsa.*

——— : *Sculpture Inspired by Kālidāsa.*

SHUKLA, H. L. : *Kālidāsa-kośa.* A Comprehensive Dictionary of Kālidāsa, based on stylo-linguistic principles, Allahabad, 1981.

SINGH, A. D. : *Kālidāsa, a critical Study*, Delhi, 1977.

SRI AUROBINDO : *Kālidāsa.*

STEN KONOW : Kālidāsa in China, *IHQ*, X.

SUBBANNA, N. R. : *Kālidāsa Citations*, Delhi, 1973.

SUMER, M. : *Les heroines de Kālidāsa.*

SURYAKANTA : *Kālidāsa's Vision of Kumārasambhava.*

THAKUR, S. : *Kālidāser Kāvye phul* (Flowers in the poems of Kālidasa, in Bengali), Calcutta.

TUCCI, G. : Note sulle fonti di kālidāsa, *Rivista degli Studi Orientali*, IX, 1921.

UPADHYAY, B. S. : On some ancient place-names in Kālidāsa, *JUPHS*, XVI.

———: *India in Kālidāsa.*

———: Ministers and the working of the secretariat as depicted by Kālidāsa, *K. V. Rangaswami Aiyangar Comm. Vol.*, Madras, 1940.

VASU, R. : Evolution of similar ideas in Kālidāsa's works, *Summaries of Papers*, 5th World Skt. Con., Varanasi, 1981, p. 232.

VEDALANKAR, C. G. : Social structure in the works of Kālidāsa, *Vikrama Vol.*, Ujjain, 1948.

VENKATASUBBIAH, A. : Kālidāsa's Social Ideals, *Quarterly Journal of the Mythical Society*, IX. Also see Kālidāsa and Painting in *Jour. of Oriental Research*, VII, Madras.

YADAV, B. R. : *A Critical Study of the Sources of Kālidāsa.*

[For the complete works of Kālidāsa, see *Kālidāser Granthāvali*, 2 vols., with Bengali trs., Calcutta. Also see the *Complete Works of Kālidāsa* (Texts with Eng. trs. by different scholars), ed. R. P. Dvivedi, Vol. I—Poetry; Vol. II—Drama; *Kālidāsagranthāvalī*, ed. with Hindi trs., S. Chaturvedi, Aligarh, Samvat 2019; C. R. Devadhar, *Works of Kālidāsa*, Vol. I, Dramas, Delhi 1966, with Eng. trs., notes. Also see V. P. Joshi, *Complete Works of Kālidāsa*, Bombay, 1976; *Kālidāsa and South Indian Literature*, Sanskrit Academy, Madras; G. Verma, *Humour in Kālidāsa*, Delhi, 1981.]

KALLAṬA : Kashmirian Śaiva philosopher and author of the work entitled *Spanda-kārikā*. He was a pupil of Vasugupta (8th or 9th century).

KALLINĀTHA : Also called Catura Kallinātha, he was the author of the *Saṃgītaratnākara-kalānidhi*, a well-known commentary on Śārṅgadeva's *Saṃgita-ratnākara*. Son of

Lakṣmīdhara and Nārāyaṇī, he was a native of Karṇāṭa in South India, and wrote his work at the instance of Immadi Devarāya, alias Mallikārjuna, king of Vijayanagara (1446-65 A.D.).

KALYĀṆASUBRAHMAṆYA : Author of the work entitled *Alaṃkāra-kaustubha* (q.v.).

KAMALĀKARA BHAṬṬA : There are several Kamalākaras of whom the most famous is Kamalākara, son of Rāmakṛṣṇa Bhaṭṭa and grandson of Nārāyaṇa Bhaṭṭa. His literary activity is assigned by P. V. Kane roughly to the period between 1610 and 1640 A.D. Kamalākara wrote on various subjects, particularly on Smṛti. His *magnum opus* is the *Nirṇaya-sindhu*. Of his other works, mention may be made of the *Śūdra-kamalākara*.

KĀMANDAKI : Author of the *Nīti-sāra*. Acc. to some, the real name was Śikhara.
[See *Nīti-sāra*.]

KAṆĀDA : Supposed author of the *Vaiśeṣika-sūtra*. He is also called Kaṇabhuj or Kaṇabhakṣa. The name etymologically means 'atom-eater'. His real name appears to have been Kāśyapa. His date is uncertain; he may have been contemporaneous with the Buddha (6th-5th century B.C.).
[See S. Prakash, *Founders of Sciences in Ancient India*, New Delhi, 1965, Chap. VIII.]

KAPILA : The sage who is supposed to have been the founder of the Sāṃkhya system of philosophy. Believed to have flourished several generations before the Buddha. For a legend connected with Kapila, see Sagara under Myths and Legends. Acc. to the *Bhāgavata*, Kapila was the fifth incarnation.

KĀŚAKṚTSNA : An ancient grammarian and philosopher referred to in the *Mahābhāṣya* (on Pāṇini I. 1, Āhnika I). The grammar written by this author is also called *Kāśakṛtsna*.

KĀTYĀYANA : Author of the *Vārtika-sūtras* or supplementary rules in Pāṇini's *Aṣṭādhyāyī*. Date uncertain; believed to have flourished some time between 500 and 350 B.C. in South India. Vararuci appears to have been his other name. One of the twenty original Smṛti writers, mentioned by Yājñavalkya, is Kātyāyana. He is supposed to have flourished some time between the 4th and the 6th century A.D. Besides a metrical Smṛti work, the following works are attributed to Kātyāyana:

Śrauta-sūtra, *Gṛhya-sūtra*, *Śulva-sūtra*, *Śrāddha-sūtra* (*or kalpa*), *Mūlyādhyāya*, *Snāna-sūtra* or *Snāna-vidhi-sūtra.*

A *Kātyāyana-smṛti-sāroddhāra*, compiled by P.V. Kane, has been published. One Kātyāyana is credited with the authorship of the *Sarvānukramaṇī* (q.v.).

[For the work of Kātyāyana, the grammarian, see F. Kielhorn, *Kātyāyana and Patañjali—their relation to each other and to Pāṇini*, Benares, 1963 (2nd ed.); *Mahābhāṣya*, Vol. VII, pub. by D.E. Society, Poona; C.V. Devasthali, Aim of the vārtikas of Kātyāyana, *Munshi Indological Felicitation Vol.*, 1960-61. See K.P. Singh, *A critical study of Kātyāyanaśrautasūtra.*]

KAUṆḌABHAṬṬA: A reputed grammarian of the 17th century. Son of Raṅgoji and nephew of Bhaṭṭoji, he wrote an extensive gloss, called *Vaiyākaraṇabhūṣaṇa*, on the *Vaiyākaraṇa-siddhānta-kārikā* of the latter. Kauṇḍa's *Vaiyākaraṇabhūṣaṇa-sāra* is a sort of abridgment of his aforesaid work. His independent works are the *Vaiyākaraṇa-siddhānta-dīpikā* and the *Sphoṭa-vāda.*

KAUṬILYA : Also called Kauṭalya or Viṣṇugupta which is regarded as another name of Cāṇakya. Author of the celebrated *Kauṭalīya Arthaśāstra*, the oldest extant work on politics and statecraft. Believed to have been Prime Minister of the Maurya King Candragupta (c. 324-300 B.C.). Some scholars have a doubt and say that the work was not composed by the Minister of Candragupta.

[On his identity and age see, P.V. Kane, *History of Dharmaśāstra*, Vol. I; R. P. Kangle's Studies in the third part of his *Arthaśāstra*; R. K. Chaudhary, *Kauṭilya's Political Ideas and Institutions*. Also see P.C. Chunder, *Kauṭilya on Love and Morals*; M. V. K. Rao, *Studies in Kauṭilya*, 1958.]

KAVIKARṆAPŪRA : His real name was Paramānanda Sen. Son of Śivānanda, a disciple of Caitanya, he was born near Naihati in West Bengal a few years before the death of Caitanya in 1533 A.D. Author of the Sanskrit *Caitanya-caritāmṛta-kāvya* and the drama *Caitanya-candrodaya*. The Kāvyas called *Kṛṣṇāhnika-kaumudī* and *Ānanda-vṛndāvana-campū* were also composed by him. His *Gauragaṇoddeśa-dīpikā* is well-known. An *Āryā-śataka* is also attributed to him.

[Ref : S. K. De, *Early History of Vaiṣṇava Faith and Movement in Bengal*, Calcutta, 1961.]

KAVIPUTRA : Mentioned by Kālidāsa, in the prologue to the *Mālavikāgnimitra*, as a dramatist.

KAVIRĀJA : Real name perhaps Mādhava Bhaṭṭa and also styled Sūri or Paṇḍita. Wrote, under the patronage of Kāmadeva who was probably the Kādamba king (1182-97) of this name, the poem called *Rāghava-pāṇḍavīya*.

KEDĀRA BHAṬṬA : Son of Pibveka (Pathvaka) and author of the *Vṛttaratnākara*, a well-known work on Prosody, written before the 15th century. Some think that he was a Kashmirian.

KEŚAVA : Author of the *Kauśika-* (or *Keśava-*) *paddhati*. He was a contemporary of Bhoja Paramāra of Dhārā (11th cent. A.D.)

KEŚAVA MIŚRA : Author of the *Tarkabhāṣā*. Probably flourished in the 13th or 14th century.

KOHALA : An immediate disciple of Bharata, he was, acc. to the *Nāṭya-śāstra* (XXVIII. 18), to write a treatise on Prastāratantra. Author of the works *Kohala-rahasya* and *Saṅgīta-meru*, both on music and both lost. A fragment, called *Tālādhyāya*, exists in MSS. From this it appears that, though following Bharata generally, Kohala improved upon the *Nāṭyaśāstra* in details of classification. Kohala is cited by later writers, notably Abhinavagupta and commentators on Śārṅgadeva. The *Abhinaya-śāstra*, attributed to Kohala (Eggeling's *India Office Cat.*, 320; *Des. Cat. of Skt. Mss. in Oriental Mss. Lib.*, Madras, XXII. 8722, 8725), may be part or an abridgment of Kohala's work. Acc. to a tradition, he was a son of Mataṅga.

KRAMADĪŚVARA : Author of the grammar called *Saṃkṣipta-sāra*, dealing chiefly with Sanskrit and partly with Prakrit, written after 1150 A.D. He was styled *Vādīndra-cakra-cūḍāmaṇi*.

KṚṢṆA-LĪLĀŚUKA : See Līlāśuka.

KṚṢṆAMIŚRA: Author of the well-known allegorical drama entitled *Prabodha-candrodaya*. Supposed to have belonged to the second half of the 11th century. Refers to one Gopāla at whose command the play is stated to have been written to commemorate the victory of his friend, King Kīrtivarman, over the Cedi king Karṇa.

To a Kṛṣṇamiśra is ascribed a minor drama entitled *Vīravijaya*.

KṚṢṆĀNANDA ĀGAMAVĀGĪŚA : A resident of Navadvīpa, in West Bengal, he was the greatest figure in the history of the Tantra literature of Bengal. Supposed by some to have been a contemporary of Caitanya (1486-1533 A.D.). Some think that Kṛṣṇānanda was the author of the celebrated *Tantra-sāra*, a digest on Tantra.

KṚṢṆAPATI : Author of a commentary on the *Meghadūta*.

KṢEMAṄKARA : Author of the Jaina recension of the *Siṃhāsana-dvātriṃśikā*. He lived early in the 14th century A.D., and wrote in prose with verse at the beginning. He condensed the tales.

KṢEMARĀJA :A Kashmirian who, in the eleventh century, commented on the *Śiva-sūtra* of Vasugupta. He was a pupil of Abhinavagupta.

[Ref : S.C. Banerji, *Cultural Heritage of Kashmir*, Calcutta, 1965.]

KṢEMENDRA (Surnamed VYĀSADĀSA) : The Kashmirian polygrapher, who flourished in the eleventh century

A.D. He wrote on a variety of subjects. His two works on poetics are the *Kavi-kaṇṭhābharaṇa* and the *Aucitya-vicāracarcā*, the latter being more well-known. His work on prosody is called *Suvṛtta-tilaka*. Among his satirical and didactic works the following are noteworthy :—

Kalā-vilāsa, *Samaya-mātṛkā*, *Sevya-sevakopadeśa*, *Narma-mālā*, *Darpa-dalana*, *Cāru-caryā*.

His *Rāmāyaṇa-māñjarī* and *Bhārata-māñjarī* are poetical works based respectively on the *Rāmāyaṇa* and the *Mahābhārata*. His *Bṛhatkathā-mañjarī* is a metrical version of the *Bṛhatkathā*. Several works of his, referred to in his works, have not yet been discovered. This Kṣemendra is to be distinguished from Kṣemendra, author of a comm. on the *Sārasvata* grammar, who flourished probably in the 16th century.

[Ref. : Suryakanta, *Kṣemendra Studies*, Poona, 1954. R. B. Dattaray, *A Critical Survey of the Life and Works of Kṣemendra*, 1974. For the short poetical works of the author, see *Kṣemendra-laghukāvya-saṃgraha*, ed. A. Sarma, V. V. Raghavacharya and D. G. Padhye, Hyderabad, 1961. Also see L. Sternbach, *Unknown verses attributed to Kṣemendra*, Lucknow, 1979.]

KṢEMĪŚVARA : Author of the dramas called *Caṇḍakauśika* and *Naiṣadhānanda*. According to a verse in the Prologue, the *Caṇḍakauśika* was composed under king Mahīpāla who is sometimes identified with Mahīpāla of Bengal, but who in reality was Mahīpāla Bhuvanaikamalla of Kānyakubja (9th-10th century A.D.).

[For an up-to-date account of the author and the work, see S. Das Gupta's ed. of the *Caṇḍakauśika*, Asiatic Society, Calcutta, 1982.]

KṢĪRASVĀMIN : Author of the oldest and most important commentary called *Amarakośodghāṭana*, on the celebrated lexicon entitled *Nāmaliṅgānuśāsana*. Probably a native of Central India, he appears to have flourished in the second half of the 11th century. Acc. to some scholars, he was son of Īśvarasvāmin and flourished in Kashmir in the 8th century A.D. Besides commenting upon the *Pāṇinīya Dhātu-pāṭha*, he appears to have commented on a few other grammatical works. To him are attributed also the works called *Avyaya-vṛtti*, *Nipātāvyayopasarga* and the *Kṣīra-taraṅgiṇī* (a sort of comm. on the *Dhātupāṭha* of Pāṇini).

KULLŪKA : Author of the *Manvartha-muktāvalī*, a famous commentary on the *Manusmṛti*. He himself states that son of Divākara Bhaṭṭa, he was born in Varendrī in Bengal and that he wrote the above commentary in collaboration with other scholars in Kāśī (Benares). Acc. to some, he wrote also a Smṛti digest called *Smṛti-sāgara*. Date uncertain; but generally believed to have flourished earlier than the 15th century A.D. Acc. to P. V. Kane, the lower terminus of his date is 1100 A.D.

KUMĀRADĀSA (Also known as KUMĀRABHAṬṬA or BHAṬṬAKUMĀRA) : Author of the long poem entitled *Jānakī-haraṇa*. There is a tradition which makes him a friend of Kālidāsa. According to a Ceylonese tradition he was a king of Ceylon (c. 517-26 A.D.).

KUMĀRALĀTA : Probably of the 2nd century A.D., he was the author of the *Kalpanāmaṇḍitikā* or *Sūtrālaṃkāra* which, according to some, was the work of Aśvaghoṣa.

KUMĀRILA : Founder of the Bhāṭṭa school of Mīmāṃsā, he was a native of South India and wrote perhaps about 700 A.D. His works are the *Śloka-vārtika*, *Tantra-vārtika* and *Ṭupṭikā*.

[See G. P. Bhatt, *Epistemology of the Bhāṭṭa School of Pūrva Mīmāṃsā*, Benares; P.S. Sarma (ed.), *Kumārila Bhaṭṭa, Anthology of works*, Delhi, 1980.]

KUMBHA (or KUMBHAKARṆA) : Ruler of Mewar at Chittorgarh (accession 1433 A.D.). Author, *inter alia*, of the *Saṃgīta-rāja* and the *Rasika-priyā* comm. on Jayadeva's *Gītagovinda*.

KUṆARAVĀḌAVA : An ancient grammarian referred to by Patañjali in his *Mahābhāṣya* on Pāṇini III. 2. 14.

KUNTAKA : Author of the *Vakrokti-jīvita*, a well-known work on poetics. Referred to in Alaṃkāra literature as Vakrokti-jīvitakāra, he was perhaps a Kashmirian. Probably flourished

in the period between the 10th century and the 11th. He posited the theory that Vakrokti (striking or charming mode of expression) is the essence of poetry.
[Ref. : *Vakroktijīvita*, ed. S. K. De, Calcutta, 1961 (Introduction).]

KUVERA : The supposed author of the *Dattaka-candrikā* (q.v.). Date uncertain. Appears to have flourished before the 16th century A.D.

LAGADHA : The first man to systematize astronomy, the name of his compilation being *Vedāṅgajyotiṣa*. Probably flourished about 900 B.C. in Kashmir. Some would assign it to the 3rd century B.C., while others would bring it down to the 5th century A.D.

LAKṢMAṆA DEŚIKA : Author of the *Śāradā-tilaka*. He flourished in the 11th century.

LAKṢMĪDHARA : There are several authors of this name. Most famous among them is Lakṣmīdhara, author of the *Kṛtya-kalpataru*, a celebrated Smṛti digest. He informs us that, son of Bhaṭṭa Hṛdayadhara, he wrote his work at the command of Govindacandra, the Gahaḍavāla or Rathor emperor of Kanauj (1114-56 A.D.). He exercised considerable influence on the early Smṛti writers of Mithilā, Bengal and of northern India in general. A Lakṣmīdhara is known as the author of the Vedāntic work *Advaitamakaranda*.

LALLA : Son of Bhaṭṭa Trivikrama, he flourished probably later than Brahmagupta. Besides a commentary on the *Khaṇḍakhādyaka*, he wrote also the astronomical work variously called *Śiṣyadhīvṛddhitantra*, *Dhīvṛddhi-tantra*, *Siṣyadhīvṛddhida* or *Mahātantra*.

LAUGĀKṢI BHĀSKARA : Author of the *Artha-saṃgraha*, a work on Mīmāṃsā philosophy, and of the *Tarka-kaumudī* on Nyāya philosophy. Probably flourished in the 14th-15th century.

LIKHITA : One of the twenty traditional writers of original Smṛti. His Smṛti work is mentioned by later writers, notably Vijñāneśvara and Aparārka.

[See Śaṅkha.]

LĪLĀŚUKA : Author of the devotional lyric entitled *Kṛṣṇa-karṇāmṛta*. May be identical with Bilvamaṅgala, otherwise known as Kṛṣṇa-līlāśuka. Variously assigned to different periods ranging from the 9th to the 15th century A.D. From the poem we learn that the poet's parents were Dāmodara and Nīvī and preceptor Īśānadeva. One Somagiri appears to have been his spiritual Guru. Some scholars think that, of the three Bilvamaṅgalas, our author was the first and probably lived in Kerala.

LOCANAKAVI or LOCANAPAṆḌITA : Author of the *Rāga-taraṅgiṇī*. Flourished in the 12th century A.D.

LOKANĀTHA BHAṬṬA : Author of the drama, *Kṛṣṇābhyudaya*.

LOLIMBARĀJA : Author of the *Vaidya-jīvana* (q. v.). Flourished in the 17th century. A Lolimbarāja appears to have written the poem called *Harivilāsa* about 1050 A.D.

LOLLAṬA : See Bhaṭṭa Lollaṭa.

MADANĀNTADEVA : Author of the medical work called *Rasa-cintāmaṇi* (q. v.).

MADANAPĀLA : To him are ascribed the Smṛti works called *Madanapārijāta*, *Smṛti-kaumudī*, *Mahārṇava-karmavipāka*, *Tithi-nirṇaya-sāra*, the medical dictionary entitled *Madanavinoda-nighaṇṭu* as well as the *Sūrya-siddhānta-viveka* or *Vāsanārṇava*, a commentary on the astronomical work called *Sūrya-siddhānta*. Madana appears to have been a king and a great patron of learning, and is supposed to have flourished about the middle of the 14th century A.D. Some of the works ascribed to him are known to have been written by scholars enjoying his patronage. For example, the *Madana-pārijāta* was compiled by Viśveśvarabhaṭṭa, a high authority in the Benares school of Hindu Law.

MĀDHAVĀCĀRYA : Son of Māyaṇa and Śrīmatī and elder brother of Sāyaṇa, and a minister of king Bukka of Vijayanagara (14th cent. A.D.), he is credited with the authorship of the Smṛti works called *Kāla-nirṇaya* and *Parāśara-*

mādhavīya (a comm. on the *Parāśara-smṛti*). The following works are also attributed to him : *Dhātu-vṛtti*, *Nyāyamālā-vistara*, *Jīvanmukti-viveka*, *Vivaraṇa-prameya-saṃgraha* and *Śaṃkara-digvijaya*. The *Tātparya-dīpikā* comm. on the Sūta-saṃhitā, included in the *Skanda-purāṇa*, is also attributed to him. He is supposed to be the part author of the *Pañcadaśī*. Mādhava, the supposed author of the *Sarva-darśanasaṃgraha*, may or may not be identical with this Mādhava. Some take Mādhava to be identical with Sāyaṇa. Mādhavācārya is said to have become an ascetic in later life under the name of Vidyāraṇya.

A Praṇava-mīmāṃsā is also attributed to him.

[On the relationship between Mādhava and Sāyaṇa, see R. Narasimhachar, *Indian Antiquary*, Vol. 45; L. Sarup, *B. C. Law Volume*, II, Poona, 1946. Also see T. Shivamurthy, Unknown works of Mādhavamantrin, *ABORI*, 1976.; P. Olivellie on *Praṇava-mīmāṃsā*, *ABORI*, LXII, 1981, pp 77ff.]

MĀDHAVAKARA : Author of the following well-known works on Āyurveda : *Rug-viniścaya* or *Gada-viniścaya* (popularly called *Nidāna*), *Paryāya-ratnamālā*, *Cikitsā*, *Kūṭa-mudgara*. It cannot be definitely said whether or not Mādhava, author of the *Rasa-kaumudī*, is identical with Mādhavakara. Some scholars suppose, not on very convincing grounds, that Mādhavakara is identical with Mādhava, author of the following Āyurvedic works : *Āyurveda-rasaśāstra*, *Bhāva-svabhāva*, *Mugdhabodha*. Vṛndamādhava, author of the *Siddhayoga*, was perhaps different from Mādhavakara. Mādhavakara, who is believed to have flourished in the 7th-8th century, is sometimes claimed to have been a Bengali, but there is no conclusive evidence about this matter.

[For identity and age of the author, see N. Das Gupta, the Vaidyaka Literature of Bengal, in *Indian Culture*, Vol. III, and S. K. De, On some Vaidyaka writers of Bengal, *Indian Culture*, Vol. IV.]

MĀDHAVA UPĀDHYĀYA : Author of the Āyurvedic treatise called *Āyurveda-prakāśa*. The author flourished in the 18th century, and wrote his work in Benares.

MADHUSŪDANA : A redactor of the *Mahānāṭaka* (q. v.).

MADHUSŪDANA SARASVATĪ : An inhabitant of Koṭālipāḍā in the district of Faridpur in East Bengal, he was son of Pramoda Purandara Ācārya and had the name Kamalaja-nayana. Having taken to asceticism quite early in life under his preceptor Viśveśvara Sarasvatī, he was given the name Madhusūdana Sarasvatī. He studied at Navadvīpa, and settled at Benares. It is said that he was highly honoured at the court of Emperor Akbar. He is supposed to have flourished in the first half of the 16th century according to one view, in the second half of the 17th according to another. He wrote a number of original works on philosophy, and commented on some works. Of his works, the *Advaita-siddhi* and *Prasthānabheda* are very well-known. His commentary called *Bhagavadgītā-gūḍhārtha-dīpikā* on the *Gītā* is famous.

[Ref. : A. Roy in *Indian Culture, II*; P. C. Divanji in *ABORI*, VIII, IX; D. C. Bhattacharya, *Sanskrit Scholars of Akbar's time*, *ABORI*, XIII. See S. Gupta, *Studies in the Philosophy of Madhusūdana Sarasvati*, Calcutta, 1966; S. K. Gupta, *Madhusūdana Sarasvatī on the Bhagavadgītā*, Delhi, 1977. For the personal history of Madhusūdana, and a list of his works, see Sureś Candra Vandyopādhyāy, *Saṃskṛta Sāhitye Vaṅgālir Dān* (in Bengali), Calcutta, 1369 B. S.]

MADHVA : Also known as Pūrṇaprajña and Ānandatīrtha, he founded the Dvaita school of Vedānta which sought to demolish the Advaita doctrine of Śaṃkara. His standpoint is called unqualified dualism. Born in 1199 or 1197 A.D. in a village near Udipi, South Canara district, early in life he became proficient in Vedic learning, and renounced the world. His preceptor was Acyutaprekṣa. He died at the age of 79. He commented on seven of the important Upaniṣads, the *Bhagavadgītā*, the *Brahmasūtra* and the *Bhāgavatapurāṇa*. He wrote also a number of independent tracts including the *Anuvyākhyāna* and *Tattva-saṅkhyāna* (*Tattva-nirṇaya*). His epitome of the Mahābhārata, called *Bhārata-tātparya-nirṇaya*, and gloss on the *Bhāgavata-purāṇa* help to elucidate his philosophy. He wrote also a commentary on the first 40 hymns of the *Ṛgveda*. His *Gītā-tātparya*, in prose and verse, gives the essence of the *Gītā*.

[See K. Narayan, *Critique of Mādhva Refutation of the Śaṅkara School of Vedānta*; B.N.K. Sharma, *Philosophy of Madhvācārya*. For the works of Madhva, see S. N. Das Gupta, *Hist. of Indian Philosophy*, IV, Chap. XXV, and S. K. Moitra, *Madhva Logic*. Also see S. Siavra, *La Doctrine de Madhva : Dvaita-vedānta* (text and trs. of the first Pāda of Madhva's *Anuvyākhyāna* on *Brahmasūtra* and detailed discussions on his epistemology, dialectic and theology).

Also the following papers :—

1. Gopalacharya, M. R. : *Sri Madhva's Philosophy*; R. R. Divakar, *Karṇāṭaka-darśana*, Bombay, 1955.
2. Narain, K : *An Outline of Madhva Philosophy*.
3. Rao, P. N. : The problems of definition and perception in Śrī Madhva's epistemology, *Winternitz Memo. No.* (ed. N. N. Law), Calcutta, 1938.
4. Sharma, B. N. K. : The life and works of Madhva, *La Vallee Poussin Memo. Vol.*, Calcutta, 1940; The Sākṣi—an original contribution of Śrī Madhvācārya to Indian thought, *Siddhabhārati* (S. Varma Vol. II), Hoshiarpur, 1950.
5. Shastri, K. T. P. : Madhva's view of life, *Ibid*.
6. Srikantha, S. : Logical system of Madhvācārya, *P. V. Kane Pres. Vol.*, Poona, 1941.]

MĀGHA : Author of the mahākāvya entitled *Śiśupāla-vadha* which betrays deep influence of Bhāravi's *Kirātārjunīya*. Mentioned by the rhetoricians Vāmana and Ānandavardhana in the 8th-9th century A.D. Māgha himself says, at the end of his work, that his grandfather was minister of a king named Varmala. Varmala is identified by some with king Varmalāta, an inscription of whom is dated 625 A.D.

MAHĀVĪRA : Flourished under the Rāṣṭrakūṭa king Amoghavarṣa in the ninth century A.D. Author of the *Gaṇitasārasaṃgraha*.

MAHENDRAVIKRAMAVARMAN : Author of the *Mattavilāsa*, and a king of the Pallava dynasty. He ruled in Kāñcī about 620 A.D.

MAHIMABHAṬṬA : Author of the *Vyakti-viveka*, a well-known work on poetics. From his title Rājānaka he appears to have been a Kashmirian. He describes himself as son of Śrī Dhairya and disciple of Mahākavi Śyāmala. Mahimabhaṭṭa is assigned to a period later than the first quarter of the 11th century and earlier than the first quarter of the 12th. His chief concern appears to have been the demolition of the Dhvani theory.

[See G. De, *Studies in Mahimabhaṭṭa*; R. Banerji, *Analysis of Literary Fault* : Mahimabhaṭṭa as a critic.]

MAITREYANĀTHA : Supposed by some to have been author of the *Saptadaśa-bhūmi-śāstra* or *Yogācāra-bhūmi-śāstra*. Also attributed to him are the following works :

Sūtrālaṃkāra, *Madhyānta-vibhaṅga*, *Dharma-dharmatā-vibhaṅga*, *Mahāyāna-uttaratantra-śāstra* and *Abhisamayālaṃkāra-kārikā*.

[See G. Tucci, *Doctrines of Maitreya*(*nātha*) *and Asaṅga*, Calcutta, 1930.]

MAITREYARAKṢITA : Author of the *Dhātupradīpa*, a grammatical work, and of the *Tantra-pradīpa*, a commentary on the *Kāśikāvivaraṇa-pañjikā* (or *Nyāsa*) of Jinendrabuddhi. Appears to have been a Buddhist and flourished in the later half of the 11th century. He is supposed by many scholars to have been a Bengali, but there is no conclusive evidence for determining his native place.

[See K. C. Shastri, Maitreya Rakṣita, *R. K. Mookerji Vol.* (Bhārata-kaumudī), Allahabad, 1945, 1947.

MALLANĀGA (MALANĀGA) : Another name of Vātsyāyana (q. v.), author of the *Kāmasūtra*.

MALLINĀTHA : A famous commentator on the poetical works of Kālidāsa, Bhāravi, Bhaṭṭi, Māgha, Śrīharṣa and on some works on poetics (notably the *Ekāvalī*), lexicography and grammar. The *Udārakāvya*, *Raghuvīra-carita-kāvya*, *Vaidyakalpataru* and *Vaidya-ratnamālā* are the original works attributed to Mallinātha. Some of these works may have been written by other scholars bearing the same name. The great commentator, Mallinātha, appears to have flourished in the later half of the 14th century or in the earlier half of the 15th. This Mallinātha, father of an erudite scholar named Kumārasvāmin, was perhaps a Telugu

Brahmin of the Kolācala family. He is believed, by some, to have written also a commentary on the grammatical work, *Śabdenduśekhara* and one, entitled *Nyāsoddyota*, on the *Nyāsa* of Jinendrabuddhi. He is credited with comms. on the *Tārkikarakṣā*, *Praśastapāda-bhāṣya* and on the *Tantravār tika*.

[See S. C. Benerji, Commentaries of Mallinātha, *S. K. De Memorial Vol.*, Calcutta; P. K. Gode, A note on the Historical-Literary importance of Mallinātha's comms, *Proc. of Third O. Conference*, Madras, 63-67; P. G. Lalye, *Mallinātha-manīṣā*, Hyderabad, 1981.]

MALLIṢEṆA : Author of the *Syādvādamañjarī*. Flourished in the 18th century.

MAMMAṬA : Author of the whole or part of the celebrated work on poetics, called *Kāvya-prakāśa*. From his title Rājānaka he appears to have been a Kashmirian. Supposed to have flourished in the period between the middle of the eleventh century and the first quarter of the twelfth. Author also of the work entitled *Śabda-vyāpāra Paricaya.* Mammaṭa synthesises the earlier doctrines of the different schools of poetics, and finally establishes the doctrines of the Dhvani school. [See R. Mukherji, *Mammṭa's Literary Theories.*]

MAṆḌANA MIŚRA : Supposed to have been a native of Bihar, he was a pupil of Kumārila, on one theory, of Śaṃkarācārya on another. He wrote the following works : *Mimāṃsānukramaṇī*, *Vidhiviveka*, *Bhāvanāviveka* and *Vibhrama-viveka*. He is traditionally identified with Sureśvara (q.v.).

[See G. Jha, Preface to ed. of *Bhāvanāviveka*, Banaras.]

MAṄKHA (MAṄKHAKA, MAṄKHUKA) : Author of the huge poem entitled *Śrīkaṇṭha-carita*, composed between 1135 and 1145 A.D. From the work we learn that the poet's brother, Alaṅkāra, was a minister of king Jayasiṃha of Kashmir (1127-50 A.D.). Author was a pupil of Ruyyaka, well-known in the history of poetics. Maṅkha was son of Viśvāvarta and grandson of Manmatha.

MANU : Foremost among the twenty great writers of original Smṛti. Traditionally regarded as author of the *Manusmṛti* In the *Ṛg-veda* Manu is spoken of as the father of mankind.

Manu has been mentioned in various other works of Vedic literature. In the *Śatapatha Brāhmaṇa* occurs the story of Manu and the Deluge. In the *Mahābhārata* Manu is referred to as Svāyambhuva Manu and Prācetasa Manu. A Dharmasūtra by Manu or his school is supposed by some scholars to have existed at one time; it is referred to as *Mānavadharmasūtra.* Manu is considered by many modern scholars to have been mythical. See Manu under Myths and Legends (Part VI).

[See R. Sathianathier, The modernity of Manu, *C. S. Śrīnivāsāchāri Vol.*, Madras, 1950; S. K. Dutta, Manu's Daṇḍanīti and its relevance to modern society, *Summaries of Papers, AIOC*, 1974.]

MATAṄGA : Author of the *Bṛhaddeśī*, a treatise on music. He mentions Bharata, and quotes passages from Kohala. He is referred to by such eminent writers as Abhinavagupta and Śārṅgadeva. There is a tradition that Mataṅga's sons were Dattila and Kohala. Mataṅga differs from Bharata at several places, particularly in the introduction of 12 Svaras in Mūrchanā. He is supposed by some to have flourished at a time not very long after Bharata. Among Prabandhas, he is said to have introduced the form Harivilāsa and among dances a species called Zakkinī. A tradition makes Dattila and Kohala sons of Mataṅga.

MATHANASIṂHA : Author of the medical work, called *Rasaratna-mālikā* (q.v.).

MĀTṚCEṬA : Identical with Aśvaghoṣa (q.v.), according to a Tibetan tradition recorded by Tāranātha. Some modern scholars think that Mātṛceṭa was confused with Aśvaghoṣa because both belonged to the same school and were perhaps contemporaneous. Mātṛceṭa is mentioned by I-tsing and in inscriptions.

MĀTṚGUPTA : Traditionally identified with Kālidāsa. Stated by Kalhaṇa as a predecessor of Pravarasena (c. 5th cent. A.D.), king of Kashmir. May or may not have been identical with Mātṛguptācārya, the dramaturgist, fragments of whose commentary on the *Nāṭyaśāstra* are preserved.

[See S. K. De, *Sanskrit Poetics*, i; T. R. Chintamani in *Jour. of Oriental Res.*, Madras, II, 1928; S. Chattopadhyay, Mātṛgupta, *Our Heritage*, Special No., 150th Anniversary Vol., Calcutta, 1979.]

MAYŪRA : Author of the *Sūrya-śataka* and of stray verses quoted in the anthologies. According to varying traditions, he was father-in-law or brother-in-law of Bāṇabhaṭṭa. According to some later writers, a rival of Bāṇa at the court of Harṣavardhana (7th century).

[For an account of Mayūra and his works, see G. P. Quackenbos, *The Sanskrit Poems* of *Mayūra*, ed. with trs. and notes together with text of Bāṇa's *Caṇḍī-śataka*, new York, 1917, Columbia University Indo-Iranian Series.]

MĀYURĀJA : Author of the Rāma-drama called *Udātta-rāghava* which is lost but cited in the *Avaloka* commentary on the *Daśarūpaka*, and is known to Abhinavagupta and Kuntaka. Probably a Rājput of the Kalacuri clan, he is supposed by some to have been a ruler of the Cedi country with its capital at Māhiṣmatī. Verses of Māyurāja are quoted in the *Sūktimuktāvalī* of Jalhaṇa.

[See B. Svami in *IA*, XLI, 1912.]

MEDHĀTITHI : Author of the *Manu-bhāṣya*, the oldest extant commentary on the *Manu-smṛti*. Supposed to have flourished in the 9th century A.D. Son of Vīrasvāmin, he is believed by some scholars to have been a writer of south India. A *Smṛti-viveka* is supposed by P. V. Kane to have been written by Medhātithi.

[See S.G. Moghe, Medhātithi as on Etymologist, *Summaries of Criticism, AIOC*, 1974.]

Name of Vedic seer known to have stated very high numerals in a systematic way. Ten and its multiples form the basis of numerals in his system of counting. The highest figure, according to him, is called *parārdha*. It is 1012.

MEDINĪKARA : Compiler of the lexicon called *Anekārtha-kośa* (*Medini-kośa*). Generally supposed to have flourished in the 14th century A.D.

On the date of the work, see P. K. Gode, *Studies in Indian Literary History*, I, p. 281 ff.]

MEṆṬHA : Also called Bhartṛmeṇṭha or Hastipaka. Author of the lost poem *Hayagrīva-vadha*. According to Kalhaṇa (III. 125 ff. and 260 ff.), he enjoyed the patronage of king Mātṛgupta (5th century A.D.)

MERUTUṄGA : Author of the *Prabandha-cintāmaṇi*. He was a Jaina of the 14th century.

MILHAṆA : Author of the *Cikitsāmṛta*.

MISARU MIŚRA : Author of the *Vivāda-candra*, a Smṛti digest of high authority in Mithilā, and of the *Padārtha-candrikā*, on the Nyāyavaiśeṣika system of philosophy. He states that he wrote the digest under orders from Lachimādevī, wife of prince Candrasiṃha of the Kāmeśvara dynasty of Mithilā. Probably flourished in the earlier half of the 15th century A.D.

MITRA MIŚRA : A celebrated Smṛti writer who exercised profound influence on the Banaras school of Hindu law. Author of the huge digest, entitled *Vīramitrodaya* and of a commentary of the same name on the *Yājñavalkya-smṛti*. Son of Paraśurāmapaṇḍita and grandson of Haṃsapaṇḍita, Mitra-Miśra states that he wrote his great digest at the behest of Vīrasiṃha, King of Orccha (1605–27 A.D.).

MUKULA : A Kashmirian writer on poetics. Author of the *Abhidhāvṛtti-mātṛkā*, a grammatico-rhetorical treatise. From his work we learn that his father was Bhaṭṭa Kallaṭa who lived, according to Kalhaṇa, in the reign of Avantivarman of Kashmir (855-884 A.D.). He had Pratihārendurāja as his pupil.

MURĀRI : Author of the Rāma-drama entitled *Anargharāghava*. From the Prologue we learn that he was son of Vardhamāṅka of Maudgalya Gotra and Tantumatī. Supposed to have flourished at the end of the ninth century or beginning of the tenth.

[See L. Sternbach, *Verses Attributed to Murāri*, Lucknow, 1978.]

MURĀRIGUPTA : A Bengali contemporary, fellow-student and associate of Caitanya (q.v.), he wrote a biography of Caitanya, called *Śrīkṛṣṇacaitanya-caritāmṛta* or *Caitanyacaritāmṛta*.

[For life and works, see S. K. De, *Early History of the Vaiṣṇava Faith and Movement in Bengal*, Calcutta, 1961.]

NĀGĀRJUNA : The Buddhist philosopher of this name, who probably flourished in the latter part of the 2nd century A.D., was author of the *Mādhyamika-kārikās*. Acc. to his biography, translated into Chinese by Kumārajīva (c. 405 A.D.), he was a Brahmin born in south India and was versed in various branches of knowledge including the Vedas. He is stated to have embraced Buddhism and propagated it. He is described also as a great magician and as one well-versed in astronomy, medicine etc. Nāgārjuna was the founder of the Mādhyamika school of Mahāyāna. The identity of a Nāgārjuna, author of the *Yogasāra* and the *Yoga-śataka*, has not yet been established. A *Catuḥstava* (collection of four hymns) is attributed to him. A Nāgārjunā wrote the *Rati-śāstra*.

Nāgārjuna, author of the *Rasa-ratnākara*, is assigned, not on absolutely convincing grounds, to the 7th or 8th century. A Nāgārjuna is credited with the redaction of the *Suśrutasaṃhitā* which is available at present. *A Ratiramaṇa* of one Siddha Nāgārjuna is available.

Alberuni, in his travel account of India (1031 A.D.) speaks of a Nāgārjuna, a native of fort Daihak near Somnath in modern Gujarat, who lived nearly a century before him.

A *Ratnāvalī* also is attributed to Nāgārjuna, the noted Buddhist philosopher. To a Nāgārjuna is ascribed the *Suhṛl-lekha* purporting to be instruction to a king about the Buddhist doctrine.

[See P. Cordier, *Nāgārjuna et l' Uttaratantra de la Suśruta-saṃhitā*, Antananarivo, 1896 : J. Filliozat, Nāgārjuna et Agastya etc. in *Actes du XX Congres inter. des Orientalistes*, 1938, Brussels, 1940; G. Tucci, Di une leggendaria biografia cinese di Nāgārjuna, Roma, "Bilychnis", 1923, S.C. Sarkar, A Tibetan account of Nāgārjuna, *Gandhi Memo. Vol.* (*Sino-Indian Jour.*, I), Santiniketana 1947-48.

M. Walleser, The life of Nāgārjuna from Tibetan and Chinese sources, *Birth Anniversary Vol.*, London, 1920; K. Venkataraman, *Nāgārjuna's Philosophy* etc. Varanasi, 1971; S. Rimpoche and C. Mani, *Mādhyamika Dialectic and the Philosophy of Nāgārjuna*, Sarnath, Varanasi, 1977; K. S. Murty, *Nāgārjuna*, New Delhi, 1978; also see H.V. Fatone, *Philosophy of Nāgārjuna*, 1981; K.D. Prithipaul. *Philosophy of Nāgārjuna*; S. Ichimura, *Nāgārjuna's Philosophy of Śūnyatā and his dialect.* R.C. Jha, *Vedāntic and Buddhist concept of Reality as interpreted by Śaṅkara and Nāgārjuna*, Calcutta, 1973; H.N. Chatterji, *The Philosophy of Nāgārjuna as contained in the Ratnāvalī*, Pt. I, Calcutta, 1977; *The Dialectical Method of Nāgārjuna* trs. by K. Bhattacharya, Text ed. by E.H. Johnston & A Kunst, Delhi, 1978. See L. Jamspal, and others, Trs. of *Nāgārjuna's letter to king Gautamīputra*, with notes based on Tibetan commentaries, Delhi, 1983.]

NĀGEŚA BHAṬṬA : Also called Nāgoji. A Mahārāṣṭra Dīkṣita, son of Śivabhaṭṭa and Satī, a resident of Banaras and a protégé of Rāmasiṃha (18th century A.D.), a local prince of Śṛṅgaverapura (=modern Singarour), a few miles north of Allahabad. A prolific writer, he wrote several works on Dharma, Yoga, Alaṃkāra, and about a dozen works on Vyākaraṇa besides commentaries on the *Vālmīki-rāmāyaṇa*, *Adhyātma-rāmāyaṇa*, *Saptaśatī*, *Gīta-govinda*, *Sudhā-laharī* and other works. The most noteworthy of his grammatical works is the *Uddyota* comm. on Kaiyyaṭa's *Mahābhāṣya-pradīpa.* His other works on grammar are:—(1) *Paribhāṣenduśekhara*, a collection of *Paribhāṣās* handed down in connection with Pāṇini's grammar and followed by a concise comment called *Śabdenduśekhara*, (2) a comm. on the *Siddhānta-kaumudī*, (3) *Śabdaratna*, a comm. on the *Prauḍha-manoramā*, (4) *Viṣamī*, a comm. on Bhaṭṭoji's *Śabda-kaustubha*, (5) *Vaiyākaraṇa-siddhāntamañjūṣā* on the philosophy of grammar.

NĀGOJI : Same as Nāgeśa (q.v.)

NAKULA : The supposed author of the *Aśva-śāstra*, a treatise on horse-lore, the diseases of horses and their treatment.

NAMISĀDHU : Also known as Nami-paṇḍita, he was a Jaina and is well-known as a commentator on Rudraṭa's work on poetics. He flourished in the 11th century.

NANDAPAṆḌITA : Also named Vināyaka Paṇḍita, he was son of Rāmapaṇḍita of Banaras, who was styled Dharmādhikārin. Appears to have written 13 works most of which are either Smṛti digests or commentaries on well-known Smṛti works. Of his works, the most famous is the *Dattaka-mīmāṃsā*. Probably flourished in the period between the close of the 16th century and the close of the 17th.

NANDIKEŚVARA : Supposed author of the *Abhinaya-darpaṇa* (q.v.).

NĀRADA : An authoritative writer on Smṛti, who is supposed to have flourished between 100 and 300 A.D. His work on Vyavahāra exists in two versions, one longer and the other shorter. Date uncertain. Appears to have been later than Yājñavalkya. To a Nārada is ascribed also the works on music called *Saṅgītamakaranda*, *Nāradaśikṣā*, *Pañcamasārasaṃhitā* and *Rāganirūpaṇa*.

NĀRĀYAṆA : Author of the *Hitopodeśa*. His patron was one Dhavalacandra. He is believed to have flourished some time in the period between 900 and 1373 A.D.

Acc. to some the *Mātaṅga-līlā* (q.v.) is by a Nārāyaṇa.

A Nārāyaṇa of the 17th century composed the *Svāhāsudhākara-campū*. To one Nārāyaṇa is ascribed the work on prosody, called *Vṛttaratnākara* (1545 A.D.), which is to be distinguished from Kedāra Bhaṭṭa's work of the same name. A Nārāyaṇa Paṇḍita appears to have written the *Navaratna-parīkṣā*.

NĀRĀYAṆABHAṬṬA : Joint author of the well-known work entitled *Mānameyodaya* (c. 1600 A.D.), an introdution to Mīmāṃsā philosophy.

NARENDRA : Probably author of the Sārasvata grammar.

NĪLAKAṆṬHA BHAṬṬA : Author of the well-known Smṛti digests called *Vyavahāra-mayūkha*, *Saṃskāra-mayūkha*, *Prāyaścitta-mayūkha* and *Pratiṣṭhā-mayūkha*. One of the foremost digest-writers, he was grandson of Nārāyaṇabhaṭṭa and appears to have flourished in the 17th century A.D.

One Nīlakaṇṭha was the author of the *Mātaṅgalīlā*, a work on elephant-lore. Gaṇapati Śāstri thinks that he was a native of Kerala or of some place near about.

To a Nīlakaṇṭha is ascribed the astronomical work called *Tājika*.

A Nilakaṇṭha is author of one of the latest commentaries on the *Mahābhārata*.

NĪLAKAṆṬHA DĪKṢITA : A noted grammarian of the 17th century A.D. and author of the *Paribhāṣā-vṛtti*. Several other works, including hymns and satires, are also attributed to him.

[See P. Filliozat, *Oeuvres Poetiques De Nīlakaṇṭha Dikṣita*, Text, trs. and notes, Pondicherry, 1967.]

NIMBĀRKA : A famous philosopher, reputed to be a pupil of Rāmānuja (q.v.), he wrote a *Vedāntapārijātasaurabha* and a *Siddhānta-ratna*. He wrote also ten philosophical verses called *Daśaślokī*. He was a Telugu Brahmin of the Vaiṣṇava faith, and flourished about the eleventh century. His doctrine is called Dvaitādvaita or dualistic non-dualism. Acc. to him, *Jīva* is the enjoyer (*bhoktṛ*), the world is the enjoyed (*bhogya*) and Īśvara or God is the supreme controller (*niyantṛ*).

[See U. Mishra; *Nimbārka School of Vedānta*, 2nd. ed., Allahabad, 1966; J. N. Sinha, *The Philosophy of Nimbārka*, Calcutta; M.M. Agrawala, *Philosophy of Nimbārka*, Mathura, 1979].

NĪTIVARMAN : Author of the *Kīcaka-vadha*. He flourished earlier than the 11th century in some eastern province.

NITYANĀTHA : Author of the Ayurvedic work *Rasaratnahāra*. He flourished in the 13th century. The work *Rasaratna-samuccaya* is also sometimes ascribed to him.

OḌAYADEVA : Author of the *Gadya-cintāmaṇi*. He was a Digambara Jaina and a pupil of Puṣpasena.

PADMAGUPTA : Also known as Parimala. Author of the historical poem entitled *Navasāhasāṅkacarita*, composed probably in 1005 A.D. in honour of the poet's patron, the Paramāra Sindurāja of Dhārā, called, Navasāhasāṅka. Author was son of Mṛgāṅkadatta.

[Reference : Bühler and Zachariae in *Sitzungsberichte d. Wiener Akademie*, pp. 583 ff.]

PADMANĀBHADATTA : A native of Mithilā, acc. to some, of Bengal, acc. to others. Author of the *Supadmavyākaraṇa* (1375 A.D.) which was very popular in East Bengal. Son of Dāmodaradatta and grandson of Śrīdatta, he is to be distinguished from another author of this name, son of Gaṇeśvara and grandson of Śrīpati, who wrote for the school the *Pṛṣodarādivṛtti*. The author of the *Supadma* states, in the Paribhāṣā section of that grammar, that he also wrote the *Chandoratna* (on metrics), the *Bhūri-prayoga* (on lexicography) and the *Ācāra-candrikā* (on Smṛti).

PADMAPĀDA : A pupil of Śaṃkarācārya (8th-9th century), he wrote the *Pañcapādikā*, an exposition of Śaṃkara's system of philosophy.

PAIṬHĪNASI : Appears to have been an ancient writer of Dharmasūtra. Date unknown.

PAKṢADHARA MIŚRA : Real name Jayadeva. An outstanding writer on neo-logic in the post-Gaṅgeśa period in Mithilā. Probably flourished in the 15th century A.D. His famous work is the *Āloka*, a comm. on Gaṅgeśa's *Tattva-cintāmaṇi*. His other works are the *Dravyaviveka*, a comm. on the *Dravya-prakāśa of* Vardhamāna, the *Līlāvati-viveka*, a scholium of the *Nyāyalīlāvatī* of Śrīvallabhācārya, the *Tippaṇī* on the *Tattva-cintāmaṇi* and the *Śaśadharavyākhyā*. His Smṛti work is called *Tithicandrikā*. The drama, *Prasanna-rāghava*, is ascribed by some to him.

PĀLAKĀPYA : Name of a sage to whom tradition attributes the *Hastyāyurveda*, an authoritative treatise on the diseases of elephants and their treatment including surgery. Date unknown.

PAÑCAŚIKHA : An authority on the Sāṃkhya philosophy. His views are preserved, and he is supposed to have flourished some time between 100 and 300 A.D.

PĀṆINI : Author of the celebrated grammar called *Aṣṭādhyāyī*. Two Kāvyas called *Pātāla-vijaya* and *Jāmbavatīvijaya* are traditionally attributed to Pāṇini. To a Pāṇini some verses are attributed in the anthologies. The date of Pāṇini, the grammarian, who may or may not be identical with Pāṇini the poet, is controversial. He is, however, generally placed in the 4th century B.C. Acc. to some, he flourished in the 6th or 7th cent. B.C., if not earlier. In later literature, Pāṇini is referred to as Śālāturīya, an inhabitant of Śālātura, identified with the present Lahaur in the Yusufzai Valley. Patañjali, author of the *Mahābhāṣya*, calls him Dākṣī-putra; thus Dākṣī appears to have been mother of Pāṇini. In his grammar Pāṇini has mentioned many earlier grammarians, e.g. Āpiśali, Śākalya, Senaka, Sphoṭāyana etc.

[For references, see under *Aṣṭādhyāyī*. See Mahavir, *Pāṇini as grammarian*, Delhi, 1978; A.C. Sarangi : *Development of Sanskrit from Pāṇini to Patañjali*; G. Cardona : *Pāṇini, a survey of research*; P.B. Junankar, *Intro. to Pāṇini*, Baroda, 1977.]

PARĀŚARA : One of the twenty traditional writers of original Smṛti. Author of the *Parāśara-smṛti*, he is to be distinguished from Parāśara, author of the *Jāti-viveka* and Parāśara, referred to as an author on politics. Date unknown, but earlier than Yājñavalkya who mentions him (I.4). The *Bṛhat-parāśara* appears to be a later recast of the *Parāśara-smṛti*. A Vṛddha-parāśara is known from references by later writers.

PARIMALA : Same as Padmagupta (q.v.).

PĀRŚVADEVA : Author of the *Saṃgīta-samayasāra*, a work on music. Perhaps flourished in the thirteenth century and was a contemporary of Śārṅgadeva.

PĀRTHASĀRATHI : A famous Mīmāṃsā writer who wrote four books, viz. *Nyāyaratnamālā*, *Tantraratna*, *Nyāyaratnākara* and *Śāstradīpikā*. He flourished in the thirteenth-fourteenth century.

PATAÑJALI : Author of the *Mahābhāṣya*, the Great Commentary on the *Aṣṭādhyāyī*. One of the three sages responsible for the *Aṣṭādhyāyī*, the other two having been Pāṇini himself and Kātyāyana. He appears to have been a contemporary of the Śuṅga King Puṣyamitra who highly honoured him for his learning. He is regarded by some as identical with Patañjali, author of the *Yoga-sūtra*. The date of Patañjali is controversial. He is, however, generally assigned to the second century B.C. Patañjali, the grammarian, is believed by some to have been a Kashmirian. The epithets Gonardīya and Goṇikāputra, mentioned in the *Mahābhāṣya*, are supposed by some to refer to Patañjali himself. Thus his mother appears to have been named Goṇikā and Gonarda seems to be his native place.

[See L. Renou, on the identity of the two Patañjalis, *La Vallée Poussin Memo. Vol.*, Calcutta, 1940; H. Aranya, *Yaga Philosophy of Patañjali.*]

PIṄGALA : Author of the *Chandassūtra*. Sometimes identified with Patañjali (c. 2nd century B.C.). Earlier than chapters XIV and XV of the *Nāṭya-śāstra* of Bharata and the section of the *Agni-purāṇa* dealing with Prosody. Piṅgala's name occurs in the *Mahābhāṣya*.

PRABHĀKARA : Nicknamed Guru, he was a famous philosopher and founder of the Prabhākara school of Mīmāṃsā philosophy. Author of the *Bṛhatī*. Probably flourished in the 6th-7th century A.D.

[See G. Jha, *Prabhākara School of Pūrvamīmāṃsā*, 1911.]

PRĀJYABHAṬṬA : One of the continuators of the *Rājataraṅgiṇī*. He was a Kashmirian and wrote the *Rājāvalīpatākā* (q.v.) jointly with Śuka.

PRAKĀŚĀTMAN : Author of the *Pañcapādikā-vivaraṇa*, a commentary on Padmapāda's *Pañcapādikā*. Flourished probably in the 13th century A.D.

PRAŚASTAPĀDA : Author of the *Padārthadharma-saṃgraha*, an exposition of the *Vaiśeṣika-sūtra*. Generally assigned to the fifth century A.D.

[See G. Chemparathy, Praśastapāda and his other names, *Indo-Iranian Jour.*, Hague, XII, No. 4, 1970.]

PRATĀPARUDRADEVA : A king of the Gajapati Dynasty that ruled at Cuttack in Orissa. Pratāparudradeva reigned from 1497 to 1539 A.D. Author of the famous Smṛti work entitled *Sarasvatī-vilāsa*. His other Smṛti works are *Pratāpa-mārtaṇḍa* or *Prauḍhapratāpamārtaṇḍa* and *Nirṇayasaṃgraha*. His *Kautuka-cintāmaṇi* is a work on erotics and magician's tricks etc.

PRATIHĀRENDURĀJA : A native of Koṅkana and a pupil of Mukula. Assigned roughly to the first half of the 10th century. Identified by some with Bhaṭṭendurāja. Author of the *Laghu-vṛtti*, a commentary on the rhetorical work of Udbhaṭa.

PṚTHUYAŚAS : Son of Varāhamihira (q.v.) and author of the *Horā-sāra* (q.v.).

PŪJYAPĀDA : See Devanandin.

PŪRṆABHADRA : Author of a version (1199 A.D.) of the *Pañcatantra*.

PŪRṆAPRAJÑA : See Madhva.

PURUṢOTTAMADEVA : Probably a Bengali scholar at the court of king Lakṣmaṇasena of Bengal in the 12th century A.D., he is the author of the *Bhāṣā-vṛtti* commentary on the *Aṣṭādhyāyī*. A Puruṣottama, who may or may not have been identical with the author of the *Bhāṣā-vṛtti*, wrote the lexicons called *Hārāvalī*, *Trikāṇḍaśeṣa*, *Varṇadeśanā* and *Dvirūpa-kośa*. To one Puruṣottama, whose identity is not known, are attributed the grammatical works *Gaṇa-vṛtti*, *Paribhāṣā-vṛtti* and *Jñāpaka-samuccaya*, the anthology called *Subhāṣitamuktāvalī*, the Stotra entitled *Viṣṇu-bhakti-kalpalatā* and the lexicon *Ekākṣara-kośa*. The *Prāṇapaṇā*, a comm. on the *Mahābhāṣya*, is attributed to Puruṣottama.

RĀGHAVABHAṬṬA : Son of Pṛthvīdharabhaṭṭa, and author of the *Arthadyotanikā*, a well known commentary on the *Abhijñāna-śākuntala*, of Kālidāsa, and of a commentary on the well known Tantra, *Śāradātilaka*. Flourished in the 15th century A.D.

RAGHUNANDANA : The foremost writer of Smṛt digests in Bengal. Born at Navadvīpa, he was son of Harihara Bhaṭṭācārya and pupil of Śrīnātha Ācāryacūḍāmaṇi. Appears to have flourished some time between 1500 and 1600 A.D. Author of twenty-eight Smṛti digests whose titles end in the word 'tattva' and which are mentioned in the beginning of his work called *Malamāsa-tattva*. Besides the above works, he wrote also the following :—

(i) *Tīrtha-yātrā-tattva* or *Tīrtha-tattva*,
(ii) *Dvādaśa-yātrā-tattva* or *Yātrā-tattva*,
(iii) *Gayā-śrāddha-paddhati*,
(iv) *Rāsa-yātrā-paddhati*,
(v) *Tripuṣkara-śānti-tattva*,
(vi) *Graha-yāga-tattva* (or *-pramāṇa-tattva*),
(vii) *Dāyabhāga-ṭikā*.

[For his life, works and postion among the writers of Smṛti digests, see Bani Chakravarti *Samāj-saṃskārak Raghunandana* in Bengali, Calcutta, 1964.]

RAGHUNĀTHADĀSA : One of the six Gosvāmıns of Vṛndāvana, reputed for their scholarship and devotion in the Bengal school of Vaiṣṇavism. Son of Govardhana, a Kāyastha of village Saptagrāma in Hughly district of West Bengal. Attracted to Vaiṣṇavism after his meeting with Caitanya. His works are the *Dānakeli-cintāmaṇi*, a poetical composition, the *Muktācarita*, a Campū-kāvya, and a number of lyrics which are either devotional or didactic.

[For life and works, see S.K.De. :*Early History of the Vaiṣṇava Faith and Movement in Bengal*, Calcutta, 1961.]

RAGHUNĀTHA ŚIROMAṆI : The foremost among the writers of the Bengal school of Navya-Nyāya. Appears to have flourished some time between the middle of the 15th century and middle of the 16th. His works are : *Tattvacintāmaṇi-dīdhiti* (one part each on Pratyakṣa, Anumāna and Śabda), *Kiraṇāvalī-prakāśa-dīdhiti* (one part each on Dravya and Guṇa), *Padārtha-khaṇḍana*, *Ātma-tattva-vivekadīdhiti*, *Ākhyāta-vāda*, *Nañvāda*, *Nyāyalīlāvatī-prakāśa-dīdhiti* and *Malimluca-viveka*.

Some other works are attributed to him by some scholars, but there is no definite evidence of his authorship of those works.

[For life and works of Raghunātha, see D.C. Bhattacarya, *Vāṅgālīr Sārasvata Avadāna*, Vol. I.]

RĀJAŚEKHARA : Author of the Prākrit drama *Karpūra-mañjarī*, the Sanskrit dramas *Bāla-rāmāyaṇa*, *Viddha-śālabhañjikā* and the *Kāvya-mīmāṃsā*, a work dealing with miscellaneous matters relating to poets and poetry. In the *Bāla-rāmāyaṇa* he refers to his six earlier works. In the *Kāvyamīmāṃsā* he refers to his work called *Bhuvana-kośa*. He probably flourished in the period covering the last quarter of the 9th century and the first quarter of the 10th.

[See B. Prakash, New Light on the Life and Work of Rājaśekhara *Jour. of G. Jha Res. Inst.*, Allahabad, XXV, Pts. 1-4, 1969; L.Sternbach, *Rājaśekhara and his unknown verses*. A work entitled *Studies on the dramas of Rājaśekhara* by M. Mitra, is being printed; it will be published from Govt. Sanskrit College Calcutta.]

A Rājaśekhara Sūri of the 14th century wrote the Jaina work called *Prabandha-kośa* (q.v.).

The *Antarakathā-saṃgraha* of Rājaśekhara is a collection of narratives. It contains a version of the judgement of Solomon.

RĀMA AMĀTYA : Author of the *Svaramelakalānidhi*, a work on music, written about 1550 A.D. He was son of Timmāmātya of the family of Todarmal. He flourished in the court of Aliya Rāmarāja (died 1565 A.D.) of Vijaynagar, and was the daughter's son of Catura Kallinātha (q.v.).

RĀMACANDRA : Author of the *Prakriyā-kaumudī* (q.v.), he was son of Kṛṣṇācārya, and probably flourished in the first half of the fifteenth century. He wrote original works also on Vedānta and Astronomy, and was probably a resident of Andhra. Another person of the same name was joint author of the *Nāṭya-darpaṇa* (q.v.). This Rāmacandra is credited with the authorship also of the dramas, *Nirbhaya-bhīma-vyāyoga* and *Raghu-vilāsa-nāṭaka*. He is sometimes described as *Prabandhaśata-kartā*; *Prabandha-śata* is supposed by some to be the title of a work of his. A pupil of Jaina Hemacandra, he perhaps flourished between 1100 and

1175 A.D. To a Rāmacandra is ascribed the medical work called *Rasendra-cintāmaṇi.*

A grammarian, Rāmacandra, wrote a small grammatical work called *Vidagdhabodha.* One Rāmacandra, a pupil of Nāgeśa, wrote a commentary, called *Vṛtti-saṃgraha*, on the *Aṣṭādhyāyī.* Another Rāmacandra was the author of the *Jyotsnā* commentary on the *Vājasaneyi prātiśākhya.*

Rāmacandra Kavibhāratī of Bengal migrated to Ceylon where he enjoyed the patronage of king Parākramabāhu (1225-60 A.D.). Besides the *Bhaktiśataka*, he wrote the *Vṛttaratnākara-pañjikā* commentary on Kedārabhaṭṭa's *Vṛtta-ratnākara.*

[For Rāmacandra, the *Prabandhaśata-kartā*, see K.N. Sharma, *Summaries of Papers*, AIOC, 1974].

RĀMĀNUJA : A famous philosopher who founded the Viśiṣṭādvaita (qualified monism) school of Vedānta philosophy. Son of Keśava and Kāntimatī, he was born in Sriperumbudur in 1017 A.D., studied at first under Yādavaprakāśa and then under Yāmunācārya whom he succeeded as head of a Vaiṣṇava sect. He became a *Saṃnyāsin* and died about 1137 A.D. Author of the *Śrībhāṣya* on the *Brahma-sūtra*. Among other works, he wrote a *Gītā-bhāṣya*, *Vedārtha-saṃgraha*, *Vedānta dīpa.*

[See K.D. Bharadwaj, *Philosophy of Rāmānuja*, Delhi, 1958; F.K. Lazarus, *Rāmānuja and Bowne*; A.S. Gupta, *A Critical Study of the Philosophy of Rāmānuja*, Banaras, 1967; S.R. Bhatt, *Studies in Rāmānuja Vedānta*, 1975; R.C. Lester, *Rāmānuja on the Yoga*, Madras, 1976; J.N. Sinha, *Philosophy of Rāmānuja*; P.B. Vidyarthi, *Divine Personality and Human Life in Rāmānuja*, New Delhi, 1978; P.B. Vidyarthi, *Śrī Rāmānuja, Philosophy and Religion*, Madras, 1977; R. Balasubramanian, *Some Problems in the Epistemology and Metaphysics of Rāmānuja*; J.J. Lipner, *The Thought of Rāmānuja*; L. Reimer, *Rāmānuja's Doctrine of Grace*: this is reported to have been submitted to Uni. of Manitoba, 1979; J.B. Carman, *Theology of Rāmānujā*, New Haven and London, 1974.]

RĀMATOṢAṆA VIDYĀLAṂKĀRA : Author of the *Prāṇatoṣiṇī* (q.v.). Flourished in the period between the later half of the nineteenth century and earlier half of the twentieth.

RATNĀKARA : Author of the Mahākāvya called *Hara-vijaya.* Son of Amṛtabhānu, he flourished under Cippaṭa Jayāpīḍa (832-44 A.D.) and Avantivarman (855-84 A.D.) of Kashmir. He wrote also the *Vakrokti-pañcāśikā.*

RATNAKĪRTI : A noted Buddhist logician who flourished in the 10th-11th cent A.D. Of his several tracts on logic, the *Apoha-siddhi* and *Kṣaṇabhaṅga-siddhi* are well-known. His other works, discovered so far, are *Sarvajña-siddhi, Īśvara-sādhana-dūṣaṇa, Pramāṇāntarbhāva-prakaraṇa. Vyāpti-nirṇaya, Sthira-siddhidūṣaṇa. Citrādvaita-prakāśa-vāda* and *Santānāntara-dūṣaṇa.* Pupil of Jñānaśrī and a senior contemporary of Atīśa Dīpaṃkara, he was a profound scholar at the University of Vikramaśīla. There appears to have been another author of this name who, patronized by King Vimalacandra, lived about 650 A.D.

[See Intro. to Tibetan Sanskrit Works Series, Vol. III. *Ratnakīrti-nibandhāvalī,* Patna, 1957; A.L. Thakur, *Ratnakīrtinibandhāvali,* Patna 1975].

RĀYAMUKUṬA : Bṛhaspati Rāyamukuṭa, a well-known scholar at the time of Jalal Uddin, son of king Gaṇeśa of Bengal, probably wrote his works in the first half of the 15th century. Mentioned in different Smṛti works of Raghunandana. Author of the Smṛti works called *Smṛti-ratna-hāra* and *Rāyamukuṭa-paddhati.* He wrote also the *Pada-candrikā* commentary on the lexicon *Nāmaliṅgānuśāsana.* Besides, he commented on the *Raghuvaṃśa,* the *Śiśupāla-vadha* etc.

[Ref: R.C. Hazra in *IHQ*, XVII, 1941. pp. 442-471]

RUCAKA : Another name of Ruyyaka (q.v.).

RUDRACANDRADEVA : See Rudradeva.

RUDRADĀMAN : See Girnar Inscription.

RUDRADEVA : Also called Candradeva or Rudracandradeva, he was author of the *Śyainika-śāstra,* a work on hunting and fowling. He is stated to have been a king of Kumaon or Kūrmācala.

RUDRADHARA : Two writers of this name flourished in Mithilā. Rudradhara I was son of Lakṣmīdhara (not the author of the *Kṛtyakalpataru*) and younger brother of Haladhara, and perhaps lived in the earlier half of the 15th century A.D. His works are *Śrāddha-viveka*, *Śuddhi-viveka*, *Varṣakṛtya* and *Vratapaddhati*.

Rudradhara II, pupil of Caṇḍeśvara who may or may not have been identical with Caṇḍeśvara Mantrin, probably flourished in the 16th century A.D. His works are *Śrāddha-candrikā*, *Kṛtya-candrikā* and *Vivāda-candrikā*.

RUDRAṬA : Author of the *Kāvyālaṃkāra*, a treatise on poetics. Also called Śatānanda, he appears from his own work to have been son of Bhaṭṭa Vāmukha. His identity with Rudrabhaṭṭa, though advocated by some, is doubted by others. Probably flourished in the period between the first quarter of the 9th century and its end. He bears a Kashmirian name.

RŪPA GOSVĀMIN : A great figure in the history of Bengal Vaiṣṇavism. Born in a Brahmin family that originally hailed from south India and settled in Bengal, Rūpa was son of Kumāra and a resident of the village called Rāmakeli. The contemporary Muslim ruler of Bengal, under whom he served, conferred on him the title of Davir Khās. Direct association of Caitanya (1486—1533) and the impact of his preachings made Rūpa a devout Vaiṣṇava, and he was respected as one of the six Gosvāmins of Vṛndāvana. Rūpa wrote several works. His two works on the Vaiṣṇava Rasa-śāstra are the *Ujjvala-nīlamaṇi* and the *Bhakti-rasāmṛta-sindhu*. His *Saṃkṣepa-bhāgavatāmṛta* deals with Vaiṣṇava theology and philosophy. His dramatic works are the *Dānakeli-kaumudī*, the *Vidagdha-mādhava* and the *Lalita-mādhava*. The *Haṃsa-dūta* and the *Uddhavasandeśa* are two poetical compositions by Rūpa. He composed also some hymns and songs, and compiled the anthology entitled *Padyāvalī*.

[Ref: S.K. De, *Early History of the Vaiṣṇava Faith and Movement in Bengal*, Calcutta 1961; Intro. to the ed. of the *Padyāvalī*, Dacca, 1934.]

RUPPAKA : Another name of Ruyyaka (q.v.).

RUYYAKA : A Kashmirian writer of works on Alaṃkāra-śāstra. Author of the *Alaṃkāra-sarvasva*, besides the *Saṃketa* commentary on Mammaṭa's *Kāvya-prakāśa*. Probably flourished in the 12th century. Maṅkhaka, author of the *Śrīkaṇṭha-carita*, appears to have been a pupil of Ruyyaka. Another work of Ruyyaka is the *Sahṛdayalīlā*. The following works of Ruyyaka are referred to either by himself or by other writers:—

Alaṃkāra-mañjarī, *Sāhitya-mīmāṃsā*, *Alaṃkārānusāriṇī*, *Nāṭaka-mīmāṃsā*, *Harṣa-carita-vārtika*, *Alaṃkāra-vārtika*, *Śrīkaṇṭha-stava* and a commentary on Mahimabhaṭṭa's *Vyakti-viveka*.

ŚABARASVĀMIN : Renowned commentator on the *Mīmāṃsā-sūtra*. Supposed to have flourished sometime between 100 and 300 A.D.

[See G. V. Devasthali, positive data for the date of Śabara-svamin, G. Jha Res. Inst., Allahabad.]

To a comparatively modern scholar of this name is attributed the grammatical work called *Liṅgānuśāsana*.

SADĀNANDA : Author of the *Vedānta-sāra*. Appears to have flourished in the 15th-16th century.

A *Śaṃkara-digvijaya-sāra* is attributed to Sadānanda.

SADYOJYOTI : Probably a Kashmirian who appears to have flourished prior to the 8th century A.D. Author of the *Nareśvaraparīkṣā*, *Bhoga-kārikās*, *Paramokṣa-kārikās*, commentaries on the *Rudra-tantra* and *Svāyambhuva-tantra*, epitomes of these Tantras, called *Tattva-saṃgraha* and *Tattva-traya*.

SĀGARANANDIN : Author of the works entitled *Nāṭaka-lakṣaṇa-ratna-koṣa*. Date uncertain. Author appears to have flourished some time between the first quarter of the 10th century and the end of the 13th.

SĀHIB KAULA : Son of Kṛṣṇa Kaula and Buddhi, he appears to have been a Kashmirian Śaiva. He wrote a number of philosophical and devotional works. Of the works of the latter class, the most noteworthy is the *Devīnāma-vilāsa*.

[For a list of his works, see S. C. Banerjee, *Cultural Heritage of Kashmir*, p. 98.]

SAHṚDAYA : See Dhvanikāra.

ŚĀKALYA : Name of an ancient grammarian and Vedic scholar who is believed to have revised the Vedic texts and written their Padapāṭhas. Referred to in the *Aṣṭādhyāyī* (e.g. viii. 3. 19).

ŚĀKAPUṆI : An ancient writer of *Nirukta*; quoted by Yāska.

ŚAKTIBHADRA : Author of the play *Āścarya-cūḍāmaṇi*. It is claimed by some that the *Abhiṣeka* and the *Pratimānāṭaka*, generally attributed to Bhāsa, were written by Śaktibhadra. The *Pratijñā-yaugandharāyaṇa*, supposed by some scholars to be a work of Bhāsa, is believed by others to have been written by Śaktibhadra under the title *Unmāda-vāsavadattā* referred to by Śaktibhadra himself as a work of his. In the prologue to his *Āścarya-cūḍāmaṇi* Śaktibhadra refers to himself as a native of Dakṣiṇāpatha (Deccan); the play is regarded by some as the oldest South Indian drama. Śaktibhadra is assigned to the 9th century; but the date is conjectural. The *Viṇāvāsava-dattā*, which is anonymous and incomplete, is regarded by some as the lost *Unmāda-vāsavadattā* referred to above.

[See M. Winternitz, Śaktibhadra's place in the history of Sanskrit literature, *Kuppuswami Sastri Comm. Vol.*, Madras, 1937.]

ŚĀKAṬĀYANA : A Jaina writer of the ninth century A.D., who lived during the reign of the Rāṣṭrakūṭa king Amogha-varṣa. To him is attributed the grammar called *Śabdā-nuśāsana*.

Name of an ancient grammarian referred to by Pāṇini (e.g. iii.4.111, viii.4.50). He is believed by some to have been the earliest author of *Uṇādi sūtras*.

[See M. Acharya, the Uṇādi-sūtras and S. Katayana, *Summaries of Papers*, *AIOC*, 1974; S. Varma, Contributions of Śākaṭāyana to Skt. Grammar, Ibid.]

ŚĀLIHOTRA : An authority on the equestrian science including the treatment of horses. Described as son of a Brahmin sage, named Hayaghoṣa, he is said by some to have lived at Śrāvastī and by others at Salatur near Kandahar. Supposed to have lived around the eighth century B.C. To him are attributed the following works : *Haya-Āyurveda* (also called *Turaṅgama-śāstra, Śālihotrasaṃhitā, Aśvalakṣaṇa-sūtra* and *Aśva-prakāśa.*

ŚĀLIKANĀTHA : Supposed to have lived in the 7th century A.D. His epithet 'Gauḍa-mīmāṃsaka' seems to hint at his having been a Bengali. He wrote the *Ṛjuvimalā* and *Dīpa-śikhā*, commentaries respectively on the *Bṛhatī* and *Laghvī* of Prabhākara.

ŚAMBHU : Author of the *Rājendra-karṇapūra* (q.v.), a poem of panegyric of King Harṣa of Kashmir (1089-1101 A.D.). He composed also a poem called *Anyokti-muktālatā.*

ŚAṂKARĀCĀRYA : A great philosopher who founded the Advaita (non-dualistic) school of Vedānta philosophy. He belonged to the Nambudri sect of Brahmins of Malabar, and is supposed to have been born at Kaladi on the Western Coast. Quite early in life he is said to have mastered Vedic learning. He described himself as a pupil of Govinda. According to tradition, he renounced the world at an early age, became a recluse and established four Mutts or monasteries, one each at Sringeri in Mysore in the south, Puri in the east, Dvārakā in the west and Badrinath on the Himalayas. He is said to have died at Kedarnath in the Himalayas at the age of 32. Supposed to have flourished between the last quarter of the 8th century and the first quarter of the 9th. Author of a commentary (*Bhāṣya*) on the *Vedāntasūtra.* He wrote also commentaries on ten Upaniṣads, viz. *Īśa, Kena, Kaṭha, Praśna, Muṇḍaka. Māṇḍūkya, Aitareya, Taittirīya, Chāndogya* and *Bṛhadāraṇyaka.* He commented also on the *Bhagavadgītā.* Also attributed to him are the following works : *Advaitānubhūti, Āgamaśāstra-vivaraṇa, Aparokṣānubhūti, Ātma-bodha, Ātmajñānopadeśa, Ātmānatma-viveka, Ātmopadeśa-vidhi, Cidānanda-stavarāja* or *Cidānandadaśaślokī, Daśaślokī* (same as *Cidānanda-daśaślokī*), *Dṛgdṛśya-prakaraṇa, Gauḍapādīya-bhāṣya* (same as *Āgamaśāstra-vivaraṇa* above), *Hastāmalaka, Laghu-*

vākya-vṛtti, *Mantraśāstra*, *Mohamudgara*, *Pañcīkaraṇa-prakriyā*, *Prauḍhānubhūti*, *Sarvadarśanasiddhānta-saṃgraha*, *Śataślokī*, *Tattvopadeśa*, *Upadeśasāhasrī*, *Vākya-vṛtti*, *Viveka-cūḍāmaṇi*.

The poems, *Ānandalaharī* and *Saundarya-Laharī* are ascribed to Śaṃkara.

[See S.S. Roy, *Heritage of Samkara*; 2nd, rev. ed., New Delhi, 1982; N.K. Devaraja, *Intro. to Śaṃkara's Theory of Knowledge*, Varanasi, 1972; S.K.R. Rao, *Śaṃkara*; I. Sheshadri, *Śaṃkarācārya*; S.R.S. Naulakha, *Shankara's Brahmavāda*; D.R. Bhandarkar, Solecisms of Śaṃkarācārya and Kālidāsa, *IA*, XLI, 1912; M. Hiriyana, Śaṃkara and Sureśvara, *C.K. Raja Pres. Vol.*, Madras, 1941; K. Narain, *Śaṃkara School of Vedānta*; S.N.L. Srivastava, *Śaṃkara and Bradley—a critical study*, Delhi, 1968. Also see R.V. Das, *Intro. to Śaṃkara*, Calcutta, 1968; P.N. Rao, *Whitehead and Advaita Vedānta of Śaṃkara*, G. Jha Res. Inst., Allahabad; K.C. Chakravarti, *Śaṃkarācārya and God-realisation*, Calcutta, 1978; N. Venkataraman, *The Great Śaṃkarācārya and his Successors*, Madras; A Kuppuswami, *Śrī Bhagavatpāda Śaṃkarācārya* (to be pub. by Chowkhamba, Benares) ; *Minor Works of Śaṃkarācārya and Shree Śaṃkara's Works* in 12 Vols.; R.C. Jha, *Vedāntic and Buddhist Concept of Reality as interpreted by Śaṃkara and Nāgārjuna*, Calcutta, 1973; S. Sarasvati, *Ādi Śaṃkara : His life and Times*, trs. into Eng. by T.M.P. Mahadevan, Bombay, 1980; *Hymns of Śaṃkara*, Delhi; N.K. Devaraja and others, *Source-book of Śaṃkara*; R.P. Singh, *Vedānta of Śaṃkara—a metaphysics of value*, Vol. I; S.G. Mangal, *Advaita of Śaṃkara*; K.S. Murty, *Revelation and Reason in Advaita Vedānta*; R. L. Singh, *Inquiry concerning Reason in Kant and Śaṃkara*, Allahabad, 1978; A. Alston, *Śaṃkara Source-book*, Vol. I, *Śaṃkara on the Absolute*, Vol. II, *Śaṃkara on the Creation*, 1980; L.S. Betty, *Vādirāja's Refutation of Śaṃkara's Non-dualism*, 1978; G. Sundararamaiah, *Philosophical Study of the Mysticism of Śaṃkara*, Calcutta, 1982; R. M. Umesh, *Śaṃkara's Date*, Madras; *Bhujaṅga-Stotra* of Ādi Śaṃkara, Eng. trs. by V. Raghavan, 1971.

U. Shastri, *Age of Shaṅkara*, trs. L.D. Dikshit, Gaziabad, 1981.

N. Subramanian, *Śaṃkara and Modern Physics*, Calcutta, 1977. For biographical accounts of Śaṃkara in Sanskrit, see under *Śaṃkara-digvijaya* and *Śaṃkara-vijaya*]

ŚAṂKARASENA : Author of the *Nāḍī-prakāśa* (q.v.). Flourished in the sixteenth century.

ŚAṂKHA : One of the twenty traditional writers of original Smṛti. Author of a *Śaṃkha-smṛti* and a *Śaṃkhadharma-śāstra* the existence of which is vouchsafed by quotations in later works. There exists a *Śaṃkhalikhita-smṛti* which seems to be the joint work of Śaṃkha and Likhita. A *Laghu-śaṃkha-smṛti* is extant. A *Śaṃkha-likhita-dharmasūtra* is known from citations in later treatises. The Dharmasūtra of Śaṃkha is assigned by P. V. Kane to the conjectural period between 300 B.C. and 100 A.D. According to the *Mahābhārata*, (Śānti, chap. 23), Śaṃkha and Likhita were brothers.

ŚAṂKHADHARA : Surnamed Kavirāja. Author of the farcical play *Laṭakamelaka*. He wrote under king Govindacandra of Kanauj in the earlier part of the 12th century A.D.

SAṂVARTA: One of the twenty traditional writers of original Smṛti. No work of Saṃvarta has survived, and his date is unknown.

SANĀTANA GOSVĀMIN: Brother of Rūpa Gosvāmin (q.v.). He was a high official at the court of the contemporary Muhammadan ruler, and was called Sāker Mālik. He came under the direct influence of Caitanya, and became one of the venerable Gosvāmins of Vṛndāvana. His celebrated work is the *Bṛhad-bhāgavatāmṛta*. It is supposed by some that Sanātana actually composed the well-known *Haribhakti-vilāsa*, and fathered it on Gopāla Bhaṭṭa.
[Ref : S.K. De, *Early History of Vaiṣṇava Faith and Movement in Bengal*, Calcutta, 1961.]

SANDHYĀKARANANDIN : Author of the historical poem entitled *Rāma-carita*. An inhabitant of Puṇḍravardhana in north Bengal, he completed the poem in the eleventh century during the reign of Madanapāla of Bengal.

ŚAṄKUKA : Famous for his interpretation of the renowned

Rasa-sūtra of Bharata, his interpretation being known as *Anumiti-vāda*. May be identical with Śaṅkuka, the poet, who and whose poem *Bhuvanābhyudaya* are mentioned by Kalhaṇa (iv. 703-5). Śaṅkuka is stated as having flourished at the time of king Ajitāpīḍa of Kashmir early in the 9th century A.D.

ŚĀNTIDEVA : Buddhist philosopher and poet, and author of the *Bodhicaryāvatāra*, a philosophical and didactic poem, and of the philosophical work *Śikṣā-samuccaya*. Lived in the 7th century A.D. Tradition represents him as son of a king. [See G. Tucci, "In cammino verso la luce di Sāntideva", tradotto dal sanscrito in italiano, G. B. Paravia, Toriho, 1925.]

ŚĀRADĀTANAYA : Son of Bhaṭṭa Gopāla and grandson of Kṛṣṇa, he was a native of north India. Assigned roughly to the period between 1100 and 1300 A.D. Author of the *Bhāvaprakāśa* (or, *-prakāśikā* or - *prakāśana*), a work on poetics.

ŚARAṆA : Mentioned in Jayadeva's *Gītagovinda* as a poet in the court of king Lakṣmaṇasena of Bengal towards the close of the 12th century. Author of the grammatical work entitled *Durghaṭavṛtti*.

ŚĀRṄGADEVA : Author of the most exhaustive and authoritative work on dance and music, entitled *Saṅgīta-ratnākara*. From his work we learn that his ancestors belonged to Kashmir. Son of Soḍhala and grandson of Bhāskara, Śārṅgadeva was a protégé of the Yādava king Siṅghana who ruled at Devagiri from 1210 to 1247 A.D. He appears to have been a resident of village Yajñapura, and describes himself as the Chief Accountant of the above king.

ŚĀRṄGADHARA : Compiler of the anthology called *Śārṅgadhara-paddhati*, compiled about 1363 A.D. He was son of Dāmodra. One Śārṅgadhara appears to have compiled the medical work called *Śārṅgadhara-saṃgraha*.

SARVAJÑĀTMAN : A pupil of Śaṃkarācārya and author of the *Saṃkṣepaśārīraka*.

SARVĀNANDA : Son of Ārtihara and belonging to the Vandyaghaṭīya section of Bengal Brāhmaṇas, he was author of the *Tīkā-sarvasva*, a famous commentary on Amara's lexicon. He appears to have lived in the 12th century, and must be distinguished from Sarvānanda, author of the Tāntric works like the *Sarvollāsa*.

ŚARVAVARMAN (or, SARVAVARMAN) : Appears to have been a protégé of Sātavāhana, a king of Sātavāhana Dynasty of South India (1st. century A.D.?). Author of the grammatical work called *Kātantra* (or, *Kaumāra* or *Kalāpa*). The story goes that he made the king, who was innocent of Sanskrit, proficient in that language within six months.

ŚĀŚVATA : Author of the lexicon called *Anekārtha-samuccaya*. He perhaps flourished about the time of Amarasiṃha (q.v.), author of the *Nāmaliṅgānuśāsana*.

ŚATĀNANDA : Author of the astronomical work called *Bhāsvati*, he appears to have flourished in the later half of the 11th century A.D. Appears to have been different from Śatānanda, father of Abhinanda (q.v.).

ŚĀTĀTAPA : One of the twenty traditional writers af original Smṛti. Several Smṛti works, of which the *Karmavipāka* is one, are ascribed to him. Of these, one is in mixed prose and verse. There are references to Vṛddhaśātātapa and Bṛhat-śātātapa; a *Vṛddha-śātātapa-smṛti* is ascribed to the former. Date uncertain.

SAUMILLA : Mentioned by Kālidāsa, in the prologue to his *Mālavikāgnimitra*, as a dramatist.

ŚAUNAKA : Supposed to have been a teacher of Āśvalāyana. Probably flourished in the 4th century B.C. or earlier. A recension of the *Atharvavedasaṃhitā* is ascribed to him. Also ascribed to Śaunaka are the *Ṛgveda-prātiśākhya* and *Anukramaṇis* relating to the *Ṛgveda*. Cited in the *Aṣṭādhyāyī* (IV. 3. 106).

SĀYAṆA : Author of commentaries on the Vedic Saṃhitās. He commented also on some Brāhmaṇa texts, notably the *Taittirīya*, *Aitareya* and *Śatapatha*. The Smṛti work, *Prāyaś-citta-sudhānidhi*, and the anthology called *Subhāṣitasudhānidhi* are also attributed to him. Son of Māyaṇa and Śrīmatī, and brother of Mādhava, he was a contemporary of king Bukka (14th cent.) of Vijayanagara. Sometimes identified, without sufficient evidence, with Mādhava.

[See *Caturveda-bhāṣya-bhūmikā*, ed. B. Upadhyay; L. Sarup, Mādhava, son of Śrī Veṅkaṭarāya and Sāyaṇācārya, *B.C. Law Vol. II*, Poona, 1946; V. Raghavan in *Jour. of G. J. Kendriya Sanskrit Vidyapīth*, Allahabad, XXIX. See S.D. Laddhu: Sāyaṇa's authorship of the Vedabhāṣya, Recent Studies etc., *J. Agrawal Fel. Vol.*, Delhi, 1982; S.R. Banerji, Sāyaṇācāryakṛta-ṛgveda-bhāṣyopakramaṇikā, ed. with notes in Bengali, Calcutta, 1969.]

SENAKA : An ancient grammarian referred to by Pāṇini (V.4.112).

SILHAṆA (ŚILHAṆA) : Author of the *Śānti-śataka*, he bears a typically Kashmirian name. Date uncertain, but supposed to have flourished before 1206 A.D.

SIṂHABHŪPĀLA : Identified by some with the author of the Alaṃkāra work *Rasārṇava-sudhākara*, who is variously called Śiṅgadharaṇīśa, Śiṅgarāja or Śiṅgamahīpatī or Śiṅgabhūpāla. He is supposed by some to have been king Śiṅgama Nāyaḍu of Veṅkaṭagiri who ruled around 1330 A.D. over the territory between the Vindhya hills and Śrīśaila, the hereditary capital having been Rājācalam (Rācakoṇda). We further learn than that he was son of Ananta or Anapota and Annamāmbā, grandson of Śiṅgaprabhu (or, Śiṅganāyaka) and great grandson of Yācama. Also styled as Sarvajña, he was author of the dramatic work *Kuvalayāvalī* or *Ratnapāñcālikā* and of the *Saṅgīta-sudhākara*, an authoritative commentary on the *Saṅgīta-ratnākara* of Śārṅgadeva.

ŚIVADĀSA : Author of the most noteworthy version of the *Vetālapañcaviṃśatikā*. Date and personal history unknown. The book of tales, called *Kathārṇava*, the religious poem *Bhikṣāṭana-kāvya* and the romantic tale *Śālivāhanakathā* are ascribed to Śivadāsa whose identity is not known.

ŚIVĀDITYA : Author of the *Saptapadārthī*, a popular tract on Nyāya philosophy. Appears, from references in later works, to have written also the *Hetu-khaṇḍana*, *Upādhi-vārtika*, *Arthāpattī-vārtika* and the *Lakṣaṇamālā*; the last of these works, to be distinguished from Udayana's work of the same title was probably his masterpiece. Flourished in Mithilā in the middle of the 12th cent. A.D.

ŚIVASVĀMIN : Author of the Mahākāvya entitled *Kapphiṇābhyudaya*. Son of Arkasvāmin, he was a court-poet of king Avantivarman of Kashmir (855-84 A.D.).

SOḌḌHALA : Author of the Campūkāvya entitled *Udayasundarī-kathā*. He was a Valabha Kāyastha of Lāṭa, and wrote (c. 1000 A.D.) under the patronage of king Mummuṇirāja of Koṅkan.

SOMADEVA : Son of Rāma and a Brahmin poet in the court of king Ananta of Kashmir (1029-64 A.D.), Somadeva wrote his work, called *Kathā-sarit-sāgara*, a version of the *Bṛhatkathā*, between 1063 and 1082 A.D.

One Somadeva, a protêgê of the Cāhamāna King Viśāladeva Vigraharāja of Śākambharī, wrote, in the first half of the 12th century A.D., the drama, called *Lalita-vigraha-rāja*, in honour of the king.

A Jaina writer, Somadeva, who was a Digambara Jaina and a contemporary of the Rāṣṭrakūṭa Kṛṣṇa and a protêgê of his feudatory, a son of the Cālukya king Arikesarin II, was the author of the Campū-kāvya called *Yaśastilaka*. (q.v.). To him is also ascribed the *Nīti-vākyāmṛta*, a treatise on royal duties.

To a Somadeva is ascribed the medical work called *Rasendra-cūḍāmaṇi*.

SOMĀNANDA : Author of the *Śiva-dṛṣṭi* which was the basis of the Pratyabhijñā-śāstra of Kashmir. He was pobably a pupil of Vasugupta, and flourished towards the end of the 9th century A.D.

A Somānanda of the 17th century wrote the *Rāga-vibodha* (q.v.)

SOMANĀTHA : Author of the *Rāgavibodha*, a work on Indian music, written in 1609 A.D. He was a Telugu Brahmin of the East Coast, probably of Rājamandry. Appears to have been a practical musician as well as a scholar and poet.

SOMAPRABHASŪRI : Author of the *Yaśastilaka-campū*. Flourished in the tenth century A.D.

SOMEŚVARA : A king of the Cālukya dynasty. He is credited with the authorship of the work called *Mānasollāsa* (1129 A.D.).

[For a biographical account, see *Vikramāṅkadevacarita* trs. Banerji and Gupta, Summary of cantos and historical gleanings].

He is to be distinguished from his namesake who composed the Mahākāvyas called *Kīrtikaumudī* and *Surathotsava*, the drama entitled *Ullāgharāghava*, the hymn called *Rāmaśataka*, the anthology, *Karṇāmṛta-prapā*. He appears to have lived about the middle of the 13th cent. A.D.

[See B.J. Sandesara, *Pro. of A.I. Oriental Conference*, 1951.]

SOMILA : Same as Saumilla (q.v.).

SPHOṬĀYANA : An ancient grammarian mentioned by Pāṇini (VI. 1.123). Acc. to Haradatta's *Padamañjarī* relating to the *Sūtra*, he was so named as he was the greatest exponent of the *Sphoṭa* theory.

ŚRĪDATTA : One of the earliest among the medieval Maithila writers ef Smṛti digests. Styled as Upādhyāya, he wrote several digests, viz. *Ācārādarśa*, *Śuddhi-nirṇaya*, *Samaya-pradīpa*, *Chandogāhnika*, *Pitṛbhakti* (also *Kṛtyācāra*), *Śrāddha-kalpa* and *Vratasāra* (also called *Vratapaddhati*). He is to be distinguished from *Śrīdatta*, son of Nāgeśvara Miśra and author of the *Puraścaraṇa-paddhati* and other works. Supposed to have flourished in the later half of the 13th century A.D.

ŚRĪDHARĀCĀRYA : A mathematician and author of the *Gaṇitasāra* and the *Pāṭīgaṇita-ṭīkā*. Probably flourished in the first half of the 13th century A.D.

ŚRIDHARADĀSA : Compiler of the anthology entitled *Sadukti karṇāmṛta*. He states that his father was Vaṭudāsa. The date of the work is given as 1206 A.D. King Lakṣmaṇasena of Bengal appears to have been a patron of the compiler and his father.

[Ref: *Sadukti-karṇāmṛta*, ed. S.C. Banerji (Introduction).]

ŚRĪDHARA BHAṬṬA : Author of the well-known *Nyāya-kandalī*. Son of Baladeva and Acchoka and grandson of Bṛhaspati, he was a resident of village Bhūriśreṣṭhi or Bhūriṛṣṭi (modern Bhūrsuṭ) in Daksiṇaṛāḍhā in West Bengal. Born some time in the 10th century A.D.

ŚRĪDHARASVĀMIN : Supposed to have flourished a little later than Vopadeva (q.v.) at Valabhi in Gujarat. Wrote learned commentaries on the *Viṣṇu-purāṇa*, the *Bhāgavata-purāṇa* and the *Bhagavadgītā*, the commentary on the *Bhāgavata*, called *Bhāvārtha-dīpikā*, being the most famous.

ŚRĪHARṢA : Two authors of this name are found in the history of Sanskrit literature. One is the author of the three dramas, entitled *Ratnāvalī*, *Priyadarśikā* and *Nāgānanda* and usually referred to simply as Harṣa. The other is the author of the Mahākāvya called *Nāiṣadhacarita* and the philosophical treatise named *Khaṇḍanakhaṇḍakhādya*. The author of the dramas is identified by some scholars with Harṣavardhana, king of Thāneśvara, who flourished in the first half of the seventh century A.D. The author of the poem informs us that he was son of Hīra and Māmalladevī. He probably flourished in the second half of the twelfth century A.D. during the reign of Vijayacandra and Jayacandra of Kānyakubja.

[For the works of the dramatist, see B. Bose, Dramas of Śrīharṣa, S.L. Katre. *Harṣa and His Three Dramas*. D.C. Bhattacharya's paper, Udayanācārya and Śrīharṣa (*Siddha Bhārati*, II) may by consulted. See S.K. Sharma, Historical Data in the Udayana Plays, *Summaries of Papers, AIOC*, 1974.]

ŚRĪKUMĀRA : Author of the *Śilpa-ratna* (q.v.), he was of Kerala in South India and, as he himself says (*Śilpa-ratna*, chap. I, verse 6), was a protégé of King Devanārāyaṇa who appears to have flourished in the 16th century A.D.

ŚRĪPATI : Son of Nagadeva and grandson of Bhaṭṭa Keśava, he flourished in the 11th cent. A.D. Author of the astronomical works called *Dhīkoṭi* (*Dhīkoṭikaraṇa* or *Dhīkoṭigraha-karaṇa*), *Dhruvamānasa*, *Siddhānta-śekhara* and also of the mathematical work called *Gaṇita-tilaka*.

ŚRĪṢEṆA : Supposed to be either the original author or the redactor of the astronomical treatise, called *Romaka-siddhānta*.

ŚRĪVALLABHA : A stalwart in the field of Navya-nyāya in the pre-Gaṅgeśa period. Probably a native of Mithilā, he appears to have flourished in the second quarter of the 12th cent. A.D. Besides a commentary on the fifth chapter of the *Nyāyasūtra*, he wrote the well-known *Nyāyalīlāvatī*, briefly called *Līlāvatī*. An *Īśvara-siddhi* is also attributed to him.

ŚRĪVARA : Compiler of the anthology called *Subhāṣitāvalī* and author of the romantic poem *Kathā-kautuka*. He wrote also the *Jaina-rājataraṅgiṇī*, a continuation of the *Rājataraṅgiṇī*. Pupil of the Kashmirian Jonarāja, he belonged to the second half of the 15th cent. A.D.

ŚRĪVATSA : Author of a commentary on the *Padārtha-dharma-saṃgraha* (q. v.) of Praśastapāda.

SṚṢṬIDHARA : Author of a commentary on Puruṣottamadeva's *Bhāṣāvṛtti* commentary on the *Aṣṭādhyāyī*. Flourished in the 15th cent. A.D.

SUBANDHU : Author of the celebrated prose romance called *Vāsavadattā*. Flourished before the 8th cent. A.D.

[See M. Sing : *Subandhu and Daṇḍin*, New Delhi, 1979.]

ŚUBHAṂKARA : Son of Śrīdhara and Subhadrā, he is the author of the *Saṃgīta-dāmodara*, a work on music. Supposed to have flourished in Bengal in the 15th cent. A.D.

SUDHĀKARA DVIVEDIN : Born towards the end of the 19th century, he has written several works, original and expository, on astronomy and mathematics. Of his works, the most noteworthy are the *Cala-rāśi-kalana* and *Gaṇaka-taraṅgiṇī*.

ŚŪDRAKA : Author of the celebrated drama *Mṛcchakaṭika*. From the introductory portion of the drama we learn that the author was a Brahmin king versed in various branches of learning and that he immolated himself in fire at the age of one hundred and ten years. Some think that it is really a work of Bhāsa, while others think that it was composed by a court-poet of a certain king Śūdraka with whose name it was associated as a token of gratitude. The drama is assigned by different scholars to different dates ranging from the second century B.C. to the sixth century A.D. The one-act play *Padmaprābhṛtaka* is also attributed to Śūdraka. He is supposed, by some scholars, to have been the author also of the play called *Viṇā-vāsavadattā* (q.v.).

[See C. Pandey, Śūdraka (Rājā and Kavi).]

ŚUKA : Joint author of the *Rājāvalī-patākā* (q.v.).

ŚŪLAPĀṆI : One of the great pre-Raghunandana Smṛti writers of Bengal. In his works, he describes himself as a Sāhuḍiyān which perhaps refers to a branch of Bengal Brahmins of the Rāḍhī-śreṇī. Date uncertain. Supposed to have flourished some time in the period between the 11th and the 15th century. There are several authors of this name. The genuine Smṛti digests by Śūlapāṇi, the Bengal writer, appear to be as follows:—

Ekādaśi-viveka, *Tithi-vīveka*, *Dattaka-viveka*, *Durgotsava-viveka*, *Dolayātrā-viveka*, *Prāyaścitta-viveka*, *Vrata-kāla-viveka*, *Rāsa-yātrā-viveka*. *Śrāddha-viveka*, *Saṃkrānti-viveka* and *Sambandha-viveka*. Of the other works, attributed to Śūlapāṇi, the most noteworthy is the *Dīpa-kalikā*, a commentary on the *Yājñavalkya-smṛti*. The works, attributed to a Śūlapāṇī, whose identity is uncertain, are the following:—

Anumaraṇa-viveka, *Kālā-viveka*, *Tithidvaita-prakaraṇa*, *Parṇana-radāha-viveka*, *Dattakaputra-viveka*, *Durgotsavaprayoga-viveka*, *Pratiṣṭhā-viveka*, *Vāsantī-viveka*, *Śuddhi-viveka*, *Samaya-vidhāna*, *Saṃvatsara-pradīpa*. A *Caturaṅga-dīpikā*, dealing with the game of chess, is also attributed to Śūlapāṅi.

SUMANTU : From citations in later Smṛti digests and commentaries, he appears to have been an authoritative writer on original Smṛti. These citations are partly in prose and partly in verse. It is not known whether or not he wrote a prose Dharmasūtra and a metrical Smṛti work separately. Date uncertain.

SURAPĀLA : See Sureśvara.

SUREŚVARA : A pupil of Śaṃkarācārya (8th-9th century), he wrote the philosophical works *Nāiṣkarmya-siddhi* and *Brahma-siddhi*. His *Mānasollāsa* is a paraphrase of the *Dakṣiṇā-mūrti-stotra* of his master. The *Sambandha-vārtika* is another well-known work by him. Sureśvara is traditionally known as Maṇḍana Miśra; this identity is, however, not universally accepted. Sureśvara was a champion of Pūrva-mīmāṃsā before he was defeated in a debate by Śaṃkara and converted to the Advaita view and way of life. [Also see Maṇḍana Miśra. Another Sureśvara, also called Surapāla, great grandson or grandson of Devagaṇa and son of Bhadreśvara, court-physician of Rāmapāla, king of Bengal, wrote, under king Bhīmapāla, the following works on Āyurveda : *Śabda-pradīpa*, *Vṛkṣāyurveda* and *Loha-paddhati* or *Loha-sarvasva*.

[See C. M. Sastri, *Sureśvara's Contribution to Advaita*, Vamur, 1973. See S. Hino, *Sureśvara on Yājñavalkya-Maitreyī Dialogue*.]

SUŚRUTA : Author or compiler of the famous *Suśruta-saṃhitā*. We are told that his teacher was king Divodāsa of Banaras. Suśruta is the earliest writer to deal with surgery among other topics of medical science. Later than Caraka, but precise date unknown.

ŚYĀMALIKA: Author of the one-act play called *Pāda-tāḍitaka*. The lower limit of his date is fixed by references in the works of writers like Abhinavagupta, Kuntaka and Kṣemendra all belonging to the end of the 10th century.

TĀRĀNĀTHA TARKAVĀCASPATI : Compiler of the famous Sanskrit lexicon called *Vācaspatya* (q.v.). Son of Kālidāsa Sārvabhauma, he was born in 1806 A.D. and became an erudite Sanskrit scholar. He worked as a teacher in Government Sanskrit College, Calcutta, and died in 1885 A.D. His other well-known dictionary is the *Śabda-stomamahānidhi*.

TARUṆAVĀCASPATI : Belonging probably to the end of

the 12th century and first half of the 13th he wrote an authoritative commentary on the *Kāvyādarśa* or Daṇḍin.

TAUTA : See Bhaṭṭa Tauta.

TĪṢATA : Author of the *Cikitsā-kalikā* (q. v.).

TRILOCANADĀSA : Author of the *Kātantra-vṛtti-pañjikā*, a commentary on Durgasiṃha's *Kātantra-vṛtti*. Son of Megha and father of Gadādhara, he was a Kāyastha and is cited by Vopadeva.

TRIVIKRAMA BHAṬṬA : Also called Siṃhāditya. Author of the *Nalacampū*, also called *Damayantī-kathā* and of the *Madālasā-campū*. Flourished in the later half of the 9th century A.D. and the first half of the 10th. He described himself as son of Nemāditya (or Devāditya) and grandson of Śrīdhara. Trivikrama was a court-poet of the Rāṣṭrakūṭa king Indra III (914-16 A.D.). He mentions Bāṇa, and is cited by Bhoja in his *Sarasvatī-kaṇṭhābharaṇa*.

UDAYANA : The earliest scholar, in fact the real founder, of the Navya-nyāya school of Mithilā. Appears to have flourished in the last three quarters of the 11th century. His works include digests, commentaries and original treatises. Of his original works, very famous are the *Nyāya-kusumāñjali*, the *Ātma-tattva-viveka* (or, *Bauddhadhikkāra*) and the *Lakṣaṇāvalī*. *Lakṣaṇamālā* is another work of Udayana. Among his commentaries, the best known is the *Kiraṇāvalī* on the *Praśastapāda-bhāṣya*. His *Nyāya-pariśiṣṭa* or *Prabodha-siddhi* is a comm. on the fifth chapter of the *Nyāyasūtra*. The *Nyāya-vārtika-tātparya-pariśuddhi*, commonly called *Nibandha*, is well-known.

UDBHAṬA : A well-known figure in the domain of poetics. The name suggests that he was a Kashmirian. According to Kalhaṇa Bhaṭṭa Udbhaṭa was a *Sabhāpati* of king Jayāpīḍā of Kashmir (about 779-813 A.D.). Author of the *Kāvyālaṃkāra-saṃgraha* (or *sāra-saṃgraha*) and of the *Bhāmaha-vivarṇa* or *vivṛti*) which is a commentary on Bhāmaha's work on poetics. It is stated by Pratihārendurāja that Udbhaṭa wrote a poem called *Kumārasambhava*.
[See C. R. Basistha, New Light on Bhaṭṭa Udbhaṭa's date, *Summaries of Papers, AIOC,* 1974.]

UDDAṆḌANĀTHA : Author of the *Mallikā-māruta* (q.v.). Flourished about the middle of the 17th century A.D.

UDDAṆḌIN : Same as Uddaṇḍanātha (q.v.).

UDDYOTAKARA: A logician whose date falls c. 620 A.D., and who wrote the *Nyāyavārtika*, a work on Nyāya philosophy. Author was a fervent sectarian of the Pāśupata belief.

UMĀPATIDHARA : A fellow-poet of Jayadeva (q.v.) in the court of Lakṣmaṇasena, king of Bengal (12th-13th century). Mentioned by Jayadeva in the *Gīta-govinda* (i.4.). Merutuṅga, in his *Prabandha-cintāmaṇi*, refers to him as a minister of Lakṣmaṇasena. Umāpati does not appear to have composed any work. But verses of this poet have been quoted in the *Sadukti-karṇāmṛta*, *Sūkti-muktāvalī* and in the *Padyāvalī*.

UMĀPATI UPĀDHYĀYA : Author of the *Pārijāta-haraṇa*, he flourished under Hariharadeva of Mithilā reigning "after the Yavana rule", and appears to have been familiar with Jayadeva's *Gīta-govinda*.

UMĀSVĀTI : Said to have been author of no less than 500 works including the *Tattvārthādhigama-sūtra*, a work on Jaina philosophy. Called Umāsvāmin by the Digambaras, he is described as a pupil of Ghoṣanandī Kṣamāśramaṇa. Given the epithet Gṛdhrapiccha by the Digambaras, he was traditionally a pupil of Kundakunda. Acc. to Digambara *Paṭṭāvalis*, he lived from c. 135 to 219 A.D.

UMEŚA GUPTA KAVIRATNA : Author of the *Vaidyaka-śabdasindhu*, an Āyurvedic medical dictionary, written in 1894.

UPAVARṢA: A commentator on the *Pūrvamīmāṃsā-sūtra* of Jaimini. Acc. to a tradition, he was brother of Varṣa and preceptor of Pāṇini.

UŚANAS : One of the twenty traditional writers of original Smṛti. Author of an *Auśanasa-dharmaśāstra*. Appears to have written also a Sūtra work on politics. Date uncertain.

UTPALADEVA: A pupil of Somānanda and teacher of Abhinavagupta. He is to be distinguished from Utpala Vaiṣṇava. Utpaladeva is credited with the authorship of the *Īśvara-pratyabhijñā-sūtra* (also called *Pratyabhijñā-sūtra* or *Pratya-bhijñākārikā*), an authoritative work on the Pratyabhijñā-śāstra of Kashmir Śaivism, and of the *Stotrāvalī*, written about 925 A.D. and consisting of a series of 20 short hymns in honour of Śiva.

An Utpala, Utpalabhaṭṭa or Bhaṭṭotpala commented on the *Bṛhatsaṃhitā* (q.v.) of Varāhamihira and on the *Khaṇḍa-khādyaka* of Brahmagupta.

VĀCASPATI MIŚRA : A great writer of Mithilā on Navya-smṛti and Navya-nyāya. Must be distinguished from the philosopher Vācaspati (c. 850 A.D.), author of the *Bhāmatī*, *Sāṃkhya-tattva-kaumudī* and other philosophical works. This Vācaspati is also different from (Candraśekhara) Vācaspati, author of the *Smṛti-sāra-saṃgraha*. Vācaspati Miśra, author of the Smṛti works, appears to have flourished in the middle of the 15th century. His works may be broadly divided into two groups, viz. (1) those whose titles end in 'cintāmaṇi' and (2) those whose titles end in 'nirṇaya'. To the former group belong the *Tīrthacintāmaṇi, Vyavahāra-cintāmaṇi, Vivāda-cintāmaṇi, Kṛtya-cintāmaṇi* etc. To the latter belong *Tithi-nirṇaya, Vivāda-nirṇaya* etc. He wrote also several other works on Smṛti which do not fall within these groups. The Nyāya works of Vācaspati are the *Nyāya-* (or, *Naya-*) *tattvāloka, Nyāyasūtroddhāra, Nyāyaratna-prakāśa, Pratyakṣa-nirṇaya, Anumāna-nirṇaya, Śabda-nirṇaya, Khaṇḍanoddhāra* and *Cintā-maṇi-prakāśa*. Perhaps different from this Vācaspati is Vācas-pati, author of the lexicon called *Śabdārṇava*.

[For Vācaspati, the Vedāntist, see S. S. Hasurkar, *Vācaspati Miśra on Advaita Vedānta*, Darbhanga, 1958. For Vācaspati, the Smṛti writer, see P. V. Kane, *History of Dharmaśāstra*, Vol. I. For Vācaspati, the logician, see D. C. Bhaṭṭāchārya, *History of Navyanyāya in Mithilā*.]

VĀGBHAṬA : Several authors of this name are known. Vāg-bhaṭa I and Vāgbhaṭa II are writers on Āyurveda, their works respectively being the *Aṣṭāṅga-saṃgraha* and the *Aṣṭāṅgahṛdaya-saṃhitā*. The elder Vāgbhaṭa, known as Vṛddha Vāgbhaṭa, was son of Siṃhagupta, grandson of Vāgbhaṭa and pupil of the Buddhist Avalokita. Some scholars think that he has been referred to by the Chinese traveller I-tsing in the 7th century A.D. The younger Vāgbhaṭa, supposed by some to be a descendant of the elder Vāgbhaṭa, is believed to have flourished about a century after his elder namesake. To a Vāgbhaṭa is sometimes ascribed the Āyurvedic work, *Rasa-ratna-samuccaya* (q.v.). Two Vāgbhaṭas are known in the domain of Alaṃkāra literature. The one, belonging to the 12th century, wrote the *Vāgbhaṭālaṃkāra* and the other, belonging to the thirteenth century, wrote the *Kāvyānuśāsana*. The *Neminirvāṇa*, a Kāvya, is probably by the earlier of these Vāgbhaṭas.

[For Vāgbhaṭa, author of the *Aṣṭāṅgahṛdaya*, and his commentators, see P. K. Gode. *Studies in Indian Literary History*, I, p. 171 ff.]

VAIDYANĀTHA PĀYAGUṆḌE : A pupil of Nāgeśa. Lived at Banaras in the later half of the 18th cent. A.D. Believed to have written commentaries on many works of Nāgeśa. The well-known among the commentaries are the *Kāśikā* (also called *Gadā*) on the *Paribhāṣenduśekhara*, the *Cidasthimālā* on the *Laghuśabdenduśekhara* and the *Chāyā* on the *Uddyota*. Sometimes identified with Bālambhaṭṭa Pāyaguṇḍe, while some regard Bālambhaṭṭa as son of Vaidyanātha.

VALLABHA: Author of the commentary, called *Aṇubhāṣya*, on the Vedānta-sūtras. He lived from 1376 to 1430 A.D. He offers a theistic interpretation of the Vedānta, which is different from those of Śaṃkara and Rāmānuja. His view is called Śuddhādvaita. A Vallabha is the author of a commentary on Praśastapāda's *Padārtha-dharma-saṃgraha*. (q.v.).

[See M. Marfatia., *The Philosophy of Vallabhācārya*, 1967; J. G. Shah, *Vallabhācārya, his philosophy and religion*; G. H. Bhatt, *Śrī Vallabhācārya and his doctrines*; G.D. Gajja, *Ācārya Vallabha and his Mission*, Jodhpur, 1979; Johannes and others, *Puṣṭimārga and Śrī Vallabhācārya*.

See J.D. Redington, *Vallabhācārya on the love-games of Kṛṣṇa*, MLBD, Delhi 1983; Sukhawal, *Philosophy of Vallabha* (Hindi), Beawar, 1980.]

VALLABHADĀSA : Author of an abbreviated version of the *Vetāla-pañcaviṃśatikā.*

VALLABHADEVA : Compiler of the anthology called *Subhāṣitāvalī.* The author was a Kashmirian. His date is uncertain. From certain evidences he appears to have flourished before the middle of the 12th century. Other evidences would point to the 13th, 14th or even the 15th century as the period of his life and activity.

A Vallabhadeva is well-known as a commentator on the *Meghadūta* of Kālidāsa.

VALLĀLASENA (VALLĀLA) : One of the greatest Hindu rulers of Bengal, having reigned in the 12th century. He assumed the proud title of Ari-rāja-niḥśaṅka-śaṅkara, and was a great social reformer and scholar. Of his social reforms, the most noteworthy is the introduction of Kulinism. A pupil of Aniruddha Bhaṭṭa, he wrote several works on Smṛti and astrology. His works are : *Dāna-sāgara*, *Adbhuta-sāgara*, *Pratiṣṭhā-sāgara* and *Ācāra-sāgara*. Another work of his, called *Vrata-sāgara*, is referred to in his *Dāna-sāgara*. Vallālasena should be distinguished from Vallāla (end of 16th century), author of the *Bhoja-prabandha*.

[Ref : *History of Bengal*, Vol. I, Dacca University; N.N. Sen, A Note on the Rāmāyaṇa and its influence on Ballālasena etc. *JOLA*, 2.3.; Sureś Vandyopadhyāya, *Smṛti Sāstre Vāngāli* (in Bengali), Calcutta]

VĀLMĪKI : Traditional author of the *Rāmāyaṇa*. The legend goes that a bandit, Ratnākara by name, gave up his vile means of livelihood at the instance of sage Nārada and started a long and arduous penance. While seated for long years at the same spot, he was covered all over with an ant-hill which is called *Valmīka* in Sanskrit; hence his name Vālmīki. Having completed his penance, he was one day moved to pity at the sight of one of a pair of curlews, engaged in erotic enjoyment, killed with an arrow by a fowler. This shocking scene made him utter a verse (*mā niṣāda pratiṣṭhāṃ tvamagamaḥ* etc.) cursing the fowler. This verse was the first piece of poetry; hence Vālmīki is designated as Ādi-kavi (the first poet). Thereafter he wrote the *Rāmāyaṇa* at the bidding of God Brahmā.

VĀMANA : Author of the well-known work on poetics, called *Kāvyālaṃkāra-sūtra-vṛtti*. Believed to have been a minister of Jayāpīḍa, king of Kashmir (779-813 A.D.). He declared, for the first time, that Rīti (a particular arrangement of words) constituted the soul of poetry. A Vāmana is supposed to be the joint author of the *Kāśikā-vṛtti* commentary on the *Aṣṭādhyāyī*.

Vāmana Bhaṭṭa Bāṇa wrote the *Vemabhūpāla-carita* (q.v.). To him is a attributed also the lexicon, *Śabdaratnākara*, ed. R. R. Sharma, Darbhanga, 1965.

VAṄGASENA : Son of Gadādhara Vaidya, he appears to have been a native of Bengal. Probably flourished in the second half of the 11th century. Author of the medical work called *Cikitsā-sāra-saṃgraha* and of the *Ākhyāta-vṛtti* on the *Kātantra* grammar.

[See. P.K. Gode, *Indian Culture*, III., pp. 535-43.]

VARADARĀJA : A pupil of Bhaṭṭoji and author of the *Madhya-siddhānta-kaumudī* and *Laghu-siddhānta-kaumudī*, two abridgments of Bhaṭṭoji's *Siddhānta-kaumudī*, meant for beginners. A Varadarāja, who flourished probably in the 12th century, wrote the polemical work entitled *Tārkikarakṣā*. Several authors of this name are known in the history of Smṛti literature. To one Varadarāja (c. 1450-1500 A.D.) is ascribed the *Vyavahāra-nirṇaya*. To another Varadarāja of the 18th century is ascribed a *Vyavahāra-mālā*.

[See P.K. Gode, Varadarāja etc. *P.V. Kane Pres. Vol.*, Poona, 1941.]

VARĀHAMIHIRA : Son of Ādityadāsa and a pupil of Ārya-bhaṭa I, he was at once an astronomer, astrologer and mathematician. Author of the celebrated work entitled *Bṛhat-saṃhitā*. He divides the science of Jyotiṣa into three branches, viz.

(i) *Tantra*—astronomical and mathematical foundations.
(ii) *Horā*—dealing with horoscopes.
(iii) *Saṃhitā*—covers the field of natural astrology.

Supposed to have flourished in the fifth and sixth century A.D. (c. 475-550 A.D.) in the city of Kāmpilya (=modern Kālpī) in Magadha. His Magadhan origin is confirmed by his commentator Bhaṭṭotpala. His other works are the *Bṛhad-jātaka*, *Laghu-jātaka*, *Pañca-siddhāntikā*, *Bṛhad-vivāhapaṭala*, *Svalpa-vivāhapaṭala* and *Yoga-yātrā*. Tradition makes him one of the Nine Jewels of the court of Vikramāditya of Avantī. In his *Pañca-siddhāntikā* he mentions the astronomers Lāṭācārya, Siṃhācārya and Āryabhaṭa.

[See P.P. Joshi, Varāhamihira, *Vikrama Vol.*, Ujjain, 1948; H.D. Velankar, Varāhamihira and Utpal (in relation to Sanskrit metres), *C.K. Raja Pres. Vol.*, Madras, 1941; J. Scheflelowitz, Varāhamihirā's Bṛhatsaṃhitā...das Bhaviṣya-purāṇa, *Festschrift M. Winternitz*, Leipzig, 1933; P. Shastri, *Vikrama Vol.*, 1948.]

VARARUCI : References are found to one Vararuci as an authority on Alaṃkāra. A *Liṅgānuśāsana* by Vararuci is known to the *Liṅgānuśāsana* of Harṣadeva (606-47 A.D.). A *Nīti-ratna* is attributed to Vararuci. A Vararuci is supposed to have been the author of the Bengal version of the *Siṃhāsana-dvātriṃśikā*. Vararuci Kātyāyana is supposed to have been the author of the Vārtika-sūtras added to the *Aṣṭādhyāyī*. A *Patra-kaumudī*, dealing with espistolography, is attributed to Vararuci. A *Vāraruca-kāvya* is mentioned in Patañjāli's *Mahābhāṣya* (c. 2nd century B.C.). To a Vararuci is ascribed a modern grammatical work called *Prayoga-mukha-maṇḍana*. It appears that there were several scholars of the name of Vararuci. Tradition makes a Vararuci one of the Nine Jewels in the court of Vikramāditya.

[To a Vararuci are attributed the Smṛti work *Aśaucāṣṭaka* and a treatise on politics called *Rāja-nīti*. The one-act play *Ubhayābhisārikā* is ascribed to a Vararuci.]

VARDHAMĀNA : Son and disciple of Gaṅgeśopādhyāya (q.v.), he was a great writer on Nyāya-Vaiśeṣika. His works are : *Anvīkṣā-nayatattva-bodha*, *Nyāyanibandha-prakāśa*, *Nyāya-pariśiṣṭa-prakāśa*, *Kusumāñjali-prakāśa*, *Līlāvatī-prakāśa*, *Khaṇḍanoddhāra*, *Bauddhadhikkāra-prakāśa*, *Tarka-prakāśa*. The Smṛti digest, called *Smṛti-paribhāṣā*, is also attributed to him. Styled as Mahāmahopādhyāya, he should be distinguished from other authors bearing the name 'Vardhamāna'. He is supposed to have flourished towards the end of the 14th century A.D. Another Vardhamāna, son of Bhaveśa and Gaurīdevī, flourished some time in the 15th century A.D. His elder brother was Gaṇḍakamiśra; Śaṅkara Miśra and Vācaspati were his *gurus*. Author of several Smṛti works, viz. *Daṇḍa-viveka* (which is a part of the *Smṛti-tattva-viveka* or *Smṛti-tattvāmṛta*), the *Gaṅgākṛtya-viveka*, *Gayāvidhi-viveka*, *Gayāpaddhati*, *Śrāddha-pradipa*, *Śāntika-pauṣṭika*, *Kṛtya-nirṇaya* and *Pratihasta-paddhati*. Mentioned by Vācaspati Miśra and Raghunandana. Vardhamāna, author of the grammatical work, called *Gaṇaratna-mahodadhi* (1140 A.D.) appears to have been a different person. The latter is believed by some to have belonged to the court of Lakṣmaṇasena of Bengal. He has written a commentary on his own *Gaṇaratna-mahodadhi*. The works on grammar, called *Kātantra-vistara* and *Kriyā-guptaka* are also attributed to him.

VAŚIṢṬHA (VASIṢṬHA) : One of the twenty great writers of original Smṛti. Author of the *Vaśiṣṭha-dharmasūtra*. P.V. Kane tentatively assigns Vaśiṣṭha to the period between 300-100 B.C.

To a Vaśiṣṭha is ascribed the astronomical work called *Vaśiṣṭha-siddhānta* (also called *Vaśiṣṭha-saṃhitā*, *Laghu-vaśiṣṭha-siddhānta*); this is supposed to date back to the 3rd cent. A.D.

VASUBANDHU : Brother of Asaṅga (4th cent. A.D. or 5th cent. acc. to some) and author of the *Abhidharmakośa*. Son of a Brāhmaṇa of Puruṣapura (Peshawar), he was originally an adherent of the Sarvāstivāda school. In the later part of his life he was converted to the Mahāyāna by his brother Asaṅga. Vasubandhu was author of a large number of treatises. Among the works commented upon by him, are the

Mahāyāna-sūtras, the *Saddharma-puṇḍarīka*, the *Mahāparinirvāṇasūtra* etc.

[See G. Tucci, Buddhist Logic before Diṅnāga, *Jour. of Royal Asiatic Society*, 1929; J. Frauwallner, On the date of the Buddhist Master of Law, Vasubandhu, Rome, 1951; G. Ono, The date of Vasubandhu etc., *G.R. Lanman Vol.*, London, 1920; F. Belaney, On the Date of Vasubandhu—a new light, *Summaries of Papers*, *AIOC*, 1969, p. 106. See S. Anacker, *Seven Works of Vasubandhu*, MLBD, Delhi, 1984.]

VASUGUPTA : A great figure in Kashmir Śaivism. He is represented as a sage to whom the Śiva-sūtras, which form the bedrock on which the edifice of the Trika system stands, are said to have been revealed. He appears to have flourished either at the end of the eighth century or beginning of the ninth.

VAṬEŚVARĀCĀRYA : Author of the astronomical work called *Vaṭeśvara-siddhānta*. Flourished in the 9th century A.D.

VATSABHAṬṬI : Author of the inscription (473 A.D.) celebrating the consecration of a Sun-temple at Dasapura (Mandasor), Gwalior State, Central India. It provides a positive evidence of the cultivation of the Kāvya style in that far off age.

VATSARĀJA : Author of six plays each illustrating a different type of drama. He calls himself minister of Paramardideva of Kālañjara, who reigned from 1163 to 1203 A.D.

VĀTSYĀYANA : Two great writers of this name are known to us. One is the author of the great *Kāmasūtra*, who is also called Mallanāga. His date is uncertain, but he appears to have been earlier than Kālidāsa and is generally assigned to different periods from third century A.D. to the sixth. According to some, he flourished about the fourth century A.D. Supposed by some to have belonged to Pāṭaliputra; according to others, he belonged to Avantī.

The other writer is known as Pakṣilasvāmin Vātsyāyana. He wrote the *Nyāya-bhāṣya*, a well-known exposition on

Gotama's *Nyāyasūtra*. The latter is supposed by some scholars to have flourished about the fourth century A.D. in Bihar.

VEDA : Author of the *Saṃgītamakaranda*, which is to be distinguished from the work of the same name attributed to Nārada. Veda was a court-poet of Shāhji, father of Śivāji, who was known as Makarandabhūpa, and a tutor to the king's son, Śambhu, elder brother of Śivāji, early in the 17th century A.D.

VEDĀṄGARĀYA : Author of the astronomical work called *Pārasika-prakāśa*. Flourished in the reign of Shahjahan.

VEDĀNTADEŚIKA : Also called Veṅkaṭanātha, he flourished in he 13th century and was one of the greatest successors of Rāmānuja. Founder of the Vaḍagalai sect. A native of Conjeevaram, he spent most of his life at Śrīraṅgam. Wrote on many subjects. His principal philosophical works are as follows: *Pañcarātrarakṣā* and *Saccaritra-rakṣā* are the two works dealing with the principles and practices of the Pañcarātra school. His *Tattvaṭīkā* and *Tātparya-candrikā* are commentaries respectively on *Rāmānuja's Śrībhāṣya* and the *Gītā*. His *Seśvara-mīmāṃsā* treats the Pūrva and Uttara-mīmāṃsās as parts of one whole. His other works are the *Nyāyasiddhāñjana*, the *Tattvamuktākalāpa* and the *Śatadūṣaṇī*, *Haṃsa-sandeśa*, *Subhāṣitanīvī* etc. He appears to have composed some *Stotras* also.

[See S. V. Singh, *Vedānta Deshika*, 1958; V.N. Hari Rao, A note on the date of Vedāntadeśika, *Śrī Veṅkeṭeśwar University Oriental Jour.*, Tirupati XII, Pts. 1-2, 1969.]

To a Vedānta Deśīka is ascribed the work called *Bhūgola-nirṇaya-savyākhyāna*.

VEDAVYĀSA : Same as Vyāsa (*infra*).

VEṄKAṬEŚA KETAKARA : Author of the astronomical work called *Jyotirgaṇita*. Appears to have flourished in the later half of the 19th cent. A.D.

VIDYĀDHARA : Author of the *Ekāvalī* (q.v.) and perhaps also of the *Kali-rahasya*, a work on erotics. Probably flourished in the thirteenth century A.D.

VIDYĀKARA: Compiler of the anthology entitled *Subhāṣita-*

ratnakoṣa which was formerly published under the title *Kavīndra-vacanasamuccaya.* Appears to have flourished in Bengal towards the first quarter of the 12th cent. A.D.

[See Intro. to ed. of the *Subhāṣita-ratnakoṣa,* HOS.]

VIDYĀKARA VĀJAPEYIN: Son of Śambhukara, Vidyākara (earlier than 1500 A.D.) was the author of the Smṛti digests called *Ācārapaddhati, Nityācāra-paddhati* and *Āhnikakṛtya.* Mentioned in some of the Smṛti digests of Raghunandana.

VIDYĀPATI: Grandson of Jayadatta and son of Gaṇapati and a court-poet of the Maithila king Kīrtisiṃha, Devasiṃha (died 1413 A.D.), Śivasiṃha and of Viśvāsadevī, queen of Padmasiṃha. He composed *Padāvalīs* in Maithilī language. His *Kīrti-latā,* a Campū-kāvya, is in Avahaṭṭa. In the same language is written the erotic poem *Kīrtipatākā.* His Sanskrit works, dealing with topics of Smṛti, are the *Gaṅgāvākyāvalī* (written under the patronage of Viśvāsadevī), *Gayāpattalaka, Dānavākyāvalī, Durgā-bhakti-taraṅgiṇī, Varṣa-kṛtya, Vibhāga-sāra* and the *Śaiva-sarvasva-sāra* or *Śambhuvākyāvalī.* His works on moral tales are the *Puruṣaparīkṣā* and the *Bhū-parikramā.* His *Likhanāvalī* is on letter-writing. A work on Āyurveda, entitled *Cikitsāñjana,* is also attributed to him. On certain literary and epigraphic evidences, his date is given as 1350-1440 A.D. There were several other learned men bearing this name or title, both preceding and following the above Vidyāpati.

[For details about his family and age, see Intro. to the ed. of the *Puruṣa-parīkṣā* of Vidyāpati, by R. Jhā, Darbhanga, 1960. Also see R. K. Choudhary, *Mithilā in the Age of Vidyāpati*; S. C. Banerji, *Contribution of Bihar to Sanskrit Literature,* Patna, 1973. For his Āyurvedic work, see V. Mishra, *Summaries of Papers, AIOC,* 1974.]

VIDYĀRAṆYA : See Mādhavācārya.

VIJÑĀNABHIKṢU : A well-known philosopher who probably flourished in the 16th century. His works are : *Sāṃkhya-pravacanabhāṣya* (comm. on the *Sāṃkhya-sūtra*), *Sāṃkhya-sāra, Yoga-vārtika, Yoga-sārasaṃgraha, Vijñānāmṛta* (comm. on the *Brahma-sūtra*). He attempts to minimize the distinction bet ween the Sāṃkhya and theistic Vedānta which, according to him, is the genuine Vedānta while Advaita Vedānta is its modern falsification.

[See J.N. Sinha, *The Philosophy of Vijñānabhikṣu*, Calcutta.]

VIJÑĀNEŚVARA : Author of the *Mitākṣarā*, a unique commentary on the *Yājñavalkya-smṛti*, he styles himself as Vijñānayogin. A Paramahaṃsa and pupil of Uttama, he was son of Padmanābhabhaṭṭa. He informs us that he wrote his work when king Vikramārka or Vikramādityadeva had been reigning in the city of Kalyāṇa. The reign period of this king, who must have been Vikramāditya VI, was c. 1076-1127 A.D.

VINĀYAKA-PAṆḌITA : See Nandapaṇḍita.

VĪRANĀGA : According to some, author of the *Kundamālā*.

VIŚĀKHADATTA : Author of the drama called *Mudrā-rākṣasa*. In this work he tells us that he was son of king Bhāskaradatta or Pṛthu and grandson of Sāmanta Vaṭeśvaradatta. In the concluding verse of the drama the author mentions a king named Avantivarman (v.l. Rantivarman or Dantivarman). Of two kings named Avantivarman, one flourished in the 7th century and the other in the 9th. In some manuscripts the name Candragupta occurs instead of the above name. This has led some scholars to associate the author with Candragupta II (4th-5th cent. A.D.) of the Gupta dynasty.

To Viśākhadeva, who appears to be identical with Viśākhadatta, is attributed the drama called *Devī-candragupta* (q.v.). Bhoja and Abhinavagupta cite the *Abhisārikā-vañcitaka* (or, *vandhitaka*) as a work of Viśākhadeva.

[See S. K. De, Viśākhadatta, *B. C. Law Volume*, I, Calcutta, 1945.]

VIṢṆU : One of the twenty traditional writers of original Smṛti. A *Viṣṇu-dharmasūtra* exists. P.V. Kane suggests 300 B.C. to 100 B.C. as the conjectural date of the older portion of this work.

VIṢṆUDEVA : Author of the medical work, called *Rasarājalakṣmī*. Appears to have flourished in the 14th cent. A.D.

VIṢṆUGUPTA : See Kauṭilya.

VIṢṆUŚARMAN : Traditionally known as the author of the *Pañcatantra.* In the introduction to this work, he is described as relating the stories to the sons of king Amaraśakti of Mahilāropya or Mihilāropya in the Deccan. Date uncertain. The original *Pañcatantra*, now lost, appears to have been written prior to 531 A.D.

VIŚVANĀTHA : There are several writers of this name. Two of them figure very prominently in the history of Sanskrit literature. One is the author of the *Sāhitya-darpaṇa*, a very well-known work on poetics. He declares that poetry consists of a sentence full of *Rasa* (sentiment). Supposed to have flourished in the first half of the fourteenth century A.D. He describes himself as son of Mahākavi Candraśekhara who was probably a high official of a king of Kaliṅga. Viśvanātha refers to several other works written by himself. He wrote a comm. on the *Kāvyaprakāśa*. Another Viśvanātha (17th century A.D.) was the author of the *Kārikāvalī* or *Bhāṣā-pariccheda* which is a noted textbook of *Nyāya-Vaiśeṣika* philosophy.

Viśvanātha Kavirāja is credited with the authorship of a *Candrakalā-nāṭikā*.

To Viśvanātha, son of Trimaladeva, is ascribed a minor drama called *Mṛgāṅkalekhā*.

A Viśvanātha, who may or may not have been identical with the author of the *Sāhitya-darpaṇa*, appears to have written the minor drama called *Saugandhikā-haraṇa*.

[See Satyavrat, *Viśvanātha-Kavirāja, his lost works*, Hoshiarpur; S. Hota, New Light on Viśvanātha—the poet-critic of Utkal, *Summaries of Papers, AIOC*, Silver Jubilee Session, 1969, p. 91. See *Candrakalā-nāṭikā*, ed. with Hindi comm., by B. Sukla Sastri. Also see R. Mukherji, *Viśvanātha's Literary Theories.*]

VIŚVARŪPA : Author of the *Bāla-krīḍā*, a well-known commentary on the *Yājñavalkya-smṛti.* Supposed to have flourished in the first half of the 9th century A.D. Identified with Sureśvara, a pupil of the great Śaṃkarācārya and author of the *Naiṣkarmya-siddhi* and several other works.

[See K. Rönnow, Viśvarūpa, *E.J. Rapson Pres. Vol.* (BSOS,

IV), London, 1931; P.P.S. Sastri, Viśvarūpa...alias Sureśvarācārya—problems of identity, *P.V. Kane Pres. Vol.*, F.8]

VIŚVEŚVARA BHAṬṬA : Author of the Smṛti work *Madanapārijāta* passing in the name of Madanapāla (q.v.).

VOPADEVA : Son of Keśava and pupil of Dhaneśa, he was author of the well-known grammatical works called *Mugdhabodha* and *Kavikalpadruma* both written after 1250 A.D. under Mahādeva of Devagiri. The medical work *Śataślokī* was written by Vopadeva, son of Hemādri (c. 1300 A.D.). Some scholars believe, not on very convincing grounds, that the *Bhāgavata-purāṇa* was the work of the grammarian Vopadeva. The great popularity of Vopadeva's grammar in Bengal has led some scholars to believe that he flourished in Bengal. To a Vopadevācārya is ascribed the astronomical work called *Tithisiddhi-kāmadhenu.*

VṚDDHAGARGA : To him is ascribed the astronomical work called *Vṛddhagarga-saṃhitā.* Supposed to have flourished in the first century A.D.

VṚDDHAVAŚIṢṬHA : To him are ascribed the mathematical work *Gaṇitaskandha* and the astronomical work *Viśvaprakāśa.* Assigned to the 2nd century A.D.

VṚNDA : Also called Vṛndakuṇḍa. Belonging probably to a period earlier than c. 1060 A.D., he was the author of the medical treatise called *Siddha-yoga* or *Vṛndamādhava.* Supposed to be the author also of the *Rugviniścaya* (8th or 9th century), generally attributed to Mādhavakara. Name of an ancient grammarian who or whose work is mentioned in *Prātiśākhyas, Mahābhāṣya, Vākyapadīya* and some other later treatises. Appears to have written a vast and learned work called *Saṃgraha.* A *Paribhāṣā-sūcana* is ascribed to him.

VYĀSA : Traditional author of the *Mahābhārata.* Often referred to as Vedavyāsa. The legend goes that he was born out of the union of sage Parāśara and the virgin girl Matsyagandhā or Satyavatī. Having been born in an island (*dvīpa*) he is also called Dvaipāyana. On account of his dark complexion he is sometimes styled Kṛṣṇa Dvaipāyana. He is said to have compiled the Vedas for the first time, and written the Purāṇas besides an excellent commentary on the philosophical work of Patañjali. While he composed the *Mahābhārata*, God

Gaṇeśa is said to have acted as his amanuensis. The condition between the author and the scribe was that the former would not stop dictating the verses till the completion of the book and that the latter would not write without understanding the meaning of the verses. Vyāsa at intervals dictated extremely difficult verses known as Vyāsa-kūṭas. During the time Gaṇeśa took to comprehend the import of these verses, Vyāsa composed new stanzas. A Vyāsa is mentioned by Yājñavalkya (I.4) among the twenty great writers of original Smṛti. While some would identify this Vyāsa with the author of the *Mahābhārata*, and with Vyāsa, the writer on several topics of Smṛti, others regard them as distinct writers. A *Vyāsasmṛti* exists, and references are found to Vṛddha-vyāsa, Bṛhad-vyāsa and Laghu-vyāsa. To Vyāsa is ascribed the work called *Vyāsa-siddhānta* (q.v.) which appears to be a part of the *Vyāsa-smṛti*.

[See P.V.S. Sastri, Is Vyāsa the same as Bādarāyaṇa? G. Jha Res. Institute, Allahabad, 7.]

YĀDAVAPRAKĀŚA : Author of the lexicon called *Vaijayantī*. He appears to have been the same as Yādavaprakāśa who was a quondam Guru of Rāmānuja, lived in the 11th century at Conjeevaram and wrote an independent commentary on the *Brahma-sūtra*, leaning to the Advaita interpretation. There is a *Yādavaprakāśa-bhāṣya* on the *Piṅgalanāga-chandoviciti* popularly called *Piṅgala-chandaḥ-sūtra*.

The commentary is still unpublished; MSS are preserved in Tübingen University Library, Adyar Library, Madras University Library and Calcutta Sanskrit College Library.

[See K. C. Varadachari, The philosophy of Yādavaprakāśa, *Siddha-bhāratī* (*S. Varma Vol.*) II, Hosiarpur, 1950.]

YĀJÑAVALKYA : One of the twenty great traditional writers of metrical Smṛti. Date uncertain. The extant *Yājñavalkya-smṛti* is supposed to have been composed during the first two centuries of the Christian era or even earlier. In matters relating to inheritance and succession the *Yājñavalkya-smṛti*, as interpreted by Vijñāneśvara, was until recently of paramount authority in the whole of India excepting Bengal where Jīmūtavāhana's interpretation of the same Smṛti prevailed. *Vṛddha Yājñavalkya*, *Yoga-yājñavalkya*, *Yogi-yājñavalkya* and *Bṛhad Yājñavalkya* appear to be different from one another and also from the *Yājñavalkya-smṛti*.

YAMA : One of the twenty great writers of original Smṛti. A *Yama-smṛti* exists in different versions. Date uncertain. *Bṛhad-yama*, *Laghu-yama* and *Svalpa-yama* are cited in later digests and commentaries.

YĀMUNĀCĀRYA : Also known as Ālavandār, he was Guru of Rāmānuja who succeeded him as the head of the Vaiṣṇava sect. Yāmunācārya (born c. 906 A.D.) struggled hard to defend the Vaiṣṇava Āgamas, and tried to make out that they had the same purport as the Vedas. His chief works are : *Āgama-prāmāṇya*, *Mahāpuruṣa-nirṇaya*, *Siddhi-traya*, *Gītārtha-saṃgraha*, *Catuśślokī and Stotra-ratna*.

[See M. Narasimhachari, *Contribution of Yāmuna to Viśiṣṭādvaita*, Banaras, 1971; *Yāmuna's Vedānta and Pañcarātra*, Missoula, Montana, 1977.]

YĀSKA : The first commentator on the *Ṛgveda*. On the basis of the *Nighaṇṭus*, wrongly ascribed to him, he explains quite a number of Vedic verses in his *Nirukta*. In interpreting the verses he depends chiefly on etymology, and sometimes suggests more meanings than one of the same word. Date uncertain. While some scholars consider him to have been a pre-Pāṇini writer, others believe that he flourished after Pāṇini.

A *Kāvyālaṃkāra-sūtra* (q.v.) appears to have been written by Yāska.

YAŚODHARA : Author of the Āyurvedic treatise called *Rasa-prakāśa-sudhākara*. He is believed to have been a Bengal Brahmin of the 13th century.

Yaśodhara wrote the *Jayamaṅgalā* comm. on the *Kāma-sūtra* of Vātsyāyana under the Chāhamāna king Vīsaladeva (middle of the 13th century).

YOGĀNANDANĀTHA : Author of the *Āyurveda-sūtra* probably of the 16th century A.D.

PART II

WORKS

ABHIDHĀNA-CINTĀMAṆI : A lexicon by Hemacandra. It deals with synonyms in six sections, and is supplemented by the botanic dictionary *Nighaṇṭuśeṣa*. Its six sections (*Kāṇḍa*) are called respectively *Devādideva*, *Deva*, *Martya*, *Bhūmi*, *Tiryak* and *Sāmānya*.

[Ed. NSP, 1946]

ABHIDHĀNA-RATNAMĀLA : A lexicon by the poet-grammarian Halāyudha, dating back to c. 950 A.D. It consists of five sections called *Kāṇḍas*, viz *Svarga-kāṇḍa*, *Bhūmi-kāṇḍa*, *Pātāla-kāṇḍa*, *Sāmānya-kāṇḍa* and *Anekārtha-kāṇḍa*.

[Ed. T. Aufrecht, London, 1861. Also ed., under the title *Halāyudha-kośa*, with a commentary, by J. Joshi, Banaras, 1879 Śaka (=1957 A.D.).]

ABHIDHARMAKOŚA : A philosophical work by Vasubandhu. It is one of the most important sources of our knowledge of the tenets of the Sarvāstivādin and other schools of Hīnayāna Buddhism. In 600 memorial verses (*kārikās*), with the author's own comm., the work deals with the entire field of ontology, psychology, cosmology, ethics and the doctrine of salvation. The last chapter deals with the Buddhist doctrine of soul, i.e. denial of a permanent soul. The work has not come down in the Sanskrit original; we know only the *Abhidharmakośa-vyākhyā* by Yaśomitra. We have its Chinese and Tibetan versions. The earliest Chinese translation is by Paramārtha (563-67 A.D.). A second Chinese translation (651-54 A.D.) is by the famous Hiuen Tsang. In this work we get glimpses of the debates between the Vaibhāṣikas and the Sautrāntikas.

[See la vallée Poussin's *Abhidharmakośa de Vasubandhu*, Paris, 1923. Translated by same scholar, 1924-31. Chapter III, dealing with cosmology, reconstructed in Sanskrit and translated into French by same scholar in Buddhisme, Etudes et Matèriaux, Cosmologie: Le Monde des Etres et le monde-Réceptacle (Mêmoires de l' Acadêmie Roy. De Belgique, classe de lettres, etc., II. Serie, t. VI. 1914-19, according to Tibetan version.]

ABHIDHĀVṚTTI-MĀTṚKĀ : Written by Mukula, in 15 Kārikās with Vṛtti, it is a work on the grammatico-rhetorical question of Abhidhā and Lakṣaṇā.

[Ed. M.R. Telang, NSP, 1916]

ABHIJÑĀNA-ŚĀKUNTALA (or, ŚAKUNTALĀ) : The most famous Sanskrit drama. Written by Kālidāsa in seven acts, it deals with the Duṣyanta-Śakuntalā legend which occurs in the *Mahābhārata* (I. 62-69) as well as in the *Padmapurāṇa* (Svarga-khaṇḍa). Into the original story Kālidāsa has introduced many changes the most prominent of which are the curse of Durvāsas and the ring-episode. Some scholars point out the similarity of the theme of the drama with the story of the *Kaṭṭhahāri-jātaka*, and think that Kālidāsa is indebted to it for the idea of the ring.

King Duṣyanta, while out on a hunting excursion, falls in love with a hermitage-girl called Śakuntalā. Eventually they are wedded by mutual consent. The king gives her a ring as a souvenir, promises to send for her in due course and returns to his capital. Śakuntalā, engrossed in thoughts about him, fails to accord a welcome to sage Durvāsas who comes as a guest. The irate sage pronounces a curse upon her to the effect that her lover will never be able to remember her. At the intercession of her friends, the sage relents a bit and makes it a condition that the curse will be ineffective if Śakuntalā's lover finds a token of recognition. Śakuntalā, *enceinte*, is sent to the king who fails to recognise her. She fails to produce the ring lost in the way. She is repudiated by the king, but is, however, carried off by a celestial being. In course of time, the lost ring is recovered and, at its sight, the king remembers all about his woodland love and pines away in grief. At Indra's request, he goes to heaven to fight the demons.

On way back, he meets Śakuntalā and her son in a hermitage. Thus, the separated lover and the beloved are reunited.

The drama has come down in several recensions of which four, viz. Bengali, Devanāgarī, Kashmiri and South Indian, are generally distinguished. A fifth recension may also be traced. The Bengali and the Devanāgarī are, however, the two main recensions.

Both Indian and Western critics have praised the work in glowing terms. The Indians praise particularly the fourth Act where Śakuntalā leaves the hermitage for her husband's house. In this Act again, four stanzas are regarded as the best; opinions differ as to which four are the best. Of Western scholars, Goethe appreciates it in superlative terms. He finds in it "the young year's blossoms and the fruits of its decline" and the "earth and heaven combined in one name" (i.e. Śakuntalā).

[Ed. Bengali recension—A.L. Chêzy, Paris, 1830; R. Pischel, Kiel, 1877.

Devanāgarī recension—Böhtlingk, Bonn, 1842; M. Williams, Oxford, 1876 (2nd. ed.).

Kashmir recension—K. Burkhard, Wien, 1884.

South Indian recension—Śrī Vāṇi Vilāsa Press, Srirangam, 1917.

See D.K. Kanjilal, *A reconstrution of the true text of the Abhijñāna-śākuntalam of Kālidāsa from six or more available recensions.* Ed. with Rāghavabhaṭṭa's comm. by N.B. Godabole and K.P. Parab, Bombay, 1883: S.K. Belvalkar, New Delhi. A. Scharpé in *Kālidāsa Lexicon*, Vol. I, Pt. 1, Brugge, België. Ed. R. Jha, with comm. of Śaṃkara and Narahari, Darbhanga, 1957. English translation by W. Jones, London, 1790; M.B. Emaneau, Berkeley, 1962 (Bengali recension). There are numerous translations into various languages, Indian and foreign; e.g. German translation by O. Böhtlingk, Bonn, 1942; Rückert, 1876; Pischel, Kiel, 1877; French translation by A.L. Chézy, 1830; Czech translation by C. Vyhnis, 1873; Russian translation by K. Balmonta, Goslitfzdat, 1955. Also tr. into Georgian (Russia). On Text-criticism, see Pischel, De *De Kālidāsa Cakuntali recensionibus* (Diss.), Breslau, 1872 and *Die Rezensionen der Cakuntalā*, Breslau, 1875; A. Weber, Die rezensionen der Śakuntalā in *Ind. Studien*, XIV; *A Reconstruction of the Abhijñānaśākuntalam of Kālidāsa*, Calcutta, 1981. For a fuller bibliography, see Sten Konow, *Indian Drama* and M. Schuyler in *JAOS*, XXII; V. Raghavan, Bibliography of translations of Kālidāsa's works, *Indian Literature*, XI, 1968. The following papers may be consulted:—

Belvalkar, S.K. : Abhijñāna-śakuntalā and the Bhagavadgītā, *C.K. Raja Pres. Vol.*, Madras, 1941.

Raghavan, V. : Women characters in Kālidāsa's dramas, *AOR*, 1940.

Emaneau, M.R. : Kālidāsa's Śakuntalā and Mahābhārata, *JAOS*, Vol. 82, No. 1, 1962.]

ABHILASITĀRTHA-CINTĀMAṆI : See Mānasollāsa.

ABHINAVA-BHĀRATĪ : A comm. by Abhinavagupta, on the *Nāṭyaśāstra* of Bharata. Regarded as a highly authoritative exposition of Bharata's work. The comments on part of Chapter VII and the whole of Chapter VIII and Chapters XXXIII-XXXIV of Bharata's text are missing; there are also short gaps (e.g. on the last verse of Chapter V).

[Ed., with text, by M.R. Kavi, GOS, 1926, 1934 etc. A revised ed. by V. Raghavan to be shortly published. See V. Raghavan, Some corrections etc. to.....the Abhinavabhāratī, *Adyar Library Bulletin*, XVIII, 3-4, 1954; More corrections etc. Ibid., XXV, 1961; A New MS of the Abhinavabhāratī, *Summaries of Papers*, *AIOC*, 1974; P.S. Filliozat, Quotations of Ratnāvalī in Abhinavabhāratī, *Sternbach Fel. Vol.*, pp. 325-330.]

ABHINAYA-DARPAṆA : A work on histrionic art, attributed to Nandikeśvara, dealing mainly with gestures and postures used in drama and dance. It appears to have been compiled later than Bharata's Nāṭyaśāstra.

[Ed., with English translation and notes, by M. Ghosh, 1975 (3rd. ed.). See *Mirror of Gesture* with Eng. trs., intro. and illustrations, by A.K. Coomaraswamy and G.K. Duggirala, 1970.]

ABHISAMAYĀLAṄKĀRA-KĀRIKĀ : Attributed to Maitreyanātha. 'Abhisamaya' has been explained as a sysnonym of *mārga*, and 'Alaṃkāra' denotes a literary form popular among the Buddhists. Written in the form of memorial verses, it deals with the Buddhist doctrine of the Path towards moral perfection and the attainment of the state of Buddhist Mahāyānist saint. Translation into Chinese between 261 and 316 A.D.

[See E. Conze, *Abhisamayālaṃkāra*—Introduction and translation from original texts, with Sanskrit-Tibetan indexes, Rome, 1954.]

ABHIṢEKA : A play, in six acts, based on the *Rāmāyaṇa*, by Bhāsa. It takes up the Rāma story at the point of the slaying of Vālin and consecration of Sugrīva. It supplies the episodes omitted in the other Rāma drama of Bhāsa, and ends with the ordeal of Sītā and consecration of Rāma. Its noteworthy feature is the sympathetic characterisation of Vālin and Rāvaṇa. The author has slightly modified the original story.

[Ed. C.R. Devadhar, Poona Oriental Series, 1937. See C. Reddy, Sources of Deviation from Vālmīki in...Abhiṣeka Nāṭaka, *Summaries of Papers, AIOC*, 1974.]

ĀCĀRĀDARŚA : A Smṛti digest by Śrīdatta Upādhyāya. It is a manual of the daily duties of the followers of the white *Yajurveda*. The topics discussed are: *Ācamana*, *Dantadhāvana*, *Snāna*, *Sandhyā*, *Japa*, *Brahma-yajña*, *Tarpaṇa*, daily worship of deities, *Vaiśvadeva*, *Atithisatkāra* etc.

[Ed. Banaras, Saṃvat 1920; Veṅkaṭeśvara Press, Bombay, 1961.]

ADBHUTA-RĀMĀYAṆA : Also called *Adbhutottara-rāmāyaṇa*, it is attributed to Vālmīki. It describes in 27 cantos, as a sequel to the *Rāmāyaṇa*, the earlier part of the story and the real nature of Sītā. In this book Sītā is represented as having killed a Rāvaṇa with 100 heads, whom Rāma could not defeat.

[Ed. Bombay, 1912 with Hindi comm; P. Tarkaratna, with Bengali translation by T. Kāvyatīrtha, Vaṅgavāsī Press, Calcutta, 1923.]

ADBHUTA-SĀGARA : A work, by Vallālasena, on omens and

portents. The work takes its name from Adbhuta which has been interpreted in two ways:

(1) that which occurs for the first time.

(2) that which existed before, but has assumed a new form.

It discusses various signs portending good or evil, and prescribes rites for averting the evil. The rites include worship of deities, feeding of Brāhmaṇas and making gifts of cows, gold etc. to them.

[Ed. M. Jha, Banaras, 1905]

ADHYĀTMA-RĀMĀYAṆA : It means 'the *Rāmāyaṇa* in which Rāma is the Supreme Ātman'. Considered as a part of the *Brahmāṇḍapurāṇa*, it teaches Vedāntic monism (*Advaita*) and Rāmabhakti as paths to salvation. Like the *Rāmāyaṇa* it is divided into seven books bearing the same titles. It is an epic in its external form, but actually it is a manual of devotion and is Tāntric in character. Like Tantras it is in the form of a dialogue between Śiva and Umā. In this work Rāma is essentially the god Viṣṇu, Sitā abducted by Rāvaṇa is only an illusion and the real Sītā, who is Lakṣmī and Prakṛti, emerges after the fire ordeal at the end of the book. Attributed to Vyāsa, it consists of about 4000 verses. Believed to have been composed in the 15th cent. A.D.

[Ed. N. Siddhantaratna, with an English intro. by P.C. Bagchi and three commentaries, Calcutta, 1935. There are other editions also. Of the several commentaries, the most note-worthy is the one by Śaṅkara. English translation by Lala Baij Nath, 2nd. ed., New Delhi, 1979. See R.M. Shastri, *Authorship of the Adhyātma-Rāmāyaṇa*, G. Jha Res. Institute, Allahabad.]

ADVAITA-SIDDHI : A work on Vedānta philosophy by Madhusūdana Sarasvatī. In it the author seems to vindicate non-dualism after vigorously refuting the antagonistic views.

[Ed., Calcutta, 1916-18, with *Gauḍabrahmānandī*, 1937; with the *Gurucandrikā*, Vol. III, ed. S.N. Sastri, Mysore, 1940; with *Bālabodhinī* comm. by J. Bagchi, Calcutta;

with *Gauḍabrahmānandī*, *Viṭṭhaleśopādhyāyī*, *Siddhivyākhyā* of Balabhadra, with critical summary, called *Caturgranthī*, by A.K. Shastri, ed. N.S.A.K. Sastri, Delhi, 1982]

ADVAITA-MAKARANDA : A work of considerable importance, by Lakṣmīdhara, on Vedānta philosophy.

ĀGAMAḌAMBARA : A four-act philosophical drama by Jayanta Bhaṭṭa. It contains discussions on the philosophical and religious doctrines prevailing at the time of the poet.

[Ed. V. Raghavan and A. Thakur, Darbhanga, 1969]

AGASTI-MATA : Attributed to sage Agastya, it deals with the origin, characteristics, qualities and mode of testing jewels like pearls, diamonds, emeralds etc.

[Text in Roman character and trs., along with other texts, under the title *Les lapidaires indiens*, by L. Finot, Paris, 1896. Also see *Ratna-rahasya*, by R.D. Sen, Calcutta, 1884. The last section has the title page: *agastimataṃ nāma ratnaśāstram.*]

AGASTYA-SAṂHITĀ : One of the earliest texts dealing exclusively with the worship of Rāma as Supreme God. It is in the form of a dialogue between Agastya and Sutīkṣṇa. It is quoted in the *Caturvarga-cintāmaṇi* of Hemādri; so it may date back to the 12th cent. A.D. at the latest.

[See H. Bakker, the *Agastya-saṃhitā* and the history of the Rāma cult, *Summaries of Papers*, 5th World Skt. Conf., Varanasi, 1981, p. 218.]

AGNI-PURĀṆA : It describes the incarnations of Viṣṇu including those as Rāma and Kṛṣṇa. A large portion is devoted to the Viṣṇu cult. But, it is essentially a Śaivite work, and deals with the mystic cult of the Liṅga and Durgā. It also mentions Tāntric rites, gives instruction for the construction and consecration of images of gods, and refers to the cult of Gaṇeśa and the sun-cult. A few chapters deal with death, transmigration and Yoga. Chapter 380 contains a summary of the doctrines of the *Bhagavadgītā*, and Chapter 381 contains a *Yama-gītā*. It is encyclopaedic in character, and deals with the following subjects :—

geography, astronomy, astrology, marriage and death, customs, omens and portents, housebuilding, iconography, usages of daily life, politics, art of war, law, medicine, metrics, poetics, grammar and lexicography.

It is a landmark in the history of poetics.

It is difficult to determine the periods or period to which the Purāṇa or parts of it belong.

[Ed. Bibliotheca Indica, 1873-1919; Ānandāśrama Skt. Series No. 41; B. Upadhyaya, with Introduction in Hindi, 1966. Translation into English by M. N. Dutt, Calcutta, 1901 (Reprint with comprehensive index, Chowkhamba Sanskrit Studies, Vol. LIV).

See S. D. Gyani, *Agni-purāṇa—a study*; B.B. Mishra, *Polity in the Agni-purāṇa*, Calcutta; M. De Mallmann, Les enseignements iconographiques de l' Agni Purāṇa, Annales du Musee Guimet, Bibliotheque d'etudes, t. 67, Paris, 1963; S.M. Bhattacharya, *Alaṃkāra Section in the Agni-purāṇa*, Calcutta, 1977; R.S. Bhattacharya, *Subject-index of the Agnipurāṇa with important proper names*, Varanasi; *Intro. to the Index of Agnipurāṇa*; S. Handa, *Agnipurāṇ ki dārśanik evam āyurvedic sāmagrī kā adhyayan* (Hindi), Varanasi, 1982.]

AHIRBUDHNYA-SAṂHITĀ : A Tantric work. One of the earlier Saṃhitās of the Viṣṇuite Pañcarātra sect. It is a Kashmirian work which probably originated soon after the 4th century A.D. The work is in the form of a conversation between Ahirbudhnya, i.e. Śiva, and Nārada. It deals largely with occultism, and partly with philosophical matters.

[Ed. M. D. Rāmānujācārya, under the supervision of F.O. Schrader, Adyar, Madras, 1916]

AIHOLE INSCRIPTION : This inscription of Pulakeśin II, dated 634 A.D., is a landmark in the history of Sanskrit literature. It is the only definite means of determining the lower terminus of the date of Kālidāsa as well as of Bhāravi both of whom are mentioned in it.

[*Epigraphia Indica*, VI. P. I.]

AINDRA VYĀKARAṆA : The supposed name of a grammatical work, believed to have been written under instructions of the great pre-Pāṇini grammarian, Indra.

[See A. C. Burnell, *The Aindra School of Sanskrit Grammarians*, 1875.]

AITAREYA ĀRAṆYAKA : : See Ārayṇyaka.

[Ed., with Sāyaṇa's comm. by N. Sastri Talekara, ASS, 1959; ed. with Intro., Eng. trans., notes, indexes and appendix, by A.B. Keith.; M.Haug has ed., trans. and explained this work. See S. Sharma, *Aitareya Āraṇyaka, ek Adhyayan* (Hindi), Delhi, 1981].

AITAREYA BRĀHMAṆA : See Brāhmaṇa.

[Ed. S. Samasrami, with Sāyaṇa's comm., Bib. Ind., 1895-1906; Pillai, with *Sukhapradā* comm. in 3 vols., TSS (Vol. III pub. 1955). Translation into English by A.B. Keith, along with the Kauṣītaki, HOS, 1920. See *Alphabetical Index of words occurring in the Aitareya Brāhmaṇa*, etc., ed. V.B. Sastri, 1916. On the Language of this Brāhmaṇa, see Liebich, *Pāṇini*.]

AITAREYOPANIṢAD : The topics discussed in it are cosmogony, rebirth and immortality. Last of all is described Brahman as the receptacle of all things.

[Ed., along with the Taittirīya, with Śaṅkara's comm. and Ānandagiri's gloss, by E. Roer, 1849-50; Satavalekar, Pardi, 1953. *Aitareya-Upaniṣad*, with Śaṅkara's comm., trs. into Eng. with critical notes by H.M. Bhadramkar, Dharwar, 1922.]

AJAḌA-PRAMĀTṚ-SIDDHI : A work on Kashmirian Śaiva philosophy, by Utpala.

ALAṂKĀRA-KAUSTUBHA : There are several works of this title, written by different authors, viz. Kavikarṇapūra, Kalyāṇa Subrahmaṇya, Viśveśvara and Veṅkatācārya. Of these, the work of Kavikarṇapūra is the most noteworthy. It is composed in 10 chapters, called Kiraṇas, which are as follows :

1. Kāvya-lakṣaṇa, 2. Śabdārtha, 3. Dhvani, 4. Guṇībhūta-vyaṅgya, 5. Rasa-bhāva-tadbheda, 6 Guṇa, 7. Śabdālaṃ-

kāra, 8. Arthālaṃkāra, 9. Rīti, 10. Doṣa. (Most of the illustrative verses are in praise of Kṛṣṇa and the subject-matter follows the *Kāvya-prakāśa* in treatment.

[Ed. with comm. of Viśvanātha Cakravartin, Murshidabad, 1899; by S. Bhattacharya, with an anonymous comm. and a gloss, Rajshahi, Vol. I (Chs. I—V), 1923.]

ALAṂKĀRA-SAṂGRAHA : Same as Jayadeva's *Candrāloka* (q.v.).

ALAṂKĀRA-SARVASVA : Three works of this title are known. One of these, not yet printed, is by an unknown author. It deals with the general topics of Alaṃkāraśāstra. One Keśava Miśra appears to have written a book of this name.

There is a work of this title by Ruyyaka. It consists of two parts, viz. *Sūtra* and *Vṛtti*. While some think that both the parts were written by Ruyyaka, according to others, the *Sūtra* was written by Ruyyaka and the *Vṛtti* by Maṅkhaka or Maṅkhuka. The work deals only with poetic figures.

[*Alaṃkāra-sarvasva* of Maṅkhaka, ed., with comm. along with Ruyyaka's *Alaṃkāra-sūtra* and *Vṛtti* thereon, T. Gaṇapati Śāstrī, TSS, 1915. Ruyyaka's *Alaṃkāra-sarvasva*, ed. G. Dvivedī, 1939; with *Saṃjīvanī* comm. of Vidyācakravartin, *Text and Study* by S.S. Janaki, ed. V. Rāghavan, Delhi, 1965.]

ALLAHABAD STONE PILLAR INSCRIPTION : It is Hariṣeṇa's panegyric of the Gupta King Samudragupta, consisting of eight verses, a long prose passage and a concluding verse. The inscription testifies to the fact that Kāvya, in a fairly developed form, existed in that remote age.

[For the inscription and notes thereon, see D. C. Sircar, *Select Inscriptions*, I, Calcutta, 1942, pp. 254 ff.]

ĀLOKA : A reputed commentary, by Pakṣadhara Miśra, on Gaṅgeśa's *Tattva-cintāmaṇi*.

AMARA-KOṢA : See *Nāmaliṅgānuśāsana*.

AMARUŚATAKA : An erotic Sanskrit lyric by Amaru or Amaruka. It exists at least in four recensions, viz. South Indian, Bengali, West Indian and Miscellaneous. The number of verses varies from 96 to 115; the verses common to all the recensions are 51. It describes the different mental states of the lover and the beloved.

[Ed. R. Simon, Kiel, 1893; Durgaprasad, with comm. of Arjunavarmadeva, NSP, 1916 (3rd. ed.) ; with Skt. comm. by Bakkanve, Delhi, 1967. Translated into French by A. Chezy, 1831. See S.K. De, The Text of the *Amaruśataka* in 'Our Heritage' (*Calcutta Sanskrit College Jour.* Vol. II, pt. I, Jan.-June, 1954).]

AMṚTAMANTHANA : In a legend occurring in the *Nāṭya-śāstra,* it is stated that God Brahmā himself wrote a play of this title.

ĀNANDALAHARĪ : A poem, in about 104 verses, attributed to Śaṃkarācārya. It is in praise of Tripurasundarī, mixed with mystical doctrine.

[Ed., with Eng. trs. and a comm. by A.Avalon, 1953 (4th ed.). Translation into French by Troyer under the title *L'onde de Beatitude.* See A.S. Tiwari, Comparative Study of *Ānandalaharī* and *Lakṣmīlaharī* of Jagannātha, *Summaries of Papers,* 5th World Skt. Con., Varanasi, 1981, p. 224.]

ANAṄGARAṄGA : A work on erotics, by Kalyāṇamalla of the 16th century A.D.

[Ed. V. P. Bhandari, CSS, 1923. English translation (anonymous) for Kamasūtra Society, London and Banaras, 1985]

ANARGHARĀGHAVA : A drama, in seven acts, by Murāri. It dramatises the traditional narrative of the *Rāmāyaṇa* with slight modifications.

[Ed. Durgaprasad and Parab, with comm. of Rucipati, NSP, 1937; R. Misra, with Sanskrit-Hindi comm., Banaras, 1960]

ANEKĀRTHA-KOŚA : It is a lexicon by Maṅkha with his own comment. It uses the lexical works of Amara, Śāśvata, Halāyudha and Dhanvantari.

[Ed. T. Zachariae, with extracts from comm. and three indices, Vienna, 1897. See B.C. Mondal, Author and date of *Maṅkha-Kośa*, *ABORI*, 1976]

ANEKĀRTHA-ŚABDAKOŚA : See *Medinī-kośa*.

ANEKĀRTHA-SAṂGRAHA : A lexicon by Hemacandra Sūri. It collects in verses Skt. words havings more meanings than one.

[Ed.J. Sastri Hoshing, 1969, with Index]

ANEKĀRTHA-SAMUCCAYA : A well-known lexicon by Śāśvata. In it homonyms are arranged according as the explanation takes a whole verse, a half verse and a quarter-verse; indeclinables conclude the work.

[Ed. Zachariae, Berlin, 1882; N.N. Kulkarni, 1930]

AṆUBHĀṢYA : A commentary, by Vallabha, on the *Brahma-sūtras* of Bādarāyaṇa.

[Ed. Bib. Ind., 1888-97, with *Bhāṣya-prakāśa* comm., by R.G. Bhaṭṭa. See B.G. Shukla, Authority of Bhāgavata Purāṇa in connection with Brahmasūtrāṇubhāṣya, *Summaries of Papers*, 5th World Skt. Con., Varanasi, 1981, p. 178.]

ANUGĪTĀ : A part of the *Mahābhārata* (Book XIV, 16—51), it describes the spiritual instructions given by Kṛṣṇa to Arjuna after the conclusion of the war of Kurukṣetra. Besides, it contains the legends of Utaṅka, the preservation of the foetus of Uttarā from the Brahmāstra hurled by Aśvatthāman and an account of the Aśvamedha sacrifice performed by Yudhiṣṭhira.

[Translation into English by K.T. Telang, SBE, Vol viii; into German by Deussen, *Vier philosophische Texte des Mahābhāratam*.]

ANUKRAMAṆĪ : Name of a class of works which are catalogues, lists or indexes giving the contexts of the Vedic saṃhitās with regard to different items. Thus, Śaunaka wrote *Anukramaṇīs* of the Ṛṣis, metres, deities and hymns of the *Ṛgveda*.

ANUMĀNA-DĪDHITI : The most renowned work of Raghunātha Śiromaṇi. It is an authoritative commentary on the Anumāna-khaṇḍa of the *Tattvacintāmaṇi* of Gaṅgeśa. Part of the author's *Tattva-cintāmaṇi-dīdhiti*.

[Ed. M. Tarkālaṃkāra, Calcutta, 1905]

ANYOKTI-MUKTĀLATĀ : It consists of 108 detached verses, in varied metres, by Śambhu. The verses are allegorical and devoted to description of natural objects, feminine grace etc. [Ed. Kāvyamālā, II.]

APARĀRKA : Written by Aparāditya or Aparārka, its full title is *Aparārkayājñavalkiya-dharma-śāstra-nibandha*. It is an authoritative commentary on the *Yājñavalkya-smṛti*. Though a commentary, it is a sort of digest because it cites numerous passages from different Smṛti works, and discusses different views finally giving its own conclusions. [Pub. in two vols. by Ānandāśrama Press, Poona, 1903-04]

APAROKṢĀNUBHŪTI : A metrical composition by Śaṃkara, in which he lays down his philosophical views.

[Eng. trs. by Vimuktānanda; also by M.N Dvivedi, Bombay]

ĀPASTAMBA-ŚRAUTASŪTRA : See Śrautasūtra.

[Ed., with Dhūrtasvāmin's comm., by C. Sastri and P.N. P. Śāstrī, GOS, 1963. Books I—VII trs. into German by W. Caland, Göttingen, 1921. See W. Caland, *Das Śrautasūtra Des Āpastamba* and A.N.K. Aiyangar, Some additional Sūtras of Āpastamba Dharmasūtra, *C. K. Raja Pres. Vol.*, Madras, 1941; B. Bhattacharya, *Studies in Śrauta-sūtras of Āpastamba*; S. Chakrabarti, The Position of Paribhāṣās in the Textual Order of Āpastamba Śrautasūtra, *JRAS*, London, No. 1, 1979.]

ĀPASTAMBA-DHARMASŪTRA : See Dharma-sūtra.

[Ed. Bühler, with extracts from the comm. *Ujjvalā* of Haradatta, Bombay, 1932; A. C. Sastri and A. R. Sastri, with the same comm., Banaras, 1932; M. Sastri, Poona, 1932. Trs. into English by Bühler, Sacred Books of the East, Vol. II.]

ĀPASTAMBA-GṚHYASŪTRA : See Gṛhyasūtra.

[Ed., with Kapardisvāmin's comm., by Sastri, Kumbhakonam, 1953]

ĀPASTAMBA-ŚULVASŪTRA : See Śulva-sūtra.

APOHA-SIDDHI : A tract on Nyāya, by Ratnakīrti. According to this work, words denote neither the positive objects nor negative ones. The essence of meaning consists in the simultaneous cognition of the positive and negative sides. All determinate objects have a positive nature which excludes others.

[Ed. in Tibetan Sanskrit Works Series, Vol. III. *Ratnakīrti-nibandhāvalī*, Patna, 1957.]

ĀRAṆYAKA : In the Brāhmaṇas, or as appendices to them, there are texts known as Āraṇyakas or forest-texts. These dealt with secret matters of uncanny character and spelt danger to the uninitiated. Hence they could be taught and learnt in the forest, and not in the village. The principal contents of these works are mysticism and symbolism of sacrifice and priestly philosophy. The Āraṇyakas belong to the various Vedic schools. For example, the *Aitareya-āraṇyaka* belongs to the *Ṛgveda*. The other prominent Āraṇyakas are the *Kauṣītaki-āraṇyaka* belonging to the *Ṛgveda* and the *Taittirīya-āraṇyaka* belonging to the *Yajurveda*.

[See Winternitz : *History of Indian Literature*, Vol. I, 1927, p. 225 ff.]

ĀRCA JYAUTIṢA : Contains a summary of the astronomical knowledge of the Vedic Hindus up to about 2nd century A.D.

[Ed., with comm. and notes, along with the *Yājuṣa-Jyautiṣa*, by S. Dvivedi, Banaras, 1908]

ARJUNA-RĀVAṆĪYA : Same as *Rāvaṇārjunīya* (q.v.).

ARTHASAMGRAHA : A well-known work on Mīmāṃsā philosophy, by Laugākṣi Bhāskara. Based on the *Mīmāṃsā-nyāyaprakāśa* of Āpadeva.

[Ed. BenSS., 1882. Text with English translation by R. D. Karmarkar; Ed., with comm. of R. Bhikṣu, and translation into English by D. V. Gokhale; Ed. & trans. by A.B. Gajendragadkar & R. D. Karmarkar, reprinted with Intro. by Motilal Banarsidass Delhi, 1984]

ARTHAŚĀSTRA : Attributed to Kauṭilya or Kauṭalya, also called Viṣṇugupta or Cāṇakya, it is the earliest extant text on politics and statecraft. In its present form it consists of fifteen large sections called Adhikaraṇas and 180 sub-divisions styled Prakaraṇas; this division is crossed by one into chapters called Adhyāyas which are marked off from the prose of the work by the insertion of verses summing up the doctrine laid down above. The contents, Adhikaraṇa-wise, are as follows :

I. Upbringing and education of a prince; appointment of ministers and ministerial officers, spies, emissaries, counsels, measures of a king's personal safety.

II. Duties of a vast army of superintendents.

III. Law is discussed.

IV. Repression of evil-doers by police action and heavy penalties; deceitful doctors and tradesmen, artificial increase of prices, adulteration, use of false weights are some of the practices condemned.

V. Means of getting rid of an undesirable minister, extortion of taxes for filling the treasury, remuneration of the royal entourage.

VI. Description of the seven elements of politics, interstate relations.

VII. The six *Guṇas* or political expedients.

VIII. Evils arisings from a king's addiction to vices; misfortunes which fire, water etc. may bring on a land.

IX-X. War.

XI. Dissension among, and destruction of the cohesion of, hostile aristocracies of warriors.

XII. Means by which a weak king may aggrandise himself.

XIII. Capture of fortified cities.

XIV. The secret part consisting of recipes to enable one to murder, to cause blindness or madness and so on.

XV. Plan of the work, 32 methodological principles used in the discussion.

The *Arthaśāstra* has often been regarded as comparable to the works of Machiavelli. Some scholars think that it is not a work of Kauṭilya, but rather of a school which followed his views.

The following commentaries on the work have been published:—*Jayamaṅgalā*, *Pratipada-pañcikā*, *Nayacandrikā*, *Nītinirṇita*, *Śrīmūlā*. Leaving aside the first one, the others are by Bhaṭṭasvāmin, Mādhava, Yogghama and Gaṇapati Śāstri respectively.

[Ed. R. Shamasastri, Mysore, 1909 (2nd. ed. 1919); T. Ganapati Sastri with his *Śrīmūlā* comm., TSS, 3 vols., 1921, 1924,

1925; J. Jolly and R. Schmidt (with *Nayacandrikā* comm.), Lahore, 1923-24; R.P. Kangle, Bombay, 1960. See Bhaṭṭasvāmin's comm., ed. K.P. Jayaswal and A. Banerji Sastri, *Jour. of Bihar and Orissa Research Soc.*, Supp. to vols. 11, 12 (1925 and 1926). Translation into English by J.J. Meyer, Manover, 1925 f; Shamasastri, Bangalore, 1915 (2nd. ed. 1923); R.P. Kangle, Bombay, 1963; S.F. Oldenberg, et. al., ed. V. Kalyanov, *Arthaśāstra ili Nauka Politiki*, Moscow, 1959; into Hindi ed. *Bhārtīya Yoga*, Bareilly, 1973.]

For various problems connected with the Arthaśāstra see P.V. Kane, *History of Dharmaśāstra* Vol. I. For studies in the Arthaśāstra, see Jolly, *Zeit f. vergl. Rechts-wissenschaft*, xii. 305-18; G.B. Bottazzi, *Precursoridi Niccolo Machiavelli in India ed, in Grecia, Kauṭilya and Thucidides* (1914); F. Wilhelm, *Politische polemiken in Staateslehrbuch Des Kauṭilya*; M.V.K. Rao, *Studies in Kauṭilya*; and R.P. Kangle in the third part of his *Kauṭilīya Arthaśāstra*, Bombay, 1965. For fish in the Arthaśāstra, see S.L. Hora in *Jour. of Asiatic Society*, Calcutta, 1948 (3rd series) and *Year Book of Asiatic Society*, Calcutta, 1949. Also see Brelser, *Kauṭilya Studien*, 3 Vols., Bonn, 1927-34; B.C. Sen, *Economics in Kauṭilya*, Sanskrit College, Calcutta, 1967; P.C. Chunder, *Kauṭilya on Love and Morals*, Calcutta, 1970; R.C. Hazra, *Kauṭilya Studies* (shortly to be published in Calcutta); N.S. Venkatanathan in publication No. 103 of Oriental Res. Institute, Mysore; T.R. Trautmann, *Kauṭilya and the Arthaśāstra*, Leiden, 1971; R.K. Chaudhary, *Kauṭilya's Political Ideas and Institutions*, Banaras; A. chatterjee, *Arthaśāstra of Kauṭilya, a new approach*, Calcutta, 1982; H. Scharfe, *Unter suchungen zur staatsrechtslehredes Kauṭilya*, Wiesbaden, Harrasowitz, 1968. For various editions of the text and commentaries, and a comprehensive list of works and papers dealing with different aspects of Arthaśāstra, see L. Sternbach's *Bibliography of Kauṭilya Arthaśāstra*, Hoshiarpur, 1973. Also see G. Harihar Sastri, Kauṭilya's Arthaśāstra: some textual problems, *V. Raghavan Felicitation Volume*, p. 315; B. Mukherjee, *Kauṭilya's Concept of Democracy*; B.P. Sinha, *Readings in Kauṭilya's Arthaśāstra*; S.N. Dhar, *Kauṭilya and the Arthaśāstra*. Also see *Index Verborum* by R. Sharma Sastri, Mysore, 1924-25; E. Ribschi and M. Schetelich, *Studien zum Kauṭilya Arthaśāstra*, Berlin, 1973.

The following papers may be consulted :—

Buddhaprakash: Kauṭilya on Slavery, *H.L. Hariyappa Mem. Vol.*, Poona, 1955.

Das Gupta, D.C.: Kauṭilya and his educational views, *B. Kakati Comm. Vol.*, Gauhati, 1953.

Deb, H.K.: On forms of Government in Kauṭilya Arthaśāstra, *Winternitz Memo. No.* (ed. N.N. Law), Calcutta, 1938.

Dikshitar, V.R.R.: Bhāsa and Kauṭilya, *P.V. Kane Pres. Vol.*, Poona, 1941.

Jolly, J.: Lexicalishes aus dem Arthaśāstra, *Festgabe Delbruck*, Strassburg, 1912-13.

: Ganapati Śāstri's Kommentar sum Kauṭilīya Arthaśāstra, *Festgabe Jacobi*, Bom. 1926.

Kane, P.V.: Kauṭilya and the Matsyapurāṇa, *B.C. Law Vol.*, II, Poona, 1946.

LAW, N.N.: The six guṇas in Kauṭilya, *K.B. Pathak Comm.* Vol., Poona, 1934.

MULLER-HESS, E. : Zum, Kauṭilya Arthaśāstra, *Festschrift* E. *Kuhn*, Breslan, 1916.

NARAHARI, H.G. : Kauṭilya and the Vedas, *K. M. Munshi Diamond Jubilee Vol.* (*Bharatiya Vidya*, Vols. 9, 10), Bombay, 1948, 1949.

PUSALKER, A.D. : Bhāsa and Kauṭilya's Arthaśāstra, *K.V.R. Aiyangar Comm. Vol.*, Madras, 1940.

RAGHAVAN, V. : Bhavabhūti and Arthaśāstra, New Indology, *Festschrift W. Ruben*, Berlin, 1970.

SINGH & SINGH : Advances...drinks etc. in Arthaśāstra, *Summaries of Papers*, 5th *World Skt. Conf.*, Varanasi, 1981, p. 207.

TAMASKAR, G.D. : The country of Kauṭilya's Arthaśāstra, *Siddhabhārati* (*S. Varma Vol.*), II, Hoshiarpur, 1950.

———: Some observations on Kauṭilya's measures of time, *P. V. Kane Pres. Vol.*, Poona, 1941.

ĀRYABHAṬĪYA : It is an astronomical and mathematical work by Āryabhaṭa. Also called *Ārya-siddhānta*. It is divided into the following broad sections : *Daśagītikā*, *Gaṇitapāda*, *Kālakriyā* and *Gola*.

[Ed. with the *Bhaṭṭadīpikā* comm. and general index by H. Kern, Leiden, 1874; with the comm. of Nīlakaṇṭhasomasutvan (*Gaṇitapāda* and *Kālakriyā-pāda*), *TSS*, 1930-31. *Golapāda* only ed. in the same Series with the same comm., 1957. *Gaṇitapāda*, trs. G. R. Kaye, *Jour. and Proceedings of Asiatic Society of Bengal*, 1908. Entire work translated by P. C. Sen Gupta, *Jour. of Deptt. of Letters*, Calcutta University, Vol. 16 (1927) ; W. E. Clark (with notes), Chicago, 1930.]

ĀRYĀ-SAPTAŚATĪ : It consists of lyrical verses in Āryā metre by Govardhana. In it we find over 700 detached verses arranged under appropriate headings. It has probably been modelled on the *Sattasaī* of Hāla. The verses are on various subjects erotic in character.

[Ed. Durgaprasad and Parab, NSP, 1895 (2nd. ed.) with comm. of Ananta; with comm. *Rasapradīpikā*, 1931.]
There is an *Āryā-saptaśatī* by Viśveśvara, composed on the model of Govardhana's work.

[Ed. Bhandari, with author's own comm., *CSS*, 1924.]

ĀRYASIDDHĀNTA : A work on astronomy, by Āryabhaṭa II. It is assigned to c. 950 A.D. In its numerical notation it differs entirely from Āryabhaṭa I. It consists of 18 chapters. Also called *Āryabhaṭa-siddhānta* or *Mahāsiddhānta*.

[Ed. S. Dvivedi, with his own comm., Banaras, 1910.]

ĀRYĀṢṬAŚATA : A work, by Āryabhaṭa I, on astronomy. Its 108 verses in Āryā metre are divided into Gaṇita (33 stanzas on mathematics), Kālakriyā (25 stanzas on measurement of time) and Gola (50 stanzas on the sphere).

ĀŚCARYACŪḌĀMAṆI : A drama, in seven acts, by Śaktibhadra. It dramatises the story of the *Rāmāyaṇa*, and betrays knowledge of Bhavabhūti's plays. It takes its name from the magic crest-jewel of Sītā used as a token of recognition.

[Ed. C. S. Sastri, with introduction by Kuppusvami Sastri, Madras, 1926. English translation by the same editor published in 1927.]

AṢṬĀDHYĀYĪ : The earliest extant and the most authoritative grammar by Pāṇini. Divided into eight *Adhyāyas* (chapters) each of which is subdivided into four sections called *Pādas*. The total number of aphorisms is nearly 4000. It consists of aphorisms by Pāṇinī and supplementary rules, called *Vārtika-sūtra*, by Kātyāyana. This work, besides dealing with classical Sanskrit, gives rules for the Vedic language as well as Vedic accents. It mentions a few earlier grammarians. It is recognised by some eminent western scholars as the most scientific of all the grammatical systems of the world.

[Ed. and translated, O.Böhtlingk, Leipzig, 1887; S.C. Vasu, Allahabad, 2 Vols., 1891 (Reprint by Motilal Banarsidass, 1962). For studies on Pāṇini and his grammar, see Agrawala, *India as known to Pāṇini*; Goldstücker, *Pāṇini and his place in Sanskrit literature*; Faddegon, *Studies in Pāṇini's Grammar*; Thieme, *Pāṇini and the Veda*; Pawate, *The Structure of the Aṣṭādhyāyī*, 1950; Buiskool, *Pūrvatrāsiddham*, Amsterdam, 1934 (Abridged recast called *The Tripādī*, Leiden, 1939), Liebich, *Pāṇini*, 1891; L. Renou, *Etudes Vediques et Pāṇineennes*, Paris, Vols. 1-13, 1955, 1957 etc. and *Le Grammaire de Pāṇini traduite du Sanskrit*, Paris, Vol. I 1948, Vol. II 1951, Vol. III 1954; H.P. Dvivedi, *Studies in Pāṇini*, Delhi, 1978; P. B. Jumarkar, *Introd. to Pāṇini*, Baroda, 1977. In connexion with the *Aṣṭādhyāyī* following works also may be consulted :—

Pāṇini—a survey of research by G. Cardona, 1980. *Word-index to Pāṇini-sūtrapāṭha and Pariśiṣṭas*, compiled by Pathak and Chitrao, followed by *Aṣṭādhyāyi-sūtra-pāṭha* with *Vārtikas, Dhātu-pāṭha*, *Gaṇapāṭha* etc., Poona, 1935; F. Kielhorn, *Kātyāyana and Patañjali—their relation to each other and to Pāṇini*, Banaras, 1963 (2nd ed.); K.M.K. Sarma, *Pāṇini, Kātyāyana and Patañjali*, Delhi, 1968; V.S. Agrawala, *Gotras in Pāṇini*; B. Shefts, *Grammatical Method in Pāṇini*. R. Birwe's *Interpolationen in Pāṇini's Aṣṭādhyāyī* (Studia Indologica; *Festschrift für W. Kirfel*, Bonn 1955), may be consulted. Also see the same author's *Studies in chaps. iii, iv, v of the Aṣṭādhyāyī*. Also see B. K. Ghosh, Pūrvācāryas in Pāṇini, *D. R. Bhandarkar Vol.*, Calcutta, 1940; A.B. Keith, Pāṇini's Vocabulary, *R.K. Mookerji Vol., Bhārata-kaumudī*, Allahabad, 1945, 1947; S.P. Chaturvedi: Pāṇini's Vocabulary and his date, *Siddhabhāratī* (*S. Varma Vol.*) II, Hoshiarpur, 1950; Pāṇini's vocabulary: its bearing on his date, *Woolner Comm. Vol.*, Lahore, 1940; Technical Terms of the *Aṣṭādhyāyī*, *Prs. and Transactions of IXth AIOC*, 1940; G. V. Devasthali, *Anubandhas of Pāṇini*, Poona, 1967; S. Sen, *Pāṇinica*, Calcutta, 1970; R. Rocher, *La Theorie Des Voix Du Verhe Dans L' ecole Pāṇineenne* (Le 14E Āhnika), Bruxelles, 1968; H. Scharfe, *Pāṇini's metalanguage*, Philadelphia, 1971; S. M. Katre, *Dictionary of Pāṇini*, 3 Vols., Poona, 1968-69: S. D. Joshi, Pāṇini's Rules 1.4.49-1.4.51, *Summaries of Papers, AIOC*, 1974; Mahavir, Some Anomalies re: the Aṣṭādhyāyī, *Ibid*; V. N. Misra, *The Descriptive Technique of Pāṇini*. Also see R. S. Sastri, *Pāṇini Vyākaraṇ Śāstra Vaiśeṣika-tattva-mīmāṃsā*, Delhi, 1976; P. K. Majumdar, *Philosophy of Language in the light of Pāṇini and Mīmāṃsaka schools of Indian Philosophy*, Calcutta, 1977; H.P. Dvivedi, *Studies in Pāṇini*, Delhi, 1978; P.B. Junnarkar, *Intro. to Pāṇini*, Baroda, 1977; M.D. Balasubramanyam, *System of kṛt accentuation in Pāṇini and the Veda*, Tirupati, 1982; P. Kiparsky, *Pāṇini as a variationist*; ed. S.D. Joshi, *Some Theoretical Problems in Pāṇini's Grammar*, Poona, 1982; J.S. Bare, *Phonetics and Phonology in Pāṇini*, University of Michigan Phontics Latoratory, 1975.]

AṢṬĀṄGAHṚDAYASAṂHITĀ : A metrical work on Āyurveda, by Vāgbhaṭa II. Some think that one Vāgbhaṭa wrote both this work and the *Aṣṭāṅga-saṃgraha*. This work deals with the usual eight topics of Āyurveda, and is, like the *Aṣṭāṅga-saṃgraha*, divided into six sections (*Sthānas*). The *Sūtra-sthāna* of this work is regarded as the best, even better than that of Caraka and Suśruta. It deals, *inter alia*, with surgery. It was quoted in the Arabic work *Kitabal Fihrist, in* 888 A.D., under the title *Asankar* or *Astankar*.

[Ed. Y. Upādhyāya, with the comm. *Vidyotinī*, *CSS*, 1959, H. Sarma Vaidya, Banaras, V.S. 2024. First five chapters of the Tibetan version of the work edited and translated by C. Vogal, Wiesbaden, 1965.]

AṢṬĀṄGA-SAṂGRAHA : A work on Āyurveda, by Vāgbhaṭa I. According to some scholars, this and the *Aṣṭāṅga-hṛdaya-saṃhitā* were written by *one* Vāgbhaṭa. It is in prose and verse, and deals with the eight topics of Āyurveda. Its six sections are as follows :—

(1) *Sūtrasthāna*—40 chapters.
(2) *Śārīra-sthāna*—12 chapters.
(3) *Nidāna-sthāna*—16 chapters.
(4) *Cikitsā-sthāna*—40 chapters.
(5) *Kalpa-sthāna*—8 chapters.
(6) *Uttara-sthāna*—50 chapters

It follows, and incidentally reproduces, portions of the *Suśruta-saṃhitā* in its present form. It also quotes verses from the *Yoga-śataka* which is a little anterior to I-tsing (7th century A.D.). The work probably originated in the period between the 7th and 10th centuries.

[Ed. G. Changani. 1954. There is a Tibetan version of it.]

AṢṬASĀHASRIKĀ PRAJÑĀPĀRAMITĀ : Probably the earliest of the writings known as *Prajñāpāramitās* (q.v.). On the one hand, it was expanded into larger works, while on the other, its contents were condensed into shorter texts. It contains in 32 chapters dialogues between the Buddha and his disciples Subhūti, Śāriputra and Pūrṇa Maitrāyaṇīputra, and often Śakra, lord of gods, and sometimes a Bodhisattva join them.

[English translation by Edward Conze, 1958. Ed. with Haribhadra's comm. by P.L. Vaidya and S. Bagchi, Darbhanga, 1960. For studies in the *Prajñāpāramitā* literature see N. Dutt, *Aspects of Mahāyāna Buddhism*, London, 1930; T. Matsumoto, Die Prajñāpāramitā Literatur nebst einem Specimen der Suvikrāntavikrami-Prajñāpāramitā (*Bonner Orientalistische Studien*, Heft 1), Stuttgart, 1932. Also see The *Āloka* of Haribhadra and the *Sāratamā* of Ratnākaraśānti—a comparative study by P.S. Jaini, *BSOAS*, xxxv, Pt. 2, 1972.]

AṢṬĀVIṂŚATI-TATTVA : Twenty-eight works, by Raghunandana, the titles of which end in the word "—tattva". These are Smṛti digests on different topics as indicated by their titles given below :—

(Arranged alphabetically)

Āhnika-tattva
Chandoga-vṛṣotsarga°
Dāya°
Deva-pratiṣṭhā°
Dīkṣā°
Divya°
Durgotsava°
Ekādaśī°
Janmāṣṭamī°
Jyotis°
Kṛtya°
Malimluca°
Maṭha-pratiṣṭhā°
Puruṣottama-kṣetra°
Prāyaścitta°
Ṛg-vṛṣotsarga°
Saṃskāra°
Sāma-śrāddha°
Śūdra-kṛtya°
Śuddhi°
Taḍāga-bhavanotsarga°
Tithi°
Udvāha°
Vāstu-yāga°
Vrata°
Vyavahāra°
Yajur-vṛṣotsarga°
Yajuḥ-śrāddha°

[Ed. Jivananda, Calcutta, in two volumes, 1895; S. Vidyabhusana (in Bengali Script), Calcutta 1347 B.S. (New ed.). *Divyatattva*, ed. R.W. Lariviere, New Delhi.]

AŚVA-CIKITSITA : A work on horse-lore, attributed to Nakula, and assigned to a period before 1000 A.D.

[Ed. *Bib. Ind.*, 1887.]

ĀŚVALĀYANA-ŚRAUTASŪTRA : See Śrautasūtra.

[Ed., with comm. of Gārgya Nārāyaṇa, in *Bib. Ind.*, 1869; with Nārāyaṇa's *Vṛtti*, by G. Sastri, 1917. See B. Bhattacharya *Studies in the Śrautasūtras of Āśvalāyana*, etc. Pt. I. trs. into Eng. by H.G. Ranade, Poona, 1981.]

ĀŚVALĀYANA-GṚHYASŪTRA : See Gṛhyasūtra.

[Ed., with comm. of Gārgya Nārāyaṇa, in *Bib. Ind.*, 1869; with comm. of Haradattācārya, by G. Sastri, *TSS*, No. 78, 1923; with German translation by A.F. Stenzler, *Indische Haus-regeln*,

AKM, III, 4, 1964 and IV, 1, 1965; translated into English by H. Oldenberg, *SBE*, Vol. 29. Ed. Sahitya Akademi, Delhi, 1965. See V.M. Apte, *Non-Ṛgvedic Mantras rubricated in the Āśvalāyana-gṛhyasūtra. Āśvalāyana-gṛhyasūtra-bhāṣya* of Devasvāmin, ed. K.P. Asthal Ayar, Madras, 1980.]

AŚVA-ŚĀSTRA : Ascribed to Nakula, one of the five Pāṇḍavas. It appears to be a compilation, and deals with the following topics :—

Praise of horses, eulogy of Raivata and others the recitation of whose names is considered to ward off evils to horses, winged horses of old and the gradual loss of their wings, good and bad signs of horses, auspicious neigh of horses, various kinds of smell on the bodies of horses indicating good or evil, gaits of horses, nature of horses, types of horses depending on the lands in which they are born, determination of the age of horses, complexion, training, rules about riding horses etc.

[Ed. Gopalan, Tanjore, 1952.]

AŚVA-VAIDYAKA : A huge treatise by Jayadatta Sūri, dealing with diseases of horses and their respective treatment.

[Ed. Bib. Ind., Calcutta, 1887.]

ATHARVAVEDA : The Veda of the Atharvans or magic formulae. It is divided into 20 books and contains 731 Sūktas, nearly 6000 verses of which about 1200 are taken from the *Ṛgveda*. Most of the Ṛgvedic stanzas have been taken from its tenth book. The contents of this Veda can be broadly divided as follows :—

Bhaiṣajyāni Sūktāni—songs and spells for the healing of diseases.

Āyuṣyāṇi Sūktāni—prayers for health and long life.

Pauṣṭikāṇi Sūktāni—benedictions by means of which farmers, shepherds and merchants hope to gain happiness and success in their undertakings.

Prāyaścittāni Sūktāni—expiatory formulae and spells for purification from guilt and sin.

Ābhicārikāṇi—curses and exorcisms against demons, wizards and enemies.

This Veda is very important, because it represents the real popular belief as yet uninfluenced by the priestly class. It is also valuable for the history of medicine and magic. This Saṃhitā probably came into being towards the end of the Saṃhitā period, but portions of it appear to hark back to the earliest times of the Vedic age. The *Atharva-veda* has no application in sacrifices. This was perhaps why it was not originally included among the Vedic Saṃhitās which are referred to as *Trayī*, the triad, viz. *Ṛk, Yajus* and *Sāman*. It exists in two recensions, viz. Śaunaka and Paippalāda.

[Ed. Roth and Whitney, Berlin, 1856 (Śaunaka recension), revised by Lindenau, Berlin, 1924; S. P. Pandit, 4 vols., Bombay, 1895-98 (with Sāyaṇa's comm.). Śaunaka recension also ed., with Sāyaṇa's comm., annotations and text comparative data, V.V. R. I., Hoshiarpur, 1960-64. A MS of the Paippalāda recension has been published in facsimile by Bloomfield and Garbe (The Kashmirian Atharvaveda), Stuttgart, 1901. Books I,II, IV-X of the Kashmirian recension pub. with critical notes on text by Le Roy Carr Barret and Edgerton in *JAOS* (Vols. 26, 30, 32, 34, 35, 37, 40-43), 1906-23.

Paippalāda-saṃhitā, ed., with notes, by D. M. Bhattacarya, in two volumes, Sanskrit College, Calcutta, 1964, Vol. III, Kāṇḍas 2-4 pub., Calcutta, 1970. Trs. into Eng. by R. T. H. Griffith, Banaras, 1895-96 (new ed., 1916); W. D. Whitney, revised and ed. C. R. Lanman (HOS, Vols. 7 and 8, Cambridge Mass. 1905); M. Bloomfield, SBE, XLII. Trs. into French by V. Henry, Paris, 1894-1916; Bengali trs. (with text) by D. Lahiri, 1919. Hindi trs. (with text) by K. Trivedi, 1912-21. Tamil trs. by M.R. Jambunathan, Bombay, 1940. Spanish trs. by F. Tola, Buenos Aires, 1968. A selection of hymns trs. into German, among others, by A. Ludwig, in the 3rd Vol. of his *Ṛgveda*, Prague, 1878; A Weber, *Ind. Stud.*, Vols. 4, 5, 13, 17, 18; Th. Aufrecht, *Ind. Stud.*, Vol. 1. Books VII-XIII trs. into French by V. Henry, Paris, 1891-96. Under Akbar the great, this Saṃhitā was translated (983 A. H.) into Persian by Mulla Ibrahimi, Fayzi and Badauni.

For studies in the *Atharvaveda*, see Bloomfield, *Grundris*, II, I; B. V. Henry, *La magie dans l' Inde antique*, Paris, 1904; Oldenberg, AR 7, 1904; Edgerton, *American Jour. of Philology*, 35, 1914; Karambelkar, *Atharvaveda and Avesta*, *Atharvaveda and Āyurveda*, *Atharvavedic Civilisation*; Shende, *The Religion and Philosophy of the Atharvaveda*, Poona, 1952; *Kavi and Kāvya in the Atharvaveda*. See V. Svami and N. Svami, *Complete Alphabetical Index of all words in the Atharvaveda*; Vishva Bandhu, *Grammatical word-index to the Atharvaveda*, Hoshiarpur, 1962-63; K. Lal, *Historical and Critical Studies in Atharvaveda*, 1981. Also see L. Renou, Linguistic remarks on the Paippalāda version of the Atharvaveda, *S. K. Belvalkar Felicitation Vol.*, Banaras, 1957; D. Bhattacharya, Influence of A. V. Black practices in later periods, *Summaries of Papers, AIOC*, 1974; Bloomfield, *Kauśika-sūtra of Atharvaveda*, Delhi; Vishva Bandhu, *Atharvavedīya Bṛhat-sarvānukramaṇikā*, Hoshiarpur, 1966; Y. Veer, *Language of the Atharvaveda*, Delhi, 1979; N. J. Shende, *Kavi and Kāvya in the Atharvaveda*, Poona, 1967; C. J. Blair, *Heat in the Ṛgveda and Atharvaveda*, New Haven, Conn., 1961. Also see M.Trivedi, *Atharvaveda:Ek Sāhityika Adhyayan*, Hoshiarpur, 1976; S. Bali, *Historical and Critical Studies in the Atharvaveda*, Delhi 1981; S. Bhattacharya, Little Tradition and Great Tradition in Atharvaveda, *ABORI* LXVIII, 1981; Mira Roy, Methods of sterilisation and sex-determination in the Atharvaveda, *Indian Jour. of History of Science* 1 (2), pp. 91-97, 1966; Family Relations of some plants in the Atharvaveda, *Indian Jour. of History of Science*, 5 (1) pp. 162-177, 1970.]

ĀTMABODHA : A philosophical poem, in 67 stanzas, by Śaṅkarācārya.

[Ed. Hall, Mirzapore, 1852; D. C. Bhattacharya, Calcutta, 1961 (with a comm. ascribed to Madhusūdana Sarasvatī). Eng. trs. by S. Nikhilananda.]

ĀTMA-TATTVA-VIVEKA : Also called *Bauddha-dhikkāra*, it is by Udayana. In it the author assails the Buddhists who developed an important school of thought which influenced the Nyāya philosophy.

[Ed. Calcutta, 1849 and 1873.]

AUCITYA-VICĀRA-CARCĀ : A unique work on poetics, by Kṣemendra. In it he develops the concept of Aucitya or propriety as essential to sentiment, indeed the life of sentiment. The value of the work lies in rich illustrations and the author's criticism of what he considers to be defects.

[Ed., with comm. *Sahṛdaya-toṣiṇi* of Śvetāraṇya-nārāyaṇa, Madras, 1906; Chowkhamba Sanskrit Series, Banaras, 1933. Trs. into Eng. by Suryakanta in *Kṣemendra Studies*, Poona, 1954. For an account of the work, see Peterson in *JBRAS*, XVI.]

AVADĀNA : Name of a class of Buddhist works in Sanskrit. The word 'Avadāna' means a noteworthy deed, and exploit. To the Buddhists it means "a religious or moral feat." These are stories of the past lives of the Bodhisattva; they illustrate the doctrine of Karman which seeks to teach that the actions of one existence are closely connected with those of former and future existences. It is stated, by way of introduction to Avadānas, where and on what occasion the Buddha related the story and, in conclusion, the lesson is deduced from the story by the Buddha. The most noteworthy works, belonging to this class of literature, are the *Avadāna-śataka*, the *Divyāvadāna*, the *Mahāvastu* and the *Lalita-vistara*. These are written in prose, sometimes in mixed Sanskrit, with occasional metrical passages. They are not of high literary merit, but afford illustration of a type of narrative literature in Sanskrit.

[See S. Sarkar, *A critical and comparative study on the Jātakas and the Avadānas*, Pt. I, Calcutta, 1981; K.A.N. Sastri, *Gleanings of Social Life from the Avadānas*, Calcutta, 1945.]

AVADĀNAKALPALATĀ : A work, in Kāvya style, by Kṣemendra. It belongs to *Avadāna* literature, and consists of 48 chapters. Its 108 th tale was added by Kṣemendra's son Somendra. It is also called *Bodhisattvāvadāna-kalpalatā*. One, Sarat Chandra Das, is said to have discovered the work in Tibet in the eighties of the 19th century A.D.

[Ed. P.L. Vaidya, Darbhanga, 1959. See M.D. Paradkar, Subhāṣitas in Bodhisattvāvadāna-kalpalatā, *Svmmaries of Papers, AIOC*, 1974. For text critical remarks, see J. W. de Jong, Tokyo, 1979.]

AVADĀNA-ŚATAKA : Perhaps the oldest work belonging to the *Avadāna* literature. The tales are arranged into ten decades, each dealing with a certain subject. The first four decades deal with stories of pious deeds by which one can become a Buddha. The fifth speaks of soul in torments. The sixth decade narrates stories of men and animals reborn as gods. The last four decades are concerned with deeds necessary for becoming an *Arhat*. The work probably belongs to the 2nd century A.D.

[Ed. J. S. Speyer, The Hague, 1958. P. L. Vaidya, Darbhanga, 1958. Trs. into French by L. Feer in *Annals du Musee Guimet*, Paris, 1891.]

AVALOKA : Commentary, by Dhanika, on the *Daśarūpaka*. It is extremely helpful in understanding the *Daśarūpaka*.

[Ed., S. Sastri, with the text of the *Daśarūpaka*, Bombay, 1927.]

AVALOKITEŚVARA-GUṆAKĀRAṆḌA-VYŪHA; : See *Kāraṇḍa-vyūha*.

AVANTISUNDARĪKATHĀ : A fragmentary prose work. Some scholars believe that it is the lost *Pūrvapīṭhikā* of the *Daśakumāracarita* of Daṇḍin. Other scholars reject the theory.

[Ed., with a metrical summary called *Avantisundarī-kathāsāra*, by M. R. Kavi, Madras, 1924; M. Sastri, *TSS*, 1954. See S. K. De in *IHQ*, I and III; M. Singh, the Sources of Daṇḍin's Avantisundarī, *ARORI*, 1976.]

AVANTISUNDARĪ-KATHĀSĀRA : See *Avantisundarīkathā*.

AVIMĀRAKA : A drama, in six acts, by Bhāsa. Based on folklore, it depicts a prince, turned by a curse into a sheep-killer, relating his love-adventures to a princess. He falls in love with Kuraṅgī, daughter of king Kuntībhoja, and eventually marries her.

There is striking similarity in the story of the drama with a story in the *Kathāsaritsāgara*, Taraṅga 112, 89-108pp.

[Ed. C. R. Devadhar in *Bhāsa-nāṭaka-cakra* for which see notes under Bhāsa. Trs. into Eng. by J. L. Masson and D. D. Kosambi, 1971. See S. P. Narang, An unknown common archetype of Bhāsa's *Avimāraka* and Somadeva's *Kathāsaritsāgara*, *Summaries of Papers*, 5th World Skt. Conf., Varanasi, 1981, p. 213]

ĀYURVEDA-DĪPĪKĀ : Comm. by Cakrapāṇidatta on the *Caraka-saṃhitā*.

[See S. M. Katre, On some Laukika words cited in the comm. of Cakrapāṇidatta etc., *Tarapurewala Memo. Vol.*, Poona, 1957 (*Bulletin of Deccan College*).]

ĀYURVEDA-PRAKĀŚA : Also called *Rasa-mādhava*, it is an Āyurvedic treatise by Mādhava Upādhyāya. It consists of six chapters, and is regarded as an authoritative work on Āyurvedic Rasa.

ĀYURVEDA SŪTRA : A medical work, probably of the 16th century, by Yogānandanātha, in 16 chapters. It attempts to connect Āyurveda with the Yoga System of Patañjali, to show how different kinds of food increase the *Sattva*, *Rajas* and *Tamas* qualities and also how Yogic practices like fasting influence the conditions of the body.

BAKHSHĀLĪ MANUSCRIPT : Discovered, in 1881 A.D., in village Bakhshālī near Peshawar, and lodged in Bodleian Library, Oxford. While some scholars assign to it a period between the 3rd and 4th century A.D., others place it in the 12th century A.D. It is a work on mathematics dealing with rules for arithmetical, algebraic and geometrical operations. Problems connected with mensuration and miscellaneous subjects have also been dealt with in it.

[See G. R. Kaye, *The Bakhshālī Manuscript*, Part I—Introduction, Part II—Text, Part III—Text re-arranged, Archaeological Survey of India, 1927-33; A study in medieval Mathematics, New Delhi, 1981.]

BĀLABHĀRATA : Also called *Pracaṇḍa-pāṇḍava*. A drama, based on the *Mahābhārata* story, by Rājaśekhara. It was left incomplete, and only two acts are available at present. The first describes Draupadī's Svayaṃvara. The second deals with the gambling scene, ill-treatment of Draupadī and departure of the Pāṇḍavas to the forest.

[Ed. C. Cappeller, Strassburg, 1885; Durgaprasad and Parab, NSP, 1887 (included in the ed. of the *Karpūra-mañjarī*).]

There is a *Bāla-bhārata* by Amaracandra Sūri (13th century). It is a close metrical adaptation, in 19 Parvans, of the *Mahābhārata*.

[Ed. Śivadatta and Parab, NSP, 1894.]

BĀLA-CARITA : A *Mahābhārata* play, in five acts, by Bhāsa. It presents a vivid picture of the feats of Kṛṣṇa culminating in the slaying of Kaṃsa.

[For ed. see under Bhāsa. With comm., grammatical notes, Eng. tra. by B. Kuslae. See S.R. Sehgal, *Bhāsa's Bālacaritam*, 1959.]

BĀLAKRĪḌĀ : The earliest commentary, by Viśvarūpa, on the *Yājñavalkya-smṛti*. It is lucid and free from prolixity.

[Pub., in two parts, by T. Gaṇapati Śāstrī, TSS.]

BĀLAMANORAMĀ : An abridgment by Bhaṭṭoji of his own commentary called *Prauḍhamanoramā* on his *Siddhāntakaumudī*. According to some, it was written by Vāsudeva-Dīkṣita of Tanjore.

One Anantadeva wrote a commentary of this name on the *Siddhānta-kaumudī*.

[Ed. with Siddhānta-kumudī, by C. S. Śāstrī, Madras, 1929 (2nd ed.).]

BĀLAMBHAṬṬI : A well-known commentary, by Bālambhaṭṭa, on Vijñāneśvara's *Mitākṣarā*, a commentary on the *Yājñavalkya-smṛti*.

[Ed. G. Das, Bib. Ind., 1904-07. Vyavahāra portion published by S. S. Setlur, Bombay, 1911. Book I (Ācāra) ed. J. R. Gharpure, Bombay, 1917; Book II (Vyavahāra) ed.

J. R. Gharpure, Bombay, 1914; Book III (Prāyaścitta), ed. J. R. Gharpure, Poona, 1924.]

BĀLA-RĀMĀYAṆA : A ten-act drama by Rājaśekhara who loosely dramatises the entire *Rāmāyaṇa* story up to Rāma's coronation. Some variations have been made in the construction of the plot. Rāvaṇa has been represented as Rāma's rival for the hand of Sītā, and his love and longing for her are more prominent than his ferocity.

[Ed. J. Vidyāsāgara, Calcutta, 1884.]

BALIBANDHA : A drama mentioned in Patañjali's *Mahābhāṣya*, but lost to us.

BAUDHĀYANA-DHARMASŪTRA : See Dharmasūtra.

[Ed. A. C. Śāstrī, with the *Vivaraṇa* comm., Banaras, 1934. Translated into English by Bühler, *SBE*, Vol. XIV.]

BAUDHĀYANA-ŚULVASŪTRA : See Śulvasūtra.

[Ed. W. Caland, *Bib. Ind.*, 1904-24; Satyaprakash and R. S. Sharma, 1980.]

BAUDDHADHIKKĀRA : See *Ātma-tattva-viveka*.

BHAGAVADAJJUKA : A farcical play attributed to Bodhāyana. It is so named because Bhagavān, named Parivrāṭ or Yogin, and Ajjukā, a courtesan, play the prominent roles. The courtesan, waiting for her lover in a garden, is bitten by a snake and dies. The Yogin, in order to display his Yogic powers, causes his soul to enter the dead body. The messenger of Yama coming to take the soul finds that a mistake has been committed. He allows the courtesan's soul to enter the dead body of the Yogin. The exchange of souls makes the saint speak and act like the courtesan and the courtesan speak and act like the saint. At last, Yama's messenger makes the souls enter their respective bodies.

[Ed., with an anonymous comm., P.A. Achan, Cochin, 1925; P. Veturi, Madras, 1925. Trs. into Eng. by C. C. Mehta, in *Three Skt. Lighter Delights*, Baroda, 1969.]

BHAGAVADGĪTĀ : Same as *Gitā* (q.v.).

BHĀGAVATA : See *Bhāgavata-purāṇa*.

BHĀGAVATA-PURĀṆA : Also called *Śrīmadbhāgavata* or simply *Bhāgavata*. It consists of nearly 18,000 verses divided into 12 Skandhas or chapters.

Supposed by some to have been written not later than 800 A.D. According to some scholars, it was written by Vopadeva, the famous grammarian. R.C. Hazra places it in the earlier half of the sixth century. According to T.S. Rukmani, its date is the fifth century.

It deals chiefly with the life and sports of Kṛṣṇa, the incarnations of Viṣṇu and prophecies about the Kali Age. It is noteworthy that, in it, there is no mention of Rādhā, the Chief of the Gopīs and Kṛṣṇa's energy of infinite bliss (*hlādinī-śakti*).

In language, style and metre, this Purāṇa occupies an important place among the Purāṇas. In contents it resembles the *Viṣṇu-purāṇa* to a great extent. This Purāṇa, especially its tenth chapter, is very popular with the Vaiṣṇavas, many of whom think that it should be recited daily.

[Ed. Tarkaratna, with Śrīdharasvāmin's comm., Vangavasi Press, Calcutta, 1920; N. Brahmachari, with seven comms. including that of Śrīdharasvāmin, notes and Hindi translation, 14 vols., 1903-08; K. S. Sastri, with several comms., Ahmedabad, Saṃvat 2022-25. Also ed. J. L. Shastri, Delhi. Translated into English by M. N. Dutt, Calcutta, 1895; K.D. Vyas and J.M. Sanyal, 5 Vols., Delhi; Bhaktivedanta, with Roman transliteration, synonyms, trs. and purport, London, Canto I (3 vols.), Canto II (2 vols.), 1972; Tapasyānanda, Madras, 1980. A French translation of its Tamil version was published at Paris in 1788 (2nd revised ed., Pondicherry, 1920) and this was rendered into German, Zurich, 1791. Also translated E. Burnouf and others, Paris, 1840-98 (up to Skandha IX). A recent translation, with annotation, is by G. V. Tagare, 1976-79. Repeatedly translated into Bengali. See *Index to Śrīmad Bhāgavatam*, T. R. Krsnacarya, 1932; S. Bhattacharyya, *Philosophy of Bhāgavata* 2. vols.; P. N. Sinha, Study of the Bhāgavata-purāṇa. Original text, with Roman transliteration, Eng. synonyms of words, Eng. translation and elaborate purport by A. Bhaktivedānta Svāmi, Vrindavan. Also see T. S. Rukmani, *A Crittcal study of the Bhāgavata Purāṇa*; A. Gail, *Bhakti in Bhāgavatapurāṇa* (in German), Wiesbaden, O. Harrassowitz, 1969; D. S. Nadkarni. G. Chattopadhyay, *Bhāgavata O Bāṅglā Sāhitya* (in Bengali), Calcutta; A. S. Biswas, Bhāgavatapurāṇa—a linguistic study particularly from the Vedic background; G. V. Bapat, *Parables of the sage* (dialogue bet. Dattātreya and King Yadu), Poona, 1970; V. Raghavan in *Purāṇa*, XV, 1973, Did the Bhāgavata know Kālidāsa; R. N. Byas, The *Synthetic philosophy of the Bhāgavata*, 1774; K. K. Shastree, Some Important Historical Ref. in the Bhāgavata Purāṇa, *Summaries of papers*, *AIOC* 1974; S. S. Prasad, Some vocables of the Bhāgavata, Ibid. Also see Nadkarni, *Textual Restoration in the Bhāgavata Purāṇa*; B. Shukla, Authority of B. Purāṇa is connection with Brahmasūtrabhāṣya, *Summaries of Papers*, 5th world Skt. Conf., Varanasi, 1981, p. 178; Satyavrat, Synonyms in the Bhāgavata Purāṇa, *ABORI*, 1,1970; K.S. Tripathi, A Critical Study of the Śrīmadbhāgavata, Varanasi. A very useful work is *Śrīmad Bhāgavata*, ed. Tapasyananda, Madras.]

BHĀGAVATA-SANDARBHA : An elaborate treatise by Jīva Gosvāmin. It consists of the following six books called *Sandarbhas*:—*Tattva-sandarbha*, *Bhagavat-sandarbha*, *Paramātma-sandarbha*, *Śrīkṛṣṇa-sandarbha*, *Bhakti-sandarbha* and *Prīti-sandarbha*. The work is based chiefly on the Bhāgavatapurāṇa. The principal topic discussed in the *Tattva-sandarbha*, is means of valid knowledge (*pramāṇa*). The *Bhagavat-sandarbha* discusses the power and qualities of the Bhagavat. The subject discussed in the *Paramātma-sandarbha* is *paramātman* which consists in the Bhagavat's relation with Prakṛti and Jīva. The *Śrīkṛṣṇa-sandarbha*, the most authoritative theological work of the Vaiṣṇavas of Bengal, deals with the nature of Kṛṣṇa who is regarded as Lord Himself. The *Bhakti-sandarbha* discusses the nature and classification of *Bhakti*, and seeks to establish the superiority of the *Bhakti-mārga* over other ways of life. The last *Sandarbha* discusses at length the nature of liberation, the love of the lord, the sentiment of *Bhakti*, the relation between Kṛṣṇa and the Gopīs, etc.

[*Tattva-*, *Bhagavat-* and *Paramātma-sandarbhas*, ed. Rādhāramaṇa Press, Murshidabad, 1317, 1324 and 1335 B.S.; *Bhaktisandarbha* (along with five other *Sandarbhas*), ed. S. Gosvāmī, Calcutta, Śaka 1822; *Śrīkṛṣṇa-sandarbha*, ed. P. Gosvāmī, Navadvīpa, 1332 B.S.; *Prīti-sandarbha*, ed. P. Gosvāmī, Noakhali.]

BHAGAVAT-SANDARBHA : See *Bhāgavata-sandarbha*.

BHĀGAVṚTTI : Name of one of the oldest commentaries on the *Aṣṭadhyāyī*. Not available at present, but copiously quoted by Puruṣottamadeva and other Eastern grammarians of the 12th and later centuries. Attributed by some to Bhartṛhari and by others to Vimalamati.

BHAIMARATHI : A prose Kāvya mentioned in Patañjali's *Mahābhāṣya*. It is lost.

BHAIRAVA-VILĀSA : A drama of the Prekṣaṇaka variety, by Brahmatra Vaidyanātha. [Ed. with Eng. trs. by N. N. Sharma]

BHAIṢAJYA-RATNĀVALĪ : An Āyurvedic compilation by Govindadāsa. Composed probably towards the end of the 16th century, it is a useful work to Āyurvedic practitioners.

BHAKTI-RASĀMṚTA-SINDHU : A huge work on Vaiṣṇava Rasa-śāstra, by Rūpa Gosvāmin. It consists of four parts called Vibhāgas each of which is sub-divided into sections called Laharīs. In it there are analysis of the *Bhakti-rasa* and definitions and subtle divisions of its constituents.

[Ed. D. Gosvāmī, Banaras, 1932 (with the *Durgama-saṃgamanī* comm. of Jīva Gosvāmin; Bon Manārāj, with translation, Part I.]

BHAKTI-SANDARBHA : See *Bhāgavata-sandarbha*.

BHAKTI-ŚATAKA : A poetical work by Rāma Candra Kavibhāratī. In it the Buddha has been eulogised according to the doctrine of the Hindus. In accordance with the manner, laid down in poetics, it is composed in 107 verses. [Pub. Buddhist Text Society, 1896.]

BHALLAṬA-ŚATAKA : Attributed to Bhallaṭa, it consists of 108 verses of varied metres. In the verses, the poet lays down his reflections on the ways of the world. Verses from this work have been quoted by Abhinavagupta, Kṣemendra and other eminent rhetoricians of Kashmir. The anthologies, called *Śārṅgadhara-paddhati*, and *Sadukti-karṇāmṛta*, quote verses from it.

[Ed. Kāvyamālā, IV]

BHĀMAHĀLAṂKĀRA : Same as Bhāmaha's *Kāvyālaṃkāra* (q.v.).

BHĀMAHA-VIVARAṆA : A commentary, by Udbhaṭa, on Bhāmaha's *Kāvyālaṃkāra*.

[Ed. from fragments by R. Gnoli, Rome, 1962.]

BHĀMATĪ : It is an exposition, by Vācaspati Miśra, of the system of Vedānta philosophy of Śaṅkarācārya contained in his commentary on the Brahma-sūtra. Also called *Śārīraka-bhāṣya-vibhāga* or *Vibhāga.*

[Ed. *Bib. Ind.*, Calcutta, 1876-80; with full notes, by D. Sastri, Kashi Skt. Series, 2nd ed.; S. S. S. Śastrī and C. K. Raja (with Eng. trs.), Madras, 1930.]

BHĀMINĪ-VILĀSA : Composed by Jagannātha, it is a poem divided into four parts, viz. Anyokti (101 verses), Śṛṅgāra (102), Karuṇa (19), and Śānta (31). Though the poet dwells on various matters, the leaning is towards the erotic and the didactic. Many verses are praiseworthy for their neatness, elegance of expression and pictorial fancy.

[Ed. H. D. Sharma with a Skt. comm., Eng. translation, Poona, 1938. English translation by S. Iyer, Bombay, 1894; French translation by A. Bergaigne, Paris, 1872.]

BHĀRADVĀJA ŚIKṢĀ : See Śikṣā.

[Ed. E. Sieg, Berlin, 1892.]

BHARAṬAKA DVĀTRIṂŚIKĀ : Of unknown date and authorship, it is a collection of 32 tales of the ridiculous

Bharaṭakas who were probably Śaiva mendicants. It seems to be of Jaina inspiration, and is designed to deride Brāhmaṇas. The vernacular verses interspersed in it probably point to the fact that it was a Sanskrit version of a vernacular work.

[Ed. T. Hertel, Leipzig, 1921. Russian trs. by I. D. Serebryakov under title *Tridtsat dve novelly O monakhakh*, Moscow, 1962.]

BHĀRATA-MAÑJARĪ : Written by Kṣemendra in 1037 A.D., it is a long poem based on the *Mahābhārata*. The author has left out certain matters of the original epic and modified others. In place of about a lac of verses in the epic, he has summed up the whole matter in about 500 stanzas. The poet has re-arranged the contents in certain cases. For example, the episode of club-duel between Bhīma and Duryodhana has been torn from the Śalya Parvan of the original, and described in what he calls Gadā-parvan.
[Ed. Śivadatta and Parab, Bombay, 1898.]

BHĀRATA-TĀTPARYA-NIRṆAYA : See *Mahābhārata-tātparya-nirṇaya*.

BHĀṢĀ-PARICCHEDA : A practical guide-book, by Viśvanātha who is to be distinguished from the author of the *Sāhitya-darpaṇa*, to Nyāya-Vaiśeṣika philosophical systems. It, like other tracts of its class, deals with the doctrines of both the systems as a whole and presents a fusion of the two traditions. It is in 166 memorial verses divided into four parts, viz. *Pratyakṣa*, *Anumāna*, *Upamāna* and *Śabda*. Some of the *Sūtras* occurring in Sureśvara's *Mānasollāsa* appear to be borrowed from older sources. It deals with the seven categories, and the four means of valid knowledge, viz. perception, inference, comparison and verbal testimony. So far as categories are concerned, it agrees with Vaiśeṣika. In regard to means of knowledge, it agrees with Nyāya philosophy.

[Ed. M.S. Jha, with *Anvitārtha-pradīpikā* comm., NSP, 1922; A. S. Jere, with comms. *Muktāvalī*, *Dinakarī* and *Rāmarudrī*,

NSP, 1927. Translated Hultzsch, *ZDMG*, LXXIV; translated into English with the *Siddhānta-muktāvalī*, by Swāmī Mādhavānanda, Calcutta, 1954.]

BHĀṢĀ-VṚTTI : A commentary, by Puruṣottamadeva, on the *Aṣṭādhyāyī* excluding the Vedic portion. It is brief but lucid.

[Ed., with comm. of Sṛṣṭidhara, *Bib. Ind.*, Calcutta, 1912; S. Chakravarti, Rajshahi, 1918.]

BHĀSKARA-BHĀṢYA : Also called *Śārīraka-mīmāṃsā-bhāṣya*, it is a commentary by Bhāskara on the *Brahmasūtra*. It upholds the Bhedābheda-vāda or the doctrine that unity and multiplicity are equally real. The author rejects the illusion theory, and believes in real evolution (*pariṇāma*). According to him, the Jīva is naturally one with Brahman, its difference from Brahman is due to limitations. He adopts the view of *Jñāna-karma-samuccaya* or the combination of knowledge and action.

[Ed., with the *Brahmasūtra*, *CSS*, 1915.]

BHĀSVATĪ or BHASVATĪKARAṆA. A well-known astronomical work chiefly based on Varāhamihira's works and the *Sūryasiddhānta*. Written by Śatānanda, it contains rules for the accurate determination of the occurrence of eclipses. Containing 8 chapters, it gives epochal positions as true for Purī.

[Ed. S. Dvivedi, Banaras, 1883.]

BHAṬṬI-KĀVYA : Composed by Bhartṛhari or Bhaṭṭi, its real title is *Rāvaṇa-vadha*. Designed to teach grammar and rhetorical principles through *Kāvya*. Based on the *Rāmāyaṇa*, it deals, in 22 cantos, with the story up to the coronation of Rāma on his return from Laṅkā. The poet himself is conscious of the fact that his work is intelligible only through a commentary (*vyākhyā-gamya*) and that it can be enjoyed only by those who are proficient in grammar.

[Ed. K. P. Trivedi, with comm. of Mallinātha, Bombay, 1898; J. N. Tarkaratna, with comm of Jayamaṅgala and Bharatamallika, Calcutta, 1871-73; with the *Candrakalā-vidyotinī*

Sanskrit Hindi comms., by S. S. Regmi, *CSS*, 1964. Translated into Eng. with notes by G.G. Leonardi, Leiden, 1972. See C. Hooykaas, On some arthālaṃkāras in the Bhaṭṭikāvya, *R. Turner Vol.* (*BSOAS*, XX), London, 1957; S. P. Narang, *Bhaṭṭikāvya, a study*, 1969; K. Bandyopadhyay, Yamakālaṃkāra in the Bhaṭṭikāvya etc., *Summaries of Papers*, *AIOC*, 1974. Also see Karandikar and Karandikar, ed. trs.]

BHĀVA-PRAKĀŚA (or, -PRAKĀŚIKĀ or, - PRAKĀŚANA) : A work on poetics, by Śāradātanaya. It consists of ten chapters called *Adhikāras*. The topics discussed are as follows :

I—II	*Bhāva*
III	*Avāntara-bhāvabheda-svarūpa*
IV	*Śṛṅgārālambana-nāyakādi-svarūpa*
V	*Nāyaka-bhedāvasthā-rasa-bhāva-vikāra*
VI	*Śabdārtha-sambandha-bheda-prakāra*
VII	*Nāṭyetivṛttādi-lakṣaṇa*
VIII	*Daśarūpaka-lakṣaṇa*
IX	*Nṛtya-bheda-svarūpa-lakṣaṇa*
X	*Nāṭya-prayoga-bheda-prakāra*

There is a compilation of Āyurveda, called *Bhāva-prakāśa*, by one Bhāva Miśra. It was composed in 1550 A. D.

[Ed., with Gujarati translation, by G. Śāstrī, Bombay, 1956; with Hindi comm., by L. Vaidya, Delhi 1958; Bengali translation by D. Sen and U. Sen, Calcutta, 1931. See Die ophthalmologie des Bhāvaprakāśa. Quallenkritisch bearbeitet von A. A. M. Esser. Teil I. Anatomie and Pathologie, 55 Leipzig, 1930. Studien zur Geschichte der Medezin, 19. (Text in Roman characters and translation of relevant sections of the text). Also see M. M. Agrawal, *Bhāvaprakāśanam of Śāradātanaya*, Mathura, 1978.]

BHĀVĀRTHA-DĪPIKĀ : A well-known commentary, by Śrīdharasvāmin, on the *Bhāgavata-purāṇa*.

BHAVIṢYA- or BHAVIṢYAT-PURĀṆA : The extant work does not seem to be the original work of this name, referred to in the *Āpastambīya-dharmasūtra.* The greater part of it deals with the Brahmanical ceremonies and feasts, the duties of castes and so on. The worship of snakes and snake-myths have been dealt with in it. A considerable part deals with the sun-worship in Śākadvīpa in which sun-priests named Bhojaka and Maga are mentioned : this is related to the Zoroastrian sun-and-fire-cult. Numerous *Māhātmyas* and other modern texts claim to be parts of this Purāṇa. The *Bhaviṣyottara-Purāṇa* is a sort of continuation of this Purāṇa.

[Ed. Veṅkaṭeśvara Press, Bombay. See L. Sternback, *Mānava-dharmaśāstras I-IV and Bhaviṣya Purāṇa.* See R. K. Arora, *Historical and Cultural Data from the Bhaviṣya Purāṇa.*]

BHELA-SAṂHITĀ : A treatise on Āyurveda, mainly in verse and partly in prose, attributed to Bhelācārya. It contains the same divisions as in the *Caraka-saṃhitā,* and knows Suśruta. The work presents a tradition inferior to that of the *Caraka-saṃhitā.*

[Ed. G. Sukla, Banaras, 1959.]

BHOJANA-KUTŪHALA : A work on Dietetics by Raghunātha, a Marāṭhā Brāhmaṇa, written in the last quarter of the 17th century A.D. It deals mainly with Deccani Dietetics and occasionally with the Dietetics of other provinces. Exists in MSS.

[For an analysis of contents and information about MSS, see P. K. Gode, *Studies in Indian Literary History,* II, pp. 380-390, Pub. in Kerala University Publications.]

BHOJA-PRABANDHA : A prose work, by Vallāla, who is to be distinguished from the Bengal king Vallālasena, belonging to the class of tales. Its principal object is to describe Bhoja, apparently Bhoja of Dhārā, in relation to many poets attached to his court for his liberal patronage. It is worthless as an historical document. Regardless of chronology, it brings together in Bhoja's court such literary figures as Kālidāsa, Bhavabhūti, Daṇḍin, Māgha and some other less known poets. There are several versions of the text.

[Repeatedly printed in India. The earliest ed. of the Southern text, pub. in Madras, 1851, Ed. V. Pansikar, NSP, 1932. An eclectic ed., with trs. of some sections, pub. by Th. Pavien, *JA,* 1854-55, t. III. Ed., with

Eng. trs., by S. Vidyābhūṣaṇa, Calcutta, 1919. Ed. with Skt. comm. and purport, Hindi and Eng. trs., vocabulary etc., by J. L. Shastri. See L. H. Gray, *Narrative of Bhoja*. There are works of the same title, by Merutuṅga, Padmagupta and Rājaśekhara, among others.]

BHUŚUṆḌI RĀMĀYAṆA : Earliest Rāma epic after *Vālmīki Rāmāyaṇa*. Supposed to be the main source of the Rāma Bhakti literature. Contains 36,000 verses divided into four parts. Believed to be a source of inspiration to medieval *Rāmāyaṇas*, eg. *Adhyātma* and the vernacular works by Kṛttivās and Tulsīdās.

[Ed. B. P. Singh, Varanasi.]

BĪJAGAṆITA : A part of Bhāskara's *Siddhāntaśiromaṇi* (q. v.). It contains elements of Hindu Algebra. [Ed., with expository notes and examples, by S. Dvivedi; with further notes, by M. Jha.]

BILHAṆA-KĀVYA : See *Caurapañcāśikā*.

BODHA-PAÑCADAŚIKĀ : A work, by Abhinavagupta, on Kashmir Śaivism. It consists of 16 verses of which 15 deal with the subject-matters and the 16th explains the purpose of such a composition. It is designed to enable the ordinary readers to have an idea of the essentials of monistic Śaivism.

[Ed. J. Jadu, 1947.]

BODHICARYĀVATĀRA : A work by Śāntideva. In this work, written in the form of Kāvya, the author sketches the career of one who seeks to attain Buddhahood as opposed to the narrow Hīnayāna ideal of saintship.

[Ed. P. L. Vaidya, Darbhanga, 1960. Trs. Paris, 1907. See *Tibetsch-Sanskritischer index zum Bodhicaryāvatāra* (Tibetan-Skt. index of *Bodhicaryāvatāra*), Berlin, 1952.]

BODHISATTVĀVADĀNA-KALPALATĀ : Same as *Avadāna-kalpalatā* (q. v.).

BOWER MANUSCRIPT : A manuscript discovered in Kashgar by Bower in 1890 A.D. Palaeographically it is assigned to the fourth century A.D. It contains seven treatises of which parts I-III deal with medical science, IV and V with cubomancy and VI and VII with *Mahāmāyurī Vidyārājñī*, a charm to be used as a remedy against snake-bite.

[See Hoernle, *The Bower Manuscript*, 1914.]

BRAHMABHARATA : The small portion, now available in six chapters, deals with *Abhinaya*. It embraces *Mārga Nāṭya*, and does not refer to *Deśi*, nor does it mention any earlier work. It is perhaps identical with the *Brahmanāṭyaśāstra* mentioned by Dāmodaragupta in his *Kuṭṭanīmata*. Padmabhū's view, mentioned by Śāradātanaya in his *Bhāvaprakāśa*, perhaps refers to this work.

[MS with M. R. Kavi, Madras. Vide Krishnamachariar, *Hist. of Class. Skt. Lit.*, 1937, p. 824, f. n. 4.]

BRĀHMAṆA : Name of a class of Vedic works which are collections of utterances and discussions of priests upon the science of sacrifice. They contain cosmogonic myths, ancient legends and narratives relating to sacrifice. Together with Mantras the Brāhmaṇas are believed to constitute what is called Veda. These are prose-works some of which are accented. There are occasional verses which are of two kinds, viz. epic song verses (*gāthā*) and songs in praise of heroes (*nārāśaṃsi*). Their contents are three-fold viz.

(1) Sacrificial directions (*Vidhi*).

(2) Explanation of meanings and purpose of sacrificial acts (*Arthavāda*).

(3) Exegetical, mythological, polemical, theological or philosophical speculations (*Upaniṣad*).

These works are indispensable for understanding the whole of the later religious and philosophical literature, and highly interesting for the science of religion and the history of sacrifice and of priesthood. There are Brāhmaṇas of each of the Vedic Saṃhitās. The *Aitareya* and *Kauṣītaki* (or *Śāṅkhāyana*) belong to the *Ṛgveda*. To the *Sāmaveda* belong the *Tāṇḍya*, *Ṣaḍviṃśa*, the *Jaiminīya* and the *Chāndogya* besides the *Sāmavidhāna*, *Devatādhyāya*, *Vaṃśa* and *Saṃhitopaniṣat*. The *Śatapatha* and the *Taittirīya* belong respectively to the *Śukla-yajurveda* and the *Kṛṣṇa-yajurveda*. The *Śatapatha* exists in two recensions, viz. *Kāṇva* and *Mādhyandina*. The *Atharvaveda* has the *Gopatha*. According to Winternitz, Brāhmaṇas were composed or compiled in the period between the "conclusion" of hymn-composition and *Ṛgveda-saṃhitā* and the rise of Buddhism.

[See A. C. Banerjee, *Studies in the Brāhmaṇas*, Delhi, 1963; V. V. Dixit, *Relation of the Epics to the Brāhmaṇa Literature*, Poona, 1950; S. Levi, *La doctrine du sacrifice dans les Brāhmaṇas* (Bibliotheque de l 'école des hautes études), Paris, 1898; H. Oldenberg, *Vorwissenschaftliche Wissenschaft, die Weltanschauung der Brāhmaṇa-Texte*, Gottingen, 1919; J. Basu, *India of the Age of Brahmanas*, Calcutta, 1969; *Ṛgveda Brāhmaṇas*, trs. into Eng. by A. B. Keith, *HOS*, 1971. See H. S. Ananthanarayana, *Verb Forms of* the *Taittirīya Brāhmaṇa*, Poona, 1970. Also see Visvabandhu and others, *Brāhmaṇoddhārakośa*, Hoshiarpur, 1966; G. Umakant Thite, *Sacrifice in the Brāhmaṇa-Texts*, Poona, 1975; G. P. Devasthali, *Religion and Mythology of the Brāhmaṇas*; R. S. S. Murthy, *A Study of the Important Brāhmaṇas*; K. S. Maclonall, *Brāhmaṇas of the Vedas*, Delhi, 1979. Also see Bodewitz and Brill, *The Daily Evening and Morning (Agnihotra) according to Brāhmaṇas*, Leiden, 1976; G. U. Thite, *Sacrifice in Brāhmaṇa Texts*, Poona, 1975; S.K. Sharma, *Kauṣītaki-brāhmaṇa*, Wiesbaden, 1968.]

BRĀHMAṆA-SARVASVA : Also called *Karmopadeśinī*, it is a work of Halāyudha. It deals with various sacraments (*Saṃskāra*). Its chief object is to explain the *mantras* used in the sacraments as well as the *mantras* used by Brāhmaṇas in daily observances from the cleansing of their teeth to going to bed.

[Ed. D. Bhattacarya, Calcutta, 1958.]

BRAHMĀṆḌA-PURĀṆA : The original form of this Purāṇa is lost. The extant manuscripts mostly contain *Māhātmyas*, *Stotras* and *Upākhyānas* which claim to be parts of this Purāṇa. The *Adhyātma-rāmāyaṇa* (q. v.) is considered to be a part of this Purāṇa.

[Published K. Srikrishnadas, Veṅkaṭeśvara Press, Bombay; by P. C. Bagchi, with an English Intro., 1935; ed. with Intro. and verse-index, J. L. Shastri, Delhi, 1971.]

BRAHMA-PURĀṆA : Also called *Brāhma* or *Ādi-purāṇa,* it deals, *inter alia,* with glorifications of sacred places, particularly of Utkala. A large section is devoted to legends about Kṛṣṇa. The last chapters contain rules for *Śrāddha*, moral life, duties of castes and stages of life, merit of Viṣṇu-worship. In conclusion, it gives explanations on Sāṃkhya and Yoga, and describes the path leading to salvation. It contains earlier and later portions. It mentions the sun-temple of Konārak (Orissa) built after 1241 A.D. So the portion dealing with sacred places in Orissa cannot be earlier than the 13th century. Perhaps the *Māhātmyas* in the Purāṇa were added later.

[Ed. P. Tarkaratna, Vaṅgavāsī Press, Calcutta, 1316 B. S.; with introduction and contents of 18 Purāṇas, Gurumaṇḍala Series, Calcutta, 1954. See S. Seth, *Religion and Society in the Brahma purāṇa*, New Delhi, 1979.]

BRĀHMA-SIDDHĀNTA : Also called *Sphuṭa Brāhma-siddhānta,* it is a famous mathematical-astronomical work by Brahmagupta. According to some, it was based on the *Brahmasiddhānta* portion of the *Viṣṇudharmottara-purāṇa.* It consists of 24 chapters. It influenced Arab astronomy and mathematics in the 8th century A.D.

[Ed., with *Siddhānta-prakāśikā* comm., by M. Ojha, Banaras, 1961. See Algebra, with arithmetic and mensuration, from the Sanskrit of Brahmagupta and Bhāskara, translated into English by H. T. Colebrooke, London, 1817.]

There is a *Brahma-siddhānta* or *Śākalya-saṃhitā* by Śākalya alias Śākapūṇi (c. 821 A.D.).

BRAHMA-SŪTRA : Also called *Śārīraka-sūtra, Vedānta-sūtra, Śārīraka-mīmāṃsā* or *Uttara-mīmāṃsā,* it is ascribed to Bādarāyaṇa. For date, see under Bādarāyaṇa. While the *Mīmāṃsā-sūtra* of Jaimini investigates the duties enjoined in the Veda, along with the rewards attached thereto, the *Brahma-sūtra* describes the philosophical-theological views of the Upaniṣads. According to Deussen, "the work of Bādarāyaṇa stands to the Upaniṣads in the same relation as the Christian Dogmatics to the New Testament." The work is in 555 cryptic Sūtras which are not intelligible without commentaries. Of the commentators, the chief are Śaṃkara, Bhāskara, Yādavaprakāśa, Rāmānuja, Nimbārka, Keśava Nīlakaṇṭha, Madhva, Baladeva, Vallabha and Vijñānabhikṣu.

[Ed., with an Eng. comm. (*Sādhana* and *Phala Adhyāyas*), by Śivānanda, Rishikesh, 1949; with Bengali trs., Bengali exposition and comm. of Śaṃkara and Rāmānuja, Calcutta, 1939; with notes and comm. *Bhāmatī*, *Kalpataru* and *Parimala*, by A.K. Sastri, Bombay, 1938; with *Śrībhāṣya* and *Śrutaprakāśikā*, by Vīrarāghavācārya, New Delhi, Govt. of India, 1967. Ed., with Bengali trs., Baladeva's *Govindabhāṣya*, Bengali trs. of the *Bhāṣya* etc., Sārasvata Gaudīyāsana Mission, Calcutta, in four vols., 1968-70; with five comms., by A. Sastri, Vol. III with nine comms., by A. K. Sastri, by B. N. K. Sharma, with principal comms., III, Bombay. Brahmasūtra, with Viśiṣṭādvaita comm., trs. into French by O. Lacombe. 1938. Trs. by G. Thibaut, under the title *The Vedānta-sūtras with the comm. of Śaṃkarācārya*, SBE, Vols. xxxiv and xxxviii, 1890-96. See Radhakrishnan, *Brahma-sūtra*; V. M. Apte, *Brahmasūtra*; P. Modi, *Critique of Brahmasūtra*, 2 vols.; G. Thibaut, *Vedānta-sūtras*; *Rāmānuja-bhāṣya*; V. J. Kirtikar, *Studies in Vedānta*; Rama Chaudhuri, *Sufism and Vedānta*; V. S. Ghate, *The Vedānta—a study of the Brahma-sūtras with comm. of Śaṃkara, Rāmānuja, Nimbārka, Madhva and Vallabha*, 2nd ed., Poona, 1960; J. L. Mehta and others, *Vedānta and Buddhism*; A. K. Guha, *Jīvātman in the Brahmasūtras*, Calcutta; S. K. Belvalkar, *Brahma-sūtra-pāṭha with word-index and Brahmasūtra of Bādarāyaṇa*; B.N.K. Sharma, *Brahmasūtras and their principal commentaries*, Bombay; S. M. Bhatkhande, *Chāndogya Upaniṣad and Brahmasūtras, a comparative study*, Bombay, 1982.]

BRAHMASŪTRA-BHĀṢYA : Comm. by Śaṃkarācārya on the *Vedānta-sūtras*. It was commented on by Vācaspati Miśra (9th cent.), Ānandajñāna (13th cent.) and Govindānanda (14th cent.). In this comm. Śaṃkara has given an exposition of Advaita Vedānta and it laid the foundation of his school.

[See N. K. Devarāja, *An Introduction to Śaṃkara's Theory of Knowledge*; ed. with comm. *Brahmavidyābharaṇa* of Advaitānanda, by S. R. Krishnamurthy Sastri, Vol. I Pts. I, II, Madras, 1976. Also see A. G. K. Warrick, *God and Advaita*, Simla, 1977.]

BRAHMAVAIVARTA- or BRAHMAKAIVARTA-PURĀṆA: The latter is the title current in South India. It is divided into four books (*Khaṇḍa*), viz. *Brahma*, *Prakṛti*, *Gaṇeśa*, *Kṛṣṇajanma*. The last is the most extensive. It deals not only with the birth, but with the whole life of Kṛṣṇa, especially his battles and his love adventures with the cowherd women (Gopīs). It is the chief part of the Purāṇa whose principal object is to glorify Kṛṣṇa and his favourite *Śakti*, *Rādhā*. A large number of *Māhātmyas* claim to belong to this Purāṇa.

[Ed. Gurumaṇḍala Series, Calcutta, 1954-55; ed. with Eng. & Skt. Intro. and verse-index, by J. L. Shastri. Eng. Trs. in *SBH*. See A. N. Rawal, *Indian Society, Religion and Mythology, a study of the B. Purāṇa*, Delhi, 1982.]

BṚHADĀRAṆYAKOPANIṢAD : Written in six chapters. The principal topics discussed in it are as follows :—

Ritualistico-philosophical description of the cosmos, poetico-physiological description of the self, the eye and the head, the Ātmanism and Solipism of Yājñavalkya, reciprocal dependence of all things etc.

This work contains some parables and accounts of philosophical discussions. For example, we have the parable of the senses in chapter six. In chapter three is an account of the great philosophical symposium at the court of king Janaka. In the same chapter we find an account of Gārgī and Yājñavalkya's discourse on the immutable Brahman. Chapter four contains Yājñavalkya's criticism of the philosophers and his own constructive philosophy. Eschatological teachings are contained in chapter six.

[Ed., with comm. of Śaṃkara and gloss of Ānandagiri, and trs. into English by E. Roer, *Bib. Ind.*, 1849-56; by S. Mādhavānanda (with comm. of Śaṃkara); by P. Lal, Calcutta; into Polish by M Iwienski, Krakau, 1924; into

French by E. Senart, Paris, 1934; into Italian by B. Filippi. See J. M. van Gelder, *Der Ātman* etc., The Hague, 1957. Also see S. Hino, *Sureśvara's Vārtika on Yājñavalkya-Maitreyī Dialogue*, Delhi, 1982. Methods of Sterilisation and Sex-determination in...... Bṛhadāraṇyakopaniṣad, *Indian Jour. of History of Science,* 1(2) pp. 91-97, 1966.]

BṚHAD-BHĀGAVATĀMṚTA : A celebrated work by Sanātana Gosvāmin. It is based on the *Bhāgavata-purāṇa,* and is written in the style of a Purāṇa. It is divided into parts. The first part contains the narrative of Nārada's quest of the dearest devotee of Kṛṣṇa. The subject-matter of the second part is Kṛṣṇa's manifestation of himself before his devotee.

[Pub. N. Brahmacharī, 1904.]

BṚHADDEŚĪ : A work on music, by Mataṅga, perhaps written some time between the 5th and the 7th century A.D. The title appears to indicate that it deals with only regional music. But, the extant work, in six chapters, discusses also *Śruti* and *Svara.* It mentions Bharata, but differs from him in several places, particularly in the introduction of 12 *Svaras* in the *Mūrchanā.*

[Ed., K. S. Sastri, *TSS* 1828.]

BṚHADDEVATĀ : A metrical work ascribed to Śaunaka. It is a large catalogue of gods worshipped in the different hymns of the *Ṛgveda.* It contains also myths and legends relating to these deities. It is one of the earliest Indian narrative works.

[Ed. and trs. into English by A. A. Macdonell, *HOS,* Vols. 5, 6, 1904. See M. Tokunga, on the racensions of the Bṛhaddevatā, *JAOS,* Vol. 101, No. 3, 1981.]

BṚHAD-DHARMA-PURĀṆA : It is an Upa-purāṇa written in three parts. It deals chiefly with duties, e.g. respect for parents, conduct in holy places, rites and practices prescribed for different castes and *Āśramas.* Various *Vratas* and *Pūjās,* main castes and mixed casts, gifts, duties of women, birth and sports of Kṛṣṇa, glorification of places of pilgrimage—these are also dealt with in it. There are many myths and legends also, e.g. the story of Sītā, the genesis of the *Rāmāyaṇa*, self-immolation of Satī and destruction of *Dakṣa-yajña* etc. It is believed by some to have been compiled in Bengal in the 13th century.

[Ed. Vaṅgavāsī Press, Calcutta, 1314 B.S. (in Bengali characters); *Bib. Ind.*, Calcutta, 1888-97 (Devanāgarī script). For a full account of this Purāṇa, see R. C. Hazra in *Jour. of University of Gauhati*, VI, 1955 and his *Studies in the Upapurāṇas*, Vol. II. Also see V. Raghavan, Music in the *Bṛhad-dharamapurāṇa*, *Jour. of the Music Academy*, Madras, IX, 1938.]

BṚHAJJĀTAKA : A work, in 25 chaps., on the *Horā* section of astrology, by Varāhamihira. Its importance lies in the use, perhaps for the first time in India, of the Zodiac, with Greek names of the Zodiacal signs and planets. Some of the names, used by the author, are *Kulīra*, *Jūka*, *Tāvuri* etc. The following are some of the Greek technical terms found in the work : *dreṣkāṇa*, *anaphā*, *sunaphā*, *kendra*, *trikoṇa*, *hibuka*, *jāmitra*, etc.

[Ed., with Skt. and Hindi comm. by S. Jha, 1944; Bāikoli, 1952; Haridāsa Skt. Series, 1957. Trs. into Eng. by S. Sastri, Mysore, 1929; by Svāmī Vijñānānanda alias H. P. Chatterji, 2nd. ed, New Delhi 1978. See Das-grosse .....(*Bṛhajjātaka*) ..... Nach der Englischen ..... Iyer ..... von W. Wulf, Hamburg, 1925.]

BṚHANNĀRADĪYA PURĀṆA : It is a purely sectarian text being devoted to the glorification of *Viṣṇu-bhakti*. A lengthy chapter (XIV) enumerates the principal sins and the corresponding punishments of hell. Several chapters deal with duties of castes and *Āśramas*, *Śrāddhas*, and *Prāyaścitta*. The last chapters deal with the misery of transmigration and with salvation by means of *Yoga* and *Bhakti*.

[Ed. P. Tarkaratna, Vaṅgavāsī Press, 2nd ed., Calcutta, 1316 B.S.]

BṚHATĪ : It is a renowned commentary by Prabhākara on the *Pūrvamīmāṃsā-sūtra* of Jaimini. It gave rise to the Prabhākara school of Mīmāṃsā philosophy.

[Ed., with the *Ṛjuvimalā Pañcikā*, by S. S. Sastri, Madras, 1962. Trs. G. Jha, *IT*, ii and iii.]

BṚHAT-ŚABDENDUŚEKHARA : Commonly known as simply *Śabdenduśekhara*, it is an exhaustive commentary by Nāgeśa on Bhaṭṭoji Dīkṣita's *Siddhānta-kaumudī*.

[Ed. Sitaram Sastri, Sarasvati Bhavana Granthamālā, Vol. 87, parts I, II, III.]

BṚHAT-SAṂHITĀ : A huge work on astronomy and astrology in 106 chapters, by Varāhamihira. The principal subjects, dealt with in it, are as follows :— effects of the movements of the sun and changes of the moon, eclipse, various constellations and their influence over the fate of man, effect of the presiding planet over the fortunes or mishaps within a year, signs of weather, means of foretelling the crop and the rise and fall of its prices, importance of astrology in relation to architecture, digging of tanks, laying out of gardens, making of images, characteristics of oxen, dogs, cocks, tortoises, horses, elephants, man, woman, parasols etc., praise of women, life in the harem, couches and seats, jewels, lamps and toothsticks, science of augury, marriage etc. Incidentally we get in it an interesting sketch of Indian geography. The work is in verses of varied metres. There are commendable poetic touches in the work. Containing as it does a large number of references to astronomers, it is important from the point of view of the history of astronomy.

[Ed. S. Dvidedi, 2 vols., Viz. SS. 1895, 97 (with Bhaṭṭotpala's comm. Ed., with trs. and notes, by M. R. Bhat, 1981 : Trs. into Eng. by C. Iyer, Madura 1884; V. S. Sastri, 1947. Chaps. on jewels (LXXX—LXXXIII), ed. and trs. L. Finot, *Les lapidaires indiens*, pp. 59 ff. See Die menschlichen Körperteile in ihrer Bedeutong für, Schicksal und Charakter...Von J. J. Meyer, *WZKM* 36 (1912). Trs. of chaps. 68 and 70 with notes by M.R. Bhat, Delhi. Also see J. Schelelowitz, *Festchrift M. Winternitz*, Leipzig, 1944; A. M. Shastri, *India as seen in the Bṛhat-*

saṃhitā of Varāhamihira, Delhi, 1969. K. K. Das Gupta (ed.), *The topographical list of the Bṛhat-saṃhitā* by Fleet, Calcutta, 1973. See M. R. Bhat, *Bṛhat-saṃhitā*.]

BṚHATKATHĀ : A work on tales traditionally attributed to Guṇāḍhya and stated to have been written in Paiśācī Prakrit. The work is lost. Its three Sanskrit metrical versions are *Bṛhatkathā-mañjarī* (1037 A.D.), *Kathā-saritsāgara* (1063-81 A.D.) and *Bṛhatkathā-śloka-saṃgraha*. The first two are Kashmirian and are by Kṣemendra and Somadeva respectively. The last one, which probably originated some time in the period between the eighth century and the tenth, is Nepalese version and is by Budhasvāmin. Many Sanskrit works, particularly dramas, are based on the *Bṛhat-kathā*, e.g. Bhāsa's *Svapnavāsavadatta* and *Pratijñā-yaugandharāyaṇa*.

[See E. P. Matin, Narrative Technique and Guṇāḍhya's Bṛhatkathā, *Summaries of papers*, 5th World Skt. Conf., Varanasi, 1981, p. 212; R. Vijayalakshmy, on the Jaina Elements in the versions of the Bṛhatkathā, *Ibid*, p. 216.]

BṚHATKATHĀ-MAÑJARĪ : Divided into 18 cantos called *Lambhakas*, it is by Kṣemendra (q.v.) and consists of over 7,000 verses. Along with the *Kathā-sarit-sāgara* it represents the lost north-western version of the *Bṛhatkathā*. Like the other two versions it describes the adventure of Naravāhanadatta, son of Udayana, his acquisition of Madanamañjukā as his bride and of the land of Vidyādharas as his empire.

Kṣemendra sometimes cuts the facts too short, but unnecessarily dilates upon erotic matters, and prolongs religious sections.

[Ed. Sivadatta, NSP. Parts (intro. and first two stories) trs., with Roman text, by S. Levi, *JA*, 1885-86. Partly trs. by L. Von Mankowski.]

BṚHATKATHĀ-ŚLOKA-SAṂGRAHA : A Nepalese version, by Budhasvāmin, of the *Bṛhatkathā*, in 28 cantos, 4539 stanzas, belonging probably to the 8th or 9th cent. A.D. Available in an incomplete form.

[Ed., with notes and French trs., by F. Lacôte, 2 tom., Paris, 1908. See V. S. Agrawala, *Bṛhatkathā-ślokasaṃgraha—a study*; E. P. Maten, *Budhasvāmin's Bṛhatkathā-ślokasaṃgraha, a literary study* etc.]

BUDDHA-CARITA : Composed by Aśvaghoṣa, it describes the life of the Buddha in elegant Sanskrit. In the present Sanskrit form, it consists of parts of cantos i and xiv and the whole of cantos ii—xiii, but it appears to have been originally composed in 28 cantos. It is one of the earliest extant Kāvyas in Sanskrit. Its Chinese and Tibetan translations are available.

[Ed. E. H. Johnston, with Eng. trs., Lahore, 1935-36; S. Chaudhuri, Hindi trs., Kathautiya, 1953-55; R. B. Akvele, with Gujarati trs., Ahmedabad, 1957; with Hindi comm., Banaras, 1962; E. B. Cowell, Oxford, 1893. An ed. is reported to be under preparation at Mithilā Institute, Darbhanga. Trs. into Eng. by E. B. Cowell in *SBE*, Vol 49; into German by C. Cappeller, Jena, 1922; into Italian by C. Formichi, Bari, 1912; into Polish (extracts) by A. Gawronski in *Aśvaghoṣa*, Ossolineum, 1966.]

CAITANYA-CANDRODAYA : A ten-act drama by Kavikarṇapūra. In it the main incidents of Caitanya's life are dramatised. Perhaps modelled on the *Prabodha-candrodaya* of Kṛṣṇamiśra.

[Ed. Bib. Ind., 1854; Kāvyamālā, Bombay, 1917; Kedarnath and W. L. S. Panashikar, NSP, Bombay, 1906.]

CAITANYA-CARITĀMṚTA : A Mahākāvya by Kavikarṇapūra. Consisting of about 2,000 verses in 20 cantos, it deals with the life and activities of Caitanya who is conceived as an incarnation of Kṛṣṇa.

[Ed. Radharamana Press, Baharampur, Murshidabad, 1884.]

There is a *Caitanya-caritāmṛta* by Murārigupta. Also styled *Śrīkṛṣṇa-caitanya-caritāmṛta*, it is a biographical poem, and is popularly known as *Kaḍacā*. In 78 cantos, divided into four sections called *Prakramas*, it deals with the entire life of Caitanya. Its date of composition is given as Śaka 1431 = 1510 A.D.

[Ed. S. Gosvami, 1317 B. S. (2nd ed.), 3rd ed. pub. 1337 B. S.]

CALARĀŚI-KALANA : By S. Dvidevin. A work on mathematics in 15 chaps. of which the first four are grouped under Part I and the rest under Part II. Part I deals with rational fractions and miscellaneous remarks. Part II treats of reduction formula, double integration, lengths of curves, areas of plane curves and surfaces, volumes of solids, definite integrals and similar problems. The author has introduced new methods and differential calculus.

[Ed. B. Misra, in 2 vols., Banaras, 1941-43.]

CAMPŪ-RĀMĀYAṆA : See *Rāmāyaṇa-campū*.

CĀṆAKYA-RĀJANĪTI-ŚĀSTRA : A work on politics and statecraft, attributed to Cāṇakya. Almost identical with the *Bṛhaspati-saṃhitā* of the *Garuḍa-purāṇa*.

[Ed. Calcutta Oriental Series, No. 2. On the text, see L. Sternbach in Indo-Iranian Jour., 1957; *ABORI*, XXXVII and XLII; S. Pathak in *Viśvabhāratī Annals* (Santiniketan) VIII, 1958; L. Sternbach, *Cāṇakya-nīti-Text-tradition*, Pts. I, II, Hoshiarpur; *Cāṇakya-rājanīti*, Adyar, 1963. G. M. Bolling's 'The recension of Cāṇakya used by Galanos' (*Studies in honour of Bloomfield*, New Haven, 1926) may be consulted.]

CĀṆAKYA-SŪTRA : A collection of Sūtras ascribed to Cāṇakya. It is a list of maxims of the didactic-moral type.

[Printed in Appendix to the second ed. of Arthaśāstra, by Shama Sastri. See L. Sternbach, *Cāṇakya-rājanīti*, Adyar, 1963; *Cāṇakyanīti Text-tradition, The Subhāṣita-saṃgrahas as treasuries of Cāṇakya's sayings*, Hoshiarpur, 1966; *The spreading of Cāṇakya's Aphorisms over Greater India*, Calcutta, 1967. Also see V. K. Subramaniam, *Maxims of Cāṇakya*, 1980.]

CAṆḌA-KAUŚIKA : A drama in five acts, by Kṣemīśvara. King Hariścandra incurs the wrath of the irascible sage Kauśika Viśvāmitra who curses him. He secures pardon by the surrender of the earth and a thousand gold pieces. To obtain the latter he sells his wife and child to a Brahmin, and himself to a Caṇḍāla as a cemetery-keeper. One day, his wife brings the dead body of their child, but it proves to be merely a trial of his character; his son regains life and is crowned king.

[Ed. and trs. into Eng. by S. Das Gupta, *Bib. Indica*, 1962.]

CAṆḌĪ : See *Mārkaṇḍeya Purāṇa*.

[Ed. and trs. into Latin by L. Poley, Berolini, 1931. Trs. into English by Pargiter, *Mārkaṇḍeya-purāṇa* trs., pp. 465-523. Extracts rendered into French by Burnouf, *JA* 4, 1824. A recent edition, with Eng. trs. under the title 'Devīmāhātmya', is by V. S. Agrawal, Varanasi. Also see *Tattvānanda*, Text and Translation. On many translations in Bengali, see D. C. Sen, Bengali Language and Literature. See M. Chaudhury, The D. Māhātmya—its antiquity, philosophy and comms., *Summaries of Papers*, *AIOC*, 1974; B. Coburn, *Crystallisation of the Goddess Tradition*; *the sources and context of the D. Māhātmya.*]

CAṆḌĪ-ŚATAKA : A poem, in 102 stanzas, by Bāṇabhaṭṭa. In *Sragdharā* metre it is a high-flown panegyric of goddess Caṇḍī who slew the buffalo-demon.

[Ed. Kāvyamālā. IV, with a Sanskrit comm.; Quackenbos, *The Sanskrit Poems of Mayūra*, New York, 1917, with Eng. trs. and notes.]

CANDRAKALĀ : A *Nāṭikā* by Viśvanātha, author of the *Sāhityadarpaṇa*.

[Ed. with Hindi Comm., B. Sukla, Banaras, 1967.]

CANDRĀLOKA : A treatise on poetics, by Jayadeva who appears to be different from the author of the *Gīta-govinda*. It is in ten chapters, called *Mayūkhas*, and consists of about 350 verses. The topics discussed, according to the Calcutta edition, are (1) *Vāgvicāra*, (2) *Doṣanirūpaṇa*, (3) *Lakṣaṇa-nirūpaṇa* (4) *Guṇa-nirūpaṇa*, (5) *Alaṃkāra-nirūpaṇa*, (6) *Rasādi-nirūpaṇa*, (7) *Dhvani-nirūpaṇa*, (8) *Guṇībhūta-vyaṅgya*, (9) *Lakṣaṇā-nirūpaṇa* (10) *Abhidhā-nirūpaṇa*.

Appayya Dīkṣita's *Kuvalayānanda* incorporates the Kārikās of the *Arthālaṃkāra* section of this work.

[Ed. V. L. Pansikar, NSP, 1907; N. S. Khiste, with the comm. called *Candrāloka-prakāśa-śaradāgama*, CSS, 1929; with *Rākāgama* comm., CSS, 1938.]

CĀNDRA-VYĀKARAṆA : A grammar attributed to Candragomin whose object appears to have been to abridge and simplify the *Aṣṭādhyāyī* of Pāṇini. In place of the eight chapters of Pāṇini's grammar, it has six chapters. While the *Aṣṭādhyāyī* contains 3981 aphorisms, this grammar has 3100. Candragomin has left out the portion of Pāṇini's grammar dealing with Vedic grammar and accents. He has not given the technical terms like *Ti*, *Ghu* etc.

[Ed. B. Liebich, Leipzig, 1902; chaps. i—iii ed. K. C. Chatterjee, Poona, 1953; Part 2 (Chaps. 4-6), ed. by same scholar, Poona, 1961; ed. N. Sastri, Delhi, 1968. For a summary of the work, see *Agni-Purāṇa*, Chaps. 248-58. Also see *Mahābhāṣya*, vol. VII, D.E. Society ed. Poona; H. Misra, *A Critical study of Cāndra Vyākaraṇa-Vṛtti*.]

CARAKA-SAṂHITĀ : The oldest of the extant Saṃhitās of Āyurveda, ascribed to Caraka. The text in its present form appears to be the result of revision by one Dṛḍhabala who admits to having added the last two chapters and to having written 17 out of 28 or 30 chapters of book vi. The work does not claim to be original; it appears to have been a revision of a number of Tantras on special topics written by Agniveśa. The contents of the work are as follows :—

Part I—*Sūtra-sthāna.*

It deals with remedies, diet, duties of a physician.

Part II—*Nidāna-sthāna.*

It deals with eight chief diseases.

Part III—*Vimāna-sthāna*

It deals with general pathology and medical studies. It also contains regulations for the conduct of the newly fledged student.

Part IV—*Śārira-sthāna*

Anatomy and embryology.

Part V—*Indriya-sthāna*

Diagnosis and prognosis.

Part VI—*Cikitsā-sthāna.*

Special therapy.

Parts VII, VIII—*Kalpa-sthāna* and *Siddhi-sthāna.*

General therapy.

The work is in prose mixed with verses. Caraka is assigned by some scholars to the second or first century B.C. It was rendered into Persian at a fairly early date, and into Arabic c. 800 A.D.

[Ed. with Eng., Hindi and Gujarati trs., in 6 vols. by Āyurvedic Soc., Jamnagar, 1949; with Eng.trs., extracts from comm. of Cakrapāṇidatta (also rendered into Eng.), R. K. Sharma and V. B. Dash, Varanasi, 1977. Trs. into Eng. by A.C. Kaviratna, 68 parts, Calcutta, 1890-1925; into Bengali (with text in Bengali script) by S. C. Sarma Kavibhūṣaṇa, Calcutta, 1903. See P. Roy and H.N. Gupta, *Caraka-saṃhitā, a scientific synopsis*, and J. Filliozat, *The Classical Doctrine of Indian Medicine*, Delhi, 1964. For flora in the *Caraka-saṃhitā*, see Satya Prakash, *Founders of Sciences in Ancient India*, New Delhi, 1965, pp. 164-176.]

CARAKA-TĀTPARYA-DĪPIKĀ : Same as *Āyurveda-dipikā* (q.v.)

CĀRUCARYĀ : A poetical work, in 100 verses, by Kṣemendra who seeks in it to inculcate morality and good conduct.

[Ed. Kāvyamālā, II.]

CATUḤŚATAKA or CATUḤŚATIKĀ: Also called *Śataśāstra*, it is a poetical work by the Buddhist Āryadeva (c. 250 A.D.). Consisting of 400 *Kārikās*, it belongs to the fundamental works of the Mādhyamika school. The author shows considerable power of irony in his attack on the Brahmanical practice of bathing in the Ganges with a view to acquiring merit and washing off sin. The author defends Nāgārjuna's doctrines against the other Buddhist schools and also against Brahmanical systems, esp. the Vaiśeṣika. The *Catuḥśataka* is one of the ground-works of the faith of the Sanron sect in Japan.

[Fragments of the text, with Candrakīrti's comm., ed. by H. P. Sastri, Asiatic Society, Calcutta, 1914. Chap. vii reconstructed with extracts of comm. and Eng. trs. by V. Bhattacharya, in *Proc. of 4th Oriental Conference II*. Chaps. viii-xvi reconstructed and ed. by the same scholar, Viśvabhāratī Series No. 2, Calcutta. 1931. Last 9 chaps., with French trs., reconstructed by P. L. Vaidya, *Etudes sur Āryadeva et son Catuḥśataka*, Paris, 1923. The complete work exists in a Tibetan version. A complete Italian trs. of the text and comm., from the Chinese, pub. by G. Tucci in *Studie materiali di storia delle religioni*, 1925. For Eng. trs. see *Pre-Diṅnāga Buddhist texts, Logic from Chinese sources.*]

There is a *Catuḥśataka-stotra* by Mātṛceṭa.

[Trs. into Eng. from Tibetan by F. W. Thomas, *Indian Antiquary*, 1905.]

CATURAṄGA-DĪPIKĀ : A work on the game of Indian Dice-Chess, ascribed to a Śūlapāṇi who may have been different from the famous Smṛti writer of Bengal bearing this name.

[Ed., with Eng. trs. and notes by M. Ghosh, Calcutta, 1936. See K. D. Kulkarni, Lexicographical notes on *Caturaṅgadīpikā* of Śūlapāṇi, *S. K. Chatterji Jubilee Vol.* (*Ind. Ling.*, XVI, 1955).]

CATURBHĀṆI : A collection of four one-act monologue dramas of the *Bhāṇa* type. In atmosphere and spirit these are closely similar to one another and to the *Mṛcchakaṭika*, The four plays are : *Ubhayābhisārikā*, *Padmaprābhṛtaka*, *Dhūrtaviṭasaṃvāda* and *Pāda-tāḍitaka* ascribed respectively to Vararuci, Śūdraka, Īśvaradatta and Śyāmalika. These are assigned by some scholars to a period later than that of Bharata's *Nāṭyaśāstra* but much earlier than the end of the 10th century. Other scholars, however, place them in the beginning of the Christian era or earlier. The scene of action of the plays is laid in the imperial cities like Ujjayinī or Kusumapura. The plays are unique in their amusing pictures of the lives and adventures, scandals and gossips of rogues and rakes who lived in imperial cities. In their literary quality and style and in the portrayal of characters they richly deserve a place of their own in the history of Sanskrit drama.

[Ed. M. R. Kavi and S. K. R. Sastri, Tricur, 1922; Motichand and V. Agravala (under the title *Śṛṅgāra-hāṭa*), Bombay, 1959. *Pādatāḍitaka*, pt. I ed. G. H. Schokker, *Indo-Iranian Monographs*, IX, Hague and Paris, 1966. For studies in these works, see F.W. Thomas in *JRAS* (Centenary Supplement), 1924; S. K. De in *JRAS*, 1926. On *Pādatāḍitaka*, see I. T. Burrow, *JRAS*, 1946; S. Mukhopadhyaya, A Glimpse of Society in Pādatāḍitaka, *Summaries of Papers*, AIOC, 1969, p. 383. *Ubhayābhisārikā* trs. into English by S. Sen in *Calcutta Review*, 1926; ed., in Roman script, with Eng. trs. and notes, by A. K. Warder and T. Venkatacarya, Madras, 1967. Also trs. into Eng. by C. C. Mehta in *Three Skt. Lighter Delights*, Baroda. 1969. See M. Ghosh, *Glimpses of Sexual Life in Nanda-Maurya India* (recent Trs. of *Caturbhāṇī*) Calcutta, 1975.]

CATURVARGA-CINTĀMAṆI : A huge Smṛti digest by Hemādri. The author himself states that he intended to deal with Dharmaśāstra in five sections called *Vrata*, *Dāna*, *Tīrtha*, *Mokṣa* and *Pariśeṣa*. The last section was divided into four parts, viz. *Devatā*, *Kāla-nirṇaya*, *Karmavipāka* and *Lakṣaṇa-samuccaya*. Of the four volumes of the work, printed so far, the fourth dealing with *Prāyaścitta* does not appear to be the work of Hemādri.

[Pub. in *Bib. Ind.* Series. Vol. I (*Dāna-khaṇḍa*); Vol. II

(*Vrata-khaṇḍa*), pts. i, ii, 1878-79; Vol. III (*Pariśeṣa-khaṇḍa*), pts. i, ii, 1895; Vol. IV (*Prāyaścitta-khaṇḍa*), 1911.]

CATURVARGA-SAṂGRAHA : A poetical work, in four chapters, by Kṣemendra. The four ends of human life are praised in these chapters in order. It is a didactic work which seeks to teach us that *Viveka* (power of discrimination) and *Vairāgya* (indifference to worldly objects) are the essential things in life.

[Ed. *Kāvyamālā*, V.]

CAURA-PAÑCĀŚIKĀ : Also called *Caura* (*Caurī*) *surata-pañcāśikā*. An erotic poem, in fifty stanzas, attributed to Bilhaṇa. It deals with secret love and the liveliness of women in different amorous situations. It exists in three recensions. In the South Indian recension, the poem appears in the framework of a longer poem called *Bilhaṇa-kāvya*. The theme of the *Bilhaṇa-kāvya* has inspired versions of the story both in Sanskrit and in Bengali. Of the versions in Bengali, that preserved in Bhāratacandra's *Annadāmaṅgala* is the most well-known.

[Ed. Haeberlin's *Kāvya-saṃgraha*, Calcutta, 1847, *Kāvyamālā*, xiii; J. Vidyāsāgara's *Kāvyasaṃgraha*, I; with Hindi comm., D. Srivastava, Banaras, 1971. Metrical rendering into English by E. Arnold, London, 1896. Ed., with Eng. trs. and notes, by S. N. Tadpatrikar. See L. Shiveshwarkar, *The Pictures of the caura pañcāśikā*.]

CHANDAḤSŪTRA : Ascribed to Piṅgala, it is a work on prosody dealing partly with Vedic metres but mainly with classical metres. The author adopts the system of algebraic symbols, using L for a short (*laghu*), G for a long (*guru*) syllable, M for a molossus, and so on. The names of the metres are interesting. Some of the metres are named after epithets of the beloved, e.g. *Kuṭilagati* (one of crooked gait), *Cañcalākṣikā* (one of the glancing eyes), *Tanumadhyā* (one of slender waist), *Cāruhāsinī* (one of sweet smile) etc. The names of some metres suggest poetic observation of animal life, e.g. *Aśvalalita*, (the gait of the horse), *Śārdūlavikrīḍita* (the tiger's play) and so on. Some of the names are suggested by the plant-kingdom, e.g. *Mañjarī* (the cluster), *Mālā* (the garland).

[Ed., with Halāyudha's comm. (c. 950 A.D.), *Kāvyamālā*, 81, 1908: V. Sastri, *Bib. Ind.* An ed., with Yādavaprakāśa's commentary, prepared by H. S. Sinha Roy, under the guidance of Sivaprasad Bhattacharya, is proposed to be published in the *Bibliotheca Indica Series*, Calcutta.]

CHĀNDOGYOPANIṢAD : Divided into eight chapters (*prapāṭhaka*), it discusses, *inter alia*, the significance of the mystic syllable *Om*, the branches of moral life, meaning of *Gāyatrī*, the problem of Being and Non-being, appearance and reality, individual and universal spirit, subtlety and immanence of Ātman, self and reality, psychological categories, spiritual hedonism, realisation of Ātman as the fulfilment of desires, the radiant world of Ātman, Brahmacarya as means to God-realisation, eschatological physiology, etc. Incidentally this Upaniṣad mentions Kṛṣṇa, son of Devakī. It contains many legends and parables of which mention may be made of the parable of the sun, the story of Satyakāma Jābāla and the story of Upakosala. In it we find also the spiritual dialogue between Śvetaketu, the aspiring disciple, and his father Āruṇi.

[Ed., with comm. of Śaṃkara and gloss of Ānandagiri, by E. Roer, 1849-50. Trs. into Eng. by R. Mitra, 1854-62, and by G. N. Jha; into Polish by Michalski-Iwienski, Krakau, 1924; into French by E. Senart, Paris, 1930. See S. M. Bhatkhande, *Chāndogya Upaniṣad and Brahmaśūtras—a comparative study*, Bombay, 1982; K. H. Post, Vedic Quotations in Chāndogya Upaniṣad, *ABORI*, Poona, 1981.]

CHANDOMAÑJARĪ : A work on prosody, by Gaṅgādāsa. As the author states, it is based on various works on prosody. It deals with *Sama-vṛtta*, *Ardha-samavṛtta*, *Viṣama-vṛtta and Mātrā-vṛtta* besides a *Gadya-prakaraṇa* (section on prose). The author himself states that he defines and illustrates only those metres which are commonly used. The majority of the illustrative verses are composed by the author, and deal with various sports of Kṛṣṇa at Vṛndāvana.

[Ed., with notes in English, by D. Kanjilal, Calcutta 1970; A. Sastri Vetala, *CSS*, 1959 (with Skt. and Hindi comm.)]

CHANDOVICITI : According to some, it is the title of a lost work of Daṇḍin. Others think that it denotes Metrics as a branch of learning, and not any particular work. In the colophons to some MSS of Yādavaprakāśa's commentary on the *Piṅgala-chandaḥsūtra*, it appears to have been the real title of Piṅgala's work.

Under *Saṅgīta-ratnākara*, IV. 248 (Adyar Library ed.), commentator Kallinātha states that *Chandoviciti* is the name of a work. In the same context, commentator Siṃhabhūpāla states it to be a work by Śārṅgadeva, author of the *Saṃgīta-ratnākara*.

[See 'Chandoviciti—a note' by S. C. Banerji in *IHQ*, XXIX. A *Chandoviciti* by Mitradhara is ed. by Schlingoff, Berlin Academy, 1957.]

CIKITSĀ-KALIKĀ : A medical work by Tiṣata (14th cent. A.D.).

CIKITSĀMṚTA : A work on Āyurveda, in 2500 verses, by Milhaṇa who wrote in Delhi in 1224 A.D.

CIKITSĀ-SĀRA-SAṂGRAHA or CIKITSĀ-SAṂGRAHA: The *magnum opus* of Cakrapāṇidatta. It deals with the diagnosis of diseases and the efficacy of minerals. Written about 1060 A.D.

[Ed. and trs. into Hindi, by S. Sastri, Lahore, 1926.]

There is also a *Cikitsā-sāra-saṃgraha* by Vaṅgasena.

CITRALAKṢAṆA : A treatise on Indian painting, Calcutta, [Ed. A. K. Bhattacharya, Calcutta. See A. K. Bhattacharya, *Technique of Indian Painting*, Calcutta.]

CITRASŪTRA : Of the *Viṣṇu dharmottara*. [*A treatise on painting* by Sivaramamurti, New Delhi, 1978.]

CITSUKHĪ : Popular name of Citsukhācārya's *Pratyak-tattva-dīpikā* or *Tattava-pradīpikā*, a work on *Advaita-vedānta*.

[See under *Tattva-pradīpikā*].

DAMAYANTĪ-KATHĀ : Another name of *Nala-campū* (q.v.).

DĀNA-KELI-KAUMUDĪ : One-act drama of the *Bhāṇikā* type, by Rūpa Gosvāmin. Vasudeva is performing a sacrifice. Rādhā, along with other Gopīs, is carrying ghee. Kṛṣṇa, accompanied by his attendants, obstructs their way and demands toll on the ground that he is the lord of the forest through which they are passing. A quarrel ensues. At last a friend of Rādhā proposes to give Rādhā as toll. But Rādhā remonstrates.

[Ed. Purīdāsa, Mymensing, 1947; ed. with Skt. comm. Madhulikā, Eng. and Hindi trs. and critical intro. by S. N. Sastri, Indore.]

DĀNA-KRIYĀ-KAUMUDĪ : Smṛti digest by Govindānanda, dealing with various gifts.

[Ed. *Bib. Ind.*, 1903.]

DĀNA-RATNĀKARA : A Smṛti digest forming a part of Caṇḍeśvara's *Smṛti-ratnākara*. Consisting of 29 chapters called *Taraṅgas*, it deals with various kinds of gifts and matters connected with them.

[For MSS see (1) Deccan College MS No. 114 of 1884—86.
(2) Mitra, *Notices*, VI, No 2069.
(3) *Mithilā MSS Cat.* I, No. 191.
(4) *India Office Cat.* III, No. 1388.]

DĀNA-SĀGARA : An extensive Smṛti digest by Vallālasena. The principal subjects, dealt with in it, are as follows : eulogy of Brāhmaṇas, merit accruing from gifts, objects of gifts, the donor, proper time and place for gifts, bad donations, rites and procedure to be followed in making and accepting gifts, the 16 Mahādānas, lesser gifts, names of various Purāṇas and their extent. The author states that he has described 1375 kinds of gifts.

[Ed. *Bib. Ind.*, Calcutta, 1953. See R. C. Hazra, Critical examination of some readings of the Dānasāgara, *Our Heritage*, Vol. VIII, 1960.]

DAṆḌAVIVEKA : A part of the *Smṛti-tattva-viveka*, a Smṛti digest by Vardhamāna. In seven chapters, it deals with penal offences, the propriety of inflicting punishments and the different forms of punishment.

[Ed. K. K. Smṛtitīrtha, *GOS*, 1931.]

DAŚAGĪTIKĀ-SŪTRA : A work on astronomy, by Āryabhaṭa I. In it the author gives his numerical notation.

DARPA-DALANA : A poetical work, in seven sections, by Kṣemendra. It denounces vanity arising out of lineage, wealth, learning, beauty, valour, charity and penance.

[Ed. *Kāvyamālā*, VI.]

DAŚAKUMĀRA-CARITA : A prose-romance by Daṇḍin. It deals with the adventures and various activities of Rājavāhana and seven other princes. The deeds of two princes are described in the introductory portion called *Pūrva-pīṭhikā*. The incomplete account of prince Viśruta has been completed in the concluding portion called *Uttara-pīṭhikā*. The *Pūrva-pīṭhikā* and the *Uttara-pīṭhikā* are generally supposed to be later additions to the original work. A Daśakumara-pūrva-kathāsāra is attributed to the Vaghela King Ramacandra (1592-1593).

[Ed. G. J. Agashe (revised version of the ed. by Bühler and Peterson), Bombay, 1919; NSP, 1925 (10th ed.); M. R. Kale, with Eng. trs. and notes, Bombay, 1925. Trs. into English by P. W. Jacob, revised by C. Rylands, London, 1928; A. W. Ryder, Chicago, 1927. Trs. into German by J. J. Meyer, Leipzig, 1902; J. Hertel in *Ind. Erzāhler* 1-3, Leipzig, 1902. Trs. into French by H. Fauche in *Une Tétrade, on drame, hymne, roman et poéme*, ii, Paris, 1862, and also by V. Henry.]

DAŚARŪPAKA (DAŚARŪPA): A work on dramaturgy, by Dhanañjaya, and takes its name from the ten *Rūpakas* or primary forms of drama recognised in it following the *Nāṭya-śāstra*. It is divided into four books the contents of which are as follows :—

I. Subject-matter and plot of the drama.

II. The hero, heroine and other characters; the language of the drama.

III. The prologue and its varieties and different kinds of drama.

IV. Emotions and sentiments.

[Ed. F. Hall. Calcutta, 1865; S. Sastri, Bombay, 1927. Ed., with Dhanika's comm., notes, Eng. trs. etc. by J. K. Shastri; with comm. of Dhanika and sub-commentary of Bhaṭṭa-nṛsiṃha, by T. Venkatacharya, University of Toronto. Trs. into English by G.C.O. Haas, New York, 1912].

DAŚAŚLOKĪ : A philosophical tract of ten verses, in which Nimbārka elucidates his view of the distinctness of *Jīva*, *Īśvara* and *Jagat*.

DAŚĀVATĀRA-CARITA : Written by Kṣemendra, in 1066 A.D., it describes and extols each of the ten incaranations of Viṣṇu in separate cantos. In canto IX Buddha has been represented as the personification of Kṛṣṇa, and the Buddha legend has been transformed into a Viṣṇu legend.

[Ed. Durgaprasad and Parab, NSP, 1891].

DATTAKA-CANDRIKĀ : A work on adoption, generally ascribed to Kuvera, but really perhaps written or compiled by Raghumaṇi, spiritual preceptor of the king of Nadīyā. It is regarded in Bengal as the most authoritative work on the subject.

[Pub. Baroda, 1899 (with Marathi rendering); ASS, 1942.]

DATTAKA-MĪMĀṂSĀ : A famous Smṛti digest by Nanda Paṇḍita. It deals with all aspects of adoption and the ceremonies connected with it. In British Indian Courts, it was looked upon as the most authoritative work on adoption particularly in Mithilā and Banaras.

[Ed. B. Śiromaṇi, with his own comm., Calcutta, 1885; R. P. Pandeya, with comm. of Madhusūdana & notes of V. V. Deshpandeya, Varanasi, 1980. Trs. into English by Sutherland (comprised in Stoke's *Hindu Law Books*).]

DATTILAM : A work on music and dancing, by Dattilācārya,

perhaps a pupil of Bharata. It comprehends music and dancing.

[Ed. K. S. Sastri, TSS, 1930; with intro., trs. and comm., Wiersman—te Nijenhuis, Leiden, 1970. See M.Lath, *A Study of Dattilam*, Delhi, 1978.]

DĀYABHĀGA : Written by Jīmūtavāhana, it was probably a part of a bigger treatise called *Dharma-ratna*. It deals with the inheritance and succession in respect of ordinary properties and *Strīdhana* (exclusive property of women), partition, etc., In matters of Hindu Law relating to inheritance, partition, *Strīdhana*, etc. it was of paramount authority in British Courts of Bengal.

[Ed. J. Vidyasagara, Calcutta, 1893; with seven commentaries by B. Śiromaṇi, Calcutta, 1863-66. *Dāyabhāga of Jīmūtavāhana*, Vol. I, ed. H. N. Chatterji, Howrah (W. Bengal), 1978. Trs. into English, with the *Mitākṣarā*, by H. T. Colebrooke, Calcutta, 1810. See I. S. Pawate, *Dāyabhāga*, Dharwar, 1975; H. N. Chatterji, *Dāyabhāga, the Institutes of Jīmūtavāhana*, Calcutta.]

DELARĀMĀ-KATHĀSĀRA : A poetical work, in 13 cantos, by Bhaṭṭa Āhlādaka. It is the Sanskrit version of a story contained in Muslim works. It deals with the story of how two youthful brothers, driven away from home by certain untoward circumstances, passed through vicissitudes of fortune and were finally re-united. The work takes its name from the courtesan, named Delarāmā to whose wiles the elder of the above brothers falls a victim, and is ultimately deserted by her.

[Ed. *Kāvyamālā*, 77. Bombay, 1902.]

DEŚOPADEŚA : A poetical work, in eight sections, by Kṣemendra. In these sections, he deals respectively with the villain, the miser, the prostitute, the old procuress, the voluptuary, the student from abroad particularly from Gauḍa, the passionate fellow, the depraved Śaiva teacher with his despicable followers.

[Ed. KSTS, 1924.]

DEVĪ-BHĀGAVATA : A Purāṇa, divided into parts, each containing six chapters called *Skandhas*. Seeks to establish the supremacy of Goddess as the Energy of all others. Appears to have had a longer version, now lost. According to Winternitz, a Śaivite work, but it appears to be a Śākta-purāṇa. Supposed by some to be the original authentic *Bhāgavata-purāṇa*. Shows henotheistic tendency in holding Viṣṇu, Śiva and Kṛṣṇa as the greatest deities in different places. But, Goddess is held to be the life and energy of all gods. Though described as a Mahāpurāṇa in chapter colophons, it is really a late work. Reflects a society in which people of various sects including heretics used to live. Generally supposed to be not earlier than the middle of the 10th cent. A.D.

[Of several editions, mention may be made of those pub. by Sanskrit Pustakalay, Varanasi, Veṅkaṭeśwar Press, Bombay, Vaṅgavāsī Press, Calcutta. Also see P. Kumar's ed. with critical Intro. and Index. For details, see R. C. Hazra, *Studies in Purāṇic Records etc.*, 1940, and his articles in *JOR*, XXI, Pts. I—IV, *IHQ*, Dec. 1953. Also P. G. Lalye, *Studies in Devī-bhāgavata*, Bombay, 1973.]

DEVĪ-CANDRAGUPTA : A drama, attributed to Viśākhadeva who is probably identical with Viśākhadatta, from which passages are quoted in the *Nāṭyadarpaṇa* of Rāmacandra and Guṇacandra (12th cent. A.D.). Abhinavagupta quotes the work, without the author's name, in his commentary on the *Nāṭya-śāstra*. It is also quoted in Bhoja's *Śṛṅgāra-prakāśa*.

[See S. K. De in *BSOS*, IV, 1926, p. 282. The work has not been recovered. The plot appears, according to Rājaśekhara's *Kāvyamīmāṃsā*, to have been the rescue, by Kumāra Candragupta, in the guise of a woman, of Dhruvadevī who was abducted by a Śaka prince. The same story is perhaps alluded to in Bāṇa's *Harṣa-carita* (See IA, LII, 1923, pp. 181-84), where this Candragupta is taken to be identical with Candragupta II of Gupta dynasty. Also see S. V. Sohoni, *ABORI*, LXII, 1981, p. 169.]

DEVĪ-MĀHĀTMYA : Same as *Caṇḍī* (q.v.).

DEVĪNĀMA-VILĀSA : Composed in 16 cantos by Sāhib Kaula, a Kashmirian, it is, as the title indicates, a devotional poem. It takes its name from the one thousand names of the goddess recounted in cantos VI to XV.

[Ed. M. Kaul, Lahore, 1942.]

DEVĪ-ŚATAKA : It is a devotional poem, in 100 verses, composed by Ānandavardhana in honour of goddess Pārvatī. [Ed. Kāvyamālā, XI.]

DHĀRAṆĪ : The word is a synonym of 'Rakṣā' and the Pali 'Paritta' meaning 'protecting magic formula, talisman'. Dhāraṇīs are protecting spells, and constitute a large and important part of Mahāyānist literature. According to the *Saddharmapuṇḍarīka*, Dhāraṇīs are taught for the protection, safety and shelter of the preachers. These are also used as amulets. These consist of invocations to female deities (as 'holder', 'supporter' etc.), to Buddhas and Bodhisattvas, between which exorcisms against snakes are inserted, and also of syllables scattered here and there (such as 'sara sara, sura sura, java java, jivi, jivi' etc.).

DHARMABINDU : A Jaina work by Haribhadra. It gives a review of ethics for laymen, monks, and the blessings of Nirvāṇa.

[Ed. & trs. *Giornale della Societa Asiatica Italiana*, xxi.]

DHARMAKĪRTI-NIBANDHĀVALĪ : Works by Dharmakīrti. [Vol. II, *Vādanyāya-prakaraṇa*, comm. of Śāntarkṣita, *Sambandha-parīkṣā*, comm. of Prabhācandra, ed. D. Sastry, Varanasi, 1972.]

DHARMA-SAṂGRAHA : A collection of technical terms relating to Buddhist philosophy, attributed to Nāgārjuna. [Ed. Oxford, 1885.]

DHARMAŚARMĀBHYUDAYA : An epic poem, in 21 cantos, on the life of Dharmanātha, the fifteenth Tīrthaṃkara of the Jainas. It is written on the model of the *Śiśupāla-vadha*. Its author is Haricandra or Hariścandra.

[Ed. Durgaprasad and Parab, NSP, 1899; with comm. of Yaśaskīrti and Hindi trs. by P. L. Jain, Varanasi, 1971.]

DHARMAŚĀSTRA : See Smṛti.

DHARMASŪTRA : The Dharmasūtras are a class of works in Smṛti literature and a species of *Kalpasūtra.* Also called *Sāmāyācārika-sūtras,* these works are written in prose which is sometimes interspersed with verses. They deal with the usual topics of Smṛti, viz. *Ācāra*, *Prāyaścitta*, *Vyavahāra*, *Rāja-dharma* etc. The major *Dharmasūtra* treatises are those attributed to Āpastamba, Baudhāyana, Gautama, Vasiṣṭha, Vaikhānasa and Viṣṇu. Dharmasūtra passages of a number of other writers are quoted in later Smṛti digests and commentaries.

[For an exhaustive account of this literature, see S. C. Banerji, *Dharmasūtras—a study in their origin and development*, Calcutta, 1962. See also Ved Mitra, *India of Dharmasūtras* and Ram Gopal's *India of Vedic Kalpasūtras*; R. C. Hazra, 'The Judicial Pramāṇas known to or mentioned in the extant Dharmasūtras of Gautama and others', *Our Heritage*, XVI, p.p. 1-56; S. K. Bharadwaj, *Linguistic Study of Dharmasūtras*, Rohtak, 1982.]

DHĀTUKĀVYA : By Nārāyaṇa Bhaṭṭa of Kerala, belonging to late 16th or early 17th century A.D. It illustrates the Dhātupāṭha. Construed as a continuation of Vāsudevakavi's *Vāśudeva-vijaya.* It takes up the story of Kṛṣṇa where the *Vāsudeva-vijaya* had left off, and describes the killing of Kaṃsa by Kṛṣṇa.

[Ed., with comms. *Kṛṣṇārpaṇa* and *Vivaraṇa*, by S. Veṅkaṭa-subramanium Iyer, Trivandrum, 1970.]

DHĀTU-PRADĪPA : A grammatical work, based on Pāṇini's *Dhātupāṭha*, by Maitreya-rakṣita.

[Ed., with notes, by S. C. Chakravarti, Calcutta, 1919.]

DHĀTU-RATNAMĀLĀ : A medical work by Devadatta. It deals with the properties of all metals and minerals and the mode of their incineration.

[For a brief account of its contents, see P. C. Roy; *History of Chemistry in Ancient and Medieval India*, Calcutta, 1956.]

DHĪKOṬI : By Śrīpati. An astronomical work of the *Karaṇa* type following the *Āryabhaṭiya* or *Āryabhaṭa* I with corrections according to Lalla. It has adopted Śaka 961 (= 1039 A.D.) as the epochal year.

[For MSS see (i) *Cat. of Skt. Mss. in Gujarat*, etc. (Bühler). (ii) *Cat. of Skt. Mss. in North-west Provinces*, (iii) Velankar's *Cat. of Skt. and Pkt. Mss. in Bombay Branch of Royal Asiatic Society*, (iv) *Cat. of Viśveśvarānand Vedic Research Institute*, Hoshiarpur.]

DHĪVṚDDHI-TANTRA : An astronomical work, by Lalla, it consists of 14 chaps., and is based on the *Āryabhaṭiya.*

[Ed. with comm. *Vivaraṇa* by Bhāskara, C. B. Pandey, Varanasi, 1981.]

DHŪRTA-SAMĀGAMA : A drama of the *Prahasana* type, by Jyotirīśvara. The religious mendicant, Viśvanagara, quarrels with his disciple Durācāra over the possession of Anaṅgasenā, a beautiful courtesan. They refer the case to a Brahmin named Asajjāti who decrees that until the real owner of Anangasenā is found out, she shall remain under his protection. While he is deliberating, his Vidūṣaka seeks to secure the prize for himself. After the case, barber Mūlanāśaka demands repayment of debt by Anaṅgasenā who refers him to Asajjāti. He pays him with his pupil's purse, and demands the barber's care; the latter ties him up and leaves him to be rescued by the Vidūṣaka.

[Ed. S. Sāmaśramī Bhaṭtacharya, Calcutta, 1874; French trs. by C. Schoebel.]

DHŪRTA-VIṬA-SAṂVĀDA : See *Caturbhāṇi.*

DHVANYĀLOKA (also called KĀVYĀLOKA or SAHṚDAYĀLOKA) : It consists of *Kārikās* and *Vṛtti* thereon, the former being the work of Dhanikāra or Sahṛdaya and the latter that of Ānandavardhana. Some scholars attribute the entire work to Ānandavardhana. It clearly and firmly asserted, for the first time, that *Dhvani* or suggested sense was the soul (*ātman*) of Kāvya after refuting contrary views. It also examined critically the existing ideas of *Rasa*, *Alaṃkāra*, *Rīti*, *Guṇa* and *Doṣa*. It exercised profound influence on the later writers on poetics.

[Ed. Durgaprasad and Parab, *Kāvyamālā*, 25, NSP, 1911 (with *Locana* comm.); K. Sastri and others (with *Locana*, *Kaumudī* and *Upalocana*), Uddyota I, Madras, 1944; B. Bhattacharya (with Eng. exposition), Calcutta, 1956, with *Locana*, Hindi trs. of both text and comm. and a *Vyākhyā*, Motilal Banarsidass, Delhi, Varanasi and Patna. K. Krishnamoorthy, with Intro., Eng. trs. and notes, Mysore, 1974. Trs. into German by H. Jacobi, Leipzig, 1903; into Eng., i-ii only, by K. R. Pisharoti in *Indian Thought*, IX-X, 1917-18 (incomplete); into Russian by Y. Alikhanova with comments); into Bengali by S. Sengupta and K. Bhattacharya, Calcutta. For detailed information about the work, see P. V. Kane, *History of Sanskrit Poetics*; S. P. Bhattacharya in *Proceedings of AIOC*, Patna, 1933; S. K. De, *History of Sanskrit Poetics*. Also see M. M. Sharma, *The Dhvani Theory of Sanskrit Poetics*, 1968; K. Krishnamoorthy, *Dhvanyāloka and its critics*, Mysore, 1968.]

DĪPA-KALIKĀ : A commentary, by Śūlapāṇi, on the *Yājña-valkya-smṛti*. It combines the merits of brevity and lucidity.

[Ed. J. R. Gharpure, Bombay, 1939. Trs. into English by the same scholar, with trs. of the *Yājñavalkya-smṛti* and two other commentaries on it, by J. R. Gharpure, 4 parts, Bombay, 1936-39.]

DĪPIKĀ : Same as *Tarkasaṃgraha-dīpikā* (q.v.)

DIVYĀVADĀNA : A work of the *Avadāna* class. Date uncertain; cannot be earlier than the Ist century A.D. It is written in prose mixed with Gāthās and pieces of ornate stanzas. The language is debased Sanskrit marked by Prākritism. In it there are some really interesting and valuable narratives, especially the cycle of Aśoka legends.

[Ed. P. L. Vaidya, Darthanga, 1959.]

DRĀHYĀYAṆA-ŚRAUTASŪTRA : See *Śrautasūtra*.

[Ed. J. N. Reuter, Part I, London, 1904.]

DURGĀBHAKTI-TARAṄGIṆĪ : Written by Vidyāpati, under

the patronage of king Dhīrasiṃha of Mithilā, it is a metrical work in 1000 verses on the ceremony of the autumnal worship of Durgā.

[Printed in Calcutta, 1909.]

DURGĀ-SAPTAŚATĪ : Same as *Caṇḍī* (q. v.).

DURGHAṬA-VṚTTI : A grammatical work by Śaraṇadeva. In it the author discusses the correctness of apparently un-Pāṇinian usages.

[Ed. and trs. into French by L. Renou, Paris, 1940-45. Ed. T. Ganapati Sastri, 1942.]

DURGOTSAVA-VIVEKA : A Smṛti digest by Śūlapāṇi. In it the author discusses the following topics :—

Durgā-pūjā whether obligatory or optional, places suitable for this *Pūjā*, the shape and materials of the image of Durgā, significance of Śāradīyā Pūja, merits accruing from this Pūja, kinds of *Durgā-pūjā*, persons fit for this *Pūjā*, rites and practices connected with this *Pūjā*, particularly the duties on the *Daśami* day.

[There is also a work of this title by Śrīnātha Ācārya-cūḍāmaṇi, teacher of Ragunandana, the most famous Smṛti writer of Bengal. Both works ed. Saṃskṛta Sāhitya Pariṣad, Calcutta, 1331 B.S.]

DŪTA-GHAṬOTKACA : A *Vyāyoga* type of drama, in one act, by Bhāsa, based on the *Mahābhārata*. The Kauravas are jubilant over the defeat of Abhimanyu at the hands of Jayadratha. Dhṛtarāṣṭra warns them against the dangers that may follow. Ghaṭotkaca appears to them, and predicts their punishment at the hands of Arjuna.

[Ed. C. R. Devadhar, Poona Oriental Series, 1937.]

DŪTA-VĀKYA : A *Vyāyoga* type of drama, in one act, by Bhāsa, based on the embassy of Kṛṣṇa, described in the *Mahābhārata* (V. 122-9).

[Ed. C. R. Devadhar, Poona Oriental Series, 1937.]

DVISANDHĀNA-KĀVYA : Same as *Rāghava-pāṇḍavīya* (q.v.)

DVITĪYA-RĀJATARAṄGIṆĪ : A continuation, by Jonarāja, of the *Rājatraṅgiṇī*. Planned to bring the history down to the time of the author's patron, Sultan Zain-ul-Ābidin, it was left incomplete due to Jonarāja's death in 1459 A.D.

[Printed, along with the other two continuations of the *Rājataraṅgiṇī*, in the *editio princeps of the Rājataraṅgiṇī*, Calcutta, 1835, and also in Durgaprasad's ed. of the same work.]

DVYĀŚRAYA-KĀVYA : See *Kumārapālacarita*.

EKĀVALĪ : A work on poetics, by Vidyādhara. It consists of *Kārikās* and *Vṛtti* in eight chapters called *Unmeṣas*. The contents, chapterwise, are as follows :—

I. Discussion of the definition of *Kāvya*.

II. Three *Vṛttis* of *Abhidhā*, *Lakṣaṇā* and *Vyañjanā*.

III-IV. *Dhvani*.

V-VI. Three *Guṇas*, three *Rītis* and *Doṣas*.

VII-VIII. Poetic figures.

[Ed. K. P. Trivedi, with the *Taralā* comm. of Mallinātha, intro. and notes, Bombay Sanskrit Series, 63, 1903.]

An *Ekāvali* on prosody, by Gokulanātha, a famous Nyāya scholar of Mithilā, is preserved in manuscript form in the Darbhanga Rāj Library.

EPICS : See *Rāmāyaṇa* and *Mahābhārata*.

[See E. W. Hopkins, *Epic Mythology*, Strassburg, 1915 (Reprint, 1968); J. Ghosh, *Epic Sources of Sanskrit Literature*, Calcutta; V. V. Dixit, *Relation of the Epics to the Brāhmaṇa Literature*, Poona, 1950; S. Jayal, *Status of Women in Epics*, Delhi, 1966; S. K. De (ed.) *Anthology of the Epics and Purāṇas*; D. P. Vora, *Evolution of Morals in the Epics*; J. C. Oman, *The Great Indian Epics*.]

GADA-VINIŚCAYA : See *Nidāna*.

GADYA-CINTĀMAṆI : A prose work by the Jaina Oḍayadeva, alias Vādībhasiṃha. It deals with the legend of Jīvaka or Jīvandhara. The author imitates the *Kādambarī* of Bāṇabhaṭṭa.

[Ed. Madras, 1902; with Hindi Intro., trs. and Skt. comm., by P. Jain, Varanasi, 1968.]

GAJA-ŚĀSTRA : Same as *Hastyāyurveda* (q.v.).

GAṆAPĀṬHA : These are separate works, based on different systems of grammar, dealing with particular classes of words mentioned or referred to in the grammatical aphorisms. Such works are attributed, *inter alia*, to Pāṇini, Śākaṭāyana etc.

[For the *Gaṇapāṭha* of Pāṇini's system (chaps. 4 and 5), see *Der Gaṇapāṭha* etc. by V. R. Birwe, 1961. Also see K. D. Sastri, *Gaṇapāṭha ascribed to Pāṇini*.]

GAṆAKA-TARAṄGIṆĪ : A work, by Sudhākara Dvivedin, on the lives and works of Hindu astronomers and mathematicians.

[Originally pub. in the *Paṇḍit*. Reprinted, Banaras, 1892.]

GAṆARATNA-MAHODADHI : A grammatical work (1140 A.D.) by Vardhamāna. It consists in a metrical enumeration of the words mentioned in the *Gaṇapāṭha* of Pāṇini.

[Ed. J. Eggeling, London, 1879. On *Gaṇapāṭha* see R. Birwe, *Der Gaṇapāṭha* etc., Wiesbaden, 1961.]

GAṆḌAVYŪHA : The *Gaṇḍavyūha-mahāyāna-sūtra* corresponds to one of the Chinese translations of the *Avataṃsaka*; no *Avataṃsaka* or *Buddhāvataṃsaka Sūtra* has come down in Sanskrit. The chief contents of the *Gaṇḍavyūha* are the wanderings of the youth Sudhana who, on the advice of the Bodhisattva Mañjuśrī, travels throughout India in quest of the highest knowledge. He seeks instructions from many people including Gopā and Māyā, wife and mother respectively of Śākyamuni, till at last he attains to perfect knowledge by the grace of Mañjuśrī through the instrumentality of the Bodhisattva Samantabhadra. It inculcates the doctrines of *Śūnyatā*, *Dharmakāya* and the redemption of the world by Bodhisattvas.

[Ed. P. L. Vaidya, Darbhanga, 1960.]

GAṆḌĪSTOTRA-GĀTHĀ : Attributed to Aśvaghoṣa, it seeks

to describe in words the religious message carried to the hearts of men by the sounds produced by beating a long strip of wood with a short club. It displays great metrical skill, and testifies to the author's comprehension of the power of music. Some scholars question the authorship of Aśvaghoṣa.

[Sanskrit text restored by A. Holstein, in *Bib. Buddh.*, No. XV, St. Petersburg, 1913, and re-edited by E. H. Johnston in *IA*, 1933. See G. Tucci in *GSAI*, XXVIII, 1916.]

GAṄGĀ-VĀKYĀVALĪ : A Smṛti digest by the poet Vidyāpati. It deals with the advantages of visiting and worshipping the Ganges and bathing in it, the efficiency of meditation on it and of its sight etc.

[Ed. J. B. Chaudhury, Calcutta.]

GAṆITASĀRA : Also called *Triśatigaṇita-sāra*, *Triśatikā*, *Pāṭi-sāra*, *Pāṭigaṇita*, *Pāṭigaṇita-sāra*, *Śrīdharapāṭi*, *Śrīdharīlīlāvatī*. It is a compendium of arithmetic.

[*Triśatī* ed. S. Dvivedin, NSP, 1899. *Pāṭigaṇita* ed. and trs. into Eng. by K. S. Shukla, Lucknow University.]

GAṆITA-SĀRA-SAṂGRAHA : By Mahāvīra. Contains many examples of solutions of indeterminates and deals with geometrical progressions, ellipses, and other things.

GAṆITA-TILAKA : A work on mathematics, by Śrīpati.

[Ed. H. R. Kapadia, with comm. of Siṃhatilaka, *GOS*, 1937.]

GARUḌA-PURĀṆA : Also called *Gāruḍa-purāṇa*, it is Viṣṇuite in character. Besides some of the typical five themes, it deals exhaustively with the worship of Viṣṇu, Viṣṇuite rites and festivals, expiatory ceremonies and glorification of sacred places. Being an encyclopaedic work, it deals with the following subjects :—

Stories of the *Rāmāyaṇa*, *Mahābhārata* and *Harivaṃśa*, cosmography, astronomy, astrology, palmistry, omens and portents, chiromancy, medicine, metrics, grammar, knowledge of precious stones, politics.

A considerable portion of the *Yājñavalkya-smṛti* is included in it.

The *Gayā-māhātmya* is one of the *Māhātmyas* which claim to be parts of the *Garuḍa-purāṇa*. It is divided into three sections dealing with Karma, Dharma and Brahma.

[Ed. P. Tarkaratna, Vaṅgavāsī Press, Calcutta, 1314 B. S.; R. S. Bhattacharya, with intro., indexes and textual criticism (in Hindi), CSS, 1964; N. R. Acarya, with a Skt. comm., NSP, 1949. Eng. trs. ed. J. L. Shastri, Motilal Banarsidass, Delhi, 1979. See E. Abegg, *Der Pretakalpa des Garuḍa Purāṇa*, Leipzig, 1921; A. P. Karmarkar, Bṛhaspati-Nītisāra in Garuḍa-Purāṇa, *Siddhabhārati* (*S. Varma Vol.*). See N. Gangadharan, *Garuḍapurāṇa—a study*, Varanasi, 1972. See L. Sternbach, *A new abridged version of the Bṛhaspati Saṃhitā of the Garuḍapurāṇa*, Varanasi, 1966 and the Journal *Purāṇa*, Vol. VIII, Varanasi, 1966; E. Wood and S. V. Subramaniam, the *Garuḍa Purāṇa*, with Eng. trs.]

GAUḌAPĀDĪYA KĀRIKĀ (GAUḌAPĀDA KĀRIKĀ) : It is a work, attributed to Gauḍapāda, in 215 memorial verses, on Vedānta philosophy. The work is divided into four chapters. The first chapter, called *Āgama*, explains the text of the *Māṇḍūkya Upaniṣad*. The second, called *Vaitathya*, explains the phenomenal nature of world, characterised as it is by duality and opposition. The third chapter establishes the *Advaita* theory. The last chapter discusses the sole reality Ātman and the relative character of our ordinary experience. The work is strongly influenced by the nihilistic school of Buddhism. Some scholars hold that the above Upaniṣad is based on the *Kārikās*.

[Ed., with Eng. trs. and notes, R. D. Karmarkar, *BORI*, 1953. Trs. P. Deussen, *Sechzig Upanishads des Veda*. Alātaśānti Prakaraṇa, with Eng. trs., notes from Buddhist sources and critical introduction by J. L. Majumdar. Gujarati trs. by A. H. Joshi, Surat, 1979.]

GAUTAMA-DHARAMASŪTRA : See Dharmasūtra.

[Ed. Stenzler, London, 1876; L. Srinivasacharya, with *Maskaribhāṣya*, Mysore, 1917; Anandasrama, with *Mitākṣarā* comm. of Haradatta, Poona, 1931. Trs. into English by Bühler, Sacred Books of the East, Vol. II.]

GHAṬAKARPARA-KĀVYA : It is a lyric in 22 stanzas attributed to a poet named Ghaṭakarpara. Some think that it was composed by Kālidāsa. It describes how a young wife, at the advent of the rainy season, sends a message through the cloud to her absent husband. The situation, dealt with in it, is the reverse of that described in the *Megha-dūta*. The poem owes its title to the fact that the author, at the close, offers to carry water in a broken jar for any one who can surpass him in *Yamakas* and alliterations.

[Ed., with extracts from comm. and a new comm., by J. B. Chaudhuri, Calcutta, 1953; a Sanskrit comm. by G. M. Dursch, Berlin, 1828, with German verse trs.; with *Abhinavagupta's* comm., by M. Kaul, Srinagar, 1945. See *Ghaṭakarpara-Kāvyam* by Sharma and Sharma, Aligarh 1975.]

GIRNAR INSCRIPTION : An inscription of Mahākṣatrapa Rudradāman I, carved on a rock at Girnar near Junagarh in Kāṭhiāwar; celebrates an event of about 150 A. D. It provides one of the earliest definite instances of high-flown Sanskrit prose composition, and thus negates Maxmüller's Renaissance theory.

[For text with notes, see D. C. Sircar, *Select Inscriptions*, I, Calcutta, 1941.]

GĪTĀ : The full title is *Bhagavadgītā*. It consists of 750 verses divided into 18 chapters, and belongs to the *Bhīṣmaparvan* of the *Mahābhārata*. It is in the form of conversation between Kṛṣṇa and Arjuna in the battlefield. The former exhorts and encourages the latter who feels dejected and reluctant to fight his own kinsmen in the opposite camp. It is a very popular book among the Indians, and highly praised by Western scholars. Humboldt placed it far above Lucretius, even above Parmenides and Empedokles. It can be interpreted in consonance with all the six systems of Indian philosophy. It suggests liberation to the followers of all the three ways of *Karma*, *Jñāna* and *Bhakti*. There are valuable suggestions in it which help man in solving the various problems of practical life. Of the several commentaries on the *Gītā* by Indian writers, the chief are those by *Vṛttikāra* (Bodhāyana), Śaṃkara, Rāmānuja, Madhva, Vallabha, Nimbārka and Jñāneśvara. Of the modern commentators, the chief are B. G. Tilak, Sri Aurobindo and M. K. Gandhi.

[Reprinted from the critical ed. of the Bhīṣma-parvan of the *Mahābhārata*, ed. S. K. Belvalkar, *BORI*, Poona, 1945. See. F. O. Schrader, *The Kashmir Recension of the Bhagavad-gītā*, Stuttgart, W. Kohlhammer, 1930; ed. A Kuppuswami, with trs. and comm. in Eng. containing the essence of comms. of Śaṃkara, Rāmānuja, Madhvācārya, Śrīdhara and Rāghavacandra; ed. B. Dvivedi, with comm. of Madhusūdana, Hindi trs. and annotations, 1975. Ed. with 11 comms. Gujarat Prt. Press, Bombay; A Kuppuswami, with Eng. transliteration, Varanasi, 1983. Trs. into various European languages. For example, trs. into English by C. Wilkins, London, 1785; E. Arnold, 1885; A. Besant and B. Das (with text), Adyar (Madras) 1962; J. E. Turner, London, 1939; S. Radhakrishnan, London, 1948; Dilip Roy (in verse), New Delhi, 1974; Bhaktivedānta, London, 1972; verse rendering by K. P. Bahadur, Lucknow, 1980. Trs. into Latin (with text) by Schlegel, 1823; into German by Deussen, Schroeder, Jena, 1912; Garbe, 1921; into French by E. Burnout, Paris, 1861. Trs. into Georgian (Russia) by T. Chkhenteli. For other translations, both in Indian and European languages, see Holtzmann, *Das Mahābhārata*, II, 129 ff., Hindi trs. by Svāmī Śrī Sanātanadeva (with text), CSS, 1962. Abul Fazl of Akbar's court rendered the work into Persian. For a historical study and interpretation of the *Gītā* see D. D. Vadekar, *Bhagavadgītā—a fresh study*, Poona, 1928. Also see B. G. Tilak, *Bhagavadgītā* with *Gītā-rahasya* in Eng., 2 Vols.; F.Edgerton, The *Bhagavadgītā*, Chicago, 1925; Aurobindo Ghosh, *Essay on the Bhagavadgītā*, Calcutta, 1928; R. Otto, *Bhagavadgītā : Der sang der Her-habenen*, Stuttgart, 1935; *Die Urgestalt der Bhagavadgita*, Tubingen, 1934; *Die Lehrtrakte der Bhagavadgītā*, Tubingen, 1935; V. G. Bhat, *The*

Bhagavadgītā : A *Study*, Dharwar, 1924; Kirfel, *Verse-index to the Bhagavadgītā*, Leipzig, 1938; P. C. Divanji, *Critical word-index to the Bhagavadgītā*; S. C. Ray, *The Bhagavadgītā and Modern Scholarship*, Book I, London, 1941. See V. Misra, *Critical study of Bhagavadgītā*; A. S. Ayyar, *Layman's Bhagavadgītā*, 2 vols.; N. Rangacarya, *Lecture on Bhagavadgītā*, *Message of the Gītā* as interpreted by Sri Aurobindo; A. Jacob, *Concordance to the Principal Upaniṣads and Bhagavadgītā*; S. Radhakrishnan, *The theism of the Bhagavad*—; J. S. Jariwalla, *Gītā, the Science of Living*; J. A. B. Van Buitenen, *Rāmānuja on the Bhagavadgītā* Delhi, 1968; G. S. Khair, *Quest for the original Gītā*, Bombay, 1969; B. S. Gaucchwal, *Concept of Prefection in the Teachings of Kant and the Gītā*, Delhi, 1967; K. N. Upadhyay, *Early Buddhism and the Bhagavadgītā*, Delhi, 1971; K.K. Shastree, *Gītā-śataśloki* (Ur Gītā), Baroda, 1971; V. H. Date, *Brahmayoga of the Gītā*, Delhi, 1971; G. W. Kaveeshwar, *The Ethics of the Gītā*, Delhi, 1971; T. G. Mainkar *Comp. study of comms. on the Gītā*, 1969 (2nd ed.); S.D. Gokhale, *The Message of the Song Celestial*; *Śrīmad Bhagavadgītā*; Maheshwar (ed.), *Bhagavadagitā in the light of Śrī Aurobindo*, Pondicherry, 1978. Also see M. Desai, *A View of the Gītā*, 2nd ed., New Delhi, 1978; R. K. Pandey, *Concept of Avatāras with special ref. to Gītā*, Delhi, 1979; M. K. Durrany, *A Comparative study of the Gītā and the Quran*. Also see R. N. Minor, *Bhagavadgītā*, an *exegetical commentary*; De Nicolas, A. T. Avatara : *The humanisation of philosophy through Bhagavadgītā*, 1976; S. N. Gupta, *Madhusūdana Sarasvatī on Bhagavadgītā*, 1977; A. K. Srivastava, *Bhagavadgītā*; Virajashwar, *Science of Bhagavadgītā*, Delhi, 1977; M. K. Iyengar, *Bhagavadgītā*, Bangalore, 1978; *Early Buddhism and the Bhagavadgītā*; A. Kuppuswami, *Bhagavadgītā*, Text, Eng. trs., exp. in Eng. based on five commentaries; H. S. Sinha, *Communism and Gītā*, Delhi, 1979; M.K. Sharma, *Bhagavadgītā and Hindu Sociology*, Delhi, 1978. An interesting work is *Realistics of Bhagavadgītā* by J. M. Joshipura, Bombay, 1980. *Gītābhāṣya of Rāmānuja*, trs. into Eng. by M. R. Sampatkumaran, Madras. See G. S. Khair, *Quest for the Original Gītā*, Bombay 1969; Yogi Mahajan *Zen Gītā*; A Kuppuswami, ed. *Bhagavadgītā*; C. R. Swaminathan, *Gītābhāṣya-vivecana*,

Lucknow, 1982; ed. with trs., comm. and comparative study of Vedānta and other religions, M. N. Burury, New Delhi, 1981.

The following papers may be consulted :

Belvalkar, S. K. : The so-called Kashmirian recension of Bhagavadgītā, *E. D. Ross Pres. Vol.* Bombay, 1939; Bhagavadgītā : Trichotomy versus Triune-unity, *Karmarkar Vol.*, Poona, 1948.

Devasthali, G. V. : Bhakti in Bhagavadgītā, *Siddhabhāratī, S. Varma Pres. Vol.* II.

Krishnamurti, B. N. : The trend of the Bhagavadgītā, *Karmarkar Comm. Vol.*, Poona, 1948.

Moitra, S. K. : Gītā's conception of Freedom as compared with that of Kant, *Comparative Studies in Philosophy,* ed. W. R. Inger and others, London, 1951.

Raghavan, V : The Bhagavadgītā and Jain Literature, *Bhāratīya Vidyā*, Vols. 9 & 10, *K. M. Munshi Diamond Jubilee Vol.*, Bombay, 1948, 1949.

Taraporewala, I. J. S. : Bhagavadgītā and the gāthās of Jarathustra, *V. S. Sukthankar Memo. Vol.* (Bulletin of Deccan College Res. Inst. V, Poona, 1944.

Yardi, M. R. : Theories of Multiple Authorship of the Bhagavadgītā, *ABORI, Diamond Jubilee Vol.*, 1977-78.

GĪTĀ-BHĀṢYA : A comm. on the *Gītā*, by Rāmānuja. (Ed. Bombay, 1969).

GĪTA GOVINDA : Composed by Jayadeva. It is a devotional lyric dealing with the vernal erotic sports of Kṛṣṇa at Vṛndāvana. Rādhā's separation, Kṛṣṇa's sports with other cowherd women, Rādhā's anguish, yearning for union and jealousy, request to Kṛṣṇa by Rādhā's friend, Kṛṣṇa's return, penitence and appeasement of Rādhā, finally the blissful re-union—these are described in the poem. It received unstinted praise not only from Indian critics, but also from eminent western scholars like Lassen, Jones, Levi, Pischel and Schroeder. The existence of over forty commentaries on the work, produced in the different provinces of India, testifies to its wide popularity. Jayadeva's work inspired a number of imitations by later writer, e.g., *Gīta-gaurīpati* of Bhānudatta, the *Gīta-gaṅgādhara* of Kalyāṇa, the *Gīta-girīśa* of Rāmabhaṭṭa, the *Gīta-digambara of* Vaṃśamaṇi, the *Gīta-gopāla* of Caturbhuja etc.

[Ed., with comm. *Rasika-priyā* and *Rasa-mañjarī* and extracts from four other comms., NSP, 1949. Also see the Tanjore ed. (Sarasvatī Mahal) and V. M. Kulkarni's ed., with Mānāṅka's comm., Ahmedabad, 1965. Trs. into Eng. by Jones, *Collected Works*, London, 1807; E. Arnold, *The Indian Song of Songs*, London, 1875 (metrical); M. Varma, Calcutta; into French by G. Courtillier, E. Leroux, Paris, 1904; into Spanish by F. Tola, Buenos Aires, 1969. Also see trs. by G. Keyt, *Śhri Jayadeva's Gīta-govinda*, Bombay, 1947; M. S. Randhawa, *Kangra Paintings of the Gītagovinda*, New Delhi, 1982.]

GĪTĀLAṂKĀRA : A work on music, attributed to Bharata. Consisting of 15 chaps., it deals respectively with the following topics :

Gīta-lakṣaṇa, Kaṇṭha-śuddhi, Gīta-doṣa, Svara-lakṣaṇa, Grāma, Mūrchanā, Tāna, Mātrā, Laya, Sthāna-lakṣaṇa, Yati, Āsya, Rasa, Varṇa, Bhāṣā-lakṣaṇa.

The editors claim that the *Nāṭya-śāstra*, ascribed to Bharata, is later than this work.

[Ed. and trs. into French by A. Daniélou and N. R. Bhatt, Pondicherry, 1959.]

GOBHILA-GṚHYASŪTRA : See *Gṛhyasūtra.*

[Ed. Bib. Ind., 1966 (2nd ed.); with German trs., by F. Knauer, Dorpat, 1884, 1886. Trs. into Eng. by H. Oldenberg, *SBE*, Vol. 30.]

GOPĀLA-CAMPŪ : A work in mixed prose and verse, by Jīva Gosvāmin. Divided into two parts, it deals with the activities of Kṛṣṇa described in the tenth chapter of the *Bhāgavata*. Its composition was completed in Śaka 1510 (= 1588 A. D.).

[Ed. R. Sāṃkhyatīrtha, Baharampur, 1910; V. Sastri, with Hindi comm., Vrindavan (U. P.) 1969.]

GOVINDA BHĀṢYA : A commentary, by Baladeva, on the *Brahma-sūtra*. It is one of those works which furnish the philosophical basis for the Vaiṣṇavas of Bengal.

[For references to ed., Bengali trs. etc., see under *Brahma-sūtra*.]

GṚHASTHA-RATNĀKARA : An extensive Smṛti digest, by Caṇḍeśvara, in 68 chapters called *Taraṅgas*, dealing with duties of house-holders, It forms a part of the author's *Smṛti-ratnākara*. Some of the topics, dealt with in it, are persons from whom gifts can be accepted by householders, duties of different castes, observances for a *Brahmacārin* and for a *Snātaka*, causes of ruin of families, proper abode for a householder, practices permitted and forbidden for a *Gṛhastha*, things not to be given to Śūdras, avoidance of anger, adultery, intermixture of castes, repayment of debts etc.

[Printed *Bib. Ind.*, 1928.]

GṚHYA-SŪTRA : A part of the *Kalpa-sūtra*. *Gṛhya-sūtras* deal with sacraments (*Saṃskāras*) and other rites meant for householders. The well-known *Gṛhya-sūtras* are those of Āpastamba, Āśvalāyana, Gobhila, Khādira, Pāraskara and Śāṅkhāyana.

[The *Gṛhya-sūtras of* Āśvalāyana, Śāṅkhāyana, Pāraskara and Khādira trs. into Eng. by H. Oldenberg, *SBE*, XXIX. The same scholar has translated those of Gobhila, Hiraṇyakeśin and Āpastamba in *SBE*, XXX. See V. M. Apte, *Social and Religious Life in the Gṛhyasūtras*, Bombay, 1953 (2nd. ed.) and *Ṛgveda-mantras in their ritual setting in the Gṛhyasūtras*.]

HALĀYUDHA-KOŚA : See under *Abhidhānaratnamālā*.

HANŪMANNĀṬAKA : Another name of the *Mahānāṭaka* (q. v.).

HARṢACARITA-CINTĀMAṆI : A huge poetical work by Jayadratha. The printed text is incomplete, and runs up to the fortyfifth verse of the thirty-second *Prakāśa* (chapter). It describes the various myths and legends connected with Śiva. The work is of the nature of a Purāṇa or *Māhātmya* rather than a Kāvya. Some of the legends are associated with places of pilgrimage in Kashmir.

[Ed. *Kāvyamālā*, 61; Reprint, Delhi, 1983.]

HĀRA-LATĀ : A Smṛti digest by Aniruddha. It deals with impurity (*aśauca*) consequent on birth, and with acts allowed or forbidden during the period of impurity.

[Ed. *Bib. Ind.*, 1909.]

HĀRĀVALĪ : A lexicon, by Puruṣottamadeva, including synonyms and homonyms. Like the author's *Trikāṇḍaśeṣa*, it contains a rich store of very rare terms many of which are from Buddhist texts.

[Ed. in *Abhidhāna-saṃgraha*, I, Bombay, 1889.]

HARA-VIJAYA : A *Mahākāvya* in 50 cantos, by Ratnākara. It deals with the story of the destruction of the demon Andhaka at the hands of Śiva. The demon was born blind, but obtained sight by hard penance. Then he proved to be a source of constant trouble to gods whereupon Śiva slew him.

The work is marked by the artificialities of the age of decadence of Sanskrit literature.

[Ed. Durgaprasad and Parab, with comm. of Alaka, Bombay, 1890. See S. K. Sharma, *Haravijaya, a study*.]

HARIBHAKTI-VILĀSA : By Gopālabhaṭṭa. according to some, by Sanātana Gosvāmin, according to others. It is the most authoritative work on the rites and practices of the Vaiṣṇavas of Bengal. It is universally recognised among the Vaiṣṇavas for the rules contained in it in connexion with *Vaidhī Bhakti*. Consisting of 20 chapters, called *Vilāsas*, it deals with the following topics :—

Spiritual preceptor, disciple, *mantra*, initiation, daily duties, worship, partaking of God's *Mahāprasāda*, Vaiṣṇava devotee and characteristics of Vaiṣṇavite rites and rituals, the glory of the recitation of God's name, fast, fortnightly and monthly duties, the rite called *Puraścaraṇa*, construction of images and temples. The work is written in verse, and is replete with quotations from Purāṇas.

[Ed. Radharaman Press, Baharampur, Murshidabad, 2nd ed., in two parts, 1889, 1891, in Bengali character, with the *Digdarśanī* comm. For a detailed account about authorship, contents etc., see S. K. De, *Early Hist. of the Vaiṣṇava Faith and Movement in Bengal*, Calcutta, 1961.]

HARINĀMĀMṚTA VYĀKARAṆA : A *Saṃkṣepa*—(*or Laghu*) *harināmāṛta-vyākaraṇa* was written by Rūpa Gosvāmin. A noteworthy feature of the work is that the definitions and illustrations, given in it, contain the names of Rādhā or Kṛṣṇa or of Kṛṣṇa's sports. In most of the rules there are the names of Viṣṇu or of gods and goddesses connected with him. A larger grammatical work, entitled *Harināmāmṛta*, written in a similar plan, is by Jīva Gosvāmin whose object was probably to remove the deficiency of the earlier work. These grammatical works are sectarian, and aim at the propagation of Vaiṣṇavism.

[Ed. Puridasa, 1947; with the *Bālatoṣiṇī* comm., G. Das (2nd ed. B. Misra), Murshidabad, 1337 B. S.]

HARIVAṂŚA : It is a supplement to the *Mahābhārata*. It consists of three great sections, viz.

(1) *Harivaṃsa-parvan*—It conains an account of creation, mythological narratives, genealogy of the lunar dynasty in which Kṛṣṇa is born. The divine previous history of Kṛṣṇa as Viṣṇu is also given.

(2) *Viṣṇu-parvan*—deals with Kṛṣṇa, the god Viṣṇu become mortal.

(3) *Bhaviṣya-parvan*—a loose collection of Purāṇa texts.

[For ed. see critical edition of the *Mahābhārata*, BORI, Poona. Trs. into French by S. A. Langlois, Paris, 1834-35; into Eng., Pts. I-VIII (incomplete). The *Harivaṃśa* was translated, under Akbar, into Persian by Mulla Shiri. See A. Holtzmann, *Das Mahābhārata*, II; E. W. Hopkins, Gleanings from the Harivaṃśa in *Festchrift Wīndisch.*]

HARṢA-CARITA : A prose-composition of the *Ākhyāyikā* type, by Bāṇabhaṭṭa, written in eight chapters. It deals with the activities of Harṣa's father, Prabhākaravardhana, the expedition of Harṣa's brother, Rājyavardhana, against the Hūṇas, but chiefly with the important incidents of the reign of Harṣavardhana. In the introductory portion of this work we get references to some earlier poets and dramatists and information about the personal history of the author.

[Ed. K. P. Parab, with Śaṃkara's comm., NPS, 1946; P. V. Kane, with notes etc., Bombay, 1918; R. Sukla, with Hindi trs. and notes, Allahabad, 1962; J. Pathak, with *Saṃketa* comm. and Hindi trs., Banaras, 1964. Trs. into Eng. by E. B. Cowell and F. W. Thomas, London, 1907. See V. S. Agrawala, *Harṣacarita ek Sāṃskritik Adhyayana*, *The Deeds of Harsha*, and U. N. Ghosal, Historical Portraits in Bāṇa's Harṣa-carita, *B.C. Law Vol.*, I; B. N. Sharma, *Harṣa and his times*; R. C. Hazra's papers on the text and interpretation of a passage in *Harṣacarita*, Ucchvāsa V, *Poona Orientalist*, XIV.]

HASTĀMALAKA : By Śaṃkarācārya. In fourteen verses it plays on the refrain that the self as the eternal apprehension is all in all.

[Ed. and trs. in *IA*, IX.]

HASTYĀYURVEDA : Traditionally attributed to sage Pālakāpya, it is a huge treatise on elephant-lore and is also called *Gaja-śāstra*. It is divided into four sections called Sthānas, viz. *Mahāroga-sthāna*, *Kṣudraroga-sthāna*, *Śalya-sthāna*, *Uttara-sthāna*. Each Sthāna is sub-divided into several chapters. The first *Sthāna* deals with major maladies of elephants with corresponding modes of treatment. The second *Sthāna* deals with minor diseases and the modes of their treatment. The third *Sthāna* lays down the rules of surgery relating to elephants' diseases. In this connexion, 10 kinds of surgical instruments are mentioned. In the last chapter, the following topics have been dealt with:— food and drink of elephants, flow of ichor, construction of elephant-stalls, description of various kinds of elephants etc.

[Ed. *ASS*, 1894; K. S. S. Sastri, with extract from other works and coloured illustrations, a summary in Eng. and Tamil trs. Tanjore, 1958.]

HĀSYĀRṆAVA : A drama of the *Prahasana* type, by Jagadīśvara. The scene is laid in the house of the go-between Bandhurā who presents her daughter Mṛgāṅkalekhā to the king. The play ends with the marriage of the damsel with old reprobates and of Bandhurā with boys.

[Ed. S. Bhattacharya (with Skt. comm.), Calcutta, 1934 (3rd ed.) ; C. Cappeller, Jena, 1883.)

HAṬHAYOGA-PRADĪPIKĀ : By Svātmārāma. A work on Yoga philosophy, it deals with the practices followed to induce the trance condition desired.

[Ed. with comm. *Jyotsnā* & Eng. trs. by S. Iyengar. Rev. by R. Burnier and Rāmanāthan, *Brahmavidyā Vol.*, Adyar Library, Madras. Also trs. P. Sinh, Delhi, 1979.]

HAYA-ĀYURVEDA : Also called *Turaṅgama-sūtra* or *Śālihotra-sūtra* and attributed to Śālihotra. It deals with the care and treatment of horses.

HAYAGRĪVA-VADHA : A lost poem by Meṇṭha. The first verse of it is quoted by Rājaśekhara in his *Kāvyamīmāṃsā* and by Kṣemendra in his *Suvṛtta-tilaka*.

HEVAJRA-TANTRA : A Buddhist Tantra, supposed to have existed towards the end of the 8th century A.D. It is an invocation of Vajra. Instead of Śakti, the term Prajñā occurs in it. Among other things, it contains rituals for gaining mastery over a young woman.

[Ed. and trs. by D. L. Snellgrove, London, 1959 (2 parts).]

HITOPADEŚA : It is the name of the Bengal version of the *Pañcatantra*. In place of the five books of the original *Pañcatantra*, it contains only four. Besides, it has made many additions to, and alterations in, the original treatise. Many gnomic verses of the *Kāmandakīya Nītisāra* occur in it. Its author is Nārāyaṇa.

[Ed. P. Peterson, Bombay Skt. Ser., 1887. Also see *Hitopadesanach Nepalischen Handschrift*, ed. H. Blatt, Berlin, 1930 (Roman characters) and edition with Eng. trs., of M. S. Apte, Poona, 1957; M. R. Kale, with Skt. comm., Eng. trs. and notes, Delhi, 1967. Earliest trs. into English by

C. Wilkins, London, 1787. See J. Herte *Uber Text and Verfassen des Hitopadeśa*, Leipzig, 1897 and *Das Pancatantra*, L. Sternbach, *Cāṇakya's Aphorisms in Hitopadeśa* and *Hitopadeśa and its sources* (New Haven, 1960) ; Ayyar, *Pañcatantra and Hitopadeśa Stories.*]

HORĀSĀRA : An astrological work by Pṛthuyaśas.

HORĀŚĀSTRA : A work on astrology, by Bhaṭṭotpala. It is in 75 verses.

[Ed. and trs. into Eng. by V. S. Shastri.]

ĪŚĀ-UPANIṢAD : Also called *Īśāvāsyopaniṣad* and *Vājasaneyi-Upaniṣad*, it teaches that both Knowledge (*vidyā*) and Action (*avidyā*) are necessary for attaining immortality after crossing death. From it we learn that both Īśvara and Prakṛti are to be known. It discusses also the knowledge of Brahman.

[Ed., along with *Kena*, *Kaṭha*, *Praśna*, *Muṇḍaka* and *Māṇḍūkya*, with comm. of Śaṃkara and gloss of Ānandagiri, by E. Roer, 1851—55. Eng. trs. (with text) and analysis by Aurobindo Ghosh, Calcutta (Ideal and Progress Series No. 5). Metrical trs. by H. Baynes, *Indian Antiquary*, 26, 1897. Eng. trs. by Bhaktivedānta, London, 1974. On text-criticism see Baynes, *l.c.*, and *Hertel*, *Die Weisheit der Upanischaden.* Also see V. V. Mudhalkar, *Analytical Survey of Īśāvāsyopaniṣad*, Dharwar, 1971; K. B. Archak, Śaṃkara and Madhva on the Īśāvāsya Upaniṣad, Dharwar, 1981.]

ĪŚVARA-PRATYABHIJÑĀ-SŪTRA : Also called *Pratyabhijñā-sūtra* or *Pratyabhijñā-kārikā*, it is an authoritative work, by Utpala, on the Śaiva philosophy of Kashmir. It superseded the earlier works on the subject; as a matter of fact, the entire Śaiva philosophy of Kashmir came to be known as *Pratyabhijñā Darśana* outside the province.

[Pub. in *KSTS*, 1918—24.]

ĪŚVARA-PRATYABHIJÑĀ-VIMARŚINĪ : Briefly called *Vimarśinī* or *Laghvī Vimarśinī*, it is commentary, by Abhinavagupta, on Utpalācārya's *Īśvara-pratyabhijñā-sūtra.*

[Ed. *Paṇḍit*, ii and iii. See K. C. Pandey (ed.), *Īśvarapratyabhijñā Vimarsinī-vyākhyā.*]

ĪŚVARA-SAṂHITĀ : An early southern Pāñcarātra-saṃhitā. It is a Tāntric work which came into being before the middle of the 11th century.

[Ed. P. B. Anantacaryasvami, Conjeevaram, 1921. Ed. with notes, by M. K. Sastri, 1921.]

ĪŚVARA-SIDDHI : A work on the Śaiva philosophy of Kashmir, by Utpala.

JAIMINI-MĪMĀṂSĀ-BHĀṢYA : See *Śabara-bhāṣya.*

JAIMINĪYA ŚRAUTASŪTRA : See Śrautasūtra.

[Text and trs. of Agniṣṭoma chap. in Bijdrage tot de Kennis can het vedische, ritueel, Jaiminīya-śrautasūtra, by D. Gaastra, Leyden, 1906; text of the Śrauta Kārikā, Ibid., pp. 36—60.]

JAIMINĪYA NYĀYAMĀLĀ : Written by Mādhavācārya, with his own commentary called *Nyāyamālā-vistara*, it is a guidebook to Pūrvamīmāṃsā. It is divided into several *Adhyāyas*, each *Adhyāya* being sub-divided into *Pādas*, each *Pāda* consisting of *Adhikaraṇas.*

[Ed. S. Sarma, *ASS*, 1892.]

JAINA RĀJATARAṄGIṆĪ : A continuation, by Śrīvara, of the *Rājataraṅgiṇī*. It covers the period 1459—86 A.D.

[See under *Dvitīya-rājataraṅgiṇī.*]

JAINENDRA-VYĀKARAṆA : Also called *Jainendra-śabdānuśāsana* or *Pañcādhyāyī* from its five chapters. An apocryphal grammatical work traditionally ascribed to Jina (Mahāvīra) who is said to have revealed it to God Indra; hence the title (Jina and Indra). As a matter of fact, it appears to have been written by one Devanandin, otherwise known as Pūjyapāda. It probably originated before the 9th century A.D. Of the two extant versions of the work, the shorter one consists of about 3,000 Sūtras while the longer one, differing in wording and arrangement, gives an additional 700 *Sūtras*. The longer version perhaps represents the original more faithfully. The work aims at simplification of Pāṇini's grammar, the 14 *Śivasūtras* and the Vedic portion of which have been omitted in it. The author has invented certain shorter technical terms.

[Ed. with comm. of Abhayanandin, by S. Tripathi and M. Caturvedi, Banaras, 1956.]

JĀMBAVATĪ-VIJAYA : Name of a poem ascribed to the grammarian Pāṇini, by a Rājaśekhara, in a verse quoted in Jahlaṇa's *Sūkti-muktāvalī*. A fragment from the *Jāmbavatī-vijaya* is preserved by Rāyamukuṭa in his commentary on the *Nāmaliṅgānuśāsana* or *Amara-kośa* (1. 2. 3. 6.). The Kāvya is lost. The title implies that it dealt with Kṛṣṇa's winning Jāmbavatī in the nether regions, as his bride. It is an evidence of the existence of Kāvya at least in the 4th century B.C., if not earlier.

JĀNAKĪ-HARAṆA : A Mahākāvya by Kumāradāsa. Twenty cantos of the work are available. From a Sinhalese commentary the original work appears to have consisted of 25 cantos. It is based on the *Rāmāyaṇa* story. The subject-matter runs beyond Jānakī-haraṇa (abduction of Jānakī). From the Ceylonese source it appears to have dealt with the incidents upto the re-installation of Rāma on the throne.

[Ed. G. R. Nandargikar, Bombay, 1907. Reconstructed and ed. (with the Sinhalese *Sanna*) cantos I—XV and one verse of XXV, by D. Sthavira (in Sinhalese characters), Colombo, 1891. See A critical study of Text, critical ed. (xvi—xx) with Eng. trs. by C. R. Swaminathan, ed. by V. Raghavan, Delhi, 1977.]

JĀTAKAMĀLĀ : Written by Ārya Śūra, it consists of a Sanskrit rendering, in prose and verse, of 34 selected legends from the Pāli *Jātakas* and the *Cariyāpiṭaka*, illustrating the *Pāramitās* or perfections of a Bodhisattva.

[Ed. P. L. Vaidya, Darbhanga, 1959. Trs. J. S. Speyer in *Sacred Books of the Buddhists*, Oxford University Press, 1895, rev. ed., 1971, First Indian ed., Delhi, 1982.]

JĪVĀNANDA : A drama, in eight acts, attributed to Ānandarāya makhi. It is based on Āyurvedic principles and terminology. It depicts a battle between the forces of diseases and the forces of the body.

JĪVANDHARA-CAMPŪ : A work, by the Jain Haribhadra who may or may not be identical with Haricandra, based on the *Uttarapurāṇa* of Guṇabhadra. It deals with the legend of Jīvaka or Jīvandhara.

[Ed. with Hindi trs., by P. Jain, Banaras, 1958.]

JĪVANMUKTI-VIVEKA : Composed by Mādhava, it is a work on Advaita Vedānta in vindication of Śaṃkara's views, [Ed. *ASS*, 20, 1889; with Eng. trs. by Sastri and Aiyangar.]

JÑANA-DĪPIKĀ : Commentary on the Mahābhārata, by Devabodha.

[On Adiparvan, ed. R. N. Dandekar, Poona, 1941. On Udyogaparvan, ed. S. K. De, Bombay, 1944.]

JÑĀNĀMṚTA-SĀRA-SAṂHITĀ : A Tāntric work published with the title *Nārada-pāñcarātra*. Entirely devoted to the glorification of Kṛṣṇa and Rādhā, it is a modern and apocryphal work. It appears to have been written before Vallabhācārya at the beginning of the 16th century.

[Ed. K. M. Banerjee, *Bib. Ind.*, 1865. Trs. into English in *SBH*, Vol. 23, 1921.]

JÑĀNĀRṆAVA-TANTRA : It deals with various Tāntric rituals and the meditation on the various forms of Devī. Kumārīpūjā or the worship of young maidens is described as the highest sacrifice.

[Ed. *ASS*, No. 69, 1912.]

JYOTIRGAṆITA : An astronomical work, by Veṅkaṭeśa Ketakara, in two broad sections of which the first consists of four chaps. and the second of seven chaps. The principal object of the author is to reform the antiquated knowledge of the Hindus and to make it up-to-date. It has utilised the astronomical discoveries and researches of the last four centuries and the works of such western astronomers as Leverrier, Hansen and Newcomb.

[Pub., with illustrations, Poona, 1898.]

JYOTIRVIDĀBHARAṆA : A work on astrology, attributed to Kālidāsa. It is the source of the tradition of the Nine Jewels in the court of Vikramāditya. It shows Arabic influence, and perhaps originated not before the 16th century. It was commented on in 1661.

[Ed. with comm. of Bhavaratna, S. Jha, Bombay, 1908. See A. Weber, Ueber das Jyotirvidābharaṇam, *ZDMG* 22(1868) and Zum Jyotirividābharaṇam, *Ibid*, 24 (1870).]

KĀDAMBARĪ : A prose-rommance of the *Kathā* type, by Bāṇabhaṭṭa. It deals with the love-story of Candrāpīḍa and Kādambarī in the present and the past lives. Parallel to this story runs the love-story of Puṇḍarīka and Mahāśvetā. It contains some biographical account of the author in the beginning. Highly praised by Indians, but deprecated by some western scholars as an artificial production.

[Ed. K. P. Parab, with comm. of Bhānuśandra and Siddhacandra, NSP, 1928; M. R. Kale, with *Bālabodhinī* comm. (Pūrvabhāga), Bombay, 1928 (with notes in English); with Eng. trs. by J. N. S. Chakravarti and notes by P. V. Kane, by P. L. Vaidya, Poona, 1959; by N. G. Shinde, with trs., comm. etc., Ahmedabad. Trs. into English by C. M. Ridding, London, 1896, and by M. R. Kale (Pūrva-bhāga), Bombay, 1924 (with text); into Bengali by P. Thakur, Calcutta. For a Dutch trs. see A. A. Maria Sharpe, *Bāṇa's Kādambarī*, Diss. N. V. de Vlaamsche, Leuven, 1937. See V. S. Agrawala, *Kādambarī ek Sanskritik adhyayan*; M. Singh, Daṇḍin's version of ... Kādambarī, *Summaries of Papers, AIUC*, 1974.]

KĀDAMBARĪ-KATHĀSĀRA : It is a versified abridgment, by the Kashmirian Abhinanda, of Bāṇabhaṭṭa's *Kādambarī*. It is in eight cantos, and is marked by the artificialities found in the works belonging to the age of decadence.

[Ed. Durgaprasad and Parab, NSP, 1888, 1899.]

KĀKACAṆḌEŚVARĪMATA : A Tantra which is important in the history of the Medical Science and Chemistry in India.

[See P. C. Roy : *History of Chemistry in Ancient and Medieval India*, Calcutta, 1956.]

KĀLA-SĀRA : A Smṛti digest by Gadādhara. It deals with the periods of time suitable for various rites and observances.

[Ed. S. Misra, *Bib. Ind.*, 1900-04.]

KALĀPA : See *Kātantra.*

KALĀ-VILĀSA : A poetical work, in ten cantos by Kṣemendra. It describes the various modes of deceit practised by people in different walks of life. It is written in the form of instructions given by Mūladeva to one Candragupta.

[Ed. *Kāvyamālā*, I.]

KĀLA-VIVEKA: A well-known Smṛti digest by Jīmūtavāhana. It discusses the following topics :—

Appropriate seasons, months and time for the performance of religious rites and duties, intercalary months, suitability of solar or lunar months for certain festivals ánd rites, proper time for commencement and cessation of Vedic studies, rise of Agastya, the four months of Viṣṇu's sleep, time for various festivals including Kojāgara and Durgotsava and the eclipses.

[Ed. *Bib. Ind.*, 1905.]

KĀLĪVILĀSA-TANTRA : We can gather from it that there were two different schools of Śāktas, one of which condemned the Pañca-tattva ritual while the other considered it compulsory. A few chapters are devoted to Kṛṣṇa as the lover of Rādhā who is identical with goddess Kālī. One chapter contains a dialect which is a mixture of Assamese and Bengali current in East Bengal.

[Ed. P. C. Tarkatīrtha in *Tāntrik Texts*, vol. VI, 1917.]

KALPA-SŪTRA : Kalpa-sūtras constitute the Vedāṅga of the ritualistic type. They comprise Śrauta-sūtras, Gṛhya-sūtras, Dharma-sūtras and Śulva-sūtras. There are Kalpa-sūtras belonging to each of the four Vedic Saṃhitās. Acc. to some approximately synchronous with the rise and fast spread of Buddhism.

[See A. Hillebrandt in *Grundriss*, III. 2 (Ritual literatur) Vedische opfer und Zauber, Strassburg, 1897. For a detailed study on the society etc. reflected in Kalpasūtras, see Ram Gopal, *India of Vedic Kalpasūtras*, Delhi. 1959. Also see L. Renou, *Vocabulaire du rituel Vedique*, Paris, 1954 and *Śrauta-kośa*, Vol. I, English section, Part I, Poona, 1958; Vol. I, Part 2, Poona, 1962; Sanskrit section, Vol. I, Poona, 1958.]

KALPANĀ-MAṆḌITIKĀ : Also called *Kalpanālaṃkṛtikā* or *Sūtrālaṃkāra*, it is ascribed to Kumāralāta by some, to Aśvaghoṣa by others. It is a collection of tales, in prose and verse, inculcating the Buddhist faith. It is preserved in a fragmentary condition in Sanskrit.

[See *Bruchstücke der Kalpanāmaṇḍitikā des Kumāralāta* in Kongl Preuss Turfan Expedition, Kleinere Sanskrit-Eexte, II, Leipzig. 1926. The Chinese version of 405 A.D. has been translated by Huber into French, Paris. 1908.]

KĀMANDAKĪYA NĪTISĀRA : Same as *Nīti-sāra* (q.v.).

KĀMASŪTRA : The earliest extant work on erotics, ascribed to Vātsyāyana. It consists of 1250 verses divided into seven *Adhikaraṇas*, 14 *Prakaraṇas* and 36 *Adhyāyas*. The contents are indicated by the titles of the *Adhikaraṇas*, given below.

I. *Sādhāraṇa* (General principles).
II. *Sāṃprayogika* (Sexual union).
III. *Kanyā-saṃprayuktaka* (courtship and marriage).
IV. *Bhāryādhikārika* (wife).
V. *Pāradārika* (wives of other people).
VI. *Vaiśika* (prostitutes).
VII. *Aupaniṣadika* (Secret love or extraneous stimulation).

The work incidentally mentions 64 arts, particulary to be learnt by women. These include dance, music, art of decoration, skill in household work etc.

The life of a Nāgaraka (man about town) has been depicted in detail. The prostitutes have been divided into various classes.

The work is important from the point of view of medical science and sociology.

[Ed. D. Sastri, with Skt. comm. *Jayamaṅgalā* and a Hindi comm., *CSS*, 1964. Ed. and illustrated by L. Dane. Trs. into Eng. by K. R. Iyengar, Lahore, 1921; R. W. Burton, London, 1883 (new ed. New York, 1962); S.C. Upadhyaya with 17 line Drawings & 96 Half-tone illustrations; into German by R. Schmidt, W. Friedrich, Leipzig, 1897 (2nd ed. L. Verlag, Berlin, 1900 etc.); into French by F. Lemairesse, G. Carré, Paris, 1891. See H. Chakladar, *Studies in Kāmasūtra of Vātsyāyana : Social Life in Ancient India*, Calcutta, 1929; J. J. Meyer, *Sexual Life in Ancient India*, 2 vols., London, 1930; S. K. De, *Ancient Indian Erotics and Erotic Literature*, Calcutta, 1959; P. Peterson, Vātsyāyana on the Duties of a Hindu Wife in *Jour. of Anthrop. Soc. of Bombay*, 1892, and Courtship in Ancient India in *Jour. of Bombay Branch of Royal Asiatic Soc.*, 1892; R. Schmidt, *Liebe und Ehe im alten Indien*, Berlin, 1904. For flora and fauna in the *Kāmasūtra*, see B. H. Kapadia in *Jour. of Oriental Institute*, XI, 1961, p. 29. See Burton & Arbuthnot, *Kāmasūtra*; F. Wilhelm, The quotations in Kāmasūtra of Vātsyāyana, *Indologica Taurinensia* 6, 1978/80.]

KAṂSAVADHA : A drama mentioned in Patañjali's *Mahābhāṣya*, but lost to us.

KANDARPA-CŪḌĀMAṆI : Composed in 1577 A.D. by king Vīrabhadra of the Vaghela dynasty. It deals exhaustively with Erotics. As the author himself states, it is only an amplified metrical exposition, in seven sections, of Vātsyāyana's *Kāmasūtra*.

[Ed. R. S. Kusala, Lahore, 1926.]

KAPPHIṆĀBHYUDAYA : A *Mahākāvya*, in 20 cantos, by Śivasvāmin. The poet takes a Buddhist story from the *Avadāna-śataka*, and changes it almost beyond recognition. The work deals with the story of the south Indian king Kapphiṇa who invades Śrāvasti, the territory of Prasenajit, and is eventually converted to Buddhism through a miracle. The poem is marked with the artificialities found in the works belonging to the age of decadence.

[Ed. Gaurishankar, Lahore, 1937.]

KARAṆAPRAKĀŚA : An astronomical work, by Brahmadeva, describing the method of calculating the positions of the places from *ahargaṇanā* following the work of Āryabhaṭa I with corrections suggested by Lalla. Written in 10 chapters.

[Ed. S. Dvivedi, with a comm. and theory of numbers, Banaras, 1899 A.D.]

KĀRAṆḌA-VYŪHA : A Buddhist Mahāyāna-sūtra, the full title being *Avalokiteśvara-guṇa-karaṇḍa-vyūha*, "the detailed description of the basket of the qualities of Avalokiteśvara. It exists in two versions, the earlier one in prose and the later in Ślokas.

[Prose text pub. by S. Samassrami, Calcutta, 1873. An edition also pub. in Serampore, 1872.]

KĀRIKĀVALI : Another name of the *Bhāṣā-pariccheda* (q.v.)

KARMĀNUṢṬHĀNA-PADDHATI : Also called *Daśa-karma-paddhati*, *Saṃskāra-paddhati* or *Chandoga-paddhati*, it is a digest by Bhavadeva Bhaṭṭa and deals with the procedure of performing the various sacraments of the followers of the Sāma-veda.

[Ed. S. Kaviratna, Calcutta, 1384 B.S.]

KARMOPADEŚINĪ : See *Brāhmaṇa-sarvasva*.

KARṆA-BHĀRA : One-act play by Bhāsa, based on the *Mahābhārata*. Karṇa has an armour, and gets ready for a fight with Arjuna. Paraśurāma's curse that Karṇa's arms would be futile in the hour of need takes effect. Indra appears in the guise of a Brāhmaṇa, and takes from Karṇa his armour and earrings. Karṇa, accompanied by Śalya, goes out to battle, and the sound of Arjuna's chariot is heard.

[Ed. C. R. Devadhar, Poona Oriental Series, 1937; S. Malaviya, with Hindi and Eng. trs., notes and Appendices, 1975.]

KARṆA-SUNDARĪ : A drama, in four acts, by Bilhaṇa who wrote his work as a compliment to the Caulukya Karṇadeva Trailokyamalla of Aṇhilvad (1064—94 A.D.), whose marriage with a princess it celebrates in the guise of a romantic story. It is a recast of the theme in the *Ratnāvalī* and the *Viddhaśāla-bhañjikā*.

[Ed. NSP, 1888.]

KASHGHAR : See *Rower Manuscript*.

KĀŚIKĀ-VIVARAṆA-PAÑJIKĀ : See *Nyāsa*.

KĀŚIKĀ-VṚTTI : A celebrated commentary on the *Aṣṭādhyāyī*. Its authorship is attributed jointly to Vāmana and Jayāditya. Books i—v seem to have been Jayāditya's and the rest Vāmana's.

[Ed. B. Sastri, Banaras, 1928 (3rd ed.); D. D. Sastri and K. P. Shukla, with *Nyāsa* and *Padamañjarī*, Banaras, 1967 (Portion only). Ed. and trs. by L. Renou and Y. Ojihara, Paris, 1960. See M. D. Sharma, *K. Vṛtti Siddhānta-kaumudyoḥ tulanātmaka Adhyayana*, Poona, 1974; Raghuvir, *Citical Study of the Kāsikā.*]

KĀŚYAPA-SAṂHITĀ : A treatise on Āyurveda. It is also called *Vṛddhajīvakīya-tantra.*

[Ed. Vaidya, J. Acharya and S. Sarma, Bombay, 1938.]

KĀTANTRA : A grammatical work by Śarvavarman. The title means a "short treatise". The legend goes that the author, in pursuance of a wager made with Guṇāḍhya, author of the *Bṛhatkathā*, wrote this simplified grammar in order to make king Sātavāhana, an ignoramus, proficient in Sanskrit within a short period. It is also called *Kaumāra* or *Kalāpa*; these names indicate the acceptance of the legend that the author wrote under Śiva's special favour. Originally of four books, it appears with supplements both in the Tibetan translation and in Durgasiṃha's commentary. It exercised much influence in Kashmir and Bengal, and deeply affected the Pāli grammar of Kaccāyana and the Dravidian grammarians. A Tibetan tradition, of little historical value, alleges that the author of the *Kātantra* used the grammar of Indragomin. It appears to be an abridgment of the *Aṣṭādhyāyī*. It omits many rules of Pāṇini, totally ignores the Vedic portion of the *Aṣṭādhyāyī* and modifies many of its rules.

[Ed., with Durgasiṃha's comm., J. Eggeling, *Bib. Ind.*, 1874-78. German trs. by B. Liebich, Heidelberg, 1919. See *Pātañjala Mahābhāṣya*, pub. D. E. Society, Poona.]

KATANTRA-VṚTTI : A commentary, by Durgasiṃha, on the *Kātantra*.

KĀTANTRA-VṚTTI-PAÑJIKĀ : It is a commentary, by

Trilocanadāsa, on Durgasiṃha's commentary on the *Kātantra*.

KATHĀ-KAUTUKA : A poetical work, in 15 chapters, by Śrīvara. It is as the poet himself states, a Sanskrit version of the story narrated in the works of the Muslims. The story is that of the well-known Yusuf and Zulaikhā as narrated by Mullā Jāmi. It was composed in 1550 A.D. for the edification of the author's patron Muhammad Shāh.

[Ed. Sivadatta and Parab, NSP, 1901.]

KATHĀ-KOŚA : A collection of pupular tales, by an unknown compiler and of uncertain date. It is an insipid production in bad Sanskrit with inserted Prakrit verses. The tales are without mutual connexion.

[Ed. J. Sastri, Lahore, 1942. Trs. into English by C. H. Tawney, London, 1895. See *Kathākośa* by A. N. Upadhye, Delhi, 1974.]

KATHĀ-RATNĀKARA : A collection of popular tales, by Hemavijayagaṇi. There are 258 miscellaneous short tales, fables and anecdotes, mostly of fools, rogues and artful women. It is in prose diversified by verses in Sanskrit, Prakrit and modern Indian languages.

[Ed. H. Haṃsarāj, Jamnagar, 1911. Trs. J. Hertel, München, 1920.]

KATHĀSARIT-SĀGARA : The most famous of the versions of the *Bṛhatkathā*. It is by the Kashmirian Somadeva (q.v.), and consists of 18 books of 124 sections (Taraṅgas) and 24,000 verses. Acc. to Speyer's estimate, the complete work of Somadeva contained 21,388 verses. It is the earliest largest collection of stories extant in the world, and is the source of many tales in the *Thousand Nights and a Night* and, through them, supplied ideas not only to Persian and Turkish authors but also to the West through Boccacio, Chaucer, La Fontaine and others. In the Preface, Somadeva gives an account of the contents of the work, naming its various chapters and lays down the wonderful origin of the tale.

[Ed. Durgaprasad and Parab, NSP, 1930; H. Brokhaus, I-V, with trs., 2 vols., Leipzig, 1943, and VI-VIII, IX-XVIII (text only) in Abh. für die Kunde d. Morgenlandes, II and IV, Leipzig, 1862, 1866. Also see the three-volume ed. published by Bihar Rāṣṭrabhāṣā Pariṣad. Eng. trs. (*Ocean of Story*) by C. H. Tawney, *Bib. Ind.*, 1880-87 (reprinted, with notes and essays etc., by N. M. Penzer in 10 vols., London, 1924-28); this book is also to be shortly pub. by Motilal Banarsidass, Delhi. Russian trs. of Udayana story by I. Screbryakov and P. Grimtser under title *Poves't' O isara Udayāne*, Moscow, 1967. See Bühler, Uberdas Zeit alter des Kasmirischen Dichters Somadeva, Wien, 1885; J. S. Speyer's Studies on Kathā-saritsāgara, *JRAS*, 1908; C. S. Sundaram, Dance in Kathāsaritsāgara, *Summaries of Papers, AIOC*, 1974; L. Sternbach, *Proverbs and...in the Kathāsaritsāgara*, 1980. Also see B. Shastri, Kathāsaritsāgara and Purāṇic Literature : the Skandapurāṇa, *Summaries of Papers*, 5th World Skt. Con., Varanasi, 1981, p. 214; J. Surya narayan, Narrative Literature of Ancient India, *Ibid*; Reddy, Kathāsaritsāgaraḥ Strī-caritra-kośaḥ, *Ibid*, p. 215; N. Trikha, Sectarian Tendencies and Rivalries in the *Kathāsaritsāgara*, Ibid., p. 215).

KAṬHOPANIṢAD : It describes the following : the visit of Naciketā to the abode of Yama, his prayer to Yama for imparting to him the knowledge of Ātman, explanation by Yama of facts about Ātman, need of the purification of the mind, the oneness of soul, the immanence of the Supreme Soul, discrimination between self and non-self and rules about Yoga.

[For ed., see under *Īśopaniṣad*. Trs. into Polish by M. Iwienski, Krakau, 1924; into Italian by B. Fillippi, 1932; into German by Otto, Berlin, 1936.]

KĀTYĀYANA-ŚRAUTASŪTRA : See Śrautasūtra.

[Ed. with the *Saralā Vṛtti*, by V. Sarma, Sam. 1937. See K. P. Singh, *Critical Study of Kātyāyana*, Stet; Eng. trs. by M. G. Ranade, Poona, 1978.]

KĀTYĀYANA-ŚULVASŪTRA : See Śulvasūtra.

[Ed. A. Weber, *The White Yajurveda*, Vol. III]

KAUMĀRA or KAUMĀRAVYĀKARAṆA : Another name of *Kātantra* (q.v.).

KAUŚIKA PADDHATI : Same as *Keśava-paddhati* (q.v.).

KAUŚIKA-SŪTRA : A treatise dealing with the magical rites of the *Atharvaveda* and the application of spells.

[Ed. M. Bloomfield, New Haven, 1890. Important sections of the work, referring to magic, have been translated into German by W. Caland in *Altindisches Zauberritual*, Amsterdam, 1900. See R. N. Dandekar (ed.), *Kauśikasūtra-dārilabhāṣya*, Poona, 1972.]

KAUṢĪTAKI BRĀHMAṆA : See Brāhmaṇa.

[Trs. into Eng. along with the *Aitareya*, by A. B. Keith, HOS, 1920.]

KAVIKALPADRUMA : A treatise on roots, attributed to Vopadeva.

KAVĪNDRA-VACANA-SAMUCCAYA : See *Subhāṣita-ratnakośa*. [Ed. F. W. Thomas, *Bib. Ind.*, 1912.]

KAVIKAṆṬHĀBHARAṆA : A work on poetics, by Kṣemendra. It deals with the following topics :—

Possibility of becoming a poet, borrowing from others, the propriety of doing so in the case of the epic and similar works, the charm of poetry with illustrations of its ten aspects, the defects and excellences pertaining to sense, sound or sentiment, the various arts with which a poet should be conversant.

[Ed. *Kāvyamālā*, 1887, 1899; *CSS*, 1933. Trs. into Eng. in Suryakanta's *Kṣemendra Studies*, Poona, 1954.]

KAVI-RAHASYA : A grammatical poem by Halāyudha. It is really meant for illustrating the modes of formation of the present tense of Sanskrit roots, but incidentally serves as an eulogy of the Rāṣṭrakūṭa king Kṛṣṇa III (c. 940—56 A.D.)

[Ed. L. Heller, in both longer and shorter recensions, Greifswald, 1900. On the author, see R. G. Bhandarkar, '*Report*', 1883—94; Heller, Halāyudha's *Kavirahasya*, Diss., Gottingen, 1894; Zachariae, *Ind. Wörterbücher* (Grundriss).]

KĀVYĀDARŚA : A work on Alaṃkara-śāstra, by Daṇḍin. It comprises three chapters, and deals with the following topics :

Chap.I. Definition and division of *Kāvya*, the two *Mārgas* (Vaidarbha and Gauḍa) and the ten *Guṇas* pertaining to them and the essential requirements of a good poet.

Chap.II. Definition of *Alaṃkāra*, enumeration and description of 35 *Arthālaṃkāras*.

Chap.III. Elaborate treatment of *Śabdālaṃkāras*.

The work defines the body of Kāvya as a number of words conveying the intended sense. The soul of the Kāvya, composed in the Vaidarbha style, is stated to be the ten *Guṇas*.

[Ed. P. Tarkavāgīśa, with his comm., *Bib. Ind.*, 1863, with trs., O. Böhtlingk, Leipzig, 1890; with Eng. trs., S.K. Belvalkar, Poona, 1924; with an original comm., R. Raddi Sastri, BORI, 1938, 2nd. ed., K. S. Potdar, *BSS*, 1970. Trs. into Russian in Leningrad.]

KĀVYALAKṢAṆA : Same as *Kāvyādarśa* (q.v.).

[Ed., with *Ratnaśrī* Comm. of Ratnaśrījñāna, by A. Thakur and U. Jha, Darbhanga, 1957.]

KĀVYĀLAṂKĀRA : Also called *Bhāmahālaṃkāra*, it is by Bhāmaha. Divided into six chapters, it emphasises Alaṃkāra or poetical embellishment as the essential element of Kāvya. The importance of the work lies in the fact that we find in it, for the first time, a definite scheme of poetics systematically elaborated and authoritatively established.

[Ed. P. V. N. Sastry with Eng. trs. and notes, Tanjore, 1927 (Rev. ed., 1970); B. N. Sarma, B. Upadhyaya, CSS, Banaras, 1928. See R. Gnoli *Udbhaṭa's Comm. on the Kāvyālaṃkāra of Bhāmaha*, ed. with critical notes.]

There is a *Kāvyālaṃkāra* also by Rudraṭa. Consisting of 16 chapters and 734 *Kārikās*, it comprehends almost all the topics of Poetics. Besides the above *Kārikās*, there are 14 after xii. 40 : but these are declared to be interpolated passages.

[Ed. Durgaprasad and Parab, NSP, 1886, 1909, with Namisādhu's comm.; B. N. Sharma and B. Upadhyay.]

KĀVYĀLAṂKĀRA-SAṂGRAHA : Also called *Kāvyālaṃkāra-sāra-saṃgraha*, it is a well-known work on poetics, by Udbhaṭa. It consists of 75 *Kārikās*, with illustrations, divided into six chapters called *Vargas*. Some of the illustrative verses are assigned to Udbhaṭa himself in the *Subhāṣitāvalī*. The author deals with 41 Alaṃkāras. Although closely following Bhāmaha in the treatment of Alaṃkāra, Udbhaṭa has certain independent views.

[Ed., with Pratihārendurāja's comm., by M. R. Telang, NSP, 1905; 1915, N. D. Banhatti, with the same comm., Poona, 1925.]

KĀVYĀLAṂKĀRA-SŪTRA : Attributed to Yāska, it deal with poetics in an aphoristic style.

[Pub., with a comm., from Haryana Sāhitya-saṃsthāna, Rohtak, 2018 Vikram Saṃvat (=1960 A. D.).]

KĀVYĀLAṂKĀRA-SŪTRA-VṚTTI : A very early work on Poetics, by Vāmana. It consists of *Sūtras* and *Vṛtti*, both composed by Vāmana. It is divided into five parts called *Adhikaraṇas*, each of which is sub-divided into chapters called *Adhyāyas*. The topics, dealt with, are indicated by the names of the *Adhikaraṇas* which are as follows :—

I. *Śārīra*

II. *Doṣa-darśana*

III. *Guṇa-vivecana*

IV. *Ālaṃkārika*

V. *Prāyogika*

Vāmana, for the first time before the Dhvanikāra and Ānandavardhana, gives a well-thought-out and carefully outlined scheme of Poetics. He declares that Rīti or particular arrangement of words is the soul of poetry.

[Ed. Durgaprasad and Parab, NSP, 1880; N. Ṅ. Kulkarni, with extracts from *Kāmadhenu* comm., Poona, 1927; N. R. Acharya, with Skt. comm. Trs. into English by G. Jha, Allahabad.]

KĀVYĀLOKA : Another name of *Dhvanyāloka* (q.v.).

KĀVYA-MĪMĀṂSĀ : A work on Poetics, by Rājaśekhara. The published text consists of 18 chapters which appear to constitute only the first part of a projected extensive volume. The extant portion deals with *Kavi-rahasya.* It was very popular with such eminent writers as Kṣemendra, Bhoja, Hemacandra and younger Vāgbhaṭa.

[Ed., with introduction and notes, by C. D. Dalal in *GOS,* 1916; M. Misra, with his own comm. and Hindi trs., *CSS,* 1931, 1932. Trs. into French by N. Stchoupak and L. Renou, Paris, 1946.]

KĀVYĀNUŚĀSANA : A work on Poetics, by Vāgbhaṭa who is to be distinguished from the author, bearing the same name, of the *Vāgbhaṭālaṃkāra.* Written in the form of *Sūtra* and a running commentary, it covers in five chapters, most of the topics of poetics.

[Ed. Sivadatta and Parab, NSP, 1894, 1915, with *Alaṃkāra tilaka.*]

There is a work on poetics, bearing the same title, by Hemacandra (q.v.). Written in the form of *Sūtra* and *Vṛtti,* it comprehends all the topics of poetics and a brief reference to dramaturgy. Despite occasional differences, the author borrows freely from Bharata, Ānandavardhana, Abhinavagupta, Mammaṭa and Rājaśekhara.

[Ed., with *Alaṃkāra-cūḍāmaṇi* and *Viveka*, and an anonymous *Tippaṇa*, by R. C. Parikh and R. B. Athavale, in 2 vols., Bombay, 1938.]

KĀVYAPRAKĀŚA : A celebrated work on Poetics, attributed to Mammaṭa. A small portion of the last chapter, left incomplete by Mammaṭa, appears to have been completed by one Alaṭa or Alaka. A tradition, chiefly current in Bengal, attributes the *Kārikās* of the work to Bharata and the *Vṛtti* to Mammaṭa. Written in 10 chapters, it attempts a synthesis of the doctrines of the different schools of Poetics, and finally establishes the doctrines of the Dhvani school. No less than 70 commentaries on this work are known, the prominent commentators being Ruyyaka or Rucaka, Viśvanātha and Nāgoji or Nāgeśa Bhaṭṭa.

[Ed. V. Jhalakikar, with his own comm., Bombay 1917; with the *Dīpikā* comm., S. P. Bhattacarya, Banaras, 1933; with the *Saṃketa* comm. by the same editor in *Calcutta Oriental Journal*, II, 1935; with the *Viveka* comm., by the same editor, Calcutta, 1959, Pt. I (chs. I-VI); *Upikā* comm., ed. T. S. Nandi, Ahmedabad, 1976; with Maheśvara's comm. by A. Thakur, Calcutta Sanskrit Series; with Rasaprakāśa's comm. There is a MS of the comm., *Śitikaṇṭha Vibodhana* of Rājanaka Ānandakaul, at Kuruksetra University, Haryana, India. Eng. exposition, by S. N. Sastri, Vol. I, Chaps. 1-5, 1973. Trs. into Eng. by G. Jha, Allahabad, 1925; by P. P. Joshi (chs. I, II, X), Bombay, 1973. See R. C. Dwivedi, *Poetic Light or Kāvyaprakāśa*.]

KENOPANIṢAD : It lays down that Brahman alone is the power that makes the senses function. By an anecdote it describes how gods, obsessed with power, were convinced of the fact that Brahman alone is the source of all power.

[For ed., see under *Īśopaniṣad*. Also ed. K. Lal, Delhi, 1980. Trs. into Polish by M. Iwienski, Krakau, 1924; ed. with word meaning, Hindi-Eng trs. and explanation, Delhi. 1982.]

KEŚAVA-PADDHATI : Based on the *Kauśikasūtra* of the

Atharvaveda, it explains the ritual of the *Kauśikasūtra*. The author characterises it as *Atharvavedīya-saṃhitā-vidher vivaraṇam*.

[Ed. R. N. Dandekar, Poona, 1982.]

KHĀDIRA GṚHYASŪTRA : See Gṛhyasūtra.

[Text and Eng. trs. by H. Oldenberg, SBE, Vol. 29.]

KHAṆḌAKHĀDYAKA : Also called *Khaṇḍakhādya*, it is an astronomical work by Brahmagupta, composed c. 655 A.D., consisting of the following chapters :—

(i) Tithyadhikāra, (ii) Grahādhikāra, (iii) Tripraśnādhikāra, (iv) Candragrahaṇādhikāra, (v) Sūryagrahaṇādhikāra, (vi) Udayāstādhikāra, (vii) Śṛṅgonnatyadhikāra, (viii) Grahayutyadhikāra.

[Ed. P. C. Sen Gupta, with the comm. of Pṛthūdakasvāmin, Calcutta, 1941; B. Misra, with *Vāsanābhāṣya* Calcutta, 1925; B. Chatterji, with comm. of Bhaṭṭotpala, Eng. trs., Intro. and notes, Delhi, 1970. Trs. into Eng. by P. C. Sen Gupta, 1934.]

The ed. of P. C. Sen Gupta gives a reconstruction of *Uttarakhaṇḍakhādyaka* under the following chapters : *Khaṇḍakhādyakottaram*, *Khaṇḍakhādyake bhaṭṭotpalapaṭhitā atiriktaślokāḥ*.

KHAṆḌANAKHAṆḌAKHĀDYA : A work on Vedānta philosophy, by Śrīharṣa, the poet. The author seeks, by proving all other views to be contradictory, to establish that all objective knowledge is vain and that the doctrine of Śaṃkara is, therefore, unassailable.

[Trs. in *Indian Thought*, Allahabad, i-v.]

KĪCAKA-VADHA : A *Yamaka-kāvya*, in 5 cantos (177 verses), by Nītivarman. It is an embellished presentation of the *Mahābhārata* episode (IV. 13-23) of Bhīma's slaying of Kīcaka. It employs *Yamaka* in all the cantos excepting canto iii in which *Śleṣa* is used.

[Ed. S. K. De, with comm. of Janārdanasena and extracts from comm. of Sarvānandanāga, Dacca, 1929.]

KIRAṆĀVALĪ : A celebrated commentary, by Udayana, on Praśastapāda's *Bhāṣya* on the *Vaiśeṣika-sūtra*.

[Ed. *Bib. Ind.*, 1911. Also ed. *CSS.* J.S. Jetly with complete Text of *Praśastapāda-bhāṣya*, GOS, 1971; Ed. & trs. G. Sastri; Varanasi, 1980.]

KIRĀTĀRJUNĪYA : A *Mahākāvya*, in 18 cantos, composed by Bhāravi. Based on the *Mahābhārata* (III. 25-42), it opens with the story of the deposed Pāṇḍavas in a forest. From a spy, engaged by himself, Yudhiṣṭhira learns how carefully Duryodhana has been carrying on administration. Draupadī in vain tries to incite Yudhiṣṭhira to declare war; Bhīma supports her. At Vyāsa's instance Arjuna pleases Indra by penance. At Indra's advice Arjuna propitiates Śiva, and, by a display of skilful archery, induces him to grant him the desired *Pāśupata* weapon to be used against the hostile Kauravas. Bhāravi has introduced slight modifications into the original story. He betrays the influence of Kālidāsa in the description of the Himālayas. Bhāravi is praised by Indian critics for profundity of sense (*arthagaurava*) in his *Kāvya*. But, modern critics, especially of the West, denounce him as laboured and guilty of errors of taste.

[Ed. Godabole and Parab, with Mallinātha's comm., NPS, 1907. Trs. into German by C. Cappeller, *HOS*, 1912. See S. Pittor, *Kirātārjunīya of Bhāravi, a critical study*, Calcutta, 1983.]

There is also a drama of this title based on Bhāravi's poem. It is a drama of the Vyāyoga type by Vatsarāja.

KOHALA-RAHASYA : A work on music, by Kohala. The work is lost excepting its thirteenth chapter (*Triennial Cat. of Skt. MSS. in Oriental Library*, Madras, I. 1039). M. Krishnamachariar says that he is informed of the existence of the complete manuscript in Vadakkuttirumalagiri in Alvantirunagari, Tinnevelly District (Vide Krishnamachariar's *History of Classical Sanskrit Literature*, 1937, p. 823, f.n. 3).

KRIYĀ-KAUMUDĪ : A Smṛti work of Govindānanda mentioned in the *Āhnika-tattva* of Raghunandana. An incomplete manuscript of this work is preserved in Asiatic Society, Calcutta (No. I B 57).

KṚṢI-PARĀŚARA : Also called *Kṛṣi-saṃgraha*, *Kṛṣi-paddhati* or *Kṛṣi-tantra*. Ascribed to Parāśara, it is a metrical work dealing with agricultural operations from the collection of seeds to the harvesting of crops. It is unique in the sense that we do not know of any other work devoted exclusively to this subject.

[Ed. G. P. Majumdar and S. C. Banerji, *Bib. Ind.*, 1960]

KṚṢṆĀBHYUDAYA : A drama of the Prekṣaṇaka type, by Lokanātha Bhaṭṭa.

[Ed. with Hindi trs. by N. N. Sharma.]

KṚṢṆA-KARṆĀMṚTA : A poem by Kṛṣṇa-līlāśuka or Bilvamaṅgala. It exists in two recensions. The southern and western manuscripts present the text in three Āśvāsas or sections of more than 100 verses each. The Bengal recension preserves the text in one Āśvāsa with 112 verses. It is a collection of detached devotional lyric stanzas in which Kṛṣṇa is the object of the poet's prayer and praise. It is an important document of the *Bhakti* cult.

[Southern recension, with a comm., pub. Srirangam. Bengal recension, with three Skt. commentaries of Bengal, ed. S. K. De, Dacca, 1938. Also ed. (*The Love of Kṛṣṇa*) by F. Wilson, Philadelphia, 1975.]

KṚTYA-CINTĀMAṆI : A Smṛti digest by Caṇḍeśvara. It deals with astronomical matters relating to the performance of various religious ceremonies and *Saṃskāras* (sacraments), the movements of Saturn, the Sun's passage from one zodiac to another, the results of ecilpses, etc. There is also a Smṛti digest by Vācaspati Miśra, called *Kṛtyacintāmaṇi*. It deals with the festivals that are celebrated on different days in the year.

[For MSS of Caṇḍeśvara's work, see (i) *I. O. Cat.*, Vi, No. 1621, (ii) Calcutta Skt. College MS. No. Smṛti 107, (iii) Sarasvatībhavana Cat. III, No 13475. Vācaspati's work ed. Banaras, Śaka 1814. Partly pub. from Sāhitya Pariṣat, Calcutta, 1924 (Title : *Vācaspatimiśra-kṛta-durgotsavaprakaraṇam*)].

KṚTYA-KALPATARU : An extensive Smṛti digest by Lakṣmīdhara, but not available in the complete form. The *Kāṇḍas* or chapters, discovered hitherto, are as follows :—

I. *Brahmacārī*
II. *Gṛhastha*
III. *Naiyatakāla*
IV. *Śrāddha*
V. *Dāna*
VI. *Pratiṣṭhā*
VIII. *Tīrtha*
X. *Śuddhi*
XI. *Rāja-dharma*
XII. *Vyavahāra*
XIII. *Śānti*
XIV. *Mokṣa*

The seventh and ninth *Kāṇḍas* are missing. The work exercised considerable influence over the early Smṛti writers of northern India.

[Ed. *GOS—Dāna-kāṇḍa*, 1941; *Tīrthavivecana-kāṇḍa*, 1942; *Rājadharma-kāṇḍa*, 1943; *Mokṣa-kāṇḍa*, 1945; *Brahmacārī-kāṇḍa*, 1948; *Śrāddha-kāṇḍa*, 1950 *Naiyatakāla*, 1950; *Śuddhī-kāṇḍa*, 1950; *Vyavahāra*, 1953—1958, *Vrata*, 1953. The other published part is the *Gṛhastha-kāṇḍa*. Also *Pratiṣṭhākāṇḍa*, 1979.]

KṚTYA-RATNĀKARA: A huge Smṛti digest, by Caṇḍeśvara, in 22 chapters called *Taraṅgas*, forming a part of his *Smṛti-ratnākara* The topics discussed are as follows :—

Dharma, various *Vratas* and observances in the several months from Caitra, observances in the intercalary month, various *Vratas* on the days of the week, *Saṃkrānti*, eclipse, new moon day etc.

[Ed. K. K. Smṛtitīrtha, *Bib. Ind.*, 1921—25.]

KṢAṆABHAṄGA-SIDDHI : A work on philosophy, by the Buddhist philosopher Ratnakīrti. As the title suggests, it seeks to establish the momentariness of things by showing that they do not require three moments for their production, continuance and destruction.

KULACŪḌĀMAṆI : A very well-known Tāntric work of the

Kaulas. It is an example of *Nigama* in which Devī proclaims doctrines, and Śiva listens as a pupil.

[Ed. G. C. Vedāntatīrtha, Calcutta and London, 1915.]

KULĀRṆAVA-TANTRA : A principal Tāntric work of the *Kaulas*, i.e. the most advanced of the *Śāktas*, in 17 chapters called *Ullāsas*. Number of verses over 2000. It teaches that there are six forms of conduct (*ācāra*), which are only an introduction to *Kulācāra* and that release from suffering and the highest salvation can only be attained through *Kulācāra* or *Kula-dharma*. Probably composed before 1000 A.D.

[Ed., T. Vidyāratna in *Tāntric Texts*, V, London, 1917. See C. Chakravarti in *ABORI*, XIII, pp. 206—11. Chowkhamba Catalogue (Banaras) shows an ed. with Eng. intro. and Readings in Eng; with comm. and Bengali trs. by U. Das, Calcutta, 1383 B. S.]

KUMĀRAPĀLA-CARITA : A historical poem, in honour of Kumārapāla, the Cālukya King of Aṇhilvad. It is by Hemacandra, and is also called *Dvyāśraya-kāvya* from the fact that it is written partly (i—xx) in Sanskrit and partly (xx—xxviii) in Prakrit. It gives, in 28 cantos, an account of the rulers of Aṇhilvad, bringing it down to the time of Kumārapāla. The work is valuable for the history of the Cālukyas of Gujarat.

[Ed. A. V. Kathvate, cantos i—xx (Sanskrit), in two parts, *Bombay Skt. Series* 1885, 1915; S. P. Pandit, cantos xxi—xxviii (Prakrit) in the same Series, 1900; 2nd revised ed. by P. L. Vaidya, with the author's Prakrit Grammar, in the same Series, 1936. See S. P. Narang, *Hemacandra's Dvyāśraya Kāvya*, Delhi, 1972.]

KUMĀRA-SAMBHAVA : A famous court-epic by Kālidāsa in 17 cantos. It opens with a fine pen-picture of the Himālayas. Umā, daughter of Himālaya, is keen upon having Śiva as her spouse. The gods, persecuted by demon Tāraka, approach Brahmā at whose behest they depute Cupid to break the deep meditation of Śiva. This is necessary to bring about the wedding of Śiva and Umā, because only a son born of their union can rescue gods from the demon's oppression. Cupid succeeds in his mission, but the enraged Śiva burns him to ashes. Umā then begins hard penance to win the hand of Śiva. Śiva, convinced of the sincerity of her love, marries her. In course of time, a son named Kumāra (Kārtikeya) is born to them. This son is the future saviour of the gods. Some of the finest gems of poetry are found in the poem.

It is difficult to determine the exact source of this work. In the *Mahābhārata* (III. 220-21) occurs the story of *Mahiṣāsura* who persecutes gods and defies everyone in the three worlds. When Śiva is attacked, he invokes the help of his son Skanda who overpowers the demon. The story of Śiva's marriage with Pārvatī occurs in several Purāṇas. Some scholars think that cantos ix to xvii are the work of a later poet. Acc. to some, the eighth canto also is spurious.

[Ed. A. F. Stenzler, with Latin trs. (i—vii), London, 1838; N. B. Parvanikar, Parab and Pansikar, with comm. of Mallinātha (i—viii) and of Sītārāma (ix—xvii), NSP, 1927 (10th ed.); Suryakanta, New Delhi, 1962 with comms. of Mallinātha, Bṛhaspati Miśra, Bharatasena and Gopālānanda; S. R. Sehgal (i—vii) with Griffith's Eng. trs and notes, extracts from five commentaries including that of Mallinātha, Pāda-index etc. Delhi, 1966; S Karandikar, with complete Eng. trs., Mallinātha's comm. and appendices. On the alleged spurious portion, see Jacobi in Verhandl. d. V. Orient. Kongress, Berlin, 1881, II. 2; Weber in *ZDMG*, xxvii and in *Ind. Streifen*, III; S. P. Bhattacharya in *Pro. of* 5th *Oriental Conference*, I, and also in *JRASB*, xx. Eng. trs. by R. T. H. Griffith, London, 1879 (2nd ed.) and also by H. H. Wilson. It has been translated into French and some other languages, Indian and foreign. For a study on the various aspects of the work, see S. Sastri, *Kālidāsa's Vision of Kumārasambhava*. An interesting book is *Kālidāsa's Vision of Kumārasambhava* by Suryakanta, Delhi, 1963. Also see *Kumārasambhava-kāya O Kavi* by M. Datta (in Bengali) Calcutta. The following papers may be consulted :—

P. S. Subrahmanya Sastri : Some riddles in the Kumārasambhava, *M. Hiriyanna Comm. Vol.*, London, 1920;

C. K. Raja : The political allegory in Kālidāsa's Kumārasambhava, *R. K. Mookerji Vol.* (*Bhārata-kaumudī*), 1945, 1947.]

Udbhaṭa, a writer on Poetics, appears to have written a poem called *Kumārasambhava* from which verses are quoted in his *Kāvyālaṃkāra-saṃgraha*.

P. K. Gode discusses the dates of comm. by Jinasamudrasūri (*ABORI*, XV & XVI), Haridāsa (Ibid, XV), Cāritravardhana (Ibid, XV), Gopāla (Ibid, XV).

KUNDAMĀLĀ : A play, in six acts, dealing with the later part of the *Rāmāyaṇa* story after Rāma's coronation, i.e. the exile of Sītā, her discovery and reunion with Rāma. It appears to be earlier than the 5th century A.D., but the question of its date has not yet been settled with certainty. The authorship of the work is attributed by some, not on conclusive evidence, to Diṅnāga (q.v.). The following are the names suggested by different scholars as the author of the drama: Dhīranāga, Vīranāga, Ravināga, Nāgayya.

[Ed. K. K. Datta, Calcutta, 1964, with a Skt. comm. and Eng. trs. by J. Sastri and S. D. Bhanot, Lahore, 1932. Trs. into Eng. by A. C. Woolner, London, 1935. On the question of date and authorship, see S. K. De in JRAS, 1924, 1935; Woolner in ABORI XV.]

KŪRMA-PURĀṆA : Also called Kaurma-purāṇa. In addition to the usual topics, it also deals with the incarnation of Śiva, glorification of Kāśī and Prayāga. There are, in it, an Īśvaragītā (teaching knowledge of Śiva through meditation) and a Vyāsa-gītā (teaching acquisition of highest knowledge through pious work and ceremonies). A few chapters deal with expiatory ceremonies for all sorts of crimes.

[Ed. P. Tarkaratna, Vangavasi Press, Calcutta, 1932, B. S. (2nd Ed.) in Bengali characters; R. S. Bhattacharya, Delhi, 1968; A. S. Gupta, with Eng. trs., Varanasi, 1971; trs. into Eng. by A. Bhattacharya (Pt. I), by S. Mukherji & G. S. Rai (Part II), both ed. A. S. Gupta, Varanasi, 1972. Ed. G. V. Tagare (Parts I & II), Delhi, 1981-82.

See P. E. Dumont, The legend of Sītā in the Kūrma-purāṇa, *Siddhabhāratī* (S. Verma Vol.), I, Hoshiarpur, 1950.]

KUSUMĀÑJALI : Same as Nyāya-kusumāñjali (q.v.).

KUṬṬANĪ-MATA : A work by Dāmodaragupta, it has created a new genre in Sanskrit literature. It is erotico-comic and satiric. A courtesan, failing to attract lovers, seeks the advice of an experienced bawd. The latter instructs her to ensnare a rich young man, and describes in detail the cunning art of winning love and gold. Incidentally she relates stories in which the erotic and the pathetic sentiments intermingle.

[Ed. Tripathi, Bombay. 1924; with Hindi trs. by N. Chaturvedi, Allahabad, 1960; with Bengali trs. and notes, by T. Ray, Calcutta, 1953. Hindi trs. by A Vidyālaṃkāra and intro. by Suryakanta, Varansi, 1961; ed K. K. Dutta, Calcutta, 1964. See *India as seen in the Kuṭṭanīmata* by A. M. Sastri, Delhi, 1975.]

KUVALAYĀNANDA : A rhetorical work by Appayya Dīkṣita. It bodily incorporates the *Kārikās* of chapter v of Jayadeva's *Candrāloka*, and adds a running prose commentary by Appayya. It is, therefore, in a sense a commentary on the *Arthālaṃkāra* chapter of the *Candrāloka.*

[Ed., with the comm. *Alaṃkāra-candrikā* and Jayadeva's *Candrāloka*, by N. R. Acarya, NSP, 1955 (10th ed.); with a Hindi comm., Banaras, 1956.]

LAGHU-JĀTAKA : A work on the Horā section of astrology, by Varāhamihira.

[Ed., with Bhaṭṭotpala's comm. and a Hindi comm., Banaras, 1921. For trs. see A. Weber, Zur Geschichte der indischen Astrologie, *Indische Studien* 2, 1853.]

LAGHU-MAÑJŪṢĀ : See *Vaiyākaraṇa-siddhānta-mañjūṣā.*

LAGHU-ŚABDENDUŚEKHARA : A well-known commentary, by Nāgeśa, on Bhaṭṭoji's *Siddhānta-kaumudī.*

[Pub. in Andhra University Series, No. 26, 1941; *Kāśī Skt. Series*, 1954.]

LAGHUSIDDHĀNTA-KAUMUDĪ : Popularly called *Laghu-kaumudī* and written by Varadarāja, it is designed to be a grammatical primer based on the *Siddhānta-kaumudī* of Bhaṭṭoji Dīkṣita.

[Ed. and trs. J. R. Ballantyne, Banaras, 1867; with comm., Eng. trs., notes and appendices, by V. V. Mirashi.]

LAGHU-YOGAVĀSIṢṬHA : See *Yogavāsiṣṭha*.

LAKṢAṆĀVALĪ : A work on Vaiśeṣika philosophy, by Udayana.

[Ed. *Paṇḍit*, N. S. xxi and xxii; with the *Prakāśa* comm. of Keśavabhaṭṭa, by S. Jha, Darbhanga, 1963.]

LALITA-MĀDHAVA : A ten-act drama by Rūpa Gosvāmin. In it are depicted Kṛṣṇa's Vṛndāvana-līlā and his life at Mathurā and Dvārakā. The old legend has been considerably altered by the author.

[Ed. Puridas, Mymensingh, 1947; B. Sukla, with Nārāyaṇa's comm. and critical notes.]

LALITA-VISTARA : An *Avadāna* work of unknown date and authorship. It gives a detailed account of the 'sport' of the Buddha, and is written in prose, with long metrical passages in mixed Sanskrit, in the style of Purāṇas.

[Ed. P. L. Vaidya, Darbhanga, 1958. Eng. trs. by the same scholar (upto Ch. XV), *Bib. Ind.* 1881-86. Re-edited by S. Lefmann, Halle, 1902, 1908. Complete French trs. of the Tibetan version by P. E. Foucaux in *Annales du Muśee* Guimet, Paris, 1884, 1892. For metres in it see A. Mitra, *Summaries of Papers, AIOC*, 1974. Also see S. Bhattacharya. The Lalitavistara, a new literary genre, *Anvīkṣā* (Jour. of Jadabpur University, Calcutta), Vol. I, pt. 2, Vol. V, pt. 1, 1970.]

LAṂKĀVATĀRA : Also called *Saddharma-laṃkāvatāra*...A well-known Mahāyāna *Sūtra*, it teaches mainly a modification of Śūnyavāda. The doctrine, taught by it, is called Vijñānavāda; though denying the reality of the external world, it at the same time recognises that the phenomena of consciousness have a subjective reality.

[Ed. P. L. Vaidya and S. Bagchi, Darbhanga, 1963.]

LĀṬYĀYANA ŚRAUTA-SŪTRA : See Śrauta-sūtra for a general description of this literature.

[Ed. *Bib. Ind.* A few chapters trs. into German by R. Simon, *ZII*, Vol. II, 1923.]

LIKHANĀVALĪ : It is by Vidyāpati, and deals with forms of letter-writting. Composed under the patronage of Purāditya, a Jāgirdār in North Mithilā, it frequently mentions L. S. 299 (=1417-18 A.D.) in the letters.

LĪLAVATĪ : (1) A well-known work, by Bhāskarācārya, on arithmetic and geometry, divided into 13 chapters. Some think that it was socalled after the name of Bhāskara's daughter, Līlāvatī, while others think that it was written by Līlāvatī herself.

[Ed., with comms. *Buddhi-vilāsinī* and *Līlāvatī-vilāsa* by Gaṇeśa Daivajña and Mahīdhara respectively, by D. Apte, Poona, 1937; with *Vāsanā* comm. of D. Misra, by D. Jha, Darbhanga, 1959; with notes, by S. Dvivedi; with *Kriyākramakāri* exposition by K. V. Sarma, Hoshiarpur, 1975. On the authorship of this comm., see K. V. Sharma, *Summaries of Papers*, *AIOC*, 1974. Colebrooke's trs., ed., with notes, by H. Banerji, Calcutta, 1927. See H. T. Colebrooke, *Algebra with Arithmetic and Mensuration from the Sanskrit of Brahmagupta and Bhāscara*, London, 1817. The *Līlāvatī* was translated into Persian by Fayzi under Akbar the Great; the translation was pub. in Calcutta, 1828.]

(2) A comm., by Śrīvatsa (alias Vallabha), on Praśastapāda's *Padārtha-dharma-saṃgraha.* It was written in the 11th cent. A.D.

LIṄGA-PURĀṆA : Also called Laiṅga-purāṇa. Its main theme is the worship of Śiva in his various forms, especially in the *Liṅga* symbol. In the account of creation, Śiva occupies the position usually accorded to Viṣṇu. Legends of 28 incarnations of Śiva are told. It shows Tāntric influence.

[Pub. Veṅkaṭeśvara Press, Bombay, 1906; ed. J. L. Shastri, 2 Vols., Eng. trs., 1973; J. Legge, *Liṅgapurāṇa*, 12 vols., 1973; N. Gangadharan, *Liṅgapurāṇa, a study*, Delhi, 1980.]

LOCANA : Its full title is *Kāvyāloka-locana*. It is a commentary, by Abhinavagupta, on the *Dhvanyāloka*. It is a highly authoritative exposition of the *Dhvani* theory of Poetics.

[See Śaṇ Tapasvī Nandī (tr.), *Dhvanyāloka-locana*, Ahmedabad, 1973.]

[Ed., with the text, P. Sastri, Banaras, 1940.]

LOKĀNANDA-NĀṬAKA : A drama attributed to Candragomin, existing only in Tibetan version.

[Ed., M. Hahn, Otto Harrassowitz, Wiesbaden, 1974 with German translation.]

MADĀLASĀ-CAMPŪ : A Campū-kāvya attributed to Trivikrama Bhaṭṭa.

[Ed. J. B. Modak and K. N. Sane, Poona, 1882.]

MADANA-PĀRIJĀTA : It is an extensive Smṛti digest attributed to Madanapāla, but, in reality supposed to have been composed by Viśveśvarabhaṭṭa. It consists of nine chapters (*Stavaka*) on Brahmacarya, duties of householders, daily duties, Saṃskāras, impurity on birth and death, purification of various substances, Śrāddha, Dāyabhāga and Prāyaścitta. [Ed. M. Smrtiratna, *Bib. Ind.*, 1887—93.]

MĀDHAVA-MAHOTSAVA : A poetical composition, in 10 cantos called Ullāsas, by Jīva Gosvāmin. Its main theme is the consecration, by Kṛṣṇa, of Rādhā as the queen of Vṛndāvana, and the festivities connected therewith.

[E. H. Das, Navadvipa, 1941.]

MADHURĀ-VIJAYA : Also called *Vīrakamparāya-carita*. A historical poem, by Gaṅgādevī, describing the heroic deeds of her husband, Kampana or Kamparāya, son of Bukka I (c. 1343-79 A.D.) of Vijayanagara, who led victorious campaigns against King Campa of Kāñcī and against Jalaluddin Hasanshah, the sultan of Madurai (Madhurā).

[Ed., with comm., by P. S. Sastri, Tenali (A.P.), 1969.]

[Mūlamadhyamaka-Kārikās (Mādhyamika-sūtra) de Nāgārjuna avec la Prasannapadā, commentaire de Candrakīrti, publiê par L. de La Vallêe Poussin, St. Petersbourg, Bib. Buddh., 1903ff; Madhyamaka-śāstra of Nāgārjuna, with comm. of Candrakīrti, ed. P. L. Vaidya, Darbhanga, 1960. Chap. I (on causality) and chap. XXV (on *Nirvāṇa*), with comm. of Candrakīrti, trs. by Th. Stcherbatsky, *The Conception of Buddhist Nirvāṇa*, Leningrad, 1927. The *Kārikās*, with Nāgārjuna's own comm., trs. from Tibetan by Max Walleser, Die mittlere Lehre (*Mādhyamika-śāstra*) des Nāgārjuna, Heidelberg, 1911. See H. Chatterji's ed. of the work (Part II, 1962).]

MADHYAMA-VYĀYOGA : A *Mahābhārata* play in one act, by Bhāsa. It deals with the story of the love of the demoness Hiḍimbā for Bhīma, their marriage, the birth of Ghaṭotkaca and the parting of the parents.

[Ed. C. R. Devadhar, *Poona Oriental Series*, 1937. This play is also trs. by E. P. Janvier, Mysore, 1921; P. E. Pavolini, *Giornale della Societa Asiatica Italiana*, xxix. 1 f.]

MADHYA-SIDDHĀNTAKAUMUDĪ : Written by Varadarāja, it is a school grammar being a simplified form of the *Siddhānta-kaumudī* of Bhaṭṭoji Dīkṣita.

[Ed., with explanatory notes, by Govindasiṃha, Veṅkaṭeśvara Press, Bombay, 1900.]

MAHĀBHĀRATA : One of the two great epics of India, traditionally ascribed to Vyāsa. It consists of 18 books called *Parvans* and a supplement called *Harivaṃśa*. The five Pāṇḍavas, of whom the eldest Yudhiṣṭhira is the ruling monarch, loses his kingdom as a result of a rash wager at a game of dice with Duryodhana, the eldest of their cousins called Kauravas. The Pāṇḍavas are moreover insulted, and go to exile along with their common wife Draupadī. After the period of exile, during which the Kauravas try in vain to persecute or even kill them, they demand their rightful kingdom which is, however, denied. A grim battle, lasting for 18 days, ensues. Through the help of Kṛṣṇa the Pāṇḍavas come out victorious in the righteous war. They perform the *Aśvamedha* sacrifice, and their rule is firmly established. In course of time, they proceed towards heaven where they finally reach after overcoming various obstacles. Around the nucleus of this story there have gathered diverse matters in the shape of ancient heroic poetry, Brāhmaṇical myths and legends, fables, parables and moral narratives. The *Mahābhārata* is said to be a repertory of the whole of the old bard poetry of India.

An important portion of the *Mahābhārata* is the *Bhagavadgītā*, popularly called *Gītā* (q.v.).

The *Mahābhārata* is not one poetic production. Its composition appears to have passed through at least three stages. Single myths and legends of this epic reach back to the time of the Veda. The transformation of the epic *Mahābhārata* into the present compilation perhaps took place between the 4th century B.C. and the 4th century A.D. The Mahābhārata War is supposed by some eminent scholars to have taken place in the tenth century B.C.

Nīlakaṇṭha is the most well-known commentator of the *Mahābhārata*. An earlier commentator is Arjunamiśra. The commentary, called *Viṣamapada-vivaraṇa*, is still earlier. Devabodha is another commentator whose comments on several *parvans* have been published by Bhandarkar Oriental Res. Institute, Poona.

[Critical ed. pub. by BORI (different *parvans* separately printed) Poona, 1927-54. Of the single volume editions of the entire text, a notable one is the Citraśālā ed., with Nīlakaṇṭha's comm., Poona, 1929-36. Virāṭaparvan IV, with all available comms.,—Gujarati Printing Press, Bombay, 1971 V. S. Trs. into Eng. prose by K. M. Ganguli, Calcutta, 1884-96; M. N. Dutt, Calcutta, 1895-1905; P. C. Roy, Calcutta, 1919-25 (2nd ed.); R. C. Datta (partly metrical and partly in prose extracts) in his *Mahābhārata*, the Epic of Ancient India condensed into English Verse, London, 1899; P. Lal in parts Calcutta (To be completed). Trs. into Bengali by H. Siddhantavagisa, Calcutta, 1338 B. S. onward. Naqib Khan, Badauni, Mulla Shiri and Fayzi of Akbar's court translated the epic into Persian, under the title *Razm Namah*, with the help of a band of Pandits. Trs. into Malayalam by K. Prakasam. The Nala-Damayantī episode was rendered into Persian by Fayzi of Akbar's court under the title *Nal wa Daman* (Pub. in Calcutta, 1831). For a summary of the entire work, see M. Williams, *Indian Epic Poetry*, London, 1863.

An outline of the story and extracts given by J. C. Oman in *The Great Indian Epics*, London, 1899. Books I-X trs. into French by H. Fauche, Paris, 1963-70; a collection of larger extracts by Ph. E. Foucaux, *Le Mahābhārata* etc., Paris, 1862. Several episodes trs. into Italian by P. E. Pavolini, 1902; into German by F. Bopp, Berlin, 1824, F. Ruckert, A. Holtzmann, Indische Sagen, 1845-47 (new ed. by M. Winternitz, Jena, 1921), J. Hertel in *Indische Marchen*, Jena, 1919, No. 10-14 and by W. Porzig in the Series *Indische Erzahler* vols. 12 and 15, Leipzig, 1923. Trs. into Eng. by P. Bal, Vols. I-IV, portions trs. into Georgian (Russia).

The philosophical portions of the work including the *Bhagavadgitā*, trs. into German by O. Strauss and P. Deussen, *Vier philosophische* etc., Leipzig, 1906. A Russion trs. by B. Smyrnov appears to have been published in seven vols., 1955-63, from Turkoman Science Academi. The author is known to have discussed Indian philosophy also. An abridged Russian trs. by Lipkin has been published.]

Agarwal, G. C. : *Age of the Bhārata War*, 1979.

Banerji, S.C.: *Smṛti Material in the Mahābhārata*, Vol. I. Calcutta, 1972.

: *Indian Society in the Mahābhāratc*, Varanasi, 1976.

Bhattacharya, S : *Imagery in the Mahābhārata*, Calcutta, 1969.

Braginsky, V. I. : Mahābhārata in Malayan Tradition, *Summaries of Papers*, Vth World Skt. Conf., Varanasi, 1981.

Buck, W. : *Mahābhārata*, Berkeley.

Chandra, A. N : *Date of Kuruksetra War*, Calcutta, 1978.

Dahlmann : *Das Mahābhārata* etc., Berlin.

Dange. S. A. : *Legends in the Mahābhārata*, 1969.

Fausböll : *Hindu Mythology acc. to the Mahābhārata*, London, 1903.

Gode, P. K : New light on the chronology of the commentators of the Mahābhārata, *ABORI*, XXV, 1944.

Held, J. J. : *The Mahābhārata, an ethnological study*, Amsterdam, 1935.

Hilgenburge, L. : *Kosmgraphische episo due in Mahābhārata and Padmapurāṇa*, Stuttgart, 1933.

Holtzmann : *Grammatisches aus dem Mahābhārata*, 1884.

Hopkins, E. W. : *The Great Epic of India*, 1901 (Reprinted, Calcutta, 1969). Also see author's paper, Professed quotations from Manu found in the Mahābhārata, JAOS, 11, 239-275.

Iyenger, M. V. : *The Mahābhārata—a short study*, Madras, 1973.

Kane, P. V. : *History of Dharmaśāstra*, Rev. ed., Vol. I, pt. I, pp. 349-408.

Katre, S. L. : *Kṛṣṇa and the Mahābhārata War*.

Kirfel, A. W. : *Beitragezur Geschicte der Nominal Komposition inden Upaniṣads und im Epos*, Bonn, 1908.

Lal, U. S. : *Some aspects of the socio-political philosophy of the Mahābhārata and Plato's Republic*, Banaras.

Lal, P. : *An annotated Mahābhārata Bibliography*, Calcutta.

Meenakshi, K. : *Epic Syntax*, unpublished Ph. D. thesis, Poona, 1963.

Misra, K. N. : *Mahābhārata Men Loka-kalyāṇ ki Rājakīya Yojanāyen* (Hindi), Varanasi, 1972.

Patil, N. B. : *Folklore in the Mahābhārata*, Delhi, 1983.

Oldenberg : *Das Mahābhārata* etc., Gottingen, 1922.

Pusalker, A. D. : *Studies in Epics and Purāṇas*, Bombay, 1955.

Rai, R. : *Mahābhārata-kośa*, Banaras, 1964 (Hindi trs. of Sorensen's work—*infra*).

Rao, N. J. : *The Age of the Mahābhārata War*, Varanasi, 1978.

Rice, E. P. : *Analysis and Index of the Mahābhārata*, London, 1834.

Roy, B. P. : *Political ideas and instructions in the Mahābhārata* (based on Poona cr. ed.)

Sastry, K. S. : *Mahābhārata Retold in Eng.*, Mysore.

Sathe, S. : *Search for the year of Bhārata War*, Hyderabad, 1983.

Sen Sharma, P. : *Kurukṣetra war—a military study*, Calcutta, 1975.

Skarma, R. K. : *Elements of Poetry in the Mahābhārata*, Berkeley and Ahmedabad, 1977.

Shastri, K. K. : (ed.) *Jayasaṃhitā, the Ur-Mahābhārata*, Vols. I-II, Los Angeles, 1964.

Seegar, E. : *The Five Sons of King Pāṇḍu.*

Sinha, J. P. : *Mahābhārata, a literary study.*

Sircar, D. C. : *Bhārata War and Purāṇic Genealogies.*

Sorensen, S. : *Index to names in the Mahābhārata*, Delhi, 1963 (Reprint).

Sukthankar, V. S. : *The meaning of the Mahābhārata*, 1942.

: *Prolegomena.*

: *Critical Studies in the Mahābhārata.*

: *Epic studies.*

Tarkatirtha, R. C. : *Mahābhārata Lakṣa-śloka-saṃgraha*, Calcutta, 1974.

Thadani, N. V. : *The Mysteries of the Mahābhārata*, Vols. I-V, Karachi, 1934-35.

Tewari, J. N. : *Disposal of the Dead in the Mahābhārata*, Varanasi, 1979.

Vaidya, C. V.: *Epic India*, Bombay, 1907,

: *The Mahābhārata—a criticism*, New Delhi, 1983.

Winternitz, M. : *A History of Indian Lit.* Vol. I, Calcutta, 1927.

The following papers are informative :

Apte, V. M.: Ṛgveda citations in the Mbh, *P. V. Kane Pres. Vol.*, Poona, 1941.

Belvalkar, S. K.: Cosmographical episodes in Mbh and Padmapurāṇa, *F. W. Thomas Pres. Vol.*, Bombay, 1939.

De, S. K. : A note on hiatus in Epic Sandhi, *IL*, 18 (*Bagchi Memo. Vol.*), 1957.

Edgerton, F. : Epic studies, 2nd series, *Bulletin of Deccan College Res. Institute*, Poona, (*Sukthankar Mem. Vol.*) 1944.

Gokhale, V. D. : Un-Pāṇinian forms and usages in the cr. ed. of the Mahābhārata, *IL* (*Taraporewala Memo. Vol.*), Calcutta, 1957.

Grintoer, P. : Mythological elements in the composition of the Mahābhārata, *Indian literatures : Articles and Information*, Moscow.

Holtzmann, A. : Grammatisches aus dem Mahābhārata, 1884.

Kane, P. V. : The Two Epics, *ABORI*, XLVII.

The Mahābhārata verses and very ancient Dharmasūtras and other works, *F. W. Thomas Pres. Vol.*, Bombay, 1939.

Karve, I. : Kinship terms and the family organisations as found in the cr. ed. of the Mahābhārata, *V. S Sukthankar Memo. Vol.*, *Bulletin of Deccan College Res. Inst. V*, Poona, 1944.

Katre, S. M. : Apropos epic *iyāt*, *Bulletin of Deccan College Res. Inst.*, Poona, 1931.

Epic *iyāt* and blends of aorist and optative forms, *JAOS*, 57; *NIA*. I.

Kulkarni, E. D. : Same as V. D. Gokhale's paper above. *V. S. Sukthankar Memo. Vol., op. cit.*

Verbs of movement and their uses in cr. ed. of Ādiparvan, *Bulletin of Deccan College Res. Inst.* Poona, 1941.

Epic Variants, Do. 1946.

Dative and its variants in cr. ed. of *Mahābhārata*, Do. 1941. Un-Pāṇinian forms and usages in *Mahābhārata*, *ABORI*, 1943; *NIA*, 1943; *Bulletin of Deccan College Res. Inst.* 1942-43, 1944, 1953.

Lal, N. S. : *Some aspects of the socio-political philosophy of the Mahābhārata and Plato's Republic*, Banaras.

Long, J. B. : *The Mahābhārata, a select annotated Bibliography*, Cornell University, 1974.
Festgruss an O. Von Böhtlingk, Stuttgart, 1888.

Ludwig, A. : *A Mahābhārata die Ironie im und im Ṛgveda.*

Mehendale, C. M. A. : Absolutives in Cr. ed. of Virāṭaparvan, *Bulletin of Deccan College Res. Inst.*, Poona, 1939.

Nevelova, S. : Names in Mahābhārata, in *Indian Literatures : Articles and Information*, Moscow.

Oldenberg : *Das Mahāthārata* etc., Gottingen, 1922.

Pisani, V. : On some peculiarities of use of cases in Ādiparvan, *NIA*, 1946.

Proudfoot, I. : Interpreting Mahābhārata episodes as sources for the History of Ideas, *ABORI*, LX, pp. 41ff.

Pusalker, A. D. : *Studies in the Epics and Purāṇas*, Bombay, 1955.

Raghavan, V. : Notes on some Mahābhārata comms., *P. V. Kane Pres. Vol.*

Ray Chaudhuri, H. C. : A note on the Ghaṭotkaca-parvādhyāya of the Mahābhārata, *K. B. Pathak Comm. Vol.* Poona, 1934.

Rao, R. : The astronomical classification of the Mahābhārata text, *K. M. Munshi Diamond Jubilee Vol.*, *Bhāratīya Vidyā*, Vols. 9, 10, Bombay, 1941-49.

Ruben, W. : Indra's fight against Vṛtra in the Mahābhārata, *S. K. Belvalkar Fel. Vol.*, Banaras, 1957.

Sen, C. : Excursions of Pandavas to Himalayas, *North Bengal University Review*, Vol. 2, Nos. 1, 2, June and December, 1981.

Sen Gupta, N. L. : Studies in Epic Grammatical Forms (?), *Dacca University Bulletin* (Vol. ?).

Shaikh, C. H. : Trs. of Mahābhārata into Arabic and Persian, *V. S. Sukthankar Mem. Vol., op. cit.*

Sil, H. C. : A list of verb-forms in cr. ed. of Ādiparvan, *Indian Linguistics, Turner Jubilee Vol.*, 1955.

Un-Pāṇiniyan Verb-forms in cr. ed. of Ādiparvan, *IHQ*, 1960.

Vartak, P. V. : Uranus, Neptune and Pluto were known to Mahābhārata (5562 years before Christ), *Sum. of Papers*, Vth World Sanskrit Conference, Varanasi, 1981, p. 210.

Vasilkov, Y. : Elements of Folklore in Mahābhārata in *Indian Literatures* : Articles and information, Moscow.

Yardi, M. R. : The problem of Multiple Authorship of the Mahābhārata : a statistical approach, *JAS*, Bombay, Vols. 52-53, 1977-78 (N.S.) and *ABORI*, LXII, Poona, 1981.

See *Mahābhāratānukramaṇikā*.

Of the *Pratīka-index* to cr. ed., several vols. pub. by BORI, Poona.

A Concordance of the *Mahābhārata* is reported to be under preparation at the University of Kurukṣetra, Haryana, India.

MAHĀBHĀRATA-TĀTPARYA-NIRṆAYA : Also called *Bhārata-tātparya-nirṇaya*; it is an epitome of the *Mahābhārata*, by Madhva. It is metrical, and consists of 32 chapters.

[Ed. T. R. Krishnacharya.]

MAHĀBHĀṢYA : The Great Commentary; the oldest extant commentary by Patañjali on Pāṇini's *Aṣṭādhyāyī*. Patañjali comments on 1228 rules of Pāṇini in the order of the *Aṣṭādhyāyī*. His commentary on each *Pāda* of the *Aṣṭādhyāyī*, however, is divided into several parts called *Āhnikas*. There are 85 such *Āhnikas* in it. Patañjali does away with some of the supplementary rules (*vārtika-sūtra*) of Kātyāyana as redundant. The *Mahābhāṣya* affords good evidence of the development of Sanskrit prose in remote antiquity (c. 2nd century B.C.). It affords a lively picture of the mode of discussion of the day.

[Ed., with *Pradīpa* and *Uddyota* and Eng. version of the opening portion. J. R. Ballantyne, Vol. I (Navāhnika), Mirzapore, 1856; Kielhorn, BSS, 1906 ff. (Vol. I, 3rd ed. by K. V. Abhyankar, 1962); with comms. of Kaiyaṭa, Nāgeśa and Rudradhara Jha, by G. Sarma Chaturvedi, Āhnikas 1-9. See P. S. S. Sastri's Lectures on Patañjali's Mahābhāṣya, Vols. I and II, Annamalai Skt. Uni. Series, Nos. 9 and 11, 1944, 1951; Vol. VI, 1962.

Also see *Paspaśāhnika*, ed. and trs. by K. C. Chatterji, Calcutta, 1953; *Samarthāhnika*, ed. with Eng. trs. and notes, by S. D. Joshi, Poona 1968; *Karmadhārayāhnika*, ed. and trs. by S. D. Joshi & J. A. F. Roodbergen, Poona, 1971; *Tatpuruṣāhnika*, ed. Do, Poona, 1974; Āhnikas I-III ed. by Abhyankar and Shukla, with Eng. trs. and notes, Poona, 1975. *Avyayībhāva* and *Bahuvrīhi* Āhnikas, also ed. by Joshi and Roodbergen. *Word-Index to the Mahābhāṣya*, BORI, Poona, 1927, and B. N. Puri, *India in the times of Patañjali*, Bombay, 1957; F. Kielhorn, *Kātyāyana and Patañjali—their relation to each other and to Pāṇini*, Banaras, 1963; V. P. Limaye, *Critical Studies in Mahābhāṣya*, Hoshiarpur, 1974; J. Filliozat, (Le) *Mahābhāṣya de Patañjali, Le Pradipa de Kaiyaṭa et Uddyota de Nageśa*, 3 Vols., trs. into French, upto nine *Āhnikas*, Pondicherry 1975-80, A. C. Sarangi, *Development of Sanskrit from Pāṇini to Patañjali.*]

MĀHABHĀṢYA-PRADĪPA : Same as Pradīpa (q.v.).

[M. S. Narasimhacharya, *Mahābhāṣya-Pradīpa-Vyākhyānāni*, *Adhy*. 2, *Pāda* 4, Pondicherry, 1978.]

MAHĀBHĀṢYA-PRADĪPODDYOTA : Same as *Uddyota* (q.v.).

MAHĀNĀṬAKA : A huge work almost wholly in verse, some of the verses being taken from most of the known, and probably some unknown, dramas having the same theme. Though called a *Nāṭaka*, it is a non-descript composition, as Wilson justly remarks. There is in it little of prose dialogue, the usual stage-directions are absent. There is no Prakrit passage in it. The number of acts, at least in one version, is beyond the limit prescribed by theory. It appears to be a loose narrative composition, and was perhaps originally written in the regular form of Kāvya. It deals with the entire Rāmāyaṇa story. It is anonymous; a verse in one recension ascribes it to the mythical Hanumat; hence it is also called *Hanumannāṭaka*. It exists in two principal recensions, viz. West Indian (in 14 acts and 548 verses) redacted by Dāmodara Miśra and East Indian (Bengal) arranged by Madhusūdana in 10 acts (720 verses). The former is styled *Hanumannāṭaka* and the latter *Mahānāṭaka*.

[*Hanumannāṭaka* ed. Veṅkaṭeśvara Press, Bombay, 1909, with the *Dīpikā* comm. *Mahānāṭaka* ed. C. B. Bhattacharya, with comm. of Candraśekhara, Calcutta, 1874. On the text-problem see A. Esteller, *Die ältest Rezension des Mahānāṭaka*, Leipzig, 1936.]

MAHĀNAYAPRAKĀŚA : A work attributed to Abhinavagupta, it deals, in 9 chapters, with the principles of the *Śākta* system of philosophy. In about 600 *Kārikās* it elucidates the paths leading to the realisation of *Mahāśakti* who pervades and preserves the universe.

[Ed. K. Sastri, *TSS*, 1937.]

There is a work of the same title by Rājānaka Śitikaṇṭha. It consists of vernacular *Kārikās* followed by commentaries in Sanskrit.

MAHĀNIRVĀṆA TANTRA : A very well-known *Śākta* Tantra. Besides Tāntric ritual, it teaches a philosophy which closely resembles the system of the Vedānta and Sāṃkhya. As regards ethics, its teachings resemble those of the *Manu-*

smṛti, the *Bhagavad-gītā* and the Buddhist sermons. It recognises the caste of *Sāmānyas* in addition to the usual four castes. Instead of four *Āśramas*, it holds that in the Kali Age there are only two, viz., that of a householder and that of an ascetic. It is a highly popular work. Some scholars think that the work originated in Bengal. Farquhar regards it as a modern work, perhaps not earlier than the 18th century. The *Nirvāṇa-tantra* is an entirely different work.

[Of several eds., the earliest is the one by Ādi Brāhma Samāj, Culcutta, 1876. Also see the ed. pub. in Madras, 1929 with comm. of H. Bharati, and ed. by Woodroffe, 1953 (3rd. ed.). Ed. with comm. and Bengali trs., M. Bhattacharya. Prose Eng. trs. by M. N. Datta, Calcutta, 1900; A. Avalon, with a comm., London, 1913.]

MAHĀSIDDHĀNTA : A treatise on astronomy, by Āryabhaṭa. [Ed., with comm., by S. Dvivedi, Banaras, 1910.]

MAHĀSUBHĀṢITA-SAṂGRAHA : By L. Sternbach, an anthology of delightful verses culled from various sources. Text with Eng. trs., critical notes, introduction and Index, Delhi, 1974. Vols. I-III already out.

MAHĀTANTRA : See *Dhīvṛddhi-tantra.*

MAHĀVASTU : A work of the *Avadāna* class. It probably belongs to the 1st century A.D. Although its principal subject is *Vinaya*, yet it contains, besides the life-story of the Buddha, some narratives of the Jātaka and Avadāna types.

[Ed. E. Senart, 3 vols., Paris, 1882-97; R. G. Basak, Sanskrit College, Calcutta, Vols. I, II. Ed. S. Bagchi Vol. I, Darbhanga, 1970; Vol. II reported to be in progress. Eng. trs. by J. J. Jones, 3 vols. See R. G. Basak, *Indian Life as Revealed in Mahāvastu Avadāna*; B. C. Law, *Study of the Mahāvastu*, Calcutta, 1930; Bhikkhu T. Rahula, *A Critical Study of the Mahāvastu*, Delhi, 1978.]

MAHĀVĪRA-CARITA : A drama, in seven acts, by Bhavabhūti. It dramatises the Rāma-story up to the time of Rāma's departure for the forest. The author introduces certain innovations in order to heighten the dramatic effect.

[Ed. Todar Mall, Punjab Uni. Pub., 1928; T. R. A. Aiyar and K. P. Parab, with Vīrarāghava's comm., NSP, 1910 (3rd ed.). Trs. into Eng. by John Pickford, London, 1871.]

MAHĀYĀNA-ŚRADDHOTPĀDA : Generally attributed to Aśvaghoṣa. Some think that it was written by some other person and attributed to the great poet for securing reputation for it. Others think that it was perhaps the work of a later scholar, named Aśvaghoṣa, who probably lived in the 5th century A.D. It attempted a synthesis of the teachings of the Mādhyamika and Vijñānavāda schools of Buddhism. The Sanskrit original is lost, and it is preserved in two Chinese versions, one by Paramārtha (c. 553 A.D.) and the other by Śikṣānanda (c. 700 A.D.).

MAHĀYĀNA-SŪTRĀLAṂKĀRA : A philosophical work, representing the Vijñānavāda school of Buddhism, by Asaṅga. It is in verse followed by a comment.

[Ed. & trs. Levi, Paris, 1907-11. Ed. S. R. Bagchi, Darbhanga, 1970.]

MAHIMNAḤ-STAVA : Eulogy of Śiva, also regarded as intended to glorify Viṣṇu. Ascribed to Puṣpadanta. Appears to have been known to Jayanta Bhaṭṭa, author of the *Nyāyamañjari*, perhaps not later than 9th century A.D.; cited by Rājaśekhara (q.v.).

[Often printed. Ed., trs. and presented in illustrations by Brown, Poona, 1965. Text with Eng. Intro. and exposition by V. Raghavan, Madras, 1972.]

MĀLATĪ-MĀDHAVA : A ten-act *Prakaraṇa* by Bhavabhūti. The theme is the love-story of the young student, Mādhava, and Mālatī, daughter of the minister. Their love has a happy finale through strange vicissitudes and the skilful intervention of the Buddhist nun, Kāmandakī.

[Ed. M. R. Kale with Jagaddhara's comm. and Eng. trs., Delhi, 1967; M. R. Telang, with same comm. and comms. of Tripurāri (i-vii) and of Nānyadeva (viii-x), NPS, 1926; K. S. M. Sastri, with comm. of Pūrṇasarasvatī, TSS, 1953. Trs. into Eng. by Wilson in *Select Specimens*, II; into French by G. Strechly, Paris, 1886; into German by L. Firze, Leipzig, 1884. Also see Eng. trs. by Coulson.]

MĀLAVIKĀGNIMITRA : A drama, in five acts, by Kālidāsa. King Agnimitra, who falls in love with Princess Mālavikā in disguise, embraces her. The youngest queen, Irāvatī, is incensed at this sight, and insults the king. The eldest queen Dhāriṇī, keeps Mālavikā confined with the help of the clever Vidūṣaka : Another meeting takes place between the king and Mālavikā, but does not last owing to the hostile attitude of Irāvatī. Eventually the true identity of Mālavikā is revealed. Dhāriṇī, delighted at the news of her son's victory over the Yavanas, fulfils her promise of reward by giving consent to the king's marriage with Mālavikā. Irāvatī's wrath is also appeased. Thus the drama has a happy denouement.

[Ed. K. P. Parab, NPS, 1915; K. A. S. Aiyar, New Delhi. Trs. into Eng. by C. H. Tawney, Calcutta, 1875 and 1891; into German by Weber, Berlin, 1856; into French by V. Henry, Paris, 1889. Also trs. into Georgian (Russia). See C. K. Raja, *Interpretation of Bharatavākya in Mālavikāgnimitra*, G. Jha Res. Institute, Allahabad. See M. D. Paradkar, *Mālavikāgnimitra, a critical study*, 1971. For full bibliography of Studies in it, see Sten Konow, *Ind. Drama.*]

MĀNAMEYODAYA : According to Keith (*Hist. of Sanskrit Lit.*, 1928, p. 474), written by Nārāyaṇa Bhaṭṭa. According to Radhakrishnan (*Indian Philosophy*, II, 1948, p. 786), section on *māna* written by Nārāyaṇa Bhaṭṭa and that on *meya* by Nārāyaṇa Paṇḍita.

Composed c. 1600 according to Keith, it is of considerable philosophical interest. It summarises, in an interesting manner, Kumārila's epistemology and metaphysics.

[Ed. T. Gaṇapati Sastri, TSS, 1912; ed. and trs. into Eng. by C. K. Raja and S. S. S. Sastri, 2nd. ed., Adyar, 1975.]

MĀNASĀRA : A well-known work on *Vāstu-vidyā*. The extant work, which appears to be a later version, perhaps came into being some time between the 11th century and the

15th. The original work may have been composed in the Gupta period.

[Ed. and trs. P. K. Acarya, in 5 vols. (vol. III Text, vol. IV Eng. trs.), 1927 etc. For *Vāstu-śāstra* in general, see T. P. Bhattacharya, *A Study on Vāstu-vidyā*. Also see P.K. Acharya, *Indian Architecture according to Mānasāra*, Oxford, 1921.]

MANASOLLĀSA : Also called *Abhilaṣitārtha-cintāmaṇi*, it is by the Cālukya king Someśvara. Composed Śaka 1051 (=1129 A.D.), it consists of 100 chapters divided into five Viṃśatis. It deals, *inter alia*, with the means of acquiring a kingdom, means of stabilising a kingdom, royal enjoyments, games and sport. It devotes 2500 verses to music and musical instruments, and touches on new phases of music especially *Prabandhas*.

[Ed. *GOS*, 1961. On its *Matsya-vinoda* chapter, see S. L. Hora in *Jour. of Asiatic Society*, 1951 (3rd. series, Letters) and *As. Soc. Year Book*, 1951. Critical edition of the Music and Dance sections by V. Raghavan, Vol. III ed. G. Shrigondekar, GOS, 1961. See S. S. Misra, *Fine Arts and Technical sciences in ancient India with special reference to Mānasollāsa*, Varanasi, 1982.]

There is a paraphrase, by Sureśvara, called *Mānasollāsa*, of Śaṃkara's *Dakṣiṇāmūrti-stotra*.

MĀNAVA-DHARMAŚĀSTRA : Same as *Manusmṛti* (q.v.).

MĀNAVA-ŚRAUTASŪTRA : Perhaps the oldest work of the kind. See *Śrautasūtra* for the general description of this literature.

[Books I—V, ed. F. Knauer, St Petersburg, 1900 ff.]

MANDASOR INSCRIPTION : See Vatsabhaṭṭi.

[For the inscription and notes thereon, see D. C. Sircar, *Select Instriptions*, I, Calcutta, 1942, pp. 281-97.]

MĀṆḌŪKYA-KĀRIKĀ : Attributed to Gauḍapāda, it is a commentary on the *Māṇḍūkyopaniṣad*.

[Ed. See C. Conio, *The Philosophy of Māṇḍukya-Kārikā*, Italy (University of Florence), 1971.]

MĀṆḌŪKYOPANIṢAD : It describes, in course of explaining Oṃkāra, the three stages of soul, known as *Jāgrat*, *Svapna* and *Suṣupti*, as well as the fourth stage which is eternal and immutable, and then explains the significance of Oṃkāra.

[For Ed. see under *Īśopaniṣad*. Trs. into Italian by Carpani, pub. in Italian Journal *Samādhi*, Bologna, 1935-36; into Eng. (with Gauḍapāda-kārikā) by S. Nikhilānanda. See Svāmi Krishnananda, *Māṇḍūkya Upaniṣad—an exposition*, Sivanandanagar, 1977; Svāmī Rama, M. Upaniṣad, Enlightenment without God, Honesdale, Pa, 1982.]

MANTRA-MAHODADHI : Written in twentyfive sections (*Taraṅgas*), it consists of *mantras* of different deities, composed in Anuṣṭubh metre by Mahīdhara who is supposed to be identical with the author of this name to whom is attributed a commentary on the *Yajurveda* and who is believed to have flourished round about 1600 A.D.

[Ed., with elaborate Intro., author's commentary, *Naukā*, Delhi, 1981. Trs. into Hindi, with a Hindi comm. by S. Chaturvedi, Varanasi, 1981.]

MANU-SMṚTI : The earliest and most authoritative versified Smṛti ascribed to Manu or to his followers. It consists of 2,694 verses divided into 12 chapters. Acc. to Bühler, followed by Kane, the extant *Manu-smṛti* was written in the period between the second century B.C. and the second century A.D. Its contents are briefly as follows :

I. Creation of the world, the cycles of ages, characteristics of the four Yugas, duties and privileges of four castes.

II. Definition and sources of *Dharma*, broad divisions of the land of India, *Saṃskāras*.

III. *Saṃskāras*, marriage, duties of husband and wife, five daily *Yajñas*, *Śrāddhas*.

IV. Conduct of householders, *Snātakas*, occasions for cessation of study, food and drink.

V. Food and drink, *Aśauca*, duties of a wife and a widow.

VI. Mode of life of a *Vānaprastha*, a *Parivrājaka*, praise of a *Gṛhastha*.

VII. *Rājadharma*

VIII. *Vyavahāra*

IX. Legal duties of husband and wife, age of marriage, partition, kinds of sons and their rights, succession, *Strīdhana*, exclusion from inheritance, impartible property, sins and modes of expiation, constituents of a state, duties of Vaiśyas and Śūdras.

X. Privileges and duties of castes, *Āpaddharma*, valid modes of acquisition and means of livelihood.

XI. Gifts, sins and Prāyaścitta.

XII. Disquisition on *Karma*, liberation, eulogy of the Veda, result of the study of *Mānavaśāstra*.

[Ed. V. N. Mandlik, with several commentaries; V. L. Pansikar, NSP, 1933 (with Kullūka's comm.); G. Jha, with *Medhātithibhāṣya*, Asiatic Soc., Cal., Vol. I, 1932, Vol. II, 1939; G. Sastri Nene, with Kullūka's comm. and *Maṇiprabhā* Hindi comm., Intro., interpolated Verses and Index etc., Varanasi, 1982 (3rd. ed.). Ed. H.K. Dave, with one comm., Bombay; J.L. Sastri with Introduction by S. C. Baneji, Kullūka' Comm., Collection of Verses attributed to Manu but missing in the present editions of the *Manusmṛti*, Index of Verses, 1975, Delhi; N. N. Banerjee, *Manu and Modern Times*, New Delhi. Trs. into English by Bühler, *SBE*, Vol. 25; and by A. C. Burnell (ed. Hopkins, London, 1884) and also by G. Strehly, Paris, 1893. For influence of the *Manu-Smṛti* in places outside India, see K. Motwani, *Manu Dharmaśāstra*, Madras, 1958. Bhagwan Das's *The Science of Social Organisation or Laws of Manu*, Adyar, Madras, 1932-33, is an important contribution. For various problems connected with the work, see P. V. Kane, *History of Dharmaśāstra*,, I, 1968. For commentaries, see *Manu-ṭikā-saṃgraha*, ed. J. Jolly, Bib. Ind., 1885; J. D. M. Derrett (ed. & trs.) *Bhāruci's Commentary on the Manusṃrti*,

Wiesbaden, 1975. Also see M. D. Paradkar, *Similes in Manu-Smṛti*; C. Tewari, *Śūdras in Manu*, 1963; R. M. Das, *Women in Manu and his seven commentators*; V. S. Agrawala, *India as described by Manu*, 1969; M. V. Patwardhan, *Manusmṛti or the ideal democratic republic of Manu*, 1968; F. Laszlo, *Die parallel version der Manusmṛti in Bhaviṣya-purāṇa*, Wiesbaden, 1971. Also see L. Sternbach, *Mānava Dharma-śāstra (i-iii) and Bhaviṣya-purāṇa*, Varanasi, 1974; R. N. Sharma, *Ancient India according to Manu*; J. W. Laine on Creation Account, *ABORI*, LXII, 1951, p. 157.]

MANVARTHA-MUKTĀVALĪ : Title of Kullūka's Commentary on *Manu-smṛti*. Brief, but lucid and very popular.

[Ed. with text of *Manu-smṛti*, NSP, 1933.]

MARKAṆḌEYA PURĀṆA : For general characteristics of Purāṇas, see Purāṇa. A large portion of it is covered by such legends and narratives as have very close connection with legends of *Mahābhārata*. Contains many didactic stories. There are also dialogues relating to housholder's duties, utility of rites and sacrifice etc. A portion is called *Devī-māhātmya, Saptaśatī, Durgāmāhātmya, Caṇḍī etc.*

It describes such glorious deeds of the goddess (*Ādyā-śakti*—Primeval Energy) as the slaughter of demons etc. The *Caṇḍī* is held in great veneration, its recitation is indispensable in *Durgā-pūjā* and in many other rites and rituals. Moreover, its recitation is believed to ward off evils and dangers. Some Brahmins consider it their daily duty to recite the whole of it or at least a part. It was probably written some time before the 6th century A.D.

[Ed. P. Tarkaratna, Calcutta, 1316 B. S. (4th. ed.); K. M. Banerji, *Bib. Ind.*, Calcutta, 1862. Trs. into Eng. by F. E. Pargiter, *Bib. Ind.*, 1904 (Reprint, 1968).]

MĀTAṄGA-LĪLĀ : A work by Nīlakaṇṭha, in 12 chapters (263 verses), on elephant-lore. Acc. to Keith, it was composed by Nārāyaṇa.

[Ed. Ganapati Sastri, Trivandrum, 1910. Trs. into Eng. by Edgerton, New Haven, 1931; into German by Zimmer, Berlin, 1929.]

MĀṬHARA-VṚTTI : Written by Māṭharācārya, it is regarded as the lost original of the *Sāṃkhya-kārikā-vṛtti*, translated into Chinese by Paramārtha (born 499 A.D.). The *Māṭharavṛtti* knows the three-membered syllogism of *pakṣa*, *hetu* and *dṛṣṭānta*. The *Gauḍapāda-bhāṣya*, an abridgment of the *Māṭhara-vṛtti*, is by one Gauḍapāda who was different from Gauḍapāda, author of the *Gauḍapāda-kārikā*, and the teacher of Śaṃkarācārya's teacher.

[For detailed information about the *Māṭhara-vṛtti* and its author, see S. K. Belvalkar in *Bhandarkar Comm. Volume*. Poona, 1917.]

MATSYAPURĀṆA : Also called *Matsya*. It conforms, in a large measure, to the traditional definition of Purāṇas. It relates the Flood Legend in which Viṣṇu, in the form of a fish, rescues Manu alone. The lists of kings, contained in it, are particularly useful for the Andhra dynasty. It is as much Śaivite as Vaiṣṇavite in character. There are many later interpolations in it.

[Ed. P. Tarkaratna, Calcutta, 1316 B. S.; B. D. Basu, *SBH*, Vol. XVII, Pts. 1-2, Allahabad, 1916-17. See V. R. R. Diksitar, *Matsyapurāṇa—a study*, Madras, 1935; V.S. Agrawala, *Matsya-purāṇa—a study*, Varanasi, 1963; A. Hohenberger, *Die indische Flutsage und das Matsyapurāṇa*, Leipzig, 1930; S. G. Kantawala, *Cultural History from the Matsyapurāṇa*, Baroda, 1964. Trs. into Eng. by one Taluqdar of Oudh. Also see V. Raghavan's Svalpa matsyapurāṇa, pub. serially in *Purāṇa* Bulletin, Varanasi; N. M. Sen, *Purāṇa*, 4. 1; Some Linguistic Aberrations in the Matsyapurāṇya, Do. 5. 2.]

MATTA-VILĀSA : A drama, in one act, belonging to the *Prahasana* class, by Mahendra-vikramavarman, a king of the Pallava dynasty, who ruled in Kāñcī about 620 A.D. It depicts the drunken revelry of a Śaiva mendicant bearing a human skull in lieu of an alms-bowl, his wandering with his wench on his way to a tavern, his scuffle with a Buddhist monk whom he accuses of theft of his bowl, his appeal to a Pāśupata to settle the dispute and the final recovery of the bowl from a mad fellow who had snatched it from a stray dog. It shows some features similar to those in the dramas attributed to Bhāsa.

[Ed. T. Ganapati Sastri, TSS, 1917; N. P. Unni with Eng. trs., 1974. Eng. trs. by L. D. Barnett *BSOS*, V. 1930; also by C. C. Mehta, in *Three Sanskrit Lighter Delights*, Baroda, 1969. On the work, see L. D. Barnett in JRAS, 1919, *BSOS*, 1920, I, pt. 3.]

MAYAMATA : A work on religious and secular architecture, and town planning.

[Ed. T. Ganapati Sastri, TSS, 1919. Ed. and trs. B. Dagens, *Mayamata* : traite Sanskrit d' architecture etc., chaps. i-xxv, Pondichery, 1970.]

MEDINĪ-KOŚA : Real title *Anekārtha-śabdakośa*. It is a lexicon, by Medinīkara, containing the meaning and gender of words. In it the words are arranged as *Ka-kārānta.*, *Kha-kārānta*, *Ga-kārānta*, etc., It contains also words having the same meaning as well as words conveying two senses.

[Ed. J. Hosinga, Banaras, 1940 (*Nānārtha-koṣa*). Also see references under Medinīkara.]

MEGHADŪTA : A love lyric or rather a monody by Kālidāsa. It is divided into two parts called Pūrva-megha and Uttara-megha, the total number of verses varying from 110 to 121 in the different versions. A Yakṣa, banished to Rāmagiri for a year for dereliction of duty, pines for his beloved staying in Alakā. At the advent of the rains, he becomes disconsolate, and chooses the cloud to carry his tidings to his beloved. At first, he gives a detailed itinerary for the cloud asking it to act en route as desired by him. In the second part, Yakṣa describes the supernatural beauty of Alakā and tells the cloud the message to be delivered to his sweat-heart. The existence of some 50 commentaries on the work is an index to its popularity. The *Meghadūta* inspired a number of imitations, e.g. the *Pavana-dūta* of Dhoyī, the *Haṃsa-dūta* of Rūpagosvāmin etc.

[Ed., with metrical Eng. trs., H. H. Wilson, 1943 (2nd ed.); with comm. of Mallinātha and Cāritravardhana, N. S.

Khiste, CSS, 1931; with Eng. trs. and extracts from comm. of Mallinātha, Dakṣiṇāvartanātha and Vallabha, R. D. Karmarkar, Poona, 1947. Critically ed., on up-to-date principles, by S. K. De, *Sāhitya Akademi*, New Delhi, 1970 (2nd rev. ed.). Ed., with *Kātyāyanī* comm. and Eng. trs. by C. Maharaj; with Kṛṣṇapati's comm., by G. M. Bhattacharya, Kuruksetra, 1974; with Bhāvānuvāda in Hindi verse, by A. Mitra, Allahabad, 1979.

Eng. trs., with transliterated text and notes, by G. H. Rooke, London, 1935. Meghadūta and Ṛtusaṃhāra of Kālidāsa, text and French trs. by R. H. Assier de Pompigman, Paris, 1938. See S. K. De, Some commentators on the Meghadūta, *Our Heritage* (Calcutta Sanskrit College jour.) III. P. K. Gode, A quotation etc......comm. on Meghadūta, by Mahimahamsagane etc., *ABORI*, XIV. On the Dūta-kāvyas in Sanskrit, see C. Chakravarti in *IHQ*, III. Also see V. K. Paranjpe, *Fresh Light on Kālidāsa's Meghadūta*, Poona; P. C. Bhattacharya, *Meghadūta of Kālidāsa*, Calcutta, 1981. S. K. De's paper on A select bibliography for the textual study of Kālidāsa's Meghadūta (*S.K. Belvalkar Felicitation Vol.*, Banaras, 1957) may be consulted. See P. Bhattacharya, *Meghadūta-puricaya* (in Bengali), Calcutta, 1376 B. S.; A.V. Subramanian, A suggested source for Meghasandeśa, *Summaries of papers*, AIOC Silver Jubilee Session, 1969, p. 65; B. Bhattacharya, A critical Re-examination of the variants *prathama-divase* and *praśama-divase* in Kālidāsa's *Meghadūta*, *V. Raghavan Felicitation Vol.*, P.509. On asthetic realisation and poetic image in the poem, see A. K. Datta, *Summaries of papers*, 1974; P. Sen, *Bhāratātmā-kavikālidāsa* (in Bengali); I. Chakravarty, Image in Meghadūta, *Summaries of papers*, *AIOC* 1974; S. Chattopadhyay, On the opening Verse of the Meghadūta, *Luderik Sternbach Fel. Vol.*, Lucknow, 1979.]

MĪMĀṂSĀNUKRAMAṆĪ : A Mīmāṃsā work by Maṇḍana Miśra.

MĪMĀṂSĀ-NYĀYA-PRAKĀŚA : Written by Āpadeva, and popularly called Āpadevī, it is a good introduction to Pūrva-mīmāṃsā philosophy. It professes to summarise the essential doctrines of the whole Mīmāṃsā system. The author generally adopts the views of Pārthasārathimiśra.

[Ed., with a Skt. comm. by T. Vīrarāghavācārya, Tirupati, 1935; with *Arthadarśanī* comm., by A. Devaśarmā, Calcutta, 1922. Eng. trs. by F. Edgerton, London, 1929.]

MĪMĀṂSĀ-SŪTRA : Attributed to Jaimini. Written in twelve chapters, it describes the various sacrifices and their purposes, the theory of Apūrva (q.v.) as well as some philosophical propositions. The first chapter discusses the sources of knowledge and the validity of the Vedas.

[Ed. *Bib. Ind.*, 1873 ff. (with comm. of Śabarasvāmin); M. Sandal (with Eng. trs.) with *Śabara Bhāṣya*, *Ślokavārtika* and *Ṭupṭīkā*, G. Sāstrī Musalagaonkar, in 4 vols., Banaras. Trs. into Eng. by G. Jha, *SBH* 10, 1910; by N. V. Thadani, 1952. See Keith, *The Karmamīmāṃsā*, 1921; K. A. Nīlakaṇṭha Sastri, *IA*, I. Also see *Mīmāṃsā-kośa* (Jaimini Mīmāṃsā-sūtra Concordance), Pts. 1-2, ed. K. Sarasvati, 1952-53; G. P. Bhatt, *Epistemology of the Bhāṭṭa School of Pūrva-mīmāṃsā*; G. Jha, *Pūrvamīmāṃsā in its sources*; A. S. N. Aiyyar, *Mīmāṃsā Jurisprudence*.]

MITĀKṢARĀ : It is a commentary, on the *Yājñavalkya-smṛti* by Vijñāneśvara. Though a commentary, yet it is a sort of Smṛti digest as it cites and discusses the views of different writers on Smṛti. It is of paramount authority in matters relating to adoption, inheritance and succession etc. all over India excepting where the *Dāyabhāga* prevails, as in Bengal. It recognises the birth-right of a son to the father's ancestral property. There are numerous commentaries on it, the very famous among them being those of Viśveśvara, Nandapaṇḍita and Bālambhaṭṭa.

[Ed., S. S. Setlur, with sub-comm. *Subodhinī* and *Bālambhaṭṭī*, Madras, 1912; with the text of the *Yājñavalkya-smṛti*, V. L. S. Pansikar, NSP, 1926 (3rd ed.). Trs. into Eng. with the *Dāyabhāga*, H. T. Colebrooke Calcutta, 1810; with the trs. of the *Yājñavalkya-smṛti*, by J. R. Gharpure, 4 pts., Bombay, 1936—39]

There is a commentary, called *Mitākṣarā*, by Haradatta, on the *Gautama-dharmasūtra*.

S. S. Svamin's comm. on Gauḍapāda's *Māṇḍūkya-kārikā* is also called *Mitākṣarā*.

MOHAMUDGARA : A short poetical composition ascribed to Śaṃkarācārya. It is lyrical in form and didactic in content. It seeks to inculcate the correct attitude to life by pointing out the common human frailties. Much of it features as the *Dvādaśa-pañjarikā-stotra*.

[Ed. Haeberlin, 265 f.f.]

MṚCCHAKAṬIKA : A ten-act drama by Śūdraka. It is unique in the sense that it breaks away from the banal theme of royal life. The drama deals with the love-story of the Brahmin Cārudatta, once very rich but now impoverished and nevertheless large-hearted, and the rich courtesan Vasantasenā. It describes how steadfast is their mutual love and how, through strange vicissitudes of life, they are united in wedlock. Parallel to this love-story runs the political story of how the bad king Pālaka was dethroned and slain by Āryaka. This social drama, breathing as it does a plebeian atmosphere, is regarded as the most Shakespearian of all Sanskrit plays. The drama has taken its name from an earthen cart (*mṛtśakaṭikā*) with which Rohasena, Cārudatta's son, was playing. He was crying for a golden cart instead, and, moved to pity, Vasantasenā gave away her golden ornaments wherewith to make a golden cart for him.

[Ed. K. P. Parab, with comm. of Pṛthvīdhara, NSP, 1922 (5th ed.); with Eng. trs. and notes, M. R. Kale, Bombay, 1924; with Skt. and Hindi comm., by R. Ojha, Banaras, 1963. Trs. into English by A. W. Ryder, *HOS*, 1905; by R. P. Oliver, Illinois, 1938; by J. A. B. van Buitenen (Two plays of Ancient India), 1971. Trs. several times into German, French and into other languages. Bengali trs. by S. Bhattacharji, Sahitya Akademi, New Delhi, 1979. See S. Purvedi, *Mṛcchakaṭika Śāstrīya, Sāmājika evaṃ Rājanītika adhyayan* (Hindi, Varanasi, 1982). The following papers may be consulted :

B. FADDEGON : Mṛcchakaṭika and King Lear, *J. P. Vogel Pres. Vol.*, Leyden, 1947.

S. Mukherjee : Ujjayinī in Mṛcchakaṭika, *B. C. Law Vol.*, II, Poona, 1946.

V. C. Sarkar : Marriage with Courtesans in Ancient India, *P. K. Gode Comm. Vol.*, Poona, 1960-I.

R. G. Basak : Indian Society as pictured in the Mṛcchakaṭika, *IHQ*, 1929, pp. 229-325.]

MUDRĀ-RĀKṢASA: A seven-act drama by Viśākhadatta. The main plot is the winning over, through astute diplomacy, by Cāṇakya, minister of the Maurya King Candragupta, of Rākṣasa, the faithful and efficient minister of the Nandas. It has certain features that distinguish it from other classical Sanskrit dramas. Contrary to the usual practice, it is written on a purely political theme. Secondly, it is practically devoid of female characters, there being a solitary female character playing an insignificant role.

[Ed. K. T. Telang, with Ḍhuṇḍirāja's comm., Bombay 1928 (7th ed.) ; K. H. Dhruva, with Eng. trs., Poona, 1923 (2nd ed.) ; A. Hillebrandt, Breslau, 1935. Trs. into Eng. by Wilson in *Select Specimens*, vol. II; French by V. Henry, Paris, 1888; into German by L. Fritze, Leipzig, 1883. See G. V. Devasthali, *Intro. to the study of the Mudrārākṣasa*; K. M. Byrski, Analysis of Mudrārākṣasa, Weimer, 1979; by Coulson; J. A. B. van Buitenen (*Two plays of Ancient India*), 1971.]

MUGDHABODHA : A grammar, designed for beginners, written by Vopadeva under Mahādeva of Devagiri. It was very popular in Bengal. The object of the author was simplicity coupled with brevity. He has adopted partly the method of the *Kātantra* and partly the system of Pāṇini's grammar. Vopadeva has omitted the Vedic portion of the *Aṣṭādhyāyī*. A striking feature of this grammar is that, in examples illustrating the rules, it uses, wherever possible, the names of gods, e.g. Hari, Hara, Rāma. Thus, it was, to a great extent, the precursor of the later sectrarian grammars.

[Ed. Böhtlingk, St. Petersburg, 1847; S. Siromani and A. N.

Nyayaratna (7 fascicules), *Bib. Ind.* 1911-13; G. Vidyaratna, with a comm. based on comm. of Durgādāsa, Rāma Tarkavāgīśa and Gaṅgādhara Tarkavāgīśa, and notes showing harmony of aphorisms with those of Pāṇini, Calcutta, 1891.]

MUGDHOPADEŚA : A didactic poem in 66 verses, by Jahlaṇa who is different from Jahlaṇa, the compiler of the anthology called *Sūkti-muktāvalī*. It contains warnings against the wiles and snares of harlots. He says that love is as impossible in a harlot as want of restlessness in a monkey.

[Ed. *Kāvyamālā*, VIII.]

MUKTĀ-CARITRA : A *Campū-kāvya* by Raghunāthadāsa. It deals with *Dāna-līlā* included under *Naimittika-līlā* of Kṛṣṇa. In Dvārakā Satyabhāmā asks Kṛṣṇa whether or not pearls grow on trees. In reply Kṛṣṇa tells her about his producing pearls on a tree at Vṛndāvana. Incidentally he mentions his sports with Rādhā and other Gopīs there.

[Ed. N. Brahmachari, Vrindavana, 1917(in Bengali characters).]

MŪLAMADHYAMAKA-KĀRIKĀ : See *Mādhyamika-kārikā.*

MUṆḌAKOPANIṢAD: Divided into three sections (*Muṇḍaka*), it deals with the following matters :—

(i) Classification of knowledge into *Parā* and *Aparā*, the perishable result obtained through *Aparā Vidyā.*

(ii) Nature and the means of meditation upon Brahman.

(iii) Meditation upon Brahman, its result and *Brahma-nirvāṇa.*

[For ed., see under *Īśopaniṣat.* Also ed. J. L. Kamboja, Delhi, 1982; S. Tiwari, with Śāṃkara-bhāṣya, New Delhi, 1981. Trs. into Eng. by Gambhirananda, Calcutta, 1978.]

NĀḌĪ-PRAKĀŚA : It is a noteworthy Āyurvedic work composed by Śaṃkara Sena in the 16th century. The author utilised the works of Kaṇāda, Gautama and Rāvaṇa.

[Ed., with comm. and Bengali trs., by N. Sen, Calcutta, 1914.]

NĀGĀNANDA : A five-act drama by Śrīharṣa, based on a Buddhist legend. Jīmūtavāhana, prince of the Vidyādharas, falls in love with Malayavatī, princess of the Siddhas, and eventually marries her. One day, moved to pity at the news of the serpents being killed by Garuḍa, Jīmūtavāhana offers himself to be devoured by Garuḍa and is killed by the latter. Brought back to life through the mercy of Gaurī, Jīmūtavāhana begins to spend his days happily with Malayavatī.

[Ed. T. Ganapati Sastri, with comm. of Śivarāma, *TSS*, 1917; *Bib. Ind.*, 1957 (with Tibetan trs.); K. Krishnamoorthy, with Intro., Eng. trs. and notes. Eng. trs. by P. Boyd, London, 1872, and by H. Wartham, London and New York, 1911; French trs. by A. Bergaigne, 1879.]

NAIṢADHA-CARITA : A *Mahākāvya*, in 22 cantos, by Śrīharṣa who is different from Śrīharṣa, author of the dramas called *Ratnāvalī*, *Priyadarśikā* and *Nāgānanda*. Based on the *Mahābhārata* (III. 50-70) story of Nala and Damayantī, it describes the events up to the marriage of Nala and Damayantī and the arrival of Kali in the capital of Nala. Among departures from the original, a notable one is the character of Nala. In the epic, he is a conscientious and selfless courier of gods to Damayantī, while, in the poem, he fails in his mission thus causing mental conflict in himself and making himself feel that his honour is compromised. The poet is traditionally praised by Indian critics for *Pada-lālitya* (gracefulness of words) in this poetical composition. Many modern scholars find in it bad taste and gross artificialities which mar its quality as a poem. There are more than 20 commentaries on the work.

[Ed. Sivadatta and Pansikar, with Nārāyaṇa's comm. and extracts from comm. of Mallinātha, Vidyādhara, Jinarāja, Cāritravardhana and Narahari, NSP, 1952 (9th ed.); J. Vidyāsāgara, with Mallinātha's comm., 2 vols., Calcutta, 1875-76. Eng. trs., with extracts from 8 commentaries, by

K. K. Handiqui, Lahore, 1934. See P. Bandyopadhyaya, *Observations on Similes in Naiṣadhacarita*, Calcutta, 1966; A. N. Jani, *Critical Survey of Śrīharṣa's Naiṣadhacaritam*. There is a comm. of Narahari a MS of which exists in Kurukṣetra University, Haryana, India.]

NAIṢKARMYA-SIDDHI : A work, by Sureśvara, on the Vedānta Philosophy of Śaṃkarācārya. In this work, written in prose and memorial verses, the author tries to prove that knowledge alone achieves release.

[Ed. Jagadānanda, 1953; S. Sarasvatī with *Kleśāpahāriṇī* comm., Holenarsipuram, 1968.]

NALA-CAMPŪ : Also called *Damayanti-kathā*, it is the earliest known *Campū-kāvya*. It is by Trivikrama Bhaṭṭa, and, in seven chapters, a small part of the epic story of Nala and Damayantī is narrated. It is full of stylistic affectations of laboured composition.

[Ed. Durgaprasad and Sivadatta, with comm. of Caṇḍapāla, Bombay, 1921; *CSS*, 1932].

NALODAYA : A *Yamaka-kāvya* ascribed to Kālidāsa by some, to Ravideva by others, to Vāsudeva, protégé of Kulaśekhara and Rāma, by yet others. The ascription to Kālidāsa is generally rejected. It deals with the well-known story of Nala.

[Ed., with *Subodhinī* comm., notes, and Latin trs., F. Benary, Berlin, 1830; W. Yates, with metrical Eng. trs., Calcutta, 1844. On the queston of authorship, see Pischel, *ZDMG*, LVI, R. G. Bhandarkar, *Report*, 1883-94; A. R. Ayyar in *JRAS*, 1925.].

NĀMALIṄGĀNUŚĀSANA : Popularly known as *Amarakośa*. A standard lexicon, by Amarasiṃha, arranged in three books, viz. *Svargādi-kāṇḍa*, *Bhūmyādi-kāṇḍa* and *Sāmānya-kāṇḍa*. The work is synonymous, and its last part contains an appendix on homonyms, indeclinables and genders. Of its many commentators, special mention is deserved by Kṣīrasvāmin (11th cent.), Sarvānanda (1159) and Rāyamukuṭa (1431). Trs. with more than fifty commentaries into

Chinese by Guṇarāta of Ujjain in the fifth century A.D. The work contains many words not usually met with in Sanskrit literature.

[Ed. Jhalakikar and Bhandarkar, BSS, 1886 (with Maheśvara's comm.); H. T. Colebrooke, Calcutta, 1891; with Bhānuji Dīkṣita's comm., NSP, Bombay, 1905; with Eng. equivalents and Kṣīrasvāmin's comm., H. D. Sharma and N. G. Sardesai, Poona, 1941; A. Barua, with comm. of Kṣīrasvāmin and Rāyamukuṭa and extracts from other comm., Berhampur (Mursidabad), 1887; T. G. Sastri, with comm. of Kṣīrasvāmin and Sarvānanda, TSS, 1914-17; K. K. Datta, with *Padacandrikā* comm. of Rāyamukuṭa, Vol. I, fasc. I. Calcutta, 1966. A. A. Ramanathan, with comm. of Liṅgayasūri and Mallinātha, Adyar Library Series, No. 101, Madras, 1971. Also see *Amarakoṣa with South Indian commentaries*, ed. by H. Sastri, with comm. of Bhānuji Dīkṣita, *Maṇiprabhā-prakāśa*, Hindi comm., Notes, etc., 1970; with comm. of Kṛṣṇamitra, Eng. equivalents etc. by S. D. Mishra. Lokesh Chandra, *Amarakoṣa in Tibet*, Delhi. Latin trs. by W. Bartholome, Rome, 1798; Chinese trs. by Guṇarāta, 6th cent. A.D. (Vide M. Muller, *India : What can it teach us*, p. 328). A Tibetan version was published in 1912. For information about agriculture in the *Nāmaliṅgānuśāsana*, see G. P. Majumdar, *Vanaspati*, Calcutta, 1927, pp. 217-219. For its value as a lexicon, see S. M. Katre, Amara's contribution to Indian lexicography, *Vikrama Volume*, Ujjain, 1948. A valuable study is by C. D. Deshmukh, New Delhi, 1981.]

NĀNĀRTHA-KOŚA : Same as *Medinī-kośa* (q.v.).

NĀRADA-PAÑCARĀTRA : A well known work of the Pāñcarātra sect. The *Bṛhad-brahma-saṃhitā* supposed to belong to this work, cannot be dated earlier the 12th cent. The *Jñānāmṛta-sāra-saṃhitā*, published with the title *Nārada-pañcarātra* and devoted entirely to the glorification of Kṛṣṇa and Rādhā is believed by some modern scholars to be apocryphal dating back to the begining of 16th cent. A.D.

NĀRADA-PURĀṆA : An important Purāṇic work of the Vaiṣṇavas containing all the characteristics of a Mahāpurāṇa it is encylopaedic. It deals with religion, philosophy mythology, Vedāṅgas, *Vratas*, *tīrthas*, geographical matter. It contains several tales illustrating ethical principles or religious precepts.

[Ed. G. V. Tagare with Eng. trs. and annotation etc.; trs. with notes by H.N. Chakrabarti, Pts. I-IV, Delhi. See *A Critical Study* by K. D. Nambier, Varanasi 1979; *A Philosophical Study* by S. S. Upadhyaya, Muzaffarpur, 1983.]

NĀRADĪYA-ŚIKṢĀ : See Śikṣā. Written in two parts, each consisting of *Khaṇḍas* or chapters, and attributed to Nārada, it deals with the music of Sāman generally and as chanted at sacrifices. It serves as a link between the Vedic and post-Vedic music, and is the earliest extant record of musical divisions and terminology.

[Ed. S. Samasrami, Bombay; with the *Vivaraṇa* and *Vivaraṇa-prakāśa*, Mysore, 1949.]

NAREŚVARAPARĪKṢĀ : A philosophical work, by Sadyajyoti, in three chapters. It examines the nature of the individual soul (*nara*) and the Supreme Being (*Īśvara*). It is virtually the sole extant source of our knowledge about the Dualistic school of Kashmir Śaivism.

[Ed. M. Kaul, with the *Prakāśa* comm., *KSTS*, No. 45, Srinagar, 1926.]

NARMAMĀLĀ : A satirical work, in three sections, by Kṣemendra. The poet's satirical diatribe is directed against wicked people, particularly against the Kāyasthas who used to hold high offices and oppress the people.

[Ed. M. Kaul, KSTS, Poona, 1923.]

NĀṬAKA-CANDRIKĀ : A dramaturgical work by Rūpa Gosvāmin. The author says that, in composing it, he consulted the *Bharata-śāstra* and the *Rasārṇava-sudhākara*, but rejected the *Sāhitya-darpaṇa* as being opposed to Bharata's views. It consists of eight sections dealing respectively with the following topics :—

General characteristics of a drama, the hero, the divisions of a *Rūpaka*, elements of the action and their classification, *Arthopakṣepakas* and their divisions (viz. *Viṣkambhaka* etc.), division of acts and scenes, distribution of dialects, styles of dramatic composition and their employment.

The illustrations are taken mostly from Vaiṣṇava works. [Ed. Puridasa, Mymensing, 1948.]

NĀṬAKA-LAKṢAṆA-RATNAKOŚA : Written by Sāgaranandin, it brings together a number of views of different notable writers on important topics of dramaturgy. The topics dealt with are :

1. *Rūpaka* and its ten varieties.
2—5. *Avasthās*, dialects to be used, *Artha-prakṛtis*.
6—10. *Upakṣepakas*, *Sandhis*, *Patākāsthānas*, *Vṛttis*.
11. Excellences of the hero.
12—13. Thirty-six *Nāṭya-lakṣaṇas*, *Guṇas*, *Nāṭyālaṃkāras*.
14—16. *Rasas* and *Bhāvas*.
17. Types of heroine and their excellences.
18. Minor forms of drama.

The work is important not only for the collection of various views on these topics, but also for its citation of a large number of dramatic and dramaturgic works.

[Ed. M. Dillon, Oxford University Press, 1937; B. L. Sukla, Banaras, 1972 with a Hindi comm. Trs. into Eng., with notes, by V. Raghavan jointly with M. Dillon and M. Fowler, American Philosophical Society, Philadelphia, 1960. On the date of its composition, see P. K. Gode, *Studies in Indian Literary History*, II, p. 48 ff. Also see S. Chattopadhyaya, *Nāṭaka-lakṣaṇa-ratna-kośa* in the perspective of Ancient Indian Drama and Dramaturgy, Vol. I, Calcutta, 1973; Text, Bengali trs. and notes, Calcutta, 1978.]

NĀṬAKA-PARIBHĀṢĀ : By Śingabhūpāla, it is a work on dramaturgy. In 268 verses, it deals with technical terms of dramaturgy in a terse but lucid language. It contains dramaturgic treatment of language, mode of address and names of major dramatic elements along with the ten types of Sanskrit. The work has some peculiarities of its own.

[See H. Dholakia, paper read at AIOC, Viśvabhārati, 1980.]

NĀṬYA-DARPAṆA : Ascribed jointly to Rāmacandra and Guṇacandra, it deals, in four chapters called *Vivekas,* with Dramaturgy. It mentions twelve varieties of *Rūpakas* and a number of *Uparūpakas.*

[Ed. G. K. Shrigondekar and L. B. Gandhi, GOS, 1929. For a discussion on its date of composition, see P. K. Gode, *Studies in Indian Literary History,* I, p. 36 ff. Also see *The Nāṭyadarpaṇa of Rāmachandra and Guṇacandra : a critical study,* by K. H. Trivedi, Ahmedabad, 1966.]

NĀṬYA-ŚĀSTRA : The earliest extant work on Dramaturgy, attributed to Bharata. The treatise, in its present form, is considered to be the result of additions by later hands. It is an elaborate work covering as it does the whole ground connected with the drama. It deals with the theatre, the religious rites to be performed at every representation, the dress and equipment of actors, the music, dance, movements and gestures of actors, the different classes of drama and the emotions and sentiments which constitute the vital element in the drama. It anticipates many of the concepts elaborated in later works on Poetics. It, for the first time, states the nature of *Rasa* and enumerates eight sentiments.

[Ed. CSS, Banaras, 1929; with Abhinavabhāratī, by M. R. Kavi, in 4 vols., GOS, 1926 onward. Also ed. M. M. Ghosh 1967; ed. Kedarnath, Delhi, 1983, Reprint, Kāvyamālā 427. Trs. into English by M. Ghosh, Bibliotheca Indica, Vols. I, II, 1951, 1961. Revised second ed. of Vol. I, Calcutta, 1967. See *Le Gitālaṃkāra* Sur la musique Edition critique traduction Francaise et introduction, Par Danielou et N. R. Bhatt, Pondicherry, 1959 and *Bharata-kośa,* compiled by M. R. Kavi, Tirupati, 1951. Rev. ed. of *Bharatakośa* by V. Raghavan. Also see A. Rangacarya, *Introduction to Bharata's Nāṭyaśāstra,* Bombay, 1966; G. K. Bhat, *Bharata-nāṭyamañjarī,* Poona, 1975; R. L. Singhal, *Aristotle and Bharata,* Chandigarh,

1977. See N. V. P. Unithiri, A critical study of the Sāmānyābhinayādhyāya of Nāṭyaśāstra...variant readings, *Summaries of Papers*, 5th World Skt. Conf., Varanasi, 1981, p. 200; C. J. Nayak, Religious Sects in the Nāṭyaśāstra etc. *Summaries of papers, AIOC*, 1974; P. S. Gupta, A Fresh Light upon...Śṛṅgāra Rasa in the N.S., Ibid; G. H. Tarlekar, *Studies in Nāṭyaśāstra*, 1975; S. A. Srinivasan, *On the composition of the Nāṭyaśāstra*, Reinbek, 1980.]

NĀṬYAŚĀSTRA-SAṂGRAHA : A collection of texts on dramaturgy, made by Uṭaka Govindāchār at the order of the Mahratta kings of Tanjore. It consists of two parts. The first part deals with the different movements of *Aṅgas, Upāṅgas* and *Pratyaṅgas*. It is based entirely on the *Saṃgīta-ratnākara* (chap. VII) of Śārṅgadeva. The second part consists of texts culled from different sources the chief of which are the *Saṃgīta-muktāvalī* of Devendra, *Śṛṅgāra-śekhara* of Bhallaṭa, *Saṃgīta-darpaṇa* of Dāmodara and *Saṃgīta-makaranda* of Vedasūri.

[Ed. with Eng. and Tamil trs. of the Marathi version, by K. V. Sastri and A. K. M. Row Sahib and G. N. Rao, Tanjore, 1953.]

NAVASĀHASĀṄKA-CARITA : A historical poem, in 18 cantos, by Padmagupta or Parimala. It is in honour of the poet's patron, the Paramāra Sindhurāja of Dhārā, called Nava-sāhasāṅka. It describes the marriage of Sindhurāja with Śaśiprabhā, daughter of the Nāga king Śaṃkhapāla through wonderful events. An account of the Paramāra dynasty is given in XI. 64—102.

[Ed. Islampurkar, Bombay, 1895. See Bühlerd and Zachariae in Sitzungsberichte d. Wiener. Akademie, pp. 583 ff., reprinted Wien, 1888, pp. 1—50; trs. into Eng. in *IA*, XXXVI, pp. 624 f.]

NAYATATTVĀLOKA : See *Nyāya-tattvāloka*.

[Ed. Islampurkar, Bombay, 1895.]

NIBANDHA-SAṂGRAHA : Name of Ḍallana's celebrated commentary on the *Suśruta-saṃhitā*.

[Ed. Calcutta, 1891. See S. M. Katre, On some Laukika words cited in the commentaries of...and Dalhana, *Taraporewala Memo. Vol.* (*Bulletin of Decean College*), Poona, 1957.]

NIDĀNA : By Mādhavakara. It is also called *Rug-viniścaya*, *Gada-viniścaya* or *Mādhava-nidāna*, and deals with the diagnosis of diseases, and, as the author states, is designed for beginners and persons of small intelligence. As Keith observes, it is of decisive importance on later Indian medicine.

[Ed., with the *Madhukośa* and *Ātaṅka-darpaṇa* comm. and notes, by V. Sarma, Venkaṭeśvara Press, Bombay, 1927; with the *Madhukośa* and Hindi comm., by Y. Upādhyāya, *CSS*, 1960, 1961 (2 vols.) ; with Hindi trs., *Madhukośa* and Hindi trs. of the same, by D. Sastri. See G. J. Meulenbeld (tr.), the Mādhavanidāna and its chief commentary, chaps. 1—10, Leiden, 1974.]

NIGHAṆṬU : Glossaries or lists of rare and obscure words occurring in the Vedic hymns. Sometimes wrongly ascribed to Yāska. But, as Yāska himself says, they were composed by the descendants of ancient sages for the easier understanding of the transmitted texts.

[Vide *The Nighaṇṭu and the Nirukta*—ed. L. Sarup, Punjab, 1927, trs. into English, Oxford, 1921.]

NĪLAMATA-PURĀṆA : A heterogeneous work of the *Māhātmya* type. It contains valuable information regarding the sacred places of Kashmir and the legends connected with them. It is one of the sources drawn upon by Kalhaṇa for his *Rājataraṅgiṇī*.

[Ed. R. Kanjilal and J. Zadoo, Lahore, 1924; K. St. J. M. de Vreese, Leiden (E. J. Brill), 1936; Ved Kumārī (with Eng. trs.), Delhi, 1973. See Ved Kumari, *Nīlamata Purāṇa, a cultural literary study*, Vol. I, Delhi, 1968.]

NIRṆAYA-SINDHU : Also called *Nirṇaya-kamalākara*, it is a famous Smṛti digest by Kamalākara. It is a voluminous work divided into three chapters (*pariccheda*). The chief topics, discussed in it, are proper time for various religious acts, *Vratas*, *Saṃskāra*, *Sapiṇḍa* relationship, consecration of images, auspicious time for sowing operations, buying horses and cattle etc., *Śrāddha*, impurities on birth and death, rites after death, rites for Satī and *Saṃnyāsa*.

[Ed. NSP, Bombay, 1905 (with Marāṭhī translation).]

NIRUKTA : A famous work by Yāska. This is the only work of the Vedāṅga *Nirukta* which we possess. It is a commentary on the *Nighaṇṭus* (lists of words) which tradition erroneously ascribes to Yāska. Corresponding to the threefold division of the contents of the *Nighaṇṭus*, there are three sections in the *Nirukta*, called *Naighaṇṭukakāṇḍa* (consisting of three lists in which Vedic words are collected under certain main ideas), *Naigama-kāṇḍa* or *Aikapadika* (containing a list of ambiguous and particularly difficult words of the Veda) and *Daivata-kāṇḍa* (classification of the deities according to the three regions of earth, sky and heaven).

[Ed. with Devarājayajvan's comm., BSS, in 2 vols., 1918 and 1942; with the *Nirkuta-vivṛti* comm. and notes, by M. Jha Bakshi, NSP, 1930; with the comm. of Durgācārya and gloss by S. Sarma, by C. Tripathy, Bombay, 1882; L. Sarup, in 6 vols., 1920-29 (with Eng. trs. and ed. of Madhva's comm.) ; B. Bhattacharya, *Yāsha's Nirukta and the Science of Etymology*, Calcutta, 1958 and H. Skold, *The Nirukta* etc., Lund, 1926; B. Sastri and S. Varma, *The Etymologies of Yāska*, Hoshiarpur, 1953. Also see P. D. Gune, Brāhmaṇa-quotations in the Nirukta, *R. G. Bhandarkar Comm. Vol.*, Poona, 1917; M. A. Mehendale, *Nirukta Notes*, Series I, Poona, 1965; Do (II), Poona, 1978; M. Prasad *Language of the Nirukta*, Delhi, 1963; Y. Devaraja, *Comm. on the Nirukta*, Calcutta, 1952; B. R. Chaubey, *Ṛṣi-mantranirvacana-bhāṣya of Yāska*, Hoshiarpur; S. Bhate, Pāṇini and Yāska—principles of derivations, *ABORI*, Vol. 62, 1981; H. Falk; Three groups of particles in Nirukta, BSOAS, XLV, Pt. 2, 192.

NĪTI-KALPATARU : A poetical work, in 138 sections, by Kṣemendra. It is a didactic work designed to give instructions on worldly wisdom and polity.
[Ed. V. P. Mahajan, Poona, 1956.]

NĪTI-RATNĀKARA : See *Rājanīti-ratnākara*.

NĪTI-SĀRA : Also called *Kāmandakīya Nīti-sara*. It is a work on polity, by Kāmandaki, based mainly on the *Arthaśāstra*, and is supposed by some to have originated in Bihar. According to K. P. Jayaswal, it was written, in the reign of the Gupta king Candragupta II, by one Śekhara whose family title was probably Kāmandaka. It is not merely a redaction of the *Arthaśāstra*. It is simplified by the omission of the details regarding administration in books II-IV of that text, and of the subject-Matter of the last two books. In book III and elsewhere it introduces much didactic matter which is absent in the *Arthaśāstra*. It is written in easy verses divided into cantos like a *Kāvya*.

[Ed. with the comm. *Jayamaṅgalā*, Trivandrum Sanskrit Series, 12, 1912; ASS, 1958 (with the comm. *Jayamaṅgalā* and *Upādhyāya-nirapekṣā*), Vol. I (up to the 7th canto). See *Kāmandakīya Nītisāra* or the elements of polity in English, ed. M. N. Dutt, Calcutta, 1896; 2nd ed. Varanasi, 1979; ed. S. K. Mitra, under title *Kāmandakīya Nītisāra*, Asiatic Society, Calcutta. *Nītisāra di Kāmandaki*, trs. by C. Formichi, *GSAI*, 12-17. On the question of authorship and date, see K. P. Jayaswal in *Jour. of Bihar and Orissa Research Society*, XVIII, 1932].

NĪTI-ŚATAKA: A lyric poem by Bhartṛhari. It seeks to inculcate worldly wisdom, and incidentally denounces material pleasure and love.

[Ed. with Skt. notes and Hindi trs. by K. C. Sukla, Allahabad, 1963. Included in the *Subhāṣitatriśatī*, NSP, 6th ed., Bombay, 1922 (1st ed., 1902). Trs. into Eng. by C. H. Tawney, *Indian Antiquary*, v. 1876; B. H. Wortham, London, 1886; J. M. Kennedy, London, 1913; C. W. Gurner, Calcutta, 1927. For ed. and trs., also see under Bhartṛhari.]

There is a *Nīti-śataka* by one Dhanadadeva.

[Ed. *Kāvyamālā*, Gucchaka XIII, A. Sastri Vetala, with the *Lalitā* comm., 1961.]

NṚTTA-RATNĀVALI : A noteworthy work on dance. Attributed to Jaya Senāpati, it contains eight chapters. Written in 1253-54 A. D.

[Ed. V. Raghavan, Madras, 1965.]

NYĀSA : Also called *Kāśikā-vivaraṇa-pañjikā*, it is a well-known commentary on the *Kāśikā-vṛtti* (q.v.). It was written by Jinendrabuddhi.

[Ed., with notes, by S. Chakravarti, Rajshahi (Bangladesh), 1913 ff.; along with *Padamañjarī* of Haradatta, by D. D. Shastri and K. P. Shukla, Varanasi, pts. I, II, 1965 (up to second section of Chap. III).]

NYĀYA-BINDU : A work on Logic, by the Buddhist logician Dharmakīrti. In it he attacks Uddyotakara in vindication of Diṅnāga. The author thinks that names and relations are imposed by the mind while the senses reveal the objects accurately unless they are themselves perverted.

[Ed., with Hindi trs., by C. Sastri, CSS, 1957. Tibetan trs., with comm. of Vinītadeva, ed. L. de la Vallée Poussin, Bib. Ind., 1907. See *Nyāyabindu-ṭīkā* by Dharmottara Ācārya, ed. Peterson, Bib. Ind., and *Nyāyabindu-Index* (Sankrit and Tibetan) by S. C. Vidyābhūṣaṇa, Bib. Ind.; Stcherbatsky, *Buddhist Logic*, vol. II, containing a trs. of the *Nyāyabindu* and of its comm. by Dharmottara, with notes etc., Leningrad, 1930. See Vinītadeva's *Ṭīkā* on *Nyāyabindu*, ed. M. K. Gangopadhyaya, Soviet Indology Series, 1971. Also see *Nyāyabindu* with comm. of Dharmottara, ed. S. N. Shastri.]

NYĀYA-BHĀṢYA : An exposition, by Vātsyāyana who is to be distinguished from the author of the *Kāmasūtra*, of Gotama's *Nyāya-sūtra*. In style it resembles the *Mahābhāṣya*. The author propounds modifications of the *Sūtra* in short sentences comparable to the *Vārtikas* in the *Aṣṭādhyāyī*.

[See E. Windisch, *Über das Nyāyābhāṣya*, 1888.]

NYĀYA-DARŚANA : See *Nyāya-sūtra*.

NYĀYA-KALIKĀ : A work on Nyāya philosophy, by Jayanta. It gives a bare outline of the author's exposition of Gotama's *Nyāya-sūtra* dealing with sixteen categories. Acc. to the author himself, it is meant for beginners. It is a commentary on Bhāsarvajña's *Nyāya-sāra*.

[Ed. Banaras, 1925.]

NAYAYAKANDALĪ : A reputed work on Nyāya-Vaiśeṣika philosophy by Śrīdhara Bhaṭṭa. It is a commentary on the *Padārtha-dharma-saṃgraha* which is an exposition, by Praśastapāda, of the *Vaiśeṣika-sūtra*. It was perhaps Śrīdhara who, for the first time in this work, set forth the theistic interpretation of the Nyāya-Vaiśeṣika view.

[Pub. at Banaras with the text of the *Padārtha-dharma-saṃgraha*, Ed. Viz. SS, Vol. IV, 1895.]

NYĀYAKOŚA : A dictionary of technical terms used mainly in Indian philosophy, by V. Jhalakikara.

[Pub. Bombay Sanskrit Series, Bombay, 1893.]

NYĀYAKUSUMĀÑJALI : Also called *Kusumāñjali*. A work on Nyāya philosophy, by Udayana. In it the author seeks to prove the existence of God. It is in *Kārikās* with a prose explanation.

[Ed. N. Misra, with Skt. and Hindi comm., Banaras, 1968; N. Vedantatirtha with comm. of Śaṃkara Miśra and Guṇānanda, Calcutta, Pt. I, 1954, Pt. II, 1964; P. Upadhyaya and D. Sastri, Varanasi, CSS, 1957 (with comm. of Varadarāja, Vardhamāna, Megha and Rucipati and short notes). An ed. with *Āmoda*, *Viveka* and *Bodhinī*, is reported to be in Press at Mithila Institute, Darbhanga; with comm. of Haridas Bhattacharya; ed. & trs. into Eng. by E. B. Cowell, Reprint, Varanasi, 1980. See *Kusumāñjali-kārikā-vyākhyā of Nārāyaṇatīrtha*, ed. S. Sastri, Kuruksetra, 1974; G. Chemparathy, *Indian Rational Theology*, 1973; M. Tachikewa, *Structure of the World in Udayana's Realism*, London, 1981.]

NYĀYAMĀLĀ-VISTARA : A work on Pūrvamīmāṃsā philosophy, by Mādhava.

[Ed. London, 1878.]

NYĀYA-MAÑJARĪ : A work on Nyāya philosophy, by Jayanta. In it he minutely discusses the nature of words and their meaning. He rejects the *Anvitābhidhāna-vāda* of the Mīnāṃsakas of the Prabhākara school, and partially accepts the *Abhihitānvaya-vāda* of the Bhāṭṭa school of Mīmāṃsakas, amending the latter view by recognising *Tātparya* as a function. Jayanta rejects the idea of *Sphoṭa*, and criticises the doctrines of *Apoha*, *Kṣaṇabhaṅga*, *Śrutyaprāmāṇya* and *Īśvarabhaṅga*. He criticises also the Buddhists' denial of soul and their doctrine of the unreality of the external world. The Buddhists' view that there are only two means of valid knowledge, viz. perception and inference, is also refuted by him.

[Ed. Viz. SS, 1895. Also pub. by Calcutta University, with Bengali trs., Vols. I-II, 1939—41. Eng. trs. by J. Bhattacharya, Delhi, 1978. Ed. with notes by S. N. Sukla, Kashi Skt. Series. See N. J. Shah, *Cakradhara's Nyāyamañjarī Granthibhaṅga*, Ahmedabad, 1982; Āhnika I (ed.) Ahmedabad, 1975; ed., with *Granthibhaṅga* Comn. of Cakradhara, by G. N. Sastri, Pt. I, Varanasi, 1982.]

NYĀYA-NIRṆAYA : A well-known *Advaita* treatise by Ānandagiri.

NYĀYA-PRAVEŚA : An introduction to logic, attributed by some scholars to the Buddhist philosopher Diṅnāga, and by others to Śaṃkarasvāmin.

[Ed. A. B. Dhruva (pt. I), GOS, 38, Baroda, 1930. On the question of authorship, see A. B. Keith in *IHQ*, 1928. The Skt. fragments, available in quotations, have been collected and translated by H. N. Randle, *Fragments from Diṅnāga*, London. 1926. See G. Tucci, Is the *Nyāya-praveśa* by Diṅnāga? in *Journal of Royal Asiatic Society*, 1928; Notes on the *Nyāya-praveśa* by Śaṃkarasvāmin, *Ibid*, 1931. Also see R. S. Y. Chi, *Buddhist Formal Logic*, London, 1969.]

NYĀYARATNAMĀLĀ : A Mīmāṃsā work by Pārthasārathi Miśra.

[Ed. with comm. of Rāmānuja, by A. Subrahmanya Sastri, Varanasi, 1982.]

NYĀYA-SĀRA : A short tract on logic, by Bhāsarvajña. It deals with only Pramāṇas or sources of valid knowledge. It recognises three *Pramāṇas*, viz. *Pratyakṣa*, *Anumāna* and *Āgama*. Incidentally the author deals with topics like fallacies, *Chala*, *Jāti*, *Vāda*, *Mokṣa* etc.

[Ed., with the *Nyāya-tātparya-dīpikā* comm., by S. C. Vidyabhusana, Asiatic Society, Calcutta, 1910; with *Padapañcikā* comm., by K. S. Sastri, TSS, 1935; with 2 commentraries and notes by S. S. Sastri, Madras, 1961; with *Padacandrikā*, notes and trs., by V. S. Abhyankar and C. R. Devadhar.]

NYĀYA-SŪTRA : The earliest work on Nyāya philosophy, ascribed to Gotama by some, to Akṣapāda by others while yet others believe that Gotama and Akṣapāda were identical. The *Nyāya-sūtra* and the *Caraka-saṃhitā* have much in common. The work is assigned by some to a period between the 2nd and the 5th century A.D., by others to the 4th century A.D. while yet others believe that it came into being in the first century A.D. Some scholars believe that, in its earliest form, it existed in the 4th century B.C.

It is divided into five books, each consisting of two sections.

Its contents are as follows :—

Book I—enumeration of the 16 topics to be dealt with in the other four books.

Book II—nature of doubt, means of proof and their validity.

Book III—nature of self, body, senses, their objects, cognition and mind.

Book IV—volition, sorrow, suffering and liberation are incidentally dealt with the theory of error and the relation of whole and parts.

Book V—*jāti* or unreal objections, and *nigrahasthānas* or occasions for rebuke.

The earlier portion of the work is assigned to the third century B.C., while the later portion is believed to have originated in the post-Christian era.

[Ed., with Vātsyāyana's comm., gloss of Viśvanātha Nyāyapañcānana and notes, by M. S. Dravida, R. S.

Bhandari and V. Dvivedi, Banaras, 1920; with comm. of Vātsyāyana, Vācaspati Miśra and Jha—Pt. I (Text), Pt. II (Trs. into Eng. with notes by G. Jha), Poona, 1929. Also ed., with the *Caturgranthikā* Vol. I. Chap. i by A. Thakur, Darbhanga, 1967. The comm., *Nyāyatātparya-dīpikā* of Bhaṭṭa Vāgīśvara, ed. K. N. Jha, 1979; *Gautamīya-sūtra-prakāśa* by Keśava Miśra ed. K. N. Jha, 1979; *Anvīkṣānaya-tattvabodha* by K. Raghunathan, 1979. See G. Jha *The Nyāyasūtras of Gotama*, Eng. Trans. Allahabad, 1917—19. (reprinted in 4 vols. by Motilal Banarsidass, Delhi, 1984). Trs. into English by S.C. Vidyabhusana, SBH Vol. VIII; Nyāya-darśana with Vātsyāyana's *Bhāṣya*, Uddyotakara's *Vārtika*, Vācaspati Miśra's *Tātparyaṭīkā* and Viśvanātha's *Vṛtti*, 2 vols., Kyoto, 1982, ed. Taranatha etc.; M. K. Gangopodhyay (Trs.) Nyāya : Gautama's Nyāyasūtra with Vātsyāyana's Comm., Calcutta, 1982. Allahabad, 1913. Literal Eng. trs. of *Nyāya-sūtra* and Vātsyāyana's Bhāṣya along with a free and abridged trs. of the elucidation by P. B. Tarkavāgīśa (Part I—First Adhyāya); by D. P. Chattopadhyaya and M. K. Gangopadhyaya, Calcutta, in 3 Vols. See G. Kaviraj, *History of Bibliography of the Nyāya-Vaiśeṣika Literature*; N. S. Junankar, *Gautama : The Nyāya Philosophy*, Delhi, 1975; K. K. Chakrabarti, *Logic of Gotama*, 1978.]

NYĀYA-TATTVALOKA : Also called *Nyāya-tattvāloka* or simply *Tattvāloka*, it is a highly authoritative commentary, by Vācaspati Miśra, on Gotama's *Nyāyasūtra*.

NYĀYA-VĀRTIKA : A work by Uddyotakara. The author explains the *Nyāya-sūtra* and Vātsyāyana's *Bhāṣya* thereon, and defends Vātsyāyana.

[Ed. V. P. Dvivedi, with the *Nyāyasūci-nibandha*, Bib. Ind., 1887-1914; V. P. Dvivedi and Dravida, CSS, 1916.]

PADA-CANDRIKĀ : A well-known commentary, on the *Amarakoṣa*, by Bṛhaspati Rāyamukuṭa. Written in 1431 A.D., it cites the *Ṭīkāsarvasva* of Sarvānanda.

[Printed, with Kṣīrasvāmin's comm., in A. Barua's ed. of the *Nāmaliṅgānuśāsana* (*Amara-koṣa*), Berhampore, 1887. Ed. K. K. Dutta, Vols. I—III, Sanskrit College, Calcutta,

1966 (Vol. I). Dutta's ed. reviewed by A. Banerji Sastri in *Jour. of Asiatic Society*, Calcutta, XI, 1969. Vol. II of K. K. Dutta's ed. pub., Calcutta, 1973.]

PADA-MAÑJARĪ : A commentary, by Haradatta, on the *Kāśikā*. It appears to be based partly on Kaiyaṭa's *Mahābhāṣya-pradīpa*.

[Ed. B. D. Shastri, Banaras, 1895; D. D. Shastri and K. P. Shukla along with the *Nyāsa* of Jinendrabuddhi, Varanasi, Pts. I, II, 1965 (up to 2nd section of Chap. III); P. Ramachandra and V. S. Sarma, Pt. 1, chaps. 1—4, Hyderabad, 1981. A critical study by T. R. Tripathi, New Delhi, 1981.]

PADĀRTHA-DHARMA-SAṂGRAHA : A work on Vaiśeṣika philosophy by Praśastapāda. It is not a comment on the *Vaiśeṣika-sūtra*, but an entirely novel exposition of the subject with important additions.

[Ed. Viz. SS, 1895. Trs. into Eng. by G. Jha, *Paṇḍit*, N.S., XXV—XXXIV.]

PĀDA-TĀḌITAKA : See *Caturbhāṇī*.

PADMA-PRĀBHṚTAKA : See *Caturbhāṇī*.

PADMA-PURĀṆA : A huge Purāṇa existing in two recensions. The older recension has survived in Bengali MS, and consists of the following five parts (*Khaṇḍa*) : *Sṛṣṭi*, *Bhūmi*, *Svarga*, *Pātāla*, *Uttara*. This Purāṇa inculcates the cult of Viṣṇu. It consists of parts which are probably centuries apart from one another. The latest portions of it are later than the *Bhāgavata-purāṇa*. It is almost certain that there is an ancient nucleus in the *Khaṇḍas* excepting the *Uttara*. The *Kriyāyogasāra* is a sort of appendix to the *Uttarakhaṇḍa* of this Purāṇa.

[Ed. ASS, Poona, 1893; Gurumaṇḍala Series, Calcutta, 1957-59. See *Padmapurāṇa and Kālidāsa* by H. Sarma, Calcutta, 1925; *Svarga Khaṇḍa*, cr. ed. by A. chatterjee, Varanasi 1972.See S. K. Belvalkar, The cosmographical episode in Mahābhārata and Padmapurāṇa, *F. W. Thomas Pres. Vol.*,

Bombay, 1939; A Chatterji, *Padmapurāṇa—a study*, Sanskrit College, Calcutta, 1967.]

PADYĀVALĪ : An anthology compiled by Rūpa Gosvāmin. It contains 386 verses culled from the works of over 125 poets. There are a few verses of Rūpa himself. It shows a devotional bias; the verses compiled in it relate to *Kṛṣṇa-līlā* or *Kṛṣṇa-bhakti*. The verses of the *Padyāvalī* are selected and arranged to exemplify the general features of the attitude of *Bhakti* as a *Rasa* or devotional sentiment.

[Ed. S. K. De, Dacca, 1934; with Hindi comm., Brindavan, 1959.]

PĀKADARPAṆA : A manual of cookery, ascribed to Mahārāja Nala.

[Ed. V. Bhattacharya, CSS, 1915.]

PAÑCADAŚĪ : Written partly by Mādhava and partly by Bhāratītīrtha, it supports Śaṃkara's views on Vedānta philosophy. Composed in verse, it brings out the metaphysical aspect of Advaita philosophy. It describes *Mūlaprakṛti* as an adjunct both of *Īśvara* and *Jīva* and clearly distinguishes between *Māyā and Avidyā.* In it four kinds of *Akāśa* are distinguished, viz. *Ghaṭākāśa*, *Jalākāśa Mahākāśa* and *Meghākāśa*. It mentions four kinds of intelligence.

[Ed., with *Padadīpikā* comm. of Rāmakṛṣṇa by N. R. Acharya, NSP, 1949. Trs. into Eng. by H. P. Sastri. Text and trs. by Svahananda. See Svami Abhedananda, *An Introduction to the Philosophy of Pañcadaśī*; T.M.P. Mahadevan, *Pañcadaśī : an interpretative exposition.*

PAÑCĀDHYĀYĪ : Same as *Jainendra-vyākaraṇa* (q.v.).

PAÑCAMASĀRASAṂHITĀ : A work on music, attributed to Nārada.

[*Calalogus Catalogorum*, I. 287.]

PAÑCAPĀDIKĀ : An elaborate gloss by Padampāda, on the first four *Sūtras* of the *Brahma-sūtra*. It is an exposition of Śaṃkara's system of Vedānta philosophy.

[Ed. Viz. SS, Vol. II, pt. 1, 1891-92. See Venkataramiah, *Pañcapādikā* (Eng. trs.), GOS, 1948.]

PAÑCARĀTRA : A *Mahābhārata* play, in three acts, by Bhāsa. It perhaps belongs to the *Samavakāra* type of drama. It selects, from the *Virāṭaparvan*, the dramatic situation of the Pāṇḍavas in hiding being forced into battle with the Kurus.

[Ed. C. R. Devadhar, Poona Oriental Series, 1937.]

PĀÑCRĀTRA-SAṂHITĀ : Viṣṇuite Tāntric works which perhaps originated in the North, circulated mainly in the South. The earliest of such works probably dates back to a period between the fifth and the ninth century A.D.

PAÑCA-SĀYAKA : A work on Erotics, by Maithila Jyotirīśvara Kaviśekhara, composed in the first half of the 14th cent. A.D.

[Ed. S. S. Ghiladia, Lahore, 1921 on minor works on erotics. See *Schmidt, Beiträge zur ind. Erotik*, pp. 25 ff.]

PAÑCA-SIDDHĀNTIKĀ : An astronomical work by Varāhamihira. It preserves information of the contents of five *Siddhāntas* of an earlier date. These are the *Vāśiṣṭha*, *Paitāmaha*, *Romaka*, *Pauliśa* and *Sūrya* or *Saura*. Of these *Siddhāntas*, two bear non-Indian names. These are the *Romaka* and the *Pauliśa*. The former must be connected with Rome, while the latter reminds one of the name of Paulus Alexandrinus of whom an astrological treatise exists. The *Romaka* contains elements of Greek (Alexandrian) astronomy. There is convincing evidence of Greek derivation in the *Siddhānta*. We find in the *Pauliśa*—perhaps also in the other *Siddhāntas*—an important contribution to Indian trigonometry.

All the above five *Siddhāntas*, different from the extant ones, are now lost.

[Ed., with comm. and Eng. trs., by G. Thibaut and S. Dvivedi, Banaras, 1889. Reprinted, Banaras, 1930. Second ed., Banaras, 1968. Ed. O. Neugebauyer and D. Pingree, Pt. I (Text and trs.), Pt. II (comm.), Pt. I, 1970, Pt. II, 1971. See V. P. Dvivedi, *Jyautiṣa-siddhānta-saṃgraha*, Banaras, 1912,

1917. *Sūryasiddhānta*, trs. by Burgess and Whitney and with notes by Whitney and a reply by Burgess in *JAOS VI*; Whitney's criticism of the views of Biot, Weber and M. Müller in *JAOS VIII*. For the *Pañca-siddhāntikā* and a study of the contents of each of the *Siddhāntas*, see S. Prakash, *Founders of Sciences in Ancient India*, New Delhi, 1965, pp. 546 – 600.]

PAÑCATANTRA : The only Sanskrit work on fables, ascribed to Viṣṇuśarman by some scholars. It consists of five books, viz. (1) *Mitrabheda* (separation of friends), (ii) *Mitra-prāpti* (acquisition of friends), (iii) *Sandhi-vigraha* (peace and war), (iv) *Labdhanāśa* (loss of what is acquired), (v) *Aparīkṣitakāritva* (rash action).

The original *Pañcatantra* is lost. It came down in three recensions, viz. North-western recension and two other lost versions. From one of its lost versions were derived the Kashmirian *Tantrākhyāyikā* (*Tantrākhyāyika*?) and the two Jaina versions, one abbreviated and the other enlarged. From another lost version were derived the South Indian *Pañcatantra*, the version of Nepal and the *Hitopadeśa* of Bengal. The *Tantrākhyāyikā* is the earliest and regarded as the nearest approach to the original. The *Pañcatantra* was rendered into Pahlavi as early as the middle of the sixth century A.D. From it were derived the Syriac and Arabic versions. Through Persian and Arabic translations the *Pañcatantra* reached many places of the East and the West. There was a Tibetan version. J. Hertel records over 200 versions of the work known to exist in more than 50 languages (three-fourths of the languages being non-Indian) spreading over the region from Java to Iceland.

Some scholars believe that there was a Prākrit original of the *Pañcatantra*. There are some who think that the fable as a type of literature or certain individual tales were borrowed by India form Greece.

[Pahlavi version made by the physician Burzoë under the patronage of Chosroes Anūshīrwān (531—79 A.D.) with the title Karaṭaka and Damanāka. Syriac version made from the Pahlavi by Büd, a Persian Christian, about 570 A.D. under the title Kalilag wa Damnag. Ed. Schulthess,

Berlin, 1911, Arabic version made from the Pahlavi by Muquffa about 750 A.D. under the title Kalila wa Damna. Ed. L. Cheikho, Beyrouth, 1923 (2nd ed.). Simplicior text (Jaina version) ed. K. P. Parab NSP, 1896 (revised 1912) ; Ornatior Text (Jaina version) ed. J. Hertel, HOS, 1908-12; trs. into German by Schmidt, Leipzig, 1901 ; into English by A. W. Ryder, Chicago, 1925, and F. Edgerton; into Georgian (Russia) in 12th century A.D.; into Russian, by A. Syrkin, 1958.

Pañcatantra, ed. with Skt. and Hindi comm., A. Sastri Vetāla, CSS, 1964; with Skt. and Hindi comm. by S. C. Pandeya; *Southern Pañcatantra* ed. J. Hertel, Leipzig, 1906; H. Blatt, Leipzig. 1930. Ed. M. R. Kale, with comm., notes and Eng. trs., Delhi, 1966. Of the Nepalese version, Books I—III included in Hertel's aforesaid ed. with Books IV-V in his ed. of *Tantrākhyāyika*.

Some of the important studies in the *Pañcatantra* are : J. Hertel, *Das Pañcatantra* etc., Leipzig and Berlin, 1914. F. Edgerton, *The Pañcatantra Reconstructed*, American Oriental Society, New Haven, Conn., 1924. R. Geib, *Zur Frage Nach Der Urfassunc Des Pañcatantra*, Wiesbaden, 1969. Penzer, Ocean of Story, Vol. V. Winternitz, *GIL*, III. For the literary history of *Kalilah and Damnah* or the *Fables of Bidpai* see Keith-Falconer's work under the same title, Cambridge, 1885. A. Venkatasubbiah's paper 'A Javanese Version of the Pañcatantra' in *ABORI*, XLVII, is interesting.]

PĀṆINĪYA ŚIKṢĀ : See Śikṣā.

Probably earlier than 500 B. C. There is a controversy as to whether or not it was the work of Pāṇini, author of the *Aṣṭādhyāyī*.

[Ed. M. Ghosh, with 2 comms., trs. and notes, Cal. Uni., 1938. On this Śikṣā see A. Weber, Ind. Stud., 4 and B. Liebich, Zur Einfuhrung in die indische einheimische Sprachwissenschaft, II. p. 20.]

PARAMA-LAGHU-MANJŪṢĀ : See *Vaiyākaraṇa-siddhānta*.

PARAMĀRTHA-SĀRA : A work by Abhinavagupta, it deals

in 100 Āryā verses, with the essential principles of the *Trika* system of Kashmir Śaivism. It is, acc. to the author himself, an adaption of the *Ādhāra-kārikās* of Śeṣa Muni.

[Ed. KSTS, Vol. 7, Srinagar, 1916; L. D. Barnett, *JRAS*, 1910, 1912; Winternitz, *GIL* III, 446.]

PARAMĀTMA-SANDARBHA : See *Bhāgavata-sandarbha.*

PARĀŚARA-SMṚTI : See *Dharmaśūtra.*

[Ed. C. Tarkaratna, with Mādhava's comm., Bib. Ind., 1883—99; with same comm., by V. S. Islampurkar, Vols. I, II, BSS, 1893—1911. Eng. trs. by K. K. Bhattacharya, Bib. Ind., 1887.]

PĀRASĪKA-PRAKĀŚA : An astronomical work, by Vedāṅgarāya, dealing with Hindu and Mohammedan methods of computing months, years, rise and setting of the sun and the moon, eclipses etc. It contains a vocabularly of Persian and Arabic terms used in astronomy, astrology etc. with corresponding Sanskrit synonyms. It was written in the reign of Shah Jahan (1627—58 A.D).

[For information about MSS, see S. N. Sen's *Bibliography of Skt. Works on Astronomy and Mathematics.*]

PĀRASKARA GṚHYASŪTRA : See *Gṛhyasūtra.*

[Ed., with German trs., by A. F. Stenzler, Indische Hausregeln, *AKM*,VI, 2 and 4, 1876—78; trs. by H. Oldenberg, SBE, Vol. 29.]

PARĀTRIṂŚIKĀ-VIVṚTI (or -VIVARAṆA) : A commentary, by Abhinavagupta, on the *Parātriṃśikā* the text of which constitutes the concluding portion of the *Rudrayāmalatantra,* and gives a résumé of the whole of it.

[Ed. M. Shastri, KSTS No. 18, Bombay, 1918.]

PARIBHĀṢĀ-VṚTTI : A grammatical work, by Nīlakaṇṭha Dīkṣita. It is referred to by Nāgeśa in his *Paribhāṣenduśekhara.* There is a grammatical work of this name by Puruṣottamadeva also.

PARIBHĀṢENDU-ŚEKHARA : A well-known comment, by

Nāgoji Bhaṭṭa, on a collection of *Paribhāṣās* or rules of interpretation in respect of Pāṇini's grammar.

[Ed. and trs. Kielhorn, BSS, 1868 (Part I, 2nd ed. K. V. Abhyankar, 1962; Part II, trs. and notes, 2nd ed. by K. V. Abhyankar, 1960). Ed. ASS, 72, with notes and introduction and comm. of V. Shastri, Banaras, 1943. Also see H. N. Mishra, *Parībhāṣenduśekhara of Nāgeśa Bhaṭṭa*, New Delhi, 1978.]

PĀRIJĀTA-HARAṆA : A work, by Umāpati Upādhyāya of Mithilā, of a semi-dramatic form and of greater operatic and melodramatic tenor. It deals with Kṛṣṇa's well-known exploit of carrying off Indra's *Pārijāta* tree and contains songs composed in the Maithili dialect.

[Ed. and trs. G. Grierson in *JBORS*, III, 1917. Also available separately. A *Pārijātaharaṇa*, attributed to Karṇapūra deals with the same theme. Ed. A Thakur , Darbhanga, 1956.]

Dealing with the same legend is the *Pārijātaharaṇa-campū* of Śeṣa Kṛṣṇa who flourished in the second half of the 16th century.

PĀTĀLA-VIJAYA : Name of a *Mahākāvya*, ascribed to Pāṇini, from which Namisādhu cites a fragment in his commentary on Rudraṭa's *Kāvyālaṃkāra*. It is lost. As the title implies, it perhaps dealt with Kṛṣṇa's descent into the lower world for winning Jāmbavatī as his bride. It provides evidence about the existence of *Kāvya* at least in the 4th century B.C.

PĀTAÑJALA YOGADARŚANA : See *Yoga sūtra.*

PATRA-KAUMUDĪ : A short work on epistolography, ascribbed to Vararuci. It deals with the art of writing letters to various persons. The modes of carrying letters, written to different persons, are also discussed in it.

[Ed. and trs. by S. C. Banerji in *Bulletin of Deccan College Research Institute*, Poona, presented to S. K. De.]

PAṬṬĀVALĪS : It is a class of Jaina works in Sanskrit, containing genealogical lists of pontiffs. They no doubt contain some exact chronological data, but they aim at attractive edification rather than serious history.

PAULIŚA-SIDDHĀNTA : See *Pañcasiddhantikā.*

PAUṢKARASĀDI (or, SĀDIN) : Referred to by Kātyāyana in his *Vārtika* on Pāṇini viii.4.48. He is supposed to have been a pre-Pāṇini grammarian acc. to some, a post-Pāṇini grammarian acc. to others. Also mentioned in *Taittirīya Prātiśākhya, Āpastamba-dharmasūtra* (i.28.1) and *Gaṇaratna-mahodadhi*. Fragment of an astronomical work is attributed, in the Weber MS, to this author. [See Keith, *History of Sanskrit Lit.*, 1928, p. 528, fr.]

PAVANA-DŪTA : The earliest among the *Dūta-kāvyas* of Bengal, discovered hitherto. Composed by Dhoyī, in 104 verses, in Mandākrāntā metre. With a mission of world-conquest king Lakṣmaṇasena of Bengal had been to South India when the Gandharva damsel Kuvalayavatī fell in love with him. At the advent of spring, the beloved, pining in separation, proposed to send a messenger to the king in Gauḍa.

[Ed. C. Chakravarti, Calcutta, 1926; G. C. Sharma, Aligarh, 1978.]

PIṄGALA-CHANDAḤSŪTRA : See *Chandaḥsūtra.*

PITṚ-DAYITĀ : Written by Aniruddha, it is intended for the followers of the *Sāmaveda*. It deals with daily duties, gifts, *Śrāddhas* and rites to be performed at the time of death and during the period of mourning. It is also called *Karmopadeśinī-paddhati*.

[Ed. Skt. Sāhitya Pariṣad Series, No. 6, Calcutta.]

PRABANDHA-CINTĀMAṆI : A work by the Jaina writer Merutuṅga. It is in prose with occasional verses. It is divided into five chapters called *Prakāśas*, each of which contains several *Prabandhas*. The contents are as follows :—

I. The legend of Vikramāditya and Sātavāhana, the story of the Caulukya kings of Aṇhilvād and of the Paramāra kings Muñja and Bhoja of Dhārā.

II. Continuation of the story of Bhoja.

III-IV. Story of the Aṇhilvād rulers down to the reign of Kumārapāla, account of the Gujarat rulers Lavṇaparasāda and Vīradhavala, the well-known minister of the latter, Tejaḥpāla and Vastupāla.

V. Collection of miscellaneous stories of Śilāditya, Lakṣmaṇasena and others.

[Ed. Jinavijaya, pt. I, Text, Santiniketan, Bengal, 1933. Eng. trs. by C. H. Tawney, Bib. Ind., 1901.]

PRABANDHA-KOŚA : A work of 24 stories, by Rājaśekhara Sūri. It was completed in 1348 A.D. It gives accounts respectively of seven royal (including Lakṣmaṇasena) and three lay personages, ten Jaina teachers (including Hemacandra) and four poets including Śrīharṣa.

[Ed. Jinavijaya, I, Text, Santiketan, Bengal, 1935.]

PRABODHA-CANDRODAYA : An allegorical drama, in six acts, by Kṛṣṇamiśra. It is devoted to the defence of the *Advaita* form of the Viṣṇu doctrine, a combination of Vedānta with Viṣṇuism. The characters in it are all abstractions, e.g. *Viveka* (discrimination), *Moha* (confusion) etc.

[Ed., with the commentaries *Candrikā* and *Dīpikā*, V. L. Pansikar, NSP, 1904 (2nd ed.). For a comm. by Rudradeva Tarkavāgīśa, see C. Lekha, *Summaries of papers, AIOC*, 1974. Trs. into Eng. by J. Taylor, Bombay, 1886, 1893 and 1916; into German by T. Goldstücker, Königsberg, 1842; into French by G. Deveze in Rev. de la Linguistique et de Philologic comp., XXXII—XXXV, Paris, 1899-1902. See S.K. Nambiar, *Prabodhacandrodaya of Kṛṣṇamiśra*, Delhi, 1971 (with Eng. trs. critical Intro. and Index).]

PRABODHA-PRAKĀŚA : A sectarian grammar of the Śaiva school by Balarāma Pañcānana. It designates vowels by the word 'Śiva'. Thus section on vowel-Sandhi is called *Śiva-sandhi-pāda*.

[Ed. D. Bhattacharya, Calcutta, 1318 B.S. (= 1911).]

PRACAṆḌA-PĀṆḌAVA : See *Bāla-bhārata*.

PRADĪPA : Comm. on the *Mahābhāṣya*, by Kaiyaṭa.

[See *Mahābhāṣya-pradipa-vyākhyānāni* (vols. i and ii), M. S. Narsiṃhācārya, Pondicherry, 1973-74; vols. vii, viii, Pondicherry 1980-81.]

PRAJÑĀ-PĀRAMITĀ : Name of a class of *Sūtras* which are in the nature of philosophical treatises. "The earliest of these *Sūtras* (i.e. Mahāyāna-Sūtras), those which are regarded with the greatest reverence, and which are of the greatest importance from the point of view of the history of religion, are the *Prajñā-Paramitās*, 'the (*Mahāyāna-sūtras* of the) Wisdom-Perfection.' They treat of the six perfections (*Pāramitās*) of a Bodhisattva, but especially of *Prajñā-pāramitā*, the highest perfection called wisdom. This wisdom consists of the knowledge of *Śūnyatā* (emptiness), i.e., the unsubstantiality of all phenomena, implying the conviction that all Dharmas or objects of thought, are only endowed with a conditional or relative existence." (Winternitz).

A *Prajñā-pāramitā* was translated into Chinese in 179 A.D. which therefore, is the lower terminus of its date.

The *Prajñā-pāramitās* probably originated in the South whence they spread to the East and the North. Some scholars think that this literature originated in Kashmir.

The following *Prajñā-pāramitās* have come down in Sanskrit:— *Śatasāhasrikā*, *Pañcaviṃśati-sāhasrikā*, *Aṣṭasāhasrikā*, *Sārdha-dvisāhasrikā*, *Saptaśatikā*, *Vajracchedikā*, *Alpākṣara-prajñā-pāramitā*, *Prajñā-pāramitā-hṛdaya-sūtra*.

[For a bibliography of editions and translations of the *Prajñā-pāramitās*, see M. Winternitz, *History of Indian Literature*, Vol. II, 1933, pp. 314-15. See E. Conze, *The Prajñāpāramitā Literature*, The Hague, 1960.]

PRAJÑĀPĀRAMITĀ-PIṆḌĀRTHA : Attributed to Diṅnāga, it is an epitome, in 58 verses of the *Aṣṭasāhasrikā-prajñā-pāramitā*; it is intended to classify the arguments expounded in this treatise and to adapt its long repetitions to the logic of a rational and intelligible scheme.

[Ed. and trs. G. Tucci, *JRAS*, 1947.]

PRAKARAṆA-PAÑCIKĀ : A popular manual by Śālikanātha, of the Prabhākara system of Mīmāṃsā philosophy.

PRAKRIYĀ-KAUMUDĪ : Also called *Kṛṣṇa-kiṃkara-prakriyā*. A grammatical work by Rāmacandra. It perhaps served as a model for Bhaṭṭoji's *Siddhānta-kaumudī*. In it the subject-matter of Pāṇini's grammar is arranged under different sections forming the different topics of grammar.

[Ed. BSS, Pt. I 1925; Pt. II, 1931.]

PRAMĀṆA-SAMUCCAYA : Written by the Buddhist philosopher Diṅnāga. The Sanskrit original is lost, but a Tibetan translation prepared by an Indian sage Hema Varma, still exists. It is divided into six chapters which are named in order :—

(i) *Pratyakṣa*
(ii) *Svārthānumāna*
(iii) *Parārthānumāna*
(iv) *Trirūpa-hetu*
(v) *Śabdānumāna-nirāsa*
(vi) *Nyāyāvayava*

PRAMĀṆA-VĀRTIKA : A well-known work on Buddhist logic, by Dharmakīrti. It first chapter, called *Svārthānumāna-pariccheda*, has been published. Its contents, broadly stated are as follows :

Hetu-cintā, *Anupalabdhi-cintā*, *Vyāpti-cintā*, *Sāmānya-cintā*, *Śabda-cintā*, *Āgama-cintā*, and *Apauruṣeya-cintā*.

There is a *Pramāṇavārtika-bhāṣya* (also called *Vārtikālaṃkāra*) by Prajñākaragupta, pub. Patna, 1953.

[Ed. R. Sāṃkṛtyāyana, Allahabad, 1943; D. D. Sastri, with Manoratha's comm. Banaras, 1968. Also see R. Gnoli, *Pramāṇa-vārtika of Dharmakīrti*, Chap. I, with the auto-commentary, text and critical notes, Rome, 1960; R. C. Pandeya, with author's own comm. on chap. iii and Manoratha's comm. on entire text.]

PRĀṆATOṢIṆĪ : A Tāntric compilation made, in Śaka 1842 (=1920 A.D.), by Rāmatoṣaṇa Vidyālaṃkāra with the patronage of Prāṇakṛṣṇa Biswas of West Bengal, India. It takes its name from the initial portion of the patron's name and the final portion of that of the compiler. It discusses the usual topics of Tantra, compiled from various Tāntric works.

[Pub. by Vasumatī Sāhitya Mandira, Calcutta, 1935 B. S.]

PRAPAÑCASĀRA-TANTRA : Ascribed to Śaṃkarācārya. The title means "the essence of the universe". The ritual and the mantras described in this Tantra are not confined to the worship of the various forms of Devī and Śiva; Viṣṇu and his *Avatāras* also are frequently referred to.

[Ed., with *Vivaraṇa* comm. of Padmapādācārya, and *Prayogakramadīpikā*, *vṛtti* on *Vivaraṇā*, Intro. by A. Avalon, A. Sarasvati, Delhi, 1981.]

PRASANNA-RĀGHAVA : A drama, in seven acts, based on the *Rāmāyaṇa* story, by Jayadeva who is to be distinguished from Jayadeva, author of the *Gītagovinda*. It imitates earlier models, particularly the *Vikramorvaśīya* of Kālidāsa. Certain changes have been introduced into the epic story. For example, in the first act, the demons Bāṇa and Rāvaṇa are brought together as Sītā's suitors and ridiculed. The last act introduces a pair of Vidyādharas who describe the battle and the purification and restoration of Sītā.

[Ed. K. P. Parab, NSP, 1914; with Skt. and Hindi comm., Varanasi, 1977.]

PRAŚASTI-KĀŚIKĀ : By Bālakṛṣṇa Tripāthin. It deals with letter-writing.

[Ed. K. V. Sharma, Hoshiarpur, 1967.]

PRAŚNOPANIṢAD : It consists of six chapters (*praśna*) in the form of answers, by sage Pippalāda, to questions put by his six disciples. It discusses various matters relating to the individual soul, supreme soul, origin of beings, the glory of *Oṃkāra* etc.

[For ed. see under *Īśopaniṣad*.]

PRASTHĀNA-BHEDA : A philosophical work by Madhusūdana Sarasvatī. It seeks to establish the supreme importance of Vedānta philosophy after laying down the essence of all kinds of knowledge. It contains useful accounts of the different systems of philosophy.

[Ed. Tarkadarśanatīrtha, Calcutta University, 1940; G. Sengupta, Calcutta. See A. Weber, *Madhusūdana Sarasvatī's encyclopädische Uebersicht der orthodoxen brahmanischen Litteratur* (Text and paraphrase), *Indische Studien*, I (1850) 1—24.]

PRATIJÑĀ-YAUGANDHARĀYAṆA : A play, in four acts, by Bhāsa. It is based on the Udayana legend of the *Bṛhatkathā*. Udayana goes out on a hunting excursion. By means of a ruse he is taken captive by his enemy, Pradyota Mahāsena. Mahāsena's daughter, Vāsavadattā, takes lessons in music from Udayana. They fall in love, and through the machination of his minister Yaugandharāyaṇa, Udayana elopes with his beloved.

[See under Bhāsa. On interpretation of some verses, see S.K. Sharma, *Summaries of Papers, AIOC*, 1974.]

PRATIMĀ-LAKṢAṆA : A work on the measurement of images and icons of the Buddhists.

[Ed. and trs. J. N. Banerji, Calcutta Uni. Press.]

PRATIMĀ-MĀNA-LAKṢAṆA : A work on the measurement of images and icons in general.

[Ed. and Eng. trs. by J. N. Banerji in an Appendix to his *Development of Hindu Iconography*, 2nd ed., Calcutta, 1956.]

PRATIMĀ-NĀṬAKA : A play, in seven acts, by Bhāsa. Based on the *Rāmāyaṇa* it seeks to dramatise, with considerable omissions and alterations, the almost entire *Rāmāyaṇa* story. Its interest centres chiefly round the character of Bharata and Kaikeyī. Bharata, the ideal brother, accuses his mother Kaikeyī of malafide motives and cruelty in getting Rāma banished. Kaikeyī defends her conduct in the interest of her husband and the step-son Rāma. Bhāsa seeks to exonerate Kaikeyī from the charges of selfishness and heartlessness that have been levelled against her through centuries. Besides changing the character of Kaikeyī, the author has created some new situations. As instances may be cited the *Valkala-*

incident in the first act and the statue-gallery in the second. The entire sixth Act has been written in a novel plan.

[Ed. C. R. Devadhar, Poona Oriental Series, 1937.]

PRĀTIŚĀKHYA : This is the name given to the oldest text-books of the exegetical Vedāṅga called *Śikṣā*. These works are so called because every *Śākhā* or recension of a *Saṃhitā* had a text-book of this nature. These works contain rules by which one can turn *Pada-pāṭha* into *Saṃhitā-pāṭha* Hence they contain instructions about the pronunciation, accentuation, the euphonic alteration of the sounds in the composition of words and in the initial and final sounds of words in the sentence. In short, theycontain instructions about the whole manner of the recitation of the *Saṃhitā*. These works are of twofold importance. First, these are valuable for the history of grammatical studies in India, which most probably commenced with these works. Secondly, they help preservation of the Vedic texts intact. The important *Prātiśākhyas* belonging to the different Vedic *Saṃhiās* are :

Ṛgveda-prātiśākhya ascribed to Śaunaka; *Taittiriya-prātiśākhya-sūtra*, *Vājasaneyi-prātiśākhya-sūtra* ascribed to Kātyāyana; *Atharvaveda-prātiśākhyā-sūtra*, *Puṣpasūtra* and *Ṛktantra* belonging to the *Sāmaveda*.

PRATYABHIJÑĀHṚDAYA : It is a compendium, by Kṣemarāja, of the *Pratyabhijñā-śāstra*, and is regarded as an important work on Kashmir Śaivism.

[Ed., with Eng. trs. and notes, by J. Singh, Delhi, 1963. Eng. trs. by K. F. Leidecker. See R. K. Kaw, *Pratyabhijñā Philosophy*, Hoshiarpur, 1967. M. Phil. thesis, on Evolution-Involution of Ultimate Reality in Kashmir Saivism with special ref. to Pratyabhijñā-hṛdaya has been approved by University of Jammu & Kashmir.]

PRATYABHIJÑĀ-KĀRIKĀ : Same as *Īśvara-pratyabhijñā-sūtra* (q.v.)

PRATYABHIJÑĀ-SŪTRA : Same is *Īśvara-pratyabhijñā* (q.v.)

PRATYABHIJÑĀ-VIMARŚINĪ : Also called *Laghvī Vṛtti*, it

is a commentary, by Abhinavagupta, on Utpala's *Pratyabhijñā-sūtra*.

PRATYABHIJÑĀ-VIVṚTI-VIMARŚINĪ : A commentary, by Abhinavagupta, on the lost portion of the exposition by Utpala.

PRATYAKṢA-MAṆI-DĪDHITI : An authoritative commentary by Raghunātha Śiromaṇi, on the *Pratyakṣa-khaṇḍa* of the *Tattva-cintāmaṇi* of Gaṅgeśa. Part of the author's *Tattva-cintāmaṇī-dīdhiti.*

PRATYAK-TATTVA-DĪPIKĀ : See *Citsukhī.*

PRAUḌHAMANORAMĀ : A lucid comment, by Bhaṭṭoji Dīkṣita, on his own *Siddhānta-kaumudī.*

[Ed., S. Shastri, Banaras, 1934; with comm. of Hari Dikṣita and *Laghu-śabdaratna* of Nāgeśa, by S. Shastri, Vol. I, Banaras, 1964.]

PRĀYAŚCITTA-PRAKARAṆA(NIRŪPAṆA) : A Smṛti digest of Bhavadeva Bhaṭṭa. It deals with various sins and the modes of their expiation.

[Ed. Varendra Research Society, Rajshahi (now in Bangladesh), 1927.]

PRĀYAŚCITTA-VIVEKA : A Smṛti digest by Śūlapāṇi. In it the author defines *Prāyaścitta* (expiation), defines and classifies sins and prescribes different modes of atonement.

[Ed. J. Vidyasagara, Calcutta, 1893.]

PRĪTI-SANDARBHA :—See *Bhāgavata-sandarbha.*

PRIYADARŚIKĀ :—A four-act drama of the *Nāṭikā* type, by Śrīharṣa. Princess Priyadarśikā, daughter of king Dṛḍhavarman, is, through strange circumstances, brought before the king of Vatsa, and is made an attendant of queen Vāsavadattā, under the assumed name of Āraṇyikā. The king falls in love with the girl, and develops intimacy with her. This enrages the queen who throws her into prison. In course of time, the queen comes to know that Āraṇyikā is a daughter of her relative and not a stranger. She then brings about the king's marriage with her.

[Ed. R. V. Krishnamchariar, Srirangam, 1906; Nariman, Jackson and Ogden, Text in Roman characters, Eng. trs. and notes etc., New York, 1923.]

PṚTHVĪRĀJA-VIJAYA :—It is a fragmentary and unfinished poem of unknown date and authorship. It deals, apparently on the model of Bilhaṇa's *Vikramāṅkadeva-carita*, with the victories of the Cāhumāna prince Pṛthvīrāja of Ajmer and Delhi, who fought with Shāhābuddin Ghori and fell in 1191 A.D., the prince being presented as an incarnation of Rāma. The printed text extends from canto I to part of canto XII, and is full of lacunae. We get in it a dependable genealogy and an account of Pṛthvīrāja's ancestors beginning with Vāsudeva. For the history of Rajasthan, during the period from the middle of the eighth century to the end of the twelfth, the poem is valuable. The work may have been composed between 1178 and 1193 A.D. Some scholars think that it was composed by the Kashmirian Jayānaka who is a figure in the poem.

[Ed., with Jonarāja's comm., by G. H. Ojha and C.S. Gulleri, Ajmer, 1941 (incomplete) in 12 cantos; S. K. Belvalkar (Facs. I), Bib. Ind. For a summary of the contents, see H. B. Sarda in *JRAS*, 1913.]

PŪJĀ-RATNĀKARA : Forming a part of Caṇḍeśvara's *Smṛti-ratnākara*, it deals with the worship of various gods and goddesses according to Tantric rules.

[See Mitra, *Notices*, VII, No. 2398.]

PURĀṆA : The Purāṇas are traditionally attributed to Vyāsa, but are in reality believed to have been the works of generations of writers or compilers. They are divided into two broad classes, viz. the *Mahāpurāṇa* (major works) and *Upapurāṇa* (minor works). These are generally meant for different sects e.g. *Śaiva*, *Śākta*, *Vaiṣṇava* etc. Traditionally these works are said to deal with the five topics of *Sarga* (creation), *Prati-sarga* (re-creation), *Vaṃśa* (genealogies of gods and sages), *Manvantara* (Manu periods of time) and *Vaṃśānucarita* (genealogies of kings). Some Purāṇas, however, actually deal with many more topics or with entirely different matters.

It is believed that the Purāṇas are 36 in number; of these, 18 are *Mahāpurāṇas* and 18 *Upa-purāṇas*.

The Purāṇic literature appears to have originated before the 5th or 4th century B. C. The extant Purāṇas appear to have come into being before the 7th century A.D.

The Purāṇas are valuable for the history of religion. They are of great importance from the points of view of literary and political history. Quite a number of poems and dramas are based on Purāṇic legends. The Purāṇas contain invaluable materials for the reconstruction of the early political history of India. They contain noteworthy information about the geography of ancient India. The *Bhāgavata-purāṇa* is the Bible of the Vaiṣṇavas. The *Devīmāhātmya*, popularly called *Caṇḍī*, included in the *Mārkaṇḍeyapurāṇa*, is a holy book of the Hindus and is recited on ceremonial occasions and also to ward off evils.

The Purāṇas in general were very popular, the reason of their popularity being mainly twofold. In the first place, these gave the Śūdras and womenfolk, who were debarred from Vedic study and the observances of Vedic rites, the liberty to read and hear the Purāṇas as also to perform Vratas and other Purāṇic rites. Secondly, these contained beautiful anecdotes written in simple language that appealled to the heart of the common man. The *Mahāpurāṇas* are: *Brahma*, *Padma*, *Viṣṇu*, *Śiva*, *Bhāgavata*, *Nārada*, *Mārkaṇḍeya*, *Bhaviṣya or Bhaviṣyat*, *Agni*, *Brahma-vaivarta*, *Liṅga*, *Varāha*, *Skanda*, *Vāmana*, *Kūrma*, *Matsya*, *Garuḍa*, *Brahmāṇḍa*. In certain lists, the name of *Vāyupurāṇa* occurs in the place of *Śiva-purāṇa*.

The Purāṇas have been classified as follows :—

A. *Rājasa* (relating to Brahmā)
Brahma, *Brahmāṇḍa*, *Brahma-vaivarta*, *Mārkaṇḍeya*, *Bhaviṣya*, *Vāmana*.

B. *Sāttvika* (extolling Viṣṇu)
Viṣṇu, Bhāgavata, Nāradīya, Garuḍa, Padma, Varāha.

C. *Tāmasa* (glorifying Śiva)
Śiva, Liṅga, Skanda, Agni, Matsya, Kūrma.

Acc. to Raghunandana, the famous Smṛti writer of Bengal, the *Upa-purāṇas* are the following :

Sanatkumāra, Narasiṃha, Vāyu, Śiva-dharma, Āścarya, Nārada, Nandikeśvara, Uśanas, Kapila, Varuṇa, Sāmba, Kālikā, Maheśvara, Kalki, Devī, Parāśara, Marīci and *Bhāskara* or *Sūrya.*

[All the Mahāpurāṇas have been ed. in *Aṣṭādaśa Mahāpurāṇa*, Bombay, loose leaves. The Purāṇa Text Series, Varanasi, has undertaken to publish the texts of all Mahāpurāṇas. Some Purāṇas have already been published. All-India Kashiraj Trust, Ramnagar, Varanasi, is publishing cr. ed. of Purāṇas and studies relating to them. An Eng. trs. of all the Mahā- and Upa-purāṇas is being published, in 50 vols., under the caption *Ancient Indian Tradition and Mythology*, by Motilal Banarsidass, Delhi. Vols. 1-4 *Śiva Purāṇa*, Vols. 5-6 *Liṅga Purāṇa*, Vols. 7-11 *Bhāgavata Purāṇa*, Vols. 12-14 *Garuḍa Purāṇa*, 15-19 *Nārada*, 20-21 *Kūrma*, 22-26 *Brahmāṇḍa*, 27-30 *Agni*, 31-32 *Varāha* and 33-36 *Brahma* have been published.

For various aspects of this literature, the following works may be consulted:

Ali, S.M.: The *Geography of the Purāṇas*, New Delhi, 1966.

Awasthi, A.B.L.: *History from the Purāṇas*

Do : *Garuḍa purāṇa* (*Ek Adhyayana*), Lucknow

Bahadur, B : *Polity in the Agnipurāṇa*, Calcutta, 1966.

Benjamin P. Solis : *The Kṛṣṇa Cycle in the Purāṇas*, Motilal Banarsidass, Delhi, 1984.

Bhandarkar, R. G : A Peep into the Early History of India *JBRAS*, 20, 1900. (New ed. 1920).

BHATTACHARJI, S.: *The Indian Theogony*: *Comparative study of Indian mythology from the Vedas to the purāṇas*, Calcutta, 1978.

CHAKRAVORTI, C.: *An Ethnic Interpretation of Paurāṇika Personages*, Calcutta 1971.

Daniélou, A and N. R. Bhatt : *Textes des Purāṇa sur la theorie musicale*, Vol. 1, Editions critique, traduction francaise of Introduction, Pondicherry, 1959.

CHAUDHURI, S. C: *Ethnic Settlements in Ancient India : a study on Purāṇic lists of peoples of Bhāratavarṣa*, Pt. 1. Northern India, Calcutta, 1955.

DE, S.K. and Hazra, R. C. (ed.) : *Anthology of Epics and purāṇas* and *Sāhitya-ratnakoṣa*, II (*Purāṇetihāsa-saṃgraha*, New Delhi, 1959).

Devi, A.K.: *A Biographical Dictionary of Purāṇic Personages.*

Diksitar, V.R.R.: *Purāṇa Index*, Vols. I-III, Madras, 1951, 1952, 1955.

———: *The Matsyapurāṇa—a study*, Madras, 1935.

GYANI, S. D: *Agni Purāṇa*, Varanasi.

Hazra, R. C. *Studies in the Purāṇic Records on Hindu Rites* and *Customs*, Dacca, 1940.

———: *Studies in the Upa-purāṇas*, Vols. I-III, Calcutta.

(Further vols. to be gradually published)

Iyer, K. N.: *The Purāṇas in the light of modern science*, Adyar.

Kanjilal, K. C.: *Philosophy of the Purāṇas.*

Kantawala, S. G.: *Cultural History from the Matsyapurāṇa*, Baroda, 1964.

Kennedy, V.: *Researches into the Nature and Affinity of Ancient and Modern Mythology*, London, 1831.

Kirfel, W.: *Das Purāṇa Puñcalakṣaṇa*, Bonn, 1927.

———: *Bhāratavarsha*, Stuttgart, 1931.

———: *Purāṇa von welt-gebaude*, (Bhuvana-vinyāsa): Die cosmographie der inder, Bonn and Leipzig, 1920.

Mani, V.: *Purāṇic Encyclopaedia*, Delhi.

Mankad, D.R.: *Purāṇic Chronology*, 1951.

Meyer: *Gesetzbuch and Purāṇa*, Breslau, 1929.

Mishra, B.B.: *Polity in Agnipurāna.*

Mishra, R.: *Polity in the Agnipurāṇa*, Calcutta, 1965.

Om Prakash: *Political Ideas of the Purāṇas*, Allahabad, 1977.

Pargiter, F. E.: *Purāṇa Text of the Dynasties of Kali Age* (ed. with Eng. trs.), Banaras, 1962.

———. *Ancient Indian Historical Tradition*, London, 1922.

Patil, D. R.: *Cultural History of the Vāyupurāṇa*.

Pradhan, S. N.: *Chronology of Ancient India*, Calcutta, 1927.

Pratyagatmananda Sarasvati: *Purāṇa O Vijñān* (in Bengali), Calcutta, 1969.

Pusalker, A.D.: *Studies in the Epics and Purāṇas*, Bombay, 1955.

Roy, S. N.: *Paurāṇika Dharma*, Allahabad.

——: *Historical and Cultural Studies in the Purāṇas*, Allahabad. 1978.

Ruben, W.: *The Bible and the Purana*, *Studies in Ancient Indian Thought*, Calcutta, 1966.

Sastri, J.: *Political Thought in the Purāṇas*, Lahore, 1944.

Sen Sarma: *Military Wisdom in the Purāṇas*, Calcutta, 1979.

Singh, N.R.: *A critical study of the Geographical data in the early Purāṇas*. Calcutta, 1972.

Singhal, J. P.: *The Sphinx Speaks*, Delhi, 1963.

Sircar, D. C.: *Bhārata War and Purāṇic Genealogies*.

Smith, R. M.: *Dates and Dynasties in the Purāṇas* (shortly to be published).

Tandon, Y: *Purāṇa-viṣaya-samanukramaṇikā*, Hoshiarpur, 1952.

Tripathi, S.: *Aṣṭādaśa-purāṇa-parichay*, ed. S. Avasthy Varanasi, 1980.

Vedālaṃkāra, R.: *Purāṇānāṃ kāvyarūpatāyā virecanam* (in Sanskrit), 1974.

Wilson, H. H.: *Eng. trs. of Viṣṇu-purāṇa* (Intro.)

———: *Essays on Sanskrit Literature*, 1832 ff.

———: Purāṇas or an account of their contents and nature.

———: *Metaphysics of Purāṇas*, ed. and enlarged by K. M. P. Verma, New Delhi, 1980.

Winternitz, M.: *History of Indian Literature*, Vol. I.

The following papers are useful:—

S.K. Chatterji: Purāṇa legends and the Prakrit tradition in *New Indo-Aryan, Grierson Pres. Vol.* (*BSOAS, VIII*) London, 1936.

J. D. L. de Vries: Purāṇa studies, *C. E. Pavry Vol.* London, 1933.

Rocher, L.: One century and half of Purāṇa Studies, *Summaries of Papers*, 5th World Skt. Con., 1981, p. 234.

W. Kirfel: Kṛṣṇa's Jugend-geschichte in den Purāṇa, *Festgabe Jacobi*, Bonn, 1926.

A. P. Karmarkar: The earliest extant Purāṇa in Indian literature, *Karmarkar Comm. Vol.*, Poona, 1948.

———: Purāṇic cosmogony, *R. K. Mookerji Vol.* (*Bhāratakaumudī*), Allahabad, 1945, 1947.

J. Wilhelm: Au fgaben der Purāṇa Forschung, *Festchrift E. Kuhn*, Breslau, 1916.

Abs. Jos.: Beiträge zur Kritik heterodoxer philosophien in der Purāṇa Literatur, *Festgabe Jacobi, op. cit.*

M. N. Ray: Notices of some of the Vidyās mentioned in the Purāṇas, *S. K. Aiyangar Comm. Vol.*, Madras, 1936.

P. V. Kane: Vedic Mantras and Legends in the Purāṇas, *C. K. Raja Pres. Vol.*, Madras, 1941.

A. D. Pusalker: Were the Purāṇas originally in Prakrit, *Dhruva Smāraka Grantha*, III, Ahmedabad, 1946.

P. L. Bhargava, Purāṇic Genealogies and Megasthenes, *Summaries of Papers*, 5th World Skt. Con., Varanasi, 1911, p. 189.

U. Schneider, On Eggmont's Purāṇic Lists of Maurya Kings, *Ibid*, p. 197.

G. Bonazzali, Sampradāyas in Purāṇic systematisation, *Ibid*, p. 218.

(For other papers, by different scholars, on various aspects of the Purāṇic literature, and problems connected with it, see issues of the *Purāṇam*, the half-yearly Bulletin of the Purāṇa Deptt. of All-India Kasiraja Trust, Fort Ramnagar, Varanasi) Also see *Summaries of Papers*, Vth World Sanskrit Conf., Varanasi, 1981, p. 219.]

PURUṢA-PARĪKṢĀ: A collection of tales, in prose and verse, by Maithila Vidyāpati, written under the order of King Śivasiṃha. It contains 44 tales on the question of what constitutes manly qualities, some of the stories having reference to historical persons and incidents. By means of the stories it describes the qualities of charity, piety, learning, truthfulness etc. Written on the plan of the *Pañcatantra*, but the characters are human beings.

[Ed. Gujarati Printing Press, Bombay, 1882, with Gujarati trs.; with Maithilī trs. in prose and verse by C. Jha and trs. into modern Maithilī prose by R. Jha, Darbhanga, 1960. Eng. trs., called the *Text of Man*, by G. A. Grierson, 1935, in Vol. XXXIII of the New Series of the Oriental Translation Fund. Bengali trs. by H. Ray, 1915 (First ed. by Serampore Missionaries), 1826 (by G. Haughton, London); subesquent editions were pub. in Calcutta].

PŪRVA-MĪMĀṂSĀ: Same as Mīmāṃsā. See *Mīmāṃsā-sūtra*. [See E. Frauwallner, Materialen zur karmamimāṃsā, Wien:Hermann Bollans Nachf, 1968.]

PUṢPA-SŪTRA: A *Prātiśākhya* of the *Sāmaveda*. See *Prātiśākhya*.

[Ed. Dravid, with comm. of Ajātaśatru, CSS, 1923; trs. into German by Simon, pub. with text.]

RĀGA-NIRŪPAṆA: A work on music, attributed to Nārada. It is a metrical description of 140 *Rāgas*.

[Ed. D. K. Joshi, Poona.]

RĀGA-TARAṄGIṆĪ: Written by Locanakavi or Locana Paṇḍita, in Śaka year 1082 (=1160 A.D.), it is a work on music. The major part of the work discusses a number of songs by poet Vidyāpati of the court of king Śivasiṃha of Tirhut (15th century A.D.). The author describes also the musical theories of his day, and groups the *Rāgas* under twelve fundamental modes.

[Ed. D. K. Joshi, Poona, 1918.]

RĀGA-VIBODHA: It is an important work on Indian music, written by Somānanda in 1609 A.D. Written in verse, it begins with the theory of musical sounds and describes the different types of *Viṇās* and the mode of using them. The author classifies the *Rāgas* into primary (*Janaka*) and derivative (*Janya*). He states a number of melodies developed from the *Rāgas*.

[Ed. S. Sastri, Madras, 1945 (with the author's own comm. *Viveka*); with a table of notations, by R. Simpson, Leipzig, 1904; with trs., by M. S. Ramasvami Iyer. Partly trs. into Eng. in *Indian Musical Journal*, Mysore, 1912-13.]

RĀGHVA-PĀṆḌAVĪYA: A *Mahākāvya*, in 18 cantos, by Dhanañjaya. Also called *Dvisaṃdhānakāvya*. Each verse of this *Kāvya* applies equally to the stories of the *Rāmāyaṇa* and the *Mahābhārata* at the same time.

[Ed. Sivadatta and Parab, with Badarīnātha's comm., NSP, 1895. There is also a *Rāghava-pāṇḍavīya* by Kavirāja. It relates, in 13 cantos, the double story of Rāghava and the Pāṇḍavas. Ed. Bib. Ind., with comm. of P. Tarkavāgīśa, Calcutta, 1854. (Reprinted 1892); Śivadatta and Parab, with Śaśadhara's comm. NSP, 1897.]

RAGHUVAṂŚA : A *Mahākāvya*, in 19 cantos, by Kālidāsa. It describes the activities of the kings of Ikṣvāku race from Dilīpa to Agnivarṇa. It takes its name from the famous king Raghu, son of Dilīpa. It contains fine specimens of poetry at various places, e.g. the description of Dilīpa's journey to Vasiṣṭha's hermitage (canto i), account of the *Svayaṃvarasabhā* of Indumatī (canto vi), description of the confluence of the Gaṅgā and the Yamunā (canto xiii), etc. It is based chiefly on the *Rāmāyaṇa*.

[Ed., with Mallinātha's comm., notes, Eng. trs. etc., K. M. Joglekar, NSP, 1916; A. F. Stenzler, with Latin trs., London, 1832; with Mallinātha's comm., S. P. Paṇḍit, BSS, 1969—74; G. R. Nandargikar. with Eng. trs., Bombay, 1897; with *Raghuvaṃśa-darpaṇa* of Hemādri, Patna, 1973. Eng. trs. by H. H. Wislon. See *Poona Orientalist*, VIII, pts. 3, 4 (pp. 188—201) for a discussion on the alleged spurious portions of the *Raghuvaṃśa*. See Buddha Prakash, for the relation of the *Raghuvaṃśa* to Iran, in the same journal, Vol. XIV, pts. 1—4 (pp. 4—12). Also see S. V. Sohony, Raghuvaṃśa as a source-book of Gupta history, *S.K. Belvalkar Felicitation Vol.*, Banaras, 1957; P. Ranganathan, *Kālidāsa's Raghuvaṃśa, a study*, New Delhi, 1964; R. D. Bandhu, *Raghukoṣa*; D. K. Kanjilal, A Study of the Raghuvaṃśa of Kālidāsa in the Light of a new MS, *Our Heritage* IX, pt. II, 1961; A. Deb, *Raghuvaṃśa-pariśīlan* (Hindi), Dew Delhi, 1982.]

RĀJAMĀRTAṆḌA : Ascribed to Bhoja, it is an important commentary on the *Yoga-sūtra*.

[Ed. and trs. R. Mitra, Bib. Ind., 1883; ed. CSS, with text and five other commentaries, Banaras, 1930; trs. into English by G. Jha, Bombay, 1907.

[Also ascribed to Bhoja is a work called *Rāja-mārtaṇḍa* on the preparation of medicated oil and other compound medicines.] [Ed. J. T. Acharya, Bombay, 1924.]

RĀJANĪTI-RATNĀKARA : It is a work by Caṇḍeśvara in 16 chapters called *Taraṅgas*, written at the command of king Bhaveśa of Mithilā. It deals with politics and statecraft, the qualification and function of councillors (*amātya*), the priest, the judge, rules regarding forts, the treasury, the army, ambassadors, allies, spies, the Political Circle (*rāja-maṇḍala*), abdication by a king, succession to the throne, the state's obligation towards the poor and the helpless, procedure of coronation etc. In short, it deals with usual topics of *Artha-śāstra* and the *Rājadharma* of Dharmaśāstra.

[Ed. K. P. Jayaswal, Patna, 1924. In the introduction, the editor deals with the personal history of Caṇḍeśvara.]

RĀJA-TARAṄGIṆĪ : The most famous historical poem by Kalhaṇa. Consisting of eight chapters, and drawing upon earlier sources, notably the *Nīlamata-purāṇa*, it deals, in the earlier part, with the legendary kings of Kashmir. In the later part, it gives accounts of the Kashmirian kings of the historical period. It is a valuable work for the political and social history of Kashmir as well as the topography of that land.

[Ed., with critical notes, M. A. Stein, Delhi, 1960; Durga-prasad, in 3 vols. including the three continuations, Bombay,

1892, 1894, 1896; with notes, Viśva Bandhu and others, Hoshiarpur, 1963-65 (Texts of Jonarāja, Śrīvara and Śuka, 1966-67). Trs. into English by M. A. Stein, Westminster, 1900 and by Pandit, Allahabad, 1935; into French, with notes, by M. Troyer, Paris, 1840—52. An interesting publication is the *Tales from the Rājataraṅgiṇī* by S. L. Sadhu, Srinagar, 1967. Also see *Rājataraṅgiṇī-kośa* by R. Ray, Banaras, 1967; M. Pathak, *Women in Rājātaraṅgiṇī.*]

RĀJĀVALĪ-PATĀKĀ : A continuation, by Prājyabhaṭṭa and Śuka, of the *Rājataraṅgiṇī.* It deals, in nearly 1,000 verses, with the story of the kings of Kashmir till the annexation of that province by Akbar (1586 A.D.).

[Included in Durgaprasad's ed. of the *Rājataraṅgiṇī* (q.v).]

RĀJENDRA-KARṆAPŪRA : A highly exaggerated panegyric, in 75 verses of varied metres, of king Harṣadeva of Kashmir (1089—1101 A.D.) by his protégé named Śambhu.

[Ed. K. S. R. Shastri, GOS, 1930.]

RĀMACARITA: It is by Abhinanda who is supposed to have been a Bengali. Based on the *Rāmāyaṇa* story, from the middle of the *Kiṣkindhā Kāṇḍa* up to the end of the *Yuddha-kāṇḍa*, it consists of 40 cantos of which the last four appear to have been composed by one Bhīma. The poet has introduced certain changes in the original story to glorify Rāma's character and to display his poetic skill.

[Ed. K. R. Shastri, GOS, 1930.]

There is also a *Kāvya* of the same name, in 220 verses, by Sandhyākara Nandin. With the help of double *entendres* it simultaneously narrates the story of Rāma, son of Daśaratha, and Rāmapāla, king of Bengal. It is also called *Rāmapāla-carita.*

[Ed., with comm., R. C. Majumdar, R. G. Basak and N.G. Banerji, Varendra Research Society, Rajshahi (Bangladesh), 1939; Revised and trs. into Eng. by R.G. Basak, Asiatic Society, Calcutta, 1969.]

RĀMAPĀLA-CARITA : See *Rāma-carita.*

RĀMĀYAṆA: One of the two great Epics, of India, and traditionally ascribed to Vālmīki who is still a legendary figure. In seven Books, called *Kāṇḍas*, it deals with the story of the birth of Rāma and his brothers, their marriage, arrangements for Rāma's coronation which is foiled by the machination of Kaikeyī, exile of Rāma who is accompanied to the forest by his wife Sītā and brother Lakṣmaṇa, Sītā's abduction by Rāvaṇa, demon-king of Laṅkā, rescue of Sītā by Rāma after killing Rāvaṇa in a bitter fight, Rāma's return to the capital, his coronation and subsequent banishment of Sītā for pleasing the subjects, delivery of two twin sons by Sītā in exile, vain bid to bring about *rapprochement* between Rāma and Sītā, Sītā's disappearance under the earth, Rāma's ascent to heaven.

Though the Rāma-legend reaches back to the Veda, yet the original *Rāmāyaṇa* epic appears to have been composed in the third century B.C. It is probable that it had its present extent and contents towards the close of the second century A.D. Books I and VII of the *Rāmāyaṇa* and parts of Book VI are believed to be later interpolations. This epic has come down in three recensions, viz. the West Indian (North-western or Kashmirian) recension, the Bengal recension and the South Indian recension. There are also other works bearing the title *Rāmāyaṇa*, e.g. *Adbhuta-rāmāyaṇa*, *Adhyātma-rāmāyaṇa* and *Yogavāsiṣṭha-rāmāyaṇa*. For their contents, see descriptions under the respective titles.

As regards Vālmīki's *Rāmāyaṇa*, some modern theories are as follows. The Rāma story was attempted by legendary sage Cyavana, mentioned in *Śatapatha Brāhmaṇa*, and given poetical shape by his descendant Vālmīki.

The epic story was modelled on the *Daśaratha-jātaka*. Originally Daśaratha was king of Vārāṇasī, Sītā was a sister of Rāma who was banished to Himālaya region. Sītā's abduction and war with Rāvaṇa was modelled on the Greek legend of Helen etc.

Acc. to some, the original epic story, written around 500 B.C. took the final shape about 2nd cent. A.D. Some, however, think that Rāma lived around 2050 B.C. Rāvaṇa's Laṅkā is believed by a few scholars to have been in north

India, somewhere in South Eastern Madhya Pradesh or in the adjoining areas of Orissa and Andhra.

Some say that Rāma had been an incarnation from a very remote period, while others hold that he was originally only a very wise man.

[Repeatedly printed. Pub. with comm. of Govindarāja, Rāmānuja, M. Tirtha and Ahobala, Veṅkaṭeśvara Press, Bombay, 1935. See critical ed., with comm. of Govindarāja, NSP, 1913. N. W. Recension critically ed., D. A. V. College, Lahore; *Bālakāṇḍa*, ed. Bhagavad Datt, 1931; *Ayodhyā-kāṇḍa*, ed. Ram Labhaya, 1928; *Araṇyakāṇḍa*, ed. V. B. Shastri; 1935; *Kiṣkindhā-kāṇḍa*, ed. Ibid, 1936; *Sundara-kāṇḍa*, ed. Ibid, 1940. Southern recension pub. by R. N. Aiyar, Madras, 1933; ed. T. R. Krishnachary, Delhi, 1982; ed. A. L. Gadgil, 2 Vols., Pune, 1982; Vol. II—Śloka-index. Bengal recension, with Lokanātha's comm. and Bengali trs., pub. in Calcutta Sanskrit Series, Calcutta, 1933 onwards. Raghuvir and Chandorkar are engaged in the preparation of a critical ed. of this epic on the lines of the *Mahābhārata* ed. BORI, Poona. The Oriental Institute under M. S. University of Baroda is also understood to be engaged in a similar project. Also see *The Kashmirian Rāmāyaṇa* (G. A. Grierson), Bib. India., 1930 and tr. ed. by P. C. Divanji, 1963. Trs. into Eng. verse by R. T. H. Griffith, Banaras, 1915 (new ed.); into Eng. prose by M. N. Dutt, Calcutta, 1892—94; by H. P. Sastri, London, 3 vols; by M. L. Sen (3 vols.); N. S. Mani; into Italian by Gorressio, Parigi, 1847—58; into French by J. Fauche, Paris, 1854—58 and by A. Roussel, Paris, 1903—09; into German by J. Menrad, Munchen, 1897 (Book I only) and a few extracts by Fr. Rückert. Trs. into Russian by A. Barannikov. Portions trs. into Georgian (Russia). The epic was translated into Persian, in 999 A. H. under emperor Akbar, by Naquib Khan and others. For a bibliography of important studies in the epic as well as a discussion of the various problems connected with it, see M. Winternitz, *History of Indian literature* I, pp. 475-517; N. A. Gore, *Bibliography of the Rāmāyaṇa*. Also see JI Xian Lin, *Preliminary Study on the Rāmāyaṇa*, Bālakāṇḍa (Chinese trs.);

L.A. van Da alen, *Vālmīki's Sanskrit*, Leiden, 1980; A.K. Majumdar, *Economic Background of the Epic Society*; M. Bhoothlingam, Bombay, 1980; R. Sharma, *Socio-Political Study of the Vālmīki Rāmāyaṇa*; P. L. A. Sweeney, *The Rāmāyaṇa and the Malay Shadow-play*, Kuala lumpur, 1972; Mira Roy, Scientific Information in the Rāmāyaṇa, *Bulletin of National Institute of Sciences of India*, No. 21, 1962; K. R. S. Iyenger, *Epic Beautiful*, Eng. verse rendering of Sundarakāṇḍa, Delhi, 1983.

ANTOINE, R. : *Rāma and the Bards on the Rāmāyaṇa.*

AGAR, P. : *Rāmāyaṇa and Laṅkā.*

BAUMYARTNER, A.: *Das Rāmāyaṇa Und die Rāma-Literaturder Inder*, Frelburg, 1894.

BHATT, G. H. : *Pada-index of Vālmīki Rāmāyaṇa.*

BHATTACHARYA, B. : The Rāmāyaṇa and its influence upon the Medieval Digests of Eastern India, *P. K. Gode Comm. Vol.* Poona, 1960.

BHATTACHARJI, S. : Validity of Rāmāyaṇa Values, *Pro. of UNESCO Seminar on Sanskrit*, New Delhi, 1972, Vol. II.

BULCKE, C. : Rāmakathā (in Hindi), Prayag, Allahabad, 1950.

CHATTERJI, S. K. : The Rāmāyaṇa, its character...and exodus, a resume, Calcutta, 1978.

DAS, N. C. : *Ancient Geography of Asia, compiled from Vālmīki Rāmāyaṇa*, Varanasi, 1971.

DASH, T. P. : The Rāmāyaṇa...the Bible of Humanity by French Thinker Michelet, *Summaries of Paper, AIOC*, 1974.

DE, S.C. : *Historicity of Rāmāyaṇa and the Indo-Aryan Society.*

DHARMA, P. C. : *The Rāmāyaṇa Polity.*

HARKARE, M. : *Rāmāyaṇa-rahasya*, Nagpur, 1977.

JACOBI, H. : The *Rāmāyaṇa* (Eng. trs.), Baroda, 1960.

KHAN, B. : *The Concept of Dharma in Vālmiki Rāmāyaṇa*, 1965.

MUKHOPADHYAY, A. : *Rāmāyaṇa Yuga Bhārat Sabhyatā* (in Bengali), Calcutta.

NAVLEKAR, N. R. : *New Approach to the Rāmāyaṇa.*

PARASHAR, S. : *Rāmāyaṇa considered from historical and Rāṣṭravādī point of view.*

PETER, I. S. : *Beowulf and the Rāmāyaṇa* London, 1924.

PROCKINGTON, J.J. : *Vālmiki Rāmāyaṇa etc. Sternbach Volume.*

RAGHAVAN, V. : *Rāmāyaṇa triveṇī*, Madras.

——— : *The Greater Rāmāyaṇa*, Varanasi, 1973 (A survey of Rāmāyaṇa story as found in the *Mahābhārata*, *Harivaṃśa*, Purāṇas and Upa-purāṇas).
Sanskrit Rāmāyaṇas other than Vālmīki's, New Delhi.

——— : *The Rāmāyaṇa in Greater India.*

RAGHUVIRA : *The Rāmāyaṇa in China*, Lahore, 1938.

RAI, R. : *Vālmīki-rāmāyaṇa Kośa*, Banaras, 1965.

RAMASVAMI SASTRI, K. S.: *Studies in the Rāmāyaṇa*, Baroda, 1944.

ROY, MIRA : Scientific Information in the Rāmāyaṇa, *Bulletin of National Institute of Sciences in India*, No. 21, pp. 58-66, 1962.

RUBEN, W. : *Studien Zur text geschichte des Rāmāyaṇa*, Stuttgart, 1936.

SATYAVRAT : *Vālmīki Rāmāyaṇa, a linguistic study*, Delhi, 1964.

SEN, Nilmadhav : *Studies in some linguistic aspects of Vālmīki's Rāmāyaṇa.*

———: The Fire Ordeal of Sītā, a later interpolation, *JOIB*, 1.3.

SHARMA, R. : *A socio-political study of Vālmīki's Rāmāyaṇa.*

TELANG, K. T. : *Was Rāmāyaṇa copied from Homer*, Bombay, 1873.

VENKETASUBRAMONIA, S. : Rāmāyaṇa and Music, *Summaries of Papers, AIOC*, 1974.

VYAS, S. N. : *India in the Rāmāyaṇa Age*, Delhi, 1967

WURM, A. : *Character Portrayals in the Rāmāyaṇa of Vālmīki.*

For books, dealing with both the epics, see under *Mahābhārata.*

The following papers are noteworthy :—

BAILEY, H. W.: The Rāma story in Khotanese, *JAOS*, Vol. 59.

——— : On Rāmāyaṇa and Rāma in Khotanese, *BSOS*, Vol. 10.

BÖHTLINGK, O. : The Kritik des Rāmāyaṇa, *ZDMG*, 43, 1889, pp. 53-68.

Bemer Kenwerthes aus Rāmāyaṇa, *Bericht der Sachsisch Akademie*, 29.

BROCKINGTON, J. L. : The Verbal system of Rāmā., *JOIB*, 19. 1-2, 1969.

Nominal system of Rām., JOIB, 19.4, 1970.

BULCKE, C. : There Recensions of the Rāmāyaṇa, *JOR*, Vol. 17.

CHAKRAVARTI, A. : Buddhist and Jain Versions of the story of Rāma, *The Jaina Gazette*, Vol. 22, 1926.

CONNOR, J. P. : The Rāmāyaṇa in Burma, *Jour. of Burma Res. Soc.*, Vol. 15, 1915.

DHANI, PRINCE : The Rāma Jātaka—a Lao Version, *Jour. of Siam Soc.*, Vol. 36, 1946.

GODA KUMBURA, C. E. : The Rāmāyaṇa. A Version of Rāma's Story from Ceylon, *JRAS*, 1946.

GORRESIO : also wrote articles on the language of the Benga recension of the Rām.

HUBER (ed.) : La Legende du Rāmāyaṇa en Annam, *BEFEO*, Vol. 5.

IYER, K. B. : Yama-pwe or the Rāmāyaṇa play in Burma, *Triveni* (Bangalore), Vol. 14.

JACOBI, H. : Uber das Alter des Rāmāyaṇa, Festgrus an O. Von Bohtlingk, Stuttgart, 1888.

JHALA, G. C. : An echo of Buddhist practice in Rāmāyaṇa (IV.6.4—Cr. ed.), *Summaries of Papers*, AIOC, Silver Jubilee Session, 1969, p. 65.

KANE, P. V. : The Two Epics, *ABORI*, XI

KEITH, A. B.: Archaisms in the Rāmāyaṇa, *JRAS*, 1910, 1911.

LALOU, M. L. : Histoire de Rāma em Tibetan, *JA*, 1936.

MASSON, J. : Who knows Rāma ? A narrative difficulty in Vālmīki Rāmāyaṇa, *ABORI*, L, 1969.

MICHELSON, T. : Linguistic archaisms of the Rāmāyaṇa, *JAOS*, 1904.

——— : On some verb forms in the Rām., *Transactions and Pro. of Americal Philological Assn.*, Series X, Vol. 34.

——— : On some irregular uses of *me* and *te* in Epic Sanskrit, and some related problems, *JRAS*, 1911.

RICHARD, W : The Malag Version of the Rāmāyaṇa, *B. C. Law Vol.* II, Poona, 1946.

ROUSSEL : Les anomalies der Rāmāyaṇa, *Journal Asiatique* 1910.

RUBEN, W.: *Uber die ethische Idealyestalt des Rāma*, *Studia Indologica, Festcchrift W. Kinfel*, Bombay, 1955.

SANKALIA, H. D. : *Rāmāyaṇa in Historical Perspective*, New Delhi, 1982.

SEN, NILMADHAVA : Un-Pāṇinian Saṃdhi in Rām, *JAS*, Letters, 16, 1950.

Some phonetical characteristics of Rām., *Do*, 17, 1951.

The Future system of Rām., *Do*, 11, 12, 1951-52.

Un-Pāṇinian Infinitive forms of Rām., *Do*, 11,12,1952-53.

Secondary conjugations in Rām., *Poona Orientalist*, 14, 1949.

Un-Pāṇinian perfect forms in Rām., *Vak*, 1, 1951.

The Vocabulary of Rām., I, *Vak*, 1, 1951; II, *Vak*, 2, 1952; III, *Vak*. 5, 1957.

The Aorist system of Rām., *Vak*, I, 1951.

A comp. study in some linguistic aspects of the diff. recensions of Rām., *JOIB* 1.2, 1951.

Syntax of the Tenses in Rām., *JOIB*, 1.4., 1952.
On syntax of the cases in Ram., *JOIB*, 2.2, 1952.
Some Epic verbal forms in Rām., *JOIB*, 3.2., 1953.
Un-Pāṇinian Nominal declension in Rām., *JOIB*, 1955.
Un-pāṇinian pronouns and numerals in Rām.
Influence of Middle Indo-Aryan on Language of Rām., *IL*, 25, 1964 (1965).
Irregular Treatment of the Augment in Rām.: *S. K. De Memo. Vol*, Calcutta, 1972.
Also see *Summaries of Papers*, vth World Sanskrit Conference, Varanasi, 1981, p. 218.

SUKTHANKAR, V. S. : The Nala Episode of the Rām., *F. N. Thomas Pres. Vol.*, Bombay, 1939.

VAIDYA, C. V. : *The Riddle of the Rāmāyaṇa.*

WURM, A. : *Genesis of the Rāmāyaṇa of Vālmīki.*]

RĀMĀYAṆA-CAMPŪ : Ascribed to Bhoja, it extends up to the Kiṣkindhā-kāṇḍa of the *Rāmāyaṇa*. The sixth book, called Yuddha-kāṇḍa, of the *Rāmāyaṇa*, was made up in this work by Lakṣmaṇa Bhaṭṭa. Some manuscripts give a seventh or Uttara-kāṇḍa by Veṅkaṭarāja.

[Ed. K. P. Parab, with comm., NSP, 1898 (including Lakṣmaṇa Bhaṭṭa's supplement with Skt-Hindi comm.), by R. Misra, Banaras, 1956.]

RĀMĀYAṆA-MAÑJARĪ : A poetical work by Kṣemendra. It gives us an abridged version of the entire Rāma-story. All the seven books of the *Rāmāyaṇa*, with the same titles, are found in this work. Kṣemendra, however, has altered the contents to a considerable extent. He has made a judicious recast of the original to suit his purpose, and reveals his unconventional attitude towards the time-honoured contents of the epic. It is poor as a specimen of Kāvya.

[Ed. Bhavadatta and Parab, 1903.]

RASA-CINTĀMAṆI : Ascribed to Madanāntadeva Sūri, it deals, *inter alia*, with the fabrication of gold, silver, preparation of copper from Blue Vitriol and extraction of Zinc from Calamine.

[For a brief account of the work, see P. C. Roy, *History of Chemistry* etc. Calcutta, 1956.]

RASAGAṄGĀDHARA : A well-known work on Alaṃkāra-śāstra, by Jagannātha. Originally appearing to have consisted of five chapters, it is at present available in an incomplete form. We get only the first chapter complete and a part of the second. It is written in the form of *Sūtra* and *Vṛtti*. The topics, dealt with in the first chapter, are: definition of *Kāvya*; its four varieties called *Uttamottama*, *Uttama*, *Madhyama* and *Adhama*; *Rasa*, *Bhāva* and *Guṇa*. In the second chapter we have divisions of *Dhvani*, with a discussion of *Abhidhā* and *Lakṣaṇā*, after which comes the treatment of *Upamā* and other poetic figures enumerated as 70.

[Ed. Durgaprasad and Parab, with Nāgojī's comm., NSP, 1947 (6th ed.); R. Ojha, with comm. *Rasacandrikā*, Varanasi 1977. See M. Shastri, *Rasagaṅgādhara* with comm. of Nāgeśa Bhaṭṭa; R. Mukherjee, *Jagannātha's literary theories*; C. P. Shukla, *Treatment of Alaṃkāras in Rasagaṅgādhara*, 1977; A. L. Gangopadhyay, *Paṇḍitarāja Jagannātha on Esthetic Problem*, Calcutta.]

RASA-HṚDAYA : A medical work by Bhikṣu Govinda, in which the author deals with mercury, other minerals and metals etc.

[For its importance, see P. C. Roy : *History of Chemistry in Ancient and Medieval India*, Calcutta, 1956.]

RASA-NAKṢATRA-MĀLIKĀ : An Āyurvedic work by Mathanasiṃha who appears to have written under a king of Mālava. It deals, *inter alia*, with mineral preparations used in medicine.

[For the work, see P. C. Roy : *History of Chemistry in Ancient and Medieval India*, Calcutta 1966.]

RASA-PRADĪPA : A medical work describing the preparation of mineral acids by distillation, and of calomel for the treatment of *Phiraṅga-roga* (Syphilis).

RASAPRAKĀŚA-SUDHĀKARA: An Āyurvedic work by Yaśodhara, belonging to the 13th century. It deals, *inter alia*, with the means of refinement of mercury, the calcination of all metals and the process of making gold and silver.

[Ed. J. T. Acharya, NSP, 1911. For the importance of the work, see P. C. Roy : *History of Chemistry in Ancient and Medieval India*, Calcutta, 1956.]

RASARĀJALAKṢMĪ : A work on medical science, by Viṣṇudeva. The author states in the colophon that it is an essence of Āyurveda (*Vaidyakasāra*). It is stated to have been written under King Bukka (d. 1376 A.D.).

[For the importance of the work, see P. C. Roy, *History of Hindu Chemistry in Ancient and Medieval India*, Calcutta, 1956.]

RASARATNĀKARA : An Āyurvedic treatise, in five parts, by Nityanātha. Its contents are as follows :

I. *Rasa-khaṇḍa.*

II. *Rasendra-khaṇḍa.*

III. *Vāda-khaṇḍa.*

IV. *Rasāyana-khaṇḍa.*

V. *Mantra-khaṇḍa.*

There is a work of this name by Nāgārjuna who may or may not be identical with the great Nāgasena, famous in Āyurvedic literature.

[Ed. J. T. Acharya, NSP, 1913. For its importance in the science of Chemistry, see P. C. Roy : *History of Chemistry in Ancient and Medieval India*, Calcutta, 1956.]

RASARATNA-PRADĪPIKĀ : Deals with the Rasa-theory in Sanskrit poetics.

[Cr. ed. by R. N. Dandekar, Bombay, 1945.]

RASARATNA-SAMUCCAYA : An authoritative Āyurvedic work ascribed to Vāgbhaṭa in some texts, to Aśvinīkumāra or Nityanātha, in others. Assigned conjecturally to 1300 A.D., it consists of 30 chapters and deals, *inter alia*, with *Mahārasa*, *Uparasa*, description of jewels and pearls and various metals.

[Ed. ASS, 19, 1910; H. Sukula, 1937. For the importance of the work, see P. C. Roy; *History of Chemistry in Ancient and Medieval India*, Calcutta, 1956.]

RASĀRṆAVA : A Tāntric-medical work, assigned by its editor to c. 1200 A.D. In the form of Tantra, it deals with Rasas (mercury and some other important minerals), Uparasas (inferior minerals), metals etc. and the various means of processing them.

[Ed. Bib. Ind., 1908-10. For its contents and importance, see P. C. Roy : *History of Chemistry in Ancient and Medieval India*, Calcutta, 1956.]

RASĀRṆAVA-KALPA : Written about the 11th century A.D., it is a work on Indian alchemy and iatro-chemistry. A part of the *Rudrayāmala-tantra* it is a curious blending of alchemical ideas and practices relating to transmutation of base metals into noble metals and transubstantiation of human body and esoteric Tāntric rites.

[Text critically ed. and trs. into Eng. by Mira Roy and Subbaryappa, Indian National Science Academy pub. New Delhi, 1976.]

RASĀRṆAVA-SUDHĀKARA : By Sīṃhabhūpāla II. A work on dramaturgy including *Rasa*.

[Cr. ed. with Intro. and notes, by. T. Venkatachariar, Madras, 1979.]

RASENDRA-CINTĀMAṆI : An Āyurvedic work by Ḍhuṇḍukanātha. It lays down 21 methods of refining Rasa.

[Ed. with Hindi trs., by B. Misra, Bombay, 1925.]

RASENDRA-CŪḌĀMAṆI : Ascribed to Somadeva, it deals with mercury, some other minerals and metals, means of processing them etc. It is important for the history of medical science and chemistry in India.

[See P. C. Roy : *History of Chemistry in Ancient and Medieval India*, Calcutta 1956.]

RASENDRA-SĀRA-SAṂGRAHA : An authoritative Āyurvedic work by Gopāla Kṛṣṇa Bhaṭṭa. It deals with the purification and calcination of mercury, jewels etc. and with medicines for various ailments. The work is written in simple language.

[Ed., with Hindi trans., by N. Mitra, Lahore, 1927.]

RATI-RAHASYA : Attributed to Kukkoka, and composed some time before the 13th century A.D., it deals with Erotics, professes to follow Vātsyāyana and claims to have used Nandikeśvara and Goṇikāputra.

[Ed., with Kāñcīnātha's comm., D. Parajuli, Lahore. Trs. into Eng. by R. Schmidt, L. Verlag, Berlin, 1903] .

RATIŚĀSTRA : A work on erotics attributed to Nāgarjuna.

[Ed., with *Smara-tattva-prakāśikā* comm. of Rāvaṇārādhya. See R. Schmidt: Liefe Und Eha in atten Indica, Berlin, 1904.]

RATNA-ŚĀSTRA (or -PARĪKṢĀ)

Science of jewels. It deals with processes of testing jewels. Varāhamihira appears to have been familiar with this science. The extant works, containing varied information about jewels and legends concerning them, are of unknown but probably late date. These include the *Agasti-mata*, the *Ratna-parīkṣā* of Buddha Bhaṭṭa, the *Navaratna-parīkṣā* of Nārāyaṇa Paṇḍita and minor texts. The *Yukti-kalpataru*, ascribed to Bhoja, deals, *inter alia*, with this topic. The subject is treated of also in the *Garuḍa-purāṇa*, lxviii-lxxx.

[Some texts ed. T. Finot, *Les lapidaires indiens*, 1896. Also see Kirfel, *Festgabe Carbe*, p. 108.]

RATNĀVALĪ: A four-act drama of the *Nāṭikā* type, by Śrīharṣa. The theme is the marriage, through various obstacles and at the clever intervention of the minister Yaugandharāyaṇa, of king Udayana and Ratnāvalī, daughter of the king of Ceylon.

[Ed. K. P. Parab, with Govinda's comm., NSP., 1895.]

It is the title also of a work attributed to the Buddhist philosopher, Nāgārjuna. It is a metrical work purporting to be an epistle, containing the essence of the Buddhist doctrine, to an unnamed king who is supposed by some to be identical with Śātavāhana. It is styled *Rāja-parikathā*, and consists of 77 verses.

[Ed. and trs. into Eng. by G. Tucci in *JRAS*, 1934. See H.N. Chatterji, *Philosophy of Nāgārjuna as contained in the Ratnāvalī*.]

RĀVAṆĀRJUNĪYA: A grammatical poem, in imitation of the *Bhaṭṭi-kāvya*, by Bhaṭṭa Bhīma (Bhauma or Bhaumaka). It relates, in 27 cantos imperfectly recovered, the story of Rāvaṇa's fight with Kārtavīryārjuna At the same time, it illustrates the rules of Pāṇini in the regular order of the *Aṣṭādhyāyī*. The poem is also called *Arjunarāvaṇīya*.

[Ed. Sivadatta and Parab, NSP, 1900.]

RĀVAṆA-VADHA : Real name of *Bhaṭṭi-kāvya* (q. v.).

ṚGVEDA : The earliest of the Vedic *Saṃhitās*. The contents are divided in two ways, viz.

(1) *Aṣṭaka*, *Adhyāya*, *Varga* and *Ṛk*.

(2) *Maṇḍala*, *Anuvāka*, *Sūkta* and *Ṛk*.

The latter division is more popular. There are ten *Maṇḍalas* of which the tenth appears to have been compiled much later than the other *Maṇḍalas*. There are altogether 1028 hymns (*Sūktas*) in it; of these 11 are called *Khilas* or supplements. Every *Sūkta* is stated to have been revealed to a particular sage, and consists of verses ((*Ṛks*) generally composed in a particular metre. Each *Sūkta* is stated to have some ritual application (*viniyoga*). Each of the hymns is addressed to a particular deity. This Veda is polytheistic, though henotheism and subsequently monotheism developed. The gods and goddesses are generally personifications of natural phenomena. There are some abstract deities also, e.g. Manyu (anger), Śraddhā (reverence) etc. Some deities are invoked in pairs, e.g. Mitra and Varuṇa. This Veda is very important for the social and literary history of prehistoric India.

There is a wide divergence of opinion among the scholars with regard to the age of this Veda. While some scholars believe that it came into being as early as 6000 B.C., others would bring it down to 1500 or even 1200 B.C. Of the 21 recensions of this Veda, that were known at one time, we have got only two, viz. *Śākala* and *Vāṣkala*.

[Of the many editions, mention may be made of the one published by Vaidika Saṃśodhana Maṇḍala, Poona, Vols. I—IV, V (Index of words and lines), with Sāyaṇa's comm., 1933—41. The text only has been published in a handy form by Satvalekar, Surat, 1957. Also ed., with available portions of the *Bhāṣyas* of Skandasvāmin and Udgīta, the *Vyākhyā* by Veṅkaṭamādhava and Mudgala's *Vṛtti* based on *Sāyaṇa-bhāṣya*, by Visvabandhu, VVRI, Hoshiarpur, Vols. I, VII, 1965; II, III, 1963; IV—VI, 1964; VIII (Indices), 1966. Ed. K. Sastry, with *Siddhāñjana* comm., Pondicherry. Complete German trs. by A. Ludwig, in 6 vols. Prag, 1876—88, utilising both orthodox and modern interpretations. Also trs. into German by F. Geldner, 3 Vols., Cambridge, Mass.,. 1951. Wilson's Eng. trs., in 6 volumes, (Poona, 1925—28), follows the orthodox interpretation. A good Eng. trs. is that of R. T. H. Griffith, Banaras, 1896-97 (2nd ed.), 1926 (3rd ed.). There are other translations of the whole of the *Ṛgveda* or of selections from it. Trs. into French by Langlois; into Spanish by F. Tola, Buenos Aires, 1968. Trs. into Bengali by R. C. Dutta, Calcutta, 1963; by Durgadasa, Calcutta. There are also translations into several other regional languages of India. For an up-to-date discussion of the age of the *Ṛgveda*, see *History and Culture of the Indian People*, Vol. I (Vedic Age), London, 1951.]

In connexion with the *Ṛgveda*, the following works also may be consulted :

AGUILAR, H. : *Sacrifice in the Ṛgveda.*

APRABUDDHA : *Message of Ṛgveda.*

ATKINS, S. D. : *Pūṣan in the Ṛgveda*, 1941.

BASU, P. C. : *Indo-Aryan Polity—Ṛgvedic Period.*

BERGAIGNE, A. : *La religion védique* etc., 3 vols. Paris 1878—83. (Rev. ed. Paris, 1963).

———: *Etude Sur le lexique du Ṛgveda*, Paris, 1884.

BHAVE, S. S.: *Soma hymns of the Ṛgveda*, Baroda, 1960.

BLAIR, C. J.: *Heat in the Ṛgveda and Atharvaveda*, New Haven, Connecticut, 1961.

BLOOMFIELD, M.: *Ṛgveda Repetitions*, Cambridge (Mass.), 1916.

BUDDHAPRAKASH: *The Ṛgveda and the Indus Valley Civilisation*, Hoshiarpur, 1967.

CHANDA, A. N.: *Ṛgvedic Culture and the Indus Valley Civilisation*, Calcutta, 1980.

CHAUBEY, B.: *Treatment of nature in the Ṛgveda*, Hoshiarpur, 1970.

CHAUHAN, D. V.: Identification of some Ṛgvedic rivers in Afghanistan, *Summaries of papers, AIOC*, 1974.

CLAYTON, A. C.: *Ṛgveda and Vedic Religion*, New Delhi, 1981 (Reprint)

DANGE, S. A.: *Pastoral symbolism from the Ṛgveda*, Poona; *Vedic concept of field and the divine fructification*, Bombay, 1971.

DAS, A. C.: *Ṛgvedic Culture.*

DESHMUKH, P. R.: *The Indus Civilisation in the Ṛgveda*, 1954.

GHOSH, E.: *Studies in Ṛgvedic deities, astronomical and meteorological*, New Delhi, 1983.

GONDA, J: *Epithets in the Ṛgveda*, The Hague, 1959.
: *The Medium in the Ṛgveda*, Leiden, 1979.

GRASSMANN, H: *Worterbuch Zum Ṛgveda*, Leipzig, 1973.

GRISWOLD, H. D.: *Religion of Ṛgveda*, London, 1923.

HARIYAPPA, H. L.: *Ṛgveda Legends through the ages*, Poona, 1953.

LAW, N. N.: *The Age of Ṛgveda*, 1965.

MAINKAR, T. G.: *Some poetical aspects of Ṛgvedic Repetitions.*
: *Ṛgvedic Foundation of Classical Poetics*, Delhi, 1977.

MANKAD, D. R.: *Date of Ṛgveda.*

MISHRA, H. M. Dravidian Plant names in RV, *Summaries of papers, AIOC*, 1974.

NEUFELDT, R. W. : *F. Max. Müller and the Ṛgveda*, Calcutta, 1980.

OIDENBERG, H. : *Ṛgveda Text-critische and exegetische*, Noten, 2 vols., 1909-12.

OTTO, R : *Varuṇa Hymen des Ṛgveda*, Bonn, 1948.

PATANJALI, D. P. : *A critical study of the Ṛgveda, particularly from the point of view of Pāṇinian Grammar*, New Delhi 1963.

POTDAR, K. T. : *Sacrifice in the Ṛgveda*, Bombay, 1953.

RAHURKAR, V. G. : *The seers of the Ṛgveda.*

RAJA, C. K. : *Poet-philosophers of the Ṛgveda.*
: The commentaries on the Ṛgveda and the Nirukta, *Pro. of* 5*th Oriental Con.*, Vol. I., 1912.

REGNAUD, P. : *Le Ṛgveda les origines de la mythologic Indo-Eurypeenne* Paris, 1892.

RAJAWADE, V. R. : *Words in the Ṛgveda*, Poona.

RENOU, L. : *Etudes Sur Le Vocabulaire Du Ṛgveda*, Pondicherry, 1958.

: *Etudes Vediques et Pāṇineennes*, Paris, Vols. 1-13, 1955—64.

ROY, P. : Satire in the Ṛgveda, *Summaries of papers*, AIOC, 1974.

SAMKARANANDA, S. : *Ṛgvedic culture of the pre-historic Indus*, 2 vols., 1943-44.

SARUP, L. : *Ṛgveda and Mohenzoḍaro*, Pres. Address, AIOC, Mysore, 1935.

SEN, U. P. : *The Ṛgvedic Era*, Calcutta, 1974.

SHASTRI, P. C. : *Ṛgvedic Esthetics.*

SRINIVASAN, D. : *Concept of Cow in the Ṛgveda*, 1979.

SWAMI, V. and SWAMI, N. : *Complete Alphabetical Index of all words in the Ṛgveda.*

TEWARI, S. : *Ṛgvedīya Āprīsūkta* (Hindi).

VARMA, M. K. : *Poetic Beauty of the Ṛgveda.*

VENKATASUBBIAH, A. : *Contributions to the interpretation of the Ṛgveda*, Mysore, 1967.

VISHVABANDHU : *Grammatical word-index to Ṛgveda*, Hoshiarpur, 1963.

WILLARD, J. : *Poetry and Speculation of the Ṛgveda*, California, 1981.

WINTERNITZ, M. : History of Indian Literature, Vol. I., 1927.

The following papers are useful:

ABHYANKAR, K.V. : References to Nakṣatras in the Ṛgveda. Date of the Ṛgveda, *ABORI*, 1976.

APTE, V. M. : Ṛgveda citations in the Mahābhārata, *P. V. Kane Pres. Vol.*, Poona, 1941.

Textual imperfection in the extant Ṛgveda, *Siddhabhāratī* (*S. Varma Vol.*) I, Hoshiarpur, 1950.

BARRET, L. C. : Paippalāda and Ṛgveda, *B. Bloomfield Vol.*, New Haven, 1926.

BHANDARKAR, D. R.: The developement of figure of speech in the Ṛgveda; *Studia Indo-Iranica* (Ehrengabe für W. Geiger), Leipzig, 1931.

BILLIMORIYA, N. B. :The Ṛgveda and the follower of Ahuramazda, *Zoroastrian Association Silver Jubilee Vol.*

DWIVEDI, R.C. : Jāra in the Ṛgveda, *Recent Studies in Sanskrit and Indology, J. Agrawal Fel. Vol.*, Delhi, 1982.

ESTELLER, A. : The Quest for the Original Ṛgveda, *ABORI*, L, 1969.

GELDNER, K. : die Ausbutterung des Oceans in Ṛgveda, *Festgruss Böhtlingk*, Stuttgart, 1888.

PALSULE, G. R. : Verbal Forms Peculiar to Ṛgveda, Maṇḍala VI, *Adyar Library Bulletin, K. K. Raja Fel. Vol.*, 1981.

WOOLNER, A. C.: The Ṛgveda and the Punjab, *Rapson Pres. Vol.*, (*BSOAS*, VI), London, 1931.

WUST, W.: ein weiterer irano-skythischer Eigennamen im Ṛgveda, *Studia Indo-Iranica* (Ehrengabe fur W. Geiger), Leipzig, 1931.

ZIMMERMANN, R. : Asha in the Gāthās of the Avesta and Ṛta in the Ṛgveda, *Modi Mem. Vol.*, Bombay, 1930.

GONDA, J.: The so-called secular, humorous and satirical hymns of the Ṛgveda, *Orientalia Neerlandica*, Leiden.

KUIPER, F. B. J. : Ṛgvedic loan-words, *Studia Indologica* (*Kerfel Vol.*), Bonn, 1955.

KULKARNI, B. R.: Association of Seeta and Pūṣan in Ṛgveda and its astronomical significance, *D. V. Potdar Comm. Vol.*, Poona, 1950.

LUDWIG, A. : die Ironie in Mahābhārata and im Ṛgveda, *Festgruss Bohtlingk*, Stuttgart, 1888.

NARAHARI, H. G. : Allusions in the Ṛgveda to the doctrine of transmigration, *C. K. Raja Pres. Vol.*, Madras, 1941.

PARANJPE, V. G. : Historicity of Asuras mentioned in the ṚV, *ARURI*, LVI, 1975, pp. 195 200.

PATIL, G. M. : Priesthood in Avesta and Ṛgveda, *Taraporewala Memo. Vol.* (*Bulletin of Deccan College*), Poona, 1957.

PUSALKER, A. D. : Mohenjo Daro and Ṛgveda, *R. K. Mookerji Vol.* (*Bharata-kaumudi*), Allahabad, 1945, 1947.

SHARMA, B. R. : Ṛgvedic rivers, *Indica*, Bombay, 1953.

SHASHIKUMAR : A study of figures of speech in the Ṛgveda etc., *Summaries of papers, AIOC*, 1969, p. 367.

STEIN, M. A. : On some river-names in the Ṛgveda, *R. G. Bhandarkar Comm. Vol.*, Poona, 1917.

VELANKAR, H. D. : Magicians in the Ṛgveda, *Ṣarūpabhāratī* (*L. Sarup Mem. Vol.*), Hoshiarpur, 1954.

WIJESEKERA : Ṛgvedic river-goddesses and an Indus Valley Seal, *C. K. Raja Pres. Vol.*, Madras, 1941.

ṚJUVIMALĀ : A commentary, by Śālikanātha, on Prabhākara's *Bṛhatī* comm. on the *Bhāṣya* of Śabara.

ṚKTANTRA : A *Prātiśākhya* of the Sāmaveda. See *Prātiśākhya.* [Ed. Suryakanta, Lahore, 1939.]

ROMAKA-SIDDHĀNTA : See *Pañca-siddhāntikā.* It is attributed to Śrīsena, and was composed earlier than 500 A.D.

ṚTU-SAṂHĀRA : A lyric poem describing the six seasons as viewed through the lover's eye. It is believed by some to belong to Kālidāsa's juvenilia, while others think that it was composed by an inferior poet who bore the name of Kālidāsa or who associated it with the master-poet's name in order to impart a halo of importance to it. The comnentators of this poem include Maṇirāma, Amarakīrti Sūri.

[Ed. and trs. into Eng. by V.R. Nerurkar, 1916; with Latin and German metrical trs., by P. Von Bohlen, Leipzig, 1840; W.L. Pansikar, with Maṇirāma's comm., NSP, 1922; M.R. Kale, with comm., notes and Eng. trs., Delhi, 1967; R.S. Pandit, *Meghadūta and Ṛtusaṃhāra of Kālidāsa*—Text and French trs. by R.H.A. de Pompignan, Paris, 1938.]

RUDRAYĀMALA : An important Tantra. Its *Rasakalpa* chapter and the section called *Dhātukriyā* or *Dhātu-mañjarī* are particularly important for the history of medical science and chemistry in India.

[For a brief account of the relevant portion, see P.C. Roy, *History of Chemistry in Ancient and Medieval India*, Calcutta, 1956.]

RUG-VINIŚCAYA : See *Nidāna.*

ŚABARA-BHĀṢYA : A celebrated commentary, by Śabarasvāmin, on the *Mīmāṃsāsūtra* of Jaimini.

[Ed., with the original and Index to the *Bhāṣya*, in 4 pts. by R.G. Bhatta, Banaras, 1910. Trs. into Eng., by G. Jha, GOS, 1933-36. See Eng. Index to the trs., by U. Misra, GOS, 1945; D.V. Garg, *Citations in Śabara-bhāṣya*; F. D'SA, *Śabdaprāmāṇyam in Śabara and Kumārila*, 1980. See O. Gachter, *Hermeneutics and Language in Pūrva-mīmāṃsā*, Delhi. See Y. Mimamsak, *Ācārya Śabara-svāmiviracitaṃ Jaimini Mīmāṃsābhāṣyam*, Bahalgadh, Sonepat, Haryana, 1980.

ŚABDA-KALPADRUMA : A well-known lexicon compiled by a few Bengali scholars at the instance of Rājā Rādhākānta Deb of Bengal. In it the words have been analysed into their base-forms and suffixes, and their genders have been determined. Then Sanskrit synonyms are noted, and, in some cases, Bengali equivalents are also given.

[Ed. K. G. Basu, Calcutta, 1310-1313 B. S. Latest reprint by Motilal Banarsidass, Delhi, Varanasi and Patna, in 5 Vols. 1961.]

ŚABDA-KAUSTUBHA : Mainly based on the *Mahābhāṣya*, it is a voluminous commentary, by Bhaṭṭoji, on the *Aṣṭādhyāyī*. It is similar in plan to the *Kāśikā*, and was left incomplete by Bhaṭṭoji who wrote probably as far as the fourth *Āhnika* of the third *Adhyāya*.

[Ed., with the *Aṣṭādhyāyī*, Banaras, 1876 (Comm. on *Pāda* I only of the *Aṣṭādhyāyī*) ; CSS, 1898. V. P. Dvivedi & G. S. Mokate, CSS, Vol. II only, Banaras, 1917.]

ŚABDA-MAṆI-DĪDHITI : A commentary, by Raghunātha Śiromaṇi, on the *Śabda-khaṇḍa* of the *Tattva-cintāmaṇi* of Gaṅgeśa. Some think that it was not written by Raghunātha. Part of the author's *Tattva-cintāmaṇi-dīdhiti*.

ŚABDĀNUŚĀSANA : See *Śakaṭāyana Śabdānuśāsana* and *Siddha-hemacandra*.

ŚABDA-ŚAKTI-PRAKĀŚIKĀ : Written by Jagadīśa Tarkālaṃkāra, it is a subtle examination of the topics of Sanskrit grammar, in accordance with the principles of Nyāya philosophy.

[Ed., with comm. of Kṛṣṇakānta and Jayacandra, Banaras, 1907; with notes, by G. Tarakadarsana-tirtha, Calcutta University, 1914, Part I; with comms. of Kṛṣṇakānta and Rāmabhadra, by D. Shastri, Kashi Skt. Series; M. Nyayacharya, Calcutta. See K. N. Chatterjee, *Word and its Meaning, in new perspective in the light of Jagadīśa's Śabdaśakti-prakāśikā*, Varanasi, 1980.]

ṢAḌDARŚANA-SAMUCCAYA : This work of the eighth century, by Haribhadra, deals with Buddhist views, Nyāya,

Sāṃkhya, Vaiśeṣika, Pūrvamīmāṃsā, Jaina metaphysics, and very briefly with Cārvāka views. It suggests that the number six was traditional, but not rigidly fixed in significance. [Ed., with *Laghuvṛtti* comm., by D. L. Gosvami, CSS, 1905; with Guṇaratna's comm., in Jaina-Ātmānanda-Granthamālā 49, Bhavnagar, 1917.]

SADDHARMA-LAṂKĀVATĀRA : See *Laṃkāvatāra.*

SADDHARMAPUṆḌARĪKA : A work of the Buddhist Mahāyāna school. It glorifies the Buddha, and displays the ideal of the *Bodhisattva.* It is in prose mixed with Sanskrit verse-sections in the older chapters. Chapters XXI-XXVI, which are comparatively late, are in prose only. The work as a whole is not earlier than 200 A.D.

[Ed. P. L. Vaidya, Darbhanga, 1960; trs. H. Kern, SBE, XXI, 1884. S. Levi, *Saddharma Puṇḍarīka,* Paris, 1925. Trs. from the Chinese of Kumārajīva by L. Hurvitz. See A. Yuyama, *A Bibliography of the Skt. texts of the S. Puṇḍarīkasūtra,* Camberra, 1970; Lokesh Chandra (ed.), *Saddharmapuṇḍarīkasūtra,* Kashgar Manuscript, Reiyukai, 1977; H. Toda, Note on Kashgar Ms. of S. P. S., Tokyo, 1977, ed. of the same, Tokushima, 1977.]

SADUKTI-KARṆĀMṚTA : An anthology compiled by Śrīdharadāsa. It consists of 2,380 verses divided into five sections called *Pravāhas,* each of which is subdivided into several sub-sections called *Vīcis.* Each *Vīci* contains five verses. The *Pravāhas* are called respectively *Amara* (or, *Deva*)*-pravāha, Śṛṅgāra-pravāha, Cāṭu-pravāha, Apadeśa-pravāha* and *Uccāvaca-pravāha.* The verses of about 500 poets are quoted in it.

[Critically ed. by S. C. Banerji, Calcutta, 1965.]

SĀHITYA-DARPAṆA : A renowned work on Poetics, by Viśvanātha. In ten chapters it deals with the following topics of Poetics and Dramaturgy :—

I. Definition of poetry

II. Three *Vṛttis* of word and sense

III. *Rasa*

IV. *Dhvani* and *Guṇībhūta Vyaṅgya*

V. Establishment of *Vyañjanā Vṛtti*

VI. Dramaturgy

VII. *Doṣa*

VIII. *Guṇa*

IX. Four *Rītis*, viz. *Vaidarbhī*, *Gauḍī*, *Pāñcālī* and *Lāṭī*

X. *Alaṃkāras*

It lays down *Rasa* as the soul of poetry. Though not of much originality, it gives a comprehensive treatment of the above topics, and is a good text-book on the subject. Its treatment of Dramaturgy is based mostly on the *Daśarūpaka*.

[Frequently published. The notable editions are by (1) Durgaprasad Dviveda, NSP, 1915, 1922; (2) P. V. Kane (Ch. i, ii, x), with notes and a History of Sanskrit Poetics, Bombay, 1951; (3) K. Kāvyatīrtha, with comms. *Vijñāna-priyā* and *Locana*, Lahore, 1938; (4) K. M. Sastri, with the comm. *Lakṣmī*, CSS, 1955. Trs. into Eng., J. R. Ballantyne and P. D. Mitra, Bib. Ind.]

SAHṚDAYĀLOKA : Another name of *Dhvanyāloka* (q.v.).

ŚĀK AṬĀYANA-ŚABDĀNUŚĀSANA (or -VYĀKARAṆA) : A grammatical work attributed to Śākaṭāyana and compiled in the reign of Amoghavarṣa (814-77). It consists of four *Adhyāyas* of four *Pādas* each, the total number of *Sūtras* being about 3,200. It does not deal with Vedic grammar. It betrays influence of the *Cāndra-vyākaraṇa* and the *Jainendra-vyākaraṇa*. Many of its *Sūtras* are the same as Pāṇini's or slightly changed. It has a full commentary.

[Ed. London, 1913.]

ŚAKUNTALĀ : See *Abhijñāna-śākuntala*.

ŚĀLIHOTRA-SAṂHITĀ : Same as *Haya-āyurveda* (q.v.)

SĀMĀNYA NIRUKTI : By Gaṅgeśa. Devoted to the exposition of fallacious reasons.

[Ed. with comm. *Dīdhiti*, *Gādādharī*, *Baladevī* and *Vimala-prabhā* by R. Jha, Darbhanga 1970.]

SAMARĀṄGANA-SŪTRADHĀRA : A work on architecture, ascribed to Bhojadeva (11th century)

[Ed. T. Ganapati Sastri, 2 vols., GOS, 1924, 1925; Rev. ed. by V. S. Agrawala, GOS, 1966; with Hindi trs. by D. Sukla, Delhi, 1965. See D. N. Shukla, *Vāstu-śāstra, with special ref. to Bhoja's Samarāṅgana-sūtradhāra*, Vols. I, II, Lucknow.]

SĀMAVEDA : The Veda of the Sāmans or melodies. Its contents are divided into Pūrvārcika and Uttarārcika. It consists of hymns used to be sung at the time of performing Vedic sacrifices. The major portion of this Veda is later than the Ṛgveda, but certain parts are older.

This Veda is indispensable for the history of Indian music. It is in this Veda that the seven basic notes of Indian songs originated.

Of the many recensions of this Veda, that appear to have originally existed, we know of only three.

[Ed. Raja, Adyar, 1941, with comms. of Mādhava and Bharatasvāmin; ed. and trs. into Eng. by Devi Chand (2nd rev. ed.), New Delhi, 1980. Saṃhitā of the Rāṇāyanīyas ed. and trs. J. Stevenson, London, 1842 (Reprint, Banaras, 1961); that of the Kauthumas by Th. Benfey, Leipzig, 1948 and by S. Samasramin, Bib. Ind., 1871 ff. *Jaiminīya-saṃhitā* ed. Raghu Vīra, Lahore, 1938 (with Sāyaṇa's comm.). Eng. metrical rendering by Griffith in two parts, 1893, 1907 (new ed. 1916, 1926). Bengali trs. by D. Lahiri (with text), 1899; S. Samashrami, 1867, 1874. Hindi trs. by J. Sharma (with text), 1890-91. Tamil trs. by M. R. Jambunathan, Bombay, 1935. For a bibliography of studies, see M. Winternitz, *History of Indian Literature*, I, pp. 163-169. Also see B. Faddegon, *Studies on the Sāmaveda*, Amsterdam, 1951; V. Svami and N. Svami, *Complete Alphabetical index of all words in the Sāmaveda*; V. Raghavan, Sāmaveda and Music, *Jour. of Music Academy*, Madras, XXXIII, 1962; W. Howard, *Sāmavedic chant*, London, 1977.]

SAMAYA-MĀTṚKĀ : A poetical work, in 8 chapters, by Kṣemendra. It relates the story of a young courtesan who, under instructions from an old bawd, traps a rich young man and fleeces his naive parents. The work depicts the social condition of Kashmir at the time of the author.

[Ed. Durgaprasad and Parab, NSP, 1925.]

SAMBANDHA-VĀRTIKA : It is the introductory part of Sureśvarācārya's—*Bṛhadāraṇyakopaniṣad-bhāṣya-vārtika*, and a metrical comment on Śaṃkarācārya's *Bṛhadāraṇyakopaniṣad-bhāṣya*. Written in 1148 verses, acc. to the author's own statement, it may be treated as an independent work on *Advaita Vedānta*. Its purpose is to set forth the relation (*sambandha*) between two sections of the Veda, viz. *Jñāna-kāṇḍa* and *Karma-kāṇḍa*. Hence it is called *Sambandha-vārtika*. Sureśvara expounds Śaṃkara's views through a criticism of the position taken by other Vedāntins and the Mīmāṃsakas.

[Ed. and trs. into Eng., with notes and extracts from 3 unpublished comm., by T. M. P. Mahadevan, Madras, 1958.]

SAṂGĪTA-DĀMODARA : A work on music, by Śubhaṃkara. It consists of 5 chapters, and deals with a variety of topics relating to dance, drama and music. The author attempts to explain music and dramaturgy as originating from Kṛṣṇa (Dāmodara). It is very popular among the Vaiṣṇavas of Bengal. The work is largely a compilation of materials from the ancient works on music and dramaturgy, and hardly shows any originality of the author.

[Ed.G.Shastri and Mukherji, Calcutta, 1960. A critical ed. by V.Raghavan to be published.]

SAṂGĪTA-DARPAṆA : A work on the northern school of Indian music, by Dāmodara, written about 1625 A.D. during the reign of Jahangir. It has borrowed freely from the *Svarādhyāya* of the *Saṃgītaratnākara*. Pictorial descriptions of the different Rāgas, given in it, are mostly based on Somanātha's *Rāga-vibodha.*

[Ed., with Gujarati trs., L. Thakkara, Chaps. 1&2 only, Bombay, 1910.]

SAṂGĪTA-MAKARANDA : Attributed to Nārada, it is in two parts, *Saṃgīta* and *Nṛtya*, of four chapters each. May be assigned to the 11th century A.D. It mentions two divisions of *Rāgas*, pricipals and their wives, and classifies musical sounds into five kinds acc. to the source of percussion. It mentions Mahāmāheśvara, i.e. Abhinavagupta. Its definition of Gāndhāra is almost bodily repeated by Śārṅgadeva.

[Ed. M.R. Telang, GOS, 1920.]

There is a large treatise of the same title by Veda. It mentions the later forms of modern dancing as influenced by European and Mohammedan art.

[*Cat. of MSS in the Palace Library*, Tanjore, XVI. 7268. MS dated 1650 A.D.]

SAṂGĪTA-PĀRIJĀTA : An important work on the northern system of Indian music, by Ahobala, written in the 17th century. It recognises 29 *Śrutis*, and gives 122 *Rāgas*, and, for the first time, describes the twelve *Svaras* in terms of the length of the string of the *Vīṇā*.

[Ed. K. Vidyāvāgīśa, Calcutta, 1936, with a Hindi comm. by Kalinda, Hathras, 1941; with a Bengali comm. by S. Mitra, Calcutta, 1959. Trs. into Persian in 1724 A.D.]

SAṂGĪTA-RĀJA : A work on music, by Kumbha or Kumbhakarṇa. Divided into five chapters (*Ratnakośa*) called respectively Pāṭhya, Gīta, Vādya, Nṛtya and Rasa. Each chapter consists of four sections called Ullāsas each of which is subdivided into four Parīkṣaṇas. Consists of 16,000 Ślokas, each Śloka comprising 32 letters.

[Ed. P. Sharma, Vol. I, Banaras, 1963.]

SAṂGĪTA-RATNĀKARA : A huge work by Śārṅgadeva. It consists of seven chapters which are named as follows :—

I. Svaragatādhyāya
II. Rāgādhyāya
III. Prakīrṇakādhyāya
IV. Prabandhādhyāya
V. Tālādhyāya
VI. Vādyādhyāya
VII. Nartanādhyāya

It deals with dance and music, both vocal and instrumental, and is looked upon as the most authoritative work on the subject.

[Ed. S. S. Shastri, Madras, Vol. I (Adhyāya 1), 1943; Vol. II (Adhyāyas 2-4), 1959; Vol. III (Adhyāyas 5-6), 1951, IV (Adhyaya 7), 1953; Adhyayas 1-4 ed. G. H. Taralokar, Bombay, 1975. Trs. into English—Chap I, by G. K. Raja, Adyar Library Series, No. 51, 1945 (Madras), Chap. VII by K. K. Raja and R. Burnier, *Brahmavidyā* (Adyar Library Bulletin), Vol. XXIII, pts. 3-4, 1959 (Madras). Bengali trs. of the entire work by S. C. Banerji, Calcutta, 1379 B. S. Hindi trs. by S. C. Banerji (Chaps. I-IV), Calcutta. Trs. P. K. Shringy and P. L. Sharma, 1976. See P.L. Sharma, *Saṃgitaratnākara*, 1978].

SAṂGĪTA-SAMAYASĀRA : A work on music, by Pārśvadeva. The author discusses music in a simple manner.

[Ed. TSS, 1925. Critical ed. to be published by Raghavan].

ŚAṂKARA-BHĀṢYA : Well-known comm., by Śaṃkara on the *Brahma-sūtra* (q.v.).

[For ed. and trs., see *Brahma-sūtra*. Also see N. K. Devarāja, *Intro. to Śaṃkara's Theory of Knowledge*; *Word-index to Brahmasūtrabhāṣya of Śaṃkara*, part I, ed. T. M. P. Mahadevan, Madras; L.T.O'Neil, *Māyā in Śaṃkara.* Also see S. R. Krishnamurthisastri, *Brahmasūtra-śaṃkarabhāṣya* with *Brahmavidyābharaṇa* comm. of Advaitānanda, Madras 1976; A. K. Sastri and Panikar, ed. with comms. *Bhāmatī*, *Kalpataru* and *Parimala*, Index etc., Varanasi, 1982.]

ŚAṂKARA-DIGVIJAYA : A biography of Śaṃkarācārya, by Mādhava.

[Ed. ASS, 22. Trs. into Eng. by Tapasyānanda, Madras]

ŚAṂKARA-VIJAYA : Also called *Prācina-śaṃkara-vijaya*. A biography of Śaṃkarācārya, ascribed by some to his pupil Ānandagiri. Other scholars doubt his authorship.

[Ed. Bib. Ind., 1864-68; with Gujarati trs., by K. G. Devasrayi, Ahmedabad, 1888. Also ed. N. Veezhinathan, Madras.]

Other works of this title are attributed to Vidyāśaṅkara (alias Śaṅkarānanda), Anantānandagiri Vallisahayakavi (also called Ācārya-dig-vijaya). A. *Bṛhat-śaṃkaravijaya* is attributed to Citsukhācārya. A Keraliya *Śaṅkara-Vijaya* is ascribed to Govindanātha; it is also known as *Ācārya-carita*. Cūḍamaṇi Dīkṣita is credited with the authorship of *Śaṅkarābhyudaya*. The *Śaṃkara-vijaya-vilāsa* is ascribed to *Cidvilāsa*.

ŚĀṂKHĀYANA-GṚHYASŪTRA : See Gṛhyasūtra, for an account of the works of this class.

[Skt. and German by H. Oldenberg, *Ind. Stu.*, Vol. 15, Eng. trs. by same scholar, SBE, Vol. 29)

ŚĀṂKHĀYANA-ŚRAUTASŪTRA : See Śrautasūtra.
[Ed. A. Hillebrandt, Bib. Ind., 1888 ff; Lokesh Chandra, Delhi, 1980. Eng. trs. by W. Caland]

SĀṂKHYA-KĀRIKĀ : It is the first definite text on Sāṃkhya philosophy, by Īśvarakṛṣṇa. Its principal object is to teach how man can get rid of the three kinds of suffering, viz. *Ādhyātmika*, *Ādhibhautika* and *Ādhidaivika*; cessation of suffering is liberation, acc. to this work.

[Ed. R. Pandeya, with *Yuktidīpikā* comm., Delhi, 1967; G.T. Deshpande 1955; R. Phukan, with Eng. trs. and notes, 1972 (Second ed.); T. G. Mainkar, with Eng. tr. and notes, Poona, 1964. J. Sastri Pandeya, with comms. of Vedāntimahādeva and Nāgeśa, Varanasi, 1973. See S. S. S. Shastri, *The Sāṃkhya-kārikā*, Madras, 1930 and J. Davies's ed. with comm. and Eng. trs. On this work and its author, see S. K. Belvalkar in *Bhandarkar Comm. Vol.* Poona, 1917. Also see E. A. Solomon, *Commentaries of the Sāṅkhya-kārikā, A study*, Ahmedabad; 1974. A. Sen Gupta, *Classical Sāṃkhya : A critical study*, 1969; *Sāṃkhya and Advaita Vedānta : A comparative Study*, 1973; E. A. Polymor, *Commentaries of the Sāṅkhya-Kārikā—a study*, Ahmedabad, 1974.]

SĀṂKHYA-PRAVACANA-BHĀṢYA : A commentary, by Vijñānabhikṣu, on the *Sāṃkhya-sūtra*.

[Ed., with Rāghava Bhaṭṭa's comm., by M. Jha Bakshi, Banaras, 1934; also in Tāntrika Texts, Vols. XVI and XVII. For analysis of contents, see A. H. Ewing, *JAOS*, 1902.]

SĀRA-SIDDHĀNTAKAUMUDĪ : An abridgment, by Varadarāja, of the *Siddhānta-kaumudī*.

SĀRASVATA-VYĀKARAṆA : A grammatical work probably by one Narendrācārya. It combines the merits of brevity and lucidity. It traverses the entire field of grammar, leaving out the Vedic portion and accents, in 700 Sūtras, and appears to have been written at the instance of the Muslim rulers of the day. This work originated probably in the thirteenth century. There is a tradition that an ascetic called Anubhūtisvarūpācārya was author of the *Vārtikas* to this grammar and that the original *Sūtras* were revealed to him by Goddess Sarasvatī.

[Ed., with the exposition of Anubhūtisvarūpācārya, three *Vṛttis* and *Subodhikā* comm. by S. Kudal and revised by V. L. Pansikar, 1926; with *Bālabodhinī* comm. and a Hindi comm., CSS, 1955; with comms. of Candrakīrti and Vāsudeva, notes, Index etc., by N. K. Sarma.]

SARASVATĪ-KAṆṬHĀBHARAṆA : Written by Bhoja in five chapters, it is chiefly a compilation, in an encyclopaedic manner, from earlier treatises on Alaṃkāra-śāstra, especially from the *Kāvyādarśa* of Daṇḍin.

[Ed. J. Vidyāsāgara, with comm. of Ratneśvara on chaps. i-iii, Calcutta, 1894; NSP, with comm. of Ramasiṃha (i-iii) and of Jagaddhara (iv), 1934; K. N. Mishra with Ratneśvara's comm., Intro., Trs., Appendices and Hindi comm., 1976.]

There is also a grammatical work of the same title attributed to Bhoja.

[Ed. K. S. Sastri, TSS, 1935-38.]

SARASVATĪ-VILĀSA : A well-known Smṛti digest by Pratāparudradeva. It consists of two parts, the *Vyavahārakāṇḍa* and the *Ācāra-kāṇḍa*. The former has been published. The principal topics, discussed in it, are as follows :

Hall of justice, judicial procedure, the plaint, the reply, documents, possession, recovery of debt, partition and inheritance, criminal acts known as *Sāhasa* and other titles of law.

It is a work of authority in South India on matters of Hindu law, though inferior to the *Mitākṣarā*.

[*Dāyabhāga* pub., with Eng. trs., by Rev. Thomas Foulkes in 1881. Whole of *Vyavahāra* section pub. in Mysore Govt. Publication Series. On authorship of the *Sarasvatīvilāsa*, see P. K. Code, *Studies in Indian Literary History*, I, p. 423 ff.]

ŚĀRIPUTRA-PRAKARAṆA : Also called *Śāradvatī-putra-prakaraṇa*, it is a drama in nine acts by Aśvaghoṣa. Its theme is the conversion, by the Buddha, of Śāriputra and Maudgalyāyana to Buddhism. Only fragments of this work have been discovered in Central Asia.

[See H. Lüders, Das Śāriputraprakaraṇa, ein Drama des Aśvaghoṣa, in *Sitzungsberichte d Berliner Akad.*, 1911.]

ŚĀRĪRAKA-MĪMĀṂSĀ-BHĀṢYA : Name of Rāmānuja's comm. on the *Brahma-sūtra.*

[Ed. T. B. Narasimhacarya, Madras, 1936.]

Also see *Bhāskara-bhāṣya.*

ŚĀRṄGADHARA-PADDHATI : A well-known anthology compiled by Śārṅgadhara. It contains 4,689 verses in 163 sections, the number of works and authors cited being about 292. Its section, called *Upavana-vinoda*, is an important text on Vṛkṣāyurveda.

[Ed. P. Peterson, BSS, 1888. See A.D. Pusalker, Śārṅgadhara-paddhati and Bṛhat-śārṅgadharapaddhati, *P. K. Code, Comm. Vol.*, Poona, 1960.]

ŚĀRṄGADHARA-SAṂGRAHA : A work on medicine, compiled by Śārṅgadhara and also called *Śārṅgadhara-saṃhitā.* It is divided into three sections called respectively *Pūrva*, *Madhya* and *Uttara.* Each section is sub-divided into several chapters, the first section containing 7, the second 12 and the last 13 chapters. In it the medicines are stated not against diseases but classed as *Svarasa*, *Kvātha*, *Kalka*, *Cūrṇa*,

Guḍikā etc. In the 11th chapter of the second section we find methods of purification and calcination of metals.

[Ed., with the *Dīpikā* and *Gūḍhārtha-dīpikā* comms., and footnotes, by P. Shastri, NSP, 1920.]

SARVA-DARŚANA-SAṂGRAHA : Attributed to Mādhava by some, to Sāyaṇa by others, jointly to Sāyaṇa and Mādhava by yet others, it deals with the systems of philosophy arranged from the point of view of relative error. The schools of philosophy are arranged in the following order :—Cārvāka, Bauddha, Jaina, Rāmānuja, Pūrṇaprajña, four Śaiva schools, Vaiśeṣika, Nyāya, Pūrvamīmāṃsā, a grammatical school ascribed to Pāṇini, Sāṃkhya and Yoga. The chapter on Vedānta appears to be a later addition.

[Ed. with an original comm. by V. S. Abhyankar, rev. by K. V. Abhyankar, Poona, 1951 (with a bibliography on each system). Trs. into English by E. B. Cowell and A. Gough, CSS, 1961 (6th ed).]

SARVA-DARŚANA-SIDDHĀNTA-SAṂGRAHA : Ascribed by some to Śaṃkara, but considered by others to have been written by some other person. In it we find accounts of the following systems of philosophy:

Six orthodox schools of philosophy, the philosophy of Vedavyāsa, i.e. the *Mahābhārata*, the Lokāyatika, the Jaina system, the four schools of Buddhist philosophy.

The Vedānta appears to be the author's own system. Its date is not certain. The *Bhāgavata Purāṇa* is known to it while Rāmānuja is ignored. The alleged allusion to the Turks in it is uncertain.

[Ed. and trs. M. Rangacharya, Madras, 1910.]

SARVĀNUKRAMAṆĪ : It is a work ascribed to Kātyāyana. The title means 'catalogue of all things.' It gives, in the form of *Sūtras*, the first words of every hymn, then the number of verses, the name and family of the *Ṛṣi* to whom the hymn is ascribed, names of deites to whom single verses are addressed and the metre or metres in which the hymn is composed. There is a Kashmirian recension of this work.

[Ed. A. A. Macdonell, Oxford, 1886. On a Kashmirian recension of this work see Scheflelowitz, *ZII*, 1,1922. *Ṛgveda-sarvānukramaṇī* of Kātyāyana and *Anuvākānukramaṇī* of Śaunaka, ed. V. C. Sharma, Aligarh, 1977.]

ŚĀSTRADĪPIKĀ : A Mīmāṃsā work by Pārthasārathi. It enables the readers to learn both the Bhāṭṭa and Prābhākara systems. An index to its popularity is the existence of several comms. on it.

[Ed., with *Prabhā*, by P. N. Bhattacharya, New Delhi, 1978.]

ŚATADŪṢAṆĪ : A polemical work, by Vedānta Deśika attacking the Advaita philosophy.

ŚATAPATHA BRĀHMAṆA : See *Brāhmaṇa*. It contains the flood-legend.

[Kāṇva recension, ed. Caland, Lahore, 1926. Mādhyandina recension, published in 5 parts, Kalyan, 1940-41 (with comms. of Sāyaṇa and Harisvāmin) : also ed. A Weber with comms. of Sāyaṇa, Harisvāmin and Dvivedaganga, Banaras, 1964 (23rd ed.). *Mādhyandina* recension, ed. C. Shastri and P. Shastri, Banaras, 1950. Trs. into Eng. by J. Eggeling, SBE, vols. XLI, XLIII, XLIV, XXVI. For Flora in this *Brāhmaṇa*, see Satya Prakash, *Founders of Sciences in Ancient India*, New Delhi, 1965, pp. 163-64. See N. Drury, *The sacrificial ritual in the Śatapatha Brāhmaṇa*, 1981. G. K. Bhatt, Vāk in Śatapatha Brāhmaṇa, *JAS*, Bombay, (N. S.), Vols. 52-53.]

ŚATAŚLOKĪ : Ascribed to Śaṃkarācārya, it is a didactic tract. In 101 *Sragdharā* verses it lays down the principles of the Vedānta.

[Ed. Select works of Śrīśaṃkarācārya, pp. 85 ff.]

A. *Śataślokī* by Hemādri is a medical work on powders, pills etc.

ṢAṬ-SANDARBHA : See *Bhāgavata-sandarbha*.

SAUNDARANANDA : Composed in eighteen cantos by Aśvaghoṣa, it deals with the conversion, by the Buddha, of his reluctant half-brother Nanda, nicknamed Sundara, to Buddhism, and the consequent lamentation of Sundarī, Nanda's wife.

[Ed., with notes and Eng. trs., by E. H. Johnston, London, 1928, 1932. Re-issue of the text, with additions by C. Chakravarti, Bib. Ind., 1939; with Hindi trs. by S. Chaudhari, Kathautiya Saṃskṛta Bhavan, 1948. An ed. is reported to be under preparation at Mithilā Institute, Darbhanga. See G. Tucci, Note Sul Saundarananda Kāvya di Aśvaghoṣa, *Revista degli Studi Orientali*, X, 1923; A. Gawronski, *Aśvaghoṣa* (extracts trs. into Polish), Ossolineum, 1966.]

SAUNDARYA-LAHARĪ : A book of verses, ascribed to Śaṃkarācārya, containing hymns in praise of goddess Tripuraśundarī, Mantras, mystic formulae and an exposition of Āgamas and Tantras. According to some scholars, it was the work of a Śaṃkarācārya of Tamilnadu.

[Ed. N. S. Venkatanathacharya, Mysore, 1969; V. K. Subramanian, Delhi, 1977; with three comms., Eng. trs. and Prayogas illustrated with Tantras, by R. A. A. Sastri and K. Ramamurthy, Madras, 1957; ed. and trs. into Eng., HOS, 1958: the trs. is called 'Wave of Beauty'. See *Saundarya-laharī* by W. N. Bro. En.]

SEVYA-SEVAKOPADEŚA : A short tract, in 61 verses, by Kṣemendra who lays down his reflections on the relation between the master and the servant, incidentally giving advice to both.

[Ed. Kāvyamālā, II.]

SIDDHAHEMACANDRA : Also called Haimavyākaraṇa, popularly known as *Śabdānuśāsana*. Consisting of eight books, it is based on the Śākaṭāyana Vyākaraṇa. Written for Jayasiṃha Siddharāja, it mainly follows the arrangement and terminology of the *Kātantra*. It omits the Vedic grammar and accents. The eighth book is devoted to Prakrit grammar.

[See Kielhorn, WZKM, ii.]

SIDDHĀNTA-KAUMUDĪ : A celebrated recast by Bhaṭṭoji

Dīkṣita, of the *Aṣṭādhyāyī*. In it the *Sūtras* of Pāṇini are arranged under appropriate heads, e.g. *Kāraka*, *Samāsa* etc. In it the *sūtras* are also explained. The exposition is orderly and easy to follow. Hemacandra's *Śabdānuśāsana* and Rāmacandra's *Prakriyā-kaumudī* may have been utilised by Bhaṭṭoji while writing his *Siddhānta-kaumudī*. For the several comms. on the work, see Aufrecht, *Catalogue Catalogorum*. P. K. Gode informs us of a comm. called *Vidyāvilāsa*, by Śivarāma Tripāṭhin (bet. 1700 and 1775 A.D.). See *Adyar Library Bulletin*.

[Ed. and trs. into Eng. by S. Vasu, Allahabad, 8 vols., 1891-98. Ed., with the comms. *Tattvabodhimī* and *Subodhinī*, by W.L.S. Pansikar, NSP, 1933 (7th ed.). *Vaidikī-prakriyā* ed. with Hindi comm. by U. Sarma, Banaras, 1962. For an analytical discussion on contents in Eng., see P. V. N. Sastry, *Vaiyākaraṇa Siddhānta Kaumudī*, Delhi, 1974. Also see M. D. Sharma, *K. Vṛtti...Siddhāntakaumudyāḥ tulanātmaka Adhyayana*, Poona, 1974.]

SIDDHĀNTA-MUKTĀVALĪ : A commentary, by Viśvanātha, on his own *Bhāṣā-pariccheda*. There is a noteworthy work on Advaita Vedānta, by Prakāśānanda, bearing the same name.

SIDDHĀNTA-RATNA: Also called *Vedānta-kāmadhenu*, *Vedānta-siddhānta-sāra-daśaślokī*, *Vedānta-daśaślokī* and *Daśa-ślokī*, it is in ten verses by Nimbārka. In it he sums up his system of Vedānta philosophy.

[Ed., with a Hindi comm., by C. Goswami, Banaras, 1913. Trs. into Eng. by M. Y. Sanam and into Hindi by M. D. Brahmachari, Vrindavana, 1915.]

SIDDHĀNTA-ŚEKHARA : A Siddhānta work on astronomy, by Śrīpati, consisting of 20 chapters.

[Part I, chap. i—iv, ed., with Makkibhaṭṭa's comm.; chaps. v—xii by B. Misra, Calcutta, 1936. Part II, chaps. xiii—xx, ed., with an original comm., by B. Misra and with an Intro. by P. C. Sen Gupta and N. C. Lahiri, Culcutta, 1947.]

SIDDHĀNTA-ŚIROMAṆI : An astronomical work by Bhāskarācārya, written in 1150 A.D. It is in two parts, viz. *Gaṇitādhyāya* or *Grahagaṇita* and *Golādhyāya* or *Grahagola*, The first part consists of 12 chaps., while the second part is divided into 14 chaps. The parts have been treated as separate works. In the *Gola*, there are a section on astronomical problems and a description of the seasons. Bhāskara does not accept the diurnal motion of the earth. In *Gola* section, the spherical shape of the earth and the power of gravitation have been indicated.

[Ed. B. Shastri, with *Vāsanābhāṣya*, Banaras, 1929; M. Jha, with *Vāsanābhāṣya*, *Vāsanāvatārikā* and *Marīci* comms., Banaras, 1917; G. Dvivedi, with a comm., extracts from earlier *Siddhāntas* etc., Ahmedabad, 1936; K. Joshi, with *Vāsanābhāṣya*, *Marīci-bhāṣya*, editor's own comm. and trs., Varanasi, 1962-64; ed. R. M. Upadhyay, Varanasi, 1981; M. D. Chaturvedi, with author's own comm., *Vāsanābhāṣya* and *Vārtika* of Nṛsiṃha Daivajña, Varanasi, 1981. Entire work trs. by L. Wilkinson, Bib. Ind., 1861. *Bījagaṇita* trs., from a Persian version, into Eng. by E. Strachey, London, 1813. For *Gaṇitādhyāya*, see E. Roer in *JASB*, 13 (1844). *Bījagaṇita* section, with Sanskrit comm., ed. ASS, 1930. *Grahagaṇitādhyāya* section ed., ASS, 1939. *Golādhyāya* section ed., with *Vāsanābhāṣya*, by B. D. Sastri, Banaras.]

SIDDHA-YOGA : Also called *Vṛndamādhava*, it is a medical work by Vṛnda. It follows the order of diseases as laid down in Mādhavakara's *Rugviniścaya*, and provides prescriptions for curing a large number of ailments from fever to poisoning. Cakrapāṇi appears to have borrowed a large portion of it in his own work. Vṛnda mentions many medicines not stated in the works of Caraka, Suśruta and Vāgbhaṭa.

[Ed., with the *Kusumāvalī* comm., by H. S. Padhye, ASS, 27, 1894.]

ŚIKṢĀ : It is one of the 6 *Vedāṅgas*. Literally it means instruction, then particularly instruction in reciting, i.e. in the correct pronunciation, accentuation etc. of *Saṃhitā* texts.

The earliest mention of this *Vedāṅga* occurs in the *Taittirīya Upaniṣad* (I. 2) where the following 6 chapters of the *Śikṣā* are mentioned:—

teaching of letters, accents, quantity (of syllables), stress, melody, combination of words in continuous recitation.

Saṃhitā-pāṭhas and *Pada-pāṭhas* of the Vedic *Saṃhitā* are the oldest productions of the *Śikṣā* schools. The oldest extant text-books of this *Vedāṅga* are the *Prātiśākhyas* (q. v.). The *Pāṇinīya Śikṣā*, the *Nāradīya Śikṣā*, the *Bhāradvāja Śikṣā* are some of the important works of the *Śikṣā Vedāṅga*. See Yudhiṣṭhira, *Siksāsūtrāṇi Āpiśali-Pāṇini-Candragomi-viracitāni*, Ajmer, 1949.

[A collection of Śikṣās (*Śikṣa-saṃgraha*) has been published in BanSS, 1893. On the Śikṣās, see F. Kielhorn, *Indian Antiquary*, 5, 1876, 141 ff., 193ff.; W. S. Allen, *Phonetics in Ancient India*, London, 1953.]

ŚIKṢĀ-SAMUCCAYA : A work by Śāntideva. It is a laborious compendium of Buddhist dogmatics of the *Mahāyāna* school.

[Ed. P. L. Vaidya, Darbhanga, 1961; C. Bendall, The Hague, 1957. Trs. C. Bendall and W. H. D. Rouse, London, 1922, 1981.]

ŚILPARATNA : Ascribed to Śrīkumāra, it is a work on Art, and belongs to the 16th cent. A.D. It consists of two parts *Pūrvabhāga* and *Uttarabhāga*. The *Pūrvabhāga*, comprising 46 chapters, deals with the construction of houses, villages and other allied subjects. The *Uttarabhāga*, consisting of 35 chapters, deals with iconography and kindred topics. The 46th chapter of the first part is called *Citra-lakṣaṇa*.

[Ed. T. Ganapati Shastri, TSS, 1922-29. See N. N. Sen, On some remarkable words from the Śilparatna, *Indian Linguistics, Taraporewala Memorial Vol.*; 1957; *Turner Jubilee Vol.*, 1958.

ŚILPAŚĀSTRA : A metrical work, in five short chapters, dealing with house-building. At places written in corrupt Sanskrit. It has a commentary in Oriyā. Apocryphal in character.

One verse of the fifth chapter ascribes it to Viśvakarman. Some attribute it to one Bāuri Mahārāṇa, an inhabitant of Orissa, of whom very little is known.

[Ed., with Eng. trs. and notes etc., by P. N. Bose, Lahore, 1928.]

SIṂHĀSANA-DVĀTRIṂŚIKĀ : Also called *Vikramacarita*, it is a well-known prose work. It consits of 32 tales, each told by an image supporting the throne of Vikramāditya, dug out from the earth when Bhoja was about to sit on it. The object of the tales, all of which are in praise of Vikramāditya, is that nobody can be able to sit on the throne before acquiring the merits of Vikramāditya. The original is lost. Two recensions of it exist, one North Indian and other South Indian. The former is represented by three works, viz. the work written by the Jain Kṣemaṅkara Muni, the Bengal version attributed to Vararuci and an abridged version which is anonymous. The South Indian recension is represented by two works, one in prose and the other poetical.

[Ed. F. Edgerton, in two parts, containing the text in transliteration and Eng. trs., in four recensions, HOS, 1926. See C. Bawden, *Tales of king Vikramāditya and thirty-two wooden men*, Delhi; *Vikramādītyā Tales from Mangolia*, Delhi.]

ŚIŚUPĀLA-VADHA : A *Mahākāvya* by Māgha, in 20 cantos. Sage Nārada directs Kṛṣṇa to slay the Cedi king Śiśupāla, a violent enemy of gods and men. At Uddhava's advice Kṛṣṇa attends the *Rājasūya* sacrifice of Yudhiṣṭhira where Śiśupāla is present. Kṛṣṇa is highly honoured by Yudhiṣṭhira. Enraged at this Śiśupala leaves the place, and prepares for war against Kṛṣṇa. In a fight that ensues Kṛṣṇa kills Śiśupāla. The story is based on an episode of the *Mahābhārata* (II. 30-42), but the poet introduces many changes. The poem betrays the influence of Bhāravi.

[Ed., NSP, with comm. of Mallinātha, 1888 (9th ed. 1927); H. Siddhāntavāgīśa, with comm. and Bengali trs., Calcutta; trs. into German by E. Hultzsch, Leipzig, 1929; into French by H. Fauche. 1861. See S. Bandyopadhyaya, Music in Māgha,

Summaries of Papers, Vth World Skt. Conf. Varanasi, 1986, p. 199.

ŚIṢYADHĪVṚDDHIDA : See *Dhīvṛddhitantra*.

ŚIṢYALEKHA-DHARMAKĀVYA : A poetical work by Candragomin. In it instruction is given in the form of an epistle to a pupil, dealing with the essential facts of the Buddhist faith. It is calculated to mend the character of the prince Ratnakīrti who is under delusion caused by wealth and power. It is in 114 verses.

[Ed. I. P. Minayeff in Zupiski IV.]

ŚIVA-DṚṢṬI : A philosophical work by Somānanda. It formed the basis of the Śaiva philosophy of Kashmir, known as *Pratyabhijñā-śāstra*. It consisted of sections, called *Āhnikas*, of which the first three and a part of the fourth have survived.

[Pb., KSTS, 1934]

ŚIVA-PURĀṆA : A title of the *Vāyupurāṇa* (q.v.). There is an Upapurāṇa of this title comprising 12 Saṃhitās.

[Complete Eng. trs. by J. L. Shastri in 4 Vols. See *Śiva Mahāpurāṇa*, ed. P. Kumar, Delhi, 1981; B. Patni, *A Poetic Analysis*, 1980.]

ŚIVA-SŪTRA : This forms the bed-rock on which the edifice of the *Trika* system of Kashmirian Śaiva philosophy stands. This is supposed to have been revealed to Vasugupta. The fourteen *Sūtras*, at the commencement of the *Aṣṭādhyāyī* of Pāṇini, which teach what are called *Pratyāhāras*, are also called *Śiva-sūtras* or *Maheśvara-sūtras*.

[Ed. with the comm. of Kṣemarāja, in KSTS, Vol. 1, NSP, 1911. The *Śiva-sūtravimarśinī* of Kṣemarāja, trs. into Eng. by P. T. S. Iyengar, Allahabad, 1912; by J. Singh, Delhi, 1979. A Ph. D. thesis on A critical and comparative study of the comms. on Vasugupta's *Śiva-sūtras* has been approved by Uni. of Kashmir.

ŚIVA-SŪTRA-VIMARŚINĪ : A comm., by Kṣemarāja, on the *Śiva-sūtra.*

SKANDA-PURĀṆA : The extant work is not the original form which appears to be lost. It appears to consist of the following *Saṃhitās* and fifty *Khaṇḍas* (books):—

Sanatkumārīya, Sūta, Brāhmī, Vaiṣṇavī, Śāṅkarī and *Saurī.* The *Sūta-saṃhitā* consists of 4 *Kāṇḍas,* the first of which is devoted wholly to the worship of Śiva.

This Purāṇa, containing various legends of Śiva, has a few chapters on the hells and *Saṃsāra* and a section on *Yoga.* There is hardly anything in it that corresponds to the traditional "five characteristics."

[Ed. Venkatesvara Press, Bombay, 1910, consists of 7 parts, called *Khaṇḍas.* See Awasthi, *Studies in the Skandapurāṇa,* Lucknow, 1966. Also see S. Sahai, Śaiva Sects as found in the Skandapurāṇa, *ABORI,* 1976.]

ŚLOKA-VĀRTIKA : It is a part of Kumārila's commentary on Jaimini's *Pūrvamīmāṃsā-sūtra.* It is on I.1 of the *Sūtra.*

[Entire comm. ed. CSS 1898-99; BanSS 1890, 1903. See *Ślokavārtika-vyākhyā Tātparyaṭīkā* of Umbeka Bhaṭṭa, ed. S. K. Ramanatha Sastri, Madras; F. D'SA, *Śabdaprāmāṇyam in Śabara and Kumārila,* 1980.

Trs. into English by G. Jha, Bib. Ind., 1900 ff. The debate about the nature of *Ātman* in *Ślokavārtika* and Śāntarakṣita's *Tattvasaṃgraha*—thesis reported to have been submitted by L. Hanotte to Uni. of Manitoba, 1980. See K. K. Diksit, *Śloka-Vārtika, a study,* Ahmedabad, 1983.]

SMṚTI : Also called Dharmaśāstra, the Smṛti literature is vast and comprises original works written in prose, mixed prose and verses or exclusively in verse, the digests of various schools and commentaries on the original works and on digests. The contents of the Smṛti works fall roughly into four divisions, viz. *Ācāra, Prāyaścitta, Vyavahāra* and *Rāja-dharma.* The *Yājñavalkya-smṛti* enumerates twenty writers on Dharmaśāstra or Smṛti. They are : Manu, Atri, Viṣṇu, Hārīta, Yājñavalkya, Uśanas, Aṅgiras, Yama, Āpastamba,

Saṃvarta, Kātyāyana, Bṛhaspati, Parāśara, Vyāsa, Śaṅkha, Likhita, Dakṣa, Gautama, Śātātapa and Vasiṣṭha.

[For an exhaustive and up-to-date occount of the Smṛti literature, see P. V. Kane, *History of Dharmaśāstra*, Vols. 1-V. For collections of Smṛti works, see *Dharmaśāstra-saṃgraha*, ed. Jivananda Bhattacharya, Calcutta, 1876; *Smṛtīnāṃ Samuccaya*, ASS, 1905; *Smṛti-sandarbha*, Gurumaṇḍala Series, Calcutta, 1952-53; *Ūnaviṃśati-Saṃthitā*, ed. P. Tarkaratna, Text with Bengali trs. Calcutta, 1909. For fish in Smṛti literature, see S. L. Hora in *Jour. of Asiatic Soc.*, Calcutta, 1953 (3rd series), Letters. See R. Lingat, *Les Sources du Droit class le systeme traditional de L. Inde*, the Hague, 1969.]

SMṚTI-CANDRIKĀ : A well-known digest on Dharmaśāstra, by Devaṇṇabhaṭṭa. It deals with *Saṃskāras* (sacraments), *Āhnika* (daily duties), *Vyavahāra* (secular law), *Śrāddha* (rite in honour of departed souls) and *Āśauca* (impurity consequent on birth and death of near relatives of certain classes). The work was, acc. to judicial decisions, of great authority in South India.

[Ed. J. R. Gharpure (upto *Śrāddha*), Bombay; Mysore Govt. Oriental Series (upto *Āśauca*), 1914-21 (5 Vols.). Trs. into English (*Dāyabhāga* portion only) by T. K. Iyer, Madras, 1867.]

SMṚTI-RATNA-HĀRA : A *Smṛti* digest by Bṛhaspati Rāyamukuṭa, not yet published. The following are broadly the topics dealt with in it : Determination of time appropriate for different *Vratas* and *Pūjās* (including *Jagaddhātrī-pūjā*); *Āśauca* consequent on birth and death, *Śrāddha* etc.

[An incomplete MS is preserved in Asiatic Society, Calcutta. See *Des. Cat. of MSS of Asiatic Society*, Vol. III, No. 2138.]

SMṚTI-RATNĀKARA : A huge *Smṛti* digest by Caṇḍeśvara, divided into seven sections, viz. *Kṛtya* (dealing with various *Vratas* and observances at different periods), *Dāna* (dealing with gifts), *Vyavahāra* (dealing with civil and criminal law), *Śuddhi* (dealing with impurity consequent upon birth and death and the corresponding purificatory rites), *Pūjā* (worship), *Vivāda* (dealing with civil and criminal law and the various subjects of dispute) and *Gṛhastha* (dealing with the proper conduct of householders).

[For editions and MSS, see under the respective parts.]

SMṚTISĀRA : Also called *Smṛti-sāra-samuccaya,* it is a *Smṛti* digest by Harinātha. It covers the entire field of *Smṛti* including *Vyavahāra.*

SMṚTI-TATTVA : Same as *Aṣṭāviṃśati-tattva* (q.v.).

SPANDA-KĀRIKĀ : It is an authoritative work on the Śaiva philosophy of Kashmir. It is the common appellation of the *Spanda-sūtra.* The *Kārikās* are, in a way, a running commentry on the *Śiva-sūtras,* the former seeking to explain the latter in greater detail. Kṣemarāja attributes the *Spanda-sūtras* to Vasugupta. In reality, however, these seem to have been composed by Kallaṭa, a pupil of Vasugupta.

[Ed., with the *Spanda-pradīpikā* comm. of Utpala, by V. S. Islampurkar. Viz.SS, No. 16, Vol. XIV, Banaras, 1898. *Kārikā* and *Spanda-nirṇaya* trs. by J. Singh, *Spandakārikās,* Delhi, 1980.]

SPANDA-SAṂDOHA : It is a commentary, by Kṣemarāja, on the first *Sūtra* of the *Spanda-sūtra* (q.v).

[Ed. M. Śāstrī, KSTS No. 16, 1917.]

SPHUṬA BRĀHMASIDDHĀNTA : See *Brahma-siddhānta.*

ŚRĀDDHA-KRIYĀ-KAUMUDĪ : It is a *Smṛti* digest by Govindānanda, dealing with the definition of *Śrāddha,* the various kinds of *Śrāddha* and the rules regarding their performance.

[Ed., Bib. Ind., 1904.]

ŚRĀDDHA-VIVEKA : A *Smṛti* digest by Śūlapāṇi. It defines *Śrāddha,* and describes the various kinds of it.

[Ed. C. Smṛtibhūṣaṇa, Calcutta, 1314 B. S.]

ŚRAUTA-KOŚA : Encylopedia of Vedic sacrificial ritual., VSM, Poona.

English Section, Vol. I : The seven Havis-sacrifices.

Pt. I, 1958, Pt. II, 1962.

English Section, Vol. II: The Agniṣṭoma and the Ekādaśinī.

Pt. I, 1973.

Pt. II, 1980.

ŚRAUTA-SŪTRA : Comprised under *Kalpa-sūtra*, the *Śrauta-sūtras* deal with Vedic rites, e.g. laying of the sacrificial fires, the various sacrifices, particularly the Soma-sacrifice with its numerous variations. They are the most important source for the understanding of the Indian sacrifice-cult, and are of great significance in the history of religion. They are also indispensable for the interpretation of the Vedas. The important *Śrauta-sūtras* are *Āpastamba-śrauta-sūtra*, *Mānava-śrauta-sūtra* and *Baudhāyana-śrauta-sūtra* belonging to *Black Yajurveda*, *Kātyāyana-śrauta-sūtra* belonging to *White Yajurveda*, *Āśvalāyana-śrauta-sūtra* and *Śāṅkhāyana-śrautra-sūtra* belonging to *Ṛgveda*, *Lāṭyāyana-śrauta-sūtra*, *Drāhyāyaṇa-śrauta-sūtra* and *Jaiminīya-śrautasūtra* belonging to *Sāmaveda.*

[See H. Bubert and M. Mauss, Essai Sur...due sacrifice, Annee Sociologique, Paris, 1897-98 and *Śrauta-kośa*, English Section-Vol. I, Part I, Poona, 1958; Vol. II, Part 2, Eng. trs. by Dandekar, Poona, 1982. Sanskrit Section-Vol. 1; Samiran Chakrabarti, *Paribhāṣās in* the *Śrautasūtras*, Calcutta, 1980. *Kātyāyana-śrauta-sūtra* trs. into Eng. by H.G. Ranade, Pune, 1978. See B. P. Bhattacharya, *Studies in Śrautasūtras of Āśvalāyana and Āpastamba*, Calcutta, 1978. R. N. Sharma, Culture and Civilisation as revealed in Śrautasūtra. C. G. Kashikar, *A Survey of the Śrautasūtras*, Bombay, 1966].

ŚRĪBHĀṢYA : A commentary, by Rāmānuja, on the *Brahma-sūtra*. In it he expounds Vedānta philosophy according to his own theory which is called Viśiṣṭādvaita-vāda or qualified monism.

[Ed. with three comms., Mysore, 1959. Trs. into Eng. by G. Thibaut, SBE, XLVIII; by M. Raṅgacarya and M.

Aiyangar with the *Vedānta-sūtras*, Madras, 1899; into French by O. Lacombe, Paris, 1938. See P. N. Srinivasachari, *Philosophy of Viśiṣṭādvaita*; R. D. Karmakar, *Śrībhāṣya of Rāmānuja* (Text, Eng. trs., Intro., notes, Appendices).]

ŚRĪKAṆṬHA-CARITA : A *Mahākāvya*, in 25 cantos, by Maṅkha. It has for its theme the Purāṇic legend of the destruction of demon Tripura by Śiva. The poet shows lack of sense of proportion and exercise is literary style.

[Ed. Durgaprasad and Parab, with Jonarāja's comm. See B. N. Bhatt, Some Noteworthy Peculiarities of Maṇkhaka's Śrtkaṇṭhacarita, *Jour. of Oriental Institute*, Baroda, XX, No. 2; *Śrīkaṇṭhacarita, a study*, Baroda 1973. On the date of the work, see B. C. Mandal, *Summaries of Papers*, AIOC, 1974.]

ŚRĪKARAṆA : An anonymous *Karaṇa*-work on astronomy consisting of 12 chaps.

[See Bendall's *British Museum Cat.*, for MS]

ŚṚĪKṚṢṆA-SANDARBHA : See *Bhāgavata-sandarbha*.

ŚṚṄGĀRA-PRAKĀŚA : Ascribed to Bhoja, it consists of 36 chapters and is the largest known work in Sanskrit poetics. It deals with both poetics and dramaturgy.

[Ed. V. Raghavan, Madras, 1963. Also trs. into Eng. by V. Raghavan. Third rev. ed. to be pub. in HOS.]

ŚṚṄGĀRA-RASĀṢṬAKA : A small poem, in 8 erotic stanzas, ascribed by some to Kālidāsa.

ŚṚṄGĀRA-ŚATAKA : A lyric poem by Bhartṛhari. It depicts the various stages of love, happiness caused by love and its cosequence. The entire poem breathes the hollowness of love.

[Ed. P. Bohlen, with Latin trs., Berlin, 1833; in Haeberlin's *Kāvyasaṃgraha*, J. Vidyāsāgara's *Kāvya-saṃgraha*, II; in *Subhāṣita-triśatī*, NSP, Bombay, 1922 (6th ed). Eng. trs. by C. H. Tawney, *Indian Antiquary*, V, 1876; B. H. Wortham, London, 1886; J. M. Kennedy, London, 1913; C. W. Gurner, Calcutta, 1927. For ed. and trs., also see under Bhartṛhari.]

There is a *Śṛṅgāra-śataka* by one Dhanadadeva.

[Ed. *Kāvyamālā-Gucchaka* XIII.]

ŚṚṄGĀRA-TILAKA : A small poem ascribed by some to Kālidāsa. Its stanzas are attractive pictures of love. The poet, while praising his beloved, mostly condemns her for her hard-hearted nature.

[Ed. Gildemeister, Bonn, 1941.]

There is a work on poetics, called *Śṛṅgāra-tilaka,* ascribed to Rudra who is generally supposed to be identical with Rudraṭa, author of the *Kāvyālaṃkāra.*

[Ed. Pischel, Kiel, 1886.]

ŚRUTABODHA : A work on prosody, ascribed to Kālidāsa by some, to Vararuci by others. Yet others think that the author was Ajitasena who may or may not have been identical with the Jaina author of this name. In verses it describes the characteristics of different meters. The descriptive verses are themselves illustrations of the metres concerned.

[Ed., with the *Vimalā* comm., by B. Misra, Banaras, 1958. On authorship, see S. K. De: *History of Poetics* (1960), i, p. 265. See, D. K. Kanjilal, A critical study of Kālidāsa's authorship of the Śrutabodha, *Jour. of Oriental Institute,* XVII, No. 1, Sep. 1967.]

SUBHĀṢITA-MUKTĀVALĪ: See *Sūkti-muktāvalī* of Jalhaṇa. An anthology of this title is attributed to Puruṣottamadeva who may or may not be the Bengali author of this name.

[Ed. R. N. Dandekar, Poona.]

SUBHĀṢITA-RATNAKOṢA : An anthology compiled by Vidyākara (q.v.) of Bengal. It contains verses culled from the works of different poets and arranged under sections called *Vrajyās.* It quotes certain poets who are not known from any other source. Mention may be made, for instance, of Vallaṇa and Buddhākaragupta. It was at first edited from an incomplete MS not containing the names of the work and the author, and was known by the assumed title of *Kavīndra-vacana-samuccaya,* the title having been conjectured from the initial words of the first verse which reads as *nānākavīndra-vacanāni* etc.

[Ed. HOS, 1967; trs. into Eng. by Danied H. H. Ingalls under the title *An Anthology of Sanskrit Court-Poetry*, HOS, 1965.]

SUBHĀṢITĀVALĪ : An anthology compiled by Vallabhadeva. It contains 3,527 verses in 101 sections or *Paddhatis*, and the number of authors and works cited is about 360. Its verses are on a wide variety of topics including love, conduct of life, natural scenery and seasons, worldly wisdom and witty sayings. It preserves from oblivion a number of Kashmirian poets. There is another anthology of the same name, attributed to Śrīvara. It is quoted by Sarvānanda in his commentary on the *Amarakośa* in 1960 A.D. The present text of the *Subhāṣitāvalī* cannot be placed earlier than the 15th century.

[Ed. Peterson and Parab, Bombay, 1886; 2nd ed. by R. D. Karmarkar, BSS, No. XXXI.]

ŚUDDHI-KAUMUDĪ : A *Smṛti* digest by Govindānanda, dealing with the means of purification from impurities consequent on the birth and death of near relatives of certain classes.

[Ed. Bib. Ind., 1905.]

ŚUDDHI-RATNĀKARA : Consisting of 34 chapters called *Taraṅgas* and forming a part of Caṇḍeśvara's *Smṛti-ratnākara*, it deals with various means of purification.

[For MSS, see (1) *I. O. Cat.*, III, No. 1389 (2) Mitra, *Notices*, VII, No. 2384, (3) Śāstri, *Calcutta Asiatic Society Cat.*, III, No. G. 3826, (4) *Mithilā MSS. Cat.*, I, No. 331A.]

SUHṚLLEKHA : The full title is *Ārya-nāgārjuna-bodhisattva-suhṛllekha*. It is a work by Nāgārjuna, and is in the form of an epistle consisting of 123 verses. It purports to set forth, for the benefit of the author's friend King Udayana according to some, king Sātavāhana according to others, the Buddhist doctrine briefly and in an attractive style. The work exists in Chinese and Tibetan versions; the Sanskrit original has not come down.

[Trs. into Eng. by Wenzel, *JPTS*, 1886, pp. 1 ff. and into German, Leipzig, 1886. Trs. into Eng. after the Chinese trs. of Guṇavarman, by S. Beal, in *Indian Antiquary*, 16, 1887.]

ŚUKA-SAPTATI : A folk-tale in prose. It exists in three versions of which one is by Devadatta. Of the remaining two, one is the Simplicior version by a Jain and the other is the Ornatior version by Cintāmaṇi Bhaṭṭa; the latter cannot be earlier than 12th century. A man goes abroad leaving his young wife in charge of his pet, a parrot. The wife is about to be seduced away from home by rogues. The parrot asks her to tarry so long as the story, told by it, is not finished. One story is followed by another which is even more amusing and curious. Thus seventy stories are narrated by the bird; meanwhile the husband comes back and a family crisis is averted.

[Ed. Delhi, 1959. Textus Simplicior ed. R. Schmidt, Leipzig, 1893; trs. into German, Kiel, 1894. A shorter version of the text also ed. by same scholar in *ZDMG*, liv and lv, 1900-1901. Textus Ornatior ed. by same scholar, München, 1898-99. Trs. into German., Stuttgart, 1899. For analysis and comparison of two texts, with trs. of some sections, see R. Schmidt in *Der Textus Ornatior der Śuka-saptati*, Stuttgart, 1896. Trs. into Eng. by G. L. Mathur under the title *Erotic Indian Tales*.]

SUKHĀVATĪ-VYŪHA : In it the splendour of Amitābha and his paradise are described in an extravagant manner. It exists in a longer and a shorter version, the latter obviously derived from the former.

[Ed. M. Müller and B. Nanjio, Oxford, 1883; trs. SBE, xlix. The earliest of the five extant Chinese translations of the longer version was made between 147 and 186 A.D. The shorter version was translated into Chinese by Kumārajīva (402 A.D.), Guṇabhradra (420-79 A.D.) and by Hiuen Tsang (c. 650 A.D.).]

ŚUKRANĪTI : A treatise on polity of a late date attributed to sage Śukrācārya. It mentions the use of gunpowder.

Acc. to some scholars it was written in the 19th century A.D.

[Ed. G. Oppert, Madras, 1882; Sarkar, New York, 1915; B. Misra, with Hindi comm. and Intro. by R. Sastri Dravid, Varanasi, 1968. Trs. into Eng. by B. K. Sarkar, SBH, 1914 (2nd. ed. 1923). A *Śukranīti-sāra* also exists. For the date of the work, see L. Gopal, *The Śukranīti—a nineteenth century text*, Varanasi, 1978.]

SŪKTI-MUKTĀVALĪ : Also called *Subhāṣita-muktāvali*, it is an anthology attributed to Jalhaṇa but really perhaps compiled by Bhānu. It appears to have existed in a shorter and a longer recension. The printed text contains 2,790 verses arranged under 133 sections; the number of authors and works cited is over 240. At the commencement there are some traditional verses on Sanskrit poet and poetry, which are interesting from the point of view of literary history.

[Ed. E. Krishnamacharya, GOS, 1938.]

ŚULVA-SŪTRA : A part of the *Kalpa-sūtra*, and directly attached to the *Śrauta-sūtra*. 'Śulva' means the 'measuring string'; and *Śulva-sūtras* contain exact rules for the measurement and building of the place of sacrific and the fire-altars. As the oldest works on Indian geometry, they are of great importance for the history of science. Of the *Śulva-sūtras*, that of Baudhāyana is the oldest and the largest. It contains three chapters. The first chapter consists of 116 aphorisms dealing with various measures, important geometrical propositions necessary for the construction of altars, relative positions and spatial magnitudes of the various altars. The second chapter contains 83 aphorisms devoted to the description of the spatial relation in the different constructions of fire-altars made of bricks. Chapter three consists of 323 aphorisms describing the construction of 17 different kinds of fire-altars for sacrifices performed with the object of attaining definite results.

[*Kātyāyana-śulva-sūtra*, with comm. of Karka and gloss of Mahīdhara, ed. CSS, Banaras, 1936; *Baudhāyana-śulva-sūtra*, ed. and trs. by G. Thibaut, *Paṇḍit*, Vols. ix ff; *Āpastamba-*

śulva-sūtra, with comms. of Kapardisvāmin, Karavinda and Sundararāja, published at Mysore, 1931; ed. and trs. into German by A. Bürk, *ZDMG*, Vols. 55, 56, 1901-2. See B. B. Datta, *The Science of the Śulba—a study in early Hindu Geometry*, Calcutta, 1932; S. Prakash, *Founders of the Sciences in Ancient India*, New Delhi, 1965, chap. XIII; M. P. Tripathi's *Survey and cartography in the Śulvasūtras*, G. Jha Res. Institute, Allahabad. Also see S. Prakash and U. Jyotiṣmatī (ed.), *Śulbasūtra* (*Baudhāyana*, *Āpastamba*, *Kātyāyana* and *Mānava Śulba-sūtras*), Allahabad, 1979.]

SUMANOTTARĀ : A prose *Kāvya* mentioned in Patañjali's *Mahābhāṣya*. It is lost.

SUPADMA-VYĀKARAṆA : A grammatical work by Padmanābhadatta. Based on the *Aṣṭādhyāyī*, it has remodelled the greater part of Pāṇini's rules and arranged them in a methodical form, adding a short explanation by the author after each *Sūtra*. Some of Pāṇini's *Sūtras*, technical terms and *Pratyāhāras* have been retained verbatim in this grammar.

[Ed., with Viṣṇumiśra's commentary and notes by T. Bhattacharya, Calcutta, 1900.]

SŪRYA-ŚATAKA : A century of verses in praise of the sun, by Mayūra who is said to have been cured of leprosy through the grace of the sun. The work has been quoted by such eminent rhetoricians as Abhinavagupta and Mammaṭa.

[Ed., with comm. of Tribhuvanapāla, by Durgaprasad and Parab, NSP, Bombay, 1889, 1927; with comm. of Yajñeśvara, Baroda, 1872 A.D. Ceylonese paraphrase (*Sanna*) by V. Mahāthera, with text, ed. D. Batuvantudave, Colombo, 1883.]

SŪRYA-SIDDHĀNTA : One of the earliest and most popular Hindu scientfic astronomical works, dating back to c. 400 A.D. The extant text appears to be the result of many corrections and interpolations. There is considerable agreement between the *Sūryasiddhānta*, described by Varāhamihira, in his *Pañcasiddhāntikā*, with the present *Sūryasiddhānta*. Varāha himself appears to have amended the old version in acc. with the teachings of Āryabhaṭa. Asura Maya, to whom the knowledge of planets is said to have been revealed, has led some scholars to think that the work originating in the west, was derived from a Greek source. Acc. to Weber, 'Asura Maya' is correlated with the 'Plolemaios' of the Greeks. Albiruni ascribed it to one Lāṭa. The work is divided into 14 chaps.

[Ed., with *Gūḍhārtha-prakāśikā* comm., by F. E. Hall and B. Śāstrī, Bib. Ind., Calcutta, 1959; with *Sauradīpikā* and *Bhāṣā-bhāṣya* comm., by M. Purohita and G. Dvivedin, Lucknow, 1904; with *Sudhāvarṣiṇī* comm., by S. Dvivedin, Bib. Ind., Calcutta, 1925 (2nd ed.); with *Tattvāmṛtabhāṣya*, by K. Choudhuri, Banaras, 1946; with Parameśvara's comm., by K. S. Shukla, Lucknow, 1957. Trs. into Eng. by E. Burgess (A Text-book of Hindu Astronomy with notes and an appendix, 1860), reprinted by University of Calcutta, 1935, with introduction; by L. Wilkinson and B. Sastri, Bib. Ind., 1860-62. Eng. trs. by E. Burgess ed. with notes and appendix by P. Gangooly, Varanasi, 1977.]

SUŚRUTA-SAṂHITĀ : A famous treatise on Āyurveda, traditionally attributed to Suśruta. Acc. to some, it is not the personal work of a certain Suśruta, but the anonymously edited manual of a school which chose Suśruta as patron. Also called *Āyurveda-prakāśa,* it is divided into sections called *Sthānas*. The sections and their corresponding contents are as follows :—

I. *Sūtrasthāna* (46 chaps.)—it deals with general questions, and gives the name of Suśruta's teacher.

II. *Nidānasthāna* (16 chaps.)—it deals with pathology.

III. *Śārīrasthāna* (10 chaps)—anatomy and embryology.

IV. *Cikitsā-sthāna* (40 chaps.)—therapeutics.

V. *Kalpasthāna* (8 chaps.)—toxicology.

The *Uttara-tantra,* which appears to be a later addition, is a supplement to the work. A Nāgārjuna is credited with having worked over the text. It is the earliest work to deal with dissection of bodies and surgery. Some eminent authorities think that the *Saṃhitā* originated in the last centuries before the Christian era, and appeared during the first centuries A.D. in an already well-defined form. The *Saṃhitā*, in its present form, appears to have been fixed by the 7th cent. A.D.

[Ed., with *Nibandha-saṃgraha* comm. of Ḍalhaṇa, by J. T. Ācārya, NSP, 1915; Bombay Sanskrit Series Lahore, 1928; with Ḍalhaṇa's comm., by J. Trikamji, Bombay, 1931. With Hindi comm. by V. G. Ghanekar; *Śārīrasthāna*, with Hindi and Eng. comm., by J. M Ācārya. Eng. trs. by K. Bhiṣagratna, Calcutta, 1907-16. Index and Appendices by same author, Calcutta, 1918. Eng. trs. by U. C. Dutt and A. C. Chattopadhyaya (3 fasc.), Bib. Ind., by Hoernle (1 fasc.), Bib. Ind., by K. L. Bhiṣagratana, Varanasi, 1963 (2nd ed.). See *Die Tridoṣa-Lehre in der indischen Medizin* by Weckerling, Gwessen, 1929 (Text in Roman characters and translation of several passages from *Suśruta-saṃhitā*). Also see J. Filliozat, *Classical Doctrine of Indian Medicine*, Delhi, 1964; P. Cordier, *Nāgārjuna et l'Uttaratantra de la Suśruta-saṃhitā*, Antananarivo, 1860; Satya Prakash, *Founders of Sciences in Ancient India*, New Delhi, 1965, Chap. VII; F. G. R. Müller, zur Zusammensetzung des Anfanges Suśruta-saṃhitā, *Festischrift M. Winternitz*, Leipzig, 1933; P.S. Sankaran, *Suśruta's Contribution to Surgery*; P. Ray, H. Gupta and Mira Roy, A Scientific Synopsis, New Delhi, 1980.]

SUVARṆATANTRA : Same as *Svarṇatantra* (q.v.).

SUVṚTTATILAKA : A work on prosody, by Kṣemendra. Its contents are as follows :

Book I—description of metres with illustrative verses from his own works.

Book II —defects in metres with useful citations.

Book III—use of metres according to the nature of the work; poetry, science or a combination in which one or the other predominates.

He concludes by demanding a variety of metres from poets, adding that great writers have preferred some special metres, e.g., Pāṇini preferred the *Upajāti*, Kālidāsa the *Mandākrāntā*, Bhāravi the *Vaṃśastha* and so on.

It is valuable for literary history as it quotes verses from different works with the names of the respective authors.

[Ed. *Kāvyamālā*, II; with Hindi comm., V.M. Jha, Varanasi, 1968. Trs. into Eng. by Suryakanta in *Kṣemendra Studies*, Poona, 1954.]

SVAPNA-VĀSAVADATTA : The best known drama of Bhāsa. It deals, in six acts, with the Udayana legend. The astute minister, Yaugandharāyaṇa, anxious to secure extension of power for Udayana, plans the king's marriage with Padmāvatī, daughter of king of Magadha. The minister spreads the rumour that Udayana's queen Vāsavadattā has died; this he does because the king would never marry another girl so long as his beloved queen is alive. The clever minister manages to persuade Padmāvatī to take charge of Vāsavadattā in disguise. Eventually Udayana and Padmāvatī are wedded, and the drama ends happily with the king's re-union with his first queen.

[Ed., with trs. and notes, by C.R. Devadhar, Poona, 1926. Trs. A. Baston, Paris, 1914 ; A.G. Shirreff and Panna Lall, Allahabad, 1918.]

SVARAMELAKALĀNIDHI : Written about 1550 A.D. by Rāma Amātya, it gives, for the first time, a detailed exposition, in five chapters, of the southern system of Indian music. It contains the first collection of Indian *Rāgas* which are fully described. All of them belong to the Carnatic system.

[Ed. M.S.R. Aiyar, Annamalainagar, 1932. See V. Raghavan, The Svaramela-kalānidhi of Rāmāmātya, *Souvenir of 34th Confce. of Music Academy*, Madras, 1960.]

SVARṆA-TANTRA : Also called *Suvarṇa-tantra*, it deals with interesting processes of transmuting base metals into gold and silver.

[For a brief account of the contents, see P. C. Roy: *History of Chemistry in Ancient and Medieval India*, Calcutta, 1956.]

SYĀDVĀDA-MAÑJARĪ : A noteworthy work by Malliṣeṇa, on Jaina philosophy. For the standpoint of the Syādvāda philosophers, see Syādvāda.

[Ed. CSS, 1900.]

ŚYAINIKA-ŚĀSTRA : Ascribed to Rudradeva (Candradeva or Rudra-candradeva), it is the only work on hunting and fowling. It is divided into seven chapters the titles and contents of which are as follows :—

I. *Karmānuṣañjana*

In it the author seeks to establish that the so-called vices, when indulged in within due limits, are conducive to well-being.

II. *Vyasana-heyatā-nirūpaṇa*

In it are enumerated 18 vices and their usefulness when resorted to within limits.

III. *Mṛgayā-vivecana*

IV. *Śyenānāṃ Vivecanam*

V. *Cikitsādhikāra*

It deals with various diseases of the hawk and their treatment.

VI. *Śyenapātetikartavyatā*

Method of hawk-fight and the delight at its sight etc.

VII. *Mṛgayānantaretikartavyatā*

King's relaxation after hawk-fight.

It is interesting to note that this work contains some Turkish and Persian words.

[Ed. and trs. into Eng. by H. P. Sastri, Bib. Ind., 1910. See Motichand, *Śyainikaśāstra of Rudradeva.*]

TAITTIRĪYĀRAṆYAKA : See Āraṇyaka.

[Ed., with comm. of Bhaṭṭa Bhāskara Miśra, by A. M. Sastri and K. rangacharya, Mysore, 1900-02. See N. M. Sen, Some remarkable words and verb forms from the *Tai. Ār.*, *Bulletin of Deccan College*, 35.1-2, 1975.]

TAITTIRĪYOPANIṢAD : Divided into three sections, called *Vallīs*, its subject-matter is as follows:—

I. *Śikṣā-vallī*
—certain *Dhyānas* and instructions as means to the realisation of Brahman.

II. *Brahmānanda-vallī*
—description of the five cells (*koṣa*), the superiority of the bliss of the realisation of Brahman over all other pleasures.

III. *Bhṛgu-vallī*
—in course of a dialogue between Bhṛgu and Varuṇa the description of the five cells (*koṣa*) and the necessity of austerities for the acquisition of knowledge about Brahman are given.

[Ed., with Eng. rendering and comments, by Svāmi Sarvānanda, Rāmakṛṣṇa Maṭh, Madras, 1921. Trs. into Eng. by Durga Parshad, Lahore, 1919; with comms. of Śaṅkara, Sureśvara, Vidyāraṇya, trs. by A. M. Sastri, Madras, 1980.]

This Upaniṣad has been studied by P. V. Vartak. In his study he has fixed the date of the work at 9109 B.C. on the basis of astronomical data.

TAITTIRĪYA PRĀTIŚĀKHYA : See *Prātiśākhya.*

[Ed. V. Sharma, Madras, 1930 (with the comm. of Māhiṣeya).]

TĀJIKA : An astrological work (1587 A.D.) by Nīlakaṇṭha. Its two parts are called *Saṃjñā-tantra* and *Varṣa-tantra*. Works of the Tājika class appeared when Arabic and Persian influence became marked under the Muslim regime. The name 'Tājika' is derived from Persian Taiji meaning 'Arabic'.

[Ed., with *Rasālā* comm., Banaras, 1936.]

TĀLĀDHYĀYA : A fragment of Kohala's book on music.

[*Catalogus Catalogorum*, I. 130. Eggeling's *Cat. of Skt. MSS. in India Office*, 3025, 3089. *Des. Cat of Skt. MSS. in Oriental MSS. Lib.*, Madras, 8725 (with Telugu comm.).]

TANTRA : The works of this class are divided into three

broad classes, viz. *Āgama, Saṃhitā* and *Tantra*. Each of these classes belongs to a particular sect. The Tāntric works of the Śāivas are called *Āgama*; those of the Vaiṣṇavas and Śāktas are respectively designated as *Saṃhitā* and *Tantra*. These works are also divided as Hindu (Brahmanical) Tantras and Bauddha Tantras. These are further divided into *Āstika* and *Nāstika* . These two classes are also styled respectively Vedic and non-Vedic according as they recognise or do not recognise Vedic authority. In accordance with the predominance of the deities in them, they are classed as *Śākta, Śaiva, Saura, Gāṇapatya* and *Vaiṣṇava*. The contents of a complete Tantra are broadly divided into four parts, viz.

(i) *Kriyā*—dealing with rites at the building of temples, erection of images of gods etc.

(ii) *Caryā*—teaching the practical cult.

(iii) *Yoga*—dealing with practice of *Yoga*.

(iv) *Anuttara-yoga*—dealing with higher mysticism.

The origin of Tantras is shrouded in obscurity so that it is difficult to ascertain exactly when they came into being. Some modern Indologists think that the original Tantras were probably composed or compiled in or after the fifth or sixth century A.D.

Nothing definite is known about the provenance of the Tantras. It is, however, supposed that the works of the *Āgama* and *Tantra* classes originated in Kashmir and Bengal respectively. The works of the *Saṃhitā* class are believed to have originated partly in Bengal and partly in the Deccan and various other regions of India. Some scholars think that the fundamental doctrines of the Tantra literature were borrowed by India from China.

There are numerous works on Tantra. The traditional number of Tantras is 64. The names of Tantras differ in different sources. Besides original treatises, there is a number of digests and commentaries.

The principal matters, dealt with in the Tantras, are origin and nature of Tantras, Cosmogony, Śiva and Śakti, the science of the body and human nature, various practices, spiritual exercises, the fivefold *Tattvas*, acquisition of superhuman power (*Siddhi*), *Mantra, Yoga*, the spiritual guide and disciple, initiation and its various stages. Rudiments of chemistry in relation to medical science and alchemy and certain other branches of modern science are found in some of the Tantras. For example, mention may be made of Television, Teletherapy etc. Cosmic ray appears to have been known to Tantras.

The Purāṇas and Tantras reveal mutual influence. Some of the principal *Āgama* works of Kashmir are *Mālinī-vijaya, Ānanda-bhairava, Vijñāna-bhairava, Rudra-yāmala.*

Closely related to *Āgamas* is the *Pratyabhijñā* literature. Some of the main works of this literature are : *Śiva-dṛṣṭi, Tantra-sāra, Paramārtha-sāra, Tantrāloka.*

A few of the chief works of the *Saṃhitā* class are : *Ahirbudhnya-saṃhitā, Īśvara-saṃhitā, Jñānāmṛta-sāra, Parama-saṃhitā.*

Some important works of the Tantra class are : *Mahānirvāṇa, Tantra-rāja, Śāradā-tilaka, Kulārṇava, Prapañcasāra, Tantrasāra, Prāṇatoṣiṇī.*

[In connexion with Tantra, the following works may be consulted :—

Avalon, A. (John Woodroffe): *The Serpent Power*, Madras, 1934. *The Great Liberation*, Madars, 1927. *Tāntrika Texts, Kāmakalā-vilāsa*, Calcutta, 1922. *The Garland of Letters*, Madras, 1922. *Shakti and Shākta*, Madras, 1929. *Principles of Tantra*, Madras, 1952. *Introduction to Tantraśāstra*, Madras, 1952. *The World as Power, Mahāmāyā*, 1953.

BAGCHI, P. C. : *Studies in the Tantras*, I, Calcutta, 1939.

BANERJI, J. N. : *Purāṇic and Tāntric Religion, Early Phase*, Calcutta University.

BANERJI, S. C. : *Tantra in Bengal*, Calcutta.

BHARATI, AGEHANANDA : *Tāntric Tradition*, London, 1965.

BASU, M. : *Tantras, a general study*.

BOSE, D. N.: *Tantras—their philosophy and Occult Secrets*, Calcutta.

CHATTOPADHYA, S.: *Reflection on the Tantras*, Patna, 1978

CULTURAL HERITAG OF INDIA, Vol. IV.

DOUGLAS, N.: *Tantrayoga*.

GUENTHER, H. V.: *Yuganaddha, the Tantrik View of Life*, CSS Studies, Vol. III. 1952.

GUHA, D. C.: *Tāntric View of Life*, 1972.

HANZE, O. M.: *Tantravidyā*, 1978.

KAVIRAJ, G.: Tantra O Āgam Śāstrer Digdarśan (in Bengali), Vol. I, Calcutta Sanskrit College Research Series No. XXV, Calcutta, 1963.

———: Tāntrik Vāṅmaya men Śāktadṛṣṭi, Patna, 1963.

LESSING, F. D. and WAYMAN, A.: *Introduction to Buddhist Tantric systems*, Delhi, 1978.

MOOKERJEE, A.: *Tantra Magic*

NAVJIVAN Rastogi: *Krama Tantricism of Kashmir*, Vol. I, 1978.

PANDIT, M. P.: *Studies in the Tantra and the Veda*.

PRATYAGATMANANDA: *Philosophy of the Tantras*, Cultural Heritage of India, Vol. III, Calcutta, 1953.

RAGHUVIRA and S. TAKI (ed.): *A Dictionary of Tāntric Syllabic Code*.

RAO, S. K. R.: *Tāntric Tradition*.

RAWSON, P. *The Art of Tantra*, London, 1973.

SASTRY, K.: *Further Lights: The Veda and the Tantra*, Madras, 1951.

SINGH, L. P.: *Tantra—Its Mystic and Scientific Basis*.

SUBBAROYAPPA, B. V. and ROY, MIRA: Mātṛkābhedatantra and its alchemical ideas, *Indian Jour. of History of Science*, 3 (1) pp. 42-43, 198, 1968.

SVAMI, S. N : *Tāntrik Abhidhān* (in Bengali), Calcutta, 1910.
WALKER, B. : *Tantrism, its secret principles and practices*, Northampton shire, 1982.

A Bibliography of published and unpublished Śaiva and Śākta Tāntric works is reported to be under preparation at Kuruksetra University, Haryana, India.]

TANTRĀKHYĀYIKĀ (or, TANTRĀKHĀYIKA) : A version of the *Pañcatantra* (q.v.). Produced in Kashmir, it is believed to have been derived from one of the lost versions of the *Pañcatantra*. It is considered to be the oldest version of the *Pañcatantra* and to have made the nearest approach to the original. Of unknown date and authorship, it appears to have added some stories, e.g. the stories of the blue jackal (i. 8), the weaver Somelaka (ii. 4), King Śibi (iii. 7) and of the old Haṃsa (iii. 11). Acc. to Winternitz, it did not come into being before the third century B. C., the age of Cāṇakya, minister of Candragupta Maurya. It shares the characteristics of ornate Sanskrit literature, e.g. long compounds, ornate metres, double entendres etc.

[Ed. J. Hertel, Berlin, 1910, with two sub-versions; by same scholar in HOS, 1915. Trs. J. Hertel, 2 Vols., Leipzig and Berlin, 1909.]

TANTRĀLOKA : An authoritative work, by Abhinavagupta, on Kashmir Śaivism. Covering 37 chapters, of which 14 have been published, it deals with all matters, ritualistic and philosophical, connected with Śaivism. It also contains valuable autobiographical information.

[Ed., with notes, KSTS, Srinagar. Vol. I, ed. M. R. Shastrī, 1918; Vols. II-XII, ed. M. Kaul Shastri, 1921-38. A new edition in 8 vols. published by Motilal Banaridass, 1986.]

TANTRARĀJA-TANTRA : The king of Tantras. It treats of the *Śrīyantra*, the "famous diagram", which consists of nine triangles and nine circles drawn one within the other, each one of which has a mystical significance. By meditation with the help of this *Śrīyantra* one is said to attain the knowledge of Unity, i.e., the knowledge that everything in the world is identical with the Devī.

[Ed., with the comm. *Sudarśana* of Prāṇamañjarī, by J. B. Chaudhuri, Calcutta, 1940. *Tāntrika Texts*, Vols. VIII and XII, with *Manoramā* comm., Madras, 1954. Ed. with A. Avalon's Intro., by L. Shastri, Delhi, 1981.]

TANTRA-SĀRA : A well-known Tantra digest by Kṛṣṇānanda Āgamavāgīśa. It deals with the usual Tantra topics, viz. *Dīkṣā*, *Pūjā*, *Homa* and other Tāntric rites, *Yantra*, *Maṇḍala*, *Cakra* etc. Besides, it contains hymns to various deities. A noteworthy feature of the work is that it contains the essence of the Tantras of all the Hindu sects, viz. *Śaiva*, *Śākta*, *Vaiṣṇava*, *Saura*, *Gāṇapatya* etc.

[Ed., comm. and Bengali trs., by P. Tarkaratna, Calcutta, 1927; with Bengali trs., by R. Chattopadhyaya, Calcutta, 1282 B. S. See D. C. Bhattacharya, The Tantasāra, *P. K. Gode Comm. Vol.*, Poona, 1960, P. Pal, *Hindu Religion and Iconology acc. to Tantrasāra*, Los Angeles, 1981.]

There is a work of the same title, by Abhinavagupta, on Kashmir Śaivism. It is an epitome of the author's *Tantrāloka* (q.v.)

[Ed., with notes, by M. R. Śāstrī, KSTS No. 17. Srinagar, 1918; Reprint, Delhi, 1983.]

TANTRA-VĀRTIKA : It is a part of Kumārila's commentary on the *Pūrvamīmāṃsā-sūtra* of Jaimini. It is a commentary on Adhyāyas I (Pāda 2, 3, 4), II & III of the *Sūtra*.

[See under *Ślokavārtika*]

TANTRAVAṬADHĀNIKĀ : It is a summary, by Abhinavagupta, of his own work called *Tantrāloka* (q.v.)

[Ed., with notes, by M. R. Śāstrī, KSTS No. 24, Srinagar, 1918.]

TARKABHĀṢĀ : A guide-book, by Keśava Miśra (1275 A.D.), to the two schools of Nyāya and Vaiśeṣika.

[Ed. S. M. Paranjape, Poona, 1909; trs. into English, by G. Jha, *Indian Throught* (Allahabad) (ii).]

There is a treatise called *Jaina-tarka-bhāṣā* by Yaśovijaya Gaṇi (17th century), on Jaina logic.

[Ed., with comm., Singhī Jaina Granthmālā, Calcutta, 1938; with Hindi Comm., B. N. Sukla, Varanasi, 1968; with annotation by S. R. Iyer, Varanasi, 1979; with Intro., Eng. trs. and notes by D. Bhargava.]

TARKA-KAUMUDĪ : A practical guide to Nyāya philosophy, by Laugākṣi Bhāskara.

[Ed. M. N. Dvivedi, BSS, 32, 1886; trs. E. Hultzsch, *AGGW*, ix, 5, 1907.]

TARKĀMṚTA : A practical guide-book, ascribed to Jagadīśa, to Nyāya-Vaiśeṣika. It appears to have been composed around 1700 A.D. Some scholars doubt Jagadīśa's authorship.

[Ed., with Skt. and Hindi comm. by R. Misra, Banaras, 1955. On authorship, see *Vaṅgīya Sāhitya Pariṣat Patrikā*, 1350 B. S. pp. 44-45.]

TARKA-SAṂGRAHA : Written by Annam Bhaṭṭa, it is a practical guide-book to the schools of Nyāya and Vaiśeṣika. It consists of four chapters called respectively *Pratyakṣa*, *Anumāna*, *Upamāna* and *Śabda*.

[Ed., with Eng. trs. and notes by A. B. Gajendragadkar and R. D. Karmarkar, Poona, 1930; with the *Dīpikā* and *Nyāyabodhinī* comm., critical and explanatory notes by Athalye and Bodas, BORI, Poona, 1963. An excellent edition, with the transliterated text, Eng. trs. and exposition is the one by S. Kuppusvami Sastri, entitled *A Primer of Indian Logic*, Madras, 1961 (3rd. ed.). There is also an ed. with nine commentaries. A portion, along with the corresponding *Dīpikā* comm., trs. into Eng. by C. Bhattacharya, Calcutta. Ed. and trs. into French by A. Foucher, Paris, 1949.]

The *Tarka-saṃgraha* of Ānandagiri or Ānandajñāna is a critical examination and a systematic refutation of the *Vaiśeṣika* system of philosophy.

[Ed. T. M. Tripathi, GOS, 1917.]

TARKA-SAṂGRAHA-DĪPIKĀ : A lucid commentary, by Annam Bhaṭṭa, on his own *Tarka-saṃgraha*.

TĀRKIKA-RAKṢĀ : Written by Varadarāja. An important treatise of the Nyāya-Vaiśeṣika systems of philosophy.

[Ed., with the gloss of Jñānapūrṇa, 1903.]

TATTVA-BINDU : A work on Mīmāṃsā philosophy, by Vācaspati Miśra. In it the author sets forth Kumārila's views.

[Ed. R. Sastri, 1936. Ed. and trs. into French by M, Biardeau, Pondicherry, 1979.]

TATTVA-BODHINĪ : A commentary, by Jñānendra Sarasvatī, on Bhaṭṭoji's *Siddhānta-kaumudī*. It omits the *Svara-prakriyā* and *Vaidikī-prakriyā*. It is very useful for beginners.

[Ed., with the *Aṣṭādhyāyī* and the *Siddhānta-kaumudī*, by W. L. Pansikar, NSP, 1933 (7th ed.)]

TATTVA-CINTĀMAṆI : An epoch-making work on Nyāya philosophy, by Gaṅgeśa. In four books it expounds, with much subtlety, the means of proof recognised in Nyāya philosophy incidentally expounding the metaphysics of the school. It was on the basis of this work that the Navya-nyāya schools of Bengal and Mithilā were founded.

[Ed., Bib. Ind., 1898-1901 with extracts from comm. and a comm., with *Āloka* and *Darpaṇa* commentaries, U. Misra, Darbhanga, 1957 (Vol. I, Prāmāṇyavāda) ; with *Āloka* and *Darpaṇa* comms., Darbhanga (Bihar), 1957, Vol. II reported to be in press of Mithilā Institute, Darbhanga. Ed., with a comm. and super. c of Rāmakṛṣṇādhvarin, Vol. I, Tirupati. See J. Mohanty, *Gaṅgeśa's Theory of Truth*.

TATTVACINTĀMAṆI-DĪDHITI : Comm., by Raghunātha Śiromaṇi, on Gaṅgesa's *Tattva-cintāmaṇi*. See *Anumāna-dīdhiti*, *Pratyakṣamaṇidīdhiti* and *Śabdamaṇi-dīdhiti*.

TATTVA-PRADĪPIKĀ : A treatise, by Citsukha, on Advaita philosophy. See *Citsukhī*.

[Ed., with a Skt. comm. and Hindi trs., by Ānandayogīndra, Banaras, 1956.]

TATTVĀRTHĀDHIGAMA-SŪTRA : The title means 'a manual for the understanding of the true nature of things'.

A philosophical work by Umāsvāti; it is also called *Daśa-sūtrī*. In this work, consisting of *Sūtras* and a commentary, there is a careful summary of the Jaina philosophical system. The logic, psychology, cosmography, ontology and ethics of the Jainas are dealt with in the *Sūtras* and the commentary appended by the author himself. The work is recognised as an authority by both the Śvetāmbara and Digambara sects of the Jainas. There is a large number of commentaries on the work by both Śvetāmbaras and Digambaras.

[Ed., Bib. Ind., 1903-5, with the comm., a few minor works of Umāsvāti; with a Hindi comm. in Rāyacandra Jaina Śāstramālā, Bombay, 1906; with trs., notes and comm. in Eng. by J. L. Jaini, Arrah, 1920; SBJ, II. Trs. into German and explained by H. Jacobi, *ZDMG*, 60.]

TATTVA-SAMĀSA : Attributed to Kapila, it is a catechism on Sāṃkhya philosophy, written before 1600 A.D.

[See A lecture on the Sāṃkhya philosophy, embracing the text of the *Tattva-samāsa* (with trs. and exegesis) by J. R. Ballantyne, Mirzapore, 1850.]

TATTVA-SAṂKHYĀNA (or, -NIRṆAYA) : A philosophical tract by Madhva. In it the author sets forth briefly his views on Vedānta philosophy. He insists on five fundamental dualisms (*dvaita*) whence his system derives its name as opposed to the *Advaita* of Śaṃkara and *Viśiṣṭādvaita* of Rāmānuja.

[Ed. and trs. H. von Glasenapp, *Festschrift Kuhn*.]

TATTVA-SANDARBHA : See *Bhāgavata-sandarbha*.

TAUTĀTITAMATA-TILAKA : A work on Mīmāṃsā, by Bhavadeva Bhaṭṭa. Following the views of Kumārila (= Tutātita) the work appears to have consisted of three chapters.

[Ed., with notes, by A. Sastri and P. Sastri etc., Allahabad, Banaras, 1939-44 (in three parts).]

ṬĪKĀ-SARVASVA : A well-known commentary, on the *Nāmaliṅgānuśāsana*, by Sarvānanda. From the commentary itself we learn that it was composed in 1159-60 A.D. It contains a number of *Deśī* (mostly Bengali) words. It is cited by Bṛhaspati Rāyamukuṭa in his commentary (1431 A.D.) on the *Nāmaliṅgānuśāsana*.

[For ed., see under *Nāmaliṅgānuśāsana*.]

TILAKA-MAÑJARĪ : A prose *Kāvya* by Dhanapāla. It is an elaborate tale of the love and union of Tilakamañjarī and Samaraketu. The work is an imitation of the *Kādambarī* to which it is, however, much inferior. The narrative is continuous, and there is no division into chapters. It contains some information about the Paramāra kings of Dhārā, whom the author eulogises in the introductory verses.

[Ed. NSP, 1938.]

TĪRTHA-CINTĀMAṆI : A *Smṛti* digest by Vācaspati Miśra. It is divided into five chapters called *Prakāśas*, viz. *Prayāga*, *Puruṣottama*, *Gaṅgā*, *Gayā*, *Vārāṇasī*. It deals with such topics as the purpose of pilgrimage, preliminaries of pilgrimage, rites to be performed at various Tīrthas etc.

[Ed. K. K. Smṛtitīrtha, Bib. Ind., 1910-12.]

TITHI-NIRṆAYA : A *Smṛti* digest by Vācaspati Miśra. It discusses the different *Tithis*, both *Śuddhā* (pure) and *Viddhā* (mixed) and the various rites to be performed in them.

TRIKĀṆḌAŚEṢA : An important supplement, by Puruṣottamadeva, of rare words to the *Nāmaliṅgānuśāsana*.

[Pub. Śrī Vāṇīvilāsa Press, 1915; with *Sārārtha-candrikā* comm., Veṅkateśvara Press, Bombay, 1916.]

TRIPURA-DĀHA : A drama stated, in the *Nāṭyaśāstra*, to have been composed by god Brahmā himself. There is a drama of the same title, in 4 acts, by Vatsarāja. It describes the destruction of the capital of Tripurāsura by Śiva. It is of the *Ḍima* type.

[Ed. C. D. Dalal, under the title *Rūpaka-ṣaṭka*, GOS, 1918.]

TRIṢAṢṬIŚALĀKĀ-PURUṢA-CARITA : An epic poem, composed between 1160 and 1172 A.D. by Hemacandra. In ten

Parvans it deals with the lives of 63 best men of the Jaina faith, the 24 Jainas, 12 Cakravartins, 9 Vāsudevas, 9 Baladevas, 9 Viṣṇudviṣas. The last *Parvan* deals with the life of Mahāvīra, and gives some definite information about him.

[Ed. Jaina-dharma-prasāraka-sabhā, Bhagnagar, 1906-13. Parvan I trs. into Eng. by H. Johnson, GOS, Vol. I, 1931, Vol. II, 1937, Vol. IV, 1954. Parvan XI ed. H. Jacobi, Bib Ind., 1891, 2nd ed. with supplement by Leumann and Tawney, 1932.]

ṬUPṬĪKĀ : A part of Kumārila's commentary on Jaimini's *Pūrvamīmāṃsā-sūtra*. It is on Adhyāyas IV-XII of the *Sūtra*.

[See under *Śloka-vārtika*.]

TURAṄGAMA-ŚĀSTRA : Same as *Haya-āyurveda* (q.v.).

UBHAYĀBHISĀRIKĀ : See *Caturbhāṇī*.

UDAYASUNDARĪ-KATHĀ : It is a work by Soḍḍhala, being sometimes classed as a *Campūkāvya*. It, however, appears to be a *Kathā* type of prose *Kāvya*, modelled on Bāṇabhaṭṭa's *Kādambarī*. Soḍḍhala, however, uses verses liberally in his prose narrative. This romance relates, in eight chapters, the imaginary story of the love-marriage of Udayasundarī, daughter of the Nāga king Śikhaṇḍatilaka, and Malayavāhana, king of Pratiṣṭhāna.

[Ed. C. D. Dalal and E. Krishnamacharya GOS, 1920.]

UDDYOTA : Also called *Mahābhāṣya-pradīpoddyota*, it is a well-known commentary, by Nāgeśa, on Kaiyaṭa's *Mahābhāṣya-pradīpa*.

[Ed. J. R. Ballantyne, Vol. I, *Navāhnika*, with Eng. trs. of the opening portion, Mirzapore, 1856. Ed. B. Sastri, Bib. Ind.]

UJJVALA-NĪLAMAṆI : A renowned work on Vaiṣṇava *Rasa-śāstra*, by Rūpa Gosvāmin. In it the author gives a subtle analysis of the *Ujjvala-rasa* (erotic sentiment), the principal sentiment in Vaiṣṇava *Rasa-śāstra*.

[Ed. *Kāvyamālā*, Bombay, 1913, with Jīva Gosvāmin's comm. called *Locanarocanī* and Viśvanātha's comm. called *Ānanda-candrikā*.]

UṆĀDI-SŪTRA: A grammatical work containing words which are derived from verbs with unusual suffixes. In some form or other it appears to have been known to Pāṇini. See under Śākaṭāyana.

[See the *Uṇādi-sūtras in various recensions* by T. R. Cintāmaṇi, University of Madras, 1933; K. M. K. Sarma, Authorship of the Uṇādi-sūtras, *P. V. Kane Pres. Vol.*, Poona, 1941.]

UPADEŚA-SĀHASRĪ : A work on Vedānta philosophy, attributed to Śaṃkarācārya. It consists of 675 stanzas divided into 19 chapters. It touches upon the well-known Vedānta topics, but lays greater emphasis on the proper realisation of the Vedāntic texts teaching unity (e.g. *tat tvam asi*), as a means to the attainment of Brahmahood.

[Ed., with *Padayojanikā* comm., NSP, 1930 (3rd. ed.); with trs. and notes by S. Mayeda, Japan, 1979; with Eng. trs. and notes, by S. Jagadanand, Madras, 1949.]

UPANIṢAD : A class of works included in the Vedic literature. These works are designated by the word Vedānta for several reasons : (1) They were the last literary products of the Vedic period. (2) These were studied last of all other Vedic works. (3) They mark the culmination of the Vedic speculation. These were esoteric works which grew out of the secret sessions of the preceptor and his disciples. The word 'Upaniṣad' is derived from the root *Sad* (to sit) preceded by the prefixes *Upa* and *Ni*; it means 'sitting down near' for confidential instructions. Each of the four Vedic Saṃhitās has its *Upaniṣads*. There are over one hundred *Upaniṣads*. Of these, the following ten, commented upon by Śaṅkarācārya, are regarded as genuine and, therefore, most authoritative :—*Īśā, Kena, Kaṭha, Praśna, Muṇḍaka, Māṇḍūkya, Taittirīya, Aitareya, Chāndogya, Bṛhadāraṇyaka*. The principal subjects, discussed in these works, are : the nature of individual soul and Supreme Soul, nature of the world, true and false knowledge, way to liberation, nature of liberation, etc.

Some of the *Upaniṣads* contain anecdotes to bring home to the readers the truth that they aim to inculcate.

The fundamental doctrine of the Upaniṣads can be summed up in the sentence : *The universe is Brahman, but Brahman is Ātman.* Thus the entire Upaniṣadic philosophy revolves around the two conceptions of Brahman and Ātman. In the *Upaniṣads* we find also the doctrine of *Karman*; according to the latter, actions in one life are responsible for the kinds of life in future births.

Though from their denunciation of the earthly pleasures, the *Upaniṣads* seem to be pessimistic, yet they are at bottom optimistic in outlook. They aim at eternal bliss and not transient pleasures. The sublime philosophy of the *Upaniṣads* has earned for them unstinted and eloquent praise from Indian and western scholars. Schopenhauer says about the Upaniṣad, "It is the most satisfying and elevating reading which is possible in the world; it has been the solace of my life and will be the solace of my death". Some Upaniṣads are deeply influenced by Tantra. Some of the Upaniṣads have been translated into various European languages.

[Pub. Adyar Library, Vol. I (ten Upaniṣads with comm. of Brahmayogin), 1935-36; Vols. II, III (Minor Upaniṣads), 1938-40. Ed. Roer, Madras, 1931-32 (12 Principal Upaniṣads with comm. of Śaṃkara, gloss of Ānandagiri, trs. and notes) ; (Twelve Principal) Upaniṣads, trs. into English by Max Müller, SBE, vols. I and 15. Thirteen Principal Upaniṣads, trs. by R. A. Hume, Oxford, 1921. *Principal Upaniṣads,* Text in Roman script and Eng. trs. by S. Radhakrishnan. Also Eng. trs. by S. Nikhilananda, 4 vols. Various Upaniṣadic texts translated into some other foreign languages like French, German and also into various regional languages of India like Hindi, Bengali, Telugu etc. *Aitareya, Kauṣītaki, Kena* and eight others trs. into Russian by A. Syrkin, 1965. L. Renou's *Upaniṣads, Texte et traduction* '*Les Upaniṣads* (1943-56), covering 16 texts (major and minor Upaniṣads) is a noteworthy work. Daftary's *Upaniṣadarthavyākhyā* (1955-56), contains fresh light on the interpretation of the principal Upaniṣads. Adyar Library, Madras, has published several minor and sectarian Upaniṣads. For collections of Upaniṣadic texts, see *Īśādy-aṣṭottara-*

śatopaniṣadaḥ, Banaras, 1938 and *Īśādi-viṃśottara-śatopaniṣadaḥ*, NSP, 1948. Sixty Upaniṣads of the Veda, Pts. I, II, German ed. by Deussen, trs. into Eng. by Bedekar and Palsule. It includes the more supplant of the later Atharvan Upaniṣads. The classical Upaniṣads, ed. P. B. Gajendragadkar, Vol. I (*Īśā, Kena*), Bombay, 1981. The following works may be consulted in connexion with the Upaniṣads :—

ABHEDANANDA : *Upaniṣadic Doctrine of the Self*, New Delhi, 1978.

BAHADURMAL : *The Religion of the Buddha and its relation to Upaniṣadic Thought*, Hoshiarpur, 1958.

BROWN, G. W.: *The Human Body in the Upaniṣads*, Jubbulpore, 1921.

DHAWAN, K. K. : *Upaniṣadon men Kāvyatattva*, Hoshiarpur, 1976.

DEUSSEN, P. : *The Philosophy of the Upaniṣads.*
: *Sixty Upaniṣads of the Veda*, Pts. I, II, trs. Bedekar and Palsule, Delhi, 1980.

FURST, A. : *Der Sprachgebrauch......alteren Upaniṣads...Sanskrit*, Diss., Gottingen, 1915.

GARG, P. K. : *Upaniṣadic Challenge to Science*, Delhi, 1975.

GOUGH, A. E. : *The Philosophy of the Upaniṣads*, London, 1982.

JACOB, G.A. : *Concordance to the Principal Upaniṣads and the Bhagavadgītā*, Delhi, 1963.

KEITH, A. B. : *Religion and Philosophy of the Veda and Upaniṣads*, HOS, 1925.

KIRFEL, W.: *Beitrage......Upaniṣads und im Epos*, Diss, Bonn, 1908.

MODAK, M. S. : *Spinoza and the Upaniṣads*, Nagpur, 1970.

MOHAN, M. V. D.: The Antiquity of the Upaniṣads, *Bhāratī Bhānam*, VII, XVIII, Pts. I, II, 1980.

OLDENBERG : *Zur Ceschichte der altindischen Prosa*, p. 28 ff.

PARRINDER, G. : *Upaniṣads, Gītā and Bible*, 2nd ed., London, 1975.

PATWARDHAN, K. A. : *Upaniṣads, and Modern Biology.*

RADHAKRISHNAN, S. : *The Philosophy of the Upaniṣads.*

SADHALE, S. S. : *Upaniṣad-vākya-mahākośa*, 1940-41.

SHARMA, T. R. : *Studies in the Sectarian Upaniṣads.*

SHARMA, B. R. : *The conception of Ātman in the Principal Upaniṣads.*

SINGH, S. P. : *Upaniṣadic Symbolism*, New Delhi, 1981.

SREERAM, L. : *The Metaphysics of the Upaniṣads.*

SYRKIN, A. : *Some Problems of the Study of Upaniṣads.*

THITE, G. : The Magico-Religious in the Principal Upaniṣads, *Summaries of papers, AIOC*, 1974.

VARENNE, J.: *Upaniṣads der Yoga*, Paris, 1971

VISHVABANDHU : *Grammatical Word Index to Principal Upaniṣads*, Hoshiarpur, 1966.

WECKER, O. : *Der Gebrauch der Kasus in der Upaniṣad Literatur*, Göttingen, 1905.]

UPA-PURĀṆA : Minor Purāṇas are called Upa-purāṇas. They do not differ essentially from the major Purāṇas. These are, however, more exclusively adapted to suit the purpose of local cults and the religious needs of separate sects. Some of them claim to be supplements to one or other of the Mahā-purāṇas. The Upa-purāṇas are traditionally known to be 18 in number.

[For number and names of Upa-purāṇas and Studies in them, see under Purāṇa.]

UPAVANA-VINODA, A text on Arbori-horticulture, being an extract from Peterson's ed. of the *Śārṅgadhara-paddhati.*

[Ed., with Eng. trs., by G. P. Majumdar, Calcutta, 1935.]

ŪRUBHAṄGA : A *Mahābhārata* play by Bhāsa, in one act. The fight between Bhīma and Duryodhana ends in the breaking of the thigh of the later who falls in agony, and eventually passes away in the presence of his parents and wives.

[Ed. C. R. Devadhar, Poona Oriental Series, 1970.]

UTTARA-RĀMACARITA : A drama, in seven acts, by Bhavabhūti. It dramatises the later portion of the Rāma-story, i.e. from Rāma's return to Ayodhyā and coronation to the end. Into the original story he has introduced certain changes, e.g. the meeting between Rāma and the sylvan deity Vāsantī, Sītā's presence in an invisible form before Rāma etc.

The drama is reputed for the artistic delineation of the pathetic sentiment.

[Ed. P. V. Kane, with comm. of Ghanaśyāma, Bombay, 1921; S.K. Belvalkar, Poona, 1921; with Hindi trs. and notes, Skt. comm., by T. Jha, Allahabad, 1961; M.R. Kale with comm. of Vīrarāghava, Delhi, 1982. Trs. into English by S.K. Belvalkar in HOS, 1915; by C.H. Tawney, Calcutta, 1871. Trs. into French by F. Neve, Bruxelles and Paris, 1880; by P.D. Alheim, Bois-le-roi, 1906. See K.K. Datta, On the Chāyā Nāma Tṛtīyo'ṅkaḥ of Bhavabhūti, *R. G. Basak Comm.*, *Vol.* 1, Calcutta.]

VĀCASPATYA : A famous lexicon by Tārānātha Tarkavācaspati. Divided into six parts, it gives synonyms of words after analysing them into their basic forms and suffixes and determining their genders. Compound words have been expounded, and at places Bengali equivalents of the words are noted. It also explains the technical terms and doctrines of the orthodox and heterodox systems of philosophy.

[Pub. in Calcutta, 1873—84. Latest reprint in Chowkhamba Sanskrit Series, Banaras, in 6 vols., 1961—62.]

VĀGBHAṬĀLAṂKĀRA : A work on poetics, by Vāgbhaṭa who must be distinguished from the author, bearing the same name, of the *Kāvyānuśāsana* and aslo from Vāgbhaṭas, authors of works on *Āyurveda*. The *Vāgbhaṭālaṃkāra*, consisting of five chapters, covers, in 260 verses most of the topics of poetics.

[Ed. Sivadatta and Parab (with Siṃhadeva Gaṇi's comm.), NSP, 1895, 1915.]

VAHNI-PURĀṆA : Another name of *Agni-purāṇa* (q.v.). There is also an *Upa-purāṇa* of the same title.

VAIDYA-JĪVANA : A medical work by Lolimbarāja (17th century).

[Ed., with Hindi comm. and notes, by B.S. Misra, CSS, 1941.]

VAIDYAKA-ŚABDASINDHU : A dictionary of medical terms, herbs, etc. used in *Āyurveda*, by Umesh Gupta Kaviratna, written in 1894 A.D.

[Pub. in Calcutta, 1894.]

VAIJAYANTĪ : A lexicon by Yādavaprakāśa, dating back to about the middle of the 11th century. It is voluminous, and arranges the words by syllables, genders and initial letters.

[Ed. G. Oppert, Madras, 1893; H. G. Sastri, with Intro., Index.]

A commentary on the *Viṣṇu-smṛti* is also called *Vaijayantī*.

VAIKHĀNASA SMĀRTASŪTRA : See Dharmasūtra.

[Ed. W. Caland, Bibliotheca Indica, Calcutta, 1927; K. Rangachari. Madras, 1930. Trs. into English by W. Caland, 1929; Eggers, Göttingen, 1929.]

VAIRĀGYA-ŚATAKA : A lyric poem by Bhartṛhari. In it the poet points out the hollowness of love and earthly happiness. It contains valuable instructions about practical life.

There is a poem of this title, by Nīlakaṇṭha Dīkṣita.

[Ed. with Hindi metrical and prose trs., Trivedi and Hostinge, Banaras, 1961; NSP (in *Subhāṣita-triśatī*), 6th ed., Bombay, 1922. Eng. trs. by C. H. Tawney in *Indian Anti-*

quary, V, 1876; B. H. Wortham, London, 1886; J. M. Kennedy, London, 1913; C. W. Gurner, Calcutta. 1927. Also see under Bhartṛhari.]

There is one work of the same title each by Janārdana Gosvāmin and Dhanadadeva.

[Both ed. in *Kāvyamālā*, Gucchaka XIII, 1916.]

VAIŚEṢIKA-SŪTRA (or DARŚANA) : Attributed to Kaṇāda, it is the first systematic work on Vaiśeṣika philosophy. It is divided into ten *Adhyāyas* or Books, each consisting of two *Āhnikas* or sections. Its contents are as follows :—

Book I—discussion of the 5 categories.

Book II—deals with different substances excepting soul and mind.

Book III—deals with soul and mind along with the objects of the senses and nature of inference.

Book IV—deals mainly with the atomic structure of the universe.

Book V—discussion on the nature and kinds of action.

Book VI—ethical problems.

Book VII—questions of quality, self and inference.

Books VIII-X—mainly logical and deal with problems of perception, inference and causality.

The date of the work is uncertain. The system may have arisen about the time of Buddha and Mahāvīra (6th-5th cent. B. C.). The work appears to have received additions from time to time.

[Ed., with the *Praśastapāda-bhāṣya*, by Lekharaja, Lahore, 1945; with the *Kiraṇāvalī* of Udayana, Banaras, by V. P. Dube, 1885-97; with the *Nyāya-kandalī* of Śrīdhara, by V. Dvivedi, Banaras, 1895; with Bhaṭṭavādīndra's comm., by A. Thakur, Darbhanga, 1957; with *Vedabhāskara* comm. and an Appendix of Hindi gloss of the *Sūtras*, by K. N. Sharma, Barchhwar, Sarkaghat (Mandi, H. P.), 1972. See H. Ui, *Vaiśeṣika Philosophy and Vaiśeṣika-sūtra* with comm. of Śaṃkara Miśra and extracts from gloss of Jayanārāyaṇa and Candrakānta, trs. into Eng. by N. Sinha. Also see G. Kaviraj, *History and Bibliography of the Nyāya-Vaiśeṣika Literature*.]

VAIYĀKARAṆA-SIDDHĀNTA-KAUMUDĪ : Same as *Siddhānta-kaumudī*.

VAIYĀKARAṆA-BHŪṢAṆA : A gloss, by Kauṇḍa Bhaṭṭa, on Bhaṭṭoji's *Vaiyākaraṇa-siddhānta-kārikā*.

VAIYĀKARAṆA-BHŪṢAṆA-SĀRA : Written by Kauṇḍa Bhaṭṭa, it is a sort of abridgment of his *Vaiyākaraṇa-bhūṣaṇa*.

VAIYĀKARAṆA-SIDDHĀNTA-MAÑJŪṢĀ : A work on the philosophy of grammar, by Nāgeśa. Exists in versions called *Laghu-mañjūṣā* and *Parama-laghu-mañjūṣa*.

[Ed., with comms. *Kāñjikā* and *Kalā*, at first by M. M. Pathak and later by P. N. Panda and S. S. Shende, CSS, 1917. *Paramalaghu-mañjūṣā*, ed. K. Sastri, Kurukṣetra, 1975.]

VĀJASANEYI-PRĀTIŚĀKHYA : See *Prātiśākhya*.

[Ed. V. Sarma, Madras, 1934 (with comms. of Uvaṭa and Ananta). Also see *Vājasaneyi-prātiśākhya*, I, by S. N. Ghosal.]

VAJRA-SŪCĪ : A clever polemic on the Brahmanical caste which is decried very cuttingly. It is sometimes ascribed to Aśvaghoṣa, but was perhaps written by Dharmakīrti to whom it is attributed by the Chinese translation (973-81 A. D.).

[Ed. and trs. by Weber, *Über die Vajrasūcī*, in Abhandl. d. Berliner Akad., 1859; with Eng. trs., by S. Mukhopadhyaya, Santiniketan, 1956.]

VAKROKTI-JĪVITA: A well-known work on poetics, by Kuntaka. In it the author seeks to establish that *Vakrokti* (charming mode of expression) is the essence (*jīvita*) of poetry. It is not known how many chapters the original treatise comprised. The first two chapters and a part of the third have been published. A part of the fourth chapter, which is supposed to be the concluding chapter of the work, exists in MS.

[Ed. S. K. De, Calcutta, 1961 (3rd ed.)—Chs i—part of iii with a résumé of the unedited portion. Cr. ed. with fresh MS material, with Eng. tr. by K. Krishnamoorthy, Karnatak University, Dharwad.]

VAKROKTI-PAÑCĀŚIKĀ : A short work by Ratnākara. It is in 50 verses written in the form of conversation and repartees between Śiva and Pārvatī in their love-sport.

[Ed. *Kāvyamālā*, I.]

VĀKYAPADĪYA : A grammatico-philosophical work by Bhartṛhari. Written in verse, it mainly deals with questions of the philosophy of speech. It is in three chapters called respectively *Brahma* or *Āgama-kāṇḍa*, *Vākya-kāṇḍa* and *Pada-* or *Prakīrṇa-kāṇḍa*. It contains evidence of thorough knowledge of contemporary philosophical disputes. It is mentioned in the *Kāśikā* comm. on Pāṇini, IV. 3. 88.

[Ed., with Puṇyarāja's comm., Banaras SS, 1887-1907; with Helārāja's comm. (3rd Kāṇḍa), TSS 1935; with *Bhāvapradīpa* comm. and notes, by S. Sukla, CSS, 1897; Chap. ii, ed. K.A.S. Iyer, Delhi, 1977. Chaps. i and ii with Eng. trs. by K. R. Pillai, Delhi, 1971; K. V. Adhyankar and Limaye, Poona, 1965; with Puṇyarāja's comm. and the ancient *Vṛtti*, by K. A. Subramania Iyer, *Kāṇḍa* II, Delhi, 1983. See G. N. Sastri, *Philosophy of Word and Meaning*, Calcutta; K. A. S. Iyer, *Bhartṛhari : A Study of the Vākyapadīya in the light of the ancient commentaries*, Poona, 1969; W. Rau : *Die handschriftliche Uberlieferung des Vākyapadīya und Seiner Kommentare*, München, 1971. Trs. into Eng. by S. K. Iyer, Poona. Also see M. Biardeau, *Theorie de.........brahmanisme classique*, The Hague, 1964; C. Deva, Bhartṛhari—a critical study with special reference to the Vākyapadīya and its comm., *Pro. of 5th Oriental Conference*, Vol. I, 1912; V. S. Rao, *The Philosophy of sentence and its parts* Delhi, 1970; S. Verma, *Vākyapadīyam* (Brahmakāṇḍa)—text, with Eng. and Hindi, Delhi, 1970; Abhyankar and Limaye, *Vākyapadīya*, ed. with Intro. and Appendices; Kāṇḍa II Eng. trs. with notes by K. A. S. Iyer, Patna, 1977; *Vākyapadīya-prameya-saṃgraha*, München, 1981.]

VĀMANA-PURĀṆA : It does not appear to have come down in the original form. It deals with Avatāras of Viṣṇu, Liṅga-worship, the origin of Gaṇeśa and the birth of Kārtikeya.

[Ed. P. Tarkaratna, Vaṅgavāsī Press, Calcutta, 1314 B. S. A. S. Gupta, All-India Kashiraj Trust, Varanasi, 1967. Eng. trs. by S. M. Mukhopadhyay and A. Bhattacharya and others., Varanasi, 1968. See V.S. Agrawala, *Vāmana-purāṇa—a study*, Varanasi, 1983.]

VARĀHA-PURĀṆA : Also called *Vārāha-purāṇa*. It is not a a Purāṇa in the ancient sense of the word. It is rather a manual of prayers and rules for Viṣṇu-worshippers. Though Viṣṇuite in character, yet it contains legends about Śiva and Durgā. Portions are devoted to female deities. It deals also with *Śrāddha*, *Prāyaścitta*, erection of gods' images and *Mathurā-māhātmya*. It tells the legend of Naciketas.

[Ed. P. Tarkaratna, Vangavasi Press, Calcutta, 1313 B.S.; S. Sharma, with Intro. in Hindi]

VĀRARUCA KĀVYA : Mentioned in Patañjali's *Mahābhāṣya*, but lost to us.

VARṢA-KRIYĀ-KAUMUDĪ : A Smṛti digest by Govindānanda, dealing with the rites to be performed in the course of a year.

[Ed., Bib. Ind., 1902]

VĀRTIKA-SŪTRA : By Kātyāyana. Such *Sūtras* are intended to be supplements to the rules of the *Aṣṭādhyāyi*.

[Printed repeatedly with the rules of Pāṇini. See *Aṣṭādhyāyī*]

VASANTA-VILĀSA : A historical poem describing the life of Vastupāla and the history of Gujarat by Bālacandrasūri (from Modheraka or Madhera in Kadi Prant, Baroda, Baroda state) contemporary of Vastupāla, composed after his death for his son in Saṃvat 1296 (1240 A.D.).

[Ed.C.D.Dalal, GOS, 1917.]

VĀSAVADATTĀ : A romantic prose *Kāvya* of the Kathā type, by Subandhu. It deals with the fictitious love-story of prince Kandarpaketu and princess Vāsavadattā.

[Ed. F. Hall, with Śivarāma's comm., Bib. Ind. 1859, reprinted almost *verbatim* by J. Vidyāsāgara, Calcutta, 1907 (3rd ed.). Ed. L. H. Gray, in Roman characters, New York, 1913; S. Śāstri, with Skt. and Hindi comm., Banaras, 1954. Eng. trs. by L.H. Gray.]

A prose *Kāvya* of this name is mentioned in Patañjali's *Mahābhāṣya* as well as in Bāṇa's *Harṣacarita* (Introductory verse 11).

VASIṢṬHA-DHARMASŪTRA (or DHARMAŚĀSTRA) : See Dharmasūtra.

[Ed. A. Führer, Bombay, 1883, Poona, 1930; K. Dharmadhikari, with his own comm. called *Vidvanmodinī*, Banaras, Śaka 1781. Trs. into English by Bühler, Sacred Books of the East, Vol. XIV.]

VĀSTU-ŚĀSTRA (or VIDYĀ) : Science of architecture. It has been cultivated in India from very early times, perhaps from the Vedic age. We have evidence of the existence of this branch of knowledge in the *Sūtra* literature, the epics and the *Arthaśāstra*. The *Matsyapurāṇa* mentions 18 preceptors of *Vāstuśāstra*. The *Bṛhat-saṃhitā* refers to other early writers. The *Agnipurāṇa*, *Garuḍa-purāṇa*, *Vāyu-purāṇa*, *Mārkaṇḍeya-purāṇa* and the *Hayaśīrṣapañcarātra* contain useful information on the subject. Viśvakarman and Maya are regarded as founders of Vāstuvidyā in the earliest period. The *Māna-sāra*, *Maya-mata*, *Samarāṅgaṇa-sūtradhāra* and *Vāstuvidyā* are noteworthy works on this science. Styles of architecture were mainly divided into North Indian or Aryan and South Indian or Dravidian. A corresponding division of styles into *Nāgara* and *Drāviḍa* is also found. Some add a third, viz. *Vesara* which was also a South Indian design. Divisions like *Kaliṅga* and *Bhūmija* are also found. Vitruvius, the Roman architect, was perhaps acquainted with some Indian texts on architecture. The broad matters, dealt with in this Śāstra, are as follows:— quality of the soil, shape of the site, facing of the structure, ground plan, measurements, size of various parts of a structure, classification of residential houses, religious structures, gateways, pillars etc., sanitary arrangements, materials, decoration, planning of villages and towns, stability of structures.

Doors, their position, dimension etc. receive careful treatment in the works on this Śāstra. The dimensions of bricks and the method of making them receive careful attention of the writers.

Vāstuvidyā includes also texts on sculpture, painting, iconography and some minor arts and crafts.

[A *Vāstuvidyā* is ed. TSS, 1913. For a detailed study of the subject, see T.P. Bhattacharya, *The Canons of Indian Art or A study on Vāstuvidyā*, Calcutta, 1963 (2nd. ed.). Also see D.N. Shukla, *Vāstuśāstra*, Vols. I, II]

VĀSTUSŪTRA-UPANIṢAD : First known text on image-making. Attributed to Pippalāda. Six chapters. It deals with stones, compositional diagram, carving disposition of parts of the image, the basic emotions connected with images, total composition of the image panel. The metaphysical question of the origin of form and its importance for the attainment of *mokṣa* is the central idea.

[Ed. with Eng. trs. and notes by A. Boner and others, MLBD, Delhi, 1982.]

VĀSTU-VIDYĀ : A work on house-building (see Vāstu-Śāstra).

[Ed., with a comm., TSS, 1940]

VAṬEŚVARA-SIDDHĀNTA : A work on astronomy, by Vaṭeśvarācārya, consisting of 15 chaps.

[Ed., R. Swarup and M. Misra, Delhi, 1962. First three chaps. only.]

VĀYUPURĀṆA : Also called *Vāyavīya-p.* Sometimes designated as Śiva or Śaiva Purāṇa due to its predominantly Śaiva character. Perhaps the oldest of extant Purāṇas. Its earliest portions appear to date back to the third century A.D. Contains the usual five topics of old Purāṇas, besides some Smṛti matters. Two chapters deal with ancient Indian music. A *Vāyupurāṇa*, quoted in the *Mahābhārata* and the *Harivaṃśa*, and the *Harivaṃśa* itself agree, in many cases, literally with the present *Vāyu*. Bāṇabhaṭṭa (7th cent. A.D.) is said to have a *Vāyu-p.* read to him. It describes Gupta rule of the 4th cent. A.D. The extant Purāṇa preserves much of an earlier version which was not perhaps later than the 5th cent. A.D. It deals, *inter alia*, with *Yoga*, art of singing.

[Ed. Bib. Ind., 1880-89; ASS No. 49, 1905. Also ed. Vaṅgavāsī, Calcutta. See R. Patil, *Cultural History from the Vāyupurāṇa.*]

VEDA : This word generally stands for the four Vedic Saṃhitās. According to orthodox opinion the term includes also the Brāhmaṇas.

The following are some of the noteworthy works:

APTE, S.S. : *Vedic Astronomical Mythology*, 1978.

APTE, U.M. : Problem of Illegitimate Children in Vedic Religion, *Summaries of Papers*, AIOC, 1974.

ARNOLD, E.V. : *Vedic Metre in Its Historical Development*, 1905.

AUROBINDO: *On the Veda*, Pondicherry, 1956.

——— : *Hymns to the Mystic Fire*, trs., Pondicherry, 1952.

BALASUBRAMANYAN, M.D. : *System of Kṛt Accentuation in Pāṇini and the Veda*, Tirupati, 1982.

BERGAIGNE : *Vedic Religion*, Vols. I-IV, Eng. trs. by V.G. Paranjape, Poona, 1969-73.

BHARATI K. TIRTHA : *Vedic Mathematics*, 1978 (Reprint), ed. V.S. Agrawala, Delhi, 1982.

——— : *Vedic Mataphysics*, Delhi, 1978

BHARGAVA, P.L. : *India in the Vedic Age*, Lucknow, 1971

BHAT, G.K. : *Vedic Times*, Delhi, 1978

BHATTACHARJI, S. : *The Indian Theogony. Comparative Study of Indian Mythology from the Vedas to the Purāṇas*, Calcutta, 1978.

———Attitude to food in the Vedas, *W. Ruben Fel. Vol.*, Calcutta, 1981.

———Gods and Demons in the Vedas, *Jour. of Asiatic Society of Bengal*, 1980

BLOOMFIELD, M. : *Vedic Concordance*, HOS, 1906.
The Religion of the Veda, New York, 1908.

BLOOMFIELD, M. and F. Edgerton : *Vedic Variants*, 2 Vols., 1930-32.

CHAKRABORTI, H.P. : *Vedic India, Political and Legal Institutions in Vedic Literature*, Calcutta, 1981.

CHANDRA, R.G. : *Ornaments and Jewellery of Vedic India*, Varanasi.

DANDEKAR, R.N. : *Vedic Bibliography*, Vol. I, Bombay, 1946; Vol. II, Poona, 1966; Vol. III, Poona, 1973.

——— : *Vedic Mythological Tracts*, Delhi, 1979

——— : *Der Vedische Mensch*, Heidelberg, 1938.

——— : *Vedic Religion and Mythology*.

DANGE, S.A. : *Vedic Concept of Field and the Divine Fructification*, Bombay, 1971.

——— : *Cultural Source from the Veda*, Bombay, 1977.

——— : *Vedic Myths in Social Perspective*, Hoshiarpur, 1982.

——— : *Sexual Symbolism from the Vedic Ritual*, Delhi.

DASU, T.U.S. : *Veda Vijñanam*, Delhi, 1980.

DATT, L. : *Vedamimāṃsā*, Delhi, 1980.

DHARMAPAL, L.G : *The Linguistic Atom* (A key to the secret of the Veda and Vedic Ritual), Calcutta, 1969.

EDGERTON AND EMANEAU : *Vedic Variants*, Vol. III. 1934

FATEH SINGH : *The Vedic Etymology*, Kota, 1952.

GHURYE, G.S. : *Vedic India*, 1979.

GIRI, MAHADEVANANDA: *Vedic Culture*.

GONDA, J.: *Stylistic Repetitions in the Vedas*, Amsterdam, 1959.

——— : *Vedic Morning Litany*, Leiden, 1981.

——— : *Vedic Ritual in Non-solemn Rites*, Leiden, 1982.

——— : *Four Studies in the Language of the Veda*, The Hague, 1959.

——— : *Vedic Literature* (Saṃhitās; Brāhmaṇas), Utto. Harrassowitz, Wiesbaden, 1975.

GOPAL, R. : *India of the Vedic Age*, Delhi, 1959.

GURUMURTY, N. S.V.R. : *Biblical Teachings in the Light of Vedic Religion and Philosophy*, 1978.

HANSRAJ : *Science in the Vedas*, Ludhiana, India.

HILLEBRANDT, A. : *Vedische Mythologie*, 3 Vols., Breslau, 1891, 1899, 1902. Eng. trs. by S.R. Sharma, Delhi, 1980.

HARDY, E. : *Die Vedische-brahmanische Periode der Religion des alten Indiens*, Munster, 1893.

——— : *History and Culture of the Indian People*, Vol. I, Vedic Age, London, 1951.

JOSHI, J.R. : *Some Minor Diversities in Vedic Mythology and Rituals*, Pune, 1977.

——— : *Minor Vedic Deities*, Pune, 1978.

KEITH, A.B. : *The Religion and Philosophy of the Veda and the Upaniṣads*, HOS, 1925.

KULKARNI, C. : *Vedic Foundation of Indian Culture*, Bombay, 1973.

LAHIRI, A.K. : *Vedic Vṛtra*, MLBD, Delhi.

LAL, K.: *Comparative and Analytical Study of the Vedas*, 1981.

MACDONELL, A.A. : *Vedic Mythology*, Strassburg, 1897.

[There is a Hindi rendering of it by Suryakanta.]

——— : *Vedic Grammar*, 1910.

——— : *Vedic Religion*, 1880 (new ed. 1881).

MACDONELL AND KEITH : *Vedic Index of Names and Subjects*, Vols. I, II, Delhi, 1958 (Reprint).

MAINKAR, T.G. : *The Upabṛṃhaṇa and the Ṛgveda Interpretation*, Ahmeda. 1975.

MEHTA, D.D. : *Medicine in the Vedas*.

——— : *Positive Sciences in the Vedas*.

(There is a Hindi rendering of it by Suryakanta.)

MITRA, P. : *Life and Society in the Vedic Age*, Calcutta, 1966.

MÜLLER, M. : *History of Ancient Sanskrit Literature.*

OLDENBERG, H. : *Religion des Veda*, Berlin, 1894. (New ed. 1917, 1925). French trs. by V. Henry, Paris, 1903.

——— : *Trials in the Veda*, Amsterdam, 1976.

——— : *Vedic Research*, Eng. tra. by V.G. Paranjape, Poona, 1973.

GONDA, J. : *The dual deities in the religion of the Veda*, London, 1974.

PANDIT, M.P. : *Studies in the Tantra and the Veda.*

PENDSE, G.S. : *Vedic Concept of Śrāddha*, Pune, 1978.

——— : *Key to Vedic Symbolism.*

PARAB, B.A. : *The Miraculous and the Mysterious in Vedic Literature.*

PISCHEL, R. AND GELDNER : *Vedische Studien*, Vols. I-III, 1889, 1892, 1901.

PURANI, A.B. : *Studies in Vedic Interpretation* (on the lines of Sri Aurobindo) CSS, 1963.

———*Sri Aurobindo's Vedic Glossary*, Pondicherry, 1962.

Raghuvir (ed.) : *Comparative and Analytical study of Vedas*, Vol. I, Delhi, 1981.

——— : *Vedic Studies*, New Delhi, 1981.

RAGOZIN : *Vedic India.*

RAJA RAO, M. : *The Vedic Octave*, Mysore, 1955.

RAM GOPAL : The Veda and the Mahābhārata, *Sternbach Fel. Vol.*, Lucknow.

RENOU, L : *Destiny of the Veda in India*, Delhi, 1965.

——— : *Philologie Vedique*, 1928.

——— : *Les ecoles Vediques*, Paris, 1947

——— : *Bibliographie Vedique*, Paris, 1950

——— : *Index Vedique*, 1934-35

——— : *Grammaire de la langue Vedīque*, 1952.

ROUSSEL : *La religion Vedique*, 1909.

ROY, MIRA : Anatomy in Vedic Literature, *Indian Jour. of History of Science*, 2 (I), pp. 35-46, 1967.

SARASVATI, D. : *Ṛgvedādi-bhāṣya-bhūmikā* (ed. Y. Mimamsaka) Amritsar, 1967.

SEN, U. : *The Ṛgvedic Era*, Calcutta, 1974.

SASTRY, K. : *Lights on the Veda*, Madras, 1948.

——— : *Further lights : Veda and Tantra*, Madras, 1951.

Satyashrava : *A Comprehensive History of Vedic Literature.*

SEN, CHITRABHANU : *Dictionary of Vedic Rituals*, New Delhi, 1976.

SHAMASASTRY, R : The Vedic Calendar, *IA*, XLL, 1912.

SHARMA, K.L. : *Vaidika Sāhitya men śakun evaṃ adbhuta ghaṭanāen*, Saharanpur (U.P.), 1970.

SHASTRI V. : *Grammatical Word-Index to the Four Vedas*, Hoshiarpur.

——— : *Vaidika-padānukramakośa*, Hoshiarpur, 1935

SATYANARAYANA, R. (ed.): The Vedic Octave and Extracts from Saṃgīta-sāra in *Abhinava Bharata-sāra-saṃgraha.* Mysore, 1954.

SINGH, R.S. : *Botanical Identity and Critical Appreciation of the Flora of Vedic Literature.*

SINGH, S.D. : *Ancient Indian Warfare with Special Reference to Vedic Period*, Leiden, 1965.

TAIREJA, K.M. : *Philosophy of Vedas*, Ulhasnagar, 1982.

TILAK, B.G. : *Orion*, Poona, 1955

——— : *Arctic Home in the Vedas*, Poona, 1956

TOPOROV, V.N. : Vedic Mythology, *Miths of the Peoples of the World*, Moscow, 1982.

Etymologies about the Vedic Vaṅku, *Etymology*, Moscow, 1982.

VARMA, V.K. : Vedic optimism and origin of doctrine of

Karman, Recent studies etc., *J. Agarwal Fel. Vol.* Delhi, 1982.

VELANKAR, R.: *A Comparative and Analytical study of the Vedas.*

VENKATESVARA, S.V. : Traces of Pre-historic Art in Vedic Texts, *Proc. of 5th Oriental Conference*, Vol. 1, 1930.

VISHVABANDHU: *A Grammatical Word-Index to the Four Vedas*, 1962-63

——— : *A Comparative and Etymological Dictionary of Vedic Interpretation*, Hoshiarpur, 1965.

WACKERNAGEL : *Altindische Grammatic*, in 3 Vols.

I. Lautlehre, 1896.

II. Einleitung Zur Wortlehre, Nominalkom-position, 1905.

III. Nominalinflexion Zahlwort, Pronomen, 1930.

WINTERNITZ, M. : *History of Indian Literature*, Vol. I, Calcutta.

YUDHISTHIRA : *Vaidika Svara-mīmāṃsā*, Amritsar, 1958.

ZYCK, K. Early Vedic Ideas of Disease and Healing etc. from Ṛgveda and Atharvaveda (Ph.D. Thesis submitted to Australian University).

All the Vedic Saṃhitās trs. into Eng. by Durgaprasad, Lahore, 1912-20; by R.T.H. Griffith. Excerpts trs. into Georgian (Russia). See A.B. Purani, *Studies in Vedic Interpretation* (on the lines of Aurobindo), CSS, 1903. The *Vaidika Padānukrama-kośa* pub. from Hoshiarpur) is a dependable Vedic dictionary. For flora in Vedic texts, see Satya Prakash, *Founders of Sciences in Ancient India*, New Delhi, 1965, pp. 161-163. For the relation between the Veda and the Avesta, see N. Gupta in *Zoroastrian Association Silver Jubilee Vol.* A *Veda-bhāṣya-kośa* is reported to be under preparation at Kendriya Vidyapith, Allahabad.

The following Papers also are interesting:

DEUSKAR, L.S. : Vrata passages in the Vedas, *Summaries of Papers*, AIOC, 1974.

KULKARNI, C : *Vedic Foundations of Indian Culture*, Bombay, 1973.

G.P. MAJUMDAR:Vedic Plants, *B.C. Law Vol.*, Pt. I, Calcutta, 1945. Also see *Sparks from the Vedic Fire.*

H.G. NARAHARI: Kauṭilya and the Vedas, *K.M. Munshi Diamond Jubilee Vol.* (*Bhāratīya Vidyā*, Vols. 9, 10), Bombay, 1948, 1949.

L. RENOU: Sur les traits liguistiques generaux de la poesie du Veda, *Kenkyusyo Silver Jubilee Vol.*, Kyoto, 1954.

V. Bhattacharya : The phallus-worship in the Veda, *Haraprasad Memo. No.*, Calcutta, 1933.

MIRA ROY : Anatomy in the Vedic Literature, *Indian Jour of History of Science*, Vol. 2, No. 1, 1967.

S. BHATTACHARJ : Attitude to food in the Vedas, *Walter Ruben Fel. Vol.*, Calcutta.]

VEDĀṄGA-JYAUTIṢA : A work on astronomy, by Lagadha. Available in two recensions, viz. Ṛg-jyautiṣa and Yajur-jyautiṣa. Appears to be the first compilation on astronomy. [See R. Shama Sastri, Light on the Vedāṅgajyotiṣa, *Kuppuswami Sastri Comm. Vol.*, Madras, 1937.]

VEDĀNTA-DĪPA : A work on Vedānta philosophy, by Rāmānuja. In it he summarises his Śrībhāṣya.

[Ed. BenSS, 69-71; with Eng. trs. and Tamil trs. Vols. I, II, Madras, 1957, 1959.]

VEDĀNTA-KALPATARU-PARIMALA : Commentary, by Appayya Dīkṣita on Amalānanda's *Vedānta-kalpataru.*

VEDĀNTA-PARIBHĀṢĀ : Written by Dharmarāja, it is well-known as a manual of *Advaita* logic and metaphysics. It has 8 chapters of which the first six deal respectively with *Pratyakṣa* (perception), *Anumāna* (inference), *Upamāna* (comparison), *Āgama* (scriptural testimony), *Arthāpatti* (implication) and *Anupalabdhi* (non-apprehension). The last two are more metaphysical in character, and discuss *Viṣaya* or the subject-matter and *Prayojana* or the purpose of the investigation. The important problems of Advaita Philosophy, e.g. nature of *pramāṇas*, relation of *Brahman*, *Īśvara* and *Jīva*, relation of *Māyā* and *Avidyā*, salvation and the way to its attainment, are discussed in the work with great skill.

[Ed. and trs. A. Venis, *Paṇḍit*, N.S. IV—VII; with *Arthadīpikā* comm. and notes by T. Sastri, Banaras, 1954. Eng. trs. by Madhavananda. See S. S. S. Śāstrī, *Vedānta-paribhāṣā*, Madras, 1971.]

VEDĀNTA-PĀRIJĀTA-SAURABHA : A commentary, by Nimbārka, on the *Brahmasūtra*.

[Trs. and annotated, with the *Vedānta-kaustubha* of Śrīnivāsa, by Rama Bose, Bib. Ind.]

VEDĀNTA-SĀRA : A work on Vedānta philosophy, by Rāmānuja. In it he gives a summary of his doctrine called *Viśiṣṭādvaitavāda*.

[Ed. G.A. Jacob, with two comms., notes and indices, NSP, 1934; with Eng. trs. by M. B. N. Iyengar, Madras, 1953. See Deussen and Jacob, *Philosophy of the Vedānta and Vedāntasāra*; M. B. N. Iyengar, *Vedāntsāra of Rāmānuja*. Bengali trs. by Y. Ramanujacharya, 1377 B.S.]

There is a work of the same name by Sadānanda. It is important because it shows the elaborate confusion of Sāṃkhya tenets with the Vedānta to form a complex and ingenious, but quite unphilosophical, whole.

[Ed. R. Tripathi, 1962, with Eng. trs., by M. Hiriyanna; with *Kaumudī* comm. and Hindi trs., Varanasi, 1971. S. N. Srivastavya, with Hindi trs. and comm., Allahabad, 1968. Bengali trs., with Comm. *Subodhinī*, *Bālabodhinī*, *Vidvan-manorañjani*, Śaka 1890.]

VEDĀNTA-SŪTRA : Another name of *Brahma-sūtra* (q.v.).

VEDĀRTHA-PRAKĀŚA : The celebrated commentary, by Sāyaṇa, on the *Ṛgveda-saṃhitā*. In it the commentator gives the prose-order of the stanzas with synonyms of the respective words, discusses the grammatical formations and the connected rules of accentuation.

[Repeatedly printed with the text.]

VEDĀRTHA-SAṂGRAHA : A work on Vedānta philosophy, by Rāmānuja. In it the author assailed the illusion theory of Śaṃkarācārya.

[Ed. *Paṇḍit*, N.S. IX—XII; with Eng. trs., by S.S. Raghavachar, Mysore, 1956. Beng. trs. by Y. Ramanujacharya, Calcutta, 1377 B.S.]

VEMABHŪPĀLA-CARITA : Written by Vāmana Bhaṭṭa Bāṇa, it purports to celebrate the Reddi ruler, Vemabhūpāla or Vīranārāyaṇa of Koṇḍaviḍu (c. 1403—20 A.D.). It is a dreary imitation of Bāṇabhaṭṭa's *Harṣa-carita*.

[Ed. R. Krisnamachariar, Srirangam, 1910.]

VEṆĪ-SAṂHĀRA : A six-act drama by Bhaṭṭanārāyaṇa, it deals with a well-known episode of the *Mahābhārata*. The slaying of Duḥśāsana by Bhīma; the tying by the latter of the loose braid of Draupadī's hair with his hand smeared with the blood of the former and the eventual destruction of Duryodhana. This in brief is the subject-matter of the drama. The author makes some additions to, and alterations in, the epic story.

[Ed. K. P. Parab, with the comm., of Jagaddhara, NSP, 1913 (3rd ed.); with Eng. notes and trs., by S. Visvanathan, Madras, 1961. English trs. by S. M. Tagore, Calcutta, 1880. On its relation to the Mahābhārata, see B.N. Acharya, *Summaries of Papers*, AIOC, 1974.]

VETĀLA-PAÑCAVIṂŚATI : A well-known prose work in which twenty-five stories are inset within the framework of the main narrative. Of its four versions, three are by Śivadāsa, Jambhaladatta and Vallabhadāsa respectively while the other one is by an unknown author. A sage used to give one fruit everyday to king Trivikramasena (or Vikramasena) who became known as Vikramāditya. In each of these fruits a jewel lay concealed. For pleasing the sage the king promised to bring him a corpse hanging from a tree. As the king approached the dead body, a vampire guarding it said that he would make over the body to the king only if he could answer his questions. One of the questions is as follows. Of three lovers, one burns himself at the funeral pyre of his beloved, another lives in grief in a hut built near the burning ground of his dear one, and the other one brings back to life his beloved with the help of charms accidentally obtained by him. Of these, who is the greatest lover? The other questions are similarly of the nature of riddles. According to Hortel, Śivadāsa's version dates back to a period not much earlier than 1487 A.D.

[Śivadāsa's version ed. H. Uhle, Leipzig, 1884 (text in transliteration). Jambhaladatta's version ed. M.B. Emaneau, with Eng. trs. and text in transliteration, American Oriental Society, New Haven, Connecticut, 1934. The work also exists in Kalmuck (ed. B. Jülg, Leipzig, 1866) and Tibetan (ed. A. H. Francke in *ZDMG*, LXXV, 1925) adaptations. Russian trs. by I.D. Serebryakov under the topic *Dvadtsat' pyat rasskazov Vetaly*, Moscow, 1958. On translations into various modern Indian languages, see Grierson, *The Modern Vernacular Literature of Hindustan*, Calcutta; Oesterly, Baitāl Pacīsī (in Bibliothek Orientalischer) *Märchen and Erzählungen*, I, Leipzig, 1873; Penzer's ed. of *Ocean of Story*, Vol.. VI. See T.Riccardi, *A Nepali version of the Vetālapañcaviṃśati*, American Oriental Services, No. 54, New Haven, 1971.]

VIDAGDHA-MĀDHAVA : A seven-act play by Rūpa Gosvāmin. In it the entire Vṛndāvana-līlā of Rādhā-Kṛṣṇa has been dramatised. Its composition was completed in Saṃvat 1589.

[Ed. *Kāvyamālā*, Bombay, 1937.]

VIDAGDHA-MUKHA-MAṆḌANA : A work in four chapters, by Dharmadāsa Sūri. Generally regarded as a work on poetics. But, in reality, it deals with enigmatology and Citra-Kāvya, and, at the same time, describes the feeling of separation from a lover. The riddles, contained in it, are generally in Sanskrit and occasionally in different Prākrits. Acc. to M. Kractz composed between 630 and 950 A.D.

[Ed., with Skt. annotations, by P. Sarma, Lahore, 1928. Ed., for the first time, in Hoeberlin's *Kāvyasaṃgraha*, 1847. The latest ed. (of chaps. I and II only) is by M. Kraatz, Marburg, 1968. There are several other eds. See V. Raghavan in *P.K. Gode Comm. Vol.*, 3.224.]

VIDDHA-ŚĀLABHAÑJIKĀ : A minor drama of the Nāṭikā

type, by Rājaśekhara. In it Vidyādharamalla, king of Karpūravarṣa, who is already married, is represented as falling in love with Mṛgāṅkāvalī, daughter of king Candravarman of Lāṭa. The king succeeds in marrying her after passing through various obstacles. The play takes its name from a statue-device used in it; a statue is called Śāla-bhañjikā in Sanskrit.

[Ed. B.R. Arte, with comm. of Nārāyaṇa Dīkṣita, Poona, 1886; J.B. Chaudhuri, with two comms. including that of Ghanaśyāma, Calcutta 1943; B. Shukla Shastri, with Nārāyaṇa's comm., Hindi Comm., Intro. and Index.]

VIDHI-VIVEKA : A work on Mimāṃsā, by Maṇḍana Miśra. It was commented upon by Vācaspati Miśra.

[Ed. *Pandit*, N.S., XXV-XXVIII]

VIDVAJJANA-VALLABHA : An astronomical work, attributed to King Bhoja of Dhārā (c.first half of 11th cent. A.D.).

[Ed. D. Pingree, Baroda, 1970.]

VIJÑĀNĀMṚTA-BHĀṢYA : Comm. on Brahmasūtra by Vijñānabhikṣu.

[Ed. K. Tripathi, Varanasi, 1979.]

VIKRAMA-CARITA : See *Siṃhāsana-dvātriṃśikā*.

VIKRAMĀṄKADEVA-CARITA : A historical poem, in 18 cantos, by Bilhaṇa. It deals with the Cālukyas of Kalyāṇa, particularly with the history of king Vikramāditya VI (c. 11th-12th century). Along with historical facts it contains fanciful accounts and exaggerations.

[Ed. M.L. Nagar, Banaras, 1945; with a comm. and Hindi trs. by V. Sastri, Banaras, 1964. Seven episodes trs. into German, by A. Haack, 1897, 1899. Fully trs. into English, with historical gleanings, summary of contents, index of place names etc. by S.C. Banerji and A.K. Gupta, Calcutta, 1965. See P.K. Gode, References to Persian oil in Bilhaṇa's *Vikramāṅkadeva-carita* etc., *Jour. of Kalinga Hist. Res. Soc.*, Vol. II, No. 1, 1947; B.N. Misra, *Studies in Bilhaṇa and his Vikramāṅkadevacarita*. For a literary estimate, see P. Chandra in *V.D. Caritasya Sāhityikam Sarvekṣaṇam*, New Delhi.]

VIKRAMORVAŚĪYA : A drama, in five acts, by Kālidāsa. The mortal king Purūravas falls in love with the celestial nymph Urvaśī. Urvaśī is permitted by Indra to live with the king on earth on condition that she must come back to heaven just when the king will look at the son to be born. One day while living with the king the nymph, as a result of entering a forbidden bower, is transformed into a creeper. The king becomes disconsolate at the separation. With the help of a magic stone, however, he succeeds in getting back his beloved. In course of time the king finds his son by Urvaśī, who was for long concealed from the king. Urvaśī feels aggrieved at the prospect of imminent separation from the king. The divine sage, Nārada, appears at that time with the happy tidings from gods that the king is to help them in their dour fight with demons and that as a reward he will be allowed to enjoy Urvaśī's company throughout his life. The text appears to have come down in two recensions, viz. northern and southern.

The love-story of Purūravas and Urvaśī occurs in the *Ṛgveda* (X. 95), *Śatapatha Brāhmaṇa* (V. 1-2), *Viṣṇupurāṇa* (IV. 6), *Bhāgavatapurāṇa* (IX. 14), *Matsyapurāṇa* (XXIV), *Harivaṃśa* (X. 26) and *Kathā-saritsāgara* (III. 3.4—30). It is difficult to determine which version of the story was the source of the *Vikramorvaśiya*. The treatment in the drama shows clear signs of Kālidāsa's departure from the versions in the *Ṛgveda*, *Śatapatha Brāhmaṇa* and *Harivaṃśa*. Some marked changes have been introduced by the dramatist in order to heighten the dramatic effect.

[Ed. Parab and Telang, with comm. of Raṅganātha, Bombay, 1914 (4th. ed.); C. Śāstrī, with comm. of Kāṭayavema, Lahore, 1929; H. D. Velankar, Delhi, 1961. Trs. into Eng. by E.B. Cowell, Hertford, 1851; into German by L. Fritze, Leipzig, 1880; into French by P.E. Foucaux, Paris, 1861 and 1879.

The recension, acc. to Dravidian MSS, ed. by Pischel in *Monatsber, d. kgl.* preuss. Akad. Zu Berlin, 1875. See S.N. Ghosal, *The Apabhraṃśa Verses of the Vikramorvaśiya from the Linguistic Standpoint*, Calcutta, 1972.]

VĪṆĀVĀSAVADATTĀ : An anonymous and incomplete play dealing with the Udayana legend. While some scholars ascribe it to Śūdraka, to whom its initial verse is assigned in the *Subhāṣitāvali* (No. 1271), others think that it is the lost drama of Śaktibhadra, called *Unmāda-vāsavadattā*, and referred to by himself. The *Viṇāvāsavadattā* reveals some characteristics of the Trivandrum plays, generally known as Bhāsa dramas. It, however, seems to be another version of the theme of the *Pratijñā-yaugandharāyaṇa*.

[Ed. Kuppusvami Sastri and C. K. Raja, Madras, 1931 (up to the beginning of the fourth act); with fuller manuscript material, by K. V. Sarma and V. Raghavan, Madras, 1962. Also see K. V. Sarma in *JOR*, XXXII, I-IV, 1965.]

VĪRAMITRODAYA : An authoritative and extensive commentary, by Mitra Miśra, on the *Yājñavalkya-smṛti*. There is also a huge *Smṛti* digest of the same name and by the same author. The latter, divided into chapters called *Prakāśas*, deals with *Paribhāṣā*, *Saṃskāra*, *Āhnika*, *Pūjā*, *Lakṣaṇa*, *Rāja-nīti*, *Tīrtha*, *Vyavahāra*, *Śrāddha*, *Samaya*, *Bhakti* and *Śuddhi*.

[The commentary ed., with the original and the *Mitākṣarā*, by N. Śāstrī, CSS, 1930. Trs. into English, with trs. of the *Yājñavalkya-smṛti* and two other comms. on it, by J.R. Gharpure, 4 parts, Bombay, 1936—39. The *Smṛti* work has been published in CSS.]

VIṢṆUDHARMOTTARA : Often referred to as *Viṣṇudharma*, it is an *Upa-purāṇa*. It is a Kashmirian Vaiṣṇava work of encyclopaedic character in three sections. Section I deals with the usual themes of Purāṇas. Section II deals with law, politics, medicine, astronomy, astrology, science of war. Section III deals with miscellaneous topics, e.g. grammar, lexicography, metrics, poetics, dancing, music, sculpture, painting and architecture. It is supposed to have been compiled between c. 450 and 650 A.D. Portions of it may be of earlier or later origin. It is occasionally given out as a part of *Garuḍa-purāṇa*, but generally regarded as an Upapurāṇa. On its *Brahmasiddhānta* portion the *Brahmasiddhānta* of Brahmagupta is supposed to have been based.

[Ed. Venkatesvara Press, Bombay, 1912. Portion on painting (Section iii) trs. into Eng. by S. Kramrisch, Calcutta, 1928 (2nd ed.). Sec. iii. ed. GOS, 1958. See S. Tadani, *V. Dharmottara*, p. III Ad. 30 and the *Nāṭyaśāstra*, Ad. 6—a comparative study, *Jour. of Indian and Buddhist Studies*, Tokyo XVIII, No. 1.35. Khaṇḍa IV, Vol. II by P. B. Shah, GOS. A Ph.D. thesis on the polity of the *Viṣṇudharmottara-purāṇa* has been approved by Uni. of Jammu and Kashmir. Also see C.S. Sivaramamurti, *Citrasūtra of the Viṣṇudharmottara*, New Delhi, 1978.]

VIṢṆU-DHARMASŪTRA (-SMṚTI) : See Dharmasūtra.

[Ed. Jolly, with extracts from the *Vaijayantī* comm., Calcutta, 1881; J. Vidyāsāgara in *Dharmaśāstra-saṃgraha*, Calcutta. Ed. with *Vaijayantī* comm., by V. Krishnamacharya, Adyar, 1964. Trs. into English by Jolly, Sacred Books of the East, Vol. VII.]

VIṢṆU-PURĀṆA : Also called *Vaiṣṇava*. Glorifying Viṣṇu as the highest being, it is the principal work of the Viṣṇu-worshippers. Its contents approach most closely the definition of Purāṇa as having five characteristics. Consisting of six sections, it is a more unified composition than most Purāṇas which are compilations made in different periods of time. Contrary to the tradition, Parāśara is called the author of the work. The power of faith in Viṣṇu is magnificently described by the legend of Prahlāda.

[Ed. P. Tarkaratna, Vaṅgavāsī Press, Calcutta, 1331 BS (2nd ed.); Bombay, 1889. An ed. is reported to be under preparation at Mithilā Institute, Darbhanga. Trs. into Eng. by H. H. Wilson, London, 1840 (Reprinted, Calcutta, 1961). See T.M.P. Mahadevan, *Advaita in the Viṣṇupurāṇa*; H. Dayal, *V. Purāṇa : Social, Economic and Religious Aspects*, Delhi, 1983.]

VIŚVAPRAKĀŚA : Also called *Vṛddhavasiṣṭha-siddhānta*, it is an astronomical work ascribed to Vṛddhavasiṣṭha, consisting of 13 chaps.

[Ed., in the *Jyautiṣa-siddhānta-saṃgraha*, by V. P. Dvivedi, Banaras, 1912, 1917.]

VIVĀDA-BHAṄGĀRṆAVA : A huge *Smṛti* digest compiled, at the instance of Sir William Jones, by Jagannātha Tarkapañcānana who is different from Jagannātha, author of *Rasa-gaṅgādhara*. The object of the work was to facilitate the understanding of Hindu law by British judges. The portions of the work, dealing with succession and contract, were translated into English by Colebrooke in 1796 A. D.; this translation is known as *Colebrooke's Digest*.

VIVĀDA-CINTĀMAṆI : A *Smṛti* digest by Vācaspati Miśra, dealing exhaustively with the eighteen titles of law (*Vyavahāra-pada*). A work of paramount authority in the Mithilā school of Hindu Law.

[Ed. L. Jha, Patna, 1937. Trs. into English by P.K. Ṭagore, 1863.]

VIVĀDA-RATNĀKARA : An extensive *Smṛti* digest by Caṇḍeśvara forming a part of his *Smṛti-ratnākara*. In 100 chapters, called *Taraṅgas*, is covers the entire field of civil and criminal law. It formed the basis, *inter alia*, of the *Vivādacintāmaṇi* of Vācaspati and the *Daṇḍaviveka* of Vardhamāna.

[Ed. D. Vidyālaṃkāra, Bib. Ind., 1885-87; and trs. into Eng. by G.C. Sarkar and D. Chatterji.]

VIVĀDĀRṆAVA-SETU : A huge digest prepared by the Bengal scholar Bāṇeśvara Vidyālaṃkāra, with the collaboration of ten other scholars, at the instance of the then Governor of Bengal, Warren Hastings, for the settlement, by British judges, of disputes arising in connexion with Hindu Law. It is divided into 21 chapters called *Urmis*; the total number of verses is 1632. It deals with matters of dispute like recovery of debts and the modes of settlement.

[Pub. Veṅkaṭeśvara Press, Bombay. It was first translated into Persian and thence into English by Halhed under the title *A Code of Gentoo Laws*, (London, 1776).]

VIVARAṆA -PRAMEYA-SAṂGRAHA: Written by Vidyāraṇya, it is a gloss on Prakāśātman's work called *Pañcapādikā-vivaraṇa*. It contains an analysis of the conclusions of Prakāśātman in the above work.

VIVEKA-CŪḌĀMAṆI : A work on Vedānta philosophy, attributed to Śaṃkarācārya. In 580 verses the author lays down the quintessence of his views on Vedānta philosophy.

[Ed., with Eng. trs., by M. Chatterji; by S. Mādhavānanda (Calcutta, 1957, 6th. ed.); with comm. and Eng. trs., Bombay 1979.]

VṚDDHAGARGA-SAṂHITĀ : One of the oldest astronomical *Saṃhitās*, ascribed to Vṛddhagarga. At present available in an incomplete form.

[See *Asiatic Society* (Calcutta) *Catalogue of MSS.*, X, pt. I, 6958, 6958 (I), 6958 (II), 6958 (III).]

VṚKṢĀYURVEDA : A work on plant diseases by Surapāla. For a work of the same name, attributed to Parāśara, see *Journal of Asiatic Soc.*, Calcutta, vol. III, No. 2, 1961, pp. 85-86. The latter assigned to the pre-Christian age by some and to about the 12th century by others.

VṚNDAMĀDHAVA : Another name of *Siddha-yoga* (q. v.).

VṚTTARATNĀKARA: A work on prosody, by Kedāra Bhaṭṭa. It describes 136 metres, and is divided into six chapters. It has been extensively quoted by commentators like Mallinātha.

[Ed., with comm., C. A. S. Mahāsthavira, NSP, 1948; ed. N. Sastri, 1971; with comm., Hindi trs. and notes, Banaras, 1966. For the date of the work, see P.K. Gode, *Studies in Indian Literary History*, I, p. 166 ff.]

VYAKTI-VIVEKA : A well-known work on poetics, by Mahimabhaṭṭa. Written in three chapters, called *Vimarśas*, it is a vigorous piece of polemical writing, the author's object being to demolish the Dhvani theory of Ānandavardhana and to establish that the function of *Vyañjanā*, posited by Ānandavardhana, is nothing more than *Anumāna* or logical inference.

[Ed. T. Ganapati Sastri, with an anonymous comm. (attributed to Ruyyaka), in TSS, 1909. Text and Ruyyaka's comm. ed., with a Hindi comm., by R.P. Dvivedi, Banaras,

1964. An exposition of the Vyaktiviveka by T. Jha, reported to be in press of Mithila Institute, Darbhanga.]

VYĀSA-SIDDHĀNTA : Also called *Vedāṅga-jyotiśśāstra*, it is ascribed to Vyāsa and deals with mythical cosmography in three chapters called respectively *Bhuvanakośa-varṇana*, *Kakṣādhyāya* and *Golādhyāya*. It appears to be a part of the *Vyāsa-smṛti*.

[For MSS see S.N. Sen, *A Bibliography* of *Sanskrit works on Astronomy and Mathematics*.]

VYAVAHĀRA-CINTĀMAṆI: A Smṛti digest by Vācaspati Miśra. It deals with judicial procedure and the four principal topics thereof, viz. *Bhāṣā* (plaint), *Uttara* (reply), *Kriyā* (evidence) and *Nirṇaya* (judgment).

VYAVAHĀRA-MAYŪKHA : A Smṛti digest by Nīlakaṇṭha. It is a work of paramount authority on matters of Hindu Law according to decisions of Bombay High Court in Gujarat, the island of Bombay and northern Konkan.

[Pub. by BORI, 1926. Eng. trs., with notes and refs. to decided cases, by P.V. Kane.]

VYAVAHĀRA-RATNĀKARA : A work forming a part of Caṇḍeśvara's *Smṛti-ratnākara* and dealing with civil and criminal law.

[See Mitra, *Notices*, VI, No. 2036.]

WEBER MSS : A bundle of MSS purchased by the missionary Weber in Leh in Kashmir containing fragments of Pauṣkaraṣādin on astronomy and of a dictionary which is perhaps the oldest work of this kind.

[See Hoernle, *JASB*, Vol. 62, a 1893. Bühler, *WZKM*, 7, 1893, 266f, Winternitz & Keith, Cat. of Skt. MSS. in Aodleian Library, II]

YĀJÑAVALKYA-SMṚTI : A famous metrical Smṛti ascribed to Yājñavalkya. It consists of a little over 1000 verses divided into three chapters, viz. *Ācārādhyāya*, *Vyavahārādhyāya* and *Prāyaścittādhyāya*. Each chapter has been sub-divided into several sections called *Prakaraṇas*. The work deals with all the usual topics of Smṛti. It is more systematic and concise than the *Manusmṛti*.

[Ed. with *Mitākṣarā* comm., NSP, 1926 [3rd. ed.); with *Bālakriḍā* comm., TSS; with *Aparārka* comm., ASS; with *Mitākṣarā* and *Vīramitrodaya*, CSS. Trs. into Eng., with trs. of the *Mitākṣarā*, *Vīramitrodaya* and *Dīpakalikā* comms., by J.R. Gharpure, Bombay, in 4 parts, 1936-39. See R.C. Hazra, Yājñavalkya's attitude to Arthaśāstra as an authority in judicial administration, *Our Heritage*, XII, pp. 19-31.]

YAJURVEDA : The Veda of the *Yajus* or sacrificial formulae. The principal subject-matter of this Veda is various *śrauta* sacrifices—when, how and by whom these should be performed. It is invaluable for the history of religion, but has very little literary value excepting the fact that, being partly composed in prose, it contains the earliest specimens of prose composition. Supposed to have come into being some time after the *Ṛgveda*. Of the many recensions of this Veda that appear to have originally existed, the following five are well-known: *Kāṭhaka*, *Kapiṣṭhala*, *Kaṭha*, *Maitrāyaṇī*, *Taittirīya* and *Vājasaneyi*. The last two are called respectively *Kṛṣṇa* (Black) and *Śukla* (White). The *Vājasaneyi-saṃhitā* exists in two versions, viz. *Kāṇva* and *Mādhyandina*.

[*Kāṭhaka-saṃhitā*, ed. Satavalekar, Aundh, 1943. *Taittirīya-saṃhitā*, ed. Dhupkar, Pardi, 1957; with Padapāṭha and comms. of Bhaṭṭabhāskara and Sāyaṇa (Kāṇḍa II) cr. ed. by Dr. T.N. Dharmādhikari *Kāṇva-saṃhitā*, ed. Satavalekar, Aundh, 1940. *Mādhyandina Śukla Yajurveda*, ed. Satavalekar, Pardi, 1957. *Maitrāyaṇī-saṃhitā*, ed. L. V. Schroeder, Leipzig, 1881—6. *Mūla Yajurveda Saṃhitā*, ed. Daivarāta, Varanasi, 1973.

Many passages trs. into German by L. V. Schroeder in *Indians Literatur und Kultur*, Leipzig, 1887. *Taittirīya Saṃhitā*, trs. into Eng. by A.B. Keith, HOS, Vols. 18 and 19, 1914; by Devi Chand, Delhi, 1980 (3rd rev and enlarged ed.). *Kapiṣṭhala-saṃhitā*, ed. Raghu Vira, Lahore. *Maitrāyaṇī-saṃhitā*, ed. Schroeder, Leipzig, 1923. *Vājasaneyi-saṃhitā*, ed. NSP, 1929; A. Weber, with Mahīdhara's comm., Berlin-London, 1852. See H. Oertel, *Zur Kapiṣṭhala-Kāṭhaka-saṃhitā*, München, 1934. Trs. into Eng. verse by R.T.H. Griffith (*The Texts of the White Yajurveda*, Banaras, 1957). See V. Svami, and N. Svami, *Complete Alphabetical Index of all words in Yajurveda*; P. Sastri, *Word-index to Taittirīya Saṃhitā*, 1930 and *Index Verborum Zu Leopold von Schroeder's Kāṭhakam*-Ausgabe, von Richard Simon, Leipzig, 1912; Vishvabandhu, *A grammatical word-index to the Taittirīya Saṃhitā*, 1963. *Śukla Yajurveda* trs. into Bengali by D. Lahiri, 1919; into Hindi by Dayananda Sarasvati, 1906. A Tamil trs. of the *Yajurveda* is by M.R. Jambunathan, Bombay, 1938. An interesting book is the *Thinking with the Yajurveda* by G.G. Desai, Calcutta, 1967.]

YĀJUṢA-JYAUTIṢA : Contains a summary of the astronomical knowledge of the Hindus up to about the 2nd cent. A.D.

[Ed., with the Bhāṣya of Somākara Śeṣa and S. Dvivedin, Banaras, 1908.]

YAŚASTILAKA-CAMPŪ : *A campū-kāvya* by Somadeva Sūri. It covers eight chapters called *Āśvāsas*. It was composed in 959 A.D. during the reign of the Rāṣṭrakūṭa king Kṛṣṇa under the patronage of his feudatory, a son of the Cālukya Arikeśarin III. It relates the legend of Yaśodhara, Lord of Avanti, the machinations of his wife, his death and repeated rebirths and final conversion to Jainism.

[Ed. Kedarnath and others, in 2 parts, with comm. of Śrutasāgara, NSP, 1916 (2nd. ed.). See K.K. Handiqui, *Yaśastilaka and Indian Culture* etc.; E.D. Kulkarni, The vocabulary of Yaśastilaka etc., *Taraporewala Mem. Vol.* (*Bulletin of Deccan College*), Poona, 1957.]

YOGABINDU : By Haribhadrasūri. Deals, in 527 verses, with *Yoga*. It classifies *Yoga* into five species, viz. *Adhyātma*, *Bhāvanā*, *Dhyāna*, *Samatā* and *Vṛtti-sāṃkṣaya*.

[Ed. Bhavanagar, 1919 and Ahmedabad, 1940; with intro., Eng. trs. and notes, by K.K. Dixit, Ahmedabad, 1968.]

YOGĀCĀRABHŪMIŚĀSTRA : Also called *Saptadaśabhūmiśāstra*, it is a work attributed by some to Asaṅga and by others to his teacher Maitreyanātha. It represents the *Yogācāra-vijñānavāda* school of Buddhism. Only a portion of the work has come down in Sanskrit, this portion being called *Bodhisattva-bhūmi*. It is a prose work written in the style of *Abhidharma* texts. The *Bodhisattva-bhūmi*, "The Bodhisattva step", is the fifteenth of the seventeen steps taught in this work. The last step is the one in which no trace of *Karman* remains.

[See U. Wogihara, *Asaṅga's Bodhisattvabhūmi*, Strassburger Diss., Leipzig, 1908. Eng. summary of the *Bodhisattvabhūmi* with notes by C. Bendall and L. de La Vallée Poussin, [Le Muséon, N.S. VI, 1905; VII, 1906; XII, 1911.]

YOGA-ŚATAKA: A medical treatise attributed to a Nāgārjuna.

[Ed. & trs. J. Filliozat, Pondicherry, 1979.]

YOGA-SŪTRA : Ascribed to Patañjali who is perhaps to be distinguished from the author of the *Mahābhāṣya*. It is divided into four parts, viz.

I. *Samādhi*—concentration

II. *Sādhana*—means of attaining *Samādhi*

III. *Vibhūti*—supernatural powers

IV. *Kaivalya*—a state which results from complete concentration.

The relation of the individual spirit to God is treated as part of the ethic of *Yoga* or *Kriyā-yoga*.

[Ed., with commentaries of Vyāsa and Vācaspati, by R. Bhattacharya, Banaras, 1963; trs. J.H. Woods, HOS, 17, 1914; Ramaprasada, SBH 1910. See H. Āraṇya, *Yoga Philosophy of Patañjali*; J.H. Woods, *Yoga System of Patañjali*, Delhi, 1966; G.M. Koelman *Pātañjala Yoga*, Poona; G. Coster, *Yoga and Western Psychology*, Delhi.]

YOGA-VĀSIṢṬHA : Reputed as an appendix to the *Rāmā-*

yaṇa, and not much distinguished from the Vedānta. It deals with all manner of topics including final release. It is moderately old, having been written before the ninth century A.D. Its six sections (*Prakaraṇa*) are called respectively *Vairāgya*, *Mumukṣu-vyavahāra*, *Utpatti*, *Sthiti*, *Upaśama* and *Nirvāṇa*. In it Vasiṣṭha is represented as the speaker and Rāma as the listener.

(Ed. Bombay, 1911; trs. Calcutta, 1909; with the comm. *Vasiṣṭha-mahārāmāyaṇa-tātparya-prakāśa*, by V.L. Mitra, Delhi, 1978; by Pansikar, 3rd ed. New Delhi, 1981; by N.R. Acharya, NSP, 1937. See B.L. Atreya's *The Philosophy of Yogavāśiṣṭha*, Madras, 1936, *Yogavāśiṣṭha and Modern Thought.* See D.N. Bose, *Yogavāśiṣṭharāmāyaṇa*, Vol. I. Under Akbar the Great, the work was translated into Persian by Naqib Khan, Abdul Fazl and Mulla Shiri. See P.C. Divanji, Yogavāśiṣṭha on the means of proof, *E.D. Ross Pres. Vol.* Bombay, 1939; S.P. Bhattacharya, The Siddhas in the Yogavāśiṣṭha Rāmāyaṇa and a peep into their creed, *Indian Culture* (*Mahendra Jayanti Vol.*), Calcutta, 1951; K.C. Chakravarty, *Vision of Reality*, Calcutta, 1969. A *Laghu-Yogavāśiṣṭha* is attributed to Gauḍa Abhinanda (9th century A.D.). Also see G.M. Koelman, *Pātañjalayoga, from related Yoga to Absolute Self*, Poona; Satya Vrat, Some Anomalies in the Language of the *Y.V.*, *V. Raghavan Felicitation Vol.*, p. 325; Venkatesananda, *Beyond Time and Space : a series of talks on the Yogavāśiṣṭha*, South Fremantle; *Supreme Yoga, a new translation of the Yogavāśiṣṭha*, South Fremantle, 1981; V. Raghavan, Author of the Laghu-Yogavāśiṣṭha, *S.K. De Vol.*, Calcutta, 1972; *Laghu Yogavāśisṭha* trs. into Eng. by K.N. Aiyar, Adyar, Madras. Also see P.P.B. Iyar, *Selected Stories from Yogavāśiṣṭha.*

YUKTI-KALPATARU : Ascribed to Bhojadeva, it deals with statecraft and politics. Building of cities, entering a dwelling house, testing of jewels and weapons, characteristics of boats are also some of the topics dealt with in it.

[Printed in Calcutta Oriental Series, No. 1, 1917.]

PART III

CHARACTERS

AGNIMITRA : King of Vidiśā and hero of Kālidāsa's play entitled *Mālavikāgnimitra* (q.v).

AJA : Son of Raghu and father of Daśaratha, he is a prominent figure in the *Raghuvaṃśa* of Kālidāsa. He married Indumatī, sister of his royal neighbour, Bhoja.

ANASŪYĀ : A character in the drama *Abhijñāna-śākuntala*. One of the two constant companions of Śakuntalā in Kaṇva's hermitage.

ĀRAṆYIKĀ (ĀRAṆYAKĀ) : The heroine of the play *Priyadarśikā*, by Śrīharṣa. Her real name is *Priyadarśikā*, and she is daughter of king Dṛḍhavarman. She is carried off by Udayana's general, and is engaged as an attendant of queen Vāsavadattā, under the pseudonym Āraṇyikā. Priyadarśikā is eventually married by Udayana.

ĀTREYA : Vidūṣaka and king's confidant in Śrīharṣa's play called *Nāgānanda*.

AUŚĪNARĪ : Queen of Purūravas, hero of Kālidāsa's play called *Vikramorvaśīya*.

AVANTISUNDARĪ :A character in Daṇḍin's *Daśakumāracarita*. Daughter of Mānasāra, king of Mālava, she was loved and finally married by Rājavāhana, king of Magadha.

AVIMĀRAKA Literally means 'sheep-killer'. He is hero of Bhāsa's drama called *Avimāraka* (q.v.). Son of a Sauvīra king, he lives as a sheep-killer as a result of a curse. Sage Nārada reveals that he is really the son of god Agni by Sudarśanā, wife of the king of Kāśī, who gave him over to Sucetanā, her sister and wife of the Sauvīra king. He falls in love with princess Kuraṅgī whom he ultimately marries.

BHĀGURĀYAṆA : A character in Viśākhadatta's drama called *Mudrārākṣasa*. Malayaketu's secretary and friend, but really an agent of Cāṇakya.

BHŪRIVASU : Minister of king of Padmāvatī. He gives his daughter Mālatī, heroine of the play *Mālatī-mādhava*, in marriage to Mādhava, son of his friend Devarāta, minister of the king of Vidarbha.

CĀṆAKYA : A Brāhmaṇa politician, also called Viṣṇugupta, in Viśākhadatta's play called *Mudrārākṣasa* (q.v.). Helper of Candragupta in gaining the throne of the Nandas, and his Prime Minister until Rākṣasa was won over.

CANDANADĀSA : Friend of Rākṣasa in Viśākhadatta's drama entitled *Mudrārākṣasa.*

CANDRAGUPTA : The hero of Viśākhadatta's drama called *Mudrarākṣasa.* He is also called Vṛṣala and Maurya. See *Mudrārākṣasa.*

CANDRĀPĪḌA : Son of king Tārāpīḍa in the *Kādambarī.* He was the lover if *Kādambarī* and the principal figure in the romance. As he was unable to do justice to his beloved, his heart broke into two and he died. His body was, however, preserved by *Kādambarī.* Meanwhile Candrāpīḍa, as the result of a curse, assumed the form of king Śūdraka. The period of curse having been over, he regained his original form and lived happily with Kādambarī without any further separation.

CĀRUDATTA : Hero of the drama *Mṛcchakaṭika* (q.v.) and also of Bhāsa's drama called *Cārudatta* (q.v.). A rich Brāhmaṇa merchant of Ujjayinī, impoverished by generosity. He falls in love with the hetaera, named Vasantasenā, whom he eventually marries.

DAMAYANTĪ : Daughter of the Vidarbha king Bhīma, she is the chief female character in Śrīharṣa's *Naiṣadhacarita.* She chose Nala as her spouse. See *Naiṣadhacarita.*

DHĀRIṆĪ : Elder queen of Agnimitra in Kālidāsa's drama entitled *Mālavikāgnimitra* (q.v.).

DILĪPA : A character in Kālidāsa's *Mahākāvya* called *Raghuvaṃśa.* King of Ayodhyā, he obtained a son through the grace of his preceptor, sage Vaśiṣṭha.

DUṢYANTA : Hero of the drama entitled *Abhijñānaśākuntala.* See *Abhijñānaśākuntala.*

GARUḌA : A character in Śrīharṣa's play *Nāgānanda.* He is the king of birds and enemy of serpents. Acc. to an agreement, he was to eat up one serpent everyday.

HARṢAVARDHANA : The principal character in Bāṇabhaṭṭa's *Harṣacarita* (q.v.). Son of Prabhākaravardhana and brother of Rājyavardhana and Rājyaśrī.

INDUMATĪ : Sister of king Bhoja. Her Svayaṃvara, in which she chooses Aja, prince of Ayodhyā, is described in *Raghuvaṃśa* (q.v.).

IRĀVATĪ : Young queen of Agnimitrain Kālidāsa's play called *Mālavikāgnimitra* (q.v.).

JĪMŪTAVĀHANA : A Vidyādhara prince and hero of Śriharṣa's drama entitled *Nagānanda.* See *Nāgānanda.*

KĀDAMBARĪ : The principal character of Bāṇabhaṭṭa's prose romance *Kādambarī.* A paragon of beauty, she is daughter of the Gandharva king Citraratha and Madirā. Candrāpīḍa falls in love with her and, after many vicissitudes, lives happily with her.

KĀMA : Same as *Madana* (q.v.).

KĀMANDAKĪ : A prominent female character of Bhavabhūti's drama *Mālatīmādhava.* She is a nun, and successfully brings about, through many obstacles, the marriage of Mālatī with Mādhava.

KANDARPAKETU : Son of king Cintāmaṇi, he is the principal character in Subandhu's *Vāsavadattā.* He marries Vāsavadattā.

KAṆVA : Also called Kāśyapa. The foster-father of Śakuntalā in the drama *Abhijñāna-śākuntala.* He was absent when she was married by Duṣyanta. On his return, he approved the marriage and sent her to Duṣyanta. His message to the king and words of advice to Śakuntalā are fine pieces of literary composition.

KAUŚIKĪ : See Parivrājikā.

KIRĀTA : Śiva in disguise in the *Kirātārjunīya*. He fights with Arjuna, is pleased with him and grants him the boon desired.

KUMĀRA : Son of Śiva and Pārvatī, and a character in Kālidāsa's *Kumārasambhava*. He slew demon Tāraka, the oppressor of gods.

KURAṄGĪ : A character in Bhāsa's drama called *Avimāraka*. She is the daughter of king Kuntībhoja. Avimāraka falls in love with her and marries her after overcoming many obstacles.

MADANA : Name of Cupid. A prominent figure in Kālidāsa's *Kumārasambhava*. At the behest of gods he tries to disturb the deep meditation of Śiva who, incensed at his audacity, burns him to ashes with the fire emanating from his eye.

MADAYANTIKĀ : A friend of Mālatī, the heroine of Bhavabhūti's play *Mālatīmādhava*. She falls in love with Makaranda, a friend of Mādhava, and elopes with her lover.

MĀDHAVA : Hero of the drama, entitled *Mālatīmādhava*, by Bhavabhūti. He is son of Devarāta, minister of the king of Vidarbha, and is sent by his father to the place called Padmāvatī. With the help of Kāmandakī, who acts at the instance of minister Bhūrivasu, Mādhava is married with Mālatī, daughter of the said Bhūrivasu.

MĀDHAVYA : Vidūṣaka and king's confidant in the drama *Abhijñāna-śākuntala*. He is witty, averse to physical hardship, gluttonous and timid by nature.

MAHĀSENA : Pradyota Mahāsena, king of Ujjayinī, figures in Bhāsa's play, entitled *Pratijñā-yaugandharāyaṇa*, as father of Vāsavadattā loved by Udayana who eventually marries her.

[See P. Pal, *King Udayana, Mahāsena Pradyota...in history, legend and dramas*, Chinsurak (W. Bengal), 1970.]

MAHĀŚVETĀ : A character in *Kādambarī*. She is daughter of a Gandharva and an Apsaras. She falls is love with Puṇḍarīka, and, after many vicissitudes, lives with him happily.

MAITREYA : Vidūṣaka in the drama *Mṛcchakaṭika.* He is a Brāhmaṇa friend and companion of Cārudatta. A sincere well-wisher of Cārudatta for whose sake he can even lay down his life.

MAKARANDA : A friend of Mādhava, the hero of Bhavabhūti's play *Mālati-mādhava.* He falls in love with Madayantikā, a friend of Mālatī, and elopes with his beloved. A Makaranda is a friend of prince Kandarpaketu in Subandhu's prose romance *Vāsavadattā.*

MĀLATĪ : Heroine of Bhavabhūti's drama called *Mālatīmādhava.* She is daughter of minister Bhūrivasu, and is married to Mādhava, with the help of Kāmandakī who overcomes formidable hurdles in the way.

MĀLAVIKĀ : Sister of Mādhavasena and heroine of Kālidāsa's play called *Mālavikāgnimitra* (q.v.).

MALAYAKETU : A character in Viśākhadatta's drama called *Mudrā-rākṣasa.* Son of Parvataka, king of mountaineers. With him Rākṣasa allied himself with a view to invading Pāṭalīputra.

MALAYAVATĪ : Daughter of the Siddha king Viśvāvasu, she is the heroine of the drama called *Nāgānanda* by Śrīharṣa. See *Nāgānanda.*

MĀNASĀRA : A character in Daṇḍin's *Daśakumāra-carita.* King of Mālava, he was hostile to king of Magadha, whom he defeated. He was, however, vanquished and slain by Rājavāhana, son of Rājahaṃsa.

MAUDGALYĀYANA : A character in Aśvaghoṣa's drama entitled *Śāriputra-prakaraṇa* (q.v.). Converted to Buddhism by Buddha.

MITRĀVASU : Son of the Siddha king Viśvāvasu and brother of Malayavatī, heroine of Śrīharṣa's play *Nāgānanda.*

MURALĀ : Name of a river in *Uttara-rāmacarita.* For her role, see Tamasā.

NALA : The principal figure in Śrīharṣa's *Naiṣadha-carita*. King of Niṣadha, he is chosen by Damayantī as her spouse. See *Naiṣadha-carita*.

NANDA : The principal figure in Aśvaghoṣa's poem called *Saundarananda*. He is half-brother of Buddha, and is nick-named Sundara for his handsome appearance. He is forcibly converted to the life of a monk, which he detests.

NANDANA : A character in Bhavabhūti's *Mālatī-mādhava*. His desire of marrying Mālatī with the approval of the king of Padmāvatī, is frustrated by Kāmandakī who brings about Mālatī's marriage with Mādhava.

NĀRADA : A sage and a prominent figure in Māgha's *Śiśupāla-vadha*. He comes to Kṛṣṇa in the house of Vasudeva, and exhorts him to slay Śiśupāla.

NARAVĀHANA DATTA: Son of Udayana and Vāsavadattā.

PADMĀVATĪ : Sister of Darśaka, king of Magadha. She is married by Udayana in the drama, called *Svapnavāsava-datta* (q.v.), by Bhāsa.

PARIVRĀJIKĀ : Referred to as Kauśikī, she is sister of Sumati, minister of Mādhavasena. She is mainly instrumental in bringing about Agnimitra's marriage with Mālavikā in Kālidāsa's play called *Mālavikāgnimitra* (q.v.).

PĀRVATĪ : The principal female character in Kālidāsa's *Kumārasambhava*. Daughter of the Himālaya mountain, she succeeds, after hard penance, in getting God Śiva as her spouse. They get a son named Kumāra (Kārtikeya).

PRABHĀKARAVARDHANA : A character in Bāṇabhaṭṭa's *Harṣa-carita*. Father of Rājyavardhana and Harṣavardhana, he dies during the absence of the former who is ordered to attack the hostile Hūṇas.

PRADYOTA : See Mahāsena.

PRIYAṂVADĀ : A character in the drama *Abhijñāna-śākuntala*. A constant companion of Śakuntalā in Kaṇva's hermitage.

PUṆḌARĪKA : A character in Bāṇabhaṭṭa's *Kādambarī*. An ascetic boy and mind-born son of goddess Lakṣmī and sage Śvetaketu. Mahāśvetā loves him, and, after many vicissitudes, lives with him happily.

PURŪRAVAS : A king and hero of the drama, entitled *Vikramorvaśīya*, by Kālidāsa. He falls in love with Urvaśī, and lives with her for some time after which she disappears. She is afterwards got back by the king who, as a result of his helping gods in their fight against demons, is granted the privilege of enjoying Urvaśī's company throughout his life.

[See D. D. Kosambi, Urvaśī and Purūravas, *Indian Studies Past and Present*, 1 (1), Calcutta, 1959; J. C. Wright, Purūravas and Urvaśī, *BSOAS*, XXX, pt. 3.; A. Wurm, Ballad of Purūravas and Urvaśī, *Summaries of Papers*, AIOC, 1974; S.G. Kantawala, Purūravas-Urvaśī Episode: a study in Vedico-Purāṇic Correlates, *Ibid.*; S.S. Janaki, in *V. Raghavan Fel. Vol.*, Delhi, 1975.]

RAGHU : A character in Kālidāsa's *Raghuvaṃśa*. Son of Dilīpa and father of Aja. He led a victorious campaign against the Hūṇas, Persians and Greeks. He also conquered various places in the north and south of India.

RĀJAHAṂSA : A character in Daṇḍin's *Daśakumāra-carita*. King of Magadha, he was engaged in war with Mānasāra, king of Mālava. At first victorious, he was finally vanquished and retired to a forest where he got a son Rājavāhana by name who, the principal figure in the work, succeeded in killing Mānasāra and annexing his kingdom to his own.

RĀJAVĀHANA : Principal figure in Daṇḍin's *Daśakumāra-carita*. Son of Rājahaṃsa, king of Magadha, he had had many adventures after which he succeeded in marrying Avantisundarī, daughter of the Mālava king Mānasāra. Eventually he defeated and killed Mānasāra, and became the king of the united kingdoms of Magadha and Mālava.

RĀJYAŚRĪ : A character in Bāṇabhaṭṭa's *Harṣa-carita*. Sister of *Harṣavardhana*, she was married to the Maukhari king Grahavarman. Her husband having been slain by the Mālava king, she was imprisoned. After her brother Rājyavardhana was slain by the Gauḍa king Śaśāṅka, she wandered about in the forest whence she was rescued by Harṣa.

RĀJYAVARDHANA : A character in *Harṣa-carita* by Bāṇa. Son of Prabhākaravardhana and brother of Harṣa, he led a successful expedition against the Hūṇas. He was treacherously murdered by Gauḍa king Śaśāṅka.

RĀKṢASA : A prominent character in the drama, called *Mudrārākṣasa*, by Viśākhadatta. Brāhmaṇa minister of the late Nanda king, and hostile to Candragupta. It was Cāṇakya's aim to win him over to the side of Candragupta. This object was achieved.

RATI : Wife of Madana, and a character of Kālidāsa's *Kumārasambhava*. She laments bitterly when her husband is burnt to ashes by Śiva.

RUMAṆVĀN: Minister of king Udayana in the drama called *Priyadarśikā* (of Śrīharṣa) and *Svapnavāsavadatta* (of Bhāsa).

SĀGARIKĀ : Pseudonym of Ratnāvalī, daughter of king of Ceylon and heroine of the play *Ratnāvalī* by Śrīharṣa. This name is given to her as she is saved from a shipwreck at sea. She is kept in the harem of Udayana who eventually marries her after overcoming many obstacles.

SAJJALAKA : A character in Bhāsa's play called *Cārudatta*. He steals the gold ornaments of Vasantasenā, deposits them in the house of Cārudatta in order to purchase the freedom of a slave girl of Vasantasenā, with whom he is in love.

ŚAKĀRA SAṂSTHĀNAKA : A character in the *Mṛcchakaṭika*. Brother-in-law of king of Ujjayinī and the villain of the play. A unique character, being a combination of the fool and the knave. Failing to gain the love of Vasantasenā, he attempted to strangle her to death. She fell unconscious. Then he spread the rumour that Cārudatta had killed her. Eventually Śakāra's guilt was established, but through Cārudatta's magnanimity he was saved from punishment.

ŚAKUNTALĀ : Heroine of the drama *Abhijñāna-śākuntala*. Daughter of a celestial nymph, she was brought up by sage Kaṇva. See *Abhijñāna-śākuntala*.

SAṂVĀHAKA : A character in the drama *Mṛcchakaṭika*. He was a professional shampooer. He took to gambling and afterwards turned a Buddhis t monk.

ŚAṄKHACŪḌA : A character in Śrīharṣa's play called *Nāgānanda*. He is a serpent, and is ready to sacrifice his life at the order of his master.

ŚĀRIPUTRA : A character in Aśvaghoṣa's drama called *Śāriputra-prakaraṇa* (q.v.), converted to Buddhism by Buddha.

ŚARVILAKA : A character in the drama *Mṛcchakaṭika*. He was a Brāhmaṇa adventurer who committed robbery in Cārudatta's house. The object of the robbery was to get money to ranson off the servant-girl Madanikā whom he used to love and who was in the employ of Vasantasenā.

ŚIŚUPĀLA : Cedi king and the principal figure in Māgha's *Śiśupāla-vadha*. He oppresses gods, so much so that Kṛṣṇa has to slay him.

ŚIVA : Also referred to as Pinākin, Hara etc. He is the principal male character in Kālidāsa's *Kumāra-sambhava*. Pleased with Parvatī's severe penance, he marries her and gets a son named Kumāra (Kārtikeya).

ŚŪDRAKA : Mentioned, in the *Kādambarī* of Bāṇa, as a king of Vidiśā before whom the parrot narrates the story. In his former life he was Candrāpīḍa.

ŚUKANĀSA : Minister of king Tārāpīḍa in Bāṇabhaṭṭa's *Kādambarī*. He was father of Vaiśampāyana.

SUNANDĀ : Confidante of Indumatī (q.v.) in *Raghuvaṃśa*.

SUNDARĪ : Wife of Nanda in Aśvaghoṣa's poem called *Saundarananda*. She laments bitterly for her husband who, being converted to the life of a Buddhist monk, is lost to her.

TAMASĀ : Name of a river in *Uttara-rāmacarita*. She is

found conversing with another river, Muralā. From the conversation we learn that Sītā, abandoned, would have killed herself but Gaṅgā saved her and entrusted her two sons, born in her sorrow, to Vālmīki for training.

TĀRAKA : Name of a demon and a character in Kālidāsa's *Kumārasambhava*. Tormented by him, gods approach Brahmā who suggests that only a son born of the union of Śiva and Pārvatī can save the gods from trouble.

UDAYANA : Ruler of the Vatsa kingdom. He is the hero of several dramas. As the hero of Śrīharṣa's play, entitled *Ratnāvalī*, he is represented as succeeding in marrying, through many obstacles and with the help of his minister Yaugandharāyaṇa, Ratnāvalī, daughter of the king of Ceylon. As the hero of the play called *Priyadarśikā* by Śrīharṣa, he is represented as marrying Priyadarśikā, daughter of king Dṛḍhavarman and disguised as Āraṇyakā (or Āraṇyikā), after overcoming great hurdles. As the hero of *Svapnavāsavadatta* of Bhāsa, Udayana marries Padmāvatī, princess of Magadha, after he believes to be true the rumour, spread by his minister Yaugandharāyaṇa, that his queen Vāsavadattā has died in a village-fire.

[See N. Adaval, *The story of king Udayana as gleaned from Sanskrit, Pāli and Prākrit sources*, 1970; G. V. Davane, The legend of Udayana, *Taraporewala Mem. Vol.* (*Bulletin of Deccan College*), Poona, 1957; P. Pal, *King Udayana and Mahāsena Pradyota in history, legends and dramas*, Chinsurak, W. Bengal, 1970.]

UDDHAVA : Counsellor of Kṛṣṇa in Māgha's *Śiśupāla-vadha*. See Myths and Legends.

UMĀ : Another name of Pārvatī (q.v.).

URVAŚĪ : A celestial nymph whom king Purūravas, hero of the drama *Vikramorvaśīya* of Kālidāsa, loves. She is temporarily lost to the king who afterwards gets her back and, through gods' grace, enjoys her company for life.

[See D.D. Kosambi, Urvaśī and Purūvavas, *Indian Studies Past and presant*, I (1), Calcutta, 1959; J. C. Wright, Purūravas and Urvaśī, *BSOAS*, xxx, pt. 3; A Wurm, Ballad of Purūravas and Urvaśī, *Summaries of Papers*, *AIOC*, 1974; S.G. Kantawala, Purūravas-Urvaśī Episode, *ABORI*, 1976.]

VAIŚAMPĀYANA: Name of the parrot which, brought by a Caṇḍāla girl, narrates before king Śūdraka the story of *Kādambarī*. In his former birth he was son of Śukanāsa, minister of king Tārāpīḍa, bore the same name and was reduced to a parrot by a curse of Mahāśvetā.

VASANTAKA: Name of the Vidūṣaka in several plays. He is a Brāhmaṇa companion and confidant of king Udayana. He figures in the following plays: *Prīyadarśikā* of Śrīharṣa, *Ratnāvalī* of Śrīharṣa, *Svapna-vāsavadatta* of Bhāsa.

VASANTASENĀ: Heroine of the play *Mṛcchakaṭika* of Śūdraka. She was a courtesan of affluent circumstances, and fell in love with Cārudatta who, though poor, commanded her affection by his virtues. See *Mṛcchakaṭika*.

[She is the heroine also of Bhāsa's play called *Cārudatta*.]

VĀSAVADATTĀ: Queen of king Udayana and daughter of Mahāsena (also called Pradyota), king of Ujjayinī. She figures in the following plays: *Priyadarśikā* of Śrīharṣa, *Ratnāvalī* of Śrīharṣa, *Svapnavāsavadatta* of Bhāsa. A Vāsavadattā, daughter of king Śṛṅgāraśekhara, is loved and married by prince Kandarpaketu in Subandhu's prose romance *Vāsavadattā*.

VIKRAMĀDITYA: A mythical king whose throne is described as supported by magic statues in the *Siṃhāsana-dvātriṃśikā*. It should be noted that several kings of ancient India, including Candragupta II assumed this title. The Cālukya king, Tribhuvanamalla, styled Vikramāditya VI, is the main figure of the poem called *Vikramāṅkadeva-carita* by Bilhaṇa.

YAKṢA: The principal character in Kālidāsa's *Meghadūta*. Owing to inadvertence in the performance of his duties, he is banished by his master for a year to Rāmagiri. See *Meghadūta*.

[Also see Yakṣa under Myths and Legends.]

YAŚOMATĪ: A character in Bāṇa's *Harṣa-carita*. Queen of king Prabhākaravardhana, she, true to the ideal of a chaste wife, burns herself to death when her husband is down with an incurable malady and is sure to die very soon.

YAUGANDHARĀYAṆA: A character in several dramas, and represented as minister or Chief Minister to king Udayana. In the *Svapnavāsavadatta*, he spreads the rumour that queen Vāsavadattā has died in a village-fire. His motive is to bring about the king's marriage with Padmāvatī with a view to securing the help of the king of Magadha against Udayana's enemy. The marriage takes place, and the king is then re-united with Vāsavadattā.

In the *Ratnāvalī* of Śrīharṣa he is represented as bringing about, after overcoming many obstacles, Udayana's marriage with Ratnāvalī, daughter of the king of Ceylon.

Yaugandharāyaṇa is also minister to Udayana in Śrīharṣa's play called *Priyadarśikā*.

Yaugandharāyaṇa is the hero of Bhāsa's drama called *Pratijñā-yaugandharāyaṇa*. It is through his machination that king Udayana escapes with princess Vāsavadattā whom he finally marries.

PART IV

TECHNICAL TERMS

The glossary that follows consists of such technical terms as are commonly met with in studying the different branches of Sanskrit literature. The terms have been culled from books on the following subjects[1], written in Sanskrit:—

(In Devanāgarī alphabetical order)

Arthaśāstra (Politics and Statecraft)—A
Alaṃkāra-śāstra (Poetics)—Al
Aśva-śāstra (Horse-lore)—As
Āyurveda[2]—Ay
Udbhid-vidyā (Botany)—U
Kāma-śāstra (Erotics)—K
Kṛṣi-śāstra (Agriculture)—Kr
Gaja-śāstra (Elephant-lore)—G
Chandaḥ-śāstra (Prosody)—C
Jyotiṣa-śāstra (Astronomy and Astrology)—J
Tantra-śāstra—T
Darśana-śāstra (Philosophy)—D
Nāṭya-śāstra (Dramaturgy)—N
Vāstu-vidyā (Architecture and Sculpture)—V
Vyākaraṇa (Grammar)[3]—Vy
Śyainika-śāstra (Hawking)—Sy
Saṅgīta-śāstra (Music)—S
Smṛti-śāstra—Sm

(The terms are in English alphabetical order.)

AB-DURGA (Sm)

A fort surrounded by deep water.

---

1. Abbreviations of the respective names of subjects have been noted against them.

2. So far as this science is concerned, we have noted chiefly the names of common diseases, the names of various herbs and medicines have been left out.

3. We have taken into account only the grammar of Pāṇini and the works belonging to his school.

ABHĀVA (D, Vy): Non-existence. It stands for all negative facts, and is of four kinds, viz. *prāgabhāva*, *dhvaṃsābhāva*, *atyantābhāva* and *anyonyābhāva*. The first means the non-existence of a thing before (*prāk*) its production, e.g. the non-existence of a pot in clay before it is made by the potter. The second means the non-existence of an object after its destruction (*dhvaṃsa*), e.g. the non-existence of a pot after it is broken up. The third is the absolute absence of a thing at all times e.g., the non-existence of colour in air. The fourth is the mutual non-existence of two different things, e.g., the jar is not the cloth and *vice versa*. The first three together are called *saṃsargābhāva*.

ABHICĀRA (Sm, T): Magic spells or rites for malevolent purposes, e.g. killing an enemy.

ABHIDHĀ (Al): Denotation. The function by which a word denotes its primary or conventional sense.

ABHIHITĀNVAYAVĀDA (D): This view of a school of Mīmāṃsakas is thus explained by Mammaṭa, the author of *Kāvyaprakāśa*: When the meanings of the words...are connected in accordance with expectancy, compatibility and proximity, another sense arises called purport, which has a distinct form and which though not constituting the sense of the words is yet the sense of the sentence. See *Kāvyaprakāśa*, ii,1. *Vrtti* as explained by S.K. De in *Sanskrit Poetics* II, p. 149 (1960).

ABHIŚASTA (Sm): Used in the following senses :—

(i) Murderer of a Brāhmaṇa.

(ii) Murderer of a woman who is *Ātreyī* (q.v.).

(iii) One guilty of a mortal sin.

(iv) Murderer of a person of the Brāhmaṇa or Kṣatriya caste, who has studied the Veda or has been initiated for some sacrifice.

(v) One who has destroyed the foetus of a Brāhmaṇa.

ABHIṢEKA (T): A kind of Tāntric *Dikṣā* (initiation). The

Guru performs different forms of *Abhiṣeka* for his disciple in the different stages of the spiritual life of the latter. *Abhiṣeka* is of eight kinds.

ABHIVIDHI (Vy) : Limit inclusive. It is of two kinds, viz. *Kālika* (relating to time) and *Daiśika* (relating to place). *Kārtikyāḥ caitraṃ yāvat śītam* is an example of the former; it means that winter lasts from Kārtika up to Caitra (inclusive). *Kāśitaḥ pāṭalīputraṃ yāvat vṛṣṭo devaḥ* is an example of the latter; it means that it rained from Kāśī up to the region called Pāṭalīputra (inclusive).

ABHIVYAKTIVĀDA (Al) : Doctrine of Abhinavagupta. Acc. to this view, *Rasa* is revealed by *Vyañjanā* (q.v.).

ABHYĀSA (D, Vy) : Reduplication, repetition. In grammar it stands for the earlier part of a reduplicated root. For example, in *bhub bhub*, the first *bhub* is called *abhyāsa*.

ABHYASTA (Vy) : That which undergoes *Abhyāsa* (q.v.) is called *Abhyasta*.

ĀCĀRYA (Sm) . (i) One who, having performed the *Upanayana* of his pupil, teaches him the Veda together with the *Kalpasūtra* and the *Upaniṣads*.

(ii) One from whom the pupil learns his duties.

ĀDEŚA (Vy) : Substitute as contradistinguished from *Sthānin*, the origin.

ĀDHĀNA (Sm) : Pledging or mortgaging.

ĀDHI (Sm) : Pledging or mortgage of a chattel or immovable property to the creditor himself with or without possession.

ADHIKĀRA-SŪTRA (Vy) : Leading or governing rule. The aphorism that serves to make the following rule or rules complete. It is of 4 kinds, viz. *Goyūtha*, *Siṃhadṛṣṭi*, *Maṇḍūkapluti* and *Gaṅgā-srotaḥ-pravāha*.

ADHIKARAṆA (D, Vy) : Substratum. A complete argument treating of one subject. Acc. to the followers of Mīmāṃsā and Vedānta, a complete Adhikaraṇa consists of five mem-bers, viz. *Viṣaya*, *Saṃśaya*, *Pūrvapakṣa*, *Uttara* and *Siddhānta*. Locative case in grammar.

ADHIMĀSA (J) : That lunar month in which the sun does not pass to a Zodiac. Or, that solar month in which there is *Kṣaya* of two New Moons. Intercalary month. See Malamāsa.

ADHI-MĀSA (Sm) : Same as *Mala-māsa* (q.v.).

ADHIVASTRA : Part of garment: outer cover or veil.

ĀDHIVEDANA (Sm) : Marrying another woman when there is already the lawfully wedded wife.

ĀDHIVEDANIKA (Sm) : A kind of *Strīdhana*, presented to a woman by her husband on his marrying another woman.

ĀDHMĀNA (Ay) : Flatulence.

ADHYAGNI (Sm) A kind of *Strīdhana*, given to a girl at the time of her marriage, before the nuptial fire.

ADHYĀHĀRA (D, Vy) : Supplying words not stated. For example, in *rathastham vāmanaṃ dṛṣṭvā punarjanma na vidyate* the words *sthitasya janasya* have to be supplied between *dṛṣṭvā* and *punarjanma* for grammatical accuracy.

ADHYAVĀHANIKA (Sm) : A kind of *Strīdhana*, obtained by a woman while taken from her father's house to that of the husband.

ADHYĀSA (D) : False attribution, wrong supposition, e.g. nacre mistaken for silver.

ĀDIBINDU (J) : In the *rāśi-cakra* the end of Revatī Nakṣatra and the beginning of Aśvinī Nakṣatra.

ADVAITA (D) : Absence of duality, non-dualism. Acc. to this doctrine, advocated by Śaṅkarācārya and his followers, Brahman is the only One Reality and the world is not real but an appearance which Brahman conjures up with His inscrutable power called *Māyā*.

[See L. S. Betty, Vādirāja's Refutation of Śaṃkara's Non-dualism, Delhi, 1978.]

AGAMA (Sm, Vy) : Valid mode of acquisition of a property, e.g. inheritance, purchase, gift etc.

Augment, added to the primitive or basic word, during the process of formation of a complete word.

AGNIHOTRA (Sm) : Oblation to Agni, the sacred fire.

[See P. E. Dumont, *Agnihotra*; P. D. Navathe, *Agnihotra of the Kaṭha Śākhā*, Poona, 1980.]

AGNIṢṬOMA (Sm) : Name of a ceremony or sacrifice forming one of the chief modifications of the *Jyotiṣṭoma* offered by one desirous of obtaining heaven. The performer is a Brāhmaṇa maintaining the sacred fire; the offering is the *Soma*; the deities are Indra etc.; the number of requisite priests is 16; the ceremonies continue for 5 days.

[See W. Caland and H. Henry, *L' Agniṣṭoma*, 2 Vols., Paris, 1906-7.]

AGRAYAṆA: A religious rite in which the first crops harvested in the season, is offered to deities.

AGREDIDHIṢU (Sm) : Younger sister married before the elder.

ĀHAVANĪYA (Sm): Name of one of the fires with which Vedic sacrifices are to be performed.

ĀHIṆḌIKA: A class of men who used to serve as gate-keepers and watchmen.

AJĀTAVĀDA (D) : A Buddhist doctrine according to which there is nothing like origin of the universe.

AKARṢA: A kind of game played on a board.

ĀKHYĀTA (Vy) : Verb, verbal form.

ĀKRANDA (Sm, A) : The king ruling over a territory just beyond that of *Pārṣṇigrāha* (q.v.). The rear friend of a neighbouring king.

ĀKRANDĀSĀRA (Sm, A): The king of the territory just beyond that of the *Pārṣṇigrāhāsāra* (q.v.). A friend of the Ākranda (q.v.).

ĀKṚTI-GAṆA (Vy) : A group or class of words in which some words are stated and there is scope for including other words undergoing the same operation.

AKṢA(A) : (i) The number five and its multiples; (ii) A weight.

AKṢAPAṬALA (A) : The records and audit office.

AKṢABHĀ (J) : Shadow of gnomon at noon or on the day of vernal equinox.

AKṢAJYĀ (J) : Sine of latitude.

ĀLĀPA (S) : Name given to the practice of demonstrating or spreading out a *Rāga* without any wording and *Tāla*.

ALPA-PRĀṆA (Vy) : Non-aspirate letter, also called unaspirate. The first and third consonants of each class or group (*Varga*) ; the nasals and the semi-vowels belong to this category.

ĀMĀŚAYA (Ay): Stomach.

ĀMĀTISĀRA (Ay) : Dysentery.

AMĀTYA (Sm, A) : In early times, a companion of a king. Later, a minister generally of a lower rank, one of the seven limbs (*aṅga*) of the State.

ĀMAVĀTA (Ay) : Acute rheumatism.

AMBAṢṬHA (Sm) : One sprung from the union of a Brāhmaṇa male and a Vaiśya female.

ĀMREḌITA (Vy) : The latter portion of a reduplicated word. For example, in 'Upary-upari', the latter portion is called *Āmreḍita*.

AṂŚA (S) The note that manifests the *Rañjakatva* (the quality of causing delight) of a song; the note whose *Saṃvādī* and *Anuvādī* are largely perceived and, being used as *Graha* (q.v.), *Nyāsa* (q.v.) in singing is abundantly felt. Abundance and pervasion in *Rāgas* are the characteristics of *Aṃśa*.

AṂŚA (J) ; 1/360 part of a circle or 1/90 of a right angle.

AṂSAPATHA (A) : Land-route, an overbridge.

ANABHIHITA (Vy) : Not specified generally by anyone of the following : Verbal affix, *Kṛt* affix, *Taddhita* affix and compound. Sometimes the specification is done by *Nipāta* (q.v.).

ĀNADDHA (S) : See *Vādya*.

ANADHYĀYA (Sm) : Suspension of study caused by a number of factors, e.g. disturbance in village, conflagration, *Amāvasyā*, *Paurṇamāsi* of certain months, storm, rainfall, eclipse, earth-quake, etc.

ANAVASTHĀ (D) : Infinite regress. Absence of finality or conclusion, an endless series of statements or causes and effects; a fault of reasoning.

ANEKAPARIGRAHA : A prostitute attached to many persons.

ANNA-PRĀŚANA (Sm) : Name of the ceremony in which a child is fed with rice for the first time after birth. It is to be held in the sixth month from the child's birth, according to Yājñavalkya.

ANTRA-VṚDDHI (Ay) : Hernia.

ANUBANDHA (D, Ay, Vy): Acc. to Vedānta, it stands for the four, viz. *Viṣaya*, *Prayojana*, *Adhikārī* and *Sambandha*. In Ay it means the absence of the excess of *Vāta*, *Pitta* etc. In grammar it stands for a letter, technically called 'it' (that which is elided), belonging to *Prakṛti*, *Pratyaya*, *Āgama* or *Ādeśa*. For example, 'k' in the suffix -*kta* is an *Anubandha*. When added to, say, the root *Bhū*, 'k' is elided and the form obtained is *Bhūta*.

ANUBHĀVA (Al) : Ensuant. It follows and strengthens a mood, and comprises such outward manifestations of feeling as sidelong glances, smile, movement of the body. It is a factor of *Rasa*.

ANŪCĀNA (Sm) : One who has mastered the Vedas and the Vedāṅgas.

ANUDĀTTA (Vy): Grave accent which is produced from the lower places of articulation in the mouth.

ANULOMA (Sm) : In regular order; generally applied to marriage between a male of the higher caste and a female of the lower.

ANUMĀNA (D) : Inference as a means of valid knowledge.

ANUMITI-VĀDA (Al) : The doctrine of Śaṅkuka, acc. to which *Rasa* is inferred.

ANUNĀSIKA (Vy) : Nasal letter, i.e. a letter uttered simultaneously through both the nose and the mouth.

ANUPALA (J) : A measure of time equal to 1/60 *vipala*.

ANUPALABDHI (D): Non-perception. It is the source, acc. to a school of Mīmāṃsā, of our immediate cognition of the non-existence of an object. For example, the non-existence of a jar is known by non-perception of it.

ANUPAPATTI (D) : Logical non-consequence, absence of validity; discord.

ANU-PĀTAKA (Sm) : A class of sins comprising falsehood, theft, adultery etc.

ANUŚAYA (Sm, A) : Revocation, annulment.

ANUVĀDĪ (S) : The note that makes the *Saṃvādi* note clearer. Literally, it means the note that follows the note called *Vādi* (q. v.). In the works on music, all notes other than *Saṃvādī* and *Vivādī* are called *Anuvādī*.

ANUVĀKYĀ (MANTRA) (D) : Formula of invitation to gods.

ANUVṚTTI (Vy) : Continuity, repetition. When a particular aphorism or a part of it is necessary for completing the sense of a following aphorism, it is said that the former has *Anuvṛtti*. The repetition is sometimes continuous when the word or words concerned are repeated in the immediately following rules. Sometimes the *anuvṛtti* applies not to the immediately following rules but to the remote ones.

ANVĀDHEYAKA (Sm) : A kind of *Strīdhana*, obtained by a woman, after her marriage, from her husband or parents.

ANVĀHITA (Sm): Sub-mortgage, i.e. mortgage of a property by the mortgagee.

ANVAṢṬAKĀ (Sm) : The ninth day in the later half of the three (or four) months following the full moon in Agrahāyaṇa, Pauṣa, Māgha and Phālguna.

ANVAYA-VYATIREKA (D): 'Anvaya' means agreement in presence between two things, e.g. where there is smoke, there is fire. 'Vyatireka' means agreement in absence between two things. For example, where there is no smoke there is no fire. Anvaya-Vyatireka, therefore holds when both the above relations are present. 'Anvaya' ordinarily means logical connexion of words.

ĀNVĪKṢIKĪ (Sm, D) : (i) *Tarka-vidyā* or Logic.
(ii) *Ātma-vidyā* or spiritual knowledge.
(iii) *Sāṃkhya*, *Yoga* and *Lokāyata* (*Kauṭilīya Arthaśāstra*, I.2).

(*Lokāyata* in this context has been taken in the sense of *Nyāyaśāstra*.)

ANVIĀBHIDHĀNAVĀDA (D) : Doctrine of a school of Mīmāṃsakas. Acc. to it, words have a power to denote not only things but also their purport or connection along with them. In other words, words do not express their sense generally but connectedly. They reject the view of the Abhihitānvayavādins, and deny the necessity of postulating the function of tātparya. See S. K. De, *Sanskrit Poetics*, II, p. 149, 1960.

APĀDĀNA (Vy): Ablative case; the limit of separation.

APA-PĀTRA (Sm) (1) *Caṇḍālas* etc. with whom no social intercourse is possible.

(2) *Rajakas* etc. born in the reverse order of marriage.

(3) One ostracised by kinsmen for the commission of some degrading sin. Literally, one not allowed to use vessels out of which members of other castes are to take food.

APARIGRAHĀ: A prostitute not attached to a particular individual.

APASARPA (A) : A secret agent, spy.

APAVĀDA (D, Vy): Special rule, exception.
False statement, acc. to Sāṃkhya.
A special injunction to bar out a false object, acc. to the philosophers advocating the doctrine of *Māyā*.

APAVARAGA (D) : Liberation. Absolute cessation of suffering, attainment of *Nirvāṇa*.

APAVIDDHA (Sm): One cast off by one's parents, and accepted by another person as his son.

APOHA (D) : Excluding all things not coming under the category in point. For example, *nīlatva* (blue-ness) excludes all things that are not *nīla*.

APŪRVA (D) : Unperceived potency generated by the performance of rites, in the soul of the performer. It bears fruit in future. Thus, the Apūrva generated by a particular rite, performed in this life, leads to the acquisition of heaven in the next world.

ĀRAKṢAKA : Guard; police megistrate.

ĀRAMBHA (N) : One of the *Avasthās* (q.v.).

ĀRDHADHĀTUKA (Vy) : Technical term used to indicate affixes other than *Sārvadhātuka* (q.v.) i.e. the conjugational signs of the eighth and tenth classes, the affixes added to form the causal base and a few denominatives, the affixes —*sya*, —*tā*, —*sa* and —*ya* added to the bases of the two future tenses, the Desiderative and the Aorist, and the Passive and the Frequentative respectively, and those forming the Past Participle (Active and Passive), the Infinitive and the verbal indeclinables, and some others. The significance of the name is that the endings of this type are added to the root without *Vikararaṇa* (q.v.), i.e. before these endings only half the root or a part thereof is discernible.

ARDHASAMA (C) : A *Vṛtta* (q.v.) in which the first and the third feet and the second and fourth feet have the same metrical scheme.

ARDHODAYA (J) : A particular conjunction which takes place if, in the month of Pauṣa or Māgha, there are New Moon, Śravaṇā Nakṣatra and *Vyatīpātayoga* (q.v.) on Sunday.

ĀROHA (S) : Ascent of the notes in a song, in the order *SA*, *RA*, *GA*, *MA*, *PA*, *DHA*, *NA*.

ARŚA (Ay) : Piles.

ĀRṢA (VIVĀHA) (Sm) : A kind of marriage in which a girl is given away after taking a pair or two of cattle as a matter of form and not as the price of the girl.

[See J. Gonda, Reflections on the Ārṣa and Āsura forms of marriage, *Sarup Comm. Vol.*, 1954.]

ARTHĀPATTI (D) : A means of valid knowledge, acc. to Mīmāṃsā philosophy. Circumstantial inference; deduction of a matter from that which could not otherwise be. For example, a rat hat eaten up the stick. So, by *Arthāpatti* we may infer that the cake also, that was on the stick, was eaten up by it.

ARTHAVĀDA (D) : Explanation or a remark in praise. It usually recommends a *Vidhi* or precept by stating the good arising from its observance and the evil following from its omission.

ARTHA-PRAKṚTI (N) : Element of the plot of a Sanskrit drama. There are five elements, viz. *Bija*, *Bindu*, *Patākā*, *Prakarī* and *Kārya*. The first is the germ whence springs the action. For example, in the *Abhijñāna-śākuntala*, the germ is cast when the hermit blesses the king that he may have a great son, and says that Kaṇva has gone away leaving Śakuntalā to perform the rites of hospitality. *Bindu* is the drop which spreads out as oil in water; the course of the drama, which has seemed to be interrupted, is again set in activity. In the same drama (Act II) we get it when the king speaks of Śakuntalā to the Vidūṣaka when the main action is interrupted by such incidents as the talk about the chase, the double call of duty to the king etc. The other three elements are the episode, the incident and the dénouement.

ARTHIN (Sm) : Plaintiff, suitor.

ARVUDA (Ay) : Swelling, tumour.

ĀRYĀVARTA (Sm) : (1) That part of India which lies between the Himalayas and the Vindhya mountain, and extends up to the eastern and western seas.

(2) The region between the rivers Gaṅgā and Yamunā.

(3) That region of India where spotted antelopes roam about naturally.

ĀSANA (Sm) : A political expedient by which a king assumes an attitude of indifference to the activities of a belligerent power.

ASATKĀRYAVĀDA (D) : The doctrine acc. to which the effect is something new and does not pre-exist in the cause.

ĀSEDHA (Sm) : Restraint under the king's order. It is of four kinds, viz. (1) Restraint as to place (e.g. you cannot go elsewhere from specified places).

(2) Restraint as to time (e.g. you must present yourself before court on specified dates).

(3) Restraint from proceeding on a journey (till the suit is disposed of).

(4) Restraint as to certain activities (e.g. you are not to sell a certain property or plough a certain field till the disposal of the suit).

AŚMARĪ (Ay) : A disease called stone (in the bladder).

AṢṬAKĀ (Sm) : The eighth day after full moon (especially that in *Hemanta* and *Śiśira*) on which the progenitors or manes are worshipped. There are three kinds of *Aṣṭakā-śrāddha*, viz.

(1) *Pūpāṣṭakā*—in which cakes are offered;

(2) *Māṃsāṣṭakā*—in which meat is offered;

(3) *Śākāṣṭakā*—to be performed with vegetables.

AṢṬAKŪṬA (J) : The eight, *varṇa etc.*, which are examined and calculated in determining the suitability of a match in marriage.

AṢṬA-SIDDHI (T) : See *Siddhi.*

ĀSTIKA : (Sm) : One believing in the existence of God, the other world etc.

ĀSURA (VIVĀHA) (Sm) : A form of marriage in which a girl is given away, at the father's will, after the bridegroom gives as much wealth as he can afford to the relatives of the girl and to the girl herself.

[See J. Gonda, Reflection on the Ārṣa and Āsura forms of marriage, *Sarup Comm. Vol.*, 1954.]

AŚVAKRĀNTA (T) : In certain Tantras, India has been divided into three regions one of which is called *Aśvakrānta* or *Gajakrānta.* Acc. to the *Śaktimaṅgala-tantra*, the tract of land from the Vindhya hill to the great ocean is called *Aśvakrānta.*

AŚVAMEDHA (Sm) : Name of a sacrifice in which a horse was to be immolated. The horse was to be placed by a king under the charge of military men and then let loose. On its return after a year the sacrifice was to be performed. The practice, which reaches back to the Vedic times, was regarded as a symbol of sovereignty and power.

[See J. Puhvel, Vedic *Aśvamedha* and Gaulish *Epomeduous*, *Language*, Linguistic Soc. of America, 31; R. C. Hajra, *The Aśvamedha* etc., *ABORI*, 36. Also see P. E. Dumont, *L'Aśvamedha*, 1927.]

ĀTATĀYIN (Sm) : Designation of the following hostile persons : incendiary, poisoner, one armed with weapons, robber, one who wrests a field or carries away one's wife.

ATICĀRA (A) : Transgression, misconduct.

(J) : Movement of a planet from one Zodiac to another before the usual time.

ATISARGA (A) : (1) Giving up, surrender.

(2) Granting permission, allowing.

ATISĀRA or ATĪSĀRA (Ay) : Diarrhoea or dysentery.

ATIKṚCCHRA (Sm) : A form of expiation in which the

sinner has to eat merely one morsel of food for three days in the morning only, for three days in the evening only, one morsel each for three days without asking for it and has to fast for three days.

ATIDEŚA (D) : Extended application, substitution. By this principle, a thing applicable at one place may be applicable at another. For example, *Gotra*, though applicable in the case of Brāhmaṇas only may be applicable, by *Atideśa*, in the case of Kṣatriyas etc. also. Again, though the word 'son' denotes the male issue of a person, yet by *Atideśa* the word may refer to the male issue of one's co-wife also.

ATIPĀTAKA (Sm) : A class of sins comprising adultery with one's mother, daughter, daughter-in-law.

ATITHI (Sm) : One not staying permanently at another's house; a Brāhmaṇa guest who stays for one night only.

ATIVYĀPTI (D) : The fault of being too wide. For example, if we define 'cow' as a quadruped having two horns, then it will include also buffaloes etc.

ĀTODYA (S) : A kind of musical instrument ; percussion instrument.

ĀTREYĪ (Sm) : A woman who has bathed after her monthly impurity.

AUCITYA (Al) : Propriety or appropriateness. Kṣemendra elaborates, in his *Aucitya-vicāra-carcā*, the view that whatever is improper in any way detracts from *Rasa* and is to be avoided.

AUḌAVA (S) : Designation of a *Rāga*. A *Rāga*, consisting of five notes, takes this name. In it the initial note *Ṣaḍja* is never given up.

AUPARIṢṬAKA (K) : Sex-act into the mouth of an eunuch.

AURASA (Sm) : A son begotten by a man on his wife.

AVAKĪRṆĪ : (Sm) : A *Brahmacārin* who has had sexual intercourse with a woman.

AVABHṚTHA (Sm) : Ablution to be performed after the conclusion of a sacrifice.

AVADĀTIKĀ : A kind of wine.

AVAMA (J) : The end of one and the beginning and end of another on the same day.

ĀVĀPA (D) : Putting in, experimental insertion.

AVAROHA (S) : The reverse order of *Āroha* (q.v.), e.g. *NA, DHA, PA, MA, GA, RA, SA.* Lit. it means 'descent'.

ĀVARTA (Kr) : A kind of cloud.

AVASTHĀ (N) : Stage of development of dramatic action. There are five stages, viz. *Ārambha, Yatna, Prāptyāśā, Niyatāpti, Phalāgama.* "There must be at the beginning (*ārambha*) the desire to attain some end, which leads on to the determined effort (*prayatna*) to secure the object of desire; this leads to the stage in which success is felt to be possible (*prāptyāśā*) having regard to the means available and the obstacles in the way of achievement; then arrives the certainty of success (*niyatāpti*), if only some specific difficulty can be surmounted; and finally, the object is attained (*phalāgama*). Thus in the *Śakuntalā* we have the king's first anticipation of seeing the heroine; then his eagerness to find a device to meet her again; in act IV we learn that the anger of the sage, Durvāsas, has in some measure been appeased, and the possibility of the reunion of the king and *Śakuntalā* now exists; in act VI the discovery of the ring brings back the king's memory and the way for a reunion is paved, to be attained in the following act."[1]

AVIDYĀ (D) : Nescience, non-knowledge often identified with ritual practices.

[See E. A. Solomon, *Avidya—a problem of truth and reality*, Ahmedabad, 1969.]

AVĪRĀ (Sm) : (I) A woman having neither husband nor son. (II) A woman who is independent, but not gone astray.

AVYAYA (Vy) : Indeclinable. A word which does not undergo

1. Keith, *Sanskrit Drama* (1924), pp. 297-98.

any change in any gender, any case-ending and in any number.

AVYĀPTI (D) : The fault of being too narrow, as opposed to *Ativyāpti*. For example, if we say that a student is one who reads in a school the definition is too narrow because it excludes those who read in a college or other educational institutions.

AVYAYĪBHĀVA (Vy) : Adverbial compound in which the sense of the first member predominates.

AYANĀNTA BINDU (J) : The maximum declination of the sun (North or South).

BAHULA (Vy) : Used in connexion with a rule, affix or the like. It denotes four kinds of operation, viz. applicable, not applicable in certain cases, optionally applicable in some cases and quite something else in others.

BAHUMŪTRA (Ay) : Diabetes.

BAHUVRĪHI (Vy) : Atributive compound in which the sense of a word other than the members of the compound is predominant.

BANDHAKA (Sm) : Pledge or mortgage.

BANDHAKĪ : A prostitute attached to many men.

BANDHAKĪ-PUṢAKA : Keeper of a brothel.

BĀNDHAVA (Sm) : The following three classes of relatives—

(I) *Ātma-bandhu*—son of one's father's sister, mother's sister and of one's maternal uncle.

(II) *Pitṛ-bandhu*—son of one's father's sister, father's mother's sister and of one's father's maternal uncle.

(III) *Mātṛ-bandhu*—son of one's mother's mother's sister, mother's father's sister and of one's mother's maternal uncle.

BANDHU (Sm) : Same as *Bāndhava* (q.v.).

BAVRI : A kind of garment.

BHARATA-VĀKYA (N) : The concluding verse of a drama. It was so called because it used to be recited by Bharatas or actors. Some think that it takes its name from Bharata, founder of Dramaturgy. In it we find prayer to God or benediction to the spectators.

BHĀṢĀ (Sm) : Plaint in a lawsuit.

BHĀVA (Al) : Emotion, feeling, complete psychosis as the basis of *Rasa* (q.v.). Divided into two kinds, viz. *Sthāyī* (permanent or principal mood) and *Sañcārī* or *Vyabhicārī* (accessory feeling).

BHRŪṆA (Sm) (i) A Brāhmaṇa conversant with the Veda, who has performed *Soma* sacrifice.

(ii) Foetus.

(iii) Any Brāhmaṇa.

(vi) A Brāhmaṇa who has studied the Veda with its six accessories.

BHUKTI (Sm) : Possession.

BHUKTIVĀDA (Al) : According to this view of Bhaṭṭa Nāyaka *Rasa* is enjoyed, and it is neither inferred nor produced.

BHŪTA-BALI (Sm) : Offering to creatures, as a part of the householder's duty.

BHŪTA-ŚUDDHI (T) : A process by which the five elements of the body are supposed to be purified.

BĪJA (N) : An *Artha-prakṛti* (q.v.).

BĪJIN (Sm) : The owner or giver of seed, the real progenitor (as opposed) to *Kṣetrin*, the nominal father or merely the husband of a woman.

BINDU (N) : One of the *Artha-prakṛtis* (q.v.).

BODHI (D) : Perfect wisdom, enlightenment. Acc. to Buddhist philosophy, the sole Absolute embracing this consciousness which in its turn, includes in itself all psychic processes, is *Bodhi*. It is the one and only truth attainable to him who practises *Yoga*, and even to him only in stages, after he has gone through all the ten stages (*daśabhūmi*) of the career of a *Bodhisattva*.

BRAHMAPURA (T) : Designation of the human body.

BRAHMA-VIHĀRA (D) : Name given by the Buddhists to *Maitrī*, *Karuṇā*, *Muditā* and *Upekṣā*, the qualities necessary for the attainment of *Nirvāṇa*. These mean respectively love, pity, sympathy in joy and equanimity.

BRAHMĀVARTA (Sm) : The part of India between the rivers Sarasvatī and Dṛṣadvatī.

BRĀHMA-VIVĀHA (Sm) : The form of marriage in which the daughter is given away, after decking her with valuable garments and honouring her with jewels etc. to a man conversant with the Vedas and of good conduct, whom the father of the girl himself invites.

BRAHMA-YAJÑA (Sm) : See *Pañca-mahāyajña*.

CAITYA (V) : In ancient times it stood for altar, holy tree, temple or palace. Later on, it came to denote temples on *Citās* (funeral places). In course of time, it was used to denote any temple.

CAKRA (T) : Mystical circle acc. to Tantras. The human body is supposed to have the following *Cakras* :—

(I) Mūlādhāra, (II) Svādhiṣṭhāna, (III) Maṇipūra, (IV) Anāhata, (V) Viśuddha and (VI) Ājñā.

CAKRA-VṚDDHI (Sm): Compound interest, i.e. interest on interest.

CAMATKĀRA (Al) : Literary delight. The supernatural and inexplicable joy produced by a literary composition. It is the essence of *Rasa*.

CAṆḌĀLA (Sm) : (I) Name of the caste sprung from the union of a Śūdra male and a Brāhmaṇa female.

(II) Offspring of an unmarried woman.

(III) One born as a result of a man's union with a *Sagotrā* girl.

(IV) Son of one who, after becoming an ascetic, comes back to the householder's life.

CĀNDRAMĀSA (Mukhya) (J) : Lunar month beginning in the first lunar mansion of the bright half of the month and ending with the conclusion of New Moon.

CĀNDRAMĀSA (Gauṇa) (J) : Lunar month beginning with the first lunar mansion of the dark half and ending with the conclusion of the Full Moon.

CĀNDRĀYAṆA (Sm) : A form of penance in which a sinner is required to eat 15 morsels of food on each day of the dark fortnight and to fast completely on the New Moon day. This is of many kinds, viz. *Pipīlikā-madhya*, *Yati-cāndrāyaṇa* and *Śiśucāndrāyaṇa*.

CĀPA (J) : A portion of the circumference of a circle, cut by a straight line.

CARITRABANDHAKA : A mortgage. In it the creditor, relying on the honesty of the debtor, lends a big amount against the mortgage of a small property. Or, the debtor, relying on the honesty of the creditor, borrows a small sum by mortgaging a big property.

CATURASRA (J) : A place within four lines.

CĀTURMĀSYA (Sm) : Name of the three sacrifices, viz. *Vaiśvadeva*, *Varuṇapraghāsa* and *Śākamedha*, performed in the beginning of the three seasons of four months each.

CHALIKYAGĀNA : A kind of chorus.

CŪḌĀKARMAN or CŪḌĀKARAṆA, CŪḌĀ (Sm) : A sacrament in which the hair on a child's head is cut for the first time. 'Cūḍā' means the tuft of hair kept on the head when the major part is shaved off.

CŪḌĀMAṆI (J) : Name of a *Yoga* when there is solar eclipse on Sunday or lunar eclipse on Monday.

DADHIMANTHA : Perhaps ghee or buttermilk.

DĀHA-JVARA (Ay) : Inflammatory fever.

DAIVA VIVĀHA (Sm) : The form of marriage in which a father gives away his daughter after decking her with ornaments etc. to a priest who duly officiates at a sacrifice, during the course of its performance.

DAKṢIṆĀYANA (J) : The period of the sun's stay in the southern hemisphere.

DĀNA (G, Sm) : A liquid substance exuding from elephant's body, ichor. Gift: one of the four means (*Upāya*) of influencing one's enemy in one's favour.

DAṆḌA (Sm) : (1) Staff, especially that held by one at the time of *Upanayana*.

(II) Punishment, sometimes personified.

(III) Fine.

(IV) Sceptre or rod as a symbol of royal power or judicial authority.

(V) A political expedient by which a king invades an enemy's country.

(VI) The army; military power and sovereignty.

(VII) 1/30 part of a day or night.

DAṆḌA (J) : 1/60 part of 24 hours, equivalent to 24 minutes. In some cases, one *Daṇḍa* is equal to 1/32 part of 24 hours.

DAṆḌA-NĪTI (Sm) : (1) Judicature as science; application of the rod; administration of justice.

(II) Artha-śāstra.

DAṆḌA-VYŪHA (Sm) : A kind of soldiers' array looking like a stick.

DARŚA (Sm) : New Moon or a sacrifice performed at that time; the day on which the moon is seen only by the sun and by no one else.

DATTAKA (Sm) : A boy who, being given by his parents, is adopted by a person as a son.

DATTĀTMĀ (Sm) : A boy who, either bereft of parents or forsaken by them, offers himself to a person as his son.

DATTRIMA (Sm) : Same as *Dattaka* (q.v.).

DEVADĀSĪ : A girl engaged for dancing in a temple.

DEVA-YAJÑA (Sm) : See Pañca-mahāyajña.

DHAIVATA (S) : The sixth note of the Indian gamut; it is denoted by DHA.

DHAMANĪ (Ay) : A tube or canal of the human body; a vein; a nerve.

DHANVA-DURGA (Sm) : A kind of fort surrounded by deserts and devoid of water for five *Yojanas*.

DHARMASTHĪYA : Prison, a sort of lock-up.

DHĀTU (S) : Element of a song. There are four principal *Dhātus*, viz. *Udgrāha*, *Melāpaka*, *Dhruva* and *Ābhoga*. A fifth, viz. *Antara* or *Antarā* is also added.

DHRUVA (NAKṢATRA or TĀRĀ) (J) : North polar star which is always fixed on the north point of the earth.

DHRUVA (S) : A kind of song. It is chiefly of three kinds, viz. *Uttama*, *Madhyama* and *Adhama*. Acc. to Bharata, it is of five kinds, viz. *Praveśa*, *Ākṣepa*, *Niṣkrama*, *Prāsādika* and *Āntara*.

DHVAJABHAṄGA (Ay) : A kind of impotency.

DHVANI (Al) : Suggested sense, the best kind of *Kāvya* according to some.

[See M.M. Sharma, *The Dhvani Theory in Sanskrit Poetics*, 1968.]

DIDHIṢU (Sm) : An elder sister before whom her younger sister has been married.

ḌIMBA (A) : An affray, a riot.

DIVYA (Sm) : Divine proof, e.g. ordeal of fire, water etc.

DRĀVIḌA (V) : Designation of the type of architecture that was current in South India.

DREKKĀṆA or DREṢKĀṆA (J) : 1/3 of a *rāśi*.

DROṆA (Kr) : A kind of cloud.

DVAIDHA or DVAIDHĪBHĀVA (Sm, A) : One of the six kinds of royal policy (*Guṇa*). According to some, it means double-dealing, keeping apparently friendly relations with the enemy. Acc. to others, it means dividing one's army and encountering the enemy in detachments. Yet others take it to mean 'making peace with one king and carrying on war with another'.

DVĀMUṢYĀYAṆA (Sm) : A son of two fathers. Usually an only son given in adoption on condition that he will be treated as the son of both the natural father and the adoptive father.

DVANDVA (Vy): Copulative compound in which the meaning of both the members is equally prominent.

DVIGU (Vy) : Numeral appositional compound, i.e. a kind of *Karmadhāraya* (q.v.) in which the first member is a numeral.

EKAPARIGRAHĀ : A prostitute attached to one person.

EKAŚEṢA (Vy) : Name of a *Vṛtti* (q.v.). It is a phenomenon in which, of the words having the same form and same case-ending, one remains, or of words of different forms but of the same meaning only one remains. For example,

(1) *naraḥ naraḥ*=narau.

(2) *vakradaṇḍaḥ kuṭiladaṇḍaḥ* (both words meaning 'curved stick') =*vakradaṇḍau* or *kuṭiladaṇḍau*.

EKODDIṢṬA (Sm) : A kind of *Śrāddha* performed in honour of one individual.

GAṆA (Sm, C) : (i) An association of merchants etc.

(ii) A guild of horse-dealers.

(iii) An association of men living in a village, etc.

(iv) An association of warriors etc. who pursue the same vocation.

(v) A tribal community.

In Metrics it is a metrical unit consisting of three syllables, represented by a letter. For example, three consecutive long syllables are represented by *Ma*, three consecutive short ones by *Na*. There are eight *Gaṇas* representing the various permutations and combinations of the long and short syllables.

GAṆḌAMĀLĀ (Ay) : Inflammation of the glands of the neck.

GĀNDHĀRA (S) : The third of the seven notes in a song. It is indicated by *GA*.

GĀNDHARVA (Sm) : That form of clandestine marriage in which the parties marry by mutual consent.
[See L. Sternbach, Juridical aspects of the Gāndharva form of marriage, *Proc. of the All India Oriental Conference* (12th Session), Vol. II, Banaras, 1946.]

GARBHĀDHĀNA (Sm) : A sacrament performed to ensure the birth of a good child. Authorities differ as to the proper time for performing it.

GARBHA-KENDRA (J) : Centre of a circle.

GARBHASRĀVA (Ay) : Abortion.

GĀRHAPATYA (Sm) : The householder's fire received from his father and transmitted to his descendants; one of the three sacred fires, being that from which sacrificial fires are lighted.

GARUḌA (Sm) : Name of a particular array (*vyūha*) of soldiers resembling the *Varāha-vyūha* (q.v.) with the only difference that, in the former, the middle part is wider.

GATI (Vy) : Another name of certain particles which are also called *Upasarga* (q.v.). Other words receiving the designation of *Gati* are those which are listed with *Ūri* leading, words formed by adding the affix *-cvi* as well as affix *-ḍāc*, provided all such words precede verbs.

GAUḌĪ (Sm, Al) : (1) Wine distilled from molasses.
(2) Name of a *Rīti* or a particular mode of arrangement of words in a literary composition.

GHA (Vy) : Technical term for the Taddhita affixes *-tarap* and *-tamap*.

GHANA (S) : See Vādya.

GHĀTA (J) : Multiplication.

GHAṬARĪ : A kind of lute.

GHAṬIKĀ (J) : Same as *Daṇḍa* (q.v.).

GHI (Vy) : Technical term for noun-bases or *Prātipadikas* ending in short *i* or short *u*, excepting the bases *Sakhi*, *Pati* and those included in *Nadī* (q.v.).

GHU (Vy) : Technical term for the roots *dā* and *dhā*; root *dāp* is excluded.

GIRI-DURGA (Sm) : A kind of royal fort situated on a hill very difficult to climb, accessible through a narrow path, with a supply of water from rivers and falls and with many productive lands and trees.

GO-DĀNA (Sm) : The ceremony of tonsure, performed in the sixteenth year of age for a Brāhmaṇa, in the twenty-second year for a Kṣatriya and in the twenty-fourth year for a Vaiśya.

GOPA : Head of five or ten villages.

GOPURA (V) : City-gate. In course of time, it came to denote the entrance to a temple. It means a particular kind of entrance acc. to South Indian works on architecture.

GOṢṬHĪ : Something like a club where people used to relax by light talks and jokes.

GOTRA (Sm) : "All persons who trace descent in an unbroken male line from a common male ancestor" (Kane). According to some authorities, *Gotra* means the earliest traceable Brāhmaṇa ancestor from whom descent is claimed through generations. *Gotras* are eight according to some, while others recognise a few more.

GRAHA (S) : Same as *Aṃśa* (q.v.) acc. to Bharata, while later writers take it to denote the secondary note in a *Rāga*.

Generally the note from which a *Rāga* is commenced is called the *Grahasvara* of that *Rāga*.

GRAHAṆA (J) : The phenomenon called eclipse, when the sun or the moon, even though remaining in the clear sky, becomes invisible.

GRAHAṆĪ or GRAHAṆI (Ay) : Diarrhoea, dysentery, esp. when the disease is old.

GRAHAYUTI (J) : Denotes the equality of two *grahas* in *rāśi*, *aṃśa* and *Kalā*.

GRĀMA (S) : A gamut, scale in music.

GRĀMAKŪṬA : Village headman.

GṚHAPATIKAVYAÑJANA : A cultivator, unable to earn a living by his own occupation, acting as a spy with Government help.

GŪḌHAJA (Sm) . A son born to a woman during the absence of her husband, the real father being unknown.

GULMA (Sm, A, Ay) : (i) A troop or guard of soldiers. (ii) A police-station, outpost. (iii) Chronic enlargement of the spleen.

GUṆA (Vy, Sm, A) : (1) A technical term denoting AR, AL, E and O in place of Ṛ, Ḷ, I (and Ī), U (and Ū) respectively. (2) A political expedient; these are six, viz. *Sandhi*, *Vigraha*, *Yāna*, *Āsana*, *Dvaidhībhāva* and *Saṃśraya*.

GURU-TALPA (Sm) : (i) Mother. (ii) Wife of a Vedic teacher. (iii) Mother, or step-mother belonging to the same caste as that of the father.

GURVAṄGANĀ (Sm) : Same as *Guru-talpa* (q.v.).

HAIYAṄGAVĪNA : Ghee made of the milk obtained on the previous day.

HASTINĪ (K) : A class of women.

HAṬHAYOGA (T) : A kind of *Yoga* in which the mind is forced to withdraw from external objects.

HAVYA (Sm) : A sacrificial gift or food.

HETVĀBHĀSA (D) ; The semblance of *Hetu* (logical reason, reason for inference, middle term) ; a fallacious reason. This fallacy is of five kinds acc. to Nyāya philosophy. These are :

(i) *Savyabhicāra* (irregular middle),

(ii) *Viruddha* (contradictory middle),

(iii) *Satpratipakṣa* (counter-balanced middle),

(iv) *Asiddha* or *Sādhyasama* (unproved middle),

(v) *Bādhita* (sublated middle).

HIKKĀ (Ay) : Hiccup.

HORĀ (J) : Considered to be a Greek word borrowed by Sanskrit. Attempts have been made to give it an Indian tinge by deriving it from the word *ahorātra* with the initial 'a' and final 'tra' dropped. It is half of a *rāśi* or 15°. At some places, it is taken to denote $2\frac{1}{2}$ *daṇḍas* or one hour.

IḌĀ (T) : Acc. to Tantras, it is the principal nerve in the human nervous system, being on the left side of the body.

INDRADHVAJA : A popular festival.

IṢṬA (Sm) : (i) Whatever is offered in the Gṛhya fire and the Śrauta fire, and gifts made inside the *Vedi* in the Śrauta sacrifices.

(ii) Honouring a guest and performance of *Vaiśvadeva*.

(iii) Oblation to fire, penance, truthfulness, Vedic study, hospitality, performance of *Vaiśvadeva*.

IṢṬĀPŪRTA (Sm) : *Iṣṭa* and *Pūrta*. Of these, *Iṣṭa* has been defined above. *Pūrta* has been defined as (i) Dedication of deep wells, oblong large wells and tanks, temples, distribution of food and maintaining public gardens. (ii) To the above are added, by some, gifts made at the time of eclipse or on the sun's passage into a Zodiacal sign or on the twelfth day of a month. (iii) Nursing of those who are ill.

ĪTI : The following six factors causing severe damage to crops : excessive rains, drought, locusts, rats, birds, a king who is very close.

JALPA (D) : A mode of argumentation in which a man carries on while knowing himself to be wrong or unable to defend himself properly against his opponents except by trickery and other unfair means of arguments. In it the main object is the overthrow of the opponent rightly or wrongly.

JAMBHAKAVIDYĀ : The Śāstra containing rites designed to destroy enemies, secure long life, love, wealth, son etc.

JANAPADA : Union of villagers.

JAṄGALA (Sm, A) : (i) A tract of land, with scanty water and grass, where there are sufficient sunshine, air, paddy etc. (ii) A place with water, trees and hills.

JĀṄGULIKA : Snake-doctor; dealer in antidotes of poison.

JĀTAKARMAN (Sm) : A sacrament performed after the birth of a son to ensure his welfare.

JĀTI (G, D, Vy) : (1) A kind of *Padya* (q. v.) in which the metre is determined by the number of mātrās.

(2) Genus, generality.

(3) In grammar it has been used in a threefold sense :

(a) Whatever is distinguishable from another (species) on account of its possessing certain form or figure (common to the individuals of that class), e.g. *Taṭī* (a bank, a place near the river).

(b) A word, which not being used in all genders, is used to denote a single individual and, therefore, is singular in number. It will apply to other individuals of the class without their being specially mentioned, e.g.

Vṛṣalī (a low-caste woman); it implies her sons, brothers etc.

(c) A word formed with a patronymic affix and expressive of a person belonging to a particular branch of Vedic school and studying a particular portion of the Vedas.

JIGHĀṂSADA : A kind of thief.

JÑĀTI (Sm): Agnatic relations.

JVARA (Ay) : Fever.

JYOTIṢṬOMA (Sm) : Name of a *Soma* ceremony.

KAIRĀTAKA : A kind of wine.

KĀKAṆI (A) : (i) A cowrie-shell (used in gambling). (ii) Name of a copper coin (1/64 of a *Paṇa*).

KALABHA (G) : It denotes a young elephant. Acc. to some, it denotes an elephant in the fifth or thirtieth year from its birth.

KĀLARĀTRI (J) : Name of the 6th, 4th, 2nd, 7th, 5th, 3rd, 1st (and 8th) *Yāmārdha* of Sunday, Monday, Tuesday, Wednesday, Thursday, Friday and Saturday respectively. One *Yāmārdha*=1/8 of the duration of a night. It is regarded as inauspicious.

KĀLAVELĀ (J) : Designation of the fifth, second, sixth, third, eighth, fourth and eighth *Yāmārdha* respectively of Sunday, Monday, Tuesday, Wednesday, Thursday, Friday and Saturday. One *Yāmārdha*=1/8 part of a day. It is considered to be inauspicious.

KĀLIKĀ (Sm) (i) Interest accruing and payable every month. (ii) In literature, a kind of wine.

KAÑCUKĪ (N) : Designation of a character in a Sanskrit drama. He is a Brāhmaṇa endowed with various good qualities, moving about in the harem and expert in all kinds of work.

KĀNĪNA (Sm) : Son of an unmarried woman.

KAPĀLA (A) : A treaty in which excessive demands are made.

KĀPAṬIKA (Sm): A student acting as a spy.

KAPIŚĀYANA : A kind of intoxicating drink.

KĀRAKA (Vy) : That which has some connection with a verb. Six Kārakas are distinguished in grammar. These are *Kartā* (Nominative), *Karma* (Objective), *Karaṇa* (Instrumental), *Saṃpradāna* (Dative), *Apādāna* (Ablative), *Adhikaraṇa* (Locative).

KARAṆA (Vy) : Instrumental case; that which is the most helpful in the accomplishment of an action.

KARAṆA (J) : Half of the duration of a *tithi.*

KĀRITĀ (Sm) : The interest stipulated by the debtor himself.

KARKARIKA : A kind of lute.

KARMA (Vy) : Accusative or objective case; that which is the most desired object of the agent.

KARMADHĀRAYA (Vy) : Appositional compound. It is a variety of Tatpuruṣa in which the members are in the same case-relation; in other words, it is a compound of an adjective with a noun.

KARMĀNTA (Sm, A): Workshop, factory.

KARMAPRAVACANĪYA (Vy) : The particles *Prati*, *Anu* etc. receive this designation when governing a substantive and modifying a verb. These are to be distinguished from *Upasarga* and *Gati*. For example, *japam anuprāvarsat*.

KARṆA (J) : The side opposite to the right angle in a right-angle.

KĀRṢĀPAṆA : A coin or weight of different values (if of gold = 16 *Paṇa*s or 1280 Kowries., if of copper = 80 *Rattikās* or about 176 grains; but acc. to some = only 1 *Paṇa* of Kowries or 80 Kowries).

KARTĀ (Vy) : Nominative case; that is independent in the performance of an action.

KĀRYA (N) : An *Artha-prakṛti* (q.v.).

KAULA (T) : Designation of one, acc. to Tantras, following *Kulācāra*. Of the various kinds of *Ācāra* (rites and practices), recognised in Tantras, *Kulācāra* is regarded as the best and is the goal of a *Sādhaka* who is believed to attain by this liberation in the very life.

KAUPĪNA (Sm, A) : (i) Private part of the body. (ii) Nakedness. (iii) Ugly cover.

KAVYA (Sm) : Oblation of food offered to deceased ancestors.

KĀYASTHA (Sm) : (i) A scribe in the revenue department of a king. (ii) Name of a caste which, according to some, is Śūdra.

KĀYIKĀ (Sm) : (i) Interest of a *Paṇa* or quarter *Paṇa* to be paid everyday without the principal being liable to be reduced whatever interest may have been recovered. (ii) Interest received from the body, e.g. milk received from a cow pledged or the work put in by a slave or by a bull pledged.

KHAṆḌITĀ (Al) : A woman angry at the sight of nail- or tooth-marks of another woman on the body of her husband.

KITAVA : Gambler in dice.

KLĪVA (Ay) : Impotent.

KOŚA (T, Sm, A) : Acc. to Tantras, the human body consists of five *Kośas* or sheaths, viz.
(i) *Annamaya-kośa*, (ii) *Prāṇamaya-kośa*, (iii) *Manomaya-kośa*, (iv) *Vijñānamaya-kośa* and (v) *Ānandamaya-kośa*.
In works dealing with politics and Rāja-dharma, it means treasury, exchequer; one of the seven constituents (*aṅga*) of the State.

KRĀNTI-VṚTTA (J) : The circular route along which Ravi is supposed to move constantly.

KṚCCHRA (Sm) : (i) Bodily mortification, penance, (ii) A particular kind of penance. For an incapable person, one cow is substituted for penance.

KRĪTA or KRĪTAKA (Sm) : One who is purchased from one's parents in order to be treated as a son.

KRIYĀ (Sm) : Proof in a law-suit.

KṚMI-ROGA (Ay) : Worms.

KṚT (Vy) : Primary affixes, added to verbs.

KṚTI (J) : Square, e.g. $a \times a = a^2$.

KṚTRIMA (Sm) : A parentless boy adopted by a person as his son after alluring him with money, land etc.

KṚTYA (A, Vy) : (1) Seducible, liable to be disaffected. (2) Designation of the following *Kṛt* suffixes: *Tavya, Anīyar, Nyat, Yat, Kyap.*

KṢĀTRA (Sm) : A form of marriage, which is the same as Rākṣasa (q.v.).

KṢAYA-MĀSA (J) : A lunar month in which there are two *ravi-saṃkrāntis.* It happens once in 19 years or 131-37 years.

KṢETRAJA (Sm) : A kind of son, begotten by a person, by means of *Niyoga,* on the wife of a sonless person.

KṢETRIN (Sm) : The husband of a woman on whom a son is begotten by another person, called *Bījin,* according to *Niyoga* (q.v.).

KṢITIJA-VṚTTA (J) : Same as *Kuja* (q.v.).

KUJA (J) : Horizon where the earth and the sky seem to meet. Planet Mars.

KULA (Sm) : (i) As much land as can be tilled with two ploughs.
(ii) A multitude.
(iii) Family.

KŪMBA : Perhaps a kind of head-dress.

KUMBHADĀSĪ : A woman in keeping.

KUṆḌALINĪ (T) : Name of the dormant spiritual energy in the human body. It is fancied to encircle, like a serpent, the *Mūlādhāra* (q.v.).

Besides the individual *Kuṇḍalinī*, the Tantras conceive also of *Mahākuṇḍalinī* at the root of the universe.

[See R.C. Prasad, *Lifting the Veil* (*Kuṇḍalinī-yoga*), Delhi, 1971; G. Krishna, *Kuṇḍalinī*: The Evolutionary Energy.]

KUPYA (Sm) : A base metal; any metal but gold, silver, brass, etc.

KURĪRA : Perhaps a dress or ornament for the head.

KUŚĪLAVA (Sm) : A professional dancer.

KUṢṬHA-ROGA (Ay) : Leprosy; elephantiasis. There are 18 kinds of it—7 *Mahākuṣṭhas* and 11 *Kṣudrakuṣṭhas*.

KUSUMA (Ay) : Ophthalmia.

KŪṬA-SĀKṢIN (Sm) : A perjurer.

KŪṬATĀNA (S) : Those complete and incomplete *Mūrcchanās* (q.v.) in which the notes are uttered in irregular order.

KUṬṬANĪ : Procuress.

KVĀTHA (Ay) : Decoction.

LAGNA (J) : Rise of a zodiac.

LAKṢAṆĀ (Al) : A function of words. By it a word expresses a sense other than its primary sense with which the former is connected. For example, in the sentence *gaṅgāyām ghoṣaḥ vasati* the word *gaṅgāyāṃ* means not in the Ganges but on the bank which is connected with the Ganges.

LAMBA (J) : Perpendicular.

LAYA (S) : Uniformity of interval of time in music. It is of three kinds, viz. *Druta* (fast), *Madhya* (medium) and *Vilambita* (delayed).

MADHUKOṢAKA : Perhaps a drinking vessel.

MADHUPARKA (Sm) : A mixture of certain delicious substances offered to deities in religious rites or to distinguished guests. Opinions of some authorities, who differ on the ingredients, are as follows :—

(i) Mixture of curd and honey.

(ii) Mixture of water (or, milk) and honey.

(iii) Meat.

Now-a-days used in the worship of deities only, it consists of a mixture of curd, ghee, water, honey and sugar.

MADHUVIDYĀ : The science which turns poison into nectar.

MĀDHVI (Sm) : A spirituous liquor distilled from honey.

MADHYAMA (S) : The fourth of the seven notes of the Indian gamut; it is indicated by *MA*.

MAHĀLAYĀ (Sm) : The later half of Bhādrapada, when the sun is in the Zodiac Kanyā, is so called.

MAHĀMĀYŪRĪ : Prayer for exorcism.

MAHĀPĀTAKA or -PĀPA (Sm) : A class of sins comprising the following: murder of a Brāhmaṇa, drinking of wine called *Surā*, theft of gold belonging to a Brāhmaṇa, incestuous connexion with one's mother and association with one who has committed one of the above sins.

MAHĀPRĀṆA (Vy) : Aspirate. Consonants requiring hard breathing for pronunciation. The second and fourth consonants of each class or group (*Varga*) and the sibilants belong to this category.

MAHĀVRATA (Sm) : Name of a *Sāman* or *Stotra*. Appointed to be sung on the last day but one of the *Gavāmayana*, a *sacrifice* performed through a year.

MAHĀVYĀHṚTI (Sm) : Name of the mystical formula *bhūrbhuvaḥ svaḥ*.

MAHĀYAJÑA (Sm) : Same as *Pañca-mahāyajña* (q.v.).

MĀHEŚVARA-SŪTRA (Vy) : See Śiva-sūtra.

MAHĪ-DURGA (Sm) : A kind of fortress which is surrounded by a wall made of stone or brick, twice the width in height, which will not be less than twelve cubits, provided at the top with sufficient space for the movement of troops and filled with covered windows.

MĀHIṢYA (Sm) : A caste sprung from the marriage of a Kṣatriya male with a Vaiśya female.

MALAMĀSA (J, Sm) : Intercalary month; an intercalated thirteenth month in which no religious ceremony should be performed. See Adhimāsa.

MAṆḌA (Ay) : Thick scum forming on the surface of any liquid; the scum of boiled rice, gruel.

MAṆḌALA (Sm, T) : (i) The circle of a king's near and distant neighbours with whom he must maintain political and diplomatic relations.

(ii) A kind of mystical diagram used in invoking a divinity.

MAṆḌŪKA-PLUTI (Vy) : 'Frog-leap'. A kind of *Adhikāra* (q.v.) in which a *Sūtra* or a part of it is to be understood in a remote *Sūtra* without being applicable in the intervening *Sūtras*.

MĀNUṢA (Sm) : A form of marriage similar to *Āsura* (q.v.).

MANUṢYA-YAJÑA (Sm) : Same as *Nṛ-yajña* (q.v.).

MĀRGA (S, Al) : (i) Classical music. Derived from the root *mṛg* (to seek), it literally means that music which Brahmā obtained after seeking. The word 'mārga' is also interpreted as way, path i.e. the path shown by the sages. The term is used to indicate that music which is performed in strict conformity with the rules laid down in authoritative works.

(ii) Same as *Rīti*.

MARYĀDĀ (Vy) : Limit exclusive. It is of two kinds acc. as it relates to time and place. For example, in *ā mukteḥ saṃsāraḥ* '*ā*' is in the sense of *maryādā* so that it excludes the time when *mukti* is obtained. Again, in *prayāgāt prabhṛti ā kāśyā vṛṣṭo devaḥ* '*ā*' excludes the region known as Kāśī.

MĀSADAGDHĀ (J) : Certain inauspicious lunar mansions in the solar month, e.g. *Śuklā ṣaṣṭhī* in Vaiśākha, *Kṛṣṇā Caturthī* in Jyeṣṭha etc.

MĀTRĀ (C) : Mora, syllabic instant. A short vowel is said to be of one *Mātrā* while a long one has two.

MĀTṚ-BANDHU (Sm) : See *Bāndhava.*

MĀTSYA-NYĀYA (A) : The rule of might; anarchy; oppression of the weak by stronger persons. The analogy is drawn from the finny world in which a big fish devours smaller ones.

MĀYĀ (D) : In Vedānta philosophy, it means illusion by virtue of which one considers the unreal universe as really existent and as distinct from the Supreme Spirit. It is regarded as a power of God. *Māyā* is considered by some to be synonymous with *Ajñāna* or *Avidyā* which is the cause of false knowledge. In Sāṃkhya philosophy it means the *Pradhāna* or *Prakṛti.*

[See A. K. Ray Chaudhury, *Doctrine of Māyā*; T. Goudrian, *Māyā: Divine and Human*, Delhi, 1978; L.T.O'Neil, *Māyā in Śaṃkara*, Delhi, 1980.]

MLECCHA (Sm): (i) Persians and the like.

(iii) Those who live in Ceylon and such other places as are devoid of the caste system and the four stages of life.

MṚGĪ (K) : A class of women.

MUDRĀ (T) : Derived from the root *mud*, it literally means 'that which causes delight'. Generally it denotes various positions of the finger made by one at the time of worship, e.g. *Matsya-mudrā*, *Śaṅkha-mudrā* etc. This word also denotes certain postures of the body at the time of practising *Yoga.* e.g. *Aśvinī-mudrā.*

MUHŪRTA (J) : Measure of time = ten *daṇḍas* or 1/16 part of a day or night. Acc. to some, it is 1/15.

MUKHEBHAGĀ (K) : A woman satisfying the carnal desire of a man by her mouth.

MŪLĀDHĀRA (T) : Name given, in the Tantras, to a mystical circle supposed to exist above the organ of generation.

MŪLAKARMAN (A) : A magical rite performed with the help of herb-roots.

MŪRCHANĀ (S) : The rising of sounds, an intonation, duly regulated rise and fall of sounds, conducting the air and the harmony through the keys in a pleasing manner, changing the key or passing from one key to another.

MŪRDHĀVAṢIKTA (Sm) : (i) A caste sprung from the marriage of a Brāhmaṇa with a Kṣatriya woman.
(ii) Offspring of the clandestine union of a Brāhmaṇa with a Kṣatriya woman.

NĀDĪ (Vy) : A technical term which generally denotes feminine words ending in long *I* and long *U*. There are exceptions.

NĀGARA (V) : Designation of the type of architecture current in North India.

NAGNIKĀ (Sm) : (i) A ten-year old girl.

(ii) A girl whose first menstruation is imminent.

(iii) A girl in whom sexual desire has not yet grown.

(iv) A girl whose menstrual flow has not yet started, and whose breasts are not yet fully developed.

(v) A girl who looks beautiful even without dress.

NAIṢṬHIKA (Sm) : A life-long Brahmacārin.

NĀLIKĀ (A) : Water-clock.

NĀMAKARMAN or NĀMADHEYA (Sm) : The sacrament in which a child is named for the first time.

NĀṆAKA (Sm) : A coin or anything stamped with an impression.

NĀNDĪ (N) : Name of one of the preliminaries of a drama. By it the gods, the twice-born or kings etc. are eulogised along with benediction to actors or spectators.

NĀNDĪMUKHA (Sm) : Designation of the *Pitṛs* (ancestors) in whose honour *Vṛddhi-śrāddha* (q.v.) is performed.

NĀNDĪ-ŚRĀDDHA : (Sm) : Same as *Vṛddhi-śrāddha* (q.v.).

NĀSTIKA (Sm) : (i) Atheist or unbeliever.

(ii) One denying the consequence of works.

(iii) One who speaks ill of the Vedas, Brāhmaṇas, Dharma etc.

(iv) One denying the existence of future life in the other world.

NĀṬYA (N) : Imitation of a condition. Drama.

NAVĀṂŚA (J) : 1/9 of a *rāśi*.

NIDHI (Sm) : Treasure-trove, i.e. gold etc. lying underground for a long time.

NIDIDHYĀSANA (D) : Constant meditation, with a concentrated mind, on what the preceptor has said.

NIGRAHASTHĀNA (D) : A flaw in an argument, a fault in a syllogism by which a disputant is defeated in an argument.

NIḤŚREYASA (D) : Liberation. Freedom from the bonds of birth and death and the complete cessation of all sufferings.

NIKṢEPA (Sm, A) : (i) A deposit entrusted to a man after counting the articles in his presence.

(ii) Deposit of one's articles with another through confidence.

(iii) Delivery of one's articles to another for handing over to a third.

(iv) A container, a storing place.

NIMITTA-KĀRAṆA (D) : Efficient cause. For example, in the making of a table, the carpenter is the *Nimitta-kāraṇa*.

NIPĀTA (Vy) : Certain particles like *ca* etc., when not denoting a substance, are known by this name.

NIRDHĀRAṆA (Vy) : Selection of one from a group by means of genus, quality, action or name.

NIRVĀṆA (D) : Acc. to the Buddhists, the highest bliss. It means purification of the mind, its restoration to its primitive simplicity or radiant transparency. Sometimes 4 kinds of *Nirvāṇa* are distinguished, viz.

(i) Synonym of *Dharmakāya*—the undefiled essence present in all things.

(ii) *Upādhiśeṣa Nirvāṇa*—that *Nirvāṇa* in which some residue is left.

(iii) *Anupādhiśeṣa Nirvāṇa*—that which has no residue.

(iv) Absolute enlightenment having for its object the benefiting of others; it is the highest kind of *Nirvāṇa*.

NIṢĀDA (Sm, S) : (i) Offspring of the marriage of a Brāhmaṇa with a Śūdra woman, such an offspring being called *Pāraśava* by some. Acc. to some authorities, *Niṣāda* is the offspring of a Brāhmaṇa from a Vaiśya woman.

(ii) The seventh note of the Indian gamut; it is indicated by *N*l.

NIṢKA : (i) A kind of coin.

(ii) Gold or silver necklace.

NIṢKRAMAṆA or NIṢKRAMA (Sm) : The sacrament by which a child is taken out of the house for the first time after birth.

NISṚṢṬĀRTHA (A) : One authorised to negotiate in a matter, plenipotentiary, envoy, *charge d'affaires*.

NIṢṬHĀ (Vy) : Designation of the *Kṛt* suffixes *-kta* and *-ktavatu*.

NIYAMA (D, Vy, Al) : (i) Restriction relating to one when another alternative is available. The Vedic sentence *Vrīhīn avahanti* (threshes paddy) is an instance of *Niyamavidhi*. When unhusking can be effected either by using the mortar and pestle or by some other method (such as by using nails), this rule restricts one to threshing only.

(ii) In *Yoga* philosophy, restraint of the mind, the second of the 8 principal steps of Yoga.

(iii) In Rhetoric, a poetical commonplace or convention; e.g. the description of the cuckoo in spring, peacocks in the rains.

NIYATĀPTI (N) : One of the *Avasthās* (q.v.).

NIYOGA (Sm) : Appointment of a wife or widow to procreate a son from intercourse with an appointed male, usually her brother-in-law younger than her husband.

NṚ-DURGA (Sm) : A kind of royal fort guarded, on all sides, by infantry, with elephants, horses and chariots.

NṚTTA (N) : Dance based on *Tāla* (q.v.) and *Laya* (q.v.).

NṚTYA (N) : It represents, by gestures, an emotion which is expressed by words. Pantomime.

NṚ-YAJÑA (Sm) : See *Pañca-mahāyajña.*

NYĀSA (Sm, T, S) : (i) An open deposit for safe custody.
(ii) Handing over to some member in the house an article in the absence of the head of the house, for delivery to the latter.

(iii) In Tantras it is the name of the process by which *Sādhaka* imagines different parts of his body as identical with the body of the deity meditated upon or worshipped by him. *Nyāsa* is of many kinds e.g. *Aṅga-nyāsa*, *Kara-nyāsa*, *Mātṛkā-nyāsa*, etc.

(iv) In music it is the note in which a song or *Rāga* being completed is concluded.

OṢADHI (U) : It denotes a tree that dies out after its fruits ripen.

PĀCANA (Ay) : (i) A medicine prepared by cooking the ingredients.

(ii) A dissolvent, digestive medicine.

PADA (Vy) : A basic form (*Prātipadika*) with *Sup* affixes

attached and a root with *Tiṅ* affixes attached are disignated as *Pada*.

PĀDA (C) : A foot of a verse.

PADMA-VYŪHA (Sm) : A kind of military array in which the king remains at the centre, and spreads the army on all sides.

PADMINĪ (K) : A class of women.

PADYA (C) : Acc. to the *Chandomañjarī*, it is a composition having four feet. It is of two kinds, viz. *Vṛtta* and *Jāti*, the former being determined by syllables and the latter by syllabic instants.

PAIŚĀCA (Sm) : The basest and most sinful form of marriage in which a man has sexual intercourse with a girl stealthily while she is asleep.

PAIṢṬĪ : (Sm) : Spirituous liquor distilled from rice or other grains.

PAKṢA (D, Sm) : (i) A point under discussion; the subject of a syllogism or conclusion (minor term) ; alternative view. A way of presenting a matter.

(ii) Plaint in a lawsuit.

PAKṢIṆĪ (Sm) : The period of one night with one day immediately preceding it and one day immediately following. It generally denotes a period of impurity (*āśauca*) consequent upon the birth and death of certain relatives.

PALA (J) : A measure of time=1/60th part of a *daṇḍa* (q.v.).

PALABHĀ (J) : Same as *Akṣabhā* (q.v.).

PAṆA (Sm.) : (i) A weight of copper used as a coin (20 *Māṣās*).

(ii) A bet or wager.

PAÑCA-GAVYA (Sm) : The five products of cow, viz., milk, curd, ghee, cow's urine, cowdung.

PAÑCĀGNI (Sm) : The five sacred fires, viz. *Āhavanīya*, *Gārhapatya*, *Dakṣinā*, *Sabhya* and *Āvasathya*.

PAÑCAKĀRUKĪ : The following five classes of people : Potter, Blacksmith, Carpenter, Barber, Washerman.

PAÑCAKṚṢṬI : Cultivation of five crops by rotation in the same field or in different fields.

PAÑCĀLIKĀ : Perhaps doll.

PAÑCAMA (S) ; The fifth note of the Indian gamut; it is indicated by *PA*.

PAÑCA-MAHĀYAJÑA or YAJÑA (Sm) : The five religious acts to be performed by a householder, viz. *Brahma-yajña* (study and teaching of the Vedas), *Pitṛyajña* (offering libation to the manes), *Daiva-yajña* (*homa*), *Bhūta-yajña* (offering of food etc. to birds, beasts etc.), *Nṛ-yajña* (rites of hospitality).

PAÑCĀMṚTA (Sm) : The five kinds of divine food, viz. milk, coagulated or sour milk, butter, honey and sugar.

PAÑCĀṄGA (J) : A book, containing details about days of the week, lunar mansions, stars, *karaṇa* (q.v.) and *Yoga* (q.v.) is called by this name. It is called *pañjikā* (almanac) in Bengali; in it there are also days of the solar month. The solar month is observed in Bengal, Orissa, Assam and Punjab.

PAÑCA-SŪNĀ (Sm) : The five things in a house, by which animal life may be accidentally destroyed, viz. the fire-place, slab for grinding condiments, broom, pestle and mortar, water-pot.

PAÑCA-TATTVA (T) : Also called *Kula-dravya* or *Kula-tattva*. In common parlance it is called *Pañca-makāra*. The five *Tattvas* or *Makāras* are :—

(i) *Madya* (wine),
(ii) *Māṃsa* (meat),
(iii) *Matsya* (fish),
(iv) *Mudrā* (position of fingers),
(v) *Maīthuna* (copulation)

'Mudrā' in this context sometimes means particular kinds of grains.

PĀṆḌU (Ay) : Jaundice.

PARĀKA (Sm) : An expiatory rite consisting in fast for 12 days and control of the senses.

PARĀMARŚA (D) : Deduction, ascertaining that the *Pakṣa* or subject possesses the *Hetu* which is concomitant with the *Sādhya*.

PARIṆĀMA (D) : Transformation, assuming new characteristics. For example, curd is the *Pariṇāma* of milk.

PARISAṂKHYĀ (D, Vy) : Restriction relating to a part when the whole may be applicable. For example, when all five-toed animals may appear to be edible, the injunction permitting the eating of five species of five-toed animals only (*pañca pañcanakhā bhakṣyāḥ*) is a *Parisaṃkhyā*.

PARISRUT : A kind of wine.

PARIVEDANA (Sm) : The act of one's marrying before one's elder brother.

PARIVETTĀ (Sm) : The younger brother who has married before the elder.

PARIVINDAKA (Sm) : Same as *Parivettā* (q.v.).

PARIVINNA (Sm) : Same as *Parivitti* (q.v.).

PARIVITTA or PARIVITTI (Sm) : The unmarried elder brother whose younger brother has married.

PĀRṢṆI-GRĀHA (Sm, A) : A king, considered to be hostile, just behind the territory of another king; the rear enemy.

PĀRṢṆI-GRĀHĀSĀRA (Sm, A) : The king ruling over the territory just behind that of the *Ākranda* (q.v.), ally of the rear enemy of a king.

PĀRŚVAKA : Cheat.

PĀRVAṆA (Sm) : (i) Name of *homa* performed on Full and New Moon days.
(ii) Name of a kind of *Śrāddha*.

PARYUDĀSA (D, Vy) : A kind of restriction. In it stress is laid on what should be done rather than on what should not be done. For example, *abrāhmaṇam ānaya*. Here, the stress is on who should be brought and not on who should not be brought. So, the negative particle in *abrāhmaṇam* is in the sense of *paryudāsa*.

PĀṢAṆḌA (Sm) : Heresy, heretic.

PATĀKĀ-STHĀNA (N) : An equivocal speech or situation in a drama, which foreshadows an event whether near at hand or distant.

PAURṆAMĀSA (Sm) : A sacrifice performed on the Full Moon day.

PHALĀGAMA (N) : One of the *Avasthās* (q.v.).

PHĀṆṬA : A sort of hot drink.

PIṄGALĀ : (T) : A principal nerve in the nervous system of the human body, being on the right side.

PĪṬHAMARDA (N) : The associate of the hero in the episode of a drama. He is a little less qualified than the hero, and helps him in sentiments other than the erotic.

PITṚ-BANDHU (Sm) : See *Bāndhava.*

PITṚ-YAJÑA (Sm) : See *Pañca-mahāyajña.*

PITTA-JVARA (Ay) : Bilious fever.

PITTA-ŚŪLA (Ay) : Colic pain.

PLAVAKA : Acrobat.

PLUTA : (Vy) : Designation of a vowel having three *Mātrās* (mora). The vowels of words used to express calling from afar, used in singing and weeping receive this name.

PRADARA : (Ay) : The disease called *Flour albus.*

PRADEṢṬĀ : Superintendent of the residence of cowherds.

PRADOṢA (Sm) : Period of six *Ghaṭikās* after sunset.

PRĀḌVIVĀKA (Sm) : A judge in a lawsuit.

PRAGṚHYA (Vy) : Certain words receive this designation, and the final vowels of such words do not enter into *Sandhi* with the following vowel. The most commonly known words of this class are those in the dual number ending in *ī*, *ū* or *e*.

PRĀJĀPATYA (Sm) : (i) That form of marriage in which the father gives the daughter after addressing the couple with the words 'may both of you perform your religious duties together', and honouring the bridegroom with *Madhuparka* (q.v.) etc.

(ii) A mode of expiation on the description of which authorities differ. Acc. to Manu, it consists of four periods of three days each following one another in which there are respectively eating once only by day, once only by night, once only without asking for food and complete fast.

PRAKARĪ (N) : An *Artha-prakṛti* (q.v).

PRAKṚTI (D, Vy, Ay, Sm) : Stem, root, primary material or form of rite. Acc. to Sāṃkhya the equilibrium of the qualities of *Sattva*, *Rajas* and *Tamas*. Acc. to Mīmāṃsā, *Prakṛti* is that for which all the accessories are ordained. For example, the chief sacrificial rites like *Darśa* and *Pūrṇamāsa* are called *Prakṛti*. Among the followers of Vedānta, the school of Śaṃkara divides *Prakṛti* into *Māyā* and *Avidyā*. The followers of Vallabha take *Prakṛti* to mean matter which is a part of God. Acc. to the followers of Madhvācārya, *Prakṛti* is twofold, viz. *Cit-prakṛti* and *Jaḍa-prakṛti*, the former is Lakṣmī or the will of God and the latter is the entire immovable world like earth, stone etc.

In grammar this word means the base-form of a word or root before the addition of suffixes.

In *Āyurveda*, it means the condition of body.

In *Rājadharma*, the following seven limbs of a state are called *Prakṛti*; king, minister, ally, treasury, territory, fortress.

PRAMEHA (Ay) : A general name for a urinary disease (such as gleet, diabetes).

PRAṆAVA (Sm) : The mystical and sacred syllable '*Om*'.

PRĀṆĀYĀMA (Sm., T) : Name of the three breath exercises, viz. *Pūraka, Kumbhaka* and *Recaka,* to be performed during daily prayers. By it the vital breath is supposed to be controlled. The Tāntric worshipper believes that this practice secures for him rousing of the energy, freedom from disease, aversion to objects of sense and bliss.

PRAṆIDHI (Sm) : Spy.

PRAṆĪTA : A son begotten on a woman by a person other than her husband.

PRĀṄ-NYĀYA (Sm) : The kind of reply in a lawsuit, in which the defendant proves that the point at issue has already been decided in his favour in a previous lawsuit.

PRAPATTI (D) : Absolute self-surrender.

PRĀPTYĀŚĀ (N) : One of the *Avasthās* (q.v.).

PRASAJYA-PRATIṢEDHA (D, Vy) : A kind of restriction. In it stress is laid on what should not be done rather than on what should be done. For example, in the grammatical rule *na nirdhāraṇe* (II. 2. 10), the emphasis is on the prohibition.

PRASAṄGA (Sm) : Name of the principle by which an act done in connexion with one thing is helpful in another also. For example, expiation for a grave sin is capable of washing off a light sin also committed by the same person.

PRASANNĀ : A kind of wine.

PRASTĀVANĀ (N) : Prologue in which the chief actress and the *Vidūṣaka* etc. converse with the stage-manager relating to their own work or the plot of the drama.

PRATIBHŪ (Sm) : Surety. *Pratibhūs* are generally of three kinds, viz.

(i) *Darśana-pratibhū*—one who stands guarantee for producing a man.

(ii) *Pratyaya-pratibhū*—one who creates confidence in the mind of the creditor etc. about the debtor and the like.

(iii) *Dāna-pratibhū*—one who gives assurance like this—if so and so fails to repay the money, I shall make the payment.

PRATIDHI : A part of female garment.

PRATILOMA (Sm) : The reverse order, usually applied to marriage between a male of the lower caste and a female of the higher caste.

PRĀTIPADIKA (Vy) : That which has some meaning, but which is neither a root nor a suffix, is so called. Words ending in *Kṛt* suffixes, *Taddhita* suffixes and *Samāsas* are also called *Prātipadikas*.

PRATIPRASAVA (D, Vy) : Counter-exception. Exception to exception.

PRATĪTYASAMUTPĀDA (D) : A Buddhist doctrine which means that the existence of everything is conditional, dependent on a cause; nothing happens fortuitously or by chance.

PRATYABHIJÑĀ (D) : Recognition. Knowledge produced by *Saṃskāras* through sense-organs. The *Pratyabhijñā Śāstra*, founded by Somānanda, is a class of literature belonging to the Śaiva philosophy of Kashmir.

[See R. K. Kaw, *Doctrine of Recognition*, Hoshiarpur, 1967.]

PRATYĀHĀRA (D, Vy) : Restraining the sense from the objects. In grammar the comprehension of several letters or affixes into one syllable, effected by combining the first letter of a *Sūtra* with the final indicatory letter, or in the case of several *Sūtras* with the final letter of the last member. For example, *AṆ* is the *Pratyāhāra* of the *Sūtra A I U Ṇ*.

PRATYARTHIN (Sm) : A defendant in a lawsuit.

PRATYAVASKANDANA (Sm): The defendant's reply of special plea or demurrer.

PRAVARA (Sm) : Also called *Ārṣa* or *Ārṣeya*, it denotes one or more illustrious *Ṛṣis* who are the ancestors of a person and are associated with his *Gotra* (q.v.).

PRAVEŚAKA (N) : It is a device used for indicating some matter in a drama. It is inserted in between two acts. In it low characters speaking Prākrit take part.

PṚṢṬHĪYA KENDRA (J) : The polar centres of a spherical body.

PUDGALA (D) : Atom. Acc. to Buddhists, something endowed with *Sparśa*, *Gandha* and *Varṇa.* It is of two kinds, viz. *Aṇu* and *Skandha.*

PŪGA (Sm, A) : Any combination or body of persons : an association, corporation, union. Assembly or group of families in the same village; assembly of townsmen.

PUṂSAVANA (Sm) : A sacrament performed before the throbbing of the foetus in the womb, for obtaining a male child.

PUṂŚCALĪ : *Demi monde* corrupting young men.

PUNARBHŪ (Sm) : It generally means a re-married widow. *Punarbhūs* are of 7 kinds :—

(i) A girl who had once been promised to be given away in marriage.

(ii) A girl round whose wrist the auspicious band was tied by the husband.

(iii) A girl already intended to be given in marriage.

(iv) A girl who had been given with water by the father.

(v) A girl whose hand was held by the bridegroom.

(vi) A girl who went round the fire.

(vii) A girl who bore a child after marriage.

The above girls are called *Punarbhū* when married to another person. Regarding the different classes of *Punarbhūs*, authorities differ.

PURAŚCARAṆA (T) : A form of *Sādhanā.* In it the *Sādhaka*, after partaking of *haviṣyānna* or *pañca-gavya*, recites, with a concentrated mind, a particular *Mantra* many times and feeds Brāhmaṇas.

PŪRTA or PŪRTAKA (Sm) : Act of pious liberality, such as feeding Brāhmaṇas, digging wells etc.

PŪRVA-NYĀYA (Sm) : Same as *Prāṅ-nyāya* (q.v.).

PUṢKARA (Kr) : A kind of cloud.

PUṬAPĀKA (Ay) : A particular method of preparing drugs, in which the various ingredients are wrapped up in leaves, and being covered with clay are roasted in the fire.

PUTRIKĀ or PUTRIKĀ-PUTRA (Sm) : One's daughter's son appointed to be one's own son. (2) One's daughter appointed as one's son.

RĀGA (S) : That which pleases (*rañjayati*) the minds of listeners is called *Rāga*. Acc. to Mataṅga, a number of notes causing delight is called *Rāga*. Generally six *Rāgas* are spoken of. As a matter of fact, however, many more *Rāgas* are described in various works on music. There are differences of opinion about the names of six *Rāgas*. Several *Rāginīs* of each *Rāga* are imagined. Authorities differ on the names and number of *Rāginīs*.

RĀJAJAKṢMĀ or RĀJAYAKṢMĀ (Ay) : Consumption, phthisis.

RĀJASŪYA (Sm) : Sacrifice performed at the coronation of a king, by himself and tributary princes; this confirms his title.

[See Heesterman, *Ancient Indian Royal Consecration*, The Hague, 1957; A. Weber, *Uber die Konigs des Rājasūya*, Berlin, 1893.]

RĀKṢASA (Sm) : A form of marriage in which a maiden is forcibly abducted.

RASA (Al, Ay) : An inexplicable inward experience of a connoisseur on witnessing a dramatic performance or reading a poetical composition. Supernatural literary delight. Acc. to Bharata, its *Niṣpatti* follows from a combination of *Vibhāvas*, *Anubhāvas* and *Vyabhicāri-bhāvas* with the *Sthāyi-bhāva*. The word *Niṣpatti* has been interpreted by different scholars as *Utpatti* (production), *Anumiti* (inference), *Bhukti* (enjoyment) and *Abhivyakti* (revelation or manifestation). The following 8 *Rasas* are generally recognised : *Śṛṅgāra* (erotic), *Vīra* (heroic), *Raudra* (furious), *Bībhatsa* (disgustful), *Hāsya* (comic), *Adbhuta* (marvellous), *Karuṇa* (pathetic) and *Bhayānaka* (terrible). *Śānta* (quietistic) is accepted by some as the ninth *Rasa*.

In the literature of the Vaiṣṇavas of Bengal *Bhakti*, which was regarded as a *Bhāva* in the earlier works on poetics, came to be regarded as *Rasa*. They divide *Bhakti-rasa* into 5 main *Rasas* and 7 subsidiary *Rasas*.

In Āyurveda it may mean any mineral or metallic salt, mercury.

[See T. P. Chakravarti, Impact of the concept of Sphoṭa on the idea of Rasa, *Summaries of Papers, AIOC*, 1969.]

RĀŚI (J) : Zodiac.

RATHAKRĀNTA (T) : Name of one of the three regions into which India is divided in certain Tantras. It extends from the Vindhya hill to *Mahācīna* including *Nepal*.

RIKTĀ (Sm) : Name of the following *Tithis* (lunar mansions) :

4th, 9th, and 14th days of the lunar fortnight.

RIKTHA (Sm) : Same as *Ṛktha* (q.v.).

RIKTHIN (Sm) : An heir.

RĪTI (Al) : Also called *Mārga*. It is defined as *viśiṣṭā padaracanā*, i.e. a particular mode of composition or arrangement of words. There are several *Rītis*, e.g. *Vaidarbhī*, *Gauḍī*, *Pāñcālī* etc. Of these, *Vaidarbhī* is generally regarded as the best.

ṚKTHA (Sm) : Any property, wealth, especially that left by one at death; inheritance.

ṚṢABHA (S) : The second of the seven notes in a song. It is so called as it is supposed to have been obtained from the bellow of a bull (*Ṛṣabha*). It is indicated by *RA*.

ṚṢI-YAJÑA : See *Pañca-mahāyajña*.

ṚTA (Sm) : (i) True, truth.

(ii) Gleaning of corns as a means of a Brāhmaṇa's livelihood.

ṚTVIK (Sm) : Priest, usually of four kinds, viz. *Hotā*, *Adhvaryu*, *Brahmā* and *Udgātā*.

RUKMA : An ornament of the neck.

ŚABARA (Sm) : An aboriginal tribe living in jungles.

SABHIKA : Keeper of a gambling house.

ṢĀḌAVA (S) : A *Rāga*, consisting of six notes, receives this designation. In *Ṣāḍava* the initial note *Ṣaḍja* is never given up.

ṢĀḌGUṆYA (Sm, A) : The six measures of royal policy, viz. *Sandhi*, *Vigraha*, *Yāna*, *Āsana*, *Dvaidhībhāva* and *Saṃśraya*.

SĀDHYA (D, Sm) : The predicate of a proposition, the major term in a syllogism. For example, in *parvato vahnimān dhūmāt*, *vahni* is *Sādhya*.

In Smṛti, *Sādhya* is that which, in disputes of various kinds, is to be established by evidence.

ṢAḌJA (S) : The first of the seven notes in a song. It is so called because it has originated from six notes. Some think that the name means 'that which has given birth to the other six notes'. It is indicated by *SA*.

SĀHASA (Sm) : (i) "Punishment, fine regarded as of three kinds, the highest being called *Uttama*, half of that *Madhyama* and half of that *Adhama*" (M. Wms.). (ii) Violence, rape, felony.

[See L. Rocher, in *V. Raghavan Fel. Vol.* Delhi, 1975.]

SAHOḌHA or SAHOḌHAJA (Sm) . A kind of son brought with a woman pregnant at her marriage.

SAHṚDAYA (Al) : Connoisseur. One having the capacity for appreciating a drama or a poetical composition.

SAIRINDHRA : A class of men who used to arrange the dress of rich people.

ŚAKAṬA (Sm) : The form of military array in which the

van is very narrow and the rear wide, such an arrangement being resorted to in the event of danger from behind.

SAKULYA (Sm) : The three paternal ancestors above the paternal great-grandfather, and the three male descendants beyond the great-grandson.

ŚAKUNAVIDYĀ : The science of omens and portents.

SĀMA (Sm) : Policy of conciliation, negotiation being one of the four *Upāyas* or means of success against the enemy.

SAMĀHARTĀ (A) : Revenue Commissioner.

SAMĀHVAYA (Sm) : Setting animals to fight for sport, betting with living creatures.

SĀMĀJIKA (Al) : Same as *Sahṛdaya* (q.v.).

SAMĀNODAKA (Sm) : "Having only libation of water to ancestors in common", distantly related (the relationship, acc. to some, extending to the 14th degree, the first 7 being both *Sapiṇḍas* and *Samānodakas*, while the remaining 7 are *Samānodakas*).

SAMĀSA (Vy) : Compound. The reducing of two or more words syntactically connected with one another, into one word.

SAMĀVARTANA (Sm) : Return home of a student after completion of Vedic studies in the preceptor's house. Also the *Saṃskāra* performed on this occasion.

SAMAVĀYA (Vy, D, Sm) : (i) Inherence. For example, the relation of fragrance to flower is one of inherence.

(ii) One of the categories in *Vaiśeṣika* philosophy.

(iii) Concourse, assemblage.

SAMA-VṚTTA (C) : A kind of *Vṛtta* (q.v.) in which all the feet have the same metrical scheme.

SAMBHALĪ : Same as *Kuṭṭanī* (q.v.)

SAMBHŪYASAMUTTHĀNA (Sm) : Partnership business.

SAṂCARA (A) : A class of roving spies.

SAṂHITĀ (Vy) : Euphonic combination, *Sandhi*.

ŚAṂKHINĪ (K) : A class of women.

(RAVI) SAṂKRĀNTI (J) : The passing of the sun from one zodiac to another.

SAṂNIDHĀTṚ (A) : Director of Stores.

SAṂNIPĀTA-JVARA (Ay) : A combined derangement of the three humours of the body, causing fever which is of a dangerous kind.

SAṂPRADĀNA (Vy) : Dative case; the person whom one wishes to connect with the object of a gift, i.e. one to whom something is given.

SAṂPRASĀRAṆA (Vy) : It means the transformation of *Y*, *V*, *R*, and *L* into *I*, *U*, *Ṛ* and *Ḷ* respectively.

SAṂPRATIPATTI (Sm) : The kind of reply in a law suit, in which the defendant admits the charge brought against him.

SAṂSĀRA (D) : Re-birth.

SAṂŚRAYA (Sm) : One of the *Guṇas* or measures of policy, acc. to which a king, pressed hard by the enemy, takes the help of a more powerful king.

SAṂSṚṢṬA or SAṂSṚṢṬIN (Sm, Al) : One re-united with coparceners after partition of the property. Simultaneous presence of figures of speech independent of one another.

SAṂSTHĀ (A) : A class of spies staying at one place.

SAMUDAYA (Sm, A) : Source of revenue, revenue.

SAṂVĀDĪ (S) : A note that helps develop a *Rāga* manifested by the *Vādi-svara* (q.v.).

SAṂVARTA (Kr) : A kind of cloud.

SANĀBHI (Sm) : Kinsmen on the paternal side.

SAÑCĀRI-BHĀVA (Al) : Same as *Vyabhicāri-bhāva* (q.v.).

SANDHI (Vy, N, Sm) : (I) Euphonic combination.

(2) Juncture in the action of a drama. There are five junctures based on the parallel sets called *Avasthās* (q.v.) and *Artha-prakṛtis* (q.v.). The junctures are *Mukha*, *Pratimukha*, *Garbha*, *Vimarśa* and *Upasaṃhṛti* meaning respectively opening, progression, development,

pause and conclusion. "Thus in the *Śakuntalā* the opening extends from Act I to the point in Act II where the general departs; the progression begins with the king's confession to the Vidūṣaka of his deep love, and extends to the close of Act III. The development occupies Acts IV and V, up to the point where Gautamī uncovers the face of Śakuntalā; at this moment the curse darkens the mind of the king who, instead of rejoicing in reunion with his wife, pauses in reflection, and this pause in the action extends to the close of Act, VI, while the conclusion is achieved in the last Act".[1]

(3) Treaty, peace; one or the six *Guṇas* or measures of policy.

SANDHYAKṢARA (Vy): Diphthong. A vowel, produced by a combination of two vowels, looked upon as a single vowel for a single effort being required for its pronunciation. The vowel *e, ai, o, au* are called diphthongs.

SAṄGĪTA (S): Vocal music, instrumental music and dance are together designated by this term.

SAṄKETA (Al) : Convention. Theorists differ as to the locus of convention in the case of words. Some think that convention lies in *jāti* (genus), *guṇa* (quality), *kriyā* (action) and *saṃjñā* (name). Others think that it lies in the genus alone.

SĀNTAPANA (Sm): A form of penance. It is of five kinds, viz. the first for two days, the second for seven days, the third for 12, the fourth for 15 days and the fifth for 21 days.

SAPIṆḌA (Sm) : It generally means one's (i) ancestors up to the sixth degree from one's father, and descendants down to the sixth degree from oneself, (ii) ancestors up to the fourth degree from mother and descendants down to the fourth degree from father.

SAPIṆḌĪKARAṆA (Sm): Name of a *Śrāddha* performed after one year from one's death. It is supposed to unite the deceased with the body (*piṇḍa*) of his ancestors.

---

1. Keith, *Sanskrit Drama* (1924), p. 299.

SĀRVADHĀTUKA (Vy): Name of the terminations of all tenses and moods, except those of the Perfect and the Benedictive, and of the affixes having the indicatory '*S*'; i.e. the various conjugational signs of the nine classes of roots (excepting the eighth) and terminations of the Present Participle (Parasmaipada and Ātmanepada). These are so called because the endings are added to the entire root. The *Vikaraṇa* (q.v.)is regarded as part and parcel of the root, so the endings before which the *Vikaraṇa* is preserved is known by this designation.

SARVANĀMAN (Vy): Pronoun like the words *Sarva*, *Viśva* etc.

SARVANĀMASTHĀNA (Vy) : In the case of masculine and feminine words, the suffixes *Su*, *Au*, *Jas*, *Am* and *Au* are so called. In the case of neuter words, *Jas* and *Śas* receive this designation.

ŚAŚAKA (K) : A class of men.

ŚĀSANA (Sm, A): An edict, royal command.

ŚATAGHNĪ : Cannon or, according to some, a huge piece of stone covered with barbed wire. It is supposed to have been wielded for killing a hundred people at a time.

SATKĀRYAVĀDA (D) : The doctrine acc. to which the effect pre-exists in the cause, and is made manifest by the operation which that cause undergoes.

SAUDĀYIKA (Sm): (i) Wealth received by a woman, whether as a maiden or as a married woman, in her father's or husband's house from her parents or relatives of the father and mother.

(ii) All property donated by the husband to a woman excepting immovable property.

ŚAUṆḌIKA : Distiller or seller of wine.

SAURAMĀSA (J) : The period from the sun's entrance into one zodiac to its passing into another.

SĀVANA-MĀSA (J) : A month counted with thirty days.

SAVARṆA (Vy, Sm) : Letters having the same place of articulation and requiring similar effort to pronounce are called *Savarṇas* of one another. A vowel cannot be a *Savarṇa* of a consonant.

In Smṛti literature, it means one of the same caste.

ŚEṢA (Vy) : Pāṇini uses this in the sense of 'the remainder after what has been said'.

[See K. C. Varadachari, The evolution of the concept of Śeṣa, *B. C. Law Volume*, II., Poona, 1946.]

SIDDHI (T) : Superhuman faculty or power which is achieved by a *Sādhaka* when he reaches the highest stage of *Sādhana*. Besides faculties or powers of little importance, the following eight are called *Aṣṭa-siddhi* :—

Aṇimā, Laghimā, Mahimā, Prāpti, Prākāmya, Īśitva, Vaśitva and *Kāmāvasāyitā*. The highest *Siddhi* is liberation.

ŚILA (Sm): Gathering stalks or ears of corn.

SĪMANTONNAYANA (Sm) : The parting or dividing of the hair; name of one of the sacraments observed by a woman in the fourth, sixth or eighth month of her pregnancy.

[See S.S. Dange, Symbolism in the rite of sīmantonnayana, *Jour. of Asiatic Soc.*, Bombay, New series, Vols. 52-53.]

ŚIŚNADEVA : A non-Aryan worshipping phallus or indulging in sexual pleasure.

ŚIVA-SŪTRA (Vy) : Also called *Māheśvara-sūtra*. The fourteen Sūtras *a i uṇ, ṛ ḷ k* etc. which are believed to have been taught by Śiva to Pāṇini by the sounds of the drum at the end of his dance.

SKANDHA (D) : Aggregate. Acc. to the Buddhists, there are five *Skandhas*, viz. *Rūpa* (form), *Vedanā* (feeling of pleasure and pain), *Saṃjñā* (perception), *Saṃskāra* (tendencies created by impressions of past experiences) and *Vijñāna* (consciousness). Acc., to them, there is no soul beyond these five *Skandhas*.

SNĀTAKA (Sm): One who has performed ablutions marking the end of studenthood.

ŚOTHA (Ay): Swelling, dropsy.

SPHOṬA (D) : The idea which bursts out or flashes on the mind when a sound is uttered; the impression produced on the mind on hearing a sound, the eternal sound. *Sphoṭa* is considered to be of eight kinds, viz., *Varṇa-sphoṭa, Pada-sphoṭa, Vākya-sphoṭa, Akhaṇḍapada-sphoṭa, Akhaṇḍavākya-sphoṭa. Varṇajāti-sphoṭa, Padajāti-sphoṭa, and Vākyajāti-sphoṭa*. Of these,

Vākya-sphoṭa alone is real and the others are unreal. This is the view of grammarians.

[*Sphoṭanirṇaya* of K. Bhaṭṭa, ed. S. D. Joshi with Intro., Eng. trs., notes. Also see H. G. Coward, *Sphoṭa Theory of Language*, Delhi, 1980; G.N. Shastri, *A Study in the Dialectics of Sphoṭa*.]

ŚREṆĪ (Sm, A) : (i) A guild or association of traders dealing in the same articles. (ii) A band (of harmful persons). (iii) Banded troops.

ŚṚṄGĀṬAKA (A) : A 'forked rod', a kind of trap for the enemy.

ŚRUTI (S) : Sound having no resonance. Acc. to some, Bharata recognised 22 *Śrutis*. *Śruti* is a unit of measurement of the gradual rise of the notes of the Indian gamut.

STHĀNA (Sm, A) : (i) Props of a kingdom, viz. army, treasury, capital city and territory. (ii) A condition of stability. (iii) Position, high position.

STHĀNIKA (A) : (i) A revenue officer in charge of a quarter of the realm. (ii) A city-officer in charge of a ward (iii) A person able to see objects buried underground.

STHĀYI-BHĀVA (Al) : Permanent or dominant feelings residing in the human mind. These are generally eight, viz. *Rati*, *Hāsa*, *Krodha*, *Utsāha*, *Bhaya*, *Jugupsā*, *Vismaya* and *Śoka*. A factor of *Rasa*. (q.v.). Acc. to those who recognise *Śānta* as the ninth *Rasa*, *Śama* or *Nirveda* is the *Sthāyi-bhāva* of this *Rasa*.

STRĪDHANA (Sm) : A woman's exclusive property. Certain special kind of property given to a woman by relatives on certain occasions or in different stages of her life, over which she has absolute right. Authorities differ on the various kinds of *Strīdhana*. Acc. to Manu, it is of the following varieties : (i) *Adhyagni*—given before the nuptial fire; (ii) *Adhyāvahanika*—given in the bridal procession; (iii) *Dattaṃ ca prītikarmaṇi*—given as a token of love; (iv) *Bhrātṛ-mātṛ-pitṛ-prāptam*—received by the girl from her parents and brothers.

STRĪ-SAṂGRAHAṆA (Sm) : Adultery, incest, rape etc.

ŚUKLAKUṢṬHA (Ay): Another name of *Śvitra* (q.v.).

ŚULKA (Sm) : (i) Bride's price, i.e. money paid by the bridegroom's side to the bride's guardians. (ii) Toll, tax, especially money levied at ferries, passes and roads.

ŚŪNĀ (SŪNĀ): See *Pañca-sūnā*.

ŚUṆḌĀ : Bar.

ŚŪNYAVĀDA (D): This doctrine of the *Mādhyamika* school of Buddhism advocates negatively the non-existence of substances and positively the ever-changing flux of *Saṃsāra*.

SURĀ (Sm): Spirituous liquor distilled from rice, molasses and honey. Primarily it denotes the first kind.

ŚUṢIRA (S) : See *Vādya*.

SUṢUMNĀ (T) : The most important nerve in the human nervous system, being in the middle of the body. It is also called *Brahma-vartma*.

SUṢUPTI (D) : Great insensibility, spiritual ignorance.

SŪTAKA (Sm) : Child-birth; impurity of parents consequent upon the birth of their child or miscarriage.

SŪTIKĀ-ROGA (Ay) : Diseases like fever, dysentery etc. of a woman delivered of a child.

SŪTRADHĀRA (N) : Experienced in music, both vocal and instrumental, and dance, and skilful in organising a dramatic performance, he largely corresponds to the modern stage-manager. He figures in the prologue of a drama, as conversing with the chief actress, *Vidūṣaka* etc.

ŚVAPĀKA or ŚVAPACA (Sm) : (i) Offspring of an Ugra male from a Kṣatṛ female.

(ii) Offspring of a Kṣatṛ male from an Ugra female.

(iii) Offspring of a Caṇḍāla male from a Vaiśya female.

(iv) Offspring of a Caṇḍāla male and a Brāhmaṇa female.

SVARA (S) : It is that which is produced immediately after *Śruti*, has resonance and is charming and delightful. There are seven *Svaras* in the Indian gamut; these are *Saḍja*, *Ṛṣabha*, *Gāndhāra*, *Madhyama*, *Pañcama*, *Dhaivata* and *Niṣāda*.

SVARITA (Vy) : Circumflex accent. Designation of the accent that is produced by the combination of *Udātta* (q.v.) and *Anudātta* (q.v.) tones.

SVAYAMDATTA (Sm) : A kind of son who, bereft of parents or forsaken by them, voluntarily offers himself to a person.

ŚVETAKUṢṬHA (Ay) : Another name of *Śvitra* (q.v.).

ŚVITRA (Ay) : Leucoderma.

SYĀDVĀDA (D) : A Jaina doctrine which is also known as *Saptabhaṅgi*. It is so called as it holds all knowledge to be only probable. Acc. to it, there are seven different ways of speaking of a thing or its attributes, in accordance with the point of view. There is a point of view from which substance or attribute (i) is (*syād asti*), (ii) is not (*syād nāsti*), (iii) is and is not (*syād asti nāsti*), (iv) is unpredicable (*syād avaktavya*), (v) is and is unpredicable (*syād asti avaktavya*), (vi) is not and is unpredicable (*syād nāsti avaktavya*) and (vii) is, is not and is unpredicable (*syād asti nāsti avaktavya*).

TADDHITA (Vy) : Secondary affixes added to substantives so as to form secondary nominal bases.

TĀLA (S) : Beating time in music.

TANTRATĀ (Sm) : The principle by which a sinner becomes free from several similar sins by performing only once the penance prescribed for the perpetrator of such a sin.

TĀPASAVYAÑJANA : A hypocritical ascetic acting as a spy.

TAPTAKṚCCHRA (Sm) : (i) A form of expiation in which the sinner has to subsist on hot water, hot milk, hot ghee for three days each and to fast for the last three days when he should inhale hot vapour or atmosphere.

(ii) A form of penance of four days' duration when the sinner has to take hot milk, hot ghee and hot water for one day each and to fast on the fourth day.

(iii) A penance of two days' duration.

(iv) A penance of 21 days' duration.

TĀRPYA : A kind of garment.

TATA (S) : See *Vādya*.

TĀTPARYA (Al) : See *Abhihitānvayavāda*.

TATPURUṢA (Vy) : Determinative compound in which the sense of the latter member predominates.

ṬI (Vy) : Part of a word, consisting of the last vowel and the consonants following it.

TIMIRA (Ay) : An optical disease.

TIRĪṬA : Perhaps a kind of head-dress.

TRETĀGNI or TRETĀ (Sm) : The sacred fires, viz. *Gārhapatya*, *Dakṣiṇa* and *Āhavanīya*.

TRIPHALĀ (Ay) : Three myrobalans together are so called. These are *Āmalaka*, *Harītakī* and *Vibhītaka*.

TRYAHASPARŚA (J) : It takes place if, from one sunrise to another, two lunar mansions end and a third begins.

TUṄGĪ (J) : A planet is called *tuṅgī* (placed in height) if it resides in a particular zodiac; e.g. Mars in Makara (Capricornus), Venus in Mīna (Pisces).

TULĀ-PURUṢA (Sm) : (i) Gift of gold etc. equal to the weight of the donor's body.

(ii) A ten-day penance.

TUNNAVĀYA : Tailor.

UBHAYAVETANA : A spy, paid by one king, serving another king in order to supply information about the latter to the former.

UDĀTTA (Vy) : Acute accent. It is produced from the higher places of articulation in the mouth.

UDAYA (Sm) : Increase, gain, interest etc.

UDDHĀRA (Sm) : (i) The best part of things obtained by conquest.

(ii) That which is set aside, e.g. for the eldest brother in the partition of patrimony among brothers.

UDVARTANA : Rubbing perfumed substances on the body.

ŪHA (D, Vy) : (1) Imagining. For example, in the sentence *agnaye juṣṭaṃ nirvapāmi* the word *sūryāya* is to be imagined for *agnaye* as occasion arises.

(2) Change, modification.

(3) Logical consequence or connexion.

UṆĀDI (Vy) : Affixes, headed by the affix *Uṇ*, similar to *Kṛ* affixes of *Pāṇini*. The *Uṇādi-sūtras* give derivation mostly of such words as cannot be derived by the rules of Pāṇini. There are, however, *Uṇādi-sūtras* of *Kātantra* and some other systems of grammar.

UÑCHA (Sm) : Gathering of abandoned corns, one by one.

UNMĀDA (A) : Mania, insanity.

UPADAṂŚA (Ay) : Venereal disease.

UPĀDĀNA-KĀRAṆA (D) : Material or inherent cause.

UPADEŚA (Vy) : Original enunciation, first or original precepts or teaching.

UPADHĀ (Vy, A): (i) Name of the penultimate letter in a word.

(ii) A secret test of loyalty and integrity.

UPĀDHI (D) : (1) A general property other than the generic attribute (*jāti*).

(2) A limiting adjunct.

(3) A vicious condition.

UPĀDHYĀYA (Sm) : One who teaches for livelihood a pupil a portion of the Veda or the Vedāṅgas.

UPĀKARMAN (Sm) : Commencement of Vedic study.

UPAKURVĀṆA (Sm) : A pupil who, on completion of Vedic

studies and becoming a *gṛhastha*, honours his religious teacher by a gift.

UPAMĀNA (D, Vy) : Comparison, analogy as a means of valid knowledge. In grammar it stands for an object with which something is compared. For example, when one's face is compared to the moon the latter is called *Upamāna*.

UPANAYANA (Sm) : Initiation of a pupil by the preceptor to Vedic studies.

[See J. Gonda, *Indologica Taurinensia*, Vol. VII. Turin (Italy), 1981].

UPANIDHI (Sm, A) : A sealed deposit, i.e, an article deposited with a person in a sealed receptacle without disclosing the contents.

UPANIKṢEPA (Sm) : An open deposit, i.e. an article kept by one with another for safe custody showing the latter the nature of what is deposited.

UPAPADA (Vy) : Such words as are indicated by the seventh case-ending in Pāṇini's rules from III.1.90 to the end of III. 4. Certain indeclinables also receive this designation.

UPAPĀTAKA (Sm) : A class of sins, lighter than *Mahāpātakas* (q.v.), and comprising such sins as incest, giving up of Vedic study, allowing the time for initiation to Vedic study to pass, following the profession of dancing, singing, acting, cow-killing, fornication, etc.

UPAPATTI (D) : Logical consequence.

UPASAṂVYĀNA : A lower garment.

UPASARGA (Vy): The particles *Pra* etc., when prefixed to verbs, receive this designation.

UPASARJANA (Vy) : (i) Name of a word indicated by the first case-ending in a grammatical rule relating to *Samāsa*.

(ii) Name of a word that is always used in the same case-ending in expounding a *Samāsa*, and does not become the first member of a compound.

UPAVĀSANA : A kind of garment.

UPĀYA (Sm) : Expedient of royal policy. The four expedients are *Sāma*, *Dāna*, *Bheda* and *Daṇḍa*. These terms mean respectively conciliation, gift, dissension and war.

ŪRUSTAMBHA (Ay) : Paralysis of the thigh.

UṢṆAKA : A labourer who works promptly.

UTPĀTA (Sm) : (i) An abnormal natural phenomenon foreboding a calamity.

(ii) Portent.

UTPATTIVĀDA (Al) : This is the view of Bhaṭṭa Lollaṭa. Acc. to it, *Rasa* is produced (*utpanna*) in the minds of persons having the capacity for appreciation.

UTSARGA (Vy, D) : A general rule as opposed to a special rule or exception. For example, the general rule is that no creature should be killed. But, an exception is that an animal may be killed in a sacrifice.

UTTARA (Sm) : (1) Defendant's reply in a law-suit. *Uttaras* are broadly of 4 kinds, viz. *Saṃpratipatti* (admission), *Mithyā* (denial), *Pratyavaskandana* (special plea) and *Pūrva-* (or, *Prāṅ-*) *nyāya* (plea of a former trial, *Res Judicata*).

(2) Obsequial rites performed after *Sapiṇḍīkaraṇa*.

(3) An indirect witness who learns from another witness who has seen or heard of a transaction, when the latter is going to a distant country or is on the point of death.

UTTARĀBHĀSA (Sm) : Vitiated reply in a law-suit.

UTTARĀYAṆA (J) : The period of the sun's stay in the northern hemisphere.

VĀDA (D) : A mode of argumentation. It consists in a number of declarations put forward by various speakers purporting to be reasons in support of several theories, leading ultimately to the acceptance of one of these theories as the demonstrated truth. The sole object of *Vāda* is to ascertain truth.

VĀDĪ (S) : The note that manifests the form of a *Rāga*. The principal note in relation to which other notes are determined.

VĀDYA (S) : Musical instrument. The instruments are divided into the following classes :—

(i) *Tata*—stringed instruments, e.g. *Viṇā* (lute).

(ii) *Śuṣira*—possessed of holes and played with the help of wind, e.g. *Vaṁśī* (flute).

(iii) *Ānaddha* (or *Vitata*)—covered with skin, e.g. *Ḍhakkā* (drum).

(iv) *Ghana*—Metallic instruments played by striking, e.g. *Ghaṇṭā* (bell), *Karatāla* (cymbal).

VAIDARBHĪ (Al) : Name of a Rīti or particular mode or arrangement of words in a literary composition. It is regarded as the Rīti par excellence. It consists of the ten *Guṇas*, viz. *Śleṣa*, *Prasāda*, *Samatā*, *Mādhurya*, *Sukumāratā*, *Arthavyakti*, *Udāratva*, *Ojas*, *Kānti* and *Samādhi*.

VAIDEHAKAVYAÑJANA (A) : A merchant, having lost his livelihood, serving as a spy.

VAIDHṚTI or VAIDHṚTA (J) : A particular conjunction of the sun and the moon, harmful to people.

VAJRA (Sm) : A kind of military array in which the army is arranged in three ways.

VĀKPĀRUṢYA (Sm) : Abuse, harsh speech.

VANASPATI (U) : A tree which bears fruits without any flower. Sometimes it means any tree.

VĀRA (J) : Day of the week, e.g. Somavāra.

VARĀHA (Sm) : A form of military array in which the army is so arranged that it is tapering at the van and rear, but wide in the middle.

VĀRAVELĀ (J) : Designation of the 4th, 7th, 2nd, 5th,

7th, 3rd, 6th (and first) *Yāmārdha* of Sunday, Monday, Tuesday, Wednesday, Thursday, Friday and Saturday respectively. One *yāmārdha*=1/8th part of a day. It is considered to be inauspicious.

VĀRDHUṢI or VĀRDHUṢIKA (Sm) : A usurer.

VĀRI-DURGA (Sm) : Same as *Ab-durga* (q.v.).

VĀRKṢA (Sm) : A kind of fortress which is surrounded, up to one *Yojana*, by huge trees, thorny shrubs, creepers and rivers.

VARṢAVARA : An eunuch generally engaged as a keeper of the royal harem.

VĀRTĀ (Sm) : Agriculture, cattle-rearing and trade etc. as a profession usually adopted by Vaiśyas.

VARTANĪ : A sort of octroi on foreign goods.

VĀRUṆĪ : A kind of wine.

VĀTA (Ay) : Wind, as one of the three humours of the body.

VESARA (V) : A type of architecture. Acc. to some, the architecture of Orissa is so called. Some think that it had two forms, viz. *Āndhra* and *Kāliṅga*.

VIBHĀVA (Al) : Excitant. A factor of *Rasa* (q.v.). It is of two kinds, viz. *Ālambana* and *Uddīpana*. For example, Sītā is the Ālambana-vibhāva of Rāma's love while moonrise, spring etc. are the Uddīpana-vibhāvas.

VIDRADHI (Ay) : Abscess.

VIDŪṢAKA (N) : A character in a drama. The hero's confidant and devoted friend. He is a Brahmin ludicrous in dress, speech and behaviour. He is generally represented as a dwarf, bald-headed, with projecting teeth and red eyes. He evokes laughter by his silly chatter in Prākrit and his ravenous greed for food.

VIGRAHA (Sm, Vy) : War. In grammar it means a sentence that expressess the meaning of a *Vṛtti* (q.v.).

VIJIGĪṢU (Sm) : 'One desiring to conquer'. The central power in the *Maṇḍala* (q.v.).

VIKĀRA (D, Vy) : (i) The transformation of *Prakṛti.* It means the assumption of a different form after giving up the original form. For example, curd, sprout, earring are the *Vikāras* respectively of milk, seed and gold.

(ii) A rite in which not all subsidiaries are directly prescribed.

(iii) Modification of a word-base or an affix, caused generally by the addition of suffixes.

VIKARAṆA (Vy) : Lit. meaning 'modification', it generally denotes the conjugational characteristic inserted between the root and the suffix or ending, or between the last vowel and the following consonant of the root. For example, *Śap* coming between the root *Bhū* and the termination *tip* (present, third person singular), is called a *Vikaraṇa.*

VIKṚTI : Same as *Vikāra* (q.v.).

VIMAṆḌALA (J) : The circular course in which a planet moves.

VINIYOGA (D) : Application.

VIPALA (J) : A measure of time=1/60th *pala* (q.v.).

VIṢAKANYĀ (A) : A poisoned woman with whom an enemy is induced to cohabit and die as a result.

VIṢAMA-VṚTTA (C) : A *Vṛtta* in which all the feet are of different metrical schemes.

VIṢKAMBHAKA (N) : A device in a drama, placed in the beginning of an act, which serves as a connecting link between what has happened and what is going to happen.

VIṢKIRA : A kind of bird that eats things after scratching the earth.

VIṢṆUKRĀNTA (T) : Name of one of the three regions into which India has been divided in certain Tantras. The tract of land from the Vindhya hill to Chittagong is called Viṣṇukrānta.

VIṢṬI (A) : Labourers who work for things instead of wages; sappers and miners.

VIṢŪCIKĀ (Ay) : Cholera.

VIṬA (N) : Paramour, passionate rogue. Associate of a king or a characterless young man. Accomplice of a prostitute.

VITATA (S) : Same as *Ānaddha* (q.v.).

VIVĀDĪ (S) : The note that causes loss of charm to a *Rāga*. If, between two notes, there exists one *Śruti*, then those two notes are *Vivādī* of each other.

VIVARTA (D) : False knowledge of a substance when the real thing remains unchanged. For example, the mistake of a rope for a serpent.

VIVĪTA (Sm) : An enclosed spot of ground (esp. pasture ground), paddock, levy on pasture.

VRĀTYA (Sm) : (i) One born to a member of the regenerate class by a wife of his own caste, on whom or on whose ancestors the sacrament of *Upanayana* has not been performed.

(ii) Anyone born of the mixture of Varṇas or Castes.

[See L.B. Keny, The Vrātyas etc., *Pro. of Indian History Congress* (9th Session), 1946, *Summary of Papers* 8th and 9th Indian History Congress; *Pro. of Indian History Congress*, 10th Session, 1947; H. P. Sastri, *Absorption of the Vrātyas*, London, 1926; R. K. Chaudhury, *Vrātyas in Ancient India*.]

VṚDDHI (Vy, Sm) : (i) A technical term denoting Ā, AI, *AU*, *AR* and *A l* in place of *A*, *I* (long and short) and *E*; *U* (long and short) and *O*; *Ṛ* and Ḷ respectively. (2) Interest.

VṚKṢA-DURGA (Sm) : Same as *Vārkṣa* (q.v.).

VṚTTA (C) : A kind of *Padya* in which the metre is determined by the number of syllables.

VṚTTI (N, Vy) : Dramatic style. *Vṛttis* are four acc. to the *Nāṭya-śāstra*, viz. *Kaiśiki* (the graceful), *Sāttvatī* (the grand), *Ārabhaṭī* (the violent), *Bhāratī* (the verbal). *Kaiśikī* is appropriate to the erotic sentiment. *Sāttvatī* is suitable for heroism, wonder, fury and in a less degree to the pathetic and erotic. *Ārabhaṭī* accords with fury, horror and terror. The verbal manner is based on sound as the other three are on sense. It is suited, acc. to *Nāṭya-śāstra*, to heroism, wonder and fury.

In grammar it means that in which a word, besides expressing its own meaning, also declares the meaning of another. Grammatical *Vṛttis* are five, viz. *Kṛt*, *Taddhita*, *Samāsa*, *Ekaśeṣa* and roots taking the affixes like *San*, *Yaṅ* etc.

VYABHICĀRĪ-BHĀVA (Al) : Transient mood, subordinate or accessory feeling such as *Śaṅkā* (apprehension). A factor of *Rasa*. (q.v.). Also called *Saṃcārī-bhāva*.

VYĀHṚTI (Sm) : The mystical utterance of the names of the seven worlds, viz. *Bhūḥ*, *Bhuvaḥ*, *Svaḥ*, *Mahaḥ*, *Janaḥ*, *Tapas* and *Satya*.

VYAÑJANĀ (Al) : A function by which a word expresses a suggested sense which is other than its primary sense.

VYĀPAKA (D) : A thing which pervades another (*vyāpya*). In *parvato vahnimān dhūmāt*, *vahni* is *Vyāpaka*.

VYĀPTI (D) : (1) Invariable concomitance between two things (*vyāpya* & *vyāpaka*). (2) A general proposition. For example, the relation of smoke to fire is one of *Vyāpti*.

VYĀPYA (D) : A thing that is pervaded by something else (*Vyāpaka*). For example, in *parvato vahnimān dhūmāt*, smoke is *Vyāpya* while fire is *Vyāpaka*.

VYATIPĀTA (Sm, J) : The day of New Moon when it falls on Sunday, and when the moon is in the Nakṣatras *Śravaṇā*, *Aśvinī*, *Dhaniṣṭhā*, *Aśleṣā* or *Ārdrā*. It is harmful to people.

VYATIREKA (D) : See *Anvaya-vyatireka*.

VYAVAHĀRA (Sm, A) : (I) Legal procedure, consisting of four stages, viz. *Bhāṣā* (plaint), *Uttara* (reply), *Kriyā* (proof or evidence) and *Nirṇaya* (judgment). (II) Administration of justice. (III) Contract. (IV) Competency to manage one's own affairs, majority.

VYAVAHĀRA-PADA (Sm) : Subject-matter of litigation or dispute.

VYŪHA (Sm) : Logistics; particular arrangements of soldiers in a battle. Manu mentions the following *Vyūhas*:— *Daṇḍa, Śakaṭa, Varāha, Makara, Sūcī, Garuḍa, Padma.*

YĀJYA-MANTRA (D) : Formula of sacrifice.

YAKṢMĀ (Ay) : Consumption, phthisis.

YAMAPAṬIKA : A class of men who used to go round showing torments of hell on a canvas.

YAMAPAṬṬAKA : A piece of canvas on which infernal torments were depicted.

YĀMYA (J) : South.

YĀMYOTTARA-REKHĀ (J) : Meridian line.

YĀNA (Sm) : One of the six *Guṇas* to be resorted to by kings; marching against the enemy.

YANTRA (T) : A mystical diagram painted with minerals on something or on the ground at the time of worship. The worshipper imagines that the deity, which is being worshipped by him, for the time being resides in the diagram in accordance with his prayer. The diagrams differ in form according as the forms of the desired deity differ.

YATI (C, S) : (i) Pause in a metre.

(ii) Pause in a song.

YATNA (N) : One of the *Avasthās* (q.v.).

YAUTUKA or YAUTAKA (Sm) : A kind of *Strīdhana*. Authorities differ on the nature of this :

(I) Wealth received, as a gift, from anybody by a woman while seated together with her husband at the time of marriage.

(II) Separate property of a woman, her *Strīdhana*.

(III) Wealth obtained from the family of the woman's father, which is separate in its characteristics.

YOGA (Sm, D) : In Smṛti literature it means—

(I) Acquisition of what has not been acquired; (II) A trick; (III) Connection, relation; (IV) Power, zeal. In philosophy it means the restraint of the functions of the mind; concentration of the mind.

YOGA-KṢEMA (Sm, A) : (I) Sacrificial acts performed with *Śrauta* or *Smārta* fire and charitable gifts such as construction of tanks, parks etc. (II) Royal minister and *Purohita* who bring about the welfare of people. (III) Umbrella, chowrie, weapons, shoes and the like. (IV) Comfortable life or easy and happy way of maintenance or annuity descending from the father (to the son) at a royal place. (V) *Yoga* means ship and *Kṣema* fort. (VI) The wealth gained by a learned Brāhmaṇa resorting to a rich man for his maintenance (VII) Acquisition of what has not been acquired and the preservation of what is acquired. Also see *Gītā* (ix. 22).

YOGA-VIBHĀGA (Vy) : A device by which a portion of a grammatical rule is cut off and treated as an independent rule. This has been adopted in the school of Pāṇini. For example, Pāṇini's rule *Saha supā* (II. 1.4), has been split up into two, viz. *Saha* and *Supā*.

PART V

GEOGRAPHICAL NAMES

The reader of Sanskrit literature often comes across the names of various places, rivers, lakes, mountains etc. It is, therefore, necessary to give brief accounts of these geographical spots and to identify them, as far as practicable, with their modern names. The geographical names are arranged below in the English alphabetical order. We have selected, for the present purpose, only the prominent names which are frequently met with. A few mythical names, which are common in Sanskrit literature, have also been included for the facility of the reader. For details, the reader may consult the works on Ancient and Medieval Indian Geography.

ACCHODA-SAROVARA : Acchāvat in Kashmir.

ADARŚANA : See Vinaśana.

AHICCHATRA : It was the capital of northern Pañcāla (q.v.). Modern Rāmnagar in Bareilly district, U. P.

ALAKĀ : The mythical abode of Kubera, supposed to be situated on the Himalayas.

AMARAKAṆṬAKA : See Āmrakūṭa.

ĀMRAKŪṬA : Identified with the hill Amarakaṇṭaka which is a part of the Mekhala hills in Gondwana in Nagpur.

ĀNARTA : Same as Saurāṣṭra (q.v.).

ANDHRA : Acc. to the *Śaktisāṃgama-tantra* (III. 7.12), it was the country having Jagannātha above and Bhramarāmbikā below. Jagannātha is the region around the shrine of Lord Jagannātha of Purī. Bhramarāmbikā is the Bhrambarāmba enshrined on the Śrīśaila (q.v.) with Mallikārjuna.

AṄGA : It was the name of the region about Bhāgalpur including Monghyr. Aṅga was one of the sixteen political divisions of India in Buddha's times. Its capital was Campā or Campāpurī. Acc. to a tradition, a sojourn in this place except for pilgrimage renders a *dvija* liable to expiation.

ANŪPA : Name of the region of river Narmadā about Nimar. Its capital was Māhiṣmatī (q.v.).

APARĀNTA : Acc. to Kālidāsa (R iv. 53), it is on the south of the river Muralā, and extends from the Sahya (Western Ghats) to the sea. Some modern scholars identify it with northern Koṅkan the capital of which was Surpāraka (= modern Supara).

ĀRYĀVARTA : Its precise extent is unknown. Acc. to the lexicon of Amara, the holy land between the Himālaya and Vindhya mountains. Acc. to the *Baudhāyana-dharmasūtra*, it is bounded on the north by the Himavat (Himālaya), on the east by the Kālaka-vana (= Prayāga acc. to some, Rāj mahal hills in Bihar, acc, to others), on the south by the Pāriyātra (q.v.) and on the west by Adarśana (q.v.). Acc. to the *Manu-smṛti* (II. 22), it is the name of the stretch of the land between the Himālaya and the Vindhya, extending up to the sea in the east and the west.

[See S. B. Chaudhuri in *IHQ*, xxv, p. 110.]

AVANTI : According to the *Mārkaṇḍeya-purāṇa*, it is included in Aparānta (North Koṅkan in Western India). Broadly speaking, in Avanti, which was one of the sixteen great *Janapadas*, were included the modern Malwa, Nimar and the places adjoining Central Provinces. Ancient Avanti is believed to have been divided into two parts; the northern part had its capital at Ujjayinī, while Māhiṣmatī was the capital of the southern part. According to the *Mahābhārata*, Avanti and Māhiṣmatī were two distinct countries, the former having been in Western India.

[See B. C. Law, Avanti in ancient India, *Vikrama Volume*, Ujjain, 1948 and S. R. Shende, Avanti-deśa, the birth-place of *Mahārāṣṭra*, *Ibid.*]

AYODHYĀ : It is the modern city of Oudh on the river Sarayū (= modern Ghagra or Gogra) in Fyzabad district, Uttarapradeśa.

[See R. Shamasastry, Ayodhyā, the city of the gods, *D. R. Bhandarkar Vol.* (Ācārya-puṣpāñjali), Calcutta, 1940; B. C.

Law, Ayodhyā in Ancient India, Allahabad; P. L. Bhargava, Ayodhyā in early Vedic literature, *ABORI*, LX, pp. 240ff.]

BĀLAVALABHI : Supposed by some to be the name of a village in Bengal (now W. Bengal), where Bhavadeva Bhaṭṭa, the famous Smṛti writer of that province lived.

BHĀGĪRATHĪ : Same as Gaṅgā (q.v.). It is so called on account of the tradition that it was caused to flow from Śiva's matted locks by Bhagīratha, a descendant of king Sagara, so that the 60000 sons of Sagara, reduced by sage Kapila to ashes, might be brought back to life.

BHARUKACCHA : Also known as Bhṛgukaccha and Bhirukaccha, it is identified with modern Barygaza of Ptolemy and the *Periplus*. Modern Broach in Kathiawar. It was a sea-port town known as Po-lu-ka-che-p'o at the time of Hiuen Tsang.

BRAHMAPUTRA : See Lauhitya.

BRAHMĀVARTA : According to the *Manusmṛti* (NSP ed. II. 17), the region between the rivers Sarasvatī and Dṛṣadvatī was called by this name. Afterwards called Kurukṣetra, it has been identified with Sirhind. Its capital was Karavirapura on the Dṛṣadvatī, according to the *Kālikā-purāṇa*, and Barhiṣmatī according to the *Bhāgavata*.

CARMAṆVATĪ : It was the name of the modern river Chambal that rises about 9 miles south-west of Mhow and falls into the Yamunā 25 miles south-west of Etawah town. Kālidāsa refers (Me. 47) to it as the fame of Rantideva in the form of a river. The legend goes that it was formed by the flood flowing from heaps of the hides of cows slaughtered by king Rantideva at his sacrifices.

CEDI : Name of a country and its people. Acc. to some, the Cedis lived in modern Bundelkhand in central India. Others think that they inhabited the modern Chandail. The Haihayas or Kalacuris ruled at Māhiṣmatī (q.v.).

CITRAKŪṬA : A hill 65 miles south-east of Prayāga in Banda district of Bundelkhand and a railway station on Jhānsi-

Mānikpur branch. Acc. to Mallinātha, it was another name of Rāmagiri (q.v.).

COLA: It appears to have been the name of the Tañjavūr-Tirucirāpalli region.

DAṆḌAKĀRAṆYA (DAṆḌAKA) : It was the name of Mahārāṣṭra including Nāgpur. According to Pargiter, it comprised all the forests from Bundelkhand or Bhopal in Central India to the river Kṛṣṇā.

DARADA : A country in the Hindukush, bordering on Kashmir.

DARDURA or DARDARA : It was the name of the Nilgiri hills in the Madras Presidency.

DAŚAPURA : Identified with Mandasor in western Malwa in the Gwalior State. Acc. to the *Kādambarī*, it was in Malwa, near Ujjayinī. The ancient Daśapura was situated on the northern bank of the Siwana, a tributary of the river Śiprā.

DAŚĀRṆA : Usually identified with Vedisā or Bhilsā region in Madhya Pradesh. Acc. to the Purāṇas, the people of this place were the Mālavas, Kāruṣas, Mekalas, Utkalas and Niṣadhas. The Daśārṇa country of the *Rāmāyaṇa* and the Purāṇas appears to have been different from that of the *Meghadūta* acc. to which (I. 23-24) the capital of the Daśārṇa country was Vidiśā and the Vetravatī (Betwa river) was near it.

It is the Dosaron of Ptolemy.

Wilson identifies the eastern and south-eastern Daśārṇa with a part of the Chhattisgarh district in Madhya Pradesh. Acc. to Buddhist sources, it was one of the sixteen great Janapadas.

There is a river called Daśārṇa. Acc. to Wilson. It is now called Dasān which rises in Bhopal and falls into the Betwā.

ḌAVĀKA: Variously identified as Daboka in Nowgong district of Assam, Kopili valley in Assam and Dacca. Some take it to refer to the districts of Bogra, Dinajpur and Rajshahi.

DEVAGIRI : Acc. to the *Meghadūta* (I. 42), it appears to have been a hill near the Chambal river between Ujjayinī and

Mandasor. Wilson identifies it with Devagara in the centre of Malwa on the south of the Chambal.

DRAVIḌA : Part of the Deccan from Madras to Seringapatam and Cape Comorin : the region south of the river Pennar or rather Tripati. Its capital was Kāñcīpura.

DṚṢADVATĪ : Cunningham identifies it with river Rākshi, 17 miles south of Thanesvar. Some scholars identify it with the Ghaggar, others with the Chittang.

DVAITAVANA : Deoband, about 50 miles north of Meerut in Saharanpur district of U.P. After the loss of his kingdom Yudhiṣṭhira is said to have retired to this place with his brothers.

DVĀRAKĀ : It appears that there were two Dvārakās, one more ancient than the other. The ancient Dvārakā was located near Kodinar. The present-day Dvārakā is near Okha in Kathiawar.

[See A.D. Pusalker, Dvārakā, *B.C. Law Vol.*, 1, Calcutta, 1945.]

DVĀRĀVATĪ : Same as Dvārakā.

EKĀMRAKA : Modern Bhuvaneswar in Orissa, about 20 miles from Cuttack.

EKAPIṄGALA : Another name of the Himālaya.

GAMBHĪRA : A tributary of the Yamunā, above the Chambal flowing east from Gaṅgāpura. Acc. to Stein (on Rājataraṅgiṇī, viii.1063), it is the name of the lowest portion of the Viśokā river before it falls into Vitastā. From the *Meghadūta* (1.40) it appears to have been a river in Central India.

GAṆḌAKĪ : A river which rises in the Himālaya, and falls into the Ganges at Sonepur in Bihar.

GANDHAMĀDANA : Acc. to some Sanskrit works it was a summit of Himālaya, while, acc. to others, it was a part of the Kailāsa range.

GĀNDHĀRA : This country lies along the Kābul river between the Khoaspes (Kunar) and the Indus, comprising the districts of Peshawar and Rawalpindi in north Punjab. Its capitals were Puruṣapura (Peshawar) and Takṣaśilā (Taxila).

[See H. Horgreaves : *Notes on Ancient Geography of Gandhāra.*]

GANDHAVATĪ : A river rising in the Udayagiri hills. Acc. to the *Śivapurāṇa,* it rises in the Vindhya. From the *Meghadūta* (I. 33) it appears to have been a small branch of the *Śiprā* (q.v.) on which stands the temple of *Mahākāla* in Ujjain.

GAṄGĀ : Also called Jahnoḥ Kanyā, Jāhnavī and Bhāgīrathī, said to have risen in Himālaya and made its first appearance in the plain of Kanakhala.

[See S. G. Darian. The Ganges in Myth and History, Calcutta; C. Sivaramamurti, *Gaṅgā,* New Delhi 1976; H. Von Stietencron, *Gaṅgā and Yamunā,* Wiesbanden, 1972.]

GAṄGĀDVĀRA : Same as Haridvāra.

GAUḌA : Designation of the whole of Bengal was Eastern Gauḍa from its capital of the same name, the ruins of which exist near Malda. Situated on the left bank of the Ganges, it was the capital of the rulers of Bengal up to about the close of the 16th century. Originally Gauḍa appers to have comprised the modern Murshidabad District excluding its southernmost part. Also see Karṇasuvarṇa.

GAURĪ-ŚIKHARA : Probably the same as Gaurī Śaṅkara, a peak of the Himālaya.

GAUTAMĪ : Another name of the river Godāvarī (q.v.). Identified by some with the Akhaṇḍa-gautamī, i.e. the Gautamī before dividing itself into seven branches collectively known as the Sapta-godāvarī.

[See S.A. Dange, Gautama and Godāvarī, *Summaries of Papers,* AIOC, Silver Jubilee Session, 1969, p. 61.; See B. M. Barua, *Gayā and Buddha Gayā,* Varanasi, 1975.]

GHARGHARA : Modern Gogra or Ghagra, a holy river that rises in Kumaon and is the great river of Oudh.

GODĀVARĪ : See Gautamī :

GOKARṆA : Identified with Gendia, a town about 30 miles south of Goa, in the Kumtā Tāluk of North Kanara District. A famous place of pilgrimage having the temple of Mahābāleśvara said to have been established by Rāvaṇa. Acc. to Kālidāsa (*Raghuvaṃśa*, viii. 33), it is situated on the shore of the southern ocean and contains a temple of Śiva.

GOMATĪ : Probably the modern river Gomal, a western tributary of the Indus. May also refer to the Gumti in Oudh, rising in the Himālaya and falling into the Gaṅgā.

GOVARDHANA : A hill in the district of Mathurā, a few miles away from Vṛndāvana. According to a legend, Kṛṣṇa held it aloft in order to protect the Gopas from the warth of Indra.

GṚDHRAKŪṬA : A hill under Gayā, now called Śailagiri, not very far from Girivraja, the ancient capital of Magadha.

GURJARA : See Saurāṣṭra.

HAIHAYA: Khandesh, parts of Aurangabad and South Malwa. It was the kingdom of Kārtavīryārjuna.

HARIDVĀRA : It is in modern Saharanpur district in Uttar Pradesh and situated on the right bank of the Ganges.

HASTINĀPURA : It was to the north-east of Delhi and situated on the right bank of the Ganges by which it was wholly diluviated. It was the capital city of the Pāṇḍavas.

HEMAKŪṬA : Another name of Kailāsa (q.v.).

HIMĀLAYA (also called HIMĀDRI, HIMAVAT, KUVERA-ŚAILA, PRĀLEYĀDRI etc.) : The greatest mountain range of India with the highest peak (29028 ft.) in the world, called Mt. Everest in English and Cho Mo Lungmā in Tibetan, and discovered by Radhanath Sikdar about 1851 A.D.

INDRAPRASTHA : Identified with the modern village of Indarpat on the Yamunā (q.v.); Old Delhi.

JAMBUDVĪPA : One of the seven islands supposed to have constituted the world with Mount Meru at its centre; it consists of the following parts (*Varṣa*) :

(i) Bhārata, (ii) Kimpuruṣa, (iii) Hari, (iv) Ilāvṛta, (v) Ramayaka, (vi) Hiraṇmaya, (vii) Uttarakuru, (viii) Bhadrāśva, (ix) Ketumāla. Of these, Bhārata-varṣa is regarded as the best.

JANASTHĀNA : A part of the Daṇḍakāraṇya appears to have been called by this name. (See Daṇḍakāraṇya.) Aurangabad and the region between the Godāvarī and the Kṛṣṇā. Pañcavaṭī of the *Rāmāyaṇa* was included in it. Acc. to Pargiter, it was probably the land around the junction of river Godāvarī with the Pranhita or Wainganga.

JVĀLĀMUKHĪ : A renowned place of pilgrimage, north of the Punjab, where fire issues from the earth. It is the fire in which Satī, consort of Śiva, is said to have burnt herself.

KAIKEYA (KAIKAYA, KEKAYA) : Name of the region from which Kaikeyī, a queen of Daśaratha, hailed. It lay in the Punjab to the east of Gāndhāra (Peshawar-Rawalpindi region). A Kekaya kingdom appears to have existed in the northern part of Mysore in the fifth century A. D. The Kaikaya country, mentioned in the *Śaktisaṃgamatantra* (III. 7. 46) appears to have been a place in North-East Bengal. D. C. Sircar thinks that Kaikaya, in this context, may indicate the land of the Kukis in Assam and Manipur. See *Studies in the Geography of Ancient and Medieval India*, p. 102.

KAILĀSA: A snow-clad peak of the Himālaya.

KĀLAÑJARA or KĀLIÑJARA: A hill and fort in Bundelkhand. From the *Rājataraṅgiṇī* (vii. 1256) it appears to have been a hilly district in Kashmir.

KALINDA-KANYĀ: Same as Kālindī (q.v.).

KĀLINDĪ: Same as Yamunā (q.v.). On the significance of the name, opinions differ. Acc. to some, the river Yamunā is so called as it is supposed to be the daughter of Kalinda or Sun-god, while others think that the river derives this name from the mountain Kalinda from which it rises.

KALIṄGA: In ancient times, it appears to have been the name of modern Orissa to the south of the river Vaitaraṇī and of the sea-coast towards the south up to Vizagapatam. Acc. to an inscription of the fifth century A.D. (*Epigraphia Indica*, Vol. xxx, p. 114), Kaliṅga appears to have extended from the Mahānadī to the river Kṛṣṇā in the south. Acc. to a tradition, a sojourn in this place, except for pilgrimage, renders a Dvija liable to expiation.

KĀMĀKHYĀ: A holy place having the temple of Tripura-bhairavī on the Nīlācala hill overhanging the Brahmaputra river. It is about two miles from Gauhati in Assam.

KĀMARŪPA: Modern Kāmarūpa in Assam is bounded on the north by Bhutan, on the east by the districts of Darrang and Nowgong, on the south by the Khasi hills and on the west by Goalpara. According to the *Yoginītantra*, the kingdom of Kāmarūpa included the entire Brahmaputra valley along with the modern districts of Rangpur and Cooch Behar. Acc. to Hiuen-Tsang, Kāmarūpa was located to the east of the river Karatoyā.

KAMBOJA: According to Buddhist sources, it was one of the sixteen Mahājanapadas and situated in the Uttarāpatha or northern India. It appears to have been so called after the people who settled here. It roughly comprised the province round about Rajaori or ancient Rājapura including the Hazara district of the North-Western Frontier Province. Some scholars place this country among the mountains either of Tibet or of the Hindukush, while others would place it in the land round modern Sind and Gujarat. The region appears to have been wellknown for fine horses.

KĀMPILYA: Capital of south Pañcāla, where Draupadī's

Svayaṃvara was held. Identified with modern Kāmpil in the Farrakhabad district to the south of the Ganges.

KANAKHALA: About two miles to the east of Haridvāra (q.v.), where the Ganges and the Nīladhārā meet. Acc. to Mallinātha (*Meghadūta*, I. 50), it was the name of a mountain.

KĀṄCĪ: Modern Conjeeveram in Madras.

[See T. V. Mahalingam, *Kāñcīpuram in Early South Indian History*, London, 1969; C. R.Srinivasan, *Kanchipuram Through the Ages*, Delhi, 1979.]

KĀNYAKUBJA: Identified with Kanoj or Kanauj on the west bank of the Kālinadī about 6 miles above its junction with the Ganges in the Farrakhabad district, U. P.

KAPIŚĀ: Mallinātha notes, under *Raghuvaṃśa* (iv. 38), Karabhā as its other name. While some think that it was the name of the river Suvarṇarekhā in Orissa, others identify it with the river Kasāi flowing through the district of Midnapur in West Bengal.

KARAHĀṬA Modern Karad in the Satara Disrict on the confluence of the Kṛṣṇā and the Koyanā.

KĀKĀPATHA : Identified with modern Kārābāgh, Kālābāgh of Bāghān on the west bank of the Indus, at the foot of the Salt Range called Nili Hill in the Bannu district. It is perhaps the Carabat of Tavernier.

KARṆASUVARṆA : Identified with Rangamati in the district of Murshidabad, on the western coast of the Ganges. About 94 miles from Bandel and a mile and a half to the south-east of Chirati railway station.

KARṆĀṬA: Part of the Carnatic between Ramnad and Seringapatam. Another name of Kuntaladeśa, the capital of which was Kalyāṇapura.

KĀŚĪ : Modern Banaras. Probably the Kassida of Ptolemy.

[See Motichandra *Kashī Janapada Kā itihas*, Bombay, 1962; L. P. Vidyarthi, *Sacred Complex of Kashi*, Delhi, 1979; B. Saraswati, *Kashi*, Simla, 1975.]

KAŚMĪRA or KĀŚMĪRA : Acc. to the *Śaktisaṃgama-tantra* (III. 7.9) Kāśmīra extended over 50 *Yojanas* between the Śāradā-maṭha and the Kuṅkumādri. Śāradā-maṭha is modern Sardi near the confluence of the Kishenganga and Kankatori rivers in Kashmir. The Kuṅkuma hill may be the saffron-growing plateau above Pampur near Srinagar.

KAUŚĀMBĪ : Modern Kosam, about 30 miles to the west of Allahabad, on the Yamunā (q.v.).

[See B. C. Law, *Kauśāmbī in ancient Literature*, Delhi, 1935; N. N. Ghosal, *Early History of Kauśāmbi*, Allahabad, 1935.]

KĀVERĪ : It rises in the western Ghats hills of Coorg, flows south-east through Mysore and falls into the Bay of Bengal in the district of Tanjore in Madras.

KEKAYA : Identified with the present Shahpur district in the Punjab. Situated between the Bias and the Sutlej, it was the kingdom of the father of Kaikeyī, a queen of king Daśaratha of Ayodhyā.

KERALA : In ancient times, it was called Ceralam which is a Tamil word meaning mountain range. Kerala is the same as Cera, and comprised the stretch of land now called Malabar, Cochin and Travancore. Broadly speaking. Kerala was the name of the coastal region inhabited by the Malayalam-speaking people.

KHĀṆḌAVA-VANA : Muzaffarnagar, not very far from Meerut included in ancient Kurukṣetra. Arjuna, a Pāṇḍava, is stated to have appeased the hunger of the god of fire in this forest.

KIṢKINDHĀ (KIṢKINDHA, KIṢKINDHYĀ): Identified with

modern Vijayanagar and Anegundi. Rāma is said to have slain Vālin here in his expedition to Laṅkā.

KOṆĀRKA : Famous for the huge Sun Temple. It is in Orissa.

[See A. Boner, S. R. Sarma and R. P. Das, *New Light on the Sun Temple of Koṇārka*.

KOṄKAṆA : The strip of land between the Western Ghats and the Arabian Sea.

KOŚALA : Acc. to Buddhist sources, it was one of the 16 Mahājanapadas. In ancient times, Kośala was divided into Uttara Kośala and Dakṣiṇa Kośala, the demarcating line having been the river Sarayū. Acc. to some sources, the capital cities of Kośala were Śrāvastī and Sāketa. Acc. to others, Ayodhyā appears to have been the earliest capital and Sāketa the next. Some think that Ayodhyā and Sāketa were identical.

[See R. B. Pandey, *Studies in the History of Kosala*, G. Jha Res. Institute, Allahabad.]

KRATHAKAIŚIKA : Same as Vidarbha (q.v.) and is so called after Kratha and Kaiśika, two sons of King Vidarbha who ruled over the province of this name.

Bhoja, the king of this land, is said to have invited Aja, son of Raghu, to the *Svayaṃvara* of Indumatī, the sister of King Bhoja.

KRAUÑCA : The Krauñca-parvata was a part of the Kailāsa mountain. Krauñca-randhra was the name of the Niti pass in the district of Garhwal, which affords a passage to Tibet from India.

KṚṢṆĀ : Generally mentioned as Kṛṣṇa-Veṇā (or Veṇyā). The third largest river in south India, rising in the Western Ghats at Mahabalesvara.

KUṆḌINA : The ancient capital of Vidarbha (q. v.). Identified by some with Kuṇḍapura about 40 miles east of

Amarāvatī. Acc. to others, it was the name of Kondavir in Berar.

KUNTALADEŚA : At the time of Cālukyas, it was bounded on the north by the Narmadā, on the south by the Tuṅgabhadrā, on the west by the Arabian Sea and on the east by the Godāvarī and the Eastern Ghats. Its capitals were Nasik and Kalyana in different periods. In later times, the Southern Mahratta country was called by this name.

KURU : One of the four *Mahādvīpas* or principal divisions of the known world. It probably extended from the Hastināpura (q.v.) region up to Kurukṣetra (q.v.) on the north and Pañcāla (q.v.) on the east. Considered by some to represent the oldest home of the Aryans.

KURUKṢETRA : The scene of the Great War in the *Mahābhārata.* The ancient Kuru land probably comprised Kurukṣetra or Thanesvar. The region included Sonpat Amin, Karnal and Panipat and was situated between the Sarasvatī on the north and the Dṛṣadvatī on the south.

[See B. C. Law, Kurukṣetra in Ancient India, *S. K. Belvalkar Felicitation Vol.*, Banaras, 1957.]

KUŚĀVATĪ : Older name of Kuśīnārā where the Buddha is said to have obtained Mahāparinibbāna. It was near the modern village of Kāsiā on the smaller Gaṇḍak, to the east of Gorakhpur and to the north-east of Bettia. Several other places bore this name, *e.g.*, (i) Dvārakā in Gujarat, (ii) ancient Darbhavatī (modern Dabhoi), 38 miles north-east of Gujarat, (iii) Kaśur in the Punjab, 32 miles south-east of Lahore, (iv) same as Kuśabhavanapura or Kuṣapura, capital of Rāma's son Kuśa; Sultanpur in Oudh, (v) a place on the Veṇā or Wain-Gaṅgā.

LAṄKĀ : Ceylon, well-known as the abode of Rāvaṇa.

[See C. E. Godakumbura, Laṅkā of classical Indian writers, *Summaries of Papers, AIOS*, 1974.]

LĀṬA : A country said to be to the west of the Narmadā. Probably included Broach, Baroda, Ahmedabad and also Kheira according some.

LAUHITYA : The river Brahmaputra was so called as it was supposed to have sprung from a lake named Lohita at the foot of Hemaśṛṅga mountain. From the *Raghuvaṃśa* (iv. 81) it appears to have formed the western boundary of Prāgjyotiṣa. Regarded as a holy river. Paraśurāma is said to have been absolved of the sin of matricide by bathing in it.

MADHURĀ : Same as Mathurā.

MADHYADEŚA : The territory of Jaipur; it included the whole of the present territory of Alwar with a portion of Bharatpur.

MADRA-DEŚA : Roughly corresponds to modern Siālkoṭ and the surrounding region between the Ravi and the Chenab rivers.

MAGADHA : Ancient name of Bihar or, more precisely, south Bihar with the river Sona as its western boundary. The ancient Magadha country comprised the modern Patna and Gaya district of South Bihar having its capital at first at Rājagṛha (q.v.) and then at Pāṭaliputra (q.v.). Acc. to a tradition, a sojourn in this place, except on pilgrimage, renders a *dvija* liable to expiation.

[See B. C. Law, *Magadhas in Ancient India*, Gwalior, 1944.]

MAHĀKĀLA : Acc. to Mallinātha (on *Meghadūta*, I.34), it was the name of a place (*Caṇḍīśvara-sthāna*). The place appears to have been in Avanti (q.v.).

MAHĀRĀṢṬRA : The Marāṭhā country lying between the Godāvarī and the Kṛṣṇā and the land watered by the Upper Godāvarī. At one time, it stood for the whole of Deccan. Its ancient capital was Pratiṣṭhāna (q.v.).

MAHENDRA : Name of the entire range of hills extending

from Orissa to the district of Madura. It included the Eastern Ghats.

MĀHIṢMATĪ : Acc. to Pargiter, it was the name of Oṃkāra Māndhātā, an island attached to Nemad district of MP Acc. to others, it was the name of Maheśvara or Mahesh on the right bank of the river Narmadā, to the south of Indore. It was the capital of Haihaya or Anūpadeśa (q.v.).

MAINĀKA : A mythical submarine mountain. Name of a mountain near Gujarat. A mountain near Sarasvatī is also so called. Acc. to some, it is the Sêwalik range. Also see Pargiter's trs. of the *Mārkaṇḍeya-purāṇa*, pp. 287-88 (note).

MĀLA : On the meaning of this word commentators differ. Some, including Mallinātha, take it to mean an elevated piece of land, while, acc. to others, it is the name of a place identified with Malda, a little to the north of Ratanpore.

MĀLAVA : Its capital was Dhārā at the time of King Bhoja. Its former capital was Avanti or Ujjayinī. Before the 7th or 8th century the country itself was called Avanti (q.v.).

[See D. C. Sircar, *Ancient Mālava and the Vikramāditya Tradition*, 1969; K. K. Das Gupta, *The Mātavas*, Calcutta; K. C. Jain, *Malwa through the Ages*, Delhi.]

MALAYA : Pargiter identifies this range of hills with the portion of the Western Ghats from the Nilgiris to Cape Comorin. Acc. to the *Raghuvaṃśa* (iv. 45—51), it was on the Kāveri where it falls into the sea. Cardamom and sandalwood are said to grow on it. The same work states (iv. 49—51) that it is a mountain of the Pāṇḍya country.

[See U. N. Day, *Medieval Malwa.*]

MĀLINĪ : It flows between the countries called Pralamba on the west and Apartala on the east, and falls into the river

Ghagra about 50 miles above Ayodhyā. Acc. to some scholars, its modern name is Chuka, the western tributary of the river Sarayū. Acc. to Hiuen Tsang, the district of Madawar in west Rohilkhand was situated on it.

MĀLYAVAT : It was the name of the Anagundi hill on the river Tuṅgabhadrā. Acc. to some, it was the same as the Prasravaṇa-giri. (q.v.).

MĀNASA : A lake stated to be on the Himālaya. Situated on the Kailāsa mountain in Hūṇadeśa in Western Tibet. Acc. to some scholars, it is 15 miles long and 11 miles wide.

MANDĀKINĪ : Acc. to some scholars, it is the western Kālī (Kālīgaṅgā) which rises in the mountain of Kedāra in Garhwal, and is a tributary of the Alakanandā. Some identify it with the Mandakin, a small tributary of the Paisundi in Bundelkhand, flowing beside the Citrakūṭa-parvata. Acc. to some texts, it is another name of the Gaṅgā.

MANDARA : A Mandara hill is situated in the Banka sub-division of the district of Bhagalpur.

MARUDVṚDDHĀ : The *Nirukta* (iv. 26) takes it as an attribute of all rivers named in the *Ṛgveda* (x. 75.5), meaning 'that are swollen by the wind'. It appears to be a river in Kashmir, called Maruwardwan, a tributary of the Chenab. The river Kāverī is called by this name in the *Padmapurāṇa* (vi. 224. 4, 19).

MATHURĀ : It was the capital of Śūrasena, and is still known by this name.

[See B. C. Law, Mathurā, *K. V. R. Aiyangar Comm. Vol.*, Madras, 1940; B. N. Mukherji, *Mathurā and its Society*, Śaka-Pahlava Phase, Calcutta, 1981.]

MATSYA-DEŚA : One of the Mahājanapadas of India. It included the whole of the present Alwar territory with parts of Jaipur and Bharatpur. Appears to have been known as Virāṭa or Vairāṭa in later times. In this kingdom the Pāṇḍavas remained *incognito* for a year.

MERU : The Rudra Himālaya in Garhwal, near Badarikāśrama, where the Gaṅgā rises, is called Sumeru-parvata. The Kedarnath mountain in Garhwal is traditionally believed to be the original Sumeru.

MITHILĀ : Name of Tirhut in Bihar.

[See Sita Ram, Mithilā, *Ganganath Jha Comm. Vol.*, Poona, 1937; B C. Law, Mithilā in Ancient India, *J. P. Vogel Pres. Vol.*, Leyden, 1947 (*India Antique*); K. K. Choudhary, *Mithilā in the Age of Vidyāpati*, Banaras, 1976; C. P. N. Sinha, *Mithilā under the Karṇāṭas.*]

MURALĀ : A river flowing in Kerala. Mallinātha notes under *Raghuvaṃśa*, iv. 55, Muravī as its other name.

NAIMIṢA : The region round Nimkhāravana or Nimsar on the Gomatī, 45 miles from Lucknow. Nimsar is not very far from the Nimsar station of the Oudh and Rohilkhand Railway. The forest in it was regarded as very holy.

NANDIGRĀMA : Nundgāon in Oudh, about 8 miles to the south of Fyzabad. Bharata is said to have lived here, guarding the kingdom as Rāma's representative during the latter's exile.

NARMADĀ : Also known as Revā. It rises from the Maikal range, and flows toward the south-west.

NĪCAIḤ : It was the name of the low range of hills in the kingdom of Bhupāl lying to the south of Bhilsa as far as Bhojapura. It is called Bhojapura hills.

NĪLĀCALA : A small hill or mound at Purī in Orissa, on which the temple of Jagannātha is considered to be situated. It is also called Nīlaparvata. Nīlācala is also the name of a hill near Gauhati, on which the temple of Satī stands.

NĪLAPARVATA : See Nīlācala.

NIṢADHA : Kālidāsa refers both to the place and the mountain of this name. It is Marwar on the right bank of the Sindh to the north-west of Gwalior. The mountain, now known as Hindu Kush, has the name Niṣadha.

OṢADHIPRASTHA : The mythical capital city of Himālaya.

PAMPĀ : Acc. to Mallinātha (*Raghuvaṃśa*, xiii. 30), it was the name of a lake or tank. It appears to be a lake near the river Pampā, a tributary of the river Tuṅgabhadrā, and is in the district of Bellary on the north of the town of Hampi.

PAÑCĀLA : It was originally the country north and west of Delhi from the foot of the Himālaya to the river Chambal. Later on, it was divided into north and south Pañcāla, separated by the Ganges. North Pañcāla roughly comprised the modern Rohilkhand Division of U. P. with Ahicchatra (q.v.) as its capital. South Pañcāla, with its capital at Kāmpilya (q.v.), was the kingdom of Drupada, father of Draupadī who was married to Pāṇḍavas.

PAÑCAVAṬĪ : Identified with Nasik on the river Godāvarī in Bombay.

PĀṆḌYA : This region comprised Madura and Tinnevelly districts. At one time, it included also Travancore.

PĀRASĪKA : Persia. Raghu is reported (*Raghuvaṃśa*, iv. 60) to have led a victorious expedition against the Persians. The Persians are supposed by some scholars to have been the Parśus of the *Ṛgveda* (vii. 83. 1).

PĀRIYĀTRA (or, PĀRIPĀTRA) : It was the name of the western part of the Vindhya range extending from the source of the Chambal to the Gulf of Cambay. It comprised the Ārāvali mountains and the hills of Rājaputānā including the Pāthar range.

PĀṬALIPUTRA : Patna built in 480 B.C. under Ajātaśatru, king of Magadha. The old capital of Magadha was removed from Girivraja (Rajgir) to Pāṭaliputra. It is the Palibothra of the Greek historians and Pa-lin-tou of the Chinese pilgrims.

[See B. C. Law, Pāṭaliputra, an Ancient Indian City, *Srinivasachari Vol.*, Madras, 1950.]

PAUṆḌRA : According to Pargiter, Pauṇḍra and Puṇḍra were different regions. Pauṇḍra was on the south side of the Ganges and Puṇḍra on the north, between Aṅga and Vaṅga. Puṇḍra is supposed to have comprised the modern districts of Santal Parganas and Birbhum and the northern portion of the Hazaribagh district.

PHALGU : A river which flows towards the north through the town of Gaya, and finally joins a branch of the Punpun.

PRABHĀSA : A holy place in Saurāṣṭra near the sea. It had the famous temple of Somanātha sacked by Sultan Mahmud of Ghazni (c. 1025 A.D.). It is also called Somanātha-paṭṭana.

PRĀGJYOTIṢA : It appears to have comprised the Kāmarūpa country and considerable parts of North Bengal and North Bihar. Some scholars identify it with the modern city of Gauhati. The king of this land is stated (*Raghuvaṃśa*, iv. 81) to have surrendered to Raghu.

PRASRAVAṆA-GIRI : Said to have been in Janasthāna, on the Tuṅgabhadrā. In a cave of it Rāma is said to have resided for some time in his exile.

PRATIṢṬHĀNA : Modern Paiṭhān on the north bank of the Godāvarī in the Aurangabad district of Hyderabad. It appears to have been the capital of Mahārāṣṭra in Hiuen Tsang's time. It is Ptolemy's Baithana and *Plithāna* of the *Periplus*. It also appears to have been the name of a place on the north bank of the Yamunā, and the capital of king Purūravas.

PRAYĀGA. Modern Allahabad. The confluence of the Gaṅgā and Yamunā here is regarded as a very holy spot. The confluence of the rivers Sindhu and Vitastā (Zhelum) is also called by this name.

PUṆḌRAVARDHANA : Pāṇḍuā, called Firuzabad in later times, 6 miles north of Malda and 20 miles north-east of Gauḍa. It was the capital of Puṇḍradeśa or Pauṇḍra (q.v.).

PURĪ : Same as Puruṣottama-kṣetra (q.v.).

PURUṢA-PURA : Peshawar, the capital of Gāndhāra.

PURUṢOTTAMA-KṢETRA : Purī in Orissa.

PUṢKALĀVATĪ : "It was probably Aṣṭanagara or Hashtanagara (Charsaddah), 18 miles north of Peshawar, on the Landi (formed by the united streams of Swat and Panjkora) near its junction with the Kabul river in the district of Peshawar" (De : *Geographical Dictionary of India*) Acc. to Kālidāsa (*Reghuvaṃśa, XV*. 89), it was named after Puṣkala, son of Bharata, whom Bharata installed as the king of the place.

PUṢKARA : Town, lake and place of pilgrimage, about six miles to the north of Ajmer in Rajasthan.

PUṢPAPURA : Also called Kusumapura, it appears to have been the capital of Magadha. Identified with modern Patna.

RĀḌHA : The part of Bengal lying to the west of the Ganges, including Tamluk, Midnapore, the districts of Hughli and Burdwan and a portion of the district of Murshidabad. It is the country af the Gangridae, Calingoe of Pliny and Gangaridai of Magasthenes and Ptolemy. Its ancient name was Suhma.

RAIVATAKA : Hill at Junagadh, opposite to Girnar. A sacred place, especially to the Jainas.

RĀJAGṚHA : Rajgir, the ancient capital of Magadha.

[See B. C. Law, *Rājagṛha in Ancient Literature*, Calcutta, 1938.]

RĀMAGIRI : Mallinātha (*Meghadūta* I. 1) identifies it with Citrakūṭa (q.v.). It is modern Ramtek, the headquarters of a Tahsil of the same name in the Nagpur district of Madhya Pradesh.

[See M. A. Mehendale, Mount Nadoda—old name of Rāmagiri, *V. Raghavan Felicitation Volume*, p. 251.]

RĀMEŚVARA : Situated on the island of Pamban in south India, it has the most venerated shrine in India. The shrine is of Śiva.

REVĀ : Same as Narmadā.

ṚKṢAVAT : Acc. to Mallinātha (*Raghuvaṃśa*, V. 44), it is a mountain on the bank of the Narmadā. It was the ancient name of the Vindhya (q.v.) mountain. Acc. to Wilson, it is the mountain of Gondwana.

ṚṢYAMŪKA : A mountain on which Sugrīva is said to have resided. See Pargiter's trs. of the *Mārkaṇḍeya-purāṇa*, (p. 289, note) for identification.

ŚACĪ-TĪRTHA : Śakuntalā is said to have bathed here *en route* to Duṣyanta's capital from the hermitage.

SAHYA : This was the name of the Western Ghats forming the western boundary of the Deccan and running continuously from the Kundaibari Pass in the Khandesh district of Bombay to Cape Comorin.

ŚĀKAMBHARĪ : Sambhara salt lake in western Rajputana on the borders of the Jaipur and Jodhpur States.

SĀKETA : Same as Ayodhyā.

It was the capital of northern Kosala.

ŚĀLAGRĀMA (ŚĀLIGRĀMA): A sacred place near the source of the Gaṇḍakī river.

ŚĀLĀTURA : Birth-place of Pāṇini. Identified by some with the village of Lahore to the north-west of Ohind in the Punjab.

SAMATAṬA : East Bengal. It appears to have comprised the districts of Comilla, Noakhali and Sylhet. Its capital was Karmānta (=modern Kamta) near Comilla in the Tippera district of East Bengal.

SARASVATĪ : The river Sarsuti. A very old river mentioned from the Vedic times. The river that survives flows between the Śatadru and the Yamunā. It rises in the hills of Sirmur in the Himālaya, and appears in the plain of Ād-Badri in Ambala (Punjab).

ŚARĀVATĪ : Identified with Fyzabad in Oudh. Some take the word as a corrupt form of Śrāvastī (=modern Sahet-Mahet) on the Rāptī.

Rāma is said (*Raghuvaṃśa*, XV. 97) to have installed his son Lava as the ruler of the kingdom of Śarāvatī.

It was also the name of a river which is probably the Rāptī in Oudh.

SARĀYŪ (SARAYU) : Ayodhyā (q.v.) is situated on this river. It is the Ghagra or Gogra in Oudh, U. P. It is the Sarabos of Ptolemy.

SAURAṢṬRA : The Peninsula of Gujarat or Kathiawar, the Syrastrene of Ptolemy. Acc. to the *Śaktisaṃgama-tantra* (III. 7.13), it covered 100 *Yojanas* on the coast from Koṅkaṇa up to Hiṅgulāja on the west. Koṅkaṇa is the strip of land between the Western Ghats and the Arabian Sea. Hiṅgulāja is the place of pilgrimage called Hiṅglāj near the Arabian Sea, over 100 miles west of Karachi. Saurāṣṭra is also called Gurjara. Acc. to a tradition, a sojourn in this place, except for pilgrimage, is said to render a *dvija* liable to expiation.

[See N. R. Majumdar, *Cultural History of Gujarat.*]

SAUVĪRA : Ancient Sauvīra lay to the east of the lower Indus and comprised Multan in the north.

[See B. D. Mirchandani, Ancient Sindhu and Sauvīra, ABORI, 1976.]

SETUBANDHA : The supposed bridge (called Adam's bridge) between Rāmeśvara and Ceylon, said to have been built by Rāma for an invasion of Laṅka. Regarded as a very holy spot.

SINDHU : Name of the country of the upper Indus. Rāma is stated (*Raghuvaṃśa*, XV. 87) to have gifted this region to Bharata.

Also the name of the river Indus (Greek Sinthos) which bore this name above its junction with the Chinab. Acc. to some, it is the Kālisindhu between the Chambal and Betwa.

Mallinātha remarks, under *Raghuvaṃśa*, IV. 67, that it is the name of a river in Kaṣhmir.

[See B. D. Mirchandani, Ancient Sindhu and Sauvīra, ABORI, 1976.]

ŚIPRĀ : A river in the Gwalior State, flowing into the Chambal. The city of Ujjain is stated to stand on its bank. Every mile of it is marked by holy spots.

SOMATĪRTHA : A holy place in Kurukṣetra (q. v.) where Tārakāsura is said to have been slain by Kārtikeya.

ŚOṆA : The river Sone which rises in the Amarakaṇṭaka mountain in Gondwana, and marks the western boundary of Magadha. It is the Soa of Ptolemy and Sonas of Arrian.

ŚRĀVASTĪ : Sahet-mahet on the Rāptī in Oudh, 58 miles north of Ayodhyā. Said to have been the capital of Lava in Uttarakosala. See Śarāvatī. Acc. to Vincent Smith, it was near Nepalganj in Nepalese territory.

[See B. C. Law, *Śrāvastī in Indian Literature*, Delhi, 1935.]

ŚRĪKṢETRA : Same as Puruṣottama-Kṣetra (q. v.).

ŚRĪŚAILA : (ŚRĪPARVATA) : A hill situated in Karnal district on the south of the river Kṛṣṇā, 50 miles from Kṛṣṇā station. There are numerous Śiva-liṅgas here including the famous Mallikārjuna.

ŚṚṄGAVERAPURA (ŚṚṄGIVERA) : Modern Sringraur or

Singor on the left bank of the Ganges, about 22 miles north-west of Prayāga. Here Rāma is said to have crossed the Ganges when going from Ayodhyā to exile.

ŚRUGHNA : Kālsi in the district of Jaunsar, on the east of Sirmur. Some identify it with Sugh near Kālsi, on the right bank of the Būḍhī Yamunā, 40 miles from Thaneswar and 20 miles north-west of Saharanpur in U.P.

SUHMA : Situated on the Ganges, it was a part of the region known as Rāḍha (q. v.). The kings of Suhma are stated (*Raghuvaṃśa*, IV. 35) to have surrendered to Raghu.

SUMERU : Same as Meru.

ŚŪRASENA : Name of a kingdom of which Mathurā was the capital. It appears to have extended from Magadha in the south-east up to the region to the west of the Vindhya.

SUVARṆA-BHŪMI : Buṛma, the Chryse Regia of Ptolemy. Acc. to some, it was the name of Thaton on the Sitang river 40 miles north of Martaban. Others identify it with Pegu of which the capital was Thaton.

TAKṢAŚILĀ : Identified with Taxila in the district of Rawalpindi in Pakistan. Some scholars locate it near Shahdheri, a little to the north-east of Kālākā-serai between Attock and Rawalpindi. Acc. to Kālidāsa, the place was so called after Takṣa who is said (*Raghuvaṃśa*, XV. 189) to have been installed as the king of this place by his father Bharata.

[See B. C. Chaudhuri, *Takṣaśilā—the ancient seat of learning*, G. Jha Res. Inst., Allahabad.]

TAMASĀ : It appears to have been the name of the river Tonse in Rewa in M.P. It flows 12 miles west of the Sarayū, and falls into the Ganges.

TĀMRALIPTI : Tamluk in the district of Midnapur in West Bengal. It was the capital of the ancient kingdom of Suhma, and formed part of the Magadha kingdom under Mauryas. It was a port famous for maritime trade.

TĀMRAPARṆĪ : Some identify it with the modern river Tāmravārī in South India, while others think it was the name of the Gundur. It is the Taprobane of Megasthenes and the Tambapaṇṇī of Aśoka's Girnar Inscription II. It appears from the *Raghuvaṃśa* (IV. 50) that pearls were found in it.

TĪRABHUKTI (TIRHUT): It comprised the modern districts of Champaran, Muzaffarpur, Darbhanga and also the strip of Nepal Terai. It is also called Vidha.

TRIGARTA : The kingdom of Jālandhara, a part of the district of Lahore. Acc. to Wilford, it was the name of Tahora situated on the river Sutlej, a few miles from Ludhiana.

TRIKŪṬA : (1) A mountain in the south-east corner of Ceylon.

(2) Trikoṭa, a mountain to the north of the Punjab and south of Kashmir.

Identified with Junnar. It is the Tagara of Ptolemy.

TRIVEṆĪ : (1) Junction of the rivers Gaṇḍakī, Devikā and Brahmaputrī.

(2) Confluence of the Ganges, Yamunā and Sarasvatī at Allahabad.

(3) Confluence of the three rivers Tamor, Arun and Sunkosi.

(4) Same as Mukta-veṇī, north of Hughli in Bengal.

TUṄGABHADRĀ : The two rivers Tuṅgā and Bhadrā. They rise in the Mysore State, and join together to form the Tungabhadra near Kudli in the same state. It falls into the Krishna near Alampur in Raichur district.

UJJAYINĪ (Also see VIŚĀLĀ) : Modern Ujjain in Madhya Pradesh. It is reported to have been a very lovely city, a veritable paradise on earth. Situated on the river Śiprā, it is said to have had in it the famous shrine of Śiva called Mahākāla. For the location of Ujjayinī, see remarks under Avanti.

See B.C. Law, *Ujjayinī in ancient India*, Gwalior, 1944; S. Mukherji, Ujjayinī in the Mṛcchakaṭika, *B.C. Law Vol.* I, Calcutta, 1945 and A.D. Pusalker, Ujjayinī in the Purāṇas, *Vikrama Volume*, Ujjain, 1948].

URAGAPURA : Uraiyor of Trichinopoly. Mallinātha (*Raghuvaṃśa*, VI. 59) identifies it with Nāgapura (Uraga = Nāga, i.e. serpent) which is very probably Nāgapatam on the river Kānyakubja (Coleroon).

UTKALA : From epigraphical evidence this land appears to have comprised the region of Purī and Bhuvaneśvara. The reference to it in the *Bṛhat-saṃhitā* denotes modern Orissa. According to the *Skandapurāṇa*, it comprises the land from the river Ṛṣikulya to the rivers Suvarṇarekhā and Mahānadī. The river Kapiśā and the territory of the Mekalas appear to have marked respectively the eastern and the western limit of Utkala.

UTTARAKOSALA : See remarks under Kosala above.

UTTARAKURU : Northern part of Garhwal and Hūṇadeśa where the river Mandākinī and the *Caitraratha-kānana* are situated. It originally comprised countries beyond the Himalayas. It is the Ottorakorra of Ptolemy.

[See S.N. Pande, Identification of the ancient land of Uttarakuru. *Jour. of G. Jha Res. Inst.*, Allahabad, XXVI, Pts. 1-3, 1970.]

VĀHĪKA or

VĀHLĪKA-DEŚA : The country of the Vāhlīkas, a tribe. Identified by some with modern Bactria or Balkh. Famous for its breed of horses and *asa foetida*.

VAITARAṆĪ : A river in Orissa, rising in the Vindhya. Regarded as a holy river. It is also the name of a river in Kurukṣetra. A river in Garhwal is also called by this name.

VALABHĪ : Perhaps one-time capital of Saurāṣṭra (q.v.). Ruins of it were discovered at Bilbi, a few miles north-west of Bhownuggar.

VARADĀ : Identified with the river Wardha in Gujarat State.

VĀRĀṆASĪ : Same as Kāśī (q.v.). Kane, however, thinks that Kāśī was on the eastern side of the Ganges and Vārāṇasī on the western.

[See *All about Varanasi, by an old resident*, Benares, 1917, and Hewall, H.A., *Benares*; *Benares* by S.N. Mishra and R. Bedi; *Sacred Complex of Kashi* by L.P. Vidyarthi, Delhi, 1979; *Banaras: City of Light* by D.L. Eck, Routledge and Kegan Paul.]

VATSA OR VATSYA : A country to the west of Allahabad. It was the kingdom of Udayana, with Kauśāmbi as its capital.

VETRAVATĪ : Identified with the modern Betwa which is a small tributary of the Gaṅgā, rising in the Bhopal and falling into the Yamunā. According to the *Meghadūta* (I. 24) Vidiśā (q.v.) was situated on this river.

VIDARBHA : It is identified with modern Berar (Madhya Pradesh).

VIDEHA : An old country of which the capital was Mithilā (q. v.). It is identified with modern Tirhut or North Bihar See Tīrabhukti.

[See Y. Mishra, *History of Videha.*]

VIDIŚĀ: Mentioned as the capital of Daśārṇa. It is reported to be situated on the river Vetravatī, and the mountain called Nīcaiḥ is said to be located in this city. It is the old name of Besnagar. It was the capital of Eastern Malwa. The river of this name has been identified with the river Bes or Basali which falls into the Betwa at Besnagar or Bhilsa. It appears to have taken its rise in the Pāripātra (q.v.) mountain.

[See B.C. Law, *Vidiśā in Ancient India*, G. Jha Res. Inst., Allahabad.]

VINAŚANA : The spot where the river Sarasvatī disappears in the desert in Ambala and Sirhind in Punjab. Many (II.21) mentions it as the eastern boundary of Madhyadeśa. The

Mahābhāṣya on Pāṇini (II.4.10 and VI.3.109) calls it 'ādarśa' and as the eastern limit of Āryāvarta. Also called 'Adarśa' it is taken by Kaiyaṭa on the *Mahābhāṣya* (on Pāṇini II. 4.10) as the name of a mountain. The *Kāśikā* on Pāṇini (IV. 2.24) speaks of Ādarśa as a *janapada* (country). Acc. to Oldham, it was perhaps not far from Sirsa.

VINDHYA : Name of the mounain range in the Deccan. It is the Ouindion of Ptolemy.

VIRĀṬA : Ancient Virāṭa or Matsya-deśa appears to have been located in Alwar-Bharatpur-Jaipur region to the south of the Delhi area and to the east of the desert. In the *Mahābhārata* Pāṇḍavas are said to have lived *incognito* in this land for one year after their exile.

VIŚĀLĀ : Name of the city of Ujjayinī (q.v.).

VṚNDĀVANA : A wood near the town Gokula in the district of Mathurā on the left bank of the river Yamunā. It is famous in Vaiṣṇava literature for Kṛṣṇa's sports. It is so called because Vṛndā, a favourite Gopī of Kṛṣṇa, is said to have shed her mortal coil here. Acc. to Cunningham, it is the Klisoboras of Arrian. The present site of Vṛndāvana on the same side of the Yamunā as the city of Mathurā, acc. to some, dates back to the time (15th-16th cent.) of Rūpa Gosvāmin's (q.v.) residence here. The original site of Vṛndāvana is believed to have been on the opposite bank.

YAMUNĀ : Name of a river which has its confluence with the Gaṅgā at Allahabad. It is the Jomanes of Pliny.

[See H. von Stictencron, *Gaṅgā und Yamunā*, Wiesbaden, 1972.]

PART VI

PRINCIPAL FIGURES
IN
MYTHS AND LEGENDS

ABHIMANYU : Son of Arjuna. On the thirteenth day of the battle of Kurukṣetra he fell fighting against heavy odds. His wife was Uttarā and son Parīkṣit.

ADITI : Called Deva-mātā. In the *Viṣṇu-purāṇa*, she is represented as daughter of Dakṣa, wife of Kaśyapa, mother of Viṣṇu and of Indra. Devakī, mother of Kṛṣṇa, is supposed to have been a manifestation of Aditi.

[See M. P. Pandit, *Aditi and other deities in the Veda.*]

ĀDITYA : Designation of the sons of Aditi. They were originally 8 celestial deities including the sun. Later on, the number was 12 representing the sun in 12 months of the year.

[See P.L. Bhargava, Ādityas in the Ṛgveda, *Bhārati Bhānam*, VIJ, XVIII, Pts. I, II, 1980.]

AGASTI : Same as Agastya.

AGASTYA : A sage with whom many legends are associated. The chief among them are as follows. In order to curb the height of the Vindhya mountain, which was obstructing the sun and the moon, Agastya, the preceptor of the mountain, hit upon a plan. He approached the mountain, and as it naturally bowed to him in obeisance the sage asked it not to raise its head till his return from journey. He never returned and the mountain remained in the same position.

The ocean having offended the sage, he drank it up.

The sage is said to have devoured the oppressive demon called Vātāpi who assumed the form of a ram.

The name of his wife was Lopāmudrā.

The sage is supposed to have been born in a jar. Hence he is called Kumbha-yoni, Kumbha-sambhava etc.

[See S. Ratna, The Legends of Agastya and Lopāmudrā, *Summaries of Papers*, AIOC, 1974.]

AHALYĀ : Wife of sage Gautama and seduced by Indra. The irate sage pronounced a curse as a result of which she was reduced to a piece of stone. Rāma restored her to her original form, and reconciled her to Gautama.

AIRĀVATA : An elephant churned out of the ocean, and taken by Indra.

AKRŪRA : Uncle of Kṛṣṇa and famed as the holder of the Syamantaka gem.

AMBĀ : 1. Name of Durgā.

2. Eldest daughter of king of Kāśī. She, along with her sisters Ambikā and Ambālikā, was carried off by Bhīṣma for marriage with Vicitravīrya. Ambā having been betrothed to the king of Śalva, Bhīṣma sent her to him. The king repudiated her. To avenge herself on Bhīṣma, Ambā, through the grace of Śiva, was reborn as Śikhaṇḍin (q.v.).

AMBĀLIKĀ : Younger widow of Vicitravīrya and mother of Pāṇḍu by Vyāsa.

AMBIKĀ : 1. Name of Umā.

2. Elder widow of Vicitravīrya and mother of Dhṛtarāṣṭra by Vyāsa.

ANAṄGA : See Kāma.

ANANTA : Name of the mythical serpent Śeṣa.

ANASŪYĀ : (1) Wife of sage Atri and mother of Durvāsas (q.v.). She was a lady of great piety and austere devotion.

(2) Friend of Śakuntalā in Kālidāsa's drama *Abhijñāna-śākuntala*.

ANDHAKA : A demon born to Kaśyapa by Diti. He was possessed of 1000 arms and heads and 2000 eyes and feet. While attempting to carry off the Pārijāta tree from the heaven he was killed by Śiva.

AṄGADA : Son of Vālin, the monkey king of Kiṣkindhā. He was protected by Rāma, and fought against Rāvaṇa.

ANIRUDDHA : Son of Pradyumna and grandson of Kṛṣṇa. He married his cousin Subhadrā. Uṣā, daughter of the demon

Bāṇa, fell in love with him. With the help of Kṛṣṇa, who defeated Bāṇa in a battle, Aniruddha carried off his beloved as his wife to Dvārakā.

AÑJANĀ : Mother of Hanūmat (q.v.).

APARṆĀ : Name of Umā (q.v.). She was so called as in her austerities to have Śiva as her husband she abstained from all food, even the leaves (*parṇa*) of trees.

ARJUNA : Name of the third Pāṇḍava. A great warrior and father of Abhimanyu. The greatest friend of Kṛṣṇa who acted as his charioteer in the battle of Kurukṣetra and gave him wise counsel. He obtained the bow called Gāṇḍīva from the god Agni. Having pleased Śiva by his prowess he obtained from him the powerful weapon Pāśupata. While staying *incognito* in the house of the king of Virāṭa he disguised himself as an eunuch and acted as music and dancing master.

He is also known as Guḍākeśa, Dhanañjaya, Kirīṭin, Phālguna, Savya-sācin and Pārtha.

ARUṆA : Son of Kaśyapa and Kadrū, he is supposed to be the charioteer of the Sun, and is conceived as thighless.

ARUNDHATĪ : The morning star fancied as the wife of sage Vaśiṣṭha, and an ideal wife.

AṢṬĀVAKRA : Name of a sage. Born with his eight (*aṣṭa*) limbs crooked (*vakra*) as a result of his father's curse,

ASURA : In the oldest parts of the *Ṛgveda* it denotes the Supreme Spirit. It was also used to apply to some chief deities, e.g. Indra, Agni, Varuṇa. In the later parts of the *Ṛgveda* and in later literature it came to signify a demon or enemy of gods.

AŚVATTHĀMAN : Son of Droṇācārya and a great fighter on the side of the Kauravas. He wrore a protective jewel on his head. Arjuna and Kṛṣṇa overpowered him, and took away the jewel from his head.

AŚVINĪ-KUMĀRA : Twins, sons of the Sun or the Sky. They are ever young and handsome and are parents of the Pāṇḍava princes, Nakula and Sahadeva. They are the physicians of gods.

ATRI : Name of a sage. Husband of Anasūyā (q.v.), and author of many Vedic hymns. Father of sage Durvāsas and supposed to be one of the stars of the Great Bear.

AVATĀRA : Literally 'descent'. Incarnation of a deity, particularly of Viṣṇu. The earliest indication of what developed into an Avatāra is contained in the mention of the three strides of Viṣṇu in the *Ṛgveda* (I. 154. 1-4). Another reference to the three steps and a kind of *Avatāra* is found in the *Taittirīya-saṃhitā* of the *Yajurveda*. The number and names of *Avatāras* differ acc. to different sources. The most commonly recognised *Avatāras* are : Matsya (Fish), Kūrma (Tortoise), Varāha (Boar), Nṛsiṃha (Man-lion), Vāmana (Dwarf), Rāma (son of Daśaratha), Paraśurāma, Balarāma, Buddha and Kalkin.

The *Bhāgavata-purāṇa* mentions 22 *Avatāras*, and adds that, in fact, these are innumerable. Jayadeva mentions 10 *Avatāras* in his *Gīta-govinda*.

The Avatāras are usually divided into three classes, viz. *Aṃśa*, *Kalā* and *Pūrṇa*.

[See K.D. Pandey, *Theory of Incarnation in Medieval Indian Literature*; A C. Sen, *The Hindu Avatāras*, Calcutta.]

BABHRŪ-VĀHANA : Son of Arjuna by his wife Citrāṅgadā. As king of Maṇipura he quarrelled with Arjuna over the latter's horse for *Aśvamedha*, and killed him.

BALABHADRA : See Balarāma.

BALARĀMA : Elder brother of Kṛṣṇa. He is represented as intoxicated and having the plough as his weapon.

BALI : A king of demons. He oppressed the gods and extended his authority over the three worlds. Viṣṇu in his Dwarf incarnation sent Bali to Pātāla, the infernal region.

BĀLIN : Monkey king of Kiṣkindhā, brother of Sugrīva and husband of Tārā. His son was Aṅgada. Hostile to Rāma who slew him. Believed to be son of Indra and born from the hair (*bāla*) of his mother.

BĀṆA : A demon, father of Uṣā (q.v.) and son of Bali. A friend of Śiva and an enemy of Viṣṇu. Also called Vairoci.

BHARADVĀJA : A sage said to have acquired Āyurvedic knowledge from Indra, and expounded it to other sages.

BHARATA : 1. Son of Śakuntalā and Duṣyanta.

2. Son of Daśaratha.

3. A sage to whom is ascribed the *Nāṭyaśāstra*, the earliest work on Dramaturgy.

4. Ancestor of the Bhāratas, a warlike race mentioned in the *Ṛgveda*.

5. A king of the first Manvantara, devoted to Viṣṇu.

BHĀRGAVA : A descendant of Bhṛgu. An epithet generally applied to Paraśurāma (q.v.).

BHĪMA : The second of the Pāṇḍava princes. A great warrior having a club as his weapon. He slew many demons, notably Hiḍimba and Vaka. While living *incognito* in the house of the king of Virāṭa he slew Kīcaka, brother-in-law of the king; Kīcaka insulted Draupadī when she refused to entertain his amorous advances. Among his mighty deeds in the battle of Kurukṣetra was his killing of Duḥśāsana, the drinking of his blood and the breaking of the thigh of Duryodhana. His last feat was the slaughter of the horse in the sacrifice performed by Yudhiṣṭhira at his accession to the throne.

BHĪṢMA: Son of Śāntanu by Gaṅgā. For the sake of his father he remained a lifelong celibate. Played a prominent part on the side of the Kauravas in the Kurukṣetra war. He fell through the treachery of Śikhaṇḍin, and embraced death at his will. Generally designated as Pitāmaha, he was a model of self-abnegation, devotion and fidelity. Acc. to the Śāntiparvan of the *Mahābhārata*, he delivered a long discourse on politics and *Rāja-dharma* as he lay dying.

BHṚGU : A Vedic sage. One of the Prajāpatis and founder of the race of Bhārgavas in which was born Paraśurāma.

BRAHMĀ: One of the famous triad in the Brahmanical pantheon, the other two being Viṣṇu and Maheśvara. Creation is believed to have emanated from Brahmā. The legend goes that, before creation, everything was enveloped in darkness. The Great Puruṣa dispelled the gloom, created water, and cast his seed into it. That seed developed into the Cosmic Egg of gold within which the Great Puruṣa resided as Brahmā. The Egg, having been into two parts, one part became the sky, while the other was the earth. Brahmā's wife was Sāvitrī. Devasenā and Daityasenā were his daughters.

[See T.P. Bhattacharya, *The Cult of Brahmā*, 2nd ed., 1969; I. Khan, *Brahmā in the Purāṇas*, Ghaziabad, 1981; *Some Graphical Purāṇic Texts on Brahmā*, Ghaziabad, 1981; G. Bailey, *Mythology of Brahmā*, Delhi, 1983. Also see T.P. Bhattacharya, The Avesta, Ṛgveda and Brahmā cult, *ABORI*, LI, 1970.]

BṚHASPATI: In the Ṛgveda, name of a deity designated as the Purohita (priest) of the gods. In later literature, he is a great sage, regent, of the planet Jupiter which itself is called Bṛhaspati. He is represented as preceptor of gods. Acc. to a legend, his wife, Tārā, was abducted by Soma (Moon).

[See H.R. Schmidt, *Bṛhaspati Und Indra*, Wiesbaden, 1968; S. Rali, *Bṛhaspati in the Vedas and Purāṇas*.]

CAITRARATHA: The garden of Kuvera on the Mandara hill; so called as it is supposed to be cultivated by Citraratha (q.v.)

CĀMUṆḌĀ: An emanation of goddess Durgā; so called from her slaying the demons Caṇḍa and Muṇḍa.

CAṆḌĪ: A form of Goddess Durgā, which she assumed for slaying the demon Mahiṣa.

CANDRAKETU: Son of Lakṣmaṇa (q.v.).

CĀRVĀKA: (1) A demon-friend of Duryodhana (q.v.).

(2) Name of a philosopher who did not accept Vedic

authority and advocated hedonism. The materialistic school of philosophy, founded by him, is called *Lokāyata*. His followers are also called Cārvākas.

CITRAGUPTA: Scribe of Yama. He records the virtues and vices of those who are dead.

CITRĀṄGADA: Elder son of Śāntanu (q.v.) by Satyavatī, brother of Vicitravīrya and half-brother of Bhīṣma.

CITRĀṄGADĀ: Daughter of a king of Maṇipura and wife of Arjuna.

CITRARATHA: King of the Gandharvas.

DAKṢA: Son of Brahmā and one of the Prajāpatis. He is famed as having performed a great sacrifice which was destroyed by Śiva, husband of Dakṣa's daughter named Satī.

DAŚARATHA: King of Ayodhyā, son of Aja. He had three wives, Kauśalyā, Kaikeyī and Sumitrā. They bore him sons called respectively Rāma, Bharata, Lakṣmaṇa and Śatrughna, the last two having been twins.
See Rāma.

DATTĀTREYA: Son of Atri and Anasūyā. A Brāhmaṇa saint sometimes regarded as an incarnation of Viṣṇu.

DEVAKĪ: Wife of Vasudeva and mother of Kṛṣṇa.

DEVAYĀNĪ: Daughter of Śukrācārya, priest of the Daityas. She fell in love with Kaca (q.v.) who rejected her. She was a companion of Śarmiṣṭhā (q.v.), daughter of the king of the Daityas. King Yayāti (q.v.) rescued her from a well into which she was thrown by Śarmiṣṭhā who became angry with her. She married Yayāti and made Śarmiṣṭhā her maid-servant.

DHANVANTARI: (1) Name of a Vedic deity. (2) Name of the physician of the gods. He was obtained at the churning of ocean. The science of *Āyurveda* is attributed to him. (3) A noted physician, one of the Nine Jewels of the court of Vikramāditya.

[See L. H. Gray, The Indian God Dhanavantari in *JAOS*, 1922.]

DHṚṢṬADYUMNA: Brother of Draupadī and commander-in-chief of the Pāṇḍava armies. He slew Droṇa and was slain by Droṇa's son Aśvatthāman.

DHṚTARĀṢṬRA: Eldest son of Vicitravīrya or Vyāsa, and brother of Pāṇḍu. By his wife Gāndhārī he had 100 sons of whom the eldest was Duryodhana. Dhṛtarāṣṭra was blind, and, along with Pāṇḍu, renounced the throne.

DHRUVA: Son of king Uttānapāda by his wife Sunīti. Through the machination of his step-mother Suruci, he was denied the throne. He performed severe austerities and obtained the grace of Viṣṇu who raised him to the sky as the Pole-star.

DHŪRJAṬI: A Name of Rudra-Śiva. Various derivative meanings of the word are suggested: one having matted locks (*jaṭā*) like a burden (*dhūr*); one who bears the burden of the three worlds; one whose matted locks are dark-red.

DITI: Daughter of Dakṣa, wife of Kaśyapa and mother of the Daityas. The Maruts are said to have been born to her.

DIVODĀSA: (1) A generous king mentioned in the *Ṛgveda*. (2) A Brāhmaṇa, twin brother of Ahalyā. (3) A king of Kāśī, son of Bhīmaratha and father of Pratardana.

DRAUPADĪ: Daughter of Drupada, king of Pañcāla, and common wife of the Pāṇḍavas. In gambling with Kauravas, Yudhiṣṭhira lost her to them. Thereupon, the Kauravas began to maltreat her. Duḥśāsana dragged her by the hair in presence of others and tore off her veil and dress. Duryodhana asked her to sit on his thigh. Highly incensed at these outrages, Bhīma promised to drink the blood of Duḥśāsana and smash the thigh of Duryodhana; promises which were eventually fulfilled.

Draupadī accompanied her husbands when they were in exile and lived *incognito*.

She is also known as Pāñcālī, Sairindhrī, Kṛṣṇā, Yājñasenī etc.

She is a model of chastity and well-known for righteous indignation.

DROṆA: A Brāhmaṇa who imparted military training to the Kauravas and Pāṇḍavas. He fought on the side of the Kauravas. He was father of Aśvatthāman.

DRUPADA: King of Pañcāla, and father of Draupadī.

DUḤŚALĀ: The only daughter of Dhṛtarāṣṭra, and wife of Jayadratha.

DUḤŚĀSANA: A brother of Duryodhana. His blood was drunk by Bhīma in the Kurukṣetra battle to take revenge for his insult to Draupadī (q.v.).

DURVĀSAS: A sage of extremely irascible temper. He cursed Śakuntalā (q.v.) for not having paid attention to him when he arrived as a guest.

DURYODHANA: Eldest son of Dhṛtarāṣtra. He defeated Yudhiṣṭhira in a game of dice, and appropriated the kingdom to himself after sending the Pāṇḍavas to exile. After Yudhiṣṭhira's defeat in the game, Duryodhana asked Draupadī to sit on his thigh. This enraged Bhīma who true to his vow, took revenge on him by smashing his thigh.
Also called Suyodhana (a good fighter).

DVAIPĀYANA: See Vyāsa.

EKALAVYA: Son of Hiraṇyadhanu, king of Niṣādas. Droṇācārya having refused to teach him archery as he was lowborn, he made a wooden image of Droṇa and began practising archery before it with devotion and zeal. Soon he became an adept in it, and surpassed even Arjuna, the most favourite pupil of Droṇa. Arjuna having resented Ekalavya's superior skill, Droṇa asked for Ekalavya's right thumb as *Guru-dakṣiṇā* (preceptor's fee) and thus curbed his capacity for skilfully wielding the bow.

GĀDHI: A king of the Kuśika race, and father of Viśvāmitra.

GĀNDHĀRĪ: Princess of Gandhāra, wife of Dhṛtarāṣṭra and mother of 100 sons of whom the eldest was Duryodhana.

GANDHARVA: The Gandharvas are regarded as semi-divine beings. In the Ṛgveda, Gandharva was a minor god living in the sky and guarding the sacred Soma.

[See S.S. Moghe, The Gandharvas in the Rāmāyaṇa, *Summaries of Papers*, AIOC, Silver Jubilee Session, 1969, p. 68.]

GAṆEŚA: A deity represented as having a human body with the head and face of an elephant. He is also described as having a rat as his mount. He is called *Siddhi-dātā* (giver of success). [See A. Getty, *Gaṇeśa*, 1972.] For Gaṇeśa and Gaṇaspati cult in India and S. Asia, see B.N. Puri in *Ṛtam*. (Lucknow Jour), X, 1, 2 pp 109 ff.

GĀṄGEYA: Epithet of Bhīṣma, derived from his mother Gaṅgā.

GĀRGĪ : Daughter of Vacaknu and a highly intellectual lady.

For her metaphysical discussion with Yājñavalkya, see the *Bṛhadāraṇyakopaniṣad*.

GARUḌA: King of birds, descended from Kaśyapa and Vinatā and used by Viṣṇu as his mount. He is supposed to have the body of a man and the head, wings, talons and the beak of an eagle.

GAUTAMA: A sage, husband of Ahalyā (q.v.).

GHAṬOTKACA: Son of Bhīma by the demoness Hiḍimbā. Killed in the great battle by Karṇa.

GṚTSAMADA: A famous seer to whom many hymns of the second book of the *Ṛgveda* are attributed. Acc. to a legend, he assumed the form of Indra and thus saved him from the demons who planned to kill him. Different versions of the story exist. The common element of the divergent versions is that the sage saved himself from the demons, who took him to be Indra, by reciting a hymn (*Ṛgveda*, II. 12) glorifying Indra who was somebody else.

GUḌĀKEŚA: An epithet of Arjuna (q.v.) and also of Mahādeva. It means one who has conquered sleep or whose hair is in tufts.

HAIHAYA: (1) A prince of the lunar race, and great-grandson of Yadu.

(2) A race of people probably of the Scythian origin. Kārtavīryārjuna, a king of the Haihayas, was defeated by Paraśurāma who chopped off his arms.

HALABHṚT: Same as Balarāma (q.v.).

HANŪMAT (HANUMAT): The famous monkey-chief who was extremely devoted to Rāma. Of divine origin, he performed many wonderful deeds and assisted Rāma in conquering Rāvaṇa. Among his exploits the more noteworthy are his burning of Laṅkā and carrying the mountain on which grew the medicine for healing wounds. Son of Marut (wind) and Añjanā, he had the patronymic Māruti and the matronymic Āñjaneya.

HARA: Name of Śiva (q.v.).

HARI: Name of Viṣṇu (q.v.).

HARIŚCANDRA: Son of Triśaṅku and a king of the solar race. He incurred the displeasure of sage Viśvāmitra who reduced him to utter destitution. Left with nothing but a bark-garment, wife and son he was obliged to sell them in order to satisfy the intransigent demand of the sage. At last he sold himself to a Caṇḍāla. Then, through the intervention of gods, he ascended heaven. For a fault he was expelled from heaven. While falling down, he was absolved of sin due to repentance and, as a result, his downward course was checked so that he began to live in an aerial city.

HIḌIMBĀ: A demoness, sister of Hiḍimba. She was enamoured of Bhīma who, at his mother's desire, married her and by her got a son named Ghaṭotkaca.

HIRAṆYAKAŚIPU: A chief of the Daityas and a twin-brother of Hiraṇyākṣa. A hater of Viṣṇu, he persecuted his son, Prahlāda, for worshipping that god. Hiraṇyakaśipu was slain by Viṣṇu in his Man-lion form.

HIRAṆYĀKṢA: A Daitya, twin brother of Hiraṇyakaśipu and killed by Viṣṇu in the Boar Incarnation.

HṚṢĪKEŚA: Literally meaning 'the lord or conqueror of the five sensory organs', it is an epithet of Kṛṣṇa or Viṣṇu.

IKṢVĀKU: Son of Manu Vaivasvata, he was founder of the solar race of kings and king of Ayodhyā at the beginning of the *Tretāyuga.*

INDRA: Lord of gods. His wife is Śacī. Often at war with the demons, he slew Vṛtra. For having seduced or attempted to seduce Ahalyā, her husband, sage Gautama, cursed Indra. As a result, he had on his body 1000 marks resembling the female organ. Later on, these marks were transformed into eyes, and he was designated Sahasrākṣa (thousand-eyed). Mahendra, Śakra, Maghavan and Vāsava are some of his other names. Of his many epithets the common are Vṛtrahan, Vajrapāṇi, Pākaśāsana, Purandara and Śatakratu. His heaven is Svarga and capital Amarāvatī. His elephant is Airāvata, horse Uccaiḥśravas and charioteer Mātali. The name of of his son is Jayanta.

[See H.P. Schmidt, *Bṛhaspati Und Indra, Wiesboden,* 1968; U. Chaudhary, *Indra and Varuṇa in Indian Mythology,* Delhi, 1981; K.D. Vajpai, Indra in early literature and art, *Pro. AIOC,* 1966; P.L. Bhargava Comparative Antiquity of Indra and Varuṇa, *Sternbach Fel. Vol.,* Lucknow.]

INDRAJIT: Rāvaṇa's son Meghanāda. He fought gallantly for Rāvaṇa against Rāma. He is stated to have been killed by Lakṣmaṇa while engaged in a sacrifice.

JAHNU: A sage who is said to have drunk up the waters of the Ganges which disturbed his devotions. Afterwards he allowed the river to flow through his ear. Hence it is called Jāhnavī (daughter of Jahnu).

JAMADAGNI: A descendant of Bhṛgu and father of Paraśurāma. He killed Kārtavīrya (q.v.) who stole the calf of his sacred cow Surabhi. In revenge the sons of Kārtavīrya slew Jamadagni.

JĀMBAVAT: King of the bears. He, with his army of bears, rendered considerable assistance to Rāma in his fight against Rāvaṇa, and gave Rāma wise counsel. Over the jewel Syamantaka there was a fight between Kṛṣṇa and Jāmbavat. The latter had to submit, gave up the jewel and presented his daughter Jāmbavatī, to the former.

JANAKA: (1) King of Mithilā, who preceded Janaka, father of Sīta, by 20 generations.

(2) King of Videha and father of Sītā. Yājñavalkya was his priest and counsellor.

JĀNAKĪ: A patronymic of Sītā (q.v.).

JANAMEJAYA: A renowned king, son of Parīkṣit and great-grandson of Arjuna. His father having died of snakebite, he performed the great serpent-sacrifice with a view to exterminating serpents.

JARĀSANDHA: A King of Magadha, son of Bṛhadratha. Each of the two wives of Bṛhadratha gave birth to half the body of the boy. These two parts, which were thrown away, were joined together by a demoness called Jarā; hence the name Jarāsandha (joined by Jarā). He fought with Kṛṣṇa, the slayer of Kaṃsa, husband of two of Jarāsandha's daughters. Jarāsandha was killed by Bhīma in an encounter.

JARATKĀRU: A sage, husband of a sister of Vāsuki (q.v.) and father of sage Āstika.

JAṬĀYU (JAṬĀYUS): Son of Garuḍa, acc. to some sources, and of Aruṇa, acc. to others. A friend of Daśaratha and an ally of Rāma. He resisted Rāvaṇa when the latter was carrying off Sītā. Rāvaṇa left him seriously wounded. It was from him that Rāma learnt what had happened to Sītā.

JAYADRATHA: King of Sindhu and husband of Duḥśalā, daughter of Dhṛtarāṣṭra. An ally of the Kauravas, he tried to seduce Draupadī from her forest-abode during the temporary absence of Pāṇḍavas. Draupadī spurned his advances, and her husband on return made him captive. He was slain by Arjuna on the fourteenth day of the Kurukṣetra battle.

JĪMŪTAVĀHANA: A prince of the Vidyādharas, and husband of Malayavatī, princess of the Siddhas. Out of sympathy for the serpents, killed by Garuḍa, he offered himself to Garuḍa with request to spare the serpents. Killed by Garuḍa, he was brought back to life by Gaurī.

KACA: Son of Bṛhaspati and disciple of Śukrācārya. Devayānī (q.v.) fell in love with him, but he rejected her. Then she cursed him to the effect, that the charms he had learnt from her father would be futile. He in his turn, cursed her that she would be the wife of a Kṣatriya, not of a Brāhmaṇa.

KADRŪ: Daughter of Dakṣa, a wife of Kaśyapa and mother of 1000 powerful serpents the chief among whom were Śeṣa and Vāsuki.

KAIKEYĪ: Princess of Kaikeya, a wife of Daśaratha and mother of Bharata. When Rāma was about to be installed on the throne she, at the instigation of her female attendant, Mantharā, asked Daśaratha for the fulfilment of the two promises he made to her as a reward for her past services. Of the two requests she made, one was that Rāma should be banished and the other that Bharata should be crowned.

KAIṬABHA: A demon who, along with Madhu, is said to have sprung from the ear of Viṣṇu who was asleep at the end of a Kalpa. When they were about to kill Brahmā lying on the lotus emanating from Viṣṇu's navel, Viṣṇu killed them. Acc. to a legend, the earth received the name of Medinī from the marrow (*medas*) of these demons.

KĀLANEMI: (1) in the *Rāmāyaṇa* he is an uncle of Rāvaṇa. At Rāvaṇa's request and offer of half of his Kingdom he tried to kill Hanūmat. He could not do so, and was rather roughly handled by Hanūmat.

(2) In the Purāṇas he is a great Asura, son of Virocana, grandson of Hiraṇyakaśipu. He was killed by Viṣṇu, but is said to have lived again as Kaṃsa and Kāliya.

KĀLAPRIYANĀTHA: Mentioned, in all the three dramas of Bhavabhūti. Identified with Śiva by some, with the sun by others.

[See V.V. Mirashi in *V. Raghavan Fel. Vol.*, Delhi, 1975.]

KALI: *Kali-yuga*, embodiment of evil spirit.

KĀLIYA: A serpent-king with five heads. Living in a pool of the Yamunā he emitted fire and smoke through his mouth and oppressed those living around him. Kṛṣṇa, even as a boy, subdued him and forced him to live in the ocean.

KALKI: The tenth incarnation of Viṣṇu who, it is believed, will appear at the end of *Kali-Age*, seated on a white horse and holding a drawn sword, for the destruction of the wicked, renovation of creation and restoration of order.

KĀMA: Also called Madana, Pañcabāṇa, Anaṅga, Kandarpa, Puṣpa-śara (or, -dhanvan), Makaraketu etc., he is Cupid having Rati as his wife. He is represented as armed with a bow; his arrows are the flowers called Aravinda, Aśoka Cūta, Navamallikā and Raktotpala. At the behest of gods, he disturbed the meditation of Śiva so that Śiva's marriage with Pārvatī might be brought about. The three-eyed Śiva having seen him on opening his eyes, burnt him to ashes by the fire emanating from his central eye. Afterwards Śiva relented and caused him to be born as Pradyumna, son of Kṛṣṇa and Rukmiṇī. He is often described as a handsome youth riding on a parrot and accompanied by nymphs one of whom carries a banner marked with the sign of Makara or a fish.

KĀMADHENU: A cow of Vaśiṣṭha, granting desires, obtained at the churning of the ocean.

KAṂSA: King of Mathurā, son of Ugrasena and cousin of Devakī, mother of Kṛṣṇa. It was predicted that a son o Devakī would kill him. So, he tried to put all the sons of Devakī to death. When her eighth son, Kṛṣṇa was born his parents fled with him. Thereupon, Kaṃsa persecuted Kṛṣṇa who at last slew him.

KANDARPA: See Kāma.

KARṆA: Son of Kuntī by the Sun-god before her marriage, and born equipped with an armour and a pair of protective ear-rings. Cast away by his mother on the Yamunā for fear of calumny, he was picked up by Adhiratha, charioteer of Dhṛtarāṣṭra, who with his wife Rādhā reared him up as their own son. He became a great warrior and a powerful ally of Kauravas who made him king of Aṅga. Indra, disguised as a Brāhmaṇa, persuaded him to part with his divine cuirass. He fought the Pāṇḍavas, and was finally killed by Arjuna. The Pāṇḍavas did not know his identity before his death.

KĀRTAVĪRYA: A patronymic of Arjuna, king of the Haihayas. Endowed with a thousand arms, he stole the calf of the cow of Jamadagni. In revenge, Paraśurāma, Jamadagni's son, severed his arms and killed him. Contemporary of Rāvaṇa, he is said to have made him captive when Rāvaṇa invaded his territory. Acc. to a legend, he invaded Laṅkā where he made Rāvaṇa a prisoner.

KĀRTIKEYA: God of war, son of Śiva and also called Kumāra, Skanda, Guha etc. Born for destroying Tāraka, a demon, who, as a result of austerities, became a formidable oppressor of gods. Represented as riding on a peacock and holding a bow in one hand and an arrow in another.

[See A.K. Chatterjee, *The Cult of Skanda-kārtikeya in ancient India*, Calcutta, 1970; V.M. Bedekar in *ABORI*, Vol. LVI, 1975, pp. 141-177; U. Thakur, *On Kārtikeya*, Varanasi, 1981.]

KAURAVA: An epithet meaning 'son or descendant of Kuru' (q.v.), applied to the sons of Dhṛtarāṣṭra (q.v.). The Kauravas are believed by some modern scholars to have flourished in the tenth century B.C.

KAUŚALYĀ: The eldest queen of Daśaratha and mother of Rāma.

KAUŚIKA: An epithet of Viśvāmitra (q.v.).

KAUSTUBHA: A renowned jewel obtained at the churning of the ocean and worn by Kṛṣṇa or Viṣṇu on his bosom.

KHARA: A Rākṣasa, younger brother of Rāvaṇa, who was killed by Rāma.

KĪCAKA: Brother-in-law of the king of Virāṭa. He made illicit advances to Draupadī during the Pāṇḍava's stay *incognito*. She rejected him, and he was slain by Bhīma.

KIMPURUṢA: 1. A part of Jambudvīpa (q.v.).

2. A synonym of Kinnara (q.v.).

KINNARA: A class of mythical beings with the bodies of men and heads of horses. Living on Kailāsa, they are celestial musicians endowed with a fine voice.

KIRĪṬIN: An epithet of Arjuna and also of Indra.

KṚPA: Adopted son of king Śāntanu. One of the trusted counsellors of the Kauravas and one of the warriors who made the nocturnal attack on the camp of the Pāṇḍavas.

KṚṢṆA: The word occurs in the *Ṛgveda*, but not as the name of a deity. Kṛṣṇa, son of Devakī, is mentioned for the first time in the *Chāndogya Upaniṣad* (III. 17.6) where he appears to be a scholar. From a Vedic hymn the word appears to refer to Rākṣasas or dark-skinned aborigines of India.

In the *Mahābhārata*, Kṛṣṇa appears to have been a great hero and diplomat siding with the Pāṇḍavas and bringing about the fall of the Kauravas. Acc. to the Vaiṣṇavas, he is none but God Himself. A mass of legends has gathered round him. The highlights of these legends are as follows. In his boyhood he enjoyed himself at Vṛndāvana in sports with the cowherd boys and wives of cowherds. Of the latter, his most favourite was Rādhā. He became king of Mathurā and Dvārakā.

Among his exploits were the subjugation in his boyhood, of the serpent-king Kāliya, the upholding of the Govardhana mountain, the killing of Śiśupāla and Kaṃsa. He was the son of Vasudeva by Devakī, and belonged to the Yadu race. He is represented in his boyhood as tending cows in Vṛndāvana with a flute in hand. Later on, he is described as holding a discus called Sudarśana.

Similarity of the two names and of some incidents in the life of both have led some scholars to believe that the legend of Kṛṣṇa originated from the life of Christ.

Stories of his life are elaborately related in the *Bhāgavata Purāṇa*. That Kṛṣṇa is God Himself is sought to be established in the *Śrīkṛṣṇa-sandarbha* of Jīva Gosvāmin of Bengal. In the Kurukṣetra war, he is represented as Charioteer of Arjuna, his bosom friend, exhorting him with what is called *Bhagavad-gītā* in order to rouse him to action when he felt dejected seeing near and dear ones among his adversaries.

On Kṛṣṇa representing a synthesis of Aryan and non-Aryan cultures, see S.K. Chatterji in *Jour. of Royal Asiatic Soc. of Bengal*, 1950. The same scholar and some other eminent scholars are inclined to assign Kṛṣṇa to the tenth century B.C.

For a résumé of different views on the question as to whether Kṛṣṇa was a historical personage or a deity, as well as for references to main works and papers dealing with the Kṛṣṇa problem, see A.D. Pusalker, *Studies in the Epics and Purāṇas*, Bombay, 1955. Also see Buddha Prakash, Kṛṣṇa, *Gode Comm. Vol.*, 1960 (III); Bankim Chattopadhyay, *Kṛṣṇa-Caritra* in Bengali.

[See K.M. Munshi, Krishṇāvatāra, 3 Vols. (ed.) M.S. Randhawa, *Krishna Legend*; M. Singer (ed.) *Krishna: Myths, Rites and attitudes*, Honolulu, 1966. (Collection of papers by different scholars). Also see D.N. Pal, *Śrī Krishna—his life and teaching*; R.S. Betai, *Place of Śrī Kṛṣṇa etc.*, G. Jha Res. Inst., Allahabad; B.B. Majumdar, *Kṛṣṇa in history and legend*, Calcutta, 1969; P. Pal, *Krishna, the cowherd King*; S.L. Katre, *Kṛṣṇa and the Mahābhārata War*; Bhaktivedantaswami, *Krishna* etc. 2 Vols., 1970; M.L. Sen, *Lord Śrī Kṛṣṇa, his life and teachings*, Vols. I-III, Calcutta; S.K. Bhattacharya, *Kṛṣṇa Cult*, New Delhi, 1978; D.R. Kinsley, *The Divine Player*, Delhi, 1979; J.D. Redington, *Vallabhācārya on the love-games of Kṛṣṇa*. B.P.-Salis, *The Kṛṣṇa Cycle in the Purāṇas*; R.K. Kubba, *Kṛṣṇakāvya in Skt. lit. with special ref. to Śrī Kṛṣṇa Vijaya, Rukmiṇi kalyāṇa* and *Harivilāsa*, Delhi, 1982.]

KṚṢṆĀ: Name of Draupadī.

KṚṢṆA DVAIPĀYANA: See Vyāsa.

KUMBHAKARṆA: Brother of Rāvaṇa. He used to sleep for six months at a stretch. In the battle against Rāma he worsted Sugrīva, but was at last slain by Rāma.

KUNTĪ: Also called Pṛthā, she was a wife of Pāṇḍu and mother of the Pāṇḍavas called Yudhiṣṭhira, Arjuna and Bhīma. She had a son, Karṇa, by the Sun-god before her marriage. After the Kurukṣetra war she retired to the forest with Dhṛtarāṣṭra and Gāndhārī. It is said that they all perished there in a forest-fire.

KURU: A king of the Lunar race, and ancestor of both Dhṛtarāṣṭra and Pāṇḍu. The patronymic Kaurava is, however, generally used to refer to the sons of Dhṛtarāṣṭra.

KUŚA: Son of Rāma. After Rāma's death he became king of South Kosala, and made Kuśāvatī his capital.

KUŚADHVAJA: Brother of Janaka, father of Sītā. His daughters Māṇḍavī and Śrutakīrti were married respectively to Bharata and Śatrughna, sons of Daśāratha.

KUVERA: Living in Alakā on Kailāsa he is the god of wealth, waited upon by Kinnaras. Half-brother of Rāvaṇa, he is said to have once got Laṅkā in his possession. Owner of the aerial car Puṣpaka, he is the regent of the northern direction. He is represented as white, deformed in body, having three legs and only eight teeth.

He has the patronymic Vaiśravaṇa and has, *inter alia*, the epithets Rāja-rāja, Yakṣa-rāja, Nara-rāja etc.

[See V.M. Bedekar, Kubera in Skt. Literature, with special ref. to the Mahābhārata, *Jour. of G. Jha Res. Inst.*, Allahabad XXV, Pts 1-4, 1969; S. G. Modhey, God Kubera in the Rāmāyaṇa, *Summaries of Papers*, AIOC, 1969, p. 93.]

LAKṢMAṆA: (1) Son of Daśaratha by Sumitrā and a half-brother of Rāma. A constant companion of Rāma whom he followed in exile. Husband of Ūrmilā, he had two sons named Aṅgada and Candraketu. He cut off the nose and ears of Śūrpaṇakhā, sister of Rāvaṇa, in the forest where he had been living with Rāma, and played an important part in the war against Rāvaṇa. (2) A son Duryodhana killed by Abhimanyu.

LAKṢMĪ: Wife of Viṣṇu and mother of Kāma, she is the goddess of fortune and arose, lotus in hand, at the churning of the ocean. She was Viṣṇu's consort in his various forms. Thus, she was Dharaṇī when he was born as Paraśurāma, Sītā when he was Rāma and Rukmiṇī when he was Kṛṣṇa. Some of her other names are Padmā, Indirā, Jaladhijā, etc.

[See D. C. Sircar, *Foreigners of Ancient India and Lakṣmī and Sarasvatī in Art and Literature*; V.S. Patil. Is Lakṣmī a metamorphosis of Vedic Uṣas, *Summaries of Papers*, AIOC, 1974: U.N. Dhol, Lakṣmī in the Purāṇapañcalakṣaṇa Texts, Ibid; *Goddess Laksmi*, New Delhi, 1978; N. Ghosh, Concept and Iconography of the Goddess of Abundance and Fortune in three religions of India, 1979; C. Sivaramamurti *Sri Lakṣmī in Indian Art and Thought*. New Delhi, 1982.]

LAVA: One of the twin sons of Rāma. After Rāma's death he became the king of Northern Kosala with Śrāvastī as his capital.

LOKAPĀLA: Guardian of the world. The guardian-deities, presiding over the eight points of the compass, are (1) Indra—east; (2) Agni—south-east; (3) Yama—south; (4) Sūrya—south-west; (5) Varuṇa—west; (6) Vāyu—north-west; (7) Kuvera—north; (4) Soma—north-east. Some substitute Nirṛti for Sūrya and Pṛthivī or Śiva (esp. in his form as Īśāna) for Soma. These guardian-deities have each an elephant. These elephants, taking part in the defence of the quarters, are themselves called Lokapālas.

LOMAPĀDA: King of Aṅga. He brought up Śāntā, daughter of Daśaratha, and gave her in marriage with sage Ṛṣyaśṛṅga.

LOPĀMUDRĀ: A girl whom sage Agastya made with the most beautiful parts of different animals and kept in the palace of the king of Vidarbha where she was brought up as the daughter of that king. Subsequently Agastya married her.

The significance of the name is that the animals sustained loss (*lopa*) by her appropriating their distinctive beauties (*mudrā*), e.g. the beauty of the eyes of a deer.

[See S. Ratna, The Legend ol Agastya and Lopāmudrā, *Summaries of Papers, AIOC,* 1974.]

MADANA: See Kāma.

MADHUSŪDANA: Slayer of Madhu, a demon. A name of Kṛṣṇa.

MĀDRĪ: Sister of king of the Madras and second wife of Pāṇḍu. Mother of the twin Pāṇḍavas, Nakula and Sahadeva, she immolated herself on the funeral pyre of her husband.

MAHĀKĀLA: A name of god Śiva.

MAHENDRA: A name of god Indra.

MAHEŚVARA: Same as Śiva (q.v.).

MAITREYĪ: Wife of sage Yājñavalkya initiated by her husband into the mysteries of religion and philosophy. For the famous conversation between the husband and the wife, see *Bṛhadāraṇyaka Upaniṣad*, II. 4.

MAKARAKETU: See Kāma.

MĀṆḌAVĪ: Daughter of Kuśadhvaja and wife of Bharata, brother of Rāma.

MĀNDHĀTṚ: A king, son of Yuvanāśva. Acc. to some Purāṇas, he issued forth from the body of Yuvanāśva. There being nobody to suckle the child, Indra gave his finger to be sucked with the words *mām ayaṃ dhāsyati*. Thus he was called Māndhātā from the words *Māṃ* and *Dhātā*.

MANDODARĪ: The favourite wife of Rāvaṇa and mother of Indrajit.

MANMATHA: Name of Kāma (q.v.).

MANTHARĀ: A hunch-backed female attendant of Kaikeyī. She instigated the queen to seek Rāma's exile and Bharata's coronation in his place.

MANU: Name borne by the fourteen mythological progenitors of mankind and rulers of the earth. Each of them is supposed to rule the earth for a *Manvantara* (age of Manu) extending over 4,320,000 years. The first of the Manus is called Svāyaṃbhuva as he is supposed to have sprung from Svayaṃbhū, the self-existent one. The *Smṛti* work, called *Manu-saṃhitā* or *Manu-smṛti* (q.v.), is attributed to this Manu who is believed also to have composed the *Mānava Kalpasūtra*. See Manu under Authors (Part I).

With Vaivasvata Manu, the seventh Manu, is connected the story of Deluge in which all but Manu are said to have perished, Manu having been rescued by a fish which he reared up from its infancy. The story occurs in the *Śatapatha Brāhmaṇa* (Mādhyandina recension), 1.8.1, the *Mahābhārata*, III. 187, the *Matsya-purāṇa*, 1. 12, the *Bhāgavata-purāṇa* viii. 24. 7 ff and in the *Agni-purāṇa*.

MANVANTARA: See under Manu.

MĀRĪCA: A Rākṣasa, son of Tārakā. He disturbed a sacrifice performed by sage Viśvāmitra. As a minister of Rāvaṇa, he accompanied him to the forest where Rāma and Sītā had been living. Mārīca assumed the form of a golden deer which Rāma chased at the request of Sītā. In the meantime Rāvaṇa carried off Sītā.

MĀRKAṆḌEYA: A sage, son of Mṛkaṇḍa, reputed as the author of the *Mārkaṇḍeya-purāṇa*.

MĀTALI: Name of Indra's charioteer.

MAYA: A Daitya and architect of the Asuras. Father of Mandodarī, wife of Rāvaṇa, he used to live on the Devagiri mountain. In the *Mahābhārata* he is said to have built a palace for the Pāṇḍavas.

MENĀ (MENAKĀ): (1) Wife of Himālaya and mother of Umā. (2) A nymph commissioned to seduce Viśvāmitra by whom she got a daughter named Śakuntalā (q.v.).

MUCUKUNDA: Son of Māndhātā, he helped the gods in their wars against the Asuras.

NACIKETAS: Son of Āruṇi. His story is told in the *Taittirīya Brāhmaṇa* and the *Kaṭhopaniṣad*. He incurred the displeasure of his father who condemned him to death. In the abode of Yama all kinds of blessings were offered to him. But, he would not be satisfied with anything but a true knowledge of the soul. Yama then started telling him the mysteries of the soul.

NAHUṢA: Father of Yayāti. By austerities and sacrifices he attained the status of Indra. There he wanted to have Śacī as his wife. As he was carried in a car drawn by sages, he spurred sage Agastya with his foot urging him to move faster. The sage, incensed at this, reduced him to a serpent. Through Yudhiṣṭhira's instrumentality he was released from this state and ascended heaven.

NAKULA: The fourth of the Pāṇḍavas, son of the Aśvins and Mādrī; twin brother of Sahadeva. He was taught by Droṇa to train and manage horses. An *Aśva-śāstra* is attributed to him.

NALA: King of Niṣadha and husband of Damayantī. The story of Nala-Damayantī is a well-known episode of the *Mahābhārata* (III. 50—70). See *Naiṣadha-carita*.

NAMUCI: A demon slain by Indra.

NANDI: Name of Śiva's bull who is the chief of his personal attendants.

NANDINĪ: Daughter of Kāmadhenu called Surabhi (q.v.), she belonged to sage Vaśiṣṭha.

NĀRADA: A sage, inventor of the lute (*viṇā*) and chief of the Gandharvas or celestial musicians. A friend and close associate of Kṛṣṇa. He is represented as very crafty and causing quarrel. A friend and associate of Kṛṣṇa, the sage induced him to take up arms against Śiśupāla (q.v.). To this sage some hymns of the *Ṛgveda* are ascribed. A *Nāradīya-dharma-śāstra* and a *Nāradīya-śikṣā* are attributed to him. He is also credited with the authorship of the *Pañcamasāra-saṃhitā*, a work on music. He is one of the Prajāpatis and one of the seven great Ṛṣis.

Legends about him occur, besides the *Ṛgveda*, in some Purāṇas, notably the *Viṣṇu-purāṇa* and the *Nārada-pañcarātra*. Acc. to the *Viṣṇu-purāṇa*, he was son of Kaśyapa and a daughter of Dakṣa.

[P.K. Savalapurkar, *Devarshi Nārada*, Nagpur, 1976.]

NARAKA: (1) An Asura, son of the Earth and king of Prāgjyotiṣa. He was a formidable enemy of the gods.

(2) Hell. A place where souls of the wicked persons and of sinners are subjected to torments in the other world. Authorities differ as to the names and number of hells. Manu (iv. 88–90) enumerates 21 hells.

NARASIṂHA: Viṣṇu in his Man-lion incarnation. See Hiraṇyakaśipu.

NĀRĀYAṆA: (1) Son of Nara, the first man. (2) Creator Brahmā, so called because waters (*nārā*) were his first shelter (*ayana*).

The word occurs, for the first time, in the *Śatapatha Brāhmaṇa*, and is generally used to denote Viṣṇu.

NIKAṢĀ: A female demon, mother of Rāvaṇa.

NIKUMBHA: (1) A Rākṣasa, son of Kumbhakarṇa, who fought against Rāma and died. (2) An Asura, brother of Tripura, who received a boon from Brahmā to the effect that he would die only at the hands of Viṣṇu. (3) A demon, brother of demon-king Vajranābha. In a fight he lost his life at the hands of Kṛṣṇa.

NIRṚTI: A malefic Vedic goddess.

[C. Chakrabarti, *Common Life in the Ṛgveda and Atharvaveda* pp. 55, 64, 69, 72, 74 etc. S. Bhattacharya, Vedic goddess Nirṛti, *Anvīkṣā* (*Jour. of Jadabpur University*, Calcutta), Vol. I, 1966.]

PĀKAŚĀSANA: Epithet of Indra.

PAÑCABĀṆA: See Kāma.

PĀÑCAJANYA: Name of Kṛṣṇa's conch made of the bones of the sea-demon Pañcajana.

PĀÑCĀLĪ: Draupadī was so called as she belonged to the region called Pañcāla.

PĀṆḌAVA: Son of Pāṇḍu (q.v.). These were five Pāṇḍavas, viz. Yudhiṣṭhira, Bhīma, Arjuna, Nakula, and Sahadeva, the first three having been born to Kuntī and the last two to Mādrī. The Pāṇḍavas are believed by some eminent modern scholars to have flourished in the tenth century B.C.

PĀṆḌU: Brother of Dhṛtarāṣṭra and father of the Pāṇḍavas. His two wives were Kuntī and Mādrī. He was begotten by Vyāsa on Ambālikā, wife of Vicitravīrya. So called from the fact that his mother turned pale (*pāṇḍu*) at the sight of Vyāsa when the latter had sexual intercourse with her.

PAṆIS: In the *Ṛgveda* they are represented as a class of aerial demons hostile to Indra. They stole cows which were recovered by Saramā (q.v.). See *Ṛgveda*, X. 108.

[See N. G. Chapekar, Paṇis, *Oriental Thought*, Nasik, 2 (2-3).

PARĀŚARA: Acc. to a legend, he was father of Kṛṣṇa Dvaipāyana Vyāsa by an amour with Satyavatī (q.v.). For Parāśara, author of a *Smṛti* work, see under Authors (Part I).

PARAŚURĀMA: Son of Jamadagni and Reṇukā, he was an incarnation of *Viṣṇu*. He was an opponent of Rāma, son of Daśaratha, who overpowered him. At his father's command he killed his mother. Kārtavīrya, a Kṣatriya king of the Haihaya dynasty, stole a sacrificial calf of Jamadagni. Paraśurāma was highly enraged and killed Kārtavīrya. In revenge, Kārtavīrya's sons killed Jamadagni. Then Paraśurāma took the vow of clearing the earth of Kṣatriyas which he did for 21 times. He is represented as carrying an axe as his weapon.

[See J. Charpentier, Paraśurāma, *Kuppuswami Sastri Vol.*, Madras, 1937.]

PĀRIJĀTA: The tree produced at the churning of the ocean

and placed in Indra's heaven. It yielded wonderfully fragrant flowers.

PARĪKṢIT: Son of Abhimanyu, grandson of Arjuna and father of Janamejaya. He was killed by Aśvatthāman in the womb of his mother. Born dead, he was restored to life by Kṛṣṇa. He succeeded Yudhiṣṭhira to the throne of Hastināpura, and died of snake-bite.

PARJANYA: God of rain.

PĀRTHA: An epithet of the three older Pāṇḍavas, sons of Pṛthā or Kuntī, but particularly applied to Arjuna.

PĀRVATĪ: Daughter of Himālaya and wife of Śiva. Also called Umā.

PAŚUPATI: 'Lord of creatures'. A name of Rudra.

PHĀLGUNA: (1) Name of Arjuna. (2) Name of a month.

PĪṬHASTHĀNA: 'Place of seat'. Fifty-one places where, acc. to Tantras, the different limbs of the body of Satī fell while it was being carried and torn to pieces. Also see Satī.

[See D.C. Sircar, *Śākta Pīṭhas*-]

PRADYUMNA : Son of Kṛṣṇa by Rukmiṇī and father of Aniruddha.

PRAHLĀDA (PRAHRĀDA) : Son of Hiraṇyakaśipu and father of Bali. Angered by his ardent devotion to Viṣṇu, his father tried to kill him by various means which, however, proved abortive. See Somaśarman.

PRAJĀPATI : Lord of creatures. In the Veda, it denotes Indra, Savitṛ, Soma, Hiraṇyagarbha and some other deities. In the *Manu-smṛti*, it stands for Brahmā. The following ten sages, supposed to be fathers of the human race, are designated as Prajāpatis: Marīci, Atri, Aṅgiras, Pulastya, Pulaha, Kratu, Vaśiṣṭha, Pracetas or Dakṣa, Bhṛgu and Nārada. The number and names of Prajāpatis vary acc. to different authorities.

[See J. Gonda, Notes on Prajāpati, *Purāṇa*, 1982; S.Banerjee, Prajāpati in the Brāhmaṇas, *Vishweshvarananda Indological Jour*; XIX, Pts. I, II, 1981; S. Bhattacharji's Prajāpati as Time the Creator, *Anvīkṣā* (Jour. of Jadabpur University, Calcutta), V.P. III, Pt. 2; Vol. IV, Pt. I, 1969-70; The Rise of Prajāpati in the Brāhmaṇas, *Pro. of Winter Seminar*, Poona, 1980.]

PRAMATHA: A class of demi-gods attending on Śiva.

PṚTHĀ: Name of Kuntī.

PṚTHU: A king of the Solar race, a descendant of Ikṣvāku.

PURAÑJAYA: Son of Vikukṣi, he was a prince of the Solar race. Seated on the hump of a bull, the form of which was assumed by Indra, Purañjaya destroyed the enemies of gods. As he sat on the hump (*kakut*), he was called Kakutstha.

PUROCANA: An emissary of Duryodhana, he tried to burn the Pāṇḍavas in their house and was himself burnt in his own house by Bhīma.

PŪRU: A king of the Lunar race, son of Yayāti and Śarmiṣṭhā.

PURŪRAVAS: She under Characters (Part III).

PURUṢOTTAMA: Epithet of Viṣṇu.

PUṢPAKA: An aerial car of huge size. Kuvera obtained it from Brahmā, but it was taken away by Rāvaṇa. Rāma took it after slaying Rāvaṇa, used it while returning from Laṅkā to Ayodhyā and restored it to Kuvera.

PUṢPA-ŚARA (or -DHANVAN): See Kāma.

PŪTANĀ: A female demon, daughter of Bali. She tried to kill Kṛṣṇa by suckling him, but was sucked to death by the child.

RĀDHĀ: (1) Wife of Adhiratha and foster-mother of Karṇa (q.v.). (2) The most favourite Gopī of Kṛṣṇa, she was wife of Āyāna Ghoṣa, a cowherd of Vṛndāvana.

RĀDHIKĀ: Another form of Rādhā (No. 2.) above.

RĀGHAVA : 'Descendant of Raghu'; a designation of Rāma.

RĀHU : Rāhu and Ketu are the ascending and descending nodes respectively in astronomy. Rāhu was a Daitya who in disguise drank some of the nectar churned from the ocean. The Sun and Moon detected it and reported the matter to Viṣṇu who severed his head and two of his arms. As he became immortal by taking nectar, his body was placed in the stellar sphere, the upper parts, represented by a dragon's head, being Rāhu, the ascending node, and the lower parts, represented by a dragon's tail, being Ketu, the descending node. Rāhu avenges himself on the Sun and the Moon by swallowing them during eclipses.

RĀMA : Eldest son of Daśaratha, king of Ayodhyā. An incarnation assumed by Lord Viṣṇu, in the Tretā age, to slay the demon Rāvaṇa. When about to be installed on the throne, he was exiled to the forest for fourteen years by Daśaratha at the machination of Kaikeyī. He was accompanied to the forest by his wife Sītā and brother Lakṣmaṇa. In his exile, Sītā was abducted by Rāvaṇa, king of Laṅkā. After killing Rāvaṇa in a war he came back to Ayodhyā with Sītā and Lakṣmaṇa and was crowned there. To please his subjects, who doubted the chastity of Sītā while in Laṅkā, Rāma banished her. In course of time, Rāma went to heaven.

[For versions of the Rāma-story from the earliest times, see K. Bulcke, *Rāmakathā*, Prayag (Allahabad), 1950.]

RAMBHĀ : A nymph produced at the churning of the ocean. She was sent by Indra to seduce sage Viśvāmitra who cursed her to become a stone and remain so for a thousand years.

RANTIDEVA : A king of the Lunar race, reputed to have been very rich and generous and said to have performed a large number of sacrifices. Acc. to a tradition, he had 200,000 cooks and had 2000 heads of cattle and other animals of the same number slaughtered daily for use in the kitchen. It is said that the river Carmaṇvatī (modern Chambal) was formed by the blood flowing from the heaps of skins of the above animals.

RATI : Wife of Kāma.

RĀVAṆA : Rākṣasa, king of Laṅkā, son of Viśravas by Nikaṣā and half-brother of Kuvera. Through Brahmā's grace he became invincible to gods and demons, but was doomed to lose his life through a woman. Endowed with ten heads and twenty arms, he persecuted and humiliated gods. He abducted Sītā from Rāma's abode in the forest. A war ensued in which, after many reverses, he was killed by Rāma. Rāvaṇa is said to have been re-born as Śiśupāla. Rāvaṇa's chief wife was Mandodarī. Of his five sons, the most famous was Meghanāda, also called Indrajit, Rāvaṇi and Akṣa. He was a great statesman versed in Śāstras. Rāma is said to have received instructions from him before the latter's death.

REṆUKĀ : Wife of Jamadagni and mother of Paraśurāma who killed her at his father's bidding.

REVATĪ : Daughter of king Raivata and wife of Balarāma.

ROHIṆĪ : (1) Daughter of Kaśyapa and Surabhi.

(2) Daughter of Dakṣa, fourth lunar asterism and the favourite wife of the Moon.

(3) A wife of Vasudeva, father of Kṛṣṇa, and mother of Balarāma.

(4) Name of a wife of Kṛṣṇa.

ROHITA : Also called Rohitāśva, he was son of Hariścandra (q.v.).

ṚṢYAŚṚṄGA : Son of Vibhāṇḍaka, he was a sage with horns of deer. He married Daśaratha's daughter, Śāntā, whom king Lomapāda, as her adoptive father, gave to him. This sage performed the sacrifice for Daśaratha, as a result of which he got Rāma as his son.

RUDRA : A Vedic god associated with disease and magic; in later times, identified with Śiva.

[See V.M. Apte, *Is Ṛgvedic Rudra a howler* ? Allahabad; M. Sen, Position of Rudra in Vedic ritual, *Summaries of papers,*

AIOC, 1974. Arbman, *Rudra*, Uppsla, 1922; I.C. Tyagi, Rudra-Śiva (in Kalpa-sūtras), *Vishweshvarananda Indological Jour.*, XIX, Pts. I, II, 1981; S. Bhattacharji, Rudra-Śiva from the Vedas to the Mahābhārata, *ABORI*, 1956; The Rudras and the Maruts, A*nvīkṣā*, *Jadavpur University Jour.*, Calcutta, Vol. III, Pt. 1, 1968.

RUKMIṆĪ : Daughter of Bhīṣmaka, king of Vidarbha. She fell in love with Kṛṣṇa who wanted to marry her but whose request was rejected by her brother. She was then betrothed to the Cedi King Śiśupāla. On the day of marriage, however, she was carried off by Kṛṣṇa to Dvārakā where he married her. She was his chief wife, and gave birth to ten sons of whom Pradyumna was one.

ŚACĪ : Wife of Indra. Also called Indrāṇī.

SĀDHYAS : A class of inferior deities whose number is 12, acc. to a source and 17, acc. to another.

SAGARA : A king of Ayodhyā. He had 60000 sons by his wife Sumati. His horse, meant for *Aśvamedha* sacrifice, was carried off to Pātāla. The 60000 sons of Sagara discovered it there; it was grazing near sage Kapila engaged in meditation. They took Kapila to be the thief and insulted him. Enraged at this, he reduced all of them to ashes. Bhagīratha, a descendant of Sagara, brought down the holy river Gaṅgā from heaven. At the touch of this river, the above sons of Sagara were brought back to life.

SAHADEVA : Twin brother of Nakula, known as a son of Pāṇḍu, but in reality perhaps a son of the Aśvins by Mādrī.

SAHASRĀKṢA : 'Thousand-eyed'. An epithet of Indra (q.v.).

ŚAIVYĀ : Wife of Hariścandra (q.v.).

ŚAKRA : Name of Indra (q.v.).

ŚAKUNI : Brother of Gāndhārī (q.v.) and thus maternal uncle of the Kauravas. It was he who made Yudhiṣṭhira stake and lose his all in a dicing contest in which both took part as opponents. He is known by the patronymic Saubala from his father Subala (q.v.).

ŚAKUNTALĀ : See under Characters (Part III).

ŚALYA : King of the Madras, brother of Mādrī, second wife of Pāṇḍu. In the Kurukṣetra war he joined the Kauravas, and acted as charioteer of Karṇa on whose death he commanded the army on the last day of the battle and was killed by Yudhiṣṭhira.

ŚĀMBA (also, Sāmba): A son of Kṛṣṇa by Jāmbavatī or Rukmiṇī. At the Svayaṃvara of Draupadī he carried her off but was captured and made prisoner by Duryodhana and his friends. Balarāma got him released and took him to Dvārakā. Under the curse of Durvāsas he was afflicted with leprosy of which he was cured by devotion to the Sun-god to whom he built a temple on the bank of the Candrabhāgā (Chināb).

ŚAMBARA : A demon mentioned in the *Ṛgveda*. In the Purāṇas, he is a Daitya who threw Pradyumna (q.v.) into the sea but was afterwards killed by him. Engaged by Hiraṇyakaśipu to slay Prahlāda.

[See R. Shamasastri, Indra's wars with Śambara, *F.W. Thomas Pres. Vol.*, Bombay, 1939.]

ŚAMBŪKA : A Śūdra sage who performed penances improper for his caste and was, therefore, slain by Rāma.

SAṂKARṢAṆA : A name of Balarāma (q.v.).

SAÑJAYA : Charioteer of Dhṛtarāṣṭra to whom he is represented as reciting the *Bhagavadgītā*.

ŚĀNTĀ : Daughter of Daśaratha, adopted by king Lomapāda and married to sage Ṛṣyaśṛṅga.

ŚĀNTANU : A king, father of Bhīṣma. Also see Satyavatī. In the *Ṛgveda* (x. 98), he is younger brother of Devāpi who occupied the throne in his stead.

SARAMĀ : 1. Dog of Indra and mother of two watchdogs of

Yama. Acc. to a legend, she recovered the cows stolen by the Paṇis.

2. Wife of Vibhīṣaṇa, she was in attendance on Śitā when she was a captive of Rāvaṇa.

3. One of the daughters of Dakṣa and mother of wild animals.

SARAṆYU : Daughter of Tvaṣṭṛ. First appears in the *Ṛgveda*. Legends about her occur in various other works, e.g. *Nirukta*, *Bṛhad-devatā* etc.

SARASVATĪ : In the Vedas, it denotes both a river and a goddess. In the Brāhmaṇas, *Madhābhārata* and later works she is identified with Vāc (Goddess of Speech) and represented as consort of Brahmā. Acc. to the Vaiṣṇavas of Bengal she is wife of Viṣṇu.

[See R.N. Airi, Etymological study of the word Sarasvatī; *Summaries of Papers*, AIOC, Silver Jubilee Session, 1969, p. 2; I. Khan, Sarasvati as a physician in the Yajurveda, *Summaries of Papers*, AIOC, 1969, p. 365; *Sarasvati in Sanskrit Literature*, Ghaziabad, 1978; D.C. Sircar, *Foreigners of Ancient India and Lakṣmī and Sarasvatī in Art and Literature* 1975. A. Vidyābhūṣaṇa, *Sarasvatī* (in Bengali), Calcutta; R. Airi, Sarasvatī in late minor Upapurāṇas, *Summaries of papers* V World Skt. Conf., Varanasi, 1981, p. 187].

ŚARMIṢṬHĀ: Daughter of Vṛṣaparvan, a demon, and second wife of Yayāti and mother of Pūru. Also see Devayānī.

ŚATAKRATU: One who has performed a hundred sacrifices. An epithet of Indra (q.v.).

SATĪ : A daughter of Dakṣa and wife of Rudra or Śiva. At the huge sacrifice, performed by Dakṣa, to which Śiva was not invited, she could not tolerate the insulting attitude of her father to her absent husband. Consequently she gave up her life. Subsequently born as Umā, daughter of the Himālaya by Menā, she was married by Śiva.

Also see *Pīṭhasthāna*.

ŚATRUGHNA: Half-brother of Rāma. He fought for Rāma, and killed the Rākṣasa-chief Lavaṇa.

SATYABHĀMĀ: One of the principal wives of Kṛṣṇa. She induced Kṛṣṇa to take away the Pārijāta tree from Indra's heaven where she was taken by Kṛṣṇa.

SATYAVĀN: See Sāvitrī.

SATYAVATĪ: (1) Daughter of Uparicara, king of Cedi. Acc. to one version, daughter of Vasurāja by Adrikā, a nymph in the form of a fish. As there was a fishy smell in her body, she was called Matsyagandhā. Vyāsa, the offspring of the illicit union of Satyavatī as a girl and Parāśara, was born on an island; hence his epithet Dvaipāyana. As wife of Śāntanu (q. v.), she gave birth to Vicitravīrya and Citrāṅgada.

(2) A daughter of king Gādhi, wife of a Brāhmaṇa named Ṛcīka, mother of Jamadagni.

SATYAVRATA: A designation of Bhīṣma; so called because of his truthfulness.

SAUBHARI: A sage who, in his old age, assumed a handsome form and married the daughter of King Māndhātṛ. He had 150 sons, and ultimately retired to the forest with his wives and was devoted solely to the worship of Viṣṇu.

SĀVITRĪ: (1) Daughter of King Aśvapati. She fell in love with and married Satyavān knowing that he had only one more year to live. On the fateful day when Satyavān died, and Yama came to take away his spirit she followed him. Her importunities and devotion induced Yama to restore her husband to life.

(2) The presiding deity of the sun. Also called Gāyatrī, she was wife of Brahmā.

SAVYASĀCIN: Puller of a bow with both hands. An epithet of Arjuna.

ŚEṢA: King of the serpent-race and of the nether regions. Represented as provided with thousand heads which serve as the couch and canopy of Viṣṇu during his sleep in the interval of creation. Sometimes represented as upholding the world. At the end of each Kalpa, he vomits fire that destroys creation. He served as a rope tied to the Mandara mountain when the ocean was churned. Generally identified with Vāsuki, but sometimes represented as distinct from him.

SIDDHAS: A class of demi-gods supposed to dwell in the sky between the earth and the sun.

ŚIKHAṆḌIN, ŚIKHAṆḌINĪ: Ambā (q.v.) was one of the two women whom Bhīṣma secured as wives of his brother, Vicitravīrya. She was re-born as Śikhaṇḍin, son of king Drupada, to wreak vengeance on Bhīṣma who was instrumental in causing misfortune in her previous life as Śikhaṇḍinī. When Bhīṣma lay in a bed of arrows in the Kurukṣetra war, the fatal arrow was discharged by him.

SIṂHIKĀ: 1. A daughter of Dakṣa and wife of Vipracitti. Rāhu (q.v.) is said to be her son.

2. A Rākṣasī who devoured Hanūmān. But Hanūmān tore her body to pieces.

SĪTĀ: Daughter of Janaka, king of Videha, and wife of Rāma. She is said to have sprung from the plough of Janaka; hence her name meaning 'furrow'. Rāma obtained her by breaking the bow of Śiva at Janaka's court. She followed Rāma to exile. There she was carried off by Rāvaṇa to Laṅkā. A war ensued in which she was rescued by Rāma and taken to Ayodhyā after a fire-ordeal in which Sītā's purity of character was proved. There, in deference to the abode of Rāvaṇa, Rāma banished her when she had been *enceinte*. In the forest, where she was given shelter by Vālmīki, she gave birth to twin sons Lava and Kuśa. One day when the two boys, now in their teens, chanced to come to Ayodhyā, Rāma having requested them recalled Sītā. She came and openly declared innocence. But, deeply aggrieved as she was, she requested mother Earth to demonstrate her purity. The Earth showed a cleft into which Sītā gradually disappeared. Thus she went back to the very source from which she sprang.

ŚIVA: One in the Brāhmaṇical triad of divinities, the other two being Brahmā and Viṣṇu. The destroying and reproducing deity Rudra of the Veda was, in later times, identified with Śiva, who is symbolised and worshipped as a phallus (*liṅga*). Also called Maheśvara.

[See C. Sivaramamurti, *Naṭarāja in Art, Thought and Literature*, Delhi; A. Sarkar, *Śiva in Medieval Indian Literature*, Calcutta, 1974; Swami Sivananda, *Lord Śiva and His Worship* 1978; F.W. Clother and J.L. Bruce, *Experiencing Śiva: Encounters with a Hindu Deity*; T. Burrow, *Problems of Śiva in Sanskrit*, London, 1979; A. M. Gaston, *The Dancing Śiva*, Oxford Uni. Press, 1981; Śiva in dance, myth and iconography; S. Kramrisch, *Manifestations of Śiva*; J. Dye, *Ways to Shiva*; G. E. Yocum, *Hymns to dancing Śiva*, New Delhi, 1982; Also see under Rudra. W.D.O'Flaherty, *Asceticism and Eroticism in the Mythology of Śiva*, London, 1973.]

ŚIVI: Son of Uśīnara, king of the country of the same name. His charity is fabulous. Agni in the form of a pigeon was followed by Indra disguised as a falcon. The pigeon fell on the king's body in quest of shelter. To spare the pigeon the falcon would take nothing but an equal quantity of the king's flesh. The king cut off some flesh from his body, and put it on the balance. But the pigeon proved heavier. He cut off more and more of flesh, but each time the pigeon grew heavier. Then he put his entire body in the balance. This time it outweighed the pigeon and the falcon fled away.

On another occasion, Viṣṇu, as a Brāhmaṇa guest, demanded as food the body of Śivi's own son. The king killed the son, cooked the dead body and placed it before the guest who asked the king to eat it himself. The king having been ready to do so, the Brāhmaṇa restored the son to life and disappeared.

There are other stories of Śivi's sacrifice and generosity.

SKANDA: Name of Kārtikeya (q.v.).

SOMA: (1) The exhilarating juice of a climbing plant (*Asclepia acida*), used by Vedic Aryans as a beverage and as libation to deities.

[See R.G. Wasson, *Soma, divine mushroom of immortality*, The Hague, 1969; J. Brough, Soma and *Amanita Muscaria*, *BSOAS*, XXXIV, Pt. 2; B. H. Kapadia, *Critical Interpretation and Investigation of Epithets of Soma in the Legends.*]

(2) Name of Moon generally said to be son of sage Atri by Anasūyā. He carried off Tārā, wife of Bṛhaspati. A war ensued. At last, through Brahmā's intervention Soma was compelled to restore Tārā to her husband.

Soma had a son, Budha, by Tārā.

Soma is also called Candra, Śaśin, Indu, Uḍupa, Śitāṃśu etc.

SOMAŚARMAN: A legendary figure mentioned in the Bhūmikhaṇḍa of the *Padmapurāṇa* in which he is stated to have been born as Prahlāda (q.v.), in a later rebirth. A Cambodian inscription reports that a Somaśarman presented the Indian epics and the Purāṇa to a temple (See Winternitz: *History of Indian Lit.*, I, p. 514).

ŚRUTAKĪRTI: Cousin of Sītā and wife of Śatrughna.

SUBALA: A King of Gandhāra, father of Gāndhārī (q.v.) and Śakuni (q.v.).

SUBHADRĀ: Daughter of Vasudeva, sister of Kṛṣṇa, wife of Arjuna and mother of Abhimanyu. She was carried off from Dvārakā by Arjuna at the instance of Kṛṣṇa.

SUGRĪVA: Brother of Bālin (q.v.) and believed to have been the son of Sun-god. An ally of Rāma who gave him the kingdom of Kiṣkindhā after slaying Bālin. His wife's name was Rumā. He took as wife Tārā, wife of Bālin, after the latter had been slain by Rāma.

ŚUKRA: Priest of the Daityas. His daughter Devayānī married Yayāti. (Also see Yayāti and Devayānī.) Identified with Uśanas, author of a Smṛti work, and regarded as author of a work on polity.

SUMANTRA: Principal adviser of Daśaratha and friend of Rāma.

ŚUMBHA: Brother of the Asura Niśumbha. Both of them, elated by Śiva's favour gained through penance, oppressed the gods and were killed by Durgā.

ŚUNAḤŚEPHAS (or, -ŚEPA): Son of sage Ṛcika and nephew (sister's son) of Viśvāmitra. Several hymns of the *Ṛgveda* (i. 24-30; ix. 3) are attributed to him. A legend about him occurs in the *Aitareya Brāhmaṇa*. It occurs also in the *Mahābhārata* and the *Viṣṇu-purāṇa* etc. with variations.

SUNDA: A Daitya, brother of Upasunda. They quarrelled over the possession of the nymph Tilottamā, sent by gods for their destruction, and killed each other.

SURABHI: The wish-yielding cow (Kāmadhenu) obtained at the churning of the ocean.

ŚŪRPAṆAKHĀ: "Having nails like winnowing fans". Sister of Rāvaṇa. Enamoured of Rāma in his forest abode, she made advances to him. Rāma directed her to Lakṣmaṇa.

SYAMANTAKA: A gem of fabulous power, given by the Sun to Satrājit. Fearing that it might be taken away by Kṛṣṇa, he gave it to his brother Prasena who, being a bad fellow, was killed by a lion. Jāmbavat, king of bears, killed the lion and carried off the gem. Kṛṣṇa defeated Jāmbavat in a contest, took the gem and restored it to Satrājit. Satrājit having been killed, it fell into the hands of Akrūra.

TĀḌAKĀ: Same as Tārakā (q.v.).

TAKṢA, TAKṢAKA: (1) Son of Bharata (q.v.)

(2) King of Gandhāra, who probably founded Takṣaśilā (=Taxila in the Punjab).

TĀRĀ: (1) Wife of monkey-king Bālin, and mother of Aṅgada. After Bālin's death she was taken by his brother Sugrīva, as his wife.

(2) Wife of Bṛhaspati. See Soma.

TĀRAKA: A Daitya who, by dint of penance, became very powerful and persecuted gods. To destroy him Skanda was born to Śiva and Umā.

TĀRAKĀ: A female Daitya and mother of Mārīca (q.v.). Rāma killed her at the bidding of sage Viśvāmitra.

TILOTTAMĀ: Originally a Brāhmaṇa female, she was reborn as a nymph for the destruction of the demons Sunda (q.v.) and Upasunda (q.v.). Created by the divine architect Viśvakarman by gathering the beauties of the world bit by bit (*tila*); hence her name.

TRIMŪRTI: The triad of gods, viz. Brahmā the creator, Viṣṇu the preserver and Śiva the destroyer.

TRIPURĀSURA: Name of the demon Bāṇa who received as gift three cities from Śiva, Brahmā and Viṣṇu. He was slain by Śiva.

TRIŚAṄKU: A king of the Solar race, father of Hariścandra. Through the favour of sage Viśvāmitra he gained access to heaven with his earthly body. The gods hurled him down. But, by the power of his penance Viśvāmitra checked his fall and began to create another heaven with Triśaṅku kept high above. The gods then allowed Triśaṅku to live in the midway to heaven, surrounded by stars.

TRIVIKRAMA: Name of Viṣṇu from his three strides.

TURVASU (Turvasa): Son of Yayāti by Devayānī. For refusing to bear the curse of premature infirmity to which his father fell a victim, he was cursed by the latter to the effect that his posterity would have no dominion.

TVAṢṬṚ: The divine architect, identified in the Purāṇas with Viśvakarman.

UCCAIḤŚRAVAS: The horse of Indra. It was white and was obtained at the churning of the ocean.

UDAYANA: See under Characters (Part III).

UDDHAVA: Friend and adviser of Kṛṣṇa. Acc. to a tradition, he was a son of a brother of Vasudeva, father of Kṛṣṇa.

UGRASENA: A king of Mathurā, father of Kaṃsa. He was deposed by his son, but Kṛṣṇa having killed Kaṃsa restored the father to the throne.

ULŪPĪ: A daughter of Kauravya, king of the Nāgas. Arjuna in a way married her.

UMĀ: Daughter of the Himālaya, wife of Śiva and mother of Skanda. The earliest mention of Umā is found in the *Kenopaniṣad* (III. 12) where she appears to mediate between Brahmā and other gods.

UPASUNDA: See Sunda.

ŪRMILĀ: Daughter of Janaka, sister of Sītā and wife of Lakṣmaṇa.

URVAŚĪ: See under Characters (Pt. III).

UṢĀ: Daughter of Bāṇa, a Daitya. See Aniruddha.

[For Vedic Uṣas, see Winternitz, *History of Indian Lit.*, Vol. I; V.S. Patil, Is Lakṣmī a metamorphosis of Vedic Uṣas, *Summaries of Papers*, AIOC, 1974.]

UTTĀNAPĀDA: Father of Dhruva (q.v.) and a son of Manu.

UTTARĀ: Daughter of the king of Virāṭa, wife of Abhimanyu, son of Arjuna.

VAIKARTANA: A patronymic of Karṇa, meaning 'son of Vikartana' (the Sun).

VAINATEYA: Name of Garuḍa; so called as he was son of Vinatā.

VAIROCANA: A name of Bali.

VAIŚAMPĀYANA: A great sage, the original teacher of the Black *Yajurveda*.

VAIŚRAVAṆA: Patronymic of Kuvera (q.v.).

VAKA: A great Asura slain by Bhīma in a dour fight.

VĀLI: Same as Bālin (q.v.).

VĀLMĪKI: Author of the *Rāmāyaṇa*, he is traditionally known as the *Ādikavi* (the first poet). It is said that the sight of a pair of curlews in sexual union pierced by the arrow of a fowler, moved him to pity and he uttered the verse *mā niṣāda* etc. which is known as the *Ādi-kāvya*. For his association with Sītā, see under Sītā. Acc. to a legend, he was, in early life, a desperado but later turned over a new leaf. He was engrossed in such deep meditation that an ant-hill (*valmīka*) grew over him; hence his name Vālmīki.

VĀMANA: The Dwarf Incarnation of Viṣṇu.

[See G.C. Tripathi, *Der Ursprung Und die Entwick long der Vāmaṇa—Legende in der Indischen Literatur*; U. Chaudhary, *Indra and Varuna in Indian Mythology*].

VARĀHA: The Boar Incarnation of Viṣṇu.

VĀRAṆĀVATA: The City where the Pāṇḍavas lived in exile.

VARUṆA: God of rain, conceived as having noose for punishing offenders.

[See H. Luders, *Varuṇa*, Vol. I, 1951; Vol;. II, 1959, Gottingen.]

VAŚIṢṬHA (Vasiṣṭha): A famous sage. There was enmity between him and Viśvāmitra. Once when the latter attempted forcibly to take away the wish-yielding cow (Kāmadhenu) of the former, a fierce fight ensued between the followers of the two parties. Viśvāmitra, a Kṣatriya, lost his 100 sons and suffered many reverses. Then he resolved to attain Brahminhood which he did by severe penance. Vaśiṣṭha was family-preceptor of the kings of the Ikṣvāku race. As the family priest of Hariścandra, he is said to have been at serious feud with Viśvāmitra. The wife of Vaśiṣṭha was Ūrjā, acc. to one tradition, and Arundhatī, acc. to another.

Vaśiṣṭha appears as a seer to whom are ascribed many hymns of the seventh book (*Maṇḍala*) of the *Ṛgveda*. Legends about him occur in the *Aitareya Brāhmaṇa*, the *Mahābhārata*, the *Rāmāyaṇa*, the *Viṣṇu-purāṇa* and the *Mārkaṇḍeya-purāṇa*.

[See U.C. Sharma, *Viśvāmitras and Vaśiṣṭhas*, Aligarh, 1975; C.S. Venkateshwaran, Vaśiṣṭha in the Ṛgveda, Pro. AIOC, 1966.]

VASUDEVA: Belonging to the Yādava race, he was father of Kṛṣṇa by Devakī and brother of Kuntī.

VĀSUDEVA: Patronymic of Kṛṣṇa, son of Vasudeva.

VĀSUKI: King of serpents living in Pātāla; also called Śeṣa.

VĀTĀPI: A Rākṣasa, son of Hrada or Vipracitti. See under Agastya.

VEṆA: Son of Aṅga and a descendant of Manu Svāyambhuva. Father of Pṛthu.

VIBHĀṆḌAKA: Son of Kaśyapa and father of Ṛṣyaśṛṅga.

VIBHĪṢAṆA: 'Terrible'. A younger brother of Rāvaṇa. An ally of Rāma who raised him to the throne of Laṅkā after killing Rāvaṇa.

VICITRAVĪRYA: Son of Satyavatī, brother of Citrāṅgada and husband of Ambikā and Ambālikā.

VIDURA: Son of Vyāsa by a Śūdra girl, and younger brother of Dhṛtarāṣṭra and Pāṇḍu. A very pious and wise man, he gave good counsel to both Kauravas and Pāṇḍavas but sided with the latter in the battle. A favourite of Kṛṣṇa.

VIDYĀDHARA: A class of inferior gods of usually benevolent character, dwelling in the region between the earth and the sky.

VIKRAMĀDITYA: See under Characters (Part III)

A cycle of legends is associated with him. The noteworthy works, in which he is mentioned, are *Siṃhāsana-dvātriṃśikā* or *Vikrama-carita*, *Prabandha-cintāmaṇi* of Merutuṅga. The *Jyotirvidābharaṇa* (c. 16th cent. A.D.), ascribed by some to Kālidāsa, in the court of a legendary king Vikramāditya, mentions Nine Jewels, including Kālidāsa. Regarding Vikramāditya, founder of Vikrama era, see Appendix XII of this book. See A.K. Chatterjee, Was there a pre-Gupta Vikramāditya?, *Summaries of Papers*, AIOC, 1974.

VIṢṆU: One of the famous Brahmanical triad of divinities, the other two being Brahmā and Maheśvara (Śiva). Partly a personification of light and of the sun, especially in his striding over the heaven in three paces. Believed to have assumed several incarnations on earth to protect it from evil.

[See G.V. Patel, Viṣṇu as an object of treatment in Vedas as Agni, *Summaries of Papers*, AIOC 1974.]

VIŚRAVAS: Father of Rāvaṇa by Nikaṣā.

VIŚVAKARMAN: The divine architect, identified with Tvaṣṭṛ (q.v.).

VIŚVĀMITRA: A renowned sage, son of king Kuśika acc. to the *Ṛgveda*, of Gāthin or Gādhi, king of Kānyakubja, acc. to later sources. Born as a Kṣatriya, he acquired Brahminhood by severe austerities. For his feud with Vaśiṣṭha, see under Vaśiṣṭha.

For his relation to Hariścandra, see under Hariścandra. See under Triśaṅku for another legend connected with him.

The gods, greatly alarmed by his severe penance, sent the nymph Menakā to seduce him. She succeeded, and his union with the nymph resulted in the birth of the famous Śakuntalā. The sage is also said to have had an amorous relation with the nymph Rambhā.

This sage is said to have induced Daśaratha to send his son, Rāma, while he was yet a boy, with him for protecting the Brāhmaṇas against the attacks of Rāvaṇa and his Rākṣasa followers. It was with this sage that Rāma went to the court of Janaka where he married Sītā. Besides the *Ṛgveda* and the *Aitareya Brāhmaṇa*, legends about Viśvāmitra occur in the epics as well as in the Purāṇas, notably the *Viṣṇu-purāṇa* and the *Mārkaṇḍeya-purāṇa*.

To Viśvāmitra is ascribed the entire third *Maṇḍala* of the *Ṛgveda*.

[See S.B. Roy, Viśvāmitra, the greatest astronomer of the ancient world, *Summaries of Papers*, AIOC, 1974; U.C. Sharma, *Viśvāmitras and Vasiṣṭhas*, Aligarh, 1975; B. H. Karadia, *Viśvāmitra*.

VṚTRA: Demon of drought in the Vedas, represented as constantly at feud with Indra, who always overpowers him.

[See Buddha Prakash, Vṛtra, *ABORI*, 30; E. Benveniste and L. Renou, *Vṛtra and Vṛtraghna*, Paris, 1934; W. Ruben, Indra's fight against Vṛtra in the Mahābhārata, *S. K. Belvalkar Felicitation Vol.*, Banaras, 1957; A. K. Lahiri, *Vedic Vṛtra*, MLBD, Delhi.]

VṚTRAHAN: Slayer of Vṛtra; an epithet of Indra (q.v.).

VYĀSA: Kṛṣṇa Dvaipāyana Vedavyāsa. Offspring of the illicit union of Satyavatī (q.v.) as a virgin and sage Parāśara. Born in island (*dvīpa*); hence called Dvaipāyana. Traditionally believed to have compiled the Vedas, composed the *Mahābhārata* as well as the Purāṇas. He is supposed by some scholars to represent a synthesis of the Aryan and non-Aryan cultures. See S. K. Chatterji in *Jour. of Asiatic Society of Bengal* 1950. The same scholar and some other eminent Indologists would assign Vyāsa to the tenth century B.C.

YADU: Son of king Yayāti (q.v.) and founder of the race of Yādavas in which Kṛṣṇa was born.

YUVANĀŚVA: A king of the Solar race, father of Māndhātṛ (q.v.).

APPENDICES

I

IMPORTANT DATES HAVING A BEARING ON THE HISTORY OF SANSKRIT LITERATURE[1]

Abhinavagupta	Last quarter of 10th cent.-first quarter of 11th
Aihole Inscription of Pulakeśin II	634 A.D.
Alberuni's visit to India	C. 1030 A.D.
Alexander's invasion of India	327-325 B.C.
Allahabad Stone Pillar Inscription by Hariṣeṇa	C. 350 A.D.
Āraṇyakas	See Brāhmaṇas below
Aśoka	C. 269-232 B.C.
Aṣṭādhyāyī	See Pāṇini.
Bhāgavata	Fifth or sixth century, according to some, not later than 800 A.D., according to others.
Bharata (Nāṭyaśāstra)	Perhaps earlier than 4th or 5th cent. A.D.
Brāhmaṇas (including Āraṇyakas)	C. 1500-1000 B.C.
Buddha	C. 563-483 B.C. (Nirvāṇa 486, acc. to tradition)
Caitanya	1486-1533 A.D.
Cālukyas of Kalyāṇi	973- C.1189 A.D.
Caulukyas of Gujarat	C. 974-1238
Fa-hien's visit to India	399 A.D.
Gāhaḍavālas of Banaras and Kānyakubja	C. 1090-1193 A.D.
Girnar Inscription	C. 150 A.D.
Gupta Age	C. 300-647 A.D.
Hariṣeṇa's inscription	See Allahabad Stone Pillar Inscription above.
Harṣavardhana's reign	606-647 A.D.
Hiuen Tsang's visit to India	630-645 A.D.
Indus Valley Civilisation or Harappa and Mohon-jo-Daro	C. 2500-1500 B.C.
I-tsing's visit to India	671-695 A.D.

1. See S.N. Pradhan *Chronology of Ancient India*; R. Singh, *A Dictionary of World Chronology*; M. Dutt, *Chronology of India*, Varanasi, 1975.

Kālidāsa	Highly controversial. Generally be-lived to have flourished around 400 A.D.
Kāmasūtra	C. 3rd cent. A.D.
Kaniṣka's reign	C. 78-101 A.D.
Kurukṣetra battle (Nucleus of the Mahābhārata)	C. 1000-900 B.C.
Lakṣmaṇasena (King of Bengal)	Accession 1178 A.D.
Mahābhārata	Present form—C. 4th century A.D.
Mahābhāṣya	See Patañjali.
Mahāvīra	d. 468 B.C. (Acc. to others, 528 B.C.)
Mandasor Inscription of Vatsabhaṭṭi	473 A.D.
Manu-smṛti	Acc. to Bühler and Kane, the extant work was composed in the period between the second century B.C. and second century A.D.
Megasthenes's visit to India	302 B.C.
Pālas of Bengal and Bihar	C. 760-1142 A.D.
Pāṇini	C. 4th century B.C.
Paramāras of Dhārā (Malwa)	C. 974-1060 A.D.
Patañjali	C. 2nd century B.C.
Pulakeśin II	See Aihole Inscription.
Purāṇas	Uncertain. Believed to have been written earlier than seventh century A.D.
Puṣyamitra	Reign—C. 187-151 B.C.
Rājataraṅgiṇī of Kalhaṇa	1148-50 A.D.
Rāmāyaṇa	Present form—C. 2nd or 3rd century A.D.
Ṛg-veda	Highly controversial. Acc. to Winternitz, 2500-2000 B.C. The dates suggested by different scholars are 6000 B.C., 3000 B.C., 1200 B.C., and 1000 B.C.
Rudradāman	See Girnar Inscription.
Senas of Bengal	C. 1118-1199 A.D.
Sūtra period	C. 600-200 B.C.
Tantras	Uncertain. Generally believed to have been composed or compiled in or after the fifth or sixth century A.D.
Upaniṣads	C. 1000-600 B.C.

Vatsabhaṭṭi	See Mandasor Inscription.
Vātsyāyana	See Kāmasūtra.
Vedic Age	See *Ṛg-veda*.
Vikramāditya (The Gupta King Candragupta II).	Accession—C. 380 A.D.
Vikrama Saṃvat (commencement)	57 B.C.
Yājñavalkya-Smṛti	C. 100-300 A.D.

II

CONTRIBUTION OF PRE-20th CENTURY OUTSTANDING WESTERN SCHOLARS TO STUDIES IN SANSKRIT LANGUAGE AND LITERATURE[1]

It is not definitely known when India came into contact with the Western world. There is, however, no doubt that India and Greece knew each other centuries before Alexander's invasion (327-26 B.C.). The Greek poet, Homer (C. 9th cent. B.C.), mentions India, and states that, even in that far-off age, the Greeks used Indian goods like ivory. We have it, on the authority of Herodotus (C. 484-425 B.C.) that the Greek Scylax was the first Greek to visit (C. 510 B.C.) India. An Indian philosopher is said to have gone to Socrates in 400 B.C. The Greeks got some information about India from the writings of Hecateus (549-486 B.C.), the father of Greek geography. More light about this country was shed by Herodotus.

With Italy, particularly Rome also India's contact was established well before the Christian era according to the testimony of the *Periplus*, Ptolemy and Pliny. Commercial relations were followed by diplomatic relations. Indian envoys were sent to the Roman Emperor, Augustus (27 B.C. to 14 A.D.).

With the passage of time, the Europeans lost contact with India. It was revived towards the close of the 13th century when Marco Polo, a Venetian traveller, visited (1288 A.D.) India. In the story of the re-discovery of India by Europe, the names of the Venetian Nicolo de Conti,[2] the Russian A. Niktin[3] and the Gonoese H. do S. Stefano[4] are prominent. John II of Portugal des-

---

1. Scholars, born before 1900 A.D., have been taken into consideration. The names of the scholars have been arranged alphabetically. The following abbreviations are used against the respective names:
   A — American
   D — Dutch
   E — English
   F — French
   G — German
   I — Italian
   G. Sen Gupta's *Videśīya Bhārat-vidyā-pathik* (Calcutta, 1965), in Bengali, contains useful information in this connexion.
2. See the fourth book of his treatise, *De Varietate Fortunae*, ed. A. Olivia (Paris, 1723).
3. His accounts were brought to Moscow by some merchants as he died, before reaching his native place, Smolensk.
4. See C.S. Singh, Holwell, Dow etc. in the Journal, *Glory of India*, Delhi Vol. VI, 1-4, 1982.

patched P. Covilham and A. de Pavya to India. Covilham[1] was the first Portuguese to reach India. He was followed by a number of Portuguese travellers.[2] The most noteworthy among them was Vasco da Gama. This sailor doubled the Cape of Good Hope, and reached Calicut in May, 1498. His accounts may be read in *Roteiro* (Haklyut Society Journal), in the *Lendas* of G. Correa, in *Castanheda* and in other Portuguese histories as also in the poetic *Lusiad* of Gamoens da Gama. da Gama was followed by N. Pinto. His book, *The Voyage and Adventure of Fernao Mendez*, appeared in 1614 A.D.

Among other early Europeans, who came to India, mention may be made of Varthoma,[3] Barbosa, Federici, Nuniz and Paes.[4] Barbosa stayed in India in 1508-9. The Italian, Federici, lived from 1513 to 1518 A.D. Nuniz wrote an account (1535 A.D.), and Paes[5] wrote his account of India in 1520 A.D.

From trade and commerce the travellers directed their attention to the spread of their own religion. The Mission, comprising chiefly R. Aquaviva, A. de Monserrato and E. Enriques, started work towards the end of 1569 A.D. Bengal and Pegu (in Burma) were the chief centres of missionary activities.

The first Dutch to venture nto the Indian waters in 1595 was C. Houtman; his voyage was made possible by J.H.V. Linschoten.[6] He met the other travellers, Fitch, Newbery and Leeds who had already been in India.

The first French sailed to India in 1601. The noteworthy French travellers to India were Bernier, Tavernier, Tavenot and Chardin. The accounts, left by the first two of them, are very important.

T. Stevens was the first Englishman to sail to Goa in 1579. Among other British celebrities, who visited India, mention may be made of R. Fitch, J. Newbery and W. Leeds, Raymond, Lancastar, Wood, Middleton, Brand, Heyood.

In the seventeenth century, the Europeans turned their attention to the collection of old Indian manuscripts which began to be preserved in European libraries,[7] e.g. Bodleian Library, Bibliotheque Royale.[8] A portion of the *Gītā*

1. He kept a journal which was lost.
2. Birdwood describes them as "hungry wolves upon a well-stocked sheap-wall" Quoted in Oaten, *European Travellers*, etc., p. 33.
3. From the original Italian his accounts were translated into five other languages and also into Latin.
4. For further information about these travellers, see *A. Dolboque-roue* (Haklyut Society Publication) and *Lusiad* of Camoeus.
5. Sewell, their English translator, says, "the two documents were sent by someone at Goa to someone in Europe". The Portuguese edition of his book is by D. Lopes, *Chronica dos Reis de Basnaga* (1897). Quoted in *Oaten, op.cit.*, p. 45. See C.S. Singh. *op.cit.*
6. His account appeared in Voyages into East and West Indies—Dutch original (1596); Eng. trs. (1598). See C.S. Singh, p. 14, f.n. 12.
7. See *Philosophical Transactions of the Royal Society*, XX (1698), p.p. 421-24.
8. Vide Lettres edifiantes et curieuses, written by French members of South Indian Missions, xxi (1734) pp. 455-56. See C.S. Singh, op. Cit., p. 15.

was translated into Portuguese[1] in the sixteenth century. The most important translation was, perhaps, by Abraham Roger who translated a hundard proverbs of Bhartṛhari. It appeared in Dutch in 1651 and in French in 1670.[2]

The opening of the sea-route facilitated the maritime trade between Europe and India. The Portuguese were the first Europeans to come into commercial contact with this country. In 1500 A.D., a Portuguese merchant sailed for India.

The Dutch followed suit. The Dutch East India Company was formed in 1602 A.D.

The English set foot on the soil of India some time about 1593 A.D.

The French Commercial Company for trade in the Orient, including India, came into being in 1664 A.D.

The English, however, gradually triumphed in their rivalry with the merchants of the other European countries.

The Battle of Plassey (1757) between the then Nawab of Bengal and the English resulted in the disastrous defeat of the former. Thus, the English got a firm foothold in Bengal. This victory laid the foundation of the total British domination of the whole of India. The measuring rod of the British merchant appeared as the royal sceptre.

The commercial quest was followed by cultural, intellectual and spiritual quest.

The formation of the East India Company (31st Dec. 1600) ushered in an era of constructive cultural exchanges between India and the West, particularly England. There was an overwhelming desire on the part of the English to understand Indian philosophy, literature and culture.

Early in the eighteenth century, a series of Jesuit *Letters edifiantes et curieuses* contained a lot of material on Hinduism.[3] P. Sonnerat published the *Voyage aux Indes Orientale* in 1782. A comprehensive account of Indian astronomy was given[4] by G. Le Gentil de la Galaisiere. E. Mignot and J. de Guignes effected a change in the orthodox point of view of earlier writers in their *Memoires de L'Academic rouale des Inscriptions et Belles Letters*;[5]

---

1. D.F. Lach, *Asia in the Making of Europe*, Chicago, 1965, I, p. 280.
2. Entitled *La Purte Ouverte Pour Parvenir a la Connoissance du Paganisme Cache*, Amsterdam, 1670, pp. 293 ff.
3. Some English translations are by J. Lockman, *Travels of the Jesuits into Various Parts of the World*, 2nd ed., 1762.
4. In two articles, published in *Memories de L'Academic Rovale des Sciences for* 1772, Pt. II.
5. Mignot published five memoires—*Sur-les anciens philosophes de L'Inde* in Tome xxxi, 1761-3. de Guignes wrote three : Researches historiques sur la religion Indienna, xl, 1773-76, Reflexions sur unlivre Indian intitule Bagavadam, xxxviii, 1750-72, Observations historique et geographiques sur la recit de Pline concernant L'origine, L' antiquite des Indiens, xlv, 1780-84.

Along the Coromondal coast were established some Danish Missions and letters were published in different collections.[1]

J. Z. Holwell (1711-1798), a surgeon in the East India Company published the following: Interesting Historical Events relative to the Provinces of Bengal and the Empire of Indostan, Festivals of the Gentoos, followers of the Shastah and a Dissertation on the Metempsychosis, commonly though erroneously called the Pythagorian doctrine, 1765. He added a second part and a third part in 1767 and 1771 respectively. In 1779, he published parts two and three with the revised title *A Review of the Original Principles religious and moral, of the Ancient Brāhmins.* In 1786, he published a short treatise, entitled *Dissertation on the Origin, Nature, and Pursuits of Intelligent Beings, and on Divine Providence, and Religious Worship.* In the chapter on the Religious Tenets of the Gentoos, taken from the *Interesting Historical Events relative to the Province of Bengal and the Empire of Indostan* (1767), Holwell quotes, *in extenso*, from a book which he calls *Saṣṭah* and the original of which has not yet been traced. "He calls it the most ancient of Hindu religious books, as ancient as any written body of Divinity that was produced to the world".[2]

Alexander Dow (1735 or 1736-1779) proceeded to Bengal as an Enoign in the East India Company. His two plays, *Zingis* and *Sethona*, were staged at the Drury Lane Theatre. He also published a *History of Hindostan* (1768) in two volumes. A continuation as a third volume was added in 1772. His observations on the Hindus appeared in the first volume; additional matter was added in the third.

The writings of Holwell and Dow were widely read and discussed in England and in the *Annual Register*, Burke paid high tribute to Holwell as enriching European literature. Holwell's treatises were translated into German in 1761[3], into French in 1768.[4] Voltaire, already familiar with Hinduism in 1760 when a copy of *Exour Vedam*[5] was presented to him, read the English works of Holwell by December, 1764.[6] He read also the *Reflections on the Government of Hindostān* (1763) by L. Scafton.

The flood-gate of Indian learning and culture was opened to the West by the establishment, in 1784, of the Asiatic Society of Bengal (now Asiatic Society,

---

1. The following are some of the important letters published in English. Several letters relating to the Protestant Danish Mission at Trabquetar in the East Indies, 1720; An Account of the Religion, Manners and Learning of the People of Malabar, trs. J. T. Phillips, 1717.
2. Vide C. S. Singh, *op.cit.*, p. 16.
3. By E. Theiel in J.T. Koehler—*Samnlung neuer Reisebeschreibungean aus fremden Sprashen*, Gottingen and Gotha, 1767-69, I.
4. *Evenements historiques, interessants, relatifs aux provinces de Bengale*, Amsterdam, 1768.
5. *Voltaire's Correspondence*, ed. T. Besterman, Geneva, 1953-65, LXVII, pp. 210, 217-18.
6. *Dissertations sur les Moeurs, les Usuages, le Language, la Religion et la philosophie des Hindous*, Paris, 1769.

Calcutta), by Sir William Jones (1746-94), a Judge of the Supreme Court of Calcutta, a polymath equally at home in Sanskrit, Arabic and Persian and a distinguished comparatist. The avowed object of the society was to carry on researches in history, geography, archaeology, arts, sciences and literatures of Asia. In short, whatever man has produced, and nature has given in this continent came into the purview of investigation.

As President of the Society, Jones delivered eleven lectures of which those on Indian subjects were entitled *On the Gods of Greece, Italy and India* (1785), *On Asiatic History, Civil and Natural* (1793) and *On the Philosophy of the Asiatics* (1794). Besides translating various Hindustāni hymns and parts of the Vedas, he translated also some Sanskrit works, as we shall see in the following list of contributions of Western scholars.

Sir Charles Wilkins (1749-1836), who came to Bengal as a writer, under East India Company, played an important role in establishing a printing press for oriental languages. On return to England, he established at Haskhurst a fount of Nāgarī type for printing books in Sanskrit. He was the first Sanskrit scholar to study Indian inscriptions. As many as four volumes of *Asiatic Researches*, in five volumes, deal with epigraphy. In 1798, he compiled a catalogue of William Jones's manuscripts.

Colebrooke published (1805) his paper, "On the Vedas or Sacred Writing of Hindus" in *Asiatic Researches.*

European scholars got the incentive to Vedic study from the fact that Colonel Antome Polier, who purchased a copy of the Vedas at Jaipur, deposited it into the British Museum in 1789 after Jones had perused it. Sir Robert Chambers, a judge, acquired a copy of the *Ṛgveda* and parts of the other Vedas.

A few Jesuits played the pioneering part in mastering Sanskrit. Father Hanxleden, who worked in Kerala from 1699 to 1732 compiled the first Sanskrit grammar in a European language. Father Coeurdoul was the first man to discover (1767) the affinity of Sanskrit with European languages. He went so far as to suggest that the Indian Brāhmins descended from one of the sons of Japhat whose brothers migrated to the West.

Attracted by Duperron's translation of the Upaniṣads, the French Govt. founded the Ecole des Langues Orientales Vivantes.

Alexander Hamilton (1762-1824), a member of the Asiatic Society of Bengal, was the first men to teach Sanskrit in Europe. His pupil was Friedrich Schlegel, the first German Sanskritist. He wrote a book on the poetry and wisdom of the Indians, *Sprache und Weisheit der indier* (1808). The first University Chair in Sanskrit was founded (1814) at the College of France, and was held by Leonard d. Chezy. In Germany, the major Universities set up Sanskrit Chairs.

In England, Sanskrit was first taught (1805) at Hertford, and Chairs for its study were founded at London, Cambridge, Edinburgh and in some other educational institutions. Horace Hayman Wilson was the first scholar to adorn the Chair at Oxford University.

Thanks to the persistent and zealous scholarly activities of Franz Bopp (1791-1867), comparative philology came to be regarded as an independent subject of study in the 19th century. The foundation of the French Society Asiatique in Paris was followed by that of the Royal Society of London.

The most remarkable achievement of Indological scholarship in the nineteenth century, not only in Europe but in the whole world, was the huge Sanskrit-German Dictionary, known as *St. Petersburg Lexicon*, compiled by the German scholars, Otto Böhtlingk and Rudolf Roth. It was also partly published by the Russian Imperial Academy of Sciences from 1852 to 1875.

The observations of the three German savants are a sufficient index to the deep impact of Sanskrit philosophy and literature on the west. The great German philospher, Schopenhauer (1788-1860) says of the *Oupnek'hat* (this is how he called the Upaniṣad):

> It is the most satisfying and elevating reading which is possible in the world; it has been the solace of my life and will be the solace of my death.[1]

We have it, on the authority of Winternitz, that the *Oupnek'hat* used to lie open on his table and that before retiring to rest he performed his devotions in it. In appreciation of Kālidāsa's masterpiece, the *Abhijñānaśākuntala*, the greatest of ancient Indian dramas, Goethe, the greatest poet of Germany and one of the greatest in the world paid glowing tributes which, in English rendering, stand as follows:

> Wouldst thou the young year's blossoms and the fruits of its decline,
> And all by which the soul is charmed, enraptured, feasted and fed?
> Wouldst thou the earth and heaven itself in one sole name combine?
> I name thee, O Śakuntalā, and all at once is said.

The great German philosopher, Humboldt, bestows a high meed of praise on the *Bhagavadgītā* by saying that it is the *only* truly philosophical poem in all the literatures known to us.

The following lines from Preface, by Warren Hastings, Governor-General under East India Company, to Wilkin's translation of the *Bhagavadgītā*, undertaken at the instance of the former, will be a fitting finale to this account:

"The writers of the Indian Philosophies will survive, when the British dominion in India shall long have ceased to exist, and when the sources which it yielded of wealth and power are lost to remembrance."

---

1. Parerga und Paralipomena, pub. by J. Frauenstadt, II, p. 427 (§ 185) Hecker, *Schopenhauer und die indische Philosophie*, pp. 6 ff. See Winternitz, *History of Indian Literature*, vol. I. (1927), p. 275.

Name of Scholar	Date	Work	Date of publication and remarks
Adelung, F (G)	1768-1843	*Versuch einer Literatur der Sanskrit sprache*	1830. A study in the literature of the Sanskrit language. It is a bibliography.
Anquetil-Duperron (F)	1731-1805	See Perron	
Aufrecht, T (G)	1822-1907	(1) *Catalogus Catalogorum*—3 Vols.	1891, 1896 and 1903. It contains an alphabetical list of all Sanskrit works and authors, based on available catalogues of MSS.
		(2) Edition of the complete text of the *Ṛgveda*.	1861-63
		(3) Trs. of *Atharvaveda*	With A. Weber in several volumes of whose *Indische Studien* it appeared from 1850 onwards. Incomplete.
Ballantyne, J.R. (E)	1813-64	(1) *Sāṃkhya Aphorisms of Kapila* (Eng. trs.).	1852
		(2) *Nyāya-sūtra*, 2 pts.	1850-53
		(3) *Vaiśeṣika-sūtra*	1851
		(4) *Mahābhāṣya*	1855
		(5) *Sāhitya-darpaṇa*	1851
		(6) *Yoga-sūtra*	1882
		(7) *Hindu Philosophy*	1879, 1881.
Barthelemy, J (F)	1805-95	*Des Vedas*	1854
Bartholome, W (Austrian)	1748-1806	(1) *Systema Brahmanicum*	Rome, 1791.
		(2) *Amarasiṃha sen Dictionari Samascrada... cum versione Latine*	Rome, 1798.
		(3) *Reise nach Ostindien.* Besides the above, Bartholome wrote two Sanskrit grammars published at	

Name of Scholar	Date	Work	Date of publication and remarks
		Rome in 1790 and 1804 respectively. These are in Tamil script, and based on the unpublished Sanskrit grammar of J.E. Hanxleden, German Jesuit Father.	
Benfey, T (G)	1809-81	(1) German trs. of the *Pañcatantra*	1859
		(2) *Handbook des Sanskrit Sprache*	Leipzig 1852-54
		(3) *A practical Grammar of Sanskrit Language*	London, 1868
		(4) *Vedica und Linguistica*	1880
		(5) *Vedica und Verwandies*	1880
		(6) *A Skt.-Eng. Dictionary with ref. to best editions of Skt. Authors*	
		(7) Ed. and German trs. of *Sāmaveda*	1848
		(8) History of *Sanskrit Philology*	
Bergaigne, A.H.J. (F)	b. 1888	(1) *Bhāminī-vilāsa* (Ed. and Fr. Trs.)	1872
		(2) *la Religion Vedique d'apres les hymns du Ṛgveda.*	1878-83
		(3) *Nāgānanda* (Fr. trs)	1879
		(4) *Śakuntalā* (Fr. trs.)	1884
		(5) *Les inscriptions Sanskrites du Cambodge*	1882
		(6) *Manuel Pour etudier lu langue Sanskrite*	1884
Bohlen, P. (G)	1796-1840	Trs. of *Ṛtu-saṃhāra*	
Böhtlingk, O (G)	1815-1904	(1) *Sanskrit Wörterbuch* (7 Vols.)	
		(2) Ed. first Chap. of *Aṣṭādhyāyī* with comm.	See under Roth, R. 1839
		(3) Whole of *Aṣṭādhyāyī* with trs. and notes.	1887
		(4) Hemcandra's *Abhidhānacintāmaṇi* (German version)	1848

Name of Scholar	Date	Work	Date of publication and remarks
		(Sanskrit-German dictionary, generally known as St. Petersburg Lexicon).	First part appeared in 1852, completed in 1875. (Russian Imperial Academy of Sciences)
Bopp, F (G)	1791—1867	(1) *Über das conjugations system der Sanskrit—sprache in Vergleichung mit jenen der griechis-chen lateinischem, persischen und germanischen sprache.*	Frankfurt, 1816. By this book he founded the new science of Comparative Philology. As an appendix to this book, he gave some episodes from the *Rāmāyaṇa* and the *Mahābhārata* in metrical translation from the original text.
		(2) *Nalus, Carmen Sanskritum e Mahābhārata, edidit*, Latine verit et adnotationibus illustravit	London, 1819. A critical ed., with a Latin rendering, of the *Mahābhārata* story of Nala and Damayatī.
		(3) *Glossarius Sanscritum*	Berolini, 1830, 1847
		(4) *Vergleichende Grammatik des Sanskrit*, Zen, Griechischen, Latcinschen etc. In 6 pts.	1833-52
		(5) Trs. of episodes of *Rāmāyaṇa*	
Bredoer, B (G)	1894-1947	*Kauṭilya Studien*	1926, 1928
Brockhaus, H (D)	1806-77	(1) *Kathāsarit-sāgara* (ed. and partly trs.)	1839-66
		(2) *Prabodha-candrodaya* (ed.)	1834—35
Bũhler, G (G)	1837-98	(1) *Grundriss der indoarischen philologie und Altertumskunde*	Encyclopaedia of Indo-Aryan philology and Archaeology. Planned by Buhler,

Name of Scholar	Date	Work	Date of publication and remarks
			and executed by a team. Had been appearing since 1896 (Strassburg). 21 vols, complete, 1920.
		(2) *Indische Palaeographie*	Strassburg, 1869.
		(3) *Detailed Report of a tour in search of Sanskrit MSS. in Kashmir, Rajputana and Central India*	1833—52.
		(4) *A Cat. of Sanskrit MSS. from Gujarat, Kutch, Sind and Khandesh*	Bombay, 1873.
		(5) *Indische Studien*	
		(6) *Aphorisms on the Sacred Laws of the Hindus by Āpastamba*	1868—71.
		(7) *Āpastamba, Gautama, Vaśiṣṭha and Baudhāyana Dharmasūtras (Eng. trs. in 2 parts)*	SBE. II and XIV, Oxford, 1879—82.
		(8) *On the origin of the Indian Brāhmī Alphabet*	Strassburg, 1898
		(9) Trs. of *Manusmṛti*	
Burnell, A.C. (E)	1840—82	(1) *The Aindra school of Skt. grammarians*	1875
		(2) *The Ordinances of Manu* (Eng. trs.)	
		(3) The Law of Partition and Succession from manuscript of Varadarāja's *Vyavahāranirṇaya*	
		(4) *Sāmavidhāna Brāhmaṇa* ed.)	1873
		(5) *Ārṣeya Brāhmaṇa* of the *Sāmaveda* (ed.)	1876
Burnouf, E. (F)	1801-52	*Le Bhāgavata Purāṇa* 3 vols. (Text and Fr. trs. upto Skandha ix)	Paris, 1840, 44-47

Name of Scholar	Date	Work	Date of publication and remarks
Caland, W. (D)	1859-1932	(1) *Die altindischen Toten etc.*	Amsterdam, 1896.
		(2) *Indische Forschungen*	Breslau, 1907
		(3) *L'Agniṣṭoma* etc.	Paris, 1906
		(4) Über Totenverehrung. volker	Amsterdam, 1888.
		(5) *Altindischer Ahnenkult*	Leyden, 1893
		(6) *Baudhāyana-śrautasūtra* (trs.)	
		(7) *Baudhāyana-śrautas ūtra* (ed.)	Calcutta, 1904-24
		(8) *Kāṭhaka-gṛhyasūtra* (ed). Besides these, he edited and translated some other works of the Kalpasūtra.	
Chezy, A.L. de (F) 1773-1832		Fr. trs. of *Śakuntalā* (1830) and *Amaru-śataka* (1831)	
Colebrooke, H.T. (F)	1765-1837	(1) *A Digest of Hindu Law on contracts and successions.*	1797-98. Trs. of a composition, prepared by native scholars, on the law of succession and contract, from the Indian law books. 4 vols., Calcutta, 1797-98.
		(2) *Miscellaneous Essays*	Madras, 1872. A German trs. pub. in 1847.
		(3) Grammar of the Sanskrit language	Calcutta, 1805.
		(4) *Hitopadeśa*, ed. with introductory remarks.	1804.
		(5) *Amarakośa*, ed. with marginal trs.	Serampore, 1808.
		(6) *Śataka-trayam* of Bhartṛhari	1804
		(7) *Sāṃkhya-kārikā* of Īśvarakṛṣṇa (trs.)	1837

Name of Scholar	Date	Work	Date of publication and remarks
		(8) Trs. of two treatises on Hindu law of inheritance	Calcutta, 1810
		(9) Algebra with Arithmetic and Mensuration from Skt. works of Brahmagupta and Bhāskara preceded by a dissertation on the state of science as known to Hindus.	London, 1817
Cunningham, A. (E)	1814-93	*Ancient Geography of India*, Vol. 1	London, 1871
Dahlmann, J. (G)		*Das Mahābhārata als Rechtsbuch*	1895
Debrunner, A. (G)	1884-1958	Continued the work left incomplete by Wackernagel	
Deussen, P. (G)	1845-1919	(1) *Die philosophie der Upaniṣads.* Part of *Allgemeine Geschichte der philosophie*	1899
		(2) Trs. of 60 Upaniṣads	1897
		(3) *Das System des Vedānta*	1883
		(4) *History of Indian Philosophy*	
		(5) Trs. of the Philosophical portions of the *Mahābhārata*	Jointly with Garbe
Duperron : See Perron			
Eggeling, J. (G)	1842-1918	(1) Trs. of *Śatapatha Brāhmaṇa*, 4 Vols. in SBE	
		(2) Studies in Pāṇini	
Fauche, H. (F)	1797-1869	French trs. gf *Gīta-govinda* (1850), *Śiśupālavadha* (1861), *Daśakumāra-carita*, *Mṛcchakaṭika*, *Rāmāyaṇa* (1854-59) and parts of the *Mahābhārata* (1863), *Rāvaṇavadha* of Bhartṛhari. Bhartṛhari et al Pantchachika de chaura.	1892

Name of Scholar	Date	Work	Date of publication and remarks
Forster, G. (G)		German trs. of William Jones' Eng. trs. of Kālidāsa's *Śakuntalā.*	1791
Forster, H.P.		An essay on the Principles of Sanskrit Grammar.	Calcutta, 1810
Foucaux P.E. (F)	1811-94	*Lalitavistara* (Tibetan version with French trs.)	
Franke, R.V. (G)	1862-1928	Studies in Pāṇini	
Garbe, R. (G)	1857-1927	(1) German trs. ot *Bhagavadgīta.* (2) *Die Sāṁkhya-philosophic cine Darstellung der indischen Rationalismus* (3) Trs. of *Sāṅkhya-tattva-kaumudī*	
Geldner, K.F.	1852-1929	Trs. of *Ṛgveda*	
Gildemeister, J (G)		*Biblotheoae Sanskritae-sive recensus librorum Sanskritorum*	1847. About 30 edited texts are mentioned in it.
Glasenapp, H.V. (G)	1891-1963	(1) *Study on Rāmānujya and Madhva* (2) *Die philosophie der India* (3) *Die Literaturen Indiens Gegenwart*	—latter in 1923. 1958 1926-27
Goldstücker, T. (G)	1821-72	(1) Pāṇini—his place in Skt. Literature, London, (2) *Prabodha-candrodaya* (German trs.) (3) Thoughts of some Brahmins	1851 1842 1792. Free translation of some anomic stanzas from Bhartṛhari; *Hitopadeśa* and *Bhagavadgītā.*
Gorresio, C.G. (1)	1808-91	*Rāmāyaṇa* (Ed. and trs. into Italian)	

Name of Scholar	Date	Work	Date of publication and remarks
Grassmann, H.G. (G)	1809-77	(1) *Wörterbuch zum Ṛg-veda*, 2 vols.	1867-77
		(2) *Uebersetzung des Ṛgveda*	1875
Grill, J. (G) :	1840-1918	Trs. of 100 songs of	*Atharvaveda*, 1776.
Halhed, N.B. (E)	1751-1830	*Gentoo Code*	Eng. trs. of the Persian version of the *Vivādārṇava-setu*, a compilation of Indian law of inheritance, family law, etc.
Hamilton, A. (E)	1762-1824	(1) *Hitopadeśa* (ed.)	1811.
		(2) *A Treatise on Skt. Grammar*	
		(3) *A Key to Chronology of the Hindus*	Cambridge, 1820.
Hanxleden, J.E. (G) [Came to India in 1699 and worked in Malabar from 1699 to 1732 A.D.]		*Grammatica Granthamia seu Samscrdumica*	First Sanskrit Grammar written by a European. It was not printed, but was used by Bartholome (q.v.).
Hastings, W. (E)	1732-1818	*Vivādārṇava-setu*	A compilation, from Indian law-books, of important matters relating to law of inheritance, family law etc. made by a number of scholars at the instance of Hastings.
Hauer, J.N. (G)	1881-1962	(1) *Anfänge der Yogapraxis*	1922
		(2) *Yoga als Heilsweg*	1932
		(3) *Mānava-kalpasūtra* (with comm. of Kumārila Svāmin)	London, 1861.
		(4) *Jaiminīya Nyāya-mālā-vistara*, 5 vols.	London, 1872. Complete vols. in 1878.
Haug, M.H. (G)	1827-76	*Aitareya Brāhmaṇa* (Eng. trs.)	Reprinted, Allahabad, 1923

Name of Scholar	Date	Work	Date of publication and remarks
Herder, J.G. (G)		(1) *Critical analysis of Kālidāsa's Śakuntalā*	
		(2) *Thoughts of Some Brahmins*	1792. Free translation of some nomic stanzas from Bhartṛhari, *Hitopodeśa* and *Bhagavadgītā*.
Hertel, J. (G)		(1) Discussion on Different Versions of *Pañcatantra*	
		(2) *Tantrākhyāyikā*	
		(3) *Hitopadeśa* (trs.)	
Hillebrandt, A. (G)	1853-1927	(1) *Vedische Mythologie*	3 Vols., Breslau, 1891, 1899, 1902.
		(2) *Das altindische Neu- und Vollmondsopfer.*	1879
		(3) *Ritual Literature*	1879
		(4) *Śāṃkhāyana-śrauta-sūtra*, Calcutta,	1888 ff.
Hohenberger, A. (G)	1881-1966	*Monograph on Rāmānuja's Philosophy.*	
Holtzmann, A. (G)	1810-70	*Indische Sagen*	
Do (Junior) (G)	1838-1914	*Das Mahābhārata und scine Tiele*	
Humboldt, W. (G)	1767-1835	*Uber die unter dem Namen Bhagavadgītā bekannte Episode des Mahābhārata*	
Jones, W. (E)	1746-94	(1) Eng. trs. of *Śakuntalā*	1789
		(2) *Ṛtu-saṃhāra* (ed)	1792. First printed work in Skt.
		(3) *Institutes of Hindu Law or the Ordinance of Manu*	Calcutta, 1794. Eng. trs. of the *Manusmṛti.* A German trs. of the work appeared in 1797 in Weimar.
		(4) *Hitopadeśa* (trs.)	1791
		(5) Eng. trs. of the *Gītagovinda*	

Name of Scholar	Date	Work	Date of publication and remarks
Kielhorn, F. (E)	1840-1908	(1) *Studies in Pāṇini* (2) *Mahābhāṣya* (ed.) (3) Ed. of *Grundriss der Indo-arischen Philologie* and *Altertumaskunde*	
Kirfel, W. (G)	1895-1964	*Das Purāṇa Pañcalakṣaṇa*	1927
Kuhn, F.F.A. (G)	1812-1894	(1) *Mythological Studies*, 2 vols.	1886-1912
		(2) *Zur altesten Geschichte der Indogermanischen Volkes*	1845
Langlois, S.A. (F)	1788-1854	(1) *Harivaṃśa* (Fr. trs.)	London, 1834
		(2) *Ṛgveda ou livre des Hymns, traduit* (Fr. trs. of *Ṛgveda*)	1848-51
		(3) *Monumens litterraies de Inde*	Paris, 1827
Lassen, C.	1800-76	*Indische Altertumskunde*, 4 vols.	1843-44. Last vol. published, 1862. It contains valuable information on various matters relating to Indian history, culture, geography and economy from after the birth of Christ down to the advent of the Muslims.
Liebich, B. (G)	1862-1939	*Studies in Pāṇini*	
Lūders, H. (G)	1869-1943	*Die Vyāsa-Śikṣā etc.* Kiel, His major work on Vedic deities, Varuṇa, was incomplete when he died. L. Alsdorf has edited the MS. in two parts.	1895
Ludwig, A. (G)	1832-1911 or 1837-1912	Trs. of *Ṛgveda*	Pub. at Prague, 1876-88

Name of Scholar	Date	Work	Date of publication and remarks
Ludwig, J.G. (G)	1792-1862	Trs. of *Nala-Damayantī* story, *Pañcatantra*, etc.	
Max Müller, F. (G)	1823-1900	(1) *Ṛgveda*, with comm. of Sāyaṇa (ed.).	1849-73 (6 vols.)
(Founder of Comparative Religion and editor of the Sacred Books of the East Series)		(2) *Hitopadeśa* (ed.) and trs. into German).	Leipzig, 1844
		(3) *Meghadūta* (ed. and trs. into German)	Konigsberg, 1847
		(4) *Ṛgveda-prātiśākhya* (Text with German trs.)	Leipzig, 1859-69
		(5) The *Upaniṣads* (Eng. trs.)	SBE, Vols. I and XV
		(6) *A History of Ancient Skt. Literature*	London, 1859
		(7) *A Sanskrit Grammar*	
		(8) *India—what can it teach us?*	
		(9) *Āpastamba-Sūtras* (Eng. trs.)	SBE, 1893
		(10) *The Six Systems of Hindu Philosophy*	London, 1890
		(11) Three Lectures on Vedānta Philosophy	London, 1894
Meter, J.J. (G)	1870-1939	*Über des .. Zu Kauṭilya*	1927
Meyer (G)		*Das altindisch Buch vom Welt-und Staats leben*	1926
Minayev, I.P.	1840-90	(1) *Declensions and Conju gations of Skt. Grammar*	St. Petersburg, 1889
		(2) *Sketches of important monuments of Skt. Literature*	St. Petersburg, 1880 Republished, 1962
		(3) *Indian Tales and Legends*	Do, 1875
Muir, J. (E)	1809-82	*Original Skt. texts on origin and history of the people of India*, 4 pts.	1858-63 (1st. ed.)
Müller, M.		See Max Müller	
Nobel, J. (A)	1887-1960	*The Foundations of Indian Poetry*	1925

Name of Scholar	Date	Work	Date of publication and remarks
Oldenberg, H. (G)	1854-1920	(1) *Religion des Veda*	Berlin, 1894
		(2) *Ṛgveda, Text-critische Und exegetische*, Noten, 2 vols.	He translated also several Gṛhyasūtras. 1902-12
		(3) Die Weltanschaung der Brāhmaṇa Texts	1919
		(4) *Die Lehre Buddhismus*	1915
Otto, R. (G)	1869-1931	*West-Östliche Mystik*	1929 Comparison of Śaṃkara's teachings with that of the German mystic Eckhart Trs. of Rāmānuja's *Siddhānta*.
Perron, A.D. (F)	1731-1805	*Oupnek'hat ou Theologia et philosophia*	Paris, 1801-02. Latin trs. of the Persian version, made in the 17th century by Dārā Shikoh, brother of Aurangzeb, of Upaniṣads.
Peterson, P. (E)	1846-1899	(1) *Vallabha's Subhāṣitāvalī* (ed.)	Bombay, 1886
		(2) *Śārṅgadhara-paddhati* (anthology) ed.	Bombay, 1886
Petrov, P.Y.	1814-75	Part of *Rāmāyaṇa*, called Sītāharaṇa, Sītāharaṇa with word-index, grammatical notes and Russian trs.	1836
Pischel, R. (G)	1849-1908	*Vedische studien*, Vol. I-III (with Geldner)	1889, 1892, 1901
Regnier, A. (F)	1804-84	(1) *Ṛgveda-prātiśākhya* (ed. and trs.)	1857-59
		(2) *Etudes sur L' idiome des Vedas et les origines de la language Sanscrite*	1885

Name of Scholar	Date	Work	Date of publication and remarks
Roer, H.H.E. (G)	1805-66	(1) *Ṛgveda* (in part ed. and trs.)	Bib. Ind., 1848
		(2) *Bṛhadāraṇyakopaniṣad* (ed. and trs.)	Bib. Ind., 1849-56
		(3) *Chāndogyopaniṣad* (ed.)	Bib. Ind. 1849-50
		(4) *Taittirīya* and *Aitareya Upaniṣads* (ed.)	Bib Ind. 1849-50
		(5) *Īśā, Kena, Kaṭha, Praśna, Muṇḍaka Upaniṣads* (ed.)	Bib. Ind., 1849
		(6) *Taittirīya, Aitareya, Śvetāśvatara, Kena, Īśā, Kaṭha, Praśna, Muṇḍaka* and *Māṇḍūkya Upaniṣads* (Eng. trs.)	Bilb. Ind., 1851-55
		(7) *The Upaniṣads* (Eng. trs.)	Bib. Ind., 1907
		(8) *Bṛhadāraṇyakopaniṣad* (Eng. trs.)	Bib. Ind., 1908
Rogerius, A. (D)	1609-?	*De Open-Deure tot het verboregen Heydendom*	In Dutch. Pub. 1651. The title means "Open door to the hidden heathendom". Dutch trs. of 200 verses from the *Nītiśataka and Vairāgyaśataka* of Bhartṛhari. First trs., into a European language, of Skt. works. Trs. into German and pub. Nuremberg, 1663. W. Caland edited and published it again in 1915.
Rosen, A.F. (G)	1805-87	(1) *Ṛgveda-saṃhitā Sanskrit et Latines*	London, 1838 Ed. of the first eighth of the *Ṛgveda*
		(2) *Corporis radicum Sanskritarum Prolusio*	Berlin, 1926.
		(3) *Radices Sanskritae*	Berlin, 1927

Name of Scholar	Date	Work	Date of publication and remarks
Rost, R. (G)	1822-96	(1) Translation of the Indian sources of the ancient Burmese Laws	1850
		(2) A Des. Cat. of Palm-leaf Mss. belonging to Imperial Library of St. Petersburg	1852
Roth, H. (G)	1610-68	His indological researches pub. in Father Arthanasisum Kircher's China illustrata	Amsterdam, 1667
Roth, R. (G)	1821-95	(1) *Zur-Literatur und Geschichte des Weds*	1846. It is on the literature and history of the Veda. Jointly with Böhtlingk, Eng. trs., Calcutta, 1880
		(2) *Nirukta* of Yāska	Göttingen, 1852.
		(3) Sanskrit Wörterbuch, 7 Vols.	St. Petersburg, 1852-75
		(4) *Atharvaveda* (ed.)	Jointly with W.D. Whitney, 1855-56
Ruben, W. (G)		Ed. of *Nyāya-sūtras*	
Ruckert, F. (G)	1788-1886		His German trs. of *Nalopākhyāna. Maitropākhyāna*, *Sāvitrī-upākhyāna*, *Gītagovinda*, *Amaruśataka*, etc. colbcted and pub. by H.V. Glasenapp in Leipzig, 1923
Schlegel, A.W.V. (G)	1767-1845	(1) *Indische Bibliothek*	First vol. appeared in 1823. It is a periodical founded and almost entirely written by this Schlegel.
		(2) First critical ed. of the *Bhagavadgītā* with Latin trs.	Bonn, 1823

Name of Scholar	Date	Work	Date of publication and remarks
		(3) *Rāmāyaṇa* (G.ed.)	1829
		(4) *Hitopadeśa*	Bonn, 1829-31
Schlegel, F. (G)	1772-1829	*Über die sprache und weisheit der Inder Ein Beitrag Zur Begründung der Altertumskunde*	1808. By this work Schlegel became the founder of Indian philology in Germany. It contains also translation of some passages from the *Rāmāyaṇa*, *Manu-smṛti*, *Bhagavadgītā* and from the Śakuntalā episode of the *Mahābhārata*. These were the first direct translations from Sanskrit into German.
Schmidt, R. (G)	1866-1939	(1) Trs. of *Gheraṇḍa Saṃhitā*.	1912
		(2) Trs. of *Śukasaptati*	
		(3) Trs. of longer version of *Tantrākhyāyikā*	
Schomerus, H.W. (G)	1879-1945	*Der Śaiva Siddhānta*	
Schrader, F.O. (G)	1876-1961	*Intro. to Pañcarātra* and the *Ahirbudhnya-saṃhitā*	
Schroeder, L. (G)	1851-1920	(1) *Black Yajurveda* (Maitrāyaṇī Saṃhitā) 2 vols.	1881-86
		(2) *Kāṭhaka-saṃhita*, 4 vols.	1900-10
Schultz, T (G)	1824-98	*Vedānta und Buddhismus*	
Schultz, (G)	1805-92	German trs. of *Bhaṭṭikāvya* (1837), *Śiśupālavadha* (1845), and *Kirātārjunīya* (1845)	
Simon, A.L. (F)	1788-1854	(1) *Harivaṃśa* (Fr. trs.)	London, 1834
		(2) Ṛgveda ou livre des Hymns. traduit (Fr. trs. of the *Ṛgveda*)	1848-51
		(3) Monuments litteraries de Inde	Paris, 1827

Name of Scholar	Date	Work	Date of publication and remarks
Stenzler, A.F. (Sweedish)	1807-87	(1) *Elementarbuch der Sanskrit Sprache* (2) *Raghuvaṃśa* (Text and Latin trs.) (3) *Kumārasambhava* (Do) (4) *Meghadūta* (Latin trs.) (5) *Brahmavaivarta-purāṇa* (Latin trs.)	
Strauss, O. (G)	1881-1940	*Indische Philosophic*	1925.
Wackernagel, J. (G)	1853-1938	*Altindische Grammatik*	
Weber, A. (G)	1825-1901	(1) *Akademische Vorlesungen Über indische Literatur geschichte*	Berlin, 1852. It is the first attempt to write a complete history of Indian literature. An Eng. trs. of it appeared in Trübner's Oriental Series.
		(2) *Indische Literatur-geschichte*	1852. It discusses about 500 works on Indian literature.
		(3) *White Yajurveda*	London and Berlin, 1852-59.
		(4) *Indische Studien* (17 vols)	1850-85
		(5) *History of Indian Literature*	1878
		(6) *Kerzeichmisse der Sanskrit and Prākrit Handschriften der Koninglichen Bibliothek*	Berlin, 1886
		(7) Varāhamihira's *Laghu-jātaka*	Ed. & trs., left incomplete.
Welter, H. (G)		Trs. of *Haṭhayoga-pradīpikā*	
Westergaard, N.L. (Danish)	1815-78	*Radices Linguae Sanskrit*	1841

Name of Scholar	Date	Work	Date of publication and remarks
Whitney, W.D. (A)	1827-94	(1) *Atharvaveda-saṃhitā* (ed.)	Berlin, 1856 (With R. Roth)
		(2) *Atharvaveda-prātiśākhya* (ed. with comm. and trs.)	*JAOS*, vol. 7, 1862
		(3) *Taittirīya Prātiśākhya* (ed. with comm. and trs.)	*JAOS*, vol. 9
		(4) *Sanskrit Grammar*	Leipzig, 1879
		(5) *The roots, verb-forms and Primary derivatives of Sanskrit language*	Leipzig, 1885
		(6) *Sūrya-siddhānta* (ed. and trs.)	*JAOS*, vol. 6
		(7) *Oriental and Linguistic Studies*, 2 vols.	1873, 1874
		(8) *Viṣṇupurāṇa* (ed.)	
Wilkins, C. (E)	1750-1836	(1) *Bhagavadgītā* (Eng. trs.)	London, 1785, with an intro. by Warren Hastings, the then Governor General of Fort William in Bengal. First Skt. book to be directly translated into a European language.
		(2) *Hitopadeśa* (Eng. trs.)	Bath, 1787
		(3) Śakuntalā episode of the *Mahābhārata*	1793
		(4) *Sanskrit Grammar*	1808. For this book, Devanāgarī type was used for the first time in Europe, a type which the author himself had made.
		(5) *Radicals of Sanskrit language*	1815

Name of Scholar	Date	Work	Date of publication and remarks
Williams, M. (E)	1819-99	(1) *An Elementary Grammar of the Skt. language*	London, 1846
		(2) *Śakuntalā*, ed. & trs.	1856 (1st. ed)
		(3) *Vikramorvaśīya*, ed. and trs.	1849
		(4) *Nalopākhyāna*, ed. and trs.	1879
		(5) *Eng.-Skt. Dictionary*	Londonm, 1851
		(6) *Skt.-Eng. Dictionary*	Oxford, 1872
		(7) *Skt. Manual for composition*	London, 1862
		(8) *A Practical Grammar of the Skt. language*	
		(9) *Indian Wisdom*	London, 1878
		(10) *Hinduism*	New York, 1877
		(11) *Religious thought and life in ancient India*	London, 1883
Wilson, H.H. (E)	1786-1860	Most important works	
		(1) *Meghadūta*, annotated text	1813
		(2) *Sanskrit-English Dictionary* (First of its kind)	1819 (2nd. ed. 1832)
		(3) *Select specimens of the Theatre of the Hindus*, 2 vols.	1826-27
		(4) *Sāṃkhya-kārikā*	1837
		(5) *Viṣṇu-purāṇa* (Eng. tr.)	1840 (Reprinted, Calcutta, 1961)
		(6) *Lectures on Religious and philosophical Systems of the Hindus*	1840
		(7) *Ṛgveda* (Eng. trs. acc. to orthodox interpretation), 6 vols.	1850
Windischmann, F.H.H. (G)	1811-61	Wrote on Śaṃkara	1833

Name of Scholar	Date	Work	Date of publication and remarks
Winternitz, M. (G)	1863-1937	(1) *Geschichte der indischen literatur*	In 3 Vols. subsequently trs. into Eng.
Zimmer, H. (G) (Senior)	1851-1910	*Altindisches Leben* (On life in Vedic India)	Berlin, 1879
Do (Junior)	1890-1943	*Hindu Medicine*	1948

III

INFLUENCE OF SANSKRIT OUTSIDE INDIA

It should not be supposed that Sanskrit literature was confined within the limits of India. Indian culture, enshrined in the ancient language of Sanskrit, had a universal appeal, and spread far beyond the geographical boundaries and political barriers of this country. Centuries before India was subjugated by the British, there had been brisk cultural and commercial intercourse between this land and various countries in Asia and Europe. Alexander's invasion of India in 326 B.C. gave a fillip to such intercourse. What is known as Hellenism was instinct with elements taken from the East. The link between Greece and India was forged as far back as the 6th century B.C. when the Persian Empire bordered on Greece at one end and India at another.

Leaving aside the unsettled question of ideas having been borrowed by India from Greece and Rome, or by the latter from the former, in the fields of astronomy, astrology, medicine, mathematics etc., we find a lot of Sanskrit works translated into various Asian and European languages. These translations are clear proofs of the influence of Sanskrit literature on the literatures written in the above languages. The translations are surely parts of the literature in the languages concerned. Besides translations, we find that certain ideas and stories of Sanskrit literature have become part and parcel of the literatures of certain countries.

For details, the following books and papers may be consulted:

Agoncills, T.A.: *The Oriental Heritage of the Philippines*, Asian History Congress, New Delhi, 1961.

Ahmed, N.: Muslim contributions etc., *Islamic Culture*, XVIII, 1944 (April).

Bag, A.K.: Binomial Theorem etc., *Indian Jour. of History of Science*, I. 1. 1966.

Bagchi, P.C.: *India and China*, New York.

———: *Bhārat O Madhya Eśiyā* (in Bengali).

Banerji, S.C.: *Sanskrit Beyond India*, Calcutta, 1976.

Bapat, P.V.: *Evidence of Indian Culture in South-East Asia*, Nagpur, 1964.

Basham, A.L.: *The Wonder that was India*, 1967.

BEFEO, particularly of 1948 and 1955 (papers by P. Damais), 1964 (paper by K. Bhattacharya).

Bethlenfalvy, G.: *India in Hungarian Learning and Literature*, Delhi, 1980,

Bhattacharya, K.: *Les Religions brāhmaniques dans l' ancien Cambodge d' apres l' epigraphile et l' iconographic*, Paris, 1961.

Bose, A.: The Wind from the East, published in the *Image of India in Western Creative Writing*, Karnatak University.

Bose, P.N.: *Indian Colony of Siam*, Lahore, 1927.

———: *The Hindu Colony of Cambodia*, Adyar, 1927.

———: *The Indian Colony of Champa*, Adyar, 1926.

Chatterji, B.R.: *Indian Cultural Influence in Cambodia*, Calcutta, 1928.

———: *India and Java*, Calcutta, 1933.

Chatterji, R. and Chakravarti, N.P. : *India and Java*.

Choudhuri, Roma: *Sufism and Vedānta*.

Coburn, K. (ed.): *The Notebooks of S.T. Coleridge*, London, 1957.

Coedes, G.: *Les Etats Hindonises d' Indonesie* etc., Paris, 1948 (Rev. ed. available).

Dasgupta, R.K.: Western Response to Indian Literature, *Indian Literature*, Sahitya Akademi, Delhi, 1967.

Datta and Singh: *History of Hindu Mathematics*.

de Casparis: *Praśasti Indonesia*, I.

Delehaye, H.: Les Saints Stylites, *Subsidia Hagiographia*.

Derrett, J.D.: *University of Ceylon Review*, Oct., 1956.

Desai, Z.A.: Story of Nala-Damayantī etc., *JOR*, VIII, 1958.

Devahuti, D.: *India and Ancient Malaya*, Singapore, 1965.

Dowden: *Life of Shelley*.

Dubey, S.: *R. Otto and Hinduism*, Benares, 1969.

Ekholm, G.F.: *American Antiquity*, XVIII, No. 3, Pt. 2, 1953.

———: *Mem. Soc. Amer. Arch.*, 9, 1953.

Evangelista, A.E.: A Preliminary Reading list of Philippine Culture and History submitted to International Conf. on Asian Archaeology, New Delhi, 1961.

Fernando, P.E.E.: *Ceylon To-day*, Jan., 1962.

Filliozat, J.: *The Classical Doctrine of Indian Medicine*, Delhi, 1964.

———: La doctrine des brāhmaṇas d' apres Saint Hippolyte, *Revue del' Histoire des Religions*, 1945.

———: *Les relations exterieures de l' inde*, 1956.

———: *A General History of Sciences*, London, 1957 (Ed. Taton).

Finot, L.: On Pañcatantra—Laotian Version, *Bulletin d' Ecole Francaise d' Extreme Orient*, XVII.

Francisco, J.R.: *Philippine Historical Review*, I. No. 1, 1965. (On the date of coming of Indian influences in the Philippines.)

———: *Historical Bulletin*, VII, No. 2, 1963. (Analogous customs etc. in India and the Philippines).

Friedrich, R.: *The civilisation and culture of Bali*, ed. E.R. Rost, Calcutta, 1959.

Furnivall, J.S.: Manu in Burma, *Jour. of Burma Res. Soc.* 30.2

Garratt, G.T. (ed.): *The Legacy of India*, Oxford, 1937.

George, P.P.S.: Vedāntic Analogies in Shelley's Poetry, unpublished Thesis, Tufts University, 1964.

Ghosh, M.: *Glimpses of Sexual Life in the Nanda-Maurya India* (Eng. trs. of the *Caturbhāṇī* and Study).

Ghosh, R.: Bhīma in Indonesia, *JAS*, X, 1968.

Gokak, V.K.: *India and World Culture*, Delhi, 1972.

Gonda, J.: *Sanskrit in Indonesia*, Nagpur, 1932.

———: *Tidschrift-volkenkunde*, 75, 1935 (On Javanese version of *Bhagavadgītā*).

———: *Die Religionen Indians.*

———: *Sanskrit Texts from Bali*, GOS, 1925.

Gorekar, N.S.: *Indo-Iranian Relations*, II, Stuttgart, 1963.

Goudriaan,: T. and C. Hooykaas: *Stuti and Stava of Balinese Brāhmaṇ Priests.*

Grader, C.J.: *Studies in Life, Thought and Ritual* (in Bali).

Groslier: *Indo-Chine, carrefour des Arts*, Paris, 1960.

———: *Angkor etc.*, Paris, 1956; London 1957; Cologne, 1958.

Hall, D.G.E.: *Hist. of S.E. Asia.*

Hatt, G.: *Det. Kal. Danske Videnskabernes Selskab, Histerisk-Filoogiske meddesler*, XXXI, 6, 1969, (Asiatic Influences in American Folklore).

Heine-Gordon, R. and G. Ekholm: *The Civilisation of Ancient American History and Culture of the Indian People* (Bhāratīya Vidyābhavana), vols. II, III.

Hoernle, A.F.R.:Manuscript remains of Buddhist Lit. found in *F.* Turkestan, Oxford, 1916.

———: *The Bower Manuscript.*

Hooykaas, C.: *Old-Javanese Rāmāyaṇa*, Amsterdam, 1958.

———: *Oldest Javanese version of Pañcatantra.*

———: Greater Indian Studies: Present Desiderata (*Vishveshvarānanda Indological Jour.*, 3, 1965). *Indian Culture*: Vol. IV (Papers on relation bet. India and Ceylon).

India's Contribution to World Thought and Culture, Madras, 1970.

Jardine, J.: *Preface to King Wagaru's Manu Dhammasattham*, Rangoon, 1934.

JASBL, 1959: paper by H.B. Sarkar; 1935, paper by Chhabra. Doctoral thesis available in print, Delhi, 1965.

DO 1881, pp. 218-19.

Jour. of Greater India Society, XII, 1945 (for inscriptions from Borneo).

Kats, J.: *Het Javanese Tooneel*, I, Batavia, 1923.

———: *Hat Rāmāyaṇa of Javansthe Temple-reliefs*, Leiden, 1925.

Kern: *Verspreide Geschriften*, vol. VII.

Kimura, H.: Sanskrit Studies in Japan; Indian Lit. in China. *JOR*, 1956-57.

Le May, R.: *The Culture of South-east Asia*, London, 1954.

Levis, S.: *Sanskrit Texts from Bali*, GOS, 1925, 1933.

Lingat, R.: *Les Regimes matrimoniaux du sud. Est Asiatique*, Paris, 1952 (Vol. I), 1954 (Vol. II).

Lokesh Chandra: *Sanskrit Texts from the Imperial Palace of Peking*, Delhi.

———: *India and Japan—a cultural symphony.*

———: *Sanskrit Culture in Turkish.*

———: *Sanskrit MSS from Tibet*, Delhi.

———: *International Rāmāyaṇa Festival in Indonesia.*

———: *An Illustrated Tibeto-Mongolian Materia Medica of Āyurveda*, Delhi.

Lokesh Chandra and Others: *India's contribution etc.* (Supra).

Lorgeau, E.: Siamese Version of Pañcatantra—*Les Entretiens d' Ecole Francaise d' Extreme Orient*, XVII.

Majumdar, R.C.: *Inscriptions of Kambuja*, Calcutta, 1953.

———: *Ancient Indian Colonies in the Far East*, 2 vols., 4 pts., Lahore, Dacca, Madras, 1927-44.

———: India and Thailand, *Indo-Asian Culture*, 2.1.

———: Hindu Law in Java and Bali, *K. Aiyangar Comm.* vol.

Mason, S.F.: *A History of Sciences*, London, 1953.

May, R. Le.: *The Culture of S.E. Asia*, London, 1954.

Meester, M.E. ed.: *Oriental influences in Eng. Lit. of 19th cent.*, Heidelberg, 1915

Mitra, S.K.: *The Vision of India*, 1949.

Motwani, K.: *Manu Dharmaśāstra.*

Mukherji, P.K.: *Indian Literature in China and the Far East,* Calcutta, 1938.

Mus, P.: *Barabudur,* Hanoi, 1935.

Mutalik, K.: *Francis William Bain,* Bombay, 1963.

Nag, K.: *Greater India,* Calcutta, 1960.

———: *India and the Middle East,* Calcutta, 1954.

Naik, M.K. and Others: *The Image of India in Western Creative Writing,* Dharwar, 1970.

Nakamura, H.: *Japan and Indian Asia,* Calcutta, 1961.

Neugebauer, O.: *The Exact Sciences in Antiquity,* Princeton, 1952.

Pande, S.N.: Geographical traces of cultural expansion from India, *Summaries of Papers, AIOC,* 1974.

Pathak, S.K.: *The Indian Nītiśāstras in Tibet,* Delhi, 1974.

Pigeaud, T.: *Literature of Java,* The Hague, 1967.

Pizzagalli, A.M.: *Indian Culture,* II (Discovery of Sanskrit and Italy in 16th cent.).

Radhakrishnan, S.: *India and China,* 3rd ed., Bombay, 1954.

Raghavan, V.: *The Rāmāyaṇa in Greater India.*

———: *Sanskrit and Indian Studies in U.S.A.*

———: *Sanskrit Studies in Russia.*

Renou, L.: *Adyar Library Bulletin,* 12(4)—Influence of Indian Thought on French Literature.

Raghuvir and C. Yamanoto: *Rāmāyaṇa and China.*

Ram Behari: *Ancient Indian contribution to Mathematics,* Delhi, 1955.

Rawlinson: *Intercourse between India and the Western World.*

Ray, N.R.: *Brāhmaṇical gods in Burma,* Calcutta, 1932.

Roy, D.N.: *The Philippines and India,* Manila, 1929.

Sachau: *Alberuni's India.*

Sadanand, S.: *Hindu Culture in Greater India,* Delhi, 1949.

Sarkar, H.B.: *Indian Influences in the literature of Java and Bali,* Calcutta, 1934.

———: *Jour. of Indian History,* 441, Language and lit. of ancient Indonesia and Malaysia.

———: *Some contributions of India to the ancient civilisation of Indonesia and Malaysia,* Calcutta, 1970.

———: *Dvīpamay Bhārater Prācīn Sāhitya* (in Bengali) Calcutta, 1970.

———: Classical Sanskrit and the beginning of Sanskritic studies in S.E. Asia, *Summaries of Papers*, AIOC., 1974.

———: *Literary Heritage of S.E. Asia*, Calcutta, 1980.

———: Paper entitled The Influence of Indian Dharmaśāstras on the evolution of the Juridical Literature of S.E. Asia—Summary pub. in *Monthly Bulletin of Asiatic Society*, May, 1977.

Sarkar, K.K.: Early Indo-Cambodian Contacts, *Viśvabhāratī Annals*, XI, 1968.

Sarton, G.: *Intro. to History of Science*, Baltimore.

Sastri, K.A.N.: *South Indian Influences in the Far East*, Bombay, 1949.

———: *in Tijdschrift* etc., Bat. G., 1936.

Schultz, S.: *Comparative Literature*, Oregon, vol. II, 1962 (On Thomas Mann).

Sehgal, S.R.: *A.N. Jha Fel. Vol.* (Skt.), III (English)—Sanskritistic Culture in S.E. Asia, India & Laos

Sen, A.K.: *History of Srīvijaya.*

———: *Shelley in Indian Thought*, Studies in Shelley, Calcutta University, 1936.

Sen, S.N.: *Bulletin of Nat. Inst. of Sciences of India*, No. 21, 1962 (Transmission of Scientific ideas).

———: *Jour. of History of Science*, I.1 (Impetus theory of the Vaiśeṣika).

Singhal, D.P.: *India and World Civilisation*, vols. I, II, Calcutta, 1972.

Sternbach, L.: *The Spreading of Cāṇakya's Aphorisms over Greater India*, Calcutta 1969.

———: Sanskrit Subhāṣita-saṃgrahas in Old-Javanese and Tibetan, *ARORI*, XLIII.

———: Influence of Sanskrit Dharma and Arthaśāstras on Nīti lit. of Burma, *Pandit Charudeva Shastri Fel. Vol.*, Delhi, 1974.

———: Hindu concept of the seven constituents of the State in S.E. Asia, *Studies in Indo-Asian Art and Culture*, Vol. III, Delhi, 1974.

———: Influence of Sanskrit Gnomic Lit. on the Gnomic Lit. of Old Java and Bali, Torino, 1979.

Pro. of VII Conf. of Int. Association of Historians of Asia, Bangkok, 1977: Influence of Sanskrit Gnomic Lit. on the Gnomic Lit. of Mongolia, *Pro. of III Int. Congress of Mongolists*, Ulan Bator, 1976.

———: Influence of Sanskrit Gnomic Literature on the Gnomic Literature of Thailand.

———: Universal Appeal of Subhāṣita literature in Sanskrit, *Pro.* of *International Sanskrit Conference*, Delhi, 1972, Vol. II; Cultural Forum, 85.2, 1973.

———: Sanskrit Nīti literature in Greater India, *Vivekananda Comm. Vol.*, Madras, 1970.

———: Purāṇic Wise Sayings in the Literature of Greater India, *Purāṇa*, XI.I.

———: On the Sanskrit Nīti literature of Old Java and Bali, *Pro. of VI Int. Conf. on Asian History*, Jogjakarta, 1974.

———On the Nīti literature of Ceylon, *Brahmavidyā*, 31, 32, 33, 35.

———: Similar social and legal Institutions in Ancient India and Ancient Mexico, *Poona Orientalist*, VII, No. 1

———: Similar thoughts in the Mahābhārata, the literature of Greater India and in the Christian Gospels, *JAOS*, Vol. 91.3.

Stutterheim, W.: *Rāma-legenden Und Rāma-reliefs in Indonesien*, 2 vols., München, 1924.

———: *Studies in Indonesian Archaeology*, The Hague, 1956 (Appendix—Ancient Javanese Bhīma cult).

Tavera, T.H. Pardo de: *El Sanskrito en la langua Tagalog*, Paris, 1887.

Thoreau, H.D.: *Writings*, vols. I, II, V, VI, VII, IX, XIV.

Toynbee, A.J.: *One World and India.*

Van Gulik, R.H.: *Siddham*, Nagpur, 1956.

Viswanath, S.V.: *Pro. of 5th Oriental Conf.*, Lahore, Vol. I (Early Migration of S. Indian Culture to Indo-China and East Indies).

Vogel: *in Bijdr.* Kon-Inst., 1918.

Wales, H.G.Q.: *The Making of Greater India*, London, 1961.

Winsiedt, W.R.: Sanskrit in Malay literature, *R. Turner Vol.*, *BSOAS*, XX, 1957.

———: Malay version of the Rāmāyaṇa, *B.C. Law Vol.*, II, Poona, 1946.

Yeats, W.B.: *Essays and Introductions*, London, 1961.

Besides the above, editions of the following texts are noteworthy:

Bṛhaspati-tattva—ed. S. Levi, 1957.

Gaṇapati-tattva— Do , 1958.

Sanskrit Texts from Bali—S. Levi, Baroda, 1933.

Ślokāntara—ed. S. Rani, Delhi, 1957.

Svara-vyañjana—ed. Raghuvir, Delhi, 1956.

Vṛtta-sañcaya—ed. H. Kern.

ORIENT

TIBET

Let us first start with the immediate neighbours of this sub-continent. It is not known precisely when cultural contact began between India and Tibet. From the Tibetan annals we learn that the ruler, Sroṅ-btsan-gam-po (629—50A.D.), the founder of Lhasa, deputed some scholars to India to study the Sanskrit language. He asked them also to invent a written language for Tibet by fitting Sanskrit alphabet to the phonetic peculiarities of the Tibetan language (See *JASB*, 1881, pp. 128-29).

There is ample evidence of contacts between Tibet and India during the Pāla rule in Bengal, extending roughly from the 8th century to the 11th. During this period, outstanding literary figures from India visited Tibet and settled there. A few noteworthy among them were Śāntarakṣita (8th century), Śīlabhadra (6th-7th cent.), Atiśa Dīpaṅkara (10th-11th cent.), and Abhayākaragupta (10th-11th cent.). They composed Sanskrit works on Buddhist philosophy and Tantra. Many such original works are lost to us and are preserved only in Tibetan translation. Tibet, Ceylon and farther India adopted Indian medicine in a very large measure. The Siddhācāryas of Bengal, to whom the *Caryāpada* is attributed, appear to have exercised considerable influence on Tibet. Four works on Vajrayāna by Tilopā or Tailikapāda are preserved in Tibetan versions. About twenty-five Tantras are associated, in the *Tanjur*, with the name of Saraha or Sarahapāda.

The Tibetans adopted Indian medicine. The *Yoga-śataka* of Nāgārjuna or Vararuci was translated into Tibetan. The voluminous treatise, *Amṛtahṛdaya*, is stated to have been translated into Tibetan in the eighth century; the original is lost. The *Tanjur* preserves also the Tibetan translation of the *Aṣṭāṅgahṛdaya* of Vāgbhaṭa, with two commentaries. It contains a Tibetan version of Śālihotra's *Aśvāyurveda* on veterinary science.

Padmasambhava (c. 750-800 A.D.) is known to have translated the *Vajramantrābhisandhi-mūla Tantra* into Tibetan.

Several Tibetan works on *Nīti*, some of which are the following, appear to be Tibetan versions (9th-11th cent.) of Sanskrit collections of wise sayings.

Prajñā-śataka-nāma-prakaraṇa by Nāgārjuna.

Gāthā-kośa-nāma or *Āryākośa* by Ravigupta.

Cāṇakya-nīti-śāstra by Cāṇakya.

Nītiśāstra by Masūrākṣa.

Subhāṣita-ratna-nidhi-nāma Śāstra, attributed to Ānandavijaya-śrībhadra (12th cent. A.D.).

The *Meghadūta*, *Kāvyādarśa*, *Nāgānanada*, *Aṣṭadhyāyī*, *Kātantra Vyākaraṇa*, *Amarakośa*, *Vetāla-pañcaviṃśati* etc. were translated into Tibetan.

The present Tibetan grammar is modelled by the Tibetan scholar, Sambhoṭa, on the pattern of Sanskrit grammer. The Tibetan versions of some Sanskrit works, notably the *Meghadūta*, *Kāvyādarśa*, *Amarakośa*, enriched Tibetan literature. The Tibetan version of the *Rāmakathā*, the exact Sanskrit original of which is not known, appears to follow, in a large measure, the *Rāma* story in the Vanaparvan of the *Mahābhārata*.

NEPAL

Nepal, though geographically an integral part of India, has had an independent political status. Nevertheless, India exercised profound cultural influence on her.

Many dramas, poems and novels in Nepāli have been written on themes derived from Sanskrit works. Several Maithili and Bengali dramas, written in Nepal, drew upon Sanskrit sources.

Innumerable Sanskrit inscriptions of Nepal date back from the 7th century or an earlier period.

Apart from contiguity, there has always been a brisk commercial contact between these two regions. The Muslim invasion of Bihar and Bengal gave a fillip to the exodus of Indians to Nepal where they sought refuge with their possessions the most precious of which were Sanskrit manuscripts, both Brāhmaṇical and Buddhistic. A very important Mahāyāna Sanskrit work, entitled *Saddharma-puṇḍarīka*, is in the Durbar library of Nepal, the original being lost in India. The other Mahāyāna Buddhist texts, preserved in Nepal, are : *Gaṇḍavyūha*, *Daśabhūmīśvara*, *Pañcaviṃśati-sāhasrikā-prajñāpāramitā*, *Śata-sāhasrikā Prajñāpāramitā*: these are lost in India. There is a Nepalese version of the *Bṛhatkathā*, called *Bṛhatakathā-śloka-saṃgraha*, by Budhasvāmin. A version of the *Cāṇakya-nītisaṃgraha* was probably composed in Nepal. Several Sanskrit works were rendered into Nepāli. Bhānubhakta's *Rāmāyaṇa*, obviously modelled on the *Adhyātma Rāmāyaṇa*, is a national epic of that land. Some of the Sanskrit dramas, composed in Nepal, are *Mahīrāvaṇavadha*, *Madālasā-jātismaraṇa* (14th cent.), *Rāmāyaṇa-nāṭaka* (14th cent.), *Bhairavānanda* and *Pāṇḍavavijaya* (14th cent.).

Sanskrit works on astronomy, Purāṇic themes, Tantra, Kāvya, Rājanīti, Kāmasūtra, Āyurveda, Saṃgīta and Nāṭyaśāstra. These works were composed in the period between the 15th and 18th centuries.

Quite a number of works was translated into Newari.

The Brāhmaṇical deity, Gaṇeśa, has been very popular there.

R.L. Mitra's work, *The Sanskrit Buddhist Literature in Nepal* and Hodgson's *Essays on the Languages, Literatures and Religion of Nepal and Tibet* throw a flood of light on the contribution of Nepal to Sanskrit literature.

BURMA

Burma has been a part of India culturally and geographically and also politically for a long time.

Some of the law-books of Burma, written in Pāli, betray the influence of the Smṛti works of Manu, Nārada, etc. Several legal treatises of that country frankly acknowledge their indebtedness to Manu. The early law-books of Burma refer to the *Wagaru Dhamma* which substantially contains the eighteen titles of law dealt with in Chapter VIII of the *Manu-smṛti*. It was introduced by king Wagaru who reigned in Martatan in 1280 A.D. Burmese texts, based on Manu's work, were compiled. These are *Dhammavilāsa*, *Dhamma-satta*, *Manu-yin*, *Mansura-show-yin*, etc. There are several Sanskrit inscriptions of Burma on stone and gold plates, dating back to the period from the third century to the tenth. These testify to the study of Kātantra grammar, and of the Vedas, particularly *Atharvaveda*. The important Burmese collections of *Nīti*, viz. *Lokanīti*, *Dhammanīti* and *Rājanīti* reveal the influence of Sanskrit gnomic and didactic works. There is a Burmese version of the *Cāṇakya-nīti-sūtra*. A Sanskrit inscription from Hamawa indicates the penetration of Hinduism to Burma long before the fifth cent. A.D. A Pagan inscription of 1442 A.D. mentions the gift, to the *Saṅgha*, of many books some of which bear Sanskrit titles. The Mon inscriptions of Burma contain many Sanskrit terms. An inscription, found in Myinpagan, opens with a Sanskrit verse from the *Mukunda-mālā* of the saint-king, Kulaśekhara. Experts in the *Atharvaveda* appear to have been present in the Burmese Court.

The *Hitopadeśa* stories were popular. Some Sanskrit texts, e.g. *Mugdhabodha*, works on astrology, palmistry, medicine and erotics etc. were translated into Burmese.

Some Brāhmaṇical deities, e.g. Brahmā, Viṣṇu, Śiva, Gaṇeśa, Durgā etc., found their way to Burma. At one place, several incarnations of Viṣṇu are represented. The Burmese chronicle, *Mahayazawin*, records the tradition that the city was founded by Viṣṇu with the help of Garuḍa, Caṇḍī and Parameśvara.

The names of some ancient cities of Burma bear Sanskrit names, e.g Arimaddanapura (ancient Pagan), Bissunomyo (city of Viṣṇu, old Prome), identified with modern town of Hamawze, also known in ancient times as Sisit or Śrikṣetra.

CEYLON

Culturally Ceylon had always been a part of India. Aśoka's attempt at the spread of Buddhism brought Ceylon into intimate contact with India.

The *Culavaṃsa*, a Pali work of Ceylon, mentions Manu's observations on royal duties. The *Mahāvaṃsa*, another work of Ceylon, mentions Cāṇakya, the four castes, Brāhmaṇas versed in the Vedic triad, the four Śāstras of *Kāma* etc. Remarkable similarity between Kandy (in Ceylon) and India is found in laws relating to property, marriage, adoption, etc. The *Sārārtha-saṃgraha* by king Buddhadāsa (4th Cent. A.D.) is one of the earliest Sanskrit works. The medical work, *Yogaśataka*, had been in use in Ceylon up to the end of the nineteenth century. A version of the *Cāṇakya-nīti-śāstra* was current in Ceylon. The Ceylonese works *Vyāsakarāya* and *Pratyayaśata-kāvya* are collections of *Nīti* sayings influenced by Sanskrit. The Sanskrit *Navaratna* was studied in schools of Ceylon. Ceylonese culture betrays the influence of Tantra.

The *Jānakīharaṇa* by Kumāradāsa (513 A.D.) is a very well-known work of Ceylon's classical Sanskrit.

The *Cāndra-vyākaraṇa* was vigorously studied, and a brief grammar, called *Padāvatāra*, was composed. The *Bālāvabodhana* of Mahākāśyapa (12th cent.) is a work on grammar. A work on lexicon, like the *Amarakośa* was written. Of works on Śilpa-śāstra, one is the *Śariputra* on statuary art. The Gauḍa scholar, Rāmacandra Kavibhāratī (13th cent.) settled in Ceylon where he wrote the *Bhakti-śataka* glorifying the Buddha.

The Ceylonese pantheon includes several Brāhmaṇical deities, e.g. Śiva, Viṣṇu, Gaṇeśa, Skanda. Sinhalese literature clearly reveals the influence of Sanskrit literary tradition. Even the language of Ceylon owes a deep debt to Sanskrit for its growth.

Inscriptions and *dhāraṇīs* in Sanskrit were composed in Ceylon. Some Sanskrit works supplied the theme and pattern of Sinhalese works. For example, the *Meghadūta* served as the model for messenger-poems in Sinhalese.

INDONESIA

Coming to the land, now known as Indonesia, we find three law-books called *Kutara Manawa*, *Dewagama* and *Swara-Jambu*. Of these, the first is the earliest and largely follows the Sanskrit *Manu-smṛti*. Of the other two, the first is wholly and the second largely based on the same Indian treatise.

CAMBODIA

Certain epigraphs of Cambodia mention such well-known Sanskrit treatises as the *Aṣṭādhyāyī*, the *Mahābhāṣya*,etc. Besides, in an inscription of Rājendravarman, four verses appear to have been composed in imitation of a few verses of the *Raghuvaṃśa* of Kālidāsa. The discovery of quite a number of Sanskrit inscriptions in Cambodia is a definite evidence of the influence of this language. Some inscriptions reveal familiarity with the Indian epics, medical works, *Artha-śāstra*, the *Raghuvaṃśa*, *Sūryaśataka*, *Kathāsarit-sāgara*, *Horāśāstra*, *Kāmasūtra*, Vedāntic ideas etc. At least four Tantras appear to have been introduced into Cambodia about 800 A.D. Under some Cambodian kings, e.g. Bhavavarman, Jayavarman, Indravarman, scholars appear to have studied and acquired proficiency in various branches of Brāhmaṇical learning. The eulogy of king Rājendravarman is in the ornate Kāvya style, and refers copiously to Vedic, epic, Purāṇic and grammatical works, the *Raghuvaṃśa*, etc. The Cambodian version of the *Rāmāyaṇa*, called *Ramakerti*, shows a curious blend of Brāhmaṇical and Buddhistic ideas. In it Rāma is called a Bodhisattva. The Śaivite temple of Angkor is a towering witness to the influence of Brāhmaṇical religion. Some temples, e.g. Baphoun Mountain Temple, Banteay Sri Temple, depict *Rāmāyaṇa* scenes. Among the Sanskrit works of Cambodia are the *Śiva-saṃhitā*,*Śivadharma*, *Guhya-ṭīkā*, mentioned in inscriptions.

Several kings and priests of this land bore Sanskrit names. The subjects of study for princes included *Siddhāntas*, Sanskrit grammar, Dharmaśāstras and Indian philosophical systems.

There are epigraphical evidences to show that the *Rāmāyaṇa* story gained currency in Indo-China and Indonesia as early as the earlier part of the first millennium of the Christian era. In the language, literature and arts of Kambuja, Campā and Siam there is marked influence of Sanskrit. The kings of

Campa and Kambuja, studied Sanskrit law-books and administered Law in their kingdoms according to these texts. Quotations from the *Manu-smṛti* have been found in Cambodian inscriptions.

THAILAND (SIAM)

The popular *Rāmāyaṇa*, current in Siam, is called *Rāmakīr* or *Rāmakien* which means Rāma-krit. One of the source-books, on which the *Rāma-kien* is based, is the old Siamese work called *Nārāyaṇa-sippam*; it contains myths and legends about the ten incarnations of *Nārāyaṇa*. The *Cāṇakya-nīti-śāstra* was translated into Siamese. The legal system of Siam appears to be based on the *Manu-smṛti*. At the instance of King Rāma I, 123 volumes of legal texts were prepared. Of these, No. I is the *Brah Dharmaśāstra* (the sacred code of Manu). A Pāli version of the Burmese *Wagaru-Dhammathat* was probably introduced into Thailand in the 16th century A.D.

A Sanskrit work, entitled *Traibhūmikathā*, dealing with Buddhist cosmology, was composed in 1345 A.D. It is preserved in Siamese translation.

A poem, *Lilit Yuen P'ay*, containing many Sanskrit words, was written in the 15th cent.

An inscription on stone points to its Barāhmaṇical character and the influence of Sanskrit learning. The cult of Agastya is very popular. The Brāhmaṇical deity, Gaṇeśa, is very prominent. A wall-painting from Phrakhee Vat, Bangkok, depicts a *Rāmāyaṇa* scene. *Rāmāyaṇa* episodes are represented in sculptures and murals, enacted on the stage and performed in the popular mask-dance. The Thai vocabulary contains some words which are either pure Sanskrit or derivatives from Sanskrit. *Vivāha*, *Velā*, etc. are instances of the former class. The following are a few examples of the latter type: *Khantha* (Skt. *grantha*), *sukhī hotu* (Skt. *sukhī bhavatu*), *Saṃkha* (Skt. *saṃgha*).

MALAYSIA

K. Motwani points out[1] that Malayan Jurisprudence was influenced by the *Manu-smṛti*. That Indian law-books were followed in this land in pre-Islamic period is borne out by several provisions of law, particularly found in the following treatises: *Adat Temenggong*, *Risalat Hukum Kanun*, *Malacca Digest*. Two Sanskrit inscriptions of Malaya probably date back to the fourth century. The *Pañcatantra* and *Hitopadeśa* were translated. At least two Malay works were inspired by the *Kathāsarit-sāgara*. The *Śukasaptati* appears to have influenced Malaya literature. The Malaya work *adat Temenggong* reveals knowledge of the works of Manu, Kauṭilya, Kāmandaka, etc. Temples and sculpture of Malaya stand as witnesses to Brāhmaṇical culture. Themes from Indian epics are used in dance, drama, puppet-shows and shadow-plays. The oldest *Rāmāyaṇa* manuscript, the *Hikayat Seri Rāma*, has a Tamil model. The Mbh. inspired the Malaya works *Hikayat Perang*, *Pāṇḍawa Jaya* and *Hikayat Maharāja Boma*. The Malaya language reveals many Sanskrit words either as they are or with phonetic variations, e.g. *Shurga* (Skt. *svarga*), *rasa*, *menteri* (*mantrī*), *geni* (*agni*) etc.

---

1. *Manu Dharmaśāstra*, p. 315.

JAVA

Among the Far Eastern neighbours of India, Java shows the most profound influence of Sanskrit literature. The chief grammatical work of Java is called *Svara-vyañjana*; the terms *Svara* and *Vyañjana* are Indian, and the work is a Sanskrit-Javanese grammar. The lexicographical works, called *Ādisvara*, *Ekalavya*, *Kṛtavasa* and *Caṇṭaka-parva* reveal the influence of Sanskrit lexicons. The most important work of this class is the Sanskrit-Kawi dictionary, available in the library of the Batavian Society of Arts and Sciences. It is of the nature of a Sanskrit *Kośa*, and offers Sanskrit synonyms of particular words. The *Amaranālā* is a Sanskrit-Old-Javanese lexicon. The *Mahābhārata*, along with the *Rāmāyaṇa*, moulded the Indo-Javanes literature to a great extent. An outstanding work in the language of Java is a prose rendering of the Indian epic *Mahābhārata.* In the same language was composed the *Arjuna-vivāha*, based on an episode of the above epic. The *Sāra-samuccaya* is a rendering, in Javanese, of many didactic verses of the Anuśāsana-parvan of the same epic. The *Sang Satyavān* is the Javanese version of the Sāvitrī-Satyavān episode of the *Mahābhārata*. The works called *Keravāśrama* and *Navaruci* (also called *Bimasuci* or *Devaruci*) are based on the same epic. Of the Old-Javanese works, the most important is the epic called *Rāmāyaṇa Kakawin* of Yogīśvara, which makes notable departures from the Indian epic. A well-known Javanese work is the *Uttara-kāṇḍa*; it is a free Old-Javanese paraphrase of the last book of the *Rāmāyaṇa* with considerable changes in the original story. The *Uttara-kāṇḍa* is, unlike in the Sanskrit *Rāmāyaṇa*, treated as an independent work. The *Serat Rāma* is a New-Javanese adaptation of the Old-Javanese *Kakawin.* Besides these works, there are many recensions of the *Rāmāyaṇa* in Java and Bali.

Most of the Old-Javanese poetical works deal with themes taken from Sanskrit literature. Some of these use Sanskrit metres and Sanskrit words and quote Sanskrit verses. The most noteworthy of such works is the *Bhārata-yuddha* based on the *Mahābhārata*, and composed mainly by Mpu Sedah in the reign of king Jayabhaya (middle of the 12th century). Sedah having fallen into disgrace in the court, the remaining portion of the work was completed by Panuluh. The *Smara-dahana* (1185 A.D.) was, perhaps, inspired by Kālidāsa's *Kumāra-sambhava*. The *Bhoma-kāvya* deals with the exploits of Kṛṣṇa. The *Harivaṃśa*, a poetical work inspired by the Sanskrit *Harivaṃśa*, has Kṛṣṇa's activities as its theme. A similar theme is found in the *Kṛṣṇāyana* (1104 A.D.) by Triguṇa, court-poet of king Varajaya. Kṛṣṇa's death and the destruction of his race form the subject-matters of the *Kṛṣṇanāṭaka*. The Kawi-works *Indravijaya*, *Bhīma-svarga*, *Pārtha-yajña*, *Ghaṭotkacāraya* and *Harivijaya* are also based on the *Mahābhārata*. The Kakawins, called *Sumanasāntaka*, *Arjuna-vijaya* and the *Hariśraya* appear to have been inspired by the *Rāmāyaṇa*; the *Raghu-vaṃśa* may have provided the model for the first-mentioned work.

The Wayang literature of Java and Bali, corresponding, to some extent, to the Sanskrit *Chāyā-nāṭaka*, shows considerable influence of the Indian epics.

Some scholars have traced the influence of Sanskrit literature on the written and unwritten legends and romances of Java and Bali.

The *Tantri-kāmandaka* and other works of the Tantri group as well as works of the Kancil group, dealing with beast-fables and other folk-tales, betray intimate influence of the Sanskrit *Pañcatantra* and *Hitopadeśa*.

Some historical works of Java, notably the *Nāgara-kṛtāgama* (1365 A.D.) reveal traces of influence of Sanskrit works.

The *Nītiśāstra-kawi* consists of detached maxims. It seems to have been modelled on the Sanskrit works called *Nītiśataka*,*Pañcatantra*, *Cāṇakya-śloka*, etc. Some of its verses are obviously translations of Sanskrit stanzas. Another noteworthy didactic work is the *Kuñjarakarṇa* which betrays marked influence of the doctrines of transmigration of souls and *Karman*, etc. which are discussed in many Sanskrit works. The *Nīti* work, *Ranayajña* contains some Sanskrit verses. The *Kāmandaka-Rājanīti* is obviously modelled on the Sanskrit work called *Nītisāra* of Kāmandaka. Many passages of *Nītipraya* remind one of Kauṭilya's *Arthaśāstra*.

On the Javanese literature on Jurisprudence too there is considerable influence of Sanskrit books, particularly of the *Manusmṛti*. The *Śivaśāsana* or *Pūrvādhigama* is suffused with the Indian spirit. It is interesting to add that the Indian term, *Āgama*, is used by the Indonesians to denote their law-codes. The *Kutāramānava* (also called *Āgama*) is, as its name indicates, largely based on the *Manu-smṛti*. It is mainly based on the eighth and ninth chapters of the *Manu-smṛti*, and contains some Sanskrit verses. The law-book, *Devāgama*, is partly based on the work of Manu. The law-code *Krama ning Sākṣi* contains some Sanskrit verses, and betrays the influence of the same Smṛti work of India. The *Svara-Jambu* is an adaptation of a large part of the eighth chapter of the *Manu-smṛti*.

L. Sternbach has shown that 36 verses, occurring in the literature of Greater India, are identical or almost identical with Skt. Dharmaśāstra verses; of these 36, 35 are verses found in the *Manu-smṛti*. Fourteen verses of the literature of Greater India, dealing with a variety of ethical and general subjects, are shown to have been influenced by Sanskrit Dharmaśāstra.

The most noteworthy religious works in Old-Javanese literature are the *Sūrya-sevana* and the *Gāruḍeya-mantra*; these betray deep influence of Sanskrit literature.

The most famous Purāṇic work of Java is called *Brahmāṇḍa-purāṇa*; it is chiefly modelled on the Indian Purāṇa of this name. The *Bhuvana-kośa* of Java contains many Sanskrit verses followed by Old-Javanese prose translation. Like this work the *Bhuvana-saṃkśepa* also is interspersed with Sanskrit verses followed by Old-Javanese translation. The very title of the *Ādi-purāṇa*, an Old-Javanese prose work, is Sanskritic. The title and contents of the *Bhuvana-purāṇa*, written in the same language and containing corrupt Sanskrit verses, are taken from Sanskrit works.

Among the Tāntric works, the most noteworthy is the *Tattva Sang Hyang Mahājñāna* which is composed in the above manner. Another Tāntric work of Java, written in the same fashion, is the *Sang Hyang Kamahayanikan*.

The *Caturpakṣopadeśa*, dealing with spiritual orders, betrays the influence of the Sanskrit religious literature.

A work, entitled *Bṛhaspati-tattva*, has been discovered in Java. It consists of 74 Sanskrit verses, written in Javanese characters, along with a commentary in Old-Javanese language. No such Sanskrit work has as yet been discovered in India. It deals with Śaiva philosophy. Another philosophical work, called *Gaṇapati-tattva*, has also been discovered in Java; no Sanskrit work of this title has been found in India.

The *Vṛttasañcaya*, a work on metrics, is avowedly based on Sanskrit works dealing with Prosody.

The Wariga (Astrology and Astronomy) literature of Java and Bali as well as the cosmogony of those lands betray deep influence of Sanskrit works.

The folk-tales and fables of Bali betray marked influence of the *Pañcatantra*. The *Caritra-rāmāyaṇa* or *Kavi Jānakī*, composed in the language of the land, is an epitome of the Indian epic *Rāmāyaṇa*. The *Manu-smṛti* appears to have exercised influence in this region too.

The Śaiva temples of Dieng in the north of Central Java, which were established in the eighth and ninth centuries A.D., are named after the prominent figures, male and female, of the *Mahābhārata*.

The work, entitled *Aṣṭādaśavyavahāra*, also reveals link with India and familiarity with Indian texts.

Some works of Java on medicine, astrology, and astronomy contain many works of Sanskrit origin.

CHAMPA
(South Annam)

A large number of inscriptions, found in this country, show that Sanskrit language and literature were cultivated at least down to the tenth century A.D. The oldest extant Sanskrit inscription in a high-flown Kāvya style, composed in the Vasantatilaka metre, dates back to the third or fourth century A.D. Some kings are stated to have been conversant with several branches of Sanskrit learning. The Indian epics, the Smṛti works, particularly of Manu, are stated to have been widely studied. The latest redaction of the *Rāmakathā* in Champa dates back to the 18th century A.D. The king of Champa assumed the title *dharma-mahārāja*. Their names Bhadravarman, Indravarman, etc. show the influence of Sanskrit which was, for some time, the official language. Several deities of the Brāhmaṇical origin found their way to Champa, e.g. Viṣṇu, Śiva, Barhmā, Skanda, Gaṇeśa, Lakṣmī.

A *Purāṇārtha* is mentioned in a record of the eleventh century.

SUMATRA

The Chinese accounts record the fact that Sanskrit was widely studied in the Śrīvijaya kingdom of this land. The Ligor inscription (775 A.D.) is in Sanskrit. The language of Sumatra contains many Sanskrit words.

BALI

The oldest extant inscriptions are in Old-Balinese mixed with Sanskrit. Several works of this land have titles ending in the word *Veda*, e.g. *Caturveda*, almost identical with *Nārāyaṇātharvaśīrṣopaniṣad*, *Buddhaveda*. Some of the

Javanese Sanskrit works, e.g. *Sārasamuccaya*, *Ślokāntara*, *Navaruci*, etc., are popular in Bali. Sanskrit compositions of Bali comprise mostly hymns some of which are protective and called *Kavaca*. A portion of the *Rāmakavaca* is almost identical with passages of *Vālmīki-rāmāyaṇa*. Some mystic *bīja-mantras*, e.g. *hrīm*, *krīm*, etc., along with their significance, are known. Some of the rites and rituals are tinged with Brāhmaṇical and Tāntric practices. The prominent Brāhmaṇical deities, popular in Bali, are Viṣṇu, Śiva, Varuṇa, etc. The folk-lore and fable literature of this land are, to a great extent, modelled on the *Pañcatantra*. The work, *Kārakasaṃgraha*, of Bali acknowledges indebtedness to the *Kātantra* grammar and Pāṇini. The *Caritra-rāmāyaṇa* or *Kavi Jatantra* is an epitome of the *Vālmīki-rāmāyaṇa*. There is marked influence of the *Manu-smṛti*. The Wayang literature corresponds, to some extent, to the Sanskrit *Chāyā-nāṭaka*, and reveals the influence of Indian epics. The Wariga (astrology and astronomy) literature and the cosmogony of Bali reveal deep influence of Sanskrit words with change of their original connotation; e.g. *mangsa* (Skt. *māṃsa*) to devour, *gumi* (Skt. *bhūmi*) kingdom, *biseka* (Skt. *abhiṣeka*) name.

BORNEO

Seven Sanskrit inscriptions, dating back to the 4th century A.D., found in this land, hint at the influence of religious and secular works in Sanskrit. Some of the inscriptions contain a few Sanskrit words, e.g. *bahusuvarṇika*, *bahudāna*, *Jivadāna*, etc. The art and architecture reveal profound Śaivite and Vaiṣṇavite influence.

LAOS

Śiva used to be worshipped here. Garuḍa and Nāga, carved on the Vat Pa Rock, and representations of *dvārapālas* at the gateways to shrines bear testimony to Brāhmaṇical influence. The earliest literature of this land contains a number of Sanskrit or Sanskritic words. It also reveals the influence of Sanskrit grammar, lexicography and prosody. The poetical literature of Laos consists mostly of translations of Sanskrit poems. The didactic and satirical literature as well as fables of this region owe much to Sanskrit literature. The title, *Mulla Tantai*, given to a collection of stories, is derived from Sanskrit Mūla Tantra. The *Rāja-savani*, the most well known work on *Rājanīti*, has obviously a Sanskritic title. Its topics, e.g. four *upāyas*, *rāja-guṇas*, etc., betray Sanskrit origin. *Rāmāyaṇa* episodes are scenically represented on the Laotian stage.

ANNAM

The form of *Rāmakathā* of this land is called 'the king of Demons'. In it Rāma and Sītā have imaginary names.

PHILIPPINE ISLANDS

Four inscriptions, dating back to a period between 682 and 686 A.D., and written in Sanskritised Malay language, were found in North Sumatra and Philippine coast. There are images of certain Brāhmaṇical deities, e.g. Śiva, Gaṇeśa, etc. The establishment of a statue of Manu, standing in the Art Gallery of the Senate chamber of Philippines Republic, shows the authority exercised by the *Manu-smṛti*. The vocabulary of this land contains some Sanskrit or Sanskritic words a few of which are noted below:

Kathā, *diwata* (Skt. *devatā*), *dukha* (*duḥkha*), *sigla* (*śīghra*), *mukha*.

The *Darangon*, the longest epic in the early literature, is essentially Indian in plot and characterisation. The tale of *Ifugao Ralituk* reminds one of a *Mahābhārata* story. The literature of the non-Christian people of the land reveals striking indebtedness to Sanskrit. For instance, the story of the *Bantugan*, a Muslim epic, is chiefly derived from the *Mahābhārata*.

The discovery of numerous Sanskrit inscriptions, both Hindu and Buddhist, in different countries of the Far East, is a conclusive evidence of the influence of Sanskrit in these regions. In some countries of the Far East, Sanskrit was used as the official language by the fourth century A.D. The Brāhmaṇical deity, Gaṇeśa, was very popular in Thailand (popularly called Siam), Cambodia, Champa, Java, Bali, Borneo.

CHINA

Many Sanskrit treatises appear to have been rendered into Chinese through ages. Hiuen-Tsang (600-664 A.D.) translated into Chinese several Indian scriptures including the *Yogācārabhūmi*, *Abhidharma-kośa* and *Vijñapti-mātratā-siddhi-śāstra*. The traveller, I-tsing, (675A.D.), was a renowned translator. According to W. Budge, in a manuscript, found in China, there is reference to the laws of Manu. Some Sanskrit works, relating to Buddhism, are preserved only in Chinese versions, the originals being lost, for example, *Satya-siddhi-śāstra*, *Ratnakūṭa*, *Mahāsannipāta*. Some *Rāmāyaṇa* stories were translated into Chinese. The *Aśokāvadāna* was translated about 300 A.D. Chinese scholars like Fa-hu (Dharmarakṣa), Seng-hui and Indians like Saṅghadeva, Buddhajīva, etc. translated into Chinese some Sanskrit works. A noteworthy Sanskrit work, translated into Chinese by the Khotanese scholar Śikṣānanda, is the now lost *Buddhāvataṃsaka* belonging to the Mahāyāna Buddhism. A notable Sanskrit work of the Hīnayāna school is the *Satyasiddhiśāstra* or, *Tattvasiddhiśāstra* by the Kashmirian Harivarman. Its Sanskrit original is lost, and it is preserved in Chinese translation only. It should be noted that most of the Sanskrit works, translated into Chinese, deal with Buddhist philosophy. The major portion of the original Sanskrit *Prajñā-pāramitā* of the Mahāyāna school is lost, and exists in Tibetan and Chinese translations. According to the *Śaktimaṅgala-tantra*, the region of Rathakrānta comprised, *inter alia*, Mahācīna; this appears to indicate the influence of Tantra on China. There are evidences of the worship of the Brāhmaṇical deity, Gaṇeśa. In recent times, Ti-Shan, the famous writer of short stories, has written in Chinese a history of Sanskrit literature. We are informed that the original *Mahābhārata* and *Rāmāyaṇa* are being rendered into Chinese. The *Śakuntalā* has been translated and staged in China.

JAPAN

It was through Buddhism that cultural contacts between India and Japan began in the sixth century A.D.

Some Sanskrit scriptures, notably the *Manu-smṛti*, were perhaps introduced in the land in pre-Christian times. There are evidences to show that the Tāntric religion, particularly Buddhist Tāntricism, was introduced quite early. Tāntric *Maṇḍalas* and *Mudrās* form an essential part of worship in Japan. The names of several sages of India, e.g. Vaśiṣṭha, Aṅgiras, Atri, etc. occur in Japanese. Sanskrit Buddhist scriptures were extensively studied. About 900 Indian deities are represented in Japanese art. The influence of Sanskrit is most marked on the *Iroha* poem. The Indian script, called *Siddhamātṛka* or *Siddham*, gained currency in Japan under the name *Shittan* for writing Sanskrit since the eighth century. K. Daishi invented the Katakana alphabet in fifty sounds based on Sanskrit alphabet. The influence of Āyurveda is manifest in the Indian names of several drugs, preserved in the Japanese Imperial Treasury since the eighth century. The discovery of certain Sanskrit manuscripts, or fragments thereof, at Horyuji monastery, testifies to the influence of Sanskrit. H. Nakamura draws our attention to the influence of Sanskrit stories on some of the Japanese stories. We are also informed that Japanese classical works betray Indian influence to a great extent.

The *Bhagavadgītā* and a few other Sanskrit works, including some Upaniṣads, have been translated into Japanese. Ikeda has written a valuable treatise in Japanese about the *Mahābhārata* and the *Rāmāyaṇa*. Kimura has translated into Japanese prose the *Ṛtu-saṃhāra* of Kālidāsa.

Sanskrit *dhāraṇīs*, *stotras*, grammars, lexicons, etc. were extensively studied. Jogan (1632-1702 A.D.) wrote a book, called *Shithan-sanmitsu* which gives an account of the Sanskrit studies in Japan.

KOREA

Influence of Sanskrit works, both Buddhist and Brāhmaṇical, is marked on Japanese classical works. Hindu theory of Karman, and transmigration of soul have exercised wide influence.

There are evidences of the visit of Indian scholars to Korea since 37 A.D. Among Korean scholars, a very eminent Sanskritist was Wanchouk (613-96 A.D.) of Silla. The Buddhist Sanskrit work, *Mahādharma-kośa*, was published in Korea in 10700 fascicules. Another edition of it was published in 1236 A.D.

The Hanggul script of Korea was adapted from Sanskrit. Sanskrit *Siddham* script was introduced to this area.

MONGOLIA

Borrowings from Sanskrit are found in Mongolian epic song and Shamanist hymns. Sanskrit names like Sumeru occur among the Mongols and in Mongolian typonomy. Shamanist Hymns (14-17th cent.) contain names of some Indian deities, e.g. Bisnu (Viṣṇu), Esrua (Brahma), etc. Among the Mongolians, Garuḍa is very familiar. The Brāhmaṇical doctrine of incantations appears to have influenced Mongolian Shamanism. There is a Mongolian version of the Arabic translation of the *Pañcatantra*. The Mongols appear to have been acquainted with the *Vetāla-pañcaviṃśati*, *Vikramacarita* and *Śukasaptati*. Many Vetāla stories have Mongolian versions in the language of the Kalmucks, a race of Mongolian origin. The Mongolian story book, *Siddikur*, contains many Vetāla stories. There is a Mongolian version of the *Rāmāyaṇa*. Some *Avadāna* stories were translated. The *Dvātriṃśatputtalikā* was rendered into Mongolian. Sanskrit was introduced into this region through Buddhism. Some *Nīti* texts found their way to this area.

KUCHA AND OTHER PARTS OF CENTRAL ASIA

In Kucha in Central Asia many treatises, written in the local language, betray the influence of Sanskrit works. Many original Buddhist works in Sanskrit were translated into the language of this place. A Sanskrit-Tocharian vocabulary (c. 700 A.D.) has been discovered. To the seventh century belongs a Sanskrit-Chinese lexicon. The find of some manuscripts of the *Kātantra Vyākaraṇa* indicates that it was studied there.

Fragments of three Sanskrit dramas, including the *Śāriputra-prakaraṇa* of Aśvaghoṣa, were found in Kucha area. Mss. of the *Buddhacarita*, *Saundarananda*, *Sūtrālaṃkāra*, etc. have also been discovered.

Manuscripts of many Buddhist hymns have been found. Brāhmī was the script of the people of ancient Agnideśa which lay on the way from Kucha to Tun Hwang. Many Sanskrit manuscripts are preserved here. At Khora, near Agnideśa, manuscripts of the *Śata-pañcāśataka* and the *Catuḥśataka* as well as two hymns of Mātṛceta have been found.

Central Asia has preserved many manuscripts of the Sanskrit *Tripiṭaka*. Among literary works are the *Jātakamālā* of Ārya Śūra and *Chandoviciti* on metrics.

The zeal of the people of this region for studying Sanskrit works led them to translate and even amplify many texts.

The language of Khotan was transformed into a literary language under the influence of Sanskrit. The *Jīrṇamūrkha-sūtra* was composed here. A versified Sanskrit medical work, with Khotanese Sáka translation has been found here. Uigurian medical texts, derived from Sanskrit, are also available. Gaṇeśa had been a popular deity here.

Some scholars discovered many Sanskrit manuscripts at various places of Central Asia. The most noteworthy of these were the frangments of the Sanskrit *Tripiṭaka*. The Bower Manuscripts, found at Kashgar in 1890 A.D., contained treatises on several subjects including medical science, cubomancy and a charm against snake-bite.

In Turfan several Sanskrit manuscripts, including parts of the *Śāriputra-prakaraṇa* and two other dramas, were discovered.

Sanskrit manuscripts, relating to Buddhism, have been found in cave-temples of Bamien.

Among Sanskrit manuscripts, discovered in Central Asia, is the *Udānavarga* of Buddhist Sarvāstivāda school. Khotanese versions of some Sanskrit manuscripts were found at Tun-huang. Seals, with the figures of Kubera and Gaṇeśa, have been found at several places, e.g. Endere and Niya. Figures of Śiva and Viṣṇu also exist.

Ancient Turkic texts are mostly adaptations and rendering of Sanskrit works. In them the Brāhmī script was used. In Uigur Turkic are preserved many remains of the Avadāna literature. The *Śaśa-jātaka* deserves mention. The philosphical texts include *Yogācārbhūmi-śāstra*, *Abhidharmakośa* and a letter from Nāgārjuna. Fragments of *Āgamas* and the *Prātimokṣa* also exist. *Udānavarga*, *Saṃvara-tantra* are some of the other Sanskrit works in Turkic. Fragments of the medical text, *Siddhasāra*, should also be mentioned. Many Sanskrit words were absorbed in ancient Turkic. For example,

Visnu (Skt. *Viṣṇu*), *Irzi* (*Ṛṣi*).

Quite a number of Kharoṣṭhī documents, found in Chinese Turkestan, reveal remarkable affinity of the local language, Niya Prākrit, with Sanskrit. For example,

maharaya (Skt. *mahārāja*), *uṭa* (*uṣṭra*), *bhoyamna* (*bhojana*).

TRANSBAIKALIAN SIBERIA

Shaman songs, current in this region, praised Indra, Agni and some other Indian deities. Śrīdevī or Kālī found her way into this area in the eighteenth century, if not earlier. The *Yisun ordeni-yin Ganjur*, the most valuable work of this region, contains over 1000 Sanskrit texts translated into the local language. Some temple-walls of this region are decorated with *aṣṭamaṅgala* emblems. Siberian folklore shows familiarity with the *Rāmāyaṇa* an abridged version of which is available in the Kalmuk language. Sanskrit incantations are recited while receiving the holy water of the Ganges. *Āyurveda* appears to have been popular in Siberia. The *aṣṭādhyāyī* is looked upon as highly authoritative. The *Meghadūta* is the first lyric of the Siberians.

WEST ASIA

Of the countries of the Middle East, Persia and Arabia show the most intimate literary contacts with India. Persian Sūfism appears to have been considerably influenced by the doctrines of the Upaniṣads. The *Avesta* reveals remarkable similarities with the Ṛgvedic language.

Though produced in India, yet the Persian poem called *Nal U Daman*[1] (1002 A.H.-1593 A.D.), based on the well-known Nala-Damayantī episode of the *Mahābhārata*, by Fayzi, a court-poet of Akbar, occupies a prominent place in the history of Persian literature. The *Kalila wa Dimna* was also translated into Persian by Abul Fazl, of Akbar's court, under the title 'Ayar-i-Danish'. According to Abul Māli, it consisted of sixteen chapters, ten having been of Indian origin and six added by Iranians.

As early as the sixth century A.D., the Sanskrit *Pañcatantra* was rendered into Pahlavi by the Persian physician Burzoë under the patronage of Chosroes Anūshīrwān (531-79 A.D.); it bore the title Kalila wa Dimna (Karaṭaka and Damanaka). The Pahlavi version was rendered into Syriac in the same century.

---

1. See F.A. Desai, The story of Nala-Damayantī as told by Faidi and its comparison with original Sanskrit version, *Jour. of Oriental Institute*, Baroda, VIII, 1958.

In the eighth century one Abdalla-Ibn-al Moqaffa rendered the above Pahlavi version into Arabic. The Arabic version was rendered into Persian by Nizamuddin under Bahram Shah of Ghazna (1153-54 A.D.). Almost at the same time the Caliph of Baghdad got the Āyurvedic treatises of Caraka and Suśruta rendered into Arabic. The treatises of Caraka and Suśruta have been quoted as authorities by the Arabian physician Al-Razi (d. 932 A.D.). When Sind was under the rule of Caliph Mansur (753-74 A.D.), some Indian scholars took to Baghdad the *Brahmasiddhānta* and the *Khaṇḍakhādyaka* of Brahmagupta with them. These astronomical works were rendered into Arabic by Alfazari and probably also by Yakub Ibn Tarik. It was through these works that the Arabs, for the first time, became acquainted with a scientific system of astronomy. The Caliphs of Baghdad often invited Indian astronomers to supervise the Arabic translation of works like the *Siddhāntas*, the works of Brahmagupta and Āryabhaṭa. The Arabic system of atomism appears to betrary the influence of the Nyāya-Vaiśeṣika system.

There was a great influx of Indian learning into Baghdad under Harun (786-808 A.D.). In this period, Indian scholars were engaged to translate into Arabic the Sanskrit works on medical science, philosophy, astrology and other subjects. The influence of Vedānta philosophy is marked in Arabian Sūfism.

The book of Sindabad and the *Arabian Nights* are believed to owe their origin, at least partly, to Indian literature.

Many Arab authors worked out Indian subjects in original compositions, commentaries and extracts. Indian mathematics was particularly fascinating to them. The decimal system of notation was, perhaps, borrowd by the Arabs from India. In fact, the Arabs called Mathematics *hindisat* (Indian art). The *Hisabul Hindi* is an Arabian tract on Indian computation.

The account of India, left by the Arabian traveller Alberuni (973-1048 A.D.), pre-supposes the author's intimate acquaintance with several branches of Sanskrit learning. Perhaps he was the first man to introduce the *Bhagavadgītā* into the world of Muslim readers. Alberuni translated into Arabic a Sanskrit treatise on loathsome diseases. Assisted by Indian scholars, he tried to translate the astronomical works of Brahmagupta and also the *Puliśa-siddhānta*. He translated into Arabic also the Sāṃkhya of Kapila and the Book of Patañjali on philosophy.

Some technical terms of Arabian music owe their origin to Indian music.

Evidences have been furnished to prove that the legal system for the empire of the Persian King Darius (6th-5th cent. B.C.) was framed on the basis of the *Manusmṛti*.

The *Bhagavadgītā* was translated into Persian by Abul Fazl under Akbar the Great. Under the patronage of the same emperor, the *Atharva-veda* was rendered (983 A.H.) into Persian by Mulla Ibrahimi, Fayzi and Badauni. The same court produced a Persian version (909 A.H.) of the *Mahābhārata*, by Naqib Khan, Badauni, Mulla Shiri and Fayzi with the assistance of a group of selected Pundits. A group of scholars, under Akbar, produced a Persian version, called *Razm Namah*, of *Mahābhārata*. Naqib Khan, Badauni and Haji Sultan translated (999 A.H.) into Persian the epic *Rāmāyaṇa*; this version was the basis of a versified form produced later by Sadullah of Panipath. *Tutinameh* is the famous Persian version of the *Śukasaptati*.

The mathematical work, *Līlāvatī*, was rendered into Persian by Fayzi of Akbar's court.

The Persian medical work, *Firdaus Ul hikmat*, contains detailed information about Indian medicine.

The *Yogavāsiṣṭha* was rendered into Persian at Akbar's court by Naqib Khan and others.

The *Harivaṃśa* was translated under the same emperor by Mulla Shiri.

The influence of Sanskrit is noticeable in the vocabulary of Afghanistan. The grammatical structure of the Afghan language also bears out this influence. The Brāhmaṇical influence is attested by the discovery of images and carvings of Brahmā, Viṣṇu, Śiva, Gaṇeśa, Kārtikeya, Mahiṣamardinī Durgā, etc.

OCCIDENT

Coming to Europe, we find that the Upaniṣads, introduced to that continent chiefly by A. Duperron's Latin translation, not only roused the admiration of the thinkers like Goethe, Schopenhauer, etc. but, to some extent, influenced the mystic-theosophical Logos doctrine of the New-Platonic School and of the Alexandrian Christians. The teachings of the Christian Mystics Eckhart and Tauler are also believed to have been influenced by the Ātman-Brahman doctrine of the Upaniṣads. The philosophy of the above-mentioned Schopenhauer, the reputed German mystic of 19th century, was, to a great extent, moulded by the Upaniṣadic philosophy. In fact, he counts the Upaniṣads among his teachers.

From the 11th century onward the *Pañcatantra* has been translated or adapted into various European languages, e.g. Greek, Latin, Italian, German, French, Spanish, Danish, Icelandic, Dutch, English, Swedish, Hungarian, etc. The first translation was from the Arabic translation into Greek. The popular narrative works of Western literature contain traces of Indian fables and tales. Of such works, mention may be made of the *Gesta Romanorum* and similar collections of monks' tales in Latin, the French fabliaux, the works of the renowned story-tellers like Boccacio and Straparola in Italy, of Chaucer in England, La Fontaine in France and the German *Household Tales* collected by Grimm brothers.

The Sanskrit *Vetāla-pañcaviṃśatikā* has considerably contributed to the narrative literature of the world. The Sanskrit *Vikrama-carita* or *Siṃhāsana-dvātriṃśikā*, translated into Persian in 1574 by order of Akbar, of which a Mongolian version is known, and the *Śuka-saptati*, known as the *Tutinameh* by its Persian and Turkish renderings, exercised considerable influence on the literature of the West. This fact led Benfey to declare, obviously in an exaggerated manner due to exuberance of enthusiasm, that India was the home of all fairy tales and stories. Nevertheless, the fact remains that quite a number of stories, current throughout the world, can be traced to Indian sources.

ITALY

There are Latin translations of some Sanskrit texts, e.g. *Pañcatantra*, *Āryabhaṭīya*, etc. The *Gesta Ramanorum* and similar collections of monks' tales in Latin reveal indebtedness to Indian fables and tales. The Roman Celsus (c. 1st cent. A.D.), Galen (131-201 A.D.) and other medical men reveal familiarity with Indian medical science. The Latin translation, by Farachi (c. 13th cent.), of al-Rhazi's *Kitab al-hawi*, which incorporated Indian medical knowledge, became an authoritative work in Europe. The work on Hindu method of calculation, by the Arabian Al-khwārizmi, was translated into Latin under the title, *Do numero indico.*

GREECE

There is much that is common between the fables in Indian literature and Greek literature. But, it is almost impossible to decide which country was the borrower. The story of Barlaam and Josaphat, written in Greek by John of Damascus who lived at the court of Caliph Almansur (753-774 A.D.) contains fables and parables most of which have been traced to Indian sources, chiefly Buddhist. Some of the Christian legends are believed,by some scholars, to have been influenced by Buddhist ones. If this is true, then it may be supposed that this influence was exerted not only by the Pāli works, but also by the Sanskrit works of the Buddhists.

In the domain of novels, a few parallels between those of Greece and India are discernible. It seems probable that some Indian motifs were borrowed by Greece, though the Greek novel might not have been wholly borrowed from India. There are numerous points of agreement between Indian and Greek philosophy. While some scholars explain this phenomenon as parallel development, others would point out definite Indian influence on some of the western philosophical systems. For example, Garbe thinks that the Sāṃkhya philosophy of India went a long way in moulding the philosophical ideas of Heraklitos, Empedokles, Anaxagoras, Demokritos and Epikuros. Some of the leading doctrines of the Eleatics, e.g. that the universe and God are identical, that everything that exists in multiplicity has no reality, that thinking and being are identical, are found in the Upaniṣads and the Vedānta system of philosophy. The assumption of Indian influence on the Greeks in this field appears to be supported by the Greek tradition that Thales, Empedokles, Anaxagoras, Democritus and others travelled in Oriental countries in order to study philosophy. Greek geometry was probably influenced by the Indian *Sulva-sūtras.*

Winternitz and others are of the opinion that Pythagoras was influenced by the Sāṃkhya school. He is certain that the Gnostic and Neo-platonic philosophies borrowed many ideas from Indian philosophy. The pessimistic philosophy of Schopenhauer and Von Hartmann is clearly influenced by Indian thought.

Turning to poetical compositions we find that some of the lyric poems of Heine and works like Arnold's *Light of Asia* betray inspiration from Sanskrit poetry.

In the domain of drama, Europe appears to have been indebted to India to some extent. In the *Suppliant Woman* of Eschylus, the first dramatist of Greece, who flourished five hundred years before Christ, we find a short pen-picture of a part of Indian Life. The Greek scholar, D. Chrysostom (c. 80 B.C.) testifies to his familiarity with Indian Mahākāvya.

Indian medical science and surgery appear to have exercised considerable influence on Greece. In the *Hippocratic Collection*, the treatment of the pneumatic system is very similar to the Indian concept of *Vāyu* or *Prāṇa*. Plato's *Timaeus* shows familiarity with the Āyurvedic doctrine of *tridoṣa*. In the above *Collection*, there are references to Indian drugs.

BRITAIN, GERMANY AND OTHER EUROPEAN COUNTRIES

The *Bhagavadgītā* appears to have exercised deep influence on European literature. Coleridge (1772-1832) read this work in translation. In some of his poetical compositions, there are traces of the influence of the *Gītā*. Wordsworth (1770-1850), in some poems, e.g. *Tintern Abbey* and *Immortality Ode*, reveals ideas very similar to those of the *Gītā*. Matthew Arnold's 'distinterested endeavour' is a literal translation of *Niṣkāma Karma* of the *Gītā*. In recent times, Yeats and Elliot appear to have been influenced by this work. The Spanish poet, Himeneth, was inspired by it. Huxley repeatedly stressed the universal value of this great work. His *Perennial Philosophy* should be particularly mentioned in this connexion. He has pointed out close similarity between certain basic ideas of the *Gītā* and those of Christianity and Islamic doctrines. William Blake's (1757-1827) writings testify to the study of the *Gītā*. Eliot, in his *Dry Salvages* and *Burnt Norton*, shows familiarity with the doctrines laid down in the *Gītā*. M. Taylor, in his *Tara*, refers to the above Indian scripture. Keats (1795-1821) in his *Endymion*, reveals his acquaintance with the *Gītā*.

Some passages of Wordsworth, e.g. in *Tintern Abbey*, *Ode on Intimations* etc., appear to reflect Vedāntic ideas. Certain ideas of Coleridge, e.g. the presence of divine spark in everyone, seem to echo Vedāntic views of life. Some works of Eliot, e.g. The *Waste Land*, *Burnt Norton*, *East Coker*, *Collected Plays*, etc., reflect intimate knowledge of Upaniṣadic ideas. Shelley's (1792-1822) *Adonais* gives expression to the doctrine of *Māyā* and some other Vedāntic concepts. Huxley's *Perennial Philosophy* reflects his knowledge of Vedānta. The Irish scholars, Yeats and Russell, were deeply influenced by the Upaniṣads. Somerset Maugham's *Razor's Edge* is a rendering of the expression *kṣurasya dhārā* occurring in the Upaniṣad. The influence of Upaniṣads on Maugham is evident also from his *Writer's Notebook* (1935).

William Jones (1746-1794) composed nine English hymns addressed to nine Brāhmaṇical deities. These reflect his erudition in Sanskrit mythology. Some of these hymns influenced other eminent English writers. For instance,Shelley's *Hymn to Intellectual Beauty* and *Hymn to Apollo* shows striking similarity with Jones' Hymns to Nārāyaṇa and Sūrya respectively. Tennyson drew upon Jones' writings in his *Lockesless Hall*.

De Qunincey (1785-1859) mentions the Brāhmaṇical deities Brahmā, Viṣṇu and Śiva; this seems to show acquaintance with Sanskrit. Gibbon,

Byron, Burrow, Southey and Moors were also attracted to Indian learnıng through the works of Jones relating to Indian thought. E. Arnold's *Light of Asia* is based on the *Lalita-vistara*, a renowned *Avadāna* work in Sanskrit.

The *Kāmasūtra* inspired writers like Carpenter,Havelock Ellis, Lawrence, etc.

A.B. Keith made outstanding contributions to Indology. His *History of Sanskrit Literature*, *Sanskrit Drama*, *Vedic Index* (jointly with Macdonell), *Religion and Philosophy of the Veda and the Upaniṣads*, etc. speak eloquently of his vast erudition. Macdonell's *History of Sanskrit Literature* was, at one time, a standard work. Monier Williams achieved undying fame by his two Dictionaries, Sanskrit to English and English to Sanskrit.

The Welsh story of *Llewellyn's Dog* appears to be an adaptation of the *Pañcatantra* story of a man who, in a fit of temper, killed a good domestic mongoose, and then repented.

The *Kādambarī*, *Daśakumāracarita* and the *Vetālapañcaviṃśati* influenced the form and content of some of F.W. Bain's works, e.g. *Indian Stories*, *A Digit of the Moon*.

GERMANY

Max Müller (1823-1900) edited the *Ṛgveda*, wrote a history of ancient Sanskrit literature besides rendering other kinds of service to Sanskrit literature. The *Pañcatantra* was rendered into German. The lyric poems of Heine reveal Sanskrit inspiration. Schopenhauer was deeply influenced by the Upaniṣads. The teaching of Eckhart and Tauler reveal the impact of the Ātman-Brahman doctrine of the Upaniṣads. The monistic ideas of Fichte and Hegel appear to be indebted to Upaniṣads. Similarity between the philosophy of Kant and that of India has been pointed out. Krause and Deussen were intimately acquainted with Vedānta. Nietzsche admired the Upaniṣads, and was influenced by the *Manusmṛti*. Hesse, in his *Game of Glass Beads* (Eng. rendering of German title), reveals the influence of the *Gītā* and Vedānta. The same remark applies to L. Bethoven. Hesse admired the three *Śatakas* of Bhartṛhari. The following are some of the noteworthy German writers who drew upon Indian materials: Dahlke, Winckler, Schaffer, Werfel, Zweig, Kasack, Neyrink and Thomas Mann. Mann, in his *Transposed Heads* (Eng. rendering of German title), gave a new interpretation of a story of the *Vetālapañcaviṃśati*. The tales by Grimm brothers betray traces of Indian fables and tales. Goethe, an ardent admirer of the *Śakuntalā*, appears to have modelled the prologue to his *Faust* on that of the Sanskrit drama. A galaxy of German scholars devoted their lives to the study of Indology—which is still actively pursued there.

FRANCE

Several eminent French scholars eg. A. Duperron, Burnouf, translated Sanskrit texts. Fauche, Regnaud, Hauvelle-Besnault, Barth, Senart, Feer are well-known Indologists. Victor Hugo, in his poem, *Suprematic*, imitated an Upaniṣad. A. de Lamartine, in his *Cours familiar de Litterature,* wrote on Sanskrit epics, drama and poetry. P. Verlaine's poem, *Sāvitrī,* drew upon the well-known episode of Satyavān-Sāvitrī in the *Mahābhārata.* In recent times, Renou distinguished himself by his erudite studies, particularly relating to the Veda and Pāṇini's grammar. J. Filliozat has done outstanding work on Indology. His work on Indian medical science is renowned.

HOLLAND

The Dutch preacher, A. Roger, wrote his *Open Door to Hidden Heathendom* which contains Dutch trs. of 200 verses from Bhartṛhari's *Nīti* and *Vairāgya-śatakas.* H. Kern practically founded Sanskrit studies in Holland. Some eminent Dutch indologists are Speyer, Vogel, Gonda and Faddegon.

HUNGARY

K. Fiolk translated some Sanskrit classical works. The activities of Aurel Stein (1862-1943) gave an impetus to Indological studies in the West.

CZECHOSLOVAKIA

J. Debrevski, J. Jungmann, A. Jungmann, A. Ludwig were eminent Indologists. The first pointed out similarities between Indian and Slav words. The second wrote on Indian prosody. The third one wrote the first Sanskrit grammar in Czech. M. Winternitz is the most renowned author of *History of Indian Literature* which was written by him in German.

RUMANIA

G. Coshbuc translated the *Śakuntalā* from a German version, and compiled a Sanskrit anthology. Anotonescu worked on the philosophy of the Upaniṣads. Eminenscu's writings reveal familiarity with Sanskrit. Among other works, he translated Bopp's *Glossarium Sanskriticum.* The title of his work *Tattvamasi* reveals his knowledge of Upaniṣadic thought.

RUSSIA

Some Russian stories appear to be adaptations of Indian ones. For example, the story of Schastio and Noschastio (Good luck and bad luck) is a modification of the story of Vīravara in the *Hitopadeśa.* The translation of the *Gītā* by Wilkins was rendered into Russian. Petrov translated the Sītāharaṇa episode of the *Rāmāyaṇa.* The famous St. Petersburg Dictionary of Sanskrit was the work of Russian Indologists. Schervatsky (1886-1941) edited some Sanskrit texts. Other noted Russian Indologists were Vasilyev (1818-1900), V.P. Minayev (1840-1890), Korsh, Fortunatov and Miller. Tolstoy (1828-1910), in his *Letter to a Hindu,* addressed to Gandhi, quoted from the Upaniṣads and the *Gītā.* It is learnt that P. Grintser's *Ancient Indian Epics* will be published in Russia. In his book, *Eating for Health,* Y. Nikolayev acknowledges his indebtedness to Āyurveda. V. Kalyanov translated the *Mahābhārata* into Russian.

In concluding our account of the influence of Sanskrit on Europe, we should mention the following eminent Indologists of different parts of this continent.

Sten Konow and Morgenstierne of Norway, J. Carpentier and H. Smith of Sweden, M. Dillon of Ireland, Majewski Lelewal, Beskowsk, Schayer of Poland, Brunnhofer, Leumann and Wackernagel of Switzerland, A. Scharpe of Belgium, L. Sternbach of (Poland?, now in Paris), Derrett, Burrow and Brough of England, L. Rocher of France (?).

Western theosophists appear to draw many ideas from the Upaniṣads and the philosophical systems of India.

AMERICA, ASIOMERICA

The Maya civilisation of South America reveals remarkable similarity with Indian civilisation. In Maya art and Architecture, Indian or Sanskrit influence is marked; e.g. the lotus-motif, the *makara*-motif, the *Kalpavṛkṣa*, etc. There are representations of Viṣṇu, Indian Nāginī of Kubera, Gaja and Nāga; these seem to indicate familiarity with Sanskrit mythology. A sort of caste system was in vogue among the Incas of Peru. The Peruvians worshipped an omnipotent Supreme Being. The poetical literature of Peru appears to betoken the influence of Sanskrit epics. A number of words of the Quichua vocabulary have analogous Sanskrit forms. Some scholars have furnished evidences of Asian migration to America.

U.S.A.

A number of eminent Indologists have made outstanding contribution to Indology. Some of them are: Salisbury, Whitney, Lanman, Hopkins, Bloomfield, Edgerton, Ryder, N. Brown and Ingalls.

Monistic and idealistic philosophies of America in the 19th cent. appear to owe a deep debt of gratitude to Sanskrit philosophical works. Outstanding American philosophers, who imbided Indian philosophical ideas, were Emerson (1803-1882), Thoreau (1817-1862) and Whitman (1819-1892).

The Christian Science movement in America drew inspiration from Vedānta.

In Mathematics it is highly probable that the system of writing numerical figures, in vogue in the whole of the civilised world, was of Indian origin. In the 8th and 9th centuries, the Indians taught the Arabs Arithmetic and Algebra. Through the Arabs this knowledge passed to the West.

In the realm of astronomy, ancient India may or may not have borrowed some ideas from Greece, but there seems to be little room for doubt that, at a later period, India influenced the West in this branch of knowledge through the Arabs.

The sciences of Comparative Philology and Comparative Mythology, which originated in the West in the 19th century, owe their genesis to the discovery of the Sanskrit language and literature.

From the foregoing pages it is clear that true culture cannot be confined within narrow limits. It is the instinct of man to receive from others what is good, however great the political and geographical barriers there may be between the two. Sanskrit language may be long dead, but Sanskrit literature is undying in the sense that the didactic teachings, sublime philosophical ideas and the human values, embodied in it are, and will continue to be, the warp and woof of the literatures of the world. Truly it has been said that the sages who meditated in the jungles of the Ganges Valley, six hundred years or more before Christ, are still forces in the world.

IV

SANSKRIT WORKS OF INDIA BASED ON THE EPICS[1]

The two epics, *Rāmāyaṇa* and *Mahābhārata,* have, to a great extent, moulded the classical Sanskrit literature in its different branches. It is, therefore, necessary to know which of the works have been influenced by them and to what extent. We give below a classified list of such works as are based on the entire epic stories,[2] on particular episodes as well as on the epic legends and myths. The titles of works are arranged in the English alphabetical order.

BASED ON THE *MAHĀBHĀRATA*

DRAMA

(a) ENTIRE STORY

Title	Author
Bāla-bhārata	Rājaśekhara
Veṇī-saṃhāra	Bhaṭṭa Nārāyaṇa

(b) EPISODES

Title	Author	Name of Episode
**Dhanañjaya-vijaya*	Kāñcanācārya	Story of Go-gṛha (Mbh. IV. 24-62).
**Draupadī-svayaṃvara*	Vijayapāla	The title indicates the episode.
**Dūta-ghaṭotkaca*	Bhāsa	Bhīma's son Ghaṭotkaca's acting as an envoy of Kṛṣṇa to Dhṛtarāṣṭra.
**Kalyāṇa-saugandhikā*	Nīlakaṇṭha	Same as that of *Saugandhikā-haraṇa.*
**Dūta-vākya*	Bhāsa	Part played by Kṛṣṇa as the messenger of Pāṇḍavas (Mbh. V. 122-9).
Karṇabhāra	Bhāsa	Karṇa's magnanimity.
**Kirātārjunīya-vyāyoga*	Vatsarāja	Same as that of Bhāravi's *Kirātārjunīya* (q.v.).
Madhyama-vyāyoga	Bhāsa	Invented by the author who introduces epic characters.

1. Minor works, not mentioned in the body of this work, are marked with asterisks.

2. Under this class are included, of course, those works which make additions to, or alterations in, the original epic stories.

Title	Author	Name of the Episode
**Nirbhaya-bhīma*	Rāmacandra Sūri	Bhīma's encounter with the demon Baka (Mbh. I. 145-52).
Pañcarātra	Bhāsa	Battle of exiled Pāṇḍavas with the Kurus in connexion with cattle-raid (Mbh. IV. 24-62).
**Pārtha-parākrama*	Prahlādana	Same as that of *Pañcarātra*.
**Saugandhikā-haraṇa*	Viśvanātha	Bhīma's effort to bring Saugandhikā flowers from a lake, strongly guarded by Kubera's men, to please Draupadī (Mbh. III. 146-53).
**Subhadrā-dhanañjaya*	Kulaśekhara Varman	Elopement of Subhadrā with Arjuna (Mbh. I. 210-13).
**Subhadrā-haraṇa*	Mādhava Bhaṭṭa	Same as that of *Subhadrā-dhanañjaya*.
**Subhadrā-pariṇayana*	Rāmadeva Vyāsa	Title indicates the theme which closely resembles that of the *Subhadrā-haraṇa*.
Ūru-bhaṅga	Bhāsa	Club-fight between Duryodhana and Bhīma (Mbh. IX).

(c) LEGENDS

Title	Author	Legend
Abhijñāna-śakuntalā	Kālidāsa	Duṣyanta and Śakuntalā (Mbh. I. 62-9).
**Nala-caritranāṭaka*	Nīlakaṇṭha Dīkṣita	Story of Nala and Damayantī.
**Nala-vilāsa*	Rāmacandra Sūri	Story of Nala and Damayantī.
**Tapatī-saṃvaraṇa*	Kulaśekhara Varman	Love-story of the Kuru king Saṃvaraṇa and Tapatī, the daughter of Sun-god (Mbh. I. 160-3).
Vikramorvaśīya	Kālidāsa	Love between the mortal king Purūravas and the celestial nymph Urvaśī. It occurs in the Mbh. (I. LXX, 16-22), besides the *Ṛgveda*, *Śatapatha Brāhmaṇa*, *Viṣṇu-purāṇa*, *Bhāgavata-purāṇa*, *Matsya-purāṇa*, *Kathā-sarit-sāgara* and *Harivaṃśa*.

(d) MYTHS

Title	Author	Myth
Tripura-dāha	Vatsarāja	See under this title in the body of this work. The myth occurs in Mbh. VIII. 24.

POEMS, PROSE COMPOSITIONS AND CAMPŪS

(a) ENTIRE STORY

Title	Author	Nature of work
Bāla-bhārata	Amaracandra Sūri	Poetical composition
**Bhārata-campū*	Ananta Bhaṭṭa	Campūkāvya
Bhārata-mañjari	Kṣemendra	Poetical composition
**Pāṇḍava-carita*	Devaprabha Sūri	Poetical composition
Rāghava-pāṇḍavīya	Dhanañjaya	Poetical composition
Rāghava-pāṇḍavīya	Kavirāja	Poetical composition
**Yudhiṣṭhira-vijaya*	Vāsudeva	Poetical composition

(b) EPISODES

Title	Author	Nature of work	Episode
**Draupadī-pariṇaya*	Cakrakavi	Campū-kāvya	Slaying of Baka demon by Bhīma and marriage of Pāṇḍavas with Draupadī
Kīcaka-vadha	Nīti-varman	Poetical composition	Title indicates the episode (Mbh. IV. 13-23)
Kirātār-junīya	Bhāravi	Poetical composition	Fight between Arjuna and Śiva in the guise of a Kirāta (Mbh. III. 35-42)
**Naranārā-yaṇānanda*	Vastupāla	Poetical composition	Friendship of Arjuna and Kṛṣṇa and the abduction of Subhadrā by the former
Śiśupāla-vadha	Māgha	Poetical composition	Slaying of Śiśupāla, king of Cedi, by Kṛṣṇa (Mbh. II. 30-42)

(c) LEGENDS

Title	Author	Nature of work	Legend
Naiṣadha-carita	Śrīharṣa	Poetical composition	Story of Nala and Damayantī (Mbh. III. 50-78)
**Nalābhyu-daya*	Vāmana Bhaṭṭa Bāṇa	Poetical composition	Story of Nala and Damayantī

Title	Author	Nature of work	Episode
Nala-campū	Trivikrama Bhaṭṭa	A Campū-kāvya	Story of Nala and Damayantī
Nalodaya	Vāsudeva (Attributed by some to Kālidāsa)	Poetical composition	Story of Nala and Damayantī
Pañca-tantra	?	Fable in prose with verses interspersed	(1) Legend of Śibi (Mbh. III. 130-1) (2) Śakunopākhyāna (Story of the three fish called Anāgata-vidhātā Yadbhaviṣya and Pratyutpanna-mati) Mbh. XII. 135
**Rāghava-naiṣadhīya*	Haradatta-Sūri	Poetical composition	Stories of Nala and Rāma
**Sahṛdayā-nanda*	Kṛṣṇā-nanda	Poetical composition	Story of Nala and Damayantī

(d) MYTHS

Kumāra-sambhava	Kālidāsa	Poetical composition	Śiva's marriage with Pārvatī, birth of Skanda who slays the demon Tāraka

BASED ON THE RĀMĀYAṆA[1]

DRAMA

Title	Author	Remarks
Abhiṣeka-nāṭaka	Bhāsa	Events from Sugrīva's coronation to consecration of Rāma at Ayodhyā
**Adbhuta-darpaṇa*	Mahādeva	The story from Aṅgada's mission to Rāvaṇa up to the coronation of Rāma
Anargha-rāghava	Murāri	
**Āścarya-cūḍāmaṇi*	Śaktibhadra	The story from Śūrpaṇakhā's appearance before Lakṣmaṇa up to Sītā's fire-ordeal
Bāla-rāmāyaṇa	Rājaśekhara	
**Dūtāṅgada*	Subhaṭa	Embassy of Aṅgada
Kundamālā	Dhīra (or, Vīra)-nāga[2]	Subject-matter similar to that of the *Uttara-rāmacarita* (q.v.)

1. The works, based on parts of the *Rāmāyaṇa* story, are very few. So these are mentioned together with those dealing with the entire story.

2. For authorship of the drama, see under *Kundamālā* (Part II).

Title	Author	Remarks
Mahānāṭaka	Madhusūdana	Events from Rāma's arrival in the hermitage of Viśvāmitra up to his return from Laṅkā and coronation.
Mahāvīra-carita	Bhavabhūti	
Prasanna-rāghava	Jayadeva	
Pratimā-nāṭaka	Bhāsa	Story from the abandonment o Rāma's coronation at Kaikeyī's demand up to Rāma's return from exile.
**Unmatta-rāghava*	Bhāskara	Imaginary situation in which Rāma turns mad at Sītā's disappearance.
* *Unmatta-rāghava*	Virūpākṣadeva	Sītā's desire for the golden deer, Rāma's chase, Sītā's abduction and consequent demented condition of Rāma, their re-union after the slaying of Rāvaṇa.
Uttara-rāmacarita	Bhavabhūti	Story from the banishment of Sītā up to final re-union with Rāma.

POEMS AND CAMPŪS

Bhaṭṭi-kāvya	Bhaṭṭi	
Bhramara-dūta-kāvya	Rudra Nyāya-pañcānana	Fictitious theme of sending a bee to Sītā with Rāma's message.
**Haṃsa-sandeśa*	Veṅkaṭanātha Vedāntācārya	Imaginary theme of Rāma's sending a swan to carry his message to Sītā in Laṅkā.
Jānakī-haraṇa	Kumāradāsa	Story up to the abduction of Sītā.
Jānakī-pariṇaya	Cakrakavi	Events up to Rāma's arrival in Ayodhyā after marrying Sītā.
Raghuvaṃśa	Kālidāsa	
Rāma-carita	Abhinanda	Story from Rāma's anxiety for the rescue of Sītā up to the destruction of Kumbha and Nikumbha.
Rāma-carita	Sandhyākara Nandin	
Rāmāyaṇa-campū	Bhoja	
Rāvaṇārjunīya	Bhaṭṭabhīma (Bhaumaka)	Conflict between Kārtavīrya, king of Haihayas, and Rāvaṇa. The story occurs in the *Rāmāyaṇa*, VII. 31-33.

V

CONTRIBUTION OF MUSLIMS TO SANSKRIT LITERATURE*

Apart from warm patronage extended by some Muslim rulers to the cultivation of Sanskrit literature, certain Muslims themselves composed works in Sanskrit dealing with various subjects.

One Kalyāṇamalla composed, in the 16th century, the work called *Anaṅgaraṅga*,[1] dealing with erotics, in order to please his patron, Lād Khān, son of Ahmad Khān Lodi. Son of Gaṇpati, Bhānukara or Bhānudatta, of the 16th century, wrote under the patronage of Sher Shāh and Nizām Shāh, the following books:

(i) *Gīta-gaurīśa*,[2] (iii) *Rasa-mañjarī*[3] (iii) *Rasa-taraṅgiṇī*[4] (iv) *Kumāra-bhārgavīya*, (v) *Alaṃkāra-tilaka* and (vi) *Śṛṅgāra-dīpikā*.

Emperor Akbar is known to have patronised quite a number of scholars who wrote works on various subjects. Govinda Bhaṭṭa alias Ākbarīya Kālidāsa is credited with the composition of many verses found in anthologies. Besides, he composed the poem *Rāmacandra-yaśaḥ-praśasti* which is in praise of Baghela Rāmacandra of Rewa. The *Vivāha-pradīpa* and *Jīvacchrāddha-prayoga* appear to have been composed by Gaurīśa (son of Dāmodara) and Nārāyaṇa Bhaṭṭa respectively under the patronage of Akbar.

Puṇḍarīka Viṭṭhala of the late 16th century, was a court-poet of Burhān Khān of the Faruqi dynasty, and wrote the *Rāgamālā* on music.

Jagannātha, author of the celebrated work on poetics, called *Rasagaṅgādhara*, enjoyed the patronage of the Mughal Court. His regard for Asaf Khan, brother of Nur Jahan, finds eloquent expression in his *Āsaphavilāsa*. There is a

---

* For details see (i) J. B. Chaudhuri, *Muslim patronage of Sanskritic learning*, Calcutta, 1945.
(ii) *Introducing India*, Vol. II, Calcutta, 1949 (J.B. Chaudhuri's paper on Muslim patronage, etc.).
(iii) *B. C. Law Volume*, Part II, Poona, 1946 (C. Chakravarti's paper on Muslim patronage, etc.).

1. Ed. Lahore, 1920; trs. London, 1885.
2. Also called *Gīta-gaurīpati*. Pub. Grantharatnamālā, Vols. I, II, Bombay, 1888; separately printed, Bombay, 1891.
3. Ed. Ben. SS. 83, 1904.
4. Ed. Benares, 1885.

tradition that Jagannātha, who wrote his works in the earlier part and middle of the 17th century, married a Muslim girl, named Lavaṅgī.

The *Rājavinoda of Udayarāja* has, as its subject-matter, the eulogy of a Sultan of Gujarat.

The Sanskrit works, composed by Muslim authors, are noted below.

(Titles in English Alphabetical order)

Title	Author	Contents	Remarks
Allopaniṣat	Shekh-bhavan	Akbar has occupied the place of Brahman, and his eulogy is the subject-matter of the work.	The author was court-poet of Akbar (1555-1605 A.D.).
Gaṅgā-stava or Gaṅgāṣṭaka	Darāf (Darāp?) Khān Gāji	Eight verses in diverse metres in honour of the Ganges.	See *Jour. of Asiatic Society of Bengal*, XVI, 1847, pp. 393ff. Author identified with Jafar Khan who conquered Saptagrāma in Bengal. Some scholars hold that he was bornin an aristocratic family, left home and settled at Triveni in West Bengal as a recluse. Appears to be mentioned in the introductory portions of the Bengali works *Dharma-maṅgala and Chahi Baḍa Jaṅg-nāmā* by Rūpa Rāma and Yākub Ali respectively. Probably flourished in the period between the later half of the 13th century and earlier half of the 14th.
Kheṭakautuka	Khān-khānān Nawab	A work on Jyotiṣa, dealing with the influence of plants on	Pub. Veṅkaṭeśvara Press, Bombay, 1908. Son of Bairam Khan

Title	Author	Contents	Remarks.
	Abdur Rahim[1]	human life. It is written in Sanskrit mixed with Persian (in verse).	Khan-khanan. Abdur Rahim was born in 1556 A.D. at Lahore. Having lost his father early in life, he was brought up by emperor Akbar who gave him eminent administrative offices under himself. He also served Jehangir. Rahim was proficient in Arabic, Persian, Turkish and Hindi besides Sanskrit. He died in 1629 A.D.
Madanāṣṭaka	Do.		See *Rahīmaratnāvali*.
Rahīmakāvya	Do.	A collection of verses in mixed Sanskrit and Hindi, dealing with the harmony existing in the contemporary Hindu and Muslim communities.	
Saṃgītamālikā	Muhmmad Shāh	Deals with music.	
Samudrasaṃgama	Dārā Shuko	Contains a comparative account of Vedānta philosophy and Sūfism.	Composed in 1655A.D. It is a Sanskrit version of his *Majma-'ul-Baharun*. Some think that it was written by a Sanskrit scholar under the patronage of Dārā Shuko. See P.K. Gode-*Bhārata-ītihā-*

1. See J. B. Chaudhuri, *Khan Khanan and Sanskrit Learning*.

			sa-saṃśodhaka-maṇḍala Quarterly, *Vol.* 94, pp. 75-88. Also see R. Chaudhuri, *Critical Study of Dārā Shikuh's Samudra-saṃgama*. The author's aim was to reconcile the Brāhmanical religion with Islam. Passages from the *Qurān* are cited to prove the several points.
Sṛṅgāra-mañjarī	Attributed to Akbar Shah, a Muslim saint of Gulbarga.	A very elaborate treatise on Nāyikā-Nāyakavibhāga, containing erudite discussions and references to other works on the subject.	Ed. V. Raghavan, Archaeological Deptt. of the Andhra Pradesh Govt., Hyderabad.

The *Rasakalpadruma* (1689 A.D.) of Caturbhuja contains some verses attributed to Śāyestā Khan, maternal uncle of Aurangzeb. A Sanskrit letter of Dārā has been published in *Adyar Library Bulletin*, Oct., 1940; May and Oct., 1943. It may have been composed by Kavīndrācārya in whose *Kavīndra-kalpadruma* it is found.

VI

CONTRIBUTION OF WOMEN TO SANSKRIT LITERATURE[1]

It is interesting to note that Sanskrit literature has been enriched by women's contributions ever since Vedic times. We find certain hymns of the *Ṛgveda* attributed to female sages who are known as Brahma-vādinīs. Of such women, well-known are Ghoṣā, Viśvavārā, Apālā, Godhā, Romaśā and Lopāmudrā. The hymns, associated with their names, are respectively X. 39, V. 28, VIII. 91, X. 134 (part), I. 126 (part), and I. 179 (part). Other female seers are Juhū (X. 109), Śāśvatī (VIII. I), Mādhavī (I. 91), Śaśiprabhā (IV. 4), Anulakṣmī (II. 78, III. 28, 63, 74 and 76), Revā (I. 87), Pahāyi (I. 83) and Rohā[1] (II. 63).

That, in the age of the *Upaniṣads*, women had unfettered right to learn and discuss *Brahma-vidyā* is amply borne out by the stories of Gārgī and Maitreyī in the *Bṛhadāraṇyakopaniṣad.*

We know only the names of Kāmalīlā, Kanakavallī, Lalitāṅgī, Madhurāṅgī, Sunandā, Vimalāṅgī, etc. who, we are told, made contributions to classical Sanskrit *Kāvya*. Unfortunately, their writings have been lost. In Sanskrit anthologies and works on *Alaṃkāra-śāstra*, we come across certain verses attributed to some poetesses. The well-known among them are Indulekhā, Śīlābhaṭṭārikā, Vikaṭanitambā, Gaurī, Caṇḍālavidyā, Candrakāntā, Jaghanacapalā, Padmāvatī, Bhāvadevī, Kuntīdevī, Madālasā, Madirekṣanā, Morikā, Nagamā, Vijjā, Sarasvatī, Cinnammā Bhikṣuṇī, Avilambita-sarasvatī, Vīra-sarasvatī, Śītā, Marulā, etc. They have written on a variety of subjects, e.g. deities, human beings, nature, love, religion, philosophy, etc. Compositions on love, however, are largest in number. Love in union and separation, love-quarrels, activities of the female messenger, union of lovers and the beloved—these topics have been dealt with by them. Female beauty has also been described by some of them. They have written on such male characters as king, poet, miser, crooked fellow, greedy person, etc.

We give below the names of poetesses and of their works with brief accounts of their contents, wherever possible.

---

1. See (1) *Sanskrit Poetesses*—J. B. Chaudhurī, Calcutta, 1939.
   (2) *Dvārakā-pattala* and *Gaṅgāvākyāvalī*—Do, Calcutta, 1940.
   (3) *Poems by Indian Women*—M. Macnicol.
   (4) *Nānā-nibandha* (In Bengali)—S.K. De, Calcutta, 1954.

Poetess	Title of work	Contents
(Sister) Balambal (of Madras)	*Āryā-rāmāyaṇa*	Based on the *Rāmāyaṇa* story.
Devakumārikā (Mother of Samgrāmasiṃha of Rājpūtānā)	*Vaidyanātha-prasāda-praśasti*	
Gaṅgādevī (14th cent.)	*Madhurā-vijaya* or *Vīrakamparāya-carita*	Celebration of the conquest of Madurā by her husband Kamparāya.
Jñānasundarī of Kumbhakonam (19th -20th cent.)	*Hālāsya-campū* (in 6 *stabakas*)	
Kāmākṣī (A Telugu Brahmin lady of Māyavaram, widowed in 1871)	*Rāma-carita*	Based on the *Rāmāyaṇa*, and employs words and phrases used by Kālidāsa. She is also known to have written glosses on some Tarka and Vedānta texts.
Lakṣmī-rājñī (Queen of Malabar, princess of Kaḍattanād. Died 1900)	*Santānagopāla-kāvya*	When of eleven sons of a Brāhmaṇa, one remained the rest having been dead, Arjuna promised to save him. Failing to do so Arjuna resolved to enter into fire. Then Kṛṣṇa brought all the sons back to life.
Priyaṃvadā (Daughter of Śivarāma and wife of Raghunātha. Lived in Faridpur, East Bengal, in the 17th cent.)	*Śyāmā-rahasya*	
Rāmabhadrāmbā (17th century)	*Raghunāthābhyudaya*	Glorification of Raghunātha Nāyaka of Tanjore, the lover of the poetess.
Subhadrā (of Cochin Royal house, 1844-1921)	Composed devotional hymns	

Poetess	Title of work	Contents
Sundaravallī (19th cent. Daughter of N. Iyengar of Mysore)	*Rāmāyaṇa-campū* (in 6 cantos)	
Tirumalāmbā (16th century)	*Varadāmbikā-pariṇaya*	Description of the marriage of Acyutarāya, ruler of Vijayanagara, with Varadāmbikā.
Triveṇī (1817-83 A.D.) Daughter of Udyendrapuram Anantācārya and wife of Veṅkaṭācārya of Śrīperumbudūr. A Vaiṣṇava lady.	(1) *Lakṣmī-sahasra*	Devotional poem.
	(2) *Raṅganātha-sahasra*	,,
	(3) *Śuka-sandeśa*	Lyric
	(4) *Bhṛṅga-sandeśa*	,, Imitation of the *Meghadūta*.
	(5) *Raṅgābhyudaya*	Epic poem.
	(6) *Sampatkumāra-vijaya*	,,
	(7) *Raṅgarāṭ-samudaya*	Drama.
	(8) *Tattvamudrābhādrodaya*	,, (Allegorical)
Vaijayantī (Daughter of Murabhaṭṭa of village Dhānukā in Faridpur district of East Bengal, and wife of Kṛṣṇanātha of Kotālīpāḍā, she lived in the middle of the 17th cent. A.D.)	*Ānandalatikā-campū*	Her husband Kṛṣṇanātha admits the fact that it was composed by him jointly with her.

To Vijjikā, also called Kiśorikā, is attributed the drama entitled *Kaumudī-mahotsava* which, acc. to some, describes the political condition of Magadha at the advent of the Gupta supremacy. While some place her during the time of Samudragupta, others would assign a much later date to her. Vijjikā was probably a South Indian.

Besides the above, there are some other Sanskrit works attributed to female authors. The *Smṛti*-work, *Dvārakā-pattala,* is associated with the name of Vinavāyī, queen of king Harasiṃha of Pāṭaliputra. She flourished sometime between the twelfth century and the sixteenth. In four chapters it deals with the glorification of Dvārakā as a place of pilgr image, the result following a visit to this place, rites to be performed there, ablution, gifts, *Mantra*, Kṛṣṇa-worship, etc.

Another *Smṛti*-work, *Gaṅgā-vākyāvali*, of the fifteenth century, is supposed by some to have been written by Viśvāsadevī, wife of Padmasiṃha, king of Mithilā. In 29 chapters it deals with such topics as ablution in the Gaṅgā, merit accruing from the worship of Gaṅgā, its sight and hearing about it, glorification of Prayāga and other places on the Gaṅgā. Some scholars are of the opinion that the work was, in reality, written by Vidyāpati.

VII

A CLASSIFIED LIST OF SANSKRIT WORKS[1]

For the convenience of readers, who want to specialise in particular branches of Sanskrit literature or require information about works written on a particular subject, the works, are classified below. The different classes, into which the works have been divided, are as follows.

(Names of subjects are in alphabetical order)

Agriculrure

Architecture, Sculpture, Painting
and Iconography

Astrology, Palmistry, Astronomy

Avadāna and Jātaka

Classical Sanskrit:

(a) Prose Works

(b) Poetical compositions

(c) Drama

(d) Campū

Dance

Dharmaśāstra

Dramaturgy

Epics

Epistles and
Epistolography

Erotics

Geography

Grammar

History

Lapidary Science

Lexicography

Medical science

---

1. Commentaries have been left out.

Military matters
(See War)
Miscellaneous
(a) Botany
(b) Elephant-lore
(c) Hawking
(d) Horse-lore
(e) Lapidary science
(f) Mathematics
(g) Omens and portents
(h) Pornography
(i) Theft
(j) Vedic miscellany
(k) Classical miscellany
(l) Culinary Science
Music
Philosophy
A. Orthodox systems
B. Heterodox schools
C. Miscellaneous
Poetics including Vaiṣṇava
Rasa-śāstra
Politics, Statecraft and Economics
Prosody
Purāṇic works
Science
Tantra
Vedic
(a) Saṃhitā
(b) Brāhmaṇa
(d) Āraṇyaka
(d) Upaniṣad
(e) Vedāṅga
(i) Śikṣā
(ii) Kalpa
(iii) Vyākaraṇa
(iv) Nirukta
(v) Chandas
(vi) Jyotiṣa
War

AGRICULTURE

Kṛṣi-parāśara

ARCHITECTURE, SCULPTURE, PAINTING AND ICONOGRAPHY

Bṛhat Saṃhitā (Chap. 53—architecture and 56, 58—sculpture)
Buddha-pratimā-lakṣaṇa
Citralakṣaṇa (in Matsya Purāṇa)
Devatā-mūrti-prakaraṇa
Kāśyapa-saṃhitā (a portion dealing with sculpture)
Mānasāra
Manuṣyālaya-candrikā
Matsyapurāṇa (for Painting)
Mayamata
Nagnacit-citralakṣaṇa
Pratimā-lakṣaṇa

Samarāṅgana-sūtradhāra

Śilparatna (I. 46—architecture. II. 35—sculputre)

Śilpaśāstra

Śukranīti (Ch. IV—sculpture)

Vāstu-vidyā

Viṣṇu-dharmottara (Chap. called *Citrasūtra*, Section III on sculpture)

Viśvakarma-prakāśa

Yukti-kalpataru (Chap. 23—architecture)

The following Purāṇas may be consulted : *Matsya* (Ch. 252-57 Architecture and Śilpaśāstra, Chap. 259-sculpture), *Agni* (Chap. 104-106 architecture and Śilpaśāstra), *Garuḍa* (ch. 46-47 architecture and śilpaśāstra, ch. 49—sculpture), *Viṣṇudharmottara* (chap. called Citrasūtra, Section III—sculpture).

ASTRONOMY AND ASTROLOGY

A rca-jyautiṣ

Ārca-jyautiṣa

Āryabhaṭīya

Bhāsvatī

Bhaviṣyottara purāṇa (a chapter on palmistry)

Brahma-siddhānta

Bṛhajjātaka

Bṛhat-saṃhitā

Daśgītikā-sūtra

Dhīkoṭi

Dhīvṛddhi-tantra

Gaṇaka-taraṅgiṇī

Horā-sāra

Jyotirvidābharaṇa

Karaṇa-prakāśa

Khaṇḍakhādyaka

Laghu-jātaka

Mahā-siddhānta

Pañca-siddhāntikā

Pārasika-prakāśa

Samudra-tilaka

Sāmudrika-cintāmaṇi

Siddhānta-śekhara

Siddhānta-śiromaṇi

Śiṣyadhīvṛddhida

Sphuṭa-brāhmasiddhānta

Śrikaraṇa

Sūrya-siddhānta

Tājika

Vaṭeśvara-siddhānta

Viśvaprakāśa

Vṛddhagarga-saṃhitā

Vyāsa-siddhānta

Yājuṣa-jyautiṣa

AVADĀNA AND JĀTAKA
Avadāna-kalapalatā
Avadāna-śataka
Bodhisattvāvadāna-kalpalatā
(Same as Avadāna-kalpalatā)
Divyāvadāna
Jātakamālā
Lalita-vistara
Mahāvastu

BOTANY
See Miscellaneous

CHEMISTRY
See Medical Science and Chemistry

CLASSICAL SANSKRIT
(a) PROSE WORKS

(Under this category are included also those works in which verses are interspersed, excluding *Campūs.*)

Avantisundarī-kathā
Bharaṭaka-dvātriṃśikā
Bhoja-prabandha
Bilhaṇa-kāvya (same as Caura-pañcāśikā)
Bṛhatkathā (prose work?)
Daśakumāra-carita
Gadya-cintāmaṇi
Harṣa-carita
Hitopadeśa
Kādambarī
Kalpanā-maṇḍitikā (also called *Sūtrālaṅkāra*)
Kathā-kośa
Kathāratnākara
Pañcatantra
Prabandha-cintāmaṇi
Prabandha-kośa
Puruṣa-parikṣā
Siṃhāsana-dvātriṃśikā (Also called *Vikrama-carita*)
Śuka-saptati
Sūtrālaṃkāra (also called *Kalpanā-maṇḍitikā*)
Tantrākhyāyikā (-ka?)
Tilaka-mañjarī
Udayasundarī-kathā
Vemabhūpāla-carita
Vetāla-pañcaviṃśati

(b) POETICAL COMPOSITIONS

Amaru-śataka
Ānanda-laharī
Anyokti-muktālatā
Aparokṣānubhūti
Arjuna-rāvaṇīya
Āryā-saptaśatī
Ātmabodha
Bhallaṭa-śataka
Bhāminī-vilāsa
Bhārata-mañjarī
Bhaṭṭi-kāvya (Same as *Rāvaṇa-vadha*)
Bodhicaryāvatāra

Bṛhatkathā-mañjarī
Bṛhatkathā-śloka-saṃgraha
Buddha-carita
Caitanya-caritāmṛta
Caṇḍī-śataka
Cāru-caryā
Catuḥśataka
Caturvarga-saṃgraha
Caura-pañcāśikā
Darpa-dalana
Daśāvatāra-carita
Delarāmā-kathāsāra
Deśopadeśa
Devīnāma-vilāsa
Devīśataka
Dharmaśarmābhyudaya
Dvisandhāna-kāvya
(Same as *Rāghava-pāṇḍavīya*)
Dvitīya-rājataraṅgiṇī
Gaṇḍīstotra-gāthā
Ghaṭakarpara-kāvya
Gītagovinda
Haracarita-cintāmaṇi
Haravijaya
Hastāmalaka
Jaina-rājataraṅgiṇī
Jāmbavatī-vijaya
Jānakī-haraṇa
Kādambarī-kathāsāra
Kalā-vilāsa
Kapphiṇābhyudaya
Kathā-kautuka
Kathāsarit-sāgara
Kavīndravacana-samuccaya
Kavirahasya
Kīcaka-vadha
Kirātārjunīya
Kṛṣṇa-karṇāmṛta
Kumārapāla-carita
Kumāra-sambhava
Mādhava-mahotsava
Mahābhārata-tātparya-nirṇaya
Meghadūta
Mohamudgara
Mugdhopadeśa
Naiṣadha-carita
Nalodaya
Narmamālā
Navasāhasāṅka-carita
Nītikalpataru
Nīti-śataka
Padyāvalī
Pavana-dūta
Pṛthvīrāja-vijaya
Rāghava-pāṇḍavīya
Raghuvaṃśa
Rājataraṅgiṇī
Rājāvalī-patākā
Rājendra-karṇapūra
Rāma-carita (Same as *Rāmapāla-carita*)
Rāmapāla-carita (Same as *Rāma-carita*)
Rāmāyaṇa-mañjarī
Rāvaṇārjunīya
Rāvaṇa-vadha (Same as *Bhaṭṭi-kāvya*)
Ṛtu-saṃhāra
Sadukti-karṇāmṛta
Samaya-mātṛkā
Śānti-śataka
Śārṅgadhara-paddhati
Saundarananda
Saundarya-laharī
Sevya-sevakopadeśa
Śiśupāla-vadha
Śrīkaṇṭha-carita
Śṛṅgāra-rasāṣṭaka

Śṛṅgāra-śataka
Śṛṅgāra-tilaka
Subhāṣita-muktāvalī (Also called *Sūkti-muktāvalī*)
Subhāṣita-ratnakoṣa
Subhāṣitāvalī
Sūkti-muktāvali (Also called *Subhāṣita-muktāvalī*)
Sūrya-śataka
Triṣaṣṭiśalākā-puruṣa-carita
Vairāgya-śataka
Vakrokti-pañcāśika
Vikramāṅkadeva-carita

(c) DRAMA

Abhijñāna-śākuntala (Also briefly called *Śakuntalā*)
Abhisārikā-vañcitaka
Abhiṣeka
Anargha-rāghava
Āścarya-cūḍāmaṇi
Avimāraka
Bāla-bhārata (Same as *Pracaṇḍa-pāṇḍava*)
Bāla-carita
Bāla-rāmāyaṇa
Bhagavadajjuka
Caitanya-candrodaya
Caṇḍa-kauśika
Caturbhāṇī
Dānakeli-kaumudī
Devī-candragupta
Dhūrta-samāgama
Dhūrta-viṭa-saṃvāda
Dūta-ghaṭotkaca
Dūta-vākya
Hanūmannāṭaka (Same as *Mahānāṭaka*)
Hāsyārṇava
Karṇa-bhāra
Karṇa-sundarī
Kundamālā
Lalita-mādhava
Laṭaka-melaka
Madhyama-vyāyoga
Mahānāṭaka (Same as *Hanūmannāṭaka*)
Mahāvīra-carita
Mālatī-mādhava
Mālavikāgnimitra
Mallikāmāruta
Mattavilāsa
Mṛcchakaṭika
Mudrārākṣasa
Nāgānanda
Pāda-tāḍitaka
Padma-prābhṛtaka
Pañcarātra
Pārijāta-haraṇa
Prabodha-candrodaya
Pracaṇḍa-pāṇḍava
Prasanna-rāghava
Pratijñā-yaugandharāyaṇa
Pratimā-nāṭaka
Priyadarśikā
Ratnāvalī
Śakuntalā (Same as *Abhijñāna-śākuntala*)
Śāriputra-prakaraṇa
Svapna-vāsavadatta
Ubhayābhisārikā
Ūrubhaṅga
Uttara-rāmacarita
Veṇī-saṃhāra
Vidagdha-mādhava
Viddhaśāla-bhañjikā
Vikramorvaśīya
Vīṇāvāsavadattā

(d) Campū

Campū-rāmāyaṇa
Damayantī-kathā (Same as *Nala-campū*)
Gopāla-campū
Jīvandhara-campū
Madālasā-campū
Muktā-caritra
Nala-campū (Same as *Damayantī-kathā*)
Rāmāyaṇa-campū
Yaśastilaka-campū

DANCE

Nāṭyaśāstra
Nṛttaratnāvali
Saṃgīta-ratnākara

DHARMAŚĀSTRA (ORIGINAL WORKS AND DIGESTS)

Ācārādarśa
Āpastamba-dharmasūtra
Āpastamba-śulvasūtra
Aṣṭāviṃśati-tattva
Baudhāyana-dharmasūtra
Baudhāyana-śrautasūtra
Baudhāyana-śulvasūtra
Brāhmaṇa-sarvasva (Same as *Karmopadeśinī*)
Caturvarga-cintāmaṇi
Dānakriyā-kaumudī
Dāna-ratnākara
Dāna-sāgara
Daṇḍa-viveka
Daśakarma-paddhati (Same as *Karmānuṣṭhāna-paddhati*)
Dattaka-candrikā
Dattaka-mīmāṃsā
Dāya-bhāga
Durgābhakti-taraṅgiṇī
Durgotsava-viveka
Gaṅgāvākyāvalī
Gautama-dharmasūtra
Gṛhastha-ratnākara
Hāralatā
Haribhakti-vilāsa
Kālasāra
Kālaviveka
Karmānuṣṭhāna-paddhati (Same as *Daśakarma-paddhati*)
Karmopadeśinī (Same as *Brāhmaṇa-sarvasva*)
Kṛtya-cintāmaṇi
Kṛtya-kalpataru
Kṛtya-ratnākara
Madana-pārijāta
Manu-smṛti
Nirṇaya-sindhu
Parāśara Smṛti
Pitṛ-dayitā
Prāyaścitta-nirūpaṇa (or,-prakaraṇa)
Prāyaścitta-viveka
Pūjā-ratnākara
Sarasvatī-vilāsa
Smṛti-candrikā
Smṛtiratna-hāra
Smṛti-ratnākara
Smṛti-sāra
Smṛti-tattva
Śrāddha-kriyā-kaumudī
Śrāddha-viveka

Śuddhi-kaumudī
Śuddhi-ratnākara
Tīrtha-cintāmaṇi
Tithi-nirṇaya
Vaikhānasa-smārtasūtra
Vasiṣṭha-dharmaśāstra
Vasiṣṭha-dharmasūtra
Viṣṇu-dharmasūtra
(or, -Smṛti)
Vivāda-bhaṅgārṇava
Vivāda-cintāmaṇi
Vivāda-ratnākara
Vivādārṇava-setu
Vyavahāra-cintāmaṇi
Vyavahāra-mayūkha
Vyavahāra-ratnākara
Yājñavalkya-smṛti

DRAMATURGY

Abhinaya-darpaṇa
Brahmabharata
Daśarūpaka
Nāṭaka-candrikā
Nāṭaka-lakṣaṇa-ratnakośa
Nāṭya-darpaṇa
Nāṭya-śāstra
Nāṭyaśāstra-saṃgraha

EPICS

(Including philosophical works bearing their title or forming their integral parts)

Adbhuta-rāmāyaṇa
Adhyātma-rāmāyaṇa
Bhagavadgītā
Gītā (same as *Bhagavadgītā*)
Harivaṃśa
Mahābhārata
Rāmāyaṇa
Yoga-vāśiṣṭha

EPISTLES & EPISTOLOGRAPHY

Likhanāvalī
Patra-kaumudī
Śiṣyalekha-dharmakāvya
Suhṛllekha

EROTICS

Anaṅgaraṅga
Kāmasūtra
Kandarpa-cūḍāmaṇi
Rati-rahasya

GEOGRAPHY

Bhūgola-khagola-varṇana
Bhū-parikramā
Brahmāṇḍa-bhūgola
Purāṇa (Brahmāṇḍa, Viṣṇu, Vāyu, Kūrma)
Siddhānta-śiromaṇi

GRAMMAR

Aindra-vyākaraṇa
Aṣṭādhyāyī
Bhāgavṛtti
Cāndra-vyākaraṇa
Dhātu-pradīpa
Durghaṭa-vṛtti
Gaṇapāṭha
Gaṇaratna-mahodadhi
Harināmāmṛta
Jainendra-vyākaraṇa
Kalāpa
Kātantra (same as *Kalāpa*)
Kaumāra
Kavikalpadruma
Mahābhāṣya

Mahābhāṣya-pradīpoddyota
Mugdhabodha
Pañcādhyāyī
Paribhāṣā-vṛtti
Prabodha-prakāśa
Prakriyā-kaumudī
Śabdānuśāsana (same as Siddhahemacandra)
Śākaṭāyana-śabdānuśāsana
Saṃkṣiptasāra
Sārasvata-vyākaraṇa
Siddhahemacandra (same as *Haima-vyākaraṇa* and *Śabdānuśāsana*)
Supadma-vyākaraṇa
Uddyota
Uṇādi-sūtra
Vaiyākaraṇa-bhūṣaṇa
Vaiyākaraṇa-bhūṣaṇa-sāra
Vaiyākaraṇa-siddhānta-kaumudī
Vākyapadīya (also see under philosophy)
Vārtika-sūtra

HISTORY

Pṛthvirājavijaya
Harṣacarita
Kumārapāla-carita
Navasāhasāṅka-carita
Nīlamata-purāṇa
Rājataraṅgiṇī
Rājāvalī-patākā
Rājendra-karṇapūra
Rāmacarita
Varadāmbikā-pariṇaya
Vasantavilāsa
Vikramāṅkadeva-carita
Vīrakamparāya-carita

LEXICOGRAPHY

Abhidhāna-cintāmaṇi
Abhidhāna-ratnamālā
Amara-kośa
Anekārtha-kośa
Anekārtha-śabdakośa
Anekārtha-samuccaya
Hārāvalī
Maṅkha-kośa (same as *Anekārtha-kośa*)
Medinī-kośa
Nāmaliṅgānuśāsana (same as *Amara-kośa* above)
Nyāya-kośa
Ṭīkā-sarvasva
Trikāṇḍaśeṣa
Vācaspatya
Vaidyaka-śabdasindhu
Vaijayantī

MATHEMATICS

See Miscellaneous

MEDICAL SCIENCE[1] AND CHEMISTRY

Aṣṭāṅgahṛdaya-saṃhitā
Aṣṭāṅga-saṃgraha
Āyurveda-prakāśa
Āyurveda-sūtra

1. See Bower Manuscript in the main body of this work.

Bhaiṣajya-ratnāvalī
Bhela-saṃhitā
Caraka-saṃhitā
Cikitsākalikā
Cikitsā-sāra-saṃgraha
Dhātu-ratnamālā
Gada-viniścaya (same as *Nidāna*)
Kāśyapa-saṃhitā
Nāḍī-parīkṣā
Nidāna (same as *Rugviniścaya*)
Rasa-cintāmaṇi
Rasa-hṛdaya
Rasa-nakṣatra-mālikā
Rasa-pradīpa
Rasaprakāśa-sudhākara
Rasarāja-lakṣmī
Rasa-ratnākara
Rasaratna-samuccaya
Rasārṇava
Rasendra-cintāmaṇi
Rasendra-cūḍāmaṇi
Rasendra-sāra-saṃgraha
Rugviniścaya (same as *Nidāna*)
Śārṅgadhara-saṃgraha
Siddha-yoga (Also called *Vṛndamādhava*)
Suśruta-saṃhitā
Svarṇa-tantra
Vaidya-jīvana
Vṛnda-mādhava (also called *Siddha-yoga*)

MISCELLANEOUS

(a) Botany
Upavana-vinoda
Vṛkṣāyurveda

(b) Elephant-lore
Gaja-śāstra
Hastyāyurveda
Mātaṅga-līlā

(c) Hawking
Śyainika-śāstra

(d) Horse-lore
Aśva-cikitsita
Aśva-śāstra
Aśva-vaidyaka

(e) Lapidary science
Agasti-mata
Garuḍa-purāṇa (Ratnaparīkṣā section)
Laghu-ratna-parīkṣā
Maṇimāhātmya
Ratna-śāstra
Ratna-parīkṣā
Ratna-saṃgraha

(f) Mathematics
Bakhshālī MS.
Calarāśikalana
Gaṇitasāra
Gaṇitatilaka
Also see Astronomy and Astrology

(g) Omens and Portents
Adbhuta-sāgara

(h) Pornography
Kuṭṭanī-mata

(i) Theft
Ṣaṇmukha-kalpa

(j) Vedic Miscellany
Bṛhaddevatā
Nighaṇṭu
Sarvānukramaṇī

(k) Classical Miscellany
Cāṇakya-sūtra
Caturaṅga-dīpikā
Malla-purāṇa
Paṭṭāvalī
Śaṃkara-digvijaya
Śaṃkara-vijaya
Sukhāvatī-vyūha

Vajrasūci
Yukti-kalpataru

(l) Culinary Science

Nalapāka
Pāka-darpaṇa
Pāka-vijñāna
Pākārṇava

MUSIC

(Instrumental and vocal; dance)

Bṛhaddeśī
Dattilam
Gītālaṃkāra
Kohala-rahasya
Pañcamasāra-saṃhitā
Rāga-nirūpaṇa
Rāga-taraṅgiṇī
Rāga-vibodha
Saṃgīta-dāmodara
Saṃgīta-darpaṇa
Saṃgīta-makaranda
Saṃgīta-pārijāta
Saṃgīta-rāja
Saṃgīta-ratnākara
Saṃgīta-samayasāra
Svaramela-kalānidhi
Tālādhyāya

PHILOSOPHY

A. Orthodox systems

(i) Nyāya and Vaiśeṣika

Āloka
Anumāna-dīdhiti
Apoha-siddhi
Ātmatattva-viveka (also called *Bauddha-dhikkāra*)
Bhāṣā-pariccheda
Jaiminīya-nyāyamālā
Kārikāvali (same as *Bhāṣā-pariccheda*)
Kṣaṇabhaṅga-siddhi
Kusumāñjali (same as *Nyāya-kusumāñjali*)
Lakṣaṇāvali
Nyāyatattvāloka
Nyāya-darśana
Nyāya-kalikā
Nyāya-kusumāñjali (same as *Kusumāñjali*)
Nyāya-māñjarī
Nyāya-praveśa
Nyāya-sāra
Nyāya-sūtra
Nyāya-tattvāloka
Padārtha-dharmasaṃgraha
Śabdaśakti-prakāśikā
Saptapadārthī
Tarkabhāṣā
Tarka-kaumudī
Tarkāmṛta
Tarka-saṃgraha
Tārkika-rakṣā
Tattva-cintāmaṇi
Tattva-cintāmaṇidīdhiti
Tattvāloka
Vaiśeṣika-sūtra

(ii) Sāṃkhya and Yoga

Pātañjala Yogadarśana
Sāṃkhya-kārikā
Sāṃkhya-pravacana-sūtra (same as *Sāṃkhya-sūtra*)
Sāṃkhya-sāra
Sāṃkhya-sūtra
Sāṃkhya-tattva-kaumudī
Tattva-samāsa
Yoga-sūtra

(iii) Mīmāṃsā and Vedānta

Advaita-siddhi
Advaita-makaranda
Arthasaṃgraha
Brahmasūtra
Brahmasūtra-bhāṣya
Citsukhī
Daśaślokī
Gauḍapāda-kārikā
Jīvanmukti-viveka
Khaṇḍanakhaṇḍa-khādya
Mānameyodaya
Mīmāṃsānukramaṇī
Mīmāṃsā-nyāyaprakāśa
Mīmāṃsā-sūtra
Naiṣkarmya-siddhi
Nyāyamālā-vistara
Nyāya-nirṇaya
Pañcadaśī
Pañcapādikā
Prakaraṇa-pañcikā
Prasthānabheda
Pratyak-tattva-dīpikā
Pūrvamīmāṃsā
Ṛjuvimalā
Śataślokī
Śatadūṣaṇī
Siddnānta-ratna (also called *Daśaślokī*)
Tattva-bindu
Tattva-pradīpikā
Tattva-saṃkhyāna
Tautātita-mata-tilaka
Upadeśa-sāhasrī
Vedānta-paribhāṣā
Vedānta-sāra
Vedānta-sūtra
Vedārtha-saṃgraha
Vidhi-viveka
Vivaraṇa-prameya-saṃgraha
Viveka-cūḍāmaṇi

(iv) Śaiva and Śākta Philosophical Systems

Ajaḍa-pramātṛ-siddhi
Bodha-pañcadaśikā
Īśvara-pratyabhijñā
Īśvara-siddhi
Nareśvara-parīkṣā
Paramārtha-sāra
Pratyabhijñā-hṛdaya
Pratyabhijñā-kārikā (same as *Īśvarapratyabhijñā-sūtra*)
Pratyabhijñā-sūtra (same as *Īśvara-pratyabhijñā*)
Śiva-dṛṣṭi
Śiva-sūtra
Spanda-kārikā
Tantrāloka
Tantrasāra
Tantravaṭadhānikā

(v) Vaiṣṇava Philosophy

Bhāgavata-sandarbha
Paramātma-sandarbha
Prīti-sandarbha
Śrīkṛṣṇa-sandarbha
Tattva-sandarbha

B. Heterodox Schools

(i) Bauddha

Abhidharma-kośa
Aṣṭasāhasrikā-prajñāpāramitā
Dharma-saṃgraha
Gaṇḍavyūha
Laṃkāvatāra
Mādhyamika-kārikā
Mahāyāna-śraddhotpāda
Mahāyāna-sūtrālaṃkāra

Mūlamadhyamaka-kārikā
Nyāyabindu
Pramāṇa-samuccaya
Pramāṇa-vārtika
Saddharma-laṃkāvatāra
Saddharma-puṇḍarīka
Śikṣā-samuccaya
Yogācārabhūmi-śāstra

(ii) Jaina

Daśa-sūtrī
Dharmabindu
Syādvāda-mañjarī
Tattvārthādhigama-sūtra

C. Miscellaneous

Ṣaḍdarśana-samuccaya
Sarvadarśana-saṃgraha
Sarvadarśana-siddhānta-saṃgraha
Vaiyākaraṇa-siddhānta-mañjūṣā
Vākyapadīya (also see under Grammar)

POETICS INCLUDING VAIṢṆAVA RASA-ŚĀSTRA

Abhidhāvṛtti-mātṛkā
Alaṃkāra-kaustubha
Alaṃkāra-saṃgraha
Alaṃkāra-sarvasva
Aucitya-vicāra-carcā
Bhakti-rasāmṛta-sindhu
Bhāmahālaṃkāra (same as *Kāvyālaṃkāra*)
Bhāva-prakāśa
Candrāloka
Dhvanyāloka
Ekāvalī
Kavikaṇṭhābharaṇa
Kāvyādarśa
Kāvyālaṃkāra
Kāvyālaṃkāra-saṃgraha
Kāvyālaṃkāra-sūtra
Kāvyālaṃkāra-sūtravṛtti
Kāvya-mīmāṃsā
Kāvyānuśāsana
Kāvya-prakāśa
Rasagaṅgādhara
Sāhitya-darpaṇa
Sarasvatī-kaṇṭhābharaṇa
Śṛṅgāra-prakāśa
Ujjvala-nīlamaṇi
Vāgbhaṭālaṃkāra
Vakrokti-jīvita
Vidagdha-mukhamaṇḍana
Vyakti-viveka

Politics and Statecraft

Abhilaṣitārtha-cintāmaṇi (same as *Mānasollāsa*)

ARTHAŚĀSTRA

Cāṇakya-rājanīti-śāstra
Kāmandakīya Nītisāra
Mānasollāsa (same as *Abhilaṣitārtha-cintāmaṇi*)
Nīti-ratnākara
Nīti-sāra
Rājanīti-ratnākara
Śukra-nīti

PROSODY

Chandaḥsūtra
Chandomañjarī
Ekāvalī
Śrutabodha
Suvṛtta-tilaka
Vṛtta-ratnākara

PURĀṆIC WORKS

Agni-purāṇa
Bhāgavata-purāṇa

Bhaviṣya (or, Bhaviṣyat-purāṇa)
Brahmāṇḍa-purāṇa
Brahma-purāṇa
Brahmavaivarta (or, Kaivarta)
Bṛhaddharmapurāṇa
Bṛhannāradīya-purāṇa
Caṇḍī
Devī-māhātmya
Durgā-saptaśatī
Garuḍa-purāṇa
Kūrma-purāṇa
Liṅga-purāṇa
Mārkaṇḍeya-purāṇa
Matsya-purāṇa
Nīlamata-purāṇa
Padma-purāṇa
Saptaśatī
Skanda-purāṇa
Vahni-purāṇa
Vāmana-purāṇa
Varāha-purāṇa
Viṣṇu-dharmottara
Viṣṇu-purāṇa

SMṚTI

See DHARMAŚĀSTRA

TANTRA

Ahirbudhnya-saṃhitā
Īśvara-saṃhitā
Jñānārṇava-tantra
Kākacaṇḍeśvarīmata
Kālīvilāsa-tantra
Kula-cūḍāmaṇi
Kulārṇava-tantra
Mahānirvāṇa-tantra
Mañjuśrī-mūlakalpa
Prāṇatoṣiṇī
Prapañcasāra-tantra
Rudrayāmala
Śāradā-tilaka
Tantrarāja-tantra

VEDIC

(a) Saṃhitā
Atharvaveda
Ṛgveda
Sāmaveda
Yajurveda
(b) Brāhmaṇa
Aitareya
Kauṣītaki
Śatapatha
(c) Āraṇyaka
Aitareya Āraṇyaka
Kauṣītaki-āraṇyaka
Taittirīya-āraṇyaka
(d) Upaniṣad
Aitareyopaniṣad
Bṛhadāraṇyakopaniṣad
Chāndogyopaniṣad
Īśopaniṣad
Kaṭhopaniṣad
Kenopaniṣad
Māṇḍūkyopaniṣad
Muṇḍakopaniṣad
Praśnopaniṣad
Taittirīyopaniṣad
(e) Vedāṅga
(i) Śikṣā
Atharvaveda-prātiśākhya
Bharadvāja-śikṣā
Nāradīya-śikṣā
Pāṇinīya-śikṣā
Puṣpa-sūtra
Ṛgveda-prātiśākhya
Ṛktantra
Taittirīya-prātiśākhya
Vājasaneyi-prātiśākhya
(ii) Kalpa (including Śrauta, Gṛhya, Dharma—and Śulva-sūtras)

Āpastamba-gṛhyasūtra
Āpastamba-śrautasūtra
Āśvalāyana-gṛhyasūtra
Āśvālāyana-śrautasūtra
Drāhyāyaṇa-śrautasūtra
Gobhila-gṛhyasūtra
Jaiminīya-śrautasūtra
Kātyāyana-śrautasūtra
Kātyāyana-śulvasūtra
Khādira-gṛhyasūtra
Lāṭyāyana-śrautasūtra
Mānava-dharmaśāstra
Mānava-śrautasūtra
Pāraskara-gṛhyasūtra
Puṣpa-sūtra
Śāṃkhāyana-gṛhyasūtra
Śāṃkhāyana-śrautasūtra

(iii) Vyākaraṇa
See Grammar
(iv) Nirukta
Nirukta
(v) Chandas
See Prosody
(vi) Jyotiṣa
See Astronomy and Astrology.

WAR

Abhilaṣitārtha-cintāmaṇi
Arthaśāstra (II. 18, 30, 33; V. 3; IX. 2; X. 1, 4, 5, 6 etc.)
Mahābhārata (See Bibliography on War)
Mānasāra (another name of *Abhilaṣitārtha-cintāmaṇi*)
Manu-smṛti (vii)

VIII

LIST OF THE IMPORTANT SERIES IN INDIA AND ABROAD, PUBLISHING SANSKRIT TEXTS AND STUDIES RELATING TO THEM OR THEIR TRANSLATION

(In English Alphabetical Order)

Adyar Library Series
American Oriental Series, New Haven, Conn.
Ānandāśrama Sanskrit Series, Poona.
Andhra Oriental Series.
Anecdota Oxonensia, Aryan Series, Oxford.
Benares Sanskrit Series.
Bibliotheca Buddhica, St. Petersburg.
Bibliotheca Indica, Calcutta.
Bibliotheca Javanica, Batavia.
Bombay Sanskrit Series.
Cahiers De La Société Asiatique, Paris.
Calcutta Oriental Series.
Calcutta Sanskrit College Reasearch Series.
Chowkhamba Sanskrit Series, Benares.
Chowkhamba Oriental Research Studies, Varanasi.
Disputationes Rheno-Trajectionae, 'S-Gravenhage, Holland.
Gaekwad's Oriental Series, Baroda.
Govt. Oriental Library Series, Madras.
Grundriss der Indo-Arischen, Philologie und Altertumskunde.
Haridāsa Sanskrit Series, Benares.
Harvard Oriental Series.
Indian Thought Series, Allahabad.
Jñānapiṭha Mūrtidevī Jaina Granthamālā, Benares.
Kāśī Sanskrit Series.
Kashmir Series of Texts and Studies.
Kāvyamālā, Bombay.
Madras Oriental Series.
Oriental Translation Fund, London.
Oriental Library Publications Sanskrit Series, University of Mysore.
Princess of Wales Sarasvatī Bhavana Texts & Studies, Benares.
Prize Publication Fund, London.
Punjab Sanskrit Series.
Purāṇa Text Series, Varanasi.
Roma Oriental Series.
Sacred Books of the East, Oxford.
Sacred Books of the Hindus, Allahabad.
Sanskrit College Series of Texts and Studies, Calcutta.
Sanskrit Sāhitya Parishad Series, Calcutta.
Sarasvatī Mahal Series, Tanjore.
Sarasvatī Bhavana Texts, Varanasi.
Singhi Jain Granthamālā (Books pub. mainly from Bombay).
Śrī Vāṇī Vilās Śāstra Series, Srīrangam.
Tāntrik Texts, ed. A. Avalon, Madras. (Sir John Woodroffe)
Trivandrum Sanskrit Series.
Vizianagram Sanskrit Series.

IX

CONTRIBUTION OF BUDDHISTS TO SANSKRIT LITERATURE[1]

The bulk of the literature of the Buddhists, both canonical and non-canonical, is in Pāli. Some of the Buddhist writers were erudite Sanskrit scholars. Moreover, Sanskrit was the language cultivated among the intelligentsia. So, the Buddhists could not ignore this language; they wrote works in Sanskrit relating to various branches of learning. We note below the titles of the note-worthy works under different heads, the names of their authors and give brief indications of their contents[2] wherever possible.

Besides works written in pure Sanskrit, there are some which are written in what is called Hybrid Sanskrit[3].

For the present purpose, we leave out of consideration the numerous *Māhātmyas* (works in glorification) and *Dhāraṇīs* (protective spells). Of the many Buddhist *Stotras*, we shall mention only the well-known ones.

The Sanskrit works, written by Buddhists, have been arranged under the following classes:—

A. Religious literature.
B. Tales and Legends.
C. Poetical compositions.
D. Tantra.

---

1. For details, see:
   (i) M. Winternitz, *History of Indian Literature*, Vol. II.
   (ii) N. Das Gupta, *Bāṅgālāy Bauddhadharma* (in Bengali).
   (iii) P.C. Bagchi, *Bhārat O Madhya Eśiyā* (in Bengali).
   (iv) S.K. De, *History of Sanskrit Literature*, Calcutta, 1947.
   (v) J.K. Nariman, *Literary History of Sanskrit Buddhism*, 1972.
   (vi) W. Lessing, *Literary History of Sanskrit Buddhism.*

2. The contents of only those works, which have not been dealt with under Works (Part II of this book), are given here. Minor works, commentaries and the Sanskrit works which are lost, and whose translations only exist in Tibetan and other languages, are not taken into account. In the cases of the works, whose titles hint at their contents, the contents have not been separately noted.

3. See F. Edgerton, *Buddhist Hybrid Sanskrit Reader*, New Haven, Yale University Press, 1953.

E. Lexicography.
F. Drama.
G. Philosophy.
H. Grammar.
I. Miscellaneous.

It is generally believed that the Buddhists wrote or compiled the *Tripiṭaka* in Pāli alone. But, recent discoveries have brought to light parts of the *Tripiṭaka* written in Sanskrit. From Tibetan and Chinese translations also we learn of the existence of this work in Sanskrit. In such works as the *Mahāvastu, Divyāvadāna, Lalita-vistara* etc., parts of Sanskrit *Tripiṭaka* have been quoted. The Sanskrit and Pāli *Tripiṭakas* appear to have been independent works; one was not the translation of the other.

There is mention of a *Mahāyāna Sūtra*, called *Buddhāvataṃsaka*, in the Buddhist lexicon called *Mahāvyutpatti* written in Sanskrit.

A Sanskrit work, called *Ratnakūṭa*, is mentioned in the Chinese *Tripiṭaka* and the Tibetan *Bstan-ḥgyur*. Parts of the *Ratnakūṭa* have been discovered near Khotan in Central Asia.

(Titles of Works arranged in English Alphabetical Order)

A. RELIGIOUS LITERATURE

Besides the *Tripiṭaka* and the other religious texts, we have the following works in Sanskrit.

Title	Author, if known	Remarks
Daśabhūmīśvara (or, Daśabhūmaka or Daśabhūmika-sūtra)		Discourse on the ten steps leading to the attainment of Buddhahood.
Daśabhūmi-vibhāṣāśāstra	Nāgārjuna	Commentary.
Gaṇḍavyūha		
Saddharma-puṇḍarīka		
Samādhirāja		Seeks to show how a Bodhisattva can acquire the highest knowledge by means of various meditations, especially the highest meditation.
Vaipulya-sūtra		Discourses of great extent belonging to Mahāyāna.

B. TALES AND LEGENDS

Akṣobhya-vyūha		An account of the land of Buddha Akṣobhya.
Aśokāvadāna-mālā		A poetical work based on Avadānas.

Title	Author, if known	Remakrs
Avadāna-kalpalatā	Kṣemendra	
Avadāna-śataka		
Avalokiteśvara-guṇa-kāraṇḍa-vyūha		Same as *Kāraṇḍavyūha*, (q.v.)
Bhadrakalpāvadāna		34 legends related by Upagupta to Aśoka.
Bodhisattvāvadānamālā		Same as *Jātakamālā*.
Divyāvadāna		
Dvāviṃśatyavadāna		Avadānas in 22 sections. Upagupta conversing with Aśoka; then they give place to Śākyamuni and Maitreya.
Jātaka-mālā	Āryaśūra	
Kalpadrumāvadānamālā		A poetical work based on Avadānas.
Kalpanā-maṇḍitikā or Kalpanālaṃkṛtikā	Kumāralāta, acc. to some. Aśvaghoṣa, acc. to others	
Kāraṇḍa-vyūha		
Karuṇā-puṇḍarīka		An account of the wonderland Padma of Buddha Padmottara.
Lalitavistara		
Mahāvastu		
Ratnāvadāna-mālā		Avadāna stories in metrical form.
Grundriss der Indo-Arischen, P		
Sukhāvatī-vyūha		
Sūtrālaṃkāra		Name of the Kalpanā-maṇḍitikā, according to Chinese version by Kumārajīva.
Vicitra-karṇikāvadāna		Varied collections of 32 narratives.
Vratāvadāna-mālā		A collection of legends, the origin of festivals or rites.

C. POETICAL COMPOSITIONS

Ārya-tārādevī-stotra-muktika-mālā	Candragomin	
Bhakti-śataka	Rāmacandra Kavi-bhāratī	100 stanzas on *Bhakti*.
Bodhicaryāvatāra	Śāntideva	
Buddha-carita	Aśvaghoṣa	
Catuḥśataka-stotra	Mātṛceta	

Title	Author, if known	Remarks
Citta-śuddhiprakarṇa	Āryadeva (?)	A didactic work containing, *inter alia*, condemnation of Brāhamaṇical rites and practices.
Gaṇḍī-stotragāthā	Aśvaghoṣa	
Mahārāja-kanikalekha	Mātṛceta (Another name of Aśvaghoṣa, according to Tāranātha, the Tibetan historian)	In 85 verses, the author instructs Kaniṣka to follow in the footsteps of the Buddha.
Mahāyāna-sūtrālaṃkāra	Asaṅga	According to some, it is by Maitreyanātha, preceptor of Asaṅga.
Manohara-kalpa	Candragomin	Contains some *Stotras*.
Padya-cūḍāmaṇi	Buddhaghoṣa	May or may not be identical with Buddhaghoṣa, the renowned commentator.
Śatapañcāśatka-stotra	Mātṛceta	Available in fragments.
Saundarananda	Aśvaghoṣa	
Śiṣyalekha-dharmakāvya	Candragomin	
Subhāṣita-muktāvalī	Puruṣottamadeva (Compiler)	Anthology of verses.
Subhāṣita-ratnakośa	Vidyākara (compiler)	
Viṣṇubhakti-kalpalatā	Puruṣottamadeva	

D. TANTRA

Besides some Mahāyāna Sūtras, which contain Tāntric sections, the following works are noteworthy. For the present purpose, we leave out the *Sādhanas* or works on magic ritual belonging to Tāntric ritual literature.

Abhicāra-karma	Candragomin	
Ādikarma-pradīpa		Describes the ceremonies and religious acts which are to be performed by the adherents of the Mahāyāna and seekers of enlightenment.
Aṣṭamī-vrata-vidhāna		
Caṇḍa-mahāroṣaṇa-tantra		It explains, on the one hand, the *Pratītya-samutpāda* according to Mahāyāna, and, on the other, the cult of Yoginīs and that of female deities with sexual actions are recommendeed.

Guhya-samāja		Same as Tathāgata-guhya (q.v.).
Mahākāla-tantra		It contains explanations as to the mystical significance of the letters in the word 'Mahākāla', and teaches means of acquiring various worldly objects and of causing harm to people and enslaving them.
Mahākāruṇika-stotra	Candragomin	
Mañjuśrī-mūlakalpa		A manual on magic.
Pañcakrama		An extract from the *Guhyasamāja.*
Rakṣā-cakra	Candragomin	
Siṃhanāda-sādhana	Candragomin	
Śrīcakra-sambhāra-tantra		Describes the ritual of *Mahāsukha.*
Suvarṇa-prabhāsa		See this title under Philosophy.
Tārā-rahasya	Brahmānanda	Teaches the cult of Tārā.
Tārā-tantra		Buddha and Vaśiṣṭha are described as great Bhairavas.
Tathāgata-guhyaka or Tathāgata-guṇajñāna		On Mahāyāna morality.

The following is a list of some more philosophical, chiefly Tāntric, works mentioned against their authors who were of Bengal.

(Names of authors are in Devanāgarī alphabetical order)

Author	Date	Title
Atiśa Dīpaṃkara	980-1053 A.D.	Bodhi-mārga-pañjikā, Ekavira-sādhana, Prajñāpāramitā-piṇḍārtha-pradipa, Ratnakaraṇḍodghāṭa-nāma-madhyamakopadeśa, Lokātītasaptāṅga-vidhi and many others totalling 200 according to a Tibetan tradition
Abhayākaragupta	11th century	Marma-kaumudī, Bodhipaddhati, Śrīmañjuvajrādi-kramābhisamaya-samuccaya-niṣpanna (Yogāvalī-nāma), Vajrayānāpatti-mañjarī, Āmnāya-mañjarī. According to the *Bstan-ḥgyur*, he wrote 20 works on Vajrayāna.
Kumāravajra	10th-11th cent.	Cakra-sambara-maṇḍana-vidhitattvāvatāra.

Jetāri (Preceptor of Atiśa)	Contemporary of king Mahīpāla	Acc. to tradition, author of 11 works on Vajrayāna-sādhana.
Divākaracandra	Earlier half of 11th century	Heruka-sādhana and some other works.
Bihbūticandra		Author of some original works and some commentaries according to Tibetan tradition.
Śīlabhadra	7th century	*Āryabuddhabhūmi-Vyākhyāna.*

From the *Bstan-ḥgyur* we learn that some of the Siddhācāryas, who are reputed as authors of the Dohās of the *Caryācarya-viniścaya*, wrote Sanskrit works on Tantra. The names of six Tantra works by Kukkuripāda are known. Ten Vajrayānī works are associated with the name of Śabari. Lui-pā is known to have written three works on Vajrayāna, besides the *Abhisamaya-vibhaṅga*. To Matsyendranātha are attributed some Tāntric works besides the *Kaula-jñāna-nirṇaya*. The *Vāyu-tattva-bhāvanopadeśa* is attributed to Gorakṣa. Four works on *Vajrayāna* are attributed to Jālandharī-pāda. Besides these, the *Bstan-ḥgyur* mentions many Buddhist Tantric works as written by Virūpa, Tilopā, Saraha etc.

E. LEXICOGRAPHY

Dharma-saṃgraha	Nāgārjuna (?)	A collection of technical terms of the Buddhists.
Dvirūpa-koṣa	Puruṣottamadeva	
Hārāvalī	Puruṣottamadeva	
Mahā-vyutpatti	?	
Nāmaliṅgānuśāsana	Amarasiṃha	
Trīkāṇḍaśeṣa	Puruṣottamadeva	
Varṇadeśanā	Puruṣottamadeva	

F. DRAMA

Lokānanda	Candragomin
Śāriputra-prakaraṇa or Śāradvatī-putra-prakaraṇa	Aśvaghoṣa

G. PHILOSOPHY

Abhīdharmakośa	Vasubandhu	Available in fragments. It treats of ontology, psychology, cosmology, ethics and the doctrine of salvation.
Abhisamayālaṃkāra-kārikā	Maitreyanātha	
Aṣṭasāhasrikā-prajñā-pāramitā		

Bodhisattva-bhūmi		Only portion of the *Yogācār-bhūmī-śāstra* that has come down in Sanskrit. It deals with the fifteenth of the seventeen steps (*bhūmī*) to the attainment of the state of Bodhisattva.
Catuḥśataka or Catuhśatikā	Āryadeva (Pupil of Nāgārjuna)	Defence of Nāgārjuna's doctrines against other Buddhist schools and Brāhmaṇical systems, especially Vaiśeṣikas.
Hastabāla-prakaraṇa	Āryadeva	It teaches that all phenomena are mere illusion, and explains distinction between two truths.
Kārya-kāraka-bhāva-siddhi	Jñānaśrīmitra (Contemporary of Dīpaṅkara)	
Kāśyapa-parivarta (Same as Ratnakūṭa (q.v.)		
Laṅkāvatāra		
Mādhyamika-kārikā or Mūlamadhyama-kārikā	Nāgārjuna	
Mahāyāna-sūtrālaṃkāra	Maitreyanātha or Asaṅga	Glorification of perfections of the Buddhas, elucidation of conception of *Bodhi* and Buddhadood.
Mahāyāna-viṃśaka	Nāgārjuna	It teaches that, from the standpoint of absolute truth, there is neither *Saṃsāra* nor *Nirvāṇa* and that everything is illusion and dream.
Muṣṭiprakaraṇa (Same as *Hastabālaprakarṇa* above)		
Nyāyabindu	Dharmakīrti	
Nyāya-praveśa	Diṅnāga	
Nyāyasiddhyāloka	Candragomin	
Prajñā-pāramitā		
Prajñā-pāramitā-sūtra-śāstra	Nāgārjuna	Commentary
Prajñā-pāramitopadeśa-śāstra		

(Same as Abhisamayālaṃkārakārikā, q.v.)		
Pramāṇa-vārtika	Dharmakirti	
Pratītya-samutpāda-hṛdaya	Nāgārjuna	
Ratnakīrti-nibandhāvalī	Ratnakīrti	
Ratnakūṭa		Sanskrit works of this title mentioned in Chinese *Tripiṭaka* and Tibetan *Bstan-ḍgyur*. Parts of it discovered near Khotan in Central Asia. It appears to proclaim repeatedly the ideal of the Bodhisattva and the doctrine of unreality.
Saptadaśa-bhūmi-śāstra (Same as *Laṅkāvatāra* above)		
Samādhirāja		A Mahāyāna-sūtra dwelling on the various meditations as a means to the attainment of the highest knowledge by Bodhisattva.
Saptadaśa-bhūmiśāstra (Same as *Yogācāra-bhūmi-śāstra*, q.v.)		
Śatasāhasrikā-prajñāpāramitā	Nāgārjuna	
Śataśāstra (Same as *Catuḥśataka* above)		
Śikṣā-samuccaya	Śāntideva	
Śūnyatā-saptati	Nāgārjuna	
Sūtra-samuccaya	Śāntideva (acc. to Tāranātha)	
Suvarṇa-prabhāsa		A later Mahāyāna-sūtra which is partly philosophical, partly ethical but largely Tāntric in character.
Tarkabhāṣā	Mokṣākaraghpta	
Tattva-saṃgraha	Śāntarakṣita	
Triṃśatikā	Vasubandhu	It refutes belief in the reality of the objective world, but defends

		the doctrine of the reality of pure consciousness.
Vigraha-vyāvartanī	Nāgārjuna	A work on logic.
Viṃśatikā	Vasubandhu	Contents same as those of the *Triṃśatikā*.
Yukti-ṣaṣṭikā	Nāgārjuna	

H. GRAMMAR

Cāndra-vyākaraṇa	Candragomin
Dhātu-pradīpa	Maitreyarakṣita
Durghaṭa-vṛtti	Śaraṇa
Kāśikā-vivaraṇa-pāñjikā	Jinendrabuddhi
Nyāsa (Same as Kāśikā-vivaraṇa-pañjikā)	
Tantra-pradīpa	Maitreyarakṣita

I. MISCELLANEOUS

Besides the above works, Buddhist scholars wrote books on various subjects. The noteworthy works are as follows.

Title	Author	Contents
Mahārāja-kanika-lekha	Maticitra (perhaps identical with Mātṛceta)	Letter to king Kanika, supposed by some to be identical with Kaniṣka, containing admonitions to lead a moral life in the spirit of the Buddha.
Maitreya-vyākaraṇa	Āryacandra	Available in fragments. In it there are prophecies about the birth and appearance of Buddhamaitreya and about peace and happiness under him. These are given in the form of a conversation between Gautama Buddha and Śāriputra or Ānanda.
Pustaka-pāṭhopāya	Dānaśīla	
Suhṛllekha	Nāgārjuna	Epistle to a friend who, according to Chinese sources, is identical with King Sātavāhana.
Vajrasūcī	Aśvaghoṣa, according to some, but Dharmakīrti, according to others.	See this title in the body of this work.

LIST OF AUTHORS OF BUDDHIST SANSKRIT WORKS

(In English alphabetical order)

Author	Date, if known
Abhayākaragupta	11th century A.D.
Amarasiṃha	Earlier than Candragomin (q.v.)
Āryacandra	?
Āryadeva	2nd-3rd century A.D.
Āryaśūra	c. 3rd or 4th century A.D.
Asaṅga	c. 4th century A.D.
Aśvaghoṣa	c. 1st century A.D.
Atīśa Dīpaṃkara	980-1053 A.D.
Bibhūticandra	Either contemporaneous with, or a little later than Abhayākaragupta (q.v.)
Candragomin	c. 7th century A.D. or earlier.
Dānaśīla	Either contemporaneous with or later than Abhayākaragupta (q.v.)
Dharmakīrti	7th cent. A.D.
Diṅnāga	Probably before 400 A.D.
Dīpaṃkara	See Atīśa
Divākaracandra	Earlier half of the 11th century A.D.
Jetāri	Contemporary of king Mahīpāla I of Bengal (c. 988-1038 A.D.)
Brahmānanda	
Buddhaghoṣa	5th century A.D.
Jñānaśrīmitra	Contemporary of Atīśa (q.v.)
Kṣemendra	11th century A.D.
Kumāralāta	Probably 2nd cent. A.D.
Kumāravajra	10th-11th cent. A.D.
Maitreyanātha	Teacher of Asaṅga (q.v.)
Maitreyarakṣita	c. 11th century A.D.
Maticitra (Probably identical with Mātṛceta below)	

Jinendrabuddhi	c. 7th-8th century A.D.	
Mokṣākaragupta	12th century A.D.	Supposed to be identical or contemporaneous with Aśvaghoṣa (q.v.)
Nāgārjuna	c. 2nd century A.D.	
Puruṣottamadeva	12th century A.D.	
Rāmacandra	About the middle of the 13th cent. A.D.	
Ratnakīrti		
Śāntarakṣita	8th century A.D.	
Śāntideva	7th century A.D.	
Śaraṇa	12th century A.D.	
Śīlabhadra	7th century A.D.	
Vasubandhu	Brother of Asaṅga (q.v.)	
Vidyākara	11th-12th cent A.D.	

X

CONTRIBUTION OF THE JAINAS TO SANSKRIT LITERATURE[1]

The canonical literature of the Jainas is written in Prākrit. Among the works of the non-canonical class, however, there are many which are written in Sanskrit. The Śvetāmbaras took to Sanskrit for their literary works at a period later than Digambaras. Broadly speaking, Sanskrit literature of the Jainas covers the period from the seventh or eighth century A.D. down to the seventeenth. In rare cases do we find Sanskrit works written by them in the third century A.D. or even a little earlier. The most noteworthy feature of the Jaina Sanskrit works is the development of an elaborate narrative literature mostly in prose. It should be noted that the Jainas appropriated to themselves quite a number of popular Brāhmaṇical themes which they often modified and used as a vehicle for the propagation of their own dogmas and doctrines. Their Sanskrit works may be divided into the following classes: Biography, Drama, Grammar, Lexicography, *Māhātmya*, Music, Philosophy, Religion, *Praśasti*, Purāṇa, Rhetoric and *Stotra*. The form of their writings is both prose and poetry and sometimes an admixture of the two.

Besides works exclusively in Sanskrit, they have also written such works as are partly in Sanskrit and partly in Prākrit.

In addition to original works in Sanskrit, the Jainas have written Sanskrit commentaries on both Prākrit and Sanskrit works.

The titles of the noteworthy works[2] of the Jainas are arranged below in the Devanāgarī alphabetical order, with the names of the respective authors. The names of the authors, with their respective dates, wherever possible, have been written in a separate list. The difficulty of preparing such a list lies in the fact that we do not know of any book dealing exclusively with the Sanskrit works written by the Jainas. All that we can do is to pick out the names of Sanskrit works, written by them, from the accounts of the literature of the Jainas given in different works. But, in these accounts the titles of Prākrit works are sometimes given in their Sanskrit forms; from their description it is not possible to

---

1. For details, see:
   (a) M. Winternitz, *History of Indian Literature*, Vol. II.
   (b) H.D. Velankar, *Jinaratnakośa*, Vol. I, Poona, 1944.
   (c) S.K. De, *History of Sanskrit Literature*, Calcutta, 1947.
   (d) Hertel, *Literature of the Śvetāmbaras of Gujarat*.

2. Works of the *Stotra* and *Māhātmya* types, as well as those dealing with *Pūjā*, *Vrata*, *Dāna*, *Dīkṣā*, etc. are not mentioned in the list. Also excluded are the minor works and commentaries.

ascertain whether they are written in Sanskrit or Prākrit. We mention here only those works which are definitely known to be in Sanskrit. The titles of those Sanskrit works which are known to be published, are marked with asterisks.

(In Devanāgarī alphabetical order)

Title	Author, if known	Remarks, if any
Atimukta-carita	Pūrṇabhadra	
**Adhyātma-tattvāloka*	Nyāyavijaya	A philosophical work.
Anekārthavāda-prakāśa	Haribhadra	
**Anekartha-saṃgraha*	Hemacandra	A lexicon.
Antaraṅga-kathā		
**Abhayakumāra-carita*	Candratilaka	There is also an anonymous work of this name.
Abhayasiṃha-kathā		
**Abhidhāna-cintāmaṇi*	Hemacandra	A lexicon.
**Abhidhāna-ratnamālā*	Nāgavarman	A lexicon.
Abhinandasvāmi-carita		
Amāmasvāmi-carita	Muniratnasūri	
**Amaradatta-mitrānanda carita*	Bhāvacandrasūri	
**Amṛtāśīta*	Yogīndra	
**Ambaḍa-carita*	Amarasundara	
Arhadgītā	See *Tattvagītā*	
Arhat-pratiṣṭhā-sāra-saṃgraha (Also called *Nemicandra saṃhitā* or *Pratiṣṭhā-tilaka*)	Nemicandra	
**Arhat-pravacana*	Prabhācandra	
**Alaṃkāra-cintāmaṇi* (-cūḍāmani?)	Ajitasena	A work on rhetoric.
Āgamapratipakṣa-nirākaraṇa		
**Ācāra-pradīpa*	Ratnaśekhara	
**Ācāra-sāra*	Vīranandin	
**Ātmānuśāsana*	Pārśvanāga	
**Ātmānuśāsana*	Guṇabhadra	
Ādinātha-caritra	Vardhamānācārya	
Ādinātha-vyākhyāna	Harṣānandanagaṇi	
Ādi-purāṇa (also see *Uttara-purāṇa*)	Jinasena	Left incomplete and completed by his pupil Guṇabhadra who is different from Guṇabhadra,

		author of the *Dhanyakumāra-carita*.
Ānandasundara-kāvya (also called *Daśa-śrāvaka-carita*)	Sarvavijayagaṇi	
Āpta-parīkṣā	Vidyānanda	
Ārāmaśobhā-kathā	Jinaharṣasūri	
* *Ālāpa-paddhati*	Devasena	
Indu-dūta	Vinayavijayagaṇi	
Ukti-ratnākara	Sādhusundara or Sādhuratna	
* *Uttamakumāra-caritra*	Cārucandra	
Uttara-purāṇa	Guṇabhadra	It is the name of the portion of the *Ādipurāṇa* left incomplete by Jinasena.
Udayana-rāja-carita	Malliṣeṇa	
* *Udayasundarī-kathā*	Soḍḍhala	
Uditodaya-carita	Śikhāmaṇi	
Upadeśa-kalpadruma (See *Vyākhyāna-paddhati*)		
Upadeśa-ratnamālā (also called *Ṣaṭ-karmopadeśa-ratnamālā*	Sakalabhūṣaṇa	
* *Upadeśa-ratnākara*	Vidyābhūṣaṇa	
Upadeśa-ratnākara	Munisundarasūri	
* *Upamitibhava-prapañcakathā*	Siddharṣi	
Ṛṣabhadeva-carita	Sakalakīrti	Vāgbhaṭa also appears to have written a poem of this name; but it is not available.
Ṛṣabhadeva-nirvāṇānanda-nāṭaka	Keśavasena	A drama.
Ṛṣidatta-kathā		
Ṛṣidatta-carita		
Ekākṣara-nāmamālā	Viśvaśambhu	
* *Ekākṣara-nāmamālā*	Sudhākalaśa	
Kathā-kośa		Different authors have written works of the same title. The works of Hariṣeṇa and Padmanandin are in Sanskrit. Also in Sanskrit prose is the anonymous *Kathākośa*. There is a *Kathākośa* (also called *Śakuna-ratnāvalī*) by

		Vardhamānasūri. A *Kathākośa* is published; Prākrit verses are inserted in it.
**Kathā-ratnākara*	Hemavijayagaṇi	
Kathā-ratna-sāgara	Naracandrasūri	
Kanaka-ratna-kathā		
Karakaṇḍu-carita	Jinendrabhūṣaṇa	
Karakaṇḍu-carita	Brahma Nemidatta	
**Karuṇā-vajrāyudha*	Bālacandrasūri	A drama.
Karṇāṭaka-śabdānuśāsana	Akalaṅkadeva	
**Karpūra-carita*	Vatsarāja	A drama.
**Karpūra-prakara* (also called *Subhāṣita-kośa* or *Sūktāvalī*)	Hari or Hariṣeṇa	
Karmakaradvaya-kathā		
Karmagrantha	Jayatilakasūri	
,,	Devendrasūri	
Karmacandra-caritra	Guṇavinaya	
Karma-prakṛti	Yaśovijaya	
Kramaprakṛti-vicāra		
Kalaśoddhāra		
Kalyāṇa-mālā	Āśādhara	
Kaviśikṣā (same as *Kāvya-kalpalatā*, q.v.)		
Kātantra-dravyāśraya-kāvya		
**Kāmaghaṭa-kathā*		
Kārakādi-vicāra		
Kāla-jñāna		
Kālikācārya-kathā		It exists in Sanskrit and Prākrit recensions. Different authors have written works of the same title. Those by Vinayacandra, Maheśvara-sūri, Pradyumna, Samayasundara, etc. are in Sanskrit. Some of these versions have been published.
Kālikācārya-kathānaka	Bhāvadeva	
Kāvya-kalpalatā (or, *Kaviśikṣā*)	Amaracandra	
Kāvya-manohara	Maheśvara	

**Kāvyānuśāsana*	Hemacandra	A work on rhetoric.
Kāvyānuśāsana	Vāgbhaṭa	A work on rhetoric.
**Kīrti-kaumudī*	Someśvara	
Kuntaladevī-kathā		
Kuntunātha-caritra	Vibuddhaprabhasūri	
Kuntunātha-caritra	Somatilakasūri	
Kuntunātha-caritra	Padmaprabha	
Kumārapāla-caritra	Somatilakasūri	
*"	Cāritrasundaragaṇi	
**Kumārapāla-carita* / (or, *Dvyāśraya-kāvya*)	Hemacandra	
**Kumārapāla-prabandha*	Jinamaṇḍanagaṇi	
Kumāra-sambhava	Jayaśekhara	
Kurucandra-kathānaka		
**Kuvalayamālā-kathā*	Ratnaprabhasūri	Sanskrit rendering of Dākṣiṇyacaritasūri's Prākrit work composed about the middle of the 13th century A.D. The author calls it a Campū.
Kuvera-purāṇa (See *Nalāyana*)		
Kūpa-dṛṣṭānta	Yaśovijayagaṇi	
Kṛtapuṇya-caritra	Pūrṇabhadra	
Kaumāra-sāra-samuccaya		
**Kṣatra-cūḍāmaṇi* (or, *Jīvandhara-campū*)	Oḍayadeva	
Kṣetra-samāsa		Several authors have written works of the same title. Those by Umāsvāti, Devānanda and Candraprabha are in Sanskrit.
**Gadya-cintāmaṇi*	Oḍayadeva	
**Gadyapāṇḍava-carita*	Devavijayagaṇi (Devarājagaṇi ?)	
**Guruguṇa-ratnākara-kāvya*	Samacāritragaṇi	
Gṛhi-dharma	Padmanandin	
Gautama-caritra	Dharmacandra	
Caturviṃśati-jina-carita		See *Padmānanda-kāvya*
Candradhavala-dharmadatta-kathā (See *Dharmadatta-kathānaka*)	Māṇikyasundara	

Candranātha-carita	Śubhacandra	
Candranṛpa-caritra		
Candraprabha-caritra	Sarvānandasūri	Some other authors also wrote works of this title, e.g. Devendra, Asaga, Vīranandin, Śubhacandra. The works by Devendra and Vīranandin have been published.
Candraprabha-caritra-vijaya	Ravigupta	
Candralekha-vijaya-prakaraṇa	Devacandra	
**Candravijaya-prabandha*	Maṇḍanakavi	
**Campaka-śreṣṭhi-kathānaka*	Jinakīrti	
Citrasena-padmāvatī-caritra		See *Padmāvatī-caritra*.
Cintāmaṇi-vyākaraṇa	Śubhacandra	
Cetodūta		
**Cauryāsiprabandha*	Rājaśekharamuni	
Jagadguru-carita	Suvarṇānanda	
**Jagadguru-kāvya*	Padmasāgaragaṇi	
**Jambūsvāmi-caritra*	Jayaśekharasūri	
Jambūsvāmi-caritra	Jinadāsa	
Jambūsvāmi-caritra	Dīpacandra	
Jayakumāra-caritra (or, *Jayapurāṇa*)	Brahmakāmarāja	
Jayapurāṇa		Same as *Jayakumāra-caritra* (q.v.).
**Jayānandakevali-caritra*	Padmvaijaya	
Jayanta-vijaya	Abhayadevasūri	
**Jalpa-mañjarī*	Jinasūra	
Jinadatta-kathā	Guṇasamudrasūri	
**Jinadatta-caritra*	Guṇabhadra	
Jinapravacana-rahasya-kośa (See *Puruṣārtha-siddhyupāya*)		
**Jinendra-carita*		See *Padmānanda-kāvya*.
Jīvaka-carita	Śubhacandra	
**Jñānārṇava* (Also called *Yogapradīpādhikāra*)	Śubhacandra	A philosophical work.

**Jīvandhara-campū*	Haribhadra	
**Jīvandhara-caritra*	Guṇabhadrācārya	
**Jaina Rāmāyaṇa*		Name of Parvan 7 of Hema candra's *Triṣaṣṭiśalākā-puruṣa-caritra.*
**Jaina Mahābhārata* (See *Pāṇḍava-purāṇa*)		
**Tattvānuśāsana*	Rāmasena	
**Tattvārtha-sāra*	Amṛtacandrasūri	A philosophical work.
Tarkabhāṣā	Yaśovijaya	
Tithi-sāraṇi	Vāghji Muni	
**Tilaka-mañjarī*	Dhanapāla	
**Tīrtha-kalpa*	Jinaprabhasūri	Partly in Prākrit and partly in Sanskrit.
Trivarṇācāra	Brahmasūri	Other authors also wrote works of the same title.
Triṣaṣṭi-mahāpurāṇa (Also called *Triṣaṣṭi-śalākā-purāṇa* or *Mahāpurāṇa*)	Malliṣeṇa	
Triṣaṣti-śalākā-purāṇa		Same as *Triṣaṣṭi-mahāpurāṇa* (q.v.)
**Triṣaṣṭi-śalākā-puruṣa-caritra*	Hemacandra	
Ttiṣaṣṭi-smṛti-śāstra	Āśādhara	
Darśanācāra-kathā	Vimalasūri	
Daśa-śrāvaka-caritra	Sarvavijayagaṇi	Also called *Ānandasundara-kāvya.*
,,	Pūrṇabhadra	
Dānaratnopākhyāna	Jayakīrti	
Dānādi-prakaraṇa	Surācārya	
Digvijaya-mahākāvya	Meghavijayagaṇi	
Dīpti-saṃhitā	Devendrakīrti	
Dṛṣṭānta-mālā	Arimalla	
**Dṛṣṭānta-śataka*	Tejasiṃha	
Devakumāra-carita		
Devakumāra-pretakumāra-kathā		
**Devadharma-parīkṣā*	Yaśovijayagaṇi	
**Deva-nṛpakathānaka*	Meghavijayagaṇi	
Deva-nṛpakathānaka		
**Dodhaka-vṛtti*		

Dvādaśa-bhāvanā		
**Dvisandhāna-kāvya* (Also called *Rāghava-pāṇḍavīya*)	Dhanañjaya Śrutakīrti	
**Dvyāśraya-kāvya* (Same as *Kumārapāla-carita* of the same author)	Hemacandra	
**Dvyāśraya-mahā-kāvya* (Also called *Śreṇīkadvyāśraya-kāvya*)	Jinaprabhasūri	
**Dhandatta-carita*	Bhāvacandra	
Dhanadevadhanamitra-kathā		
Dhana-dharma-kathā	Munisundarasūri	
Dhanapati-kathā		
Dhanyakathā		
Dhanyakumāra-caritra	Bilhaṇa	
Dhanyakumāra-caritra	Jayānanda	
Dhanyakumāra-caritra	Sakalakirti	
Dhanya-caritra	Jñānasāgaragaṇi	
Dhanya-caritra	Somasundaragaṇi	
Dhanya-caritra	Jinakirti	
Dhanya-vilāsa	Dharmasiṃhasūri	
Dhanya-śālibhadra-caritra	Pūrṇabhadra	
**Dhammilla-kathā*		
**Dharma-kalpadruma*	Udayadharma	
Dharma-caritra	Nemicandra	
**Dharma-datta-kathānaka* (Also called *Candra-dhavala-dharmadatta-kathānaka*	Māṇikyasundara	
Dharmanātha-mahā-kāvya	Haricandra	
Dharma-parīkṣā	Saubhāgya-sāgara	
Dharma-parīkṣā	Amitagati	Dogmatic-polemical work.
Dharma-parīkṣā-kathā	Rāmacandra	
**Dharma-parīkṣā-kathā*	Padmasāgara	
Dharmapāla-kathā		

**Dharmaratnākara*	Jayasena	
**Dharmavilāsa*	Matinandanagaṇi	
**Dharmaśarmābhyudaya*	Hariścandra (Haricandra?)	
**Dharmasarvasvādhikāra*	Jayaśekharasūri	
Dhūrtākhyāna		
Nandīśvara-kathā	Śubhacandra	
**Nayacakra*	Mallavādin	
**Naya-vivaraṇa*	Vidyānandin	
**Naranārāyaṇānanda*	Vastupāla	
Narmadāsundarī-kathā		
Nalacaritra	Hitaruci	
**Nalavilāsa*	Rāmacandra	A drama.
**Nalāyana* (or, *Kuvera-purāṇa*)	Māṇikyasūri	
Navatattva-prakaraṇa	Ambaka-prasāda	
Nāgakumāra-caritra	Ratnayogīndra	Other authors, who wrote works of the same title, are Śikhāmaṇi, Malliṣeṇa, Śrīdharasena and Vādirāja.
Nābheya-nemi-kāvya	Hemacandra	
Nāma-mālā	Dhanañjaya	
**Nāracandra-jyautiṣa-sāra*	Naracandrasūri	
**Nighaṇṭuśeṣa*	Hemacandra	It is a botanical glossary.
Nimirāja-kāvya	Kavi Rāyacandra	
Nemicandra-Saṃhitā (See *Arhat-pratiṣṭhā-sāra-saṃgraha*)		
**Nemidūta*	Vikrama	
Neminātha-carita	Surācārya	Eighth book of Hemacandra's *Triṣaṣṭi-śalākāpuruṣa-caritra* also bears this title. There are other works of this title in prose as well as in verse. The authors are Udayaprabhasūri, Kīrtirāja, Upādhyāya, Guṇavijaya, Narasiṃha, Vādidevasūri, Hariṣeṇa, Tilakācārya and Ratnaprabha.
**Neminātha-mahākāvya*	Kīrtirāja	

**Nemi-nirvāṇa*	Vāgbhaṭa	This Vāgbhaṭa may not be identical with Vāgbhaṭa, author of the rhetorical work *Vāgbhaṭālaṃkāra*.
**Nyāya-kusumāñjali*	Nyāyavijaya	A philosophical work.
Nyāya-maṇi-dīpikā	Ajitasena	
Nyāyāvatāra-sūtra	Siddhasena Divākara	A work on logic.
**Pañcatantra*	Pūrṇabhadra's version	
**Pañcasaṃgraha*	Amitagati	
Pañcasaṃgraha-dīpikā	Indravāmadeva	
Pañca-sandhāna-kāvya	Śāntirājakavi	
Pañcādhyāyī	Rājamallakavi (?)	
Pañcārtha-saṃdhāna-kāvya	Śāntirāja	
Padmacarita	Raviṣeṇa	
Padmacarita (Also called *Rāmacaritra*)	Vimala	
**Padmacarita*	Śubhavardhana	
Padmanāthacarita	Śubhacandra	
**Padmapurāṇa*	Raviṣeṇa	
**Padmapurāṇa*	Candrasāgara	
**Padmānanda-kāvya* (Also called *Caturviṃśati-jina-carita* or *Jinendra-carita*)	Amaracandra	
**Padmāvatī-caritra* (Also known as *Citrasena-padmāvatī-caritra*)	Pāṭhaka	
Paramahaṃsa-caritra	Nayaraṅga	
Paramātma-prakāśa	Padmanandin	
**Paramātma-prakāśa*	Yogīndrācārya	
Parigraha-pramāṇa	Mānatuṅga	
**Pariśiṣṭa-parva* (Also called *Sthavirā-valī-carita*)		Eleventh book of Hemacandra's *Triṣaṣṭi-śalākā-puruṣa-caritra* (q.v.)
**Parīkṣā-mukha-sūtra*	Māṇikyanandin	A work on logic.
**Pavana-dūta*	Vādicandra	

**Pāṇḍava-caritra*	Devavijayagaṇi	It is in prose with inserted verses many of which have been taken verbatim from Devaprabha's work.
Do	Devaprabhasūri	
**Pāṇḍava-purāṇa* (Also called *Bhārata* or *Jaina Mahābhārata*)	Śubhacandra	
Pāṇḍavapurāṇa	Vādicandra	
Pāṇḍitya-darpaṇa	Udayacandra	
Pāpaliptasūri-kathā		
**Pāpabuddhi-dharmabuddhi-kathānaka*		
Pārasī-bhāṣānuśāsana	Vikramasiṃha	
Pārśvacaritra	Devabhadra	
Pārśvanātha-kāvya	Padmasundara	
Pārśvanātha-carita	Māṇikyacandra	
* "	Vādirājasūri	
* "	Bhāvadeva	
* "	Hemavijaya	
—*purāṇa*	Sakalakīrti	
**Pārśvābhyudaya*	Jinasenācārya	
Puṇyadhana-kathā		
—*caritra*	Śubhaśīlagaṇi	
**Punyasāra-kathā*	Ajitaprabhasūri	
Puṇyasāra-kathānaka	Vivekasamudragaṇi	
**Puruṣārtha-siddhyupāya* (Also called *Jinapravacana-rahasyakośa*)	Amṛtacandrasūri	A philosophical work.
Pṛthvīcandra-caritra	Jayasāgarasūri	Other works of this title are by Satyarājagaṇi, Śāntisūri and Māṇikyasundara. There is also an anonymous work of this name. The work of Satyarāja has been published.
Pratiṣṭhā-tilaka (See *Arhat-pratiṣṭhā-sārasaṃgraha*)		

Pratyekabuddha-caritra	Lakṣmītilaka	
* ,,	Indrahaṃsagaṇi	
**Pradeśi-nṛpa-caritra*	Hīrālāla	
**Pradyumna-caritra*	Mahāsenācārya or Pappadaguru	
,,	Yaśodhara	
,,	Somakīrti	
,,	Ratnacandra	
,, (See *Manmatha-mahimā*)	Śubhacandra	
**Prabandha-cintāmaṇi*	Merutuṅga	
**Prabandha-rāja* (Also known as *Bhoja-prabandha*)	Ratnamandiragaṇi	
**Prabandha-kośa*		
**Prabodha-cintāmaṇi*	Jayaśekharasūri	
**Prabodha-sāra*	Yaśaḥkīrti	
**Prabhāvaka-carita*	Prabhācandra	
**Prabhāvatīcaritra*	Candraprabha	
**Praṃāṇa-naya-tattvā-lokālaṃkāra*	Vādidevasūri	
**Pramāṇa-parīkṣā*	Vidyānandin	A philosophical work.
* —*mīmāṃsā*	Hemacandra	A philosophical work.
Pramāṇāntaruci	Yaśodeva	
**Pramā-lakṣaṇa*	Jineśvara	
**Prameya-ratnakośa*	Candraprabha	
Pravacana-vicāra-sāra	Nayakuñjara Upādhyāya	
—*sāra-prakaraṇa*	Haribhadrasūri	
**Praśama-rati* (Religio-philosophical)	Umāsvāti (or Umā svāmin)	
**Praśnacintāmaṇi*	Vīravijayagaṇi	
Praśnottara-māṇikya-mālā	Jayasāgara	
,,	Devagaṇi	
* —*ratna-mālā*	Vimalasūri	
—*śataka*	Umedacandra	
Prāyaścitta	Vidyānanda	
**Priyaṃkara-kathā*	Jinasūra	

Prītikara-caritra	Narendrakīrti	
,,*-mahāmuni-caritra*	Brahma Nemidatta	
**Balabhadra-carita*	Śubhavardhanagaṇi	
**Bali-narendra-kathānaka*	Indrahaṃsagaṇi	
**Bāla-bhārata*	Amaracandra	
Bāhubali-carita	Cārukīrti	There is also an anonymous work of this name.
Buddhi-prakāśa	Jīvarāja	
Bṛhatkathā	(King) Durvinīta	Revised and written by Brahma Śrīpāla.
Bṛhatkathākośa	Hariṣeṇa	Composed 931 A.D.
Bṛhat-pāṇḍava-purāṇa (Also called *Mahābhārata*)	Śubhacandra	
Bṛhad-vāgbhūṣaṇa		
Bodha-pradīpikā		
Bhaktāmara-kathā	Royamalla	
**Bhadrabāhu-caritra*	Ratnanandin	
,,	Ratnacandra Bhaṭṭāraka	
Bhadraśreṣṭhi-kathā		
**Bharaṭaka-dvātriṃśikā*		
Bhavīṣyadattacaritra	Śrīdhara	
Bhavya-kuṭumba-kathānaka		
**Bhānucandragaṇi-carita*	Siddhicandragaṇi	
Bhārata (See *Pāṇḍava-purāṇa*)		
Bhāvanābhānu-kevali-caritra	Haṃsagaṇi	
Bhāvanā-prakaraṇa		
Bhīmakumāra-kathā		
Bhujabaliśataka	Doḍayya	
**Bhuvanabhānucaritra*	Haṃsagaṇi	
Bhūpāvalī	Raṅgavijaya	
Bhoja-prabandha (See *Prabandha-rāja*)		
Madanasiṃha-kathā		
Madanarekha-kathā		
Mantri-dāsī-kathā		

Manmatha-mahimā (or, *Pradyumna-carita*)	Śubhacandara	
* *Malayasundarī-kathā*	Māṇikyasundarasūri	
,, *-caritra*	Jayatilaka	
* *Mallinātha-caritra*	Vinayacandra	
Mahāpurāṇa		Same as *Triṣaṣṭi-mahāpurāṇa* (q.v.)
Mahābala-malaya-sundarī-kathā	See *Malayasundarī-kathā*	
Mahābhārata (See *Bṛhat-pāṇḍava-purāṇa*)		
Mahābhiṣeka	Guṇabhadra	Other works of this title are by Jinasena and Pūjyapāda.
* *Mahāvīra-carita*	Nemicandra	
,,-purāṇa*	Sakalakīrti	
* *Mahīpāla-carita*	Cāritrasundaragaṇi	
Mārga-prakāśa		
Mālākāra-kathā		
Mitra-kathā		
* *Mitra-catuṣṭaya-kathā*	Munisundarasūri	
Mitra-traya-kathā		
Mitrānanda-kathā		
Miśraliṅga-kośa (Also called *Miśraliṅga-nirṇaya*)	Kalyāṇasāgara	
Miśra-liṅga-nirṇaya, (See *Mśraliṅga-kośa*)		
Mīnaketūdaya	Devanātha	
Munipati-caritra	Jambūnāga or Jambūkavi	
Munipati-caritra-sāroddhāra		
Muni-suvrata-caritra	Muniratnasūri	
,,	Padmaprabha	
,,	Keśavasena	
,,*-kāvya*	Arhaddāsa	
* *Mṛgavatīcaritra*	Devaprabha	
* *Mṛgāṅka-caritra*	Ṛddhicandra	

Meghadūta-samasyā-lekha	Meghavijaya	
Maunavrata-kathā	Guṇacandrācārya	
Yakṣa-Yakṣiṇī-vicāra		
Yatidinacaryā	Hariprabhasūri	
**Yaśastilaka-campū*	Somadeva Sūrī	(Somaprabhasūri ?)
**Yaśodhara-caritra*	Kṣamājalyāṇa	Other works of this title are by Somakirti, Hemakuñjara, Māṇikyasūri, Kalyāṇasūri, Padmanābha and Vādirāja. Of these, the works of Māṇikyasūri and Vādirāja have been published.
Yajitakalpavṛtti	Sādhusundara or Sadhuratna	
Yukti-prabodha	Meghavijayagaṇi	A drama.
**Yuktyanuśāsana*	Samantabhadra	A philosophical work.
Yudhiṣṭhira-vijaya		
Yogakalpadruma		
Yogapradīpa	Devānanda	
Yogapradīpādhikāra		Same as *Jñānārṇava* (q.v.).
**Yoga-sāra*	Vītarāga	There is also a work of the same name by Amitagati. It is a poetical composition and is published.
**Yoga-śāstra*	Hemacandra	A philosophical work.
**Ratnakaraṇḍaka-śrāvakācāra*	Samantabhadra	A philosophical work.
**Ratnacūḍakathā*	Jñānasāgara	
**Ratna-mālā*	Śivakoṭi	
Ratnapāla-nṛpakathānaka	Somanandana	
Ratnaśekhara-carita	Dayavardhanagaṇi	
**Rāghava-pāṇḍavīya* (Same as *Dvisandhāna-kāvya*, q.v.)	Dhanañjaya	There is also a Sanskrit work of this title by Arala Śreṣthin.
Rāddhānta	Āryadeva	
Rāmacarita	Devavijayagaṇi	
Rāmacarita	Hemacandra	It is the name of Parvan 7 of Hemacandra's *Triṣaṣṭi-śalākā-pruṣacaritra.*
Rāmacarita (See *Padma-carita*)	Vimala	

Rāyamallābhyudaya	Padmasundara	
**Rūpasena-caritra*	Jinasūri	
Revatīśrāvī-kathā		
**Rauhiṇeya-kathā* (*carita*?)	Devamūrti	
Liṅga-nirṇaya (See *Miśra-liṅgakośa*)		
**Liṅgānuśāsana*	Hemacandra	A work on grammar.
Līlāvatī-kāvya	Kuñjarakavi	
Līlāvatīsāra-kāvya	Jinaratnasūri	
**Lokatattvanirṇaya*	Haribhadra	A philosopphical work.
Loka-vibhāga	Siṃhasūri	
Lokāpavāda-kathā		
Vajrāyudhādhi-kathā		
Vatsarāja-kathā	Sarvasundarasūri	
Varadattakumāra-caritra		
Varadatta-caritra		
**Varāṅga-nṛpa-caritra*	Jaṭācārya or Jaṭasiṃhanandin or Jaṭila Muni	
Vardhamāna-carita	Asaga	
Vardhamānadeśanā	Rājakīrti	
**Vasanta-vilāsa*	Bālacandrasūri	
Vasumatī-catrasena	Gaṅgādhara	
Vasurāja-kathā		
**Vastupāla-tejapāla-prabandha*		A work on rhetoric.
Vāgbhaṭālaṃkāra	Vāgbhaṭa	See remakrs against *Nemi-nirvāṇa*.
Vārṣika-kathā-saṃgraha		
**Vāsupūjya-carita*	Vardhamāna	
Vikrama-carita	Rājameru	
Vijayacandra-carita	Candraprabha	
Vidyāvinoda	Pūjyapāda	
Vidyāvilāsa-kathā		
Vidyāvilāsanṛpa-kathā	Malayahaṃsa	
Vidyāsāgara-śreṣṭhi-kathā	Guṇākarasūri	
Vidvanmanohara-kāvya	Tārānātha	
Vinayaṃdhara-caritra	Śīladeva	
**Vimala-caritra*	Indrahaṃsagaṇi	There is also an anonymous work of this title.

**Vimalanātha-caritra*	Jñānasāgara	
Vimalanātha-purāṇa	Ratnanandin	
Viveka-kalikā	Narendra-prabha	
Vimalasaha carita		Same as *Vimalacarita*
Vimalasaha-carita		See *Sūkta-samuccaya*
Vīrollāsa	Bhrusundi	
Vṛddha-prastāvokti-ratnākara	Siddhicandra	
Vṛṣabhānu-carita	Sakalakīrti	
Vedādi-mata-khaṇḍana	Kīrticandra	
Vaidyāmṛta	Śrīdharadeva	
**Vairāgyaśataka*	Padmānanda	
Śatañjaya-mahātīrthod-dhāra-prabandha	Kakkasūri	
Śabda-candrikā	Meghavijayagaṇi	
Śabdabrahmollāsa	Udayaprabha	
**Śabdānuśāsana* (Also called *Siddhahema-candra*)	Hemacandra	A grammar. Its eighth book deals with Prākrit grammar.
**Śāntasudhārasa-bhāvanā-kāvya*	Vinayavijayagaṇi	
**Śāntinātha-mahākāvya*	Munibhadra	
**Śāntinātha-carita*	Ajitaprabhasūri	Other works of this title are by Munidevasūri, Munisundara, Bhāvacandra, Māṇikyacandra, Munibhadra, Kanaka-prabha, Meghavijaya and Udaya-sāgara. Of these, the works of Bhāvacandra, Munibhadra and Meghavijaya have been published. The work of Kana-kaprabha is also called *Śāntivṛtta*.
Śāmba-caritra		
**Śālibhadra-caritra*	Dharmakumāra	
**Śāstrasāra-samuccaya*	Māghanandin	
Śivakumāra-kathā		
Śītalanātha-carita		
Śītalabhaṭṭārakapurāṇa	Malliṣeṇa	
**Śīla-dūta*	Cāritrasundaragaṇi	
Śīlavatī-kathā	Udayaprabhasūri	
Śīlavatī-kathā	Ājñāsundara	

Śukarāja-kathā	Śubhaśīla	
Śuka-saṃvāda-kathā		
**Śṛṅgāra-mañjarī*	Ajitsena	A work on rhetroric.
**Śṛṅgāra-vairāgyataraṅgiṇī*	Somaprabhācārya	
Śrāvakācāra	Bhadrabāhu	
Śrāvakācāra	Māghanandin	
**Śrīcandra-caritra*	Śīlasiṃhagaṇi	
Śrīcittacūḍāmaṇi	Pūrṇamala Kavi	
Śrīpāla-kathā	Labdhisāgaragaṇi	
Śrīpāla-caritra	Satyarājagaṇi	Other works of this title are by Dharmadhīra, Jñānavimalasūri, Jayakīrtisūri, Somacandragaṇi, Sakalakīrti and Labdhimuni. Of these, the works of Jñānavimalasūri, Jayakīrtisūri and Labdhimuni have been published.
Śrīpurāṇa	Hastimalla	
Śruta-jñānodayāpana	Vāmadeva	
Śruta-jñānodayāpana	Śivajilāla	
Śrutabandhu		
**Śrutabodha* (*Prosody*)	Ajitasena	The author may or may not be identical with Ajitasena, author of the rhetorical works called *Alaṃkāra-cintāmaṇi* and *Śṛṅgāramañjarī*. The *Śrutabodha* is generally ascribed to Kālidāsa.
**Śrutāvatāra*	Śrīdhara	
Śreṇika-dvyāśraya-kāvya		Same as *Dvyāśryamahākāvya* (q.v.)
Śreṇika-purāṇa	Bāhubali	
Śreṇika-caritra	Gajadharlāl	
Śreyāṃsa-carita	Mānatuṅga	
Ṣaṭkarmopadeśa-ratnamālā (See *Upadeśa-ratnamālā*)		
Ṣaṭ-samaya-sāralakṣaṇa		
**Ṣaḍ-darśana-samuccaya*	Haribhadrasūri	A philosophical work.
**Ṣaḍ-darśana-samuccaya*	Rājaśekharasūri	A philosophical work.
**Saṃvāda-sundara*	Samayasundara (?)	
Saṃvega-druma-kandalī	Vimalācārya	

Saṃśaya-vacana-viccheda	Ratnabhūṣaṇa	
Saṃkramakaraṇa	Premavijayagaṇi	
* *Saṃgītā-samaya-sāra*	Pārśvadeva	A work on music.
Saṃgīta-sāroddhāra (or, *Saṃgītopaniṣatsāra*)	Sudhākalaśa	
Saṃgītopaniṣad	Sudhākalaśa	A work on music.
Saṃgītopaniṣat-sāra		See *Saṃgīta-sāroddhāra.*
Saṃgrahaṇī	Rāmacandra	
Satyasthāna-bhaṅga-prarūpaṇā	Kanakanandin	
Sadbodha-candrodaya	Padmānanda	
Sapta-vyasana-carita	Somakīrti	
* *Sapta-sandhānamahā-kāvya*	Meghavijayagaṇi	The author states that Hemacandra also wrote a poem of this name, but it was lost.
* *Samayasāra-nāṭaka-kalaśa*	Amṛtacandrasūri	
* *Samarāditya-caritra* (or, *Samarādityasaṃkṣepa*)	Pradyumnasūri	
Samarāditya-caritra	Sumativardhana	
Samarāditya-saṃkṣepa		See *Samarāditya-caritra*
* *Samādhi-śataka*	Pūjyapāda	
Samyaktva-kaumudī	Somadevasūri	
Samyakatva-kaumudī	A Digambara Jaina	
Samyaktva-kaumudīkathā-kośa		
Samyaktva-tattvakaumudī		
Samyag-darśana-vicāra		
Sarasa-jana-cintāmaṇi-kāvya	Brahmasūri	
Sāgara-śreṣṭhi-kathā		
Sāmudrika		
* *Sāra-samuccaya*	Kulabhadra	
Sāra-Sūktāvalī		
Sārasvata-candrikā	Meghavijaya	
Sāhasāṅka-carita	Maheśvara	There are two other works of this name.
* *Siṃhāsana-dvātriṃśikā*	Kṣemaṃkaragaṇi (or, Kṣemaṃkara-muni)	
Siddhacakra-kathānaka		

Siddhadattakapilākhyāna	Munisundara	
Siddha-hemacandra (See *Śabdānuśāsana*)		
Siddhānta-sāra	Bhāvasena	
Siddhānta-sāra-dīpaka	Sakalakīrti	
* *Sindūra-prakara*	Somaprabhācārya	
Sītā-caritra	Brahma Nemidatta	There is also an anonymous work of this name.
Sītāprabandha		
Sukumālasvāmi-caritra	Sakalakīrti	
* *Sukṛta-kīrti-kallolinī*	Udayaprabha	
* *Sukṛta-saṃkīrtana*	Arisiṃha	
Sukṛta-sāgara	Ratnamaṇḍanagaṇi	
Sukosala-caritra	Narendrakīrti	
Sukosala-caritra	Brahma Nemidatta	
Sukha-nidhāna		
* *Sudarśana-caritra*	Sakalakīrti	
Sundara-nṛpa-kathā		
Supārśvanātha-caritra		
Subhāṣita-kośa		Same as *Karpūraprakara* (q.v.)
* *Subhāṣita-ratnasaṃdoha*	Amitagati	
Subhāsita-ratnāvali	Sakalakīrti	
Sumatinātha-caritra	Somaprabha	It is written mainly in Prākrit.
Sumitra-caritra	Harṣakuñjaropādhyāya	
* *Suratnotsava*	Someśvara	
Sulasācaritra	Jayatilakasūri	
Suvidhinātha-caritra		
Sūkta-ratnākara	Māghasiṃha (also called Manmathasiṃha)	Other works of this title are by Ratnasiṃhasūri and Siddhicandragaṇi.
Sūkta-samuccaya (Also called *Viveka-pādapa*)	Vibudhacandra	
Sūktāvalī	Lakṣmaṇa	
Sūktāvalī (Same as *Karpūraprakara*, q.v.)	Tattvavallabha	
Sūkti-muktāvalī (Same as *Sindūraprakara*, q.v.)		

Soma-śataka (same as *Sindūra-prakara, q.v.*)		
Stambhana-pārśvanātha-prabandha	Merutuṅgasūri	
Stambhana-pārśvanātha-kathā		
Sthavirāvalī-carita (Same as *Pariśiṣṭa-parva*, q.v.)		
Sthūlabhadra-caritra	Jayānandasūri	There is also an anonymous work of this title.
Snātra-pañcāśikā	Dharmavimalasūri	
Syādvāda-carcā		
Syādvāda-mañjarī	Vimaladāsa	
* *Hammīra-mahākāvya*	Nayacandrasūri	
Hammīra-madamardana	Jayasiṃhasūri	A drama.
* *Haribhadrasūri-carita*	Harigovindadāsa	
Haricandra-kathā		
Harivaṃśa	Sakalakīrti	
* *Harivaṃśa-purāṇa*	Jinasena	
Harivikrama-carita	Jayatilaka	
Hira-saubhāgya-kāvya	Devavimala	
Hira-praśna	Kirtivijayagaṇi	
Hetubindu		

LIST OF JAINA AUTHORS OF SANSKRIT WORKS

(In English alphabetical order)

AUTHOR	DATE, IF KNOWN
Abhayacandra	c. 12th cent. A.D.
Abhayadeva	11th century A.D.
Ajitaprabha	
Ajitasena	10th cent. A.D.
Ājñāsundara	
Amaracandra	Earlier than Rājaśekhara (q.v.)
Ambaka-prasāda	
Amitagati	11th century A.D.
Amṛtacandra	9th-10th cent. A.D.
Arcela Śreṣṭhin	
Arhaddāsa	
Arimalla	
Arisiṃha	
Āryadeva	
Āśādhara	13th century A.D.
Asaga	
Bāhubali	
Bālacandrasūrī	
Bhadrabāhu	
Bhāskaranandin	
Bhāvacandra	
Bhāvadeva	c. 13th cent. A.D.
Bhāvasena	
Bhrusundi	
Bilhaṇa (Different from Bilhaṇa, the Kashmirian poet and author of the *Vikramāṅkadeva-carita*)	
Brahma Kāmāraja	
Brahma Nemidatta	16th cent. A.D.
Brahmasūri	
Candraprabha (Same as Prabhācandra, q.v.)	

AUTHOR	DATE, IF KNOWN
Candrasāgara	
Candratilaka	
Cāritrasundaragaṇi	15th cent. A.D.
Cārucandra	
Cārukīrti	
Dayavardhana	
Devabhadra	
Devacandra	Teacher of Hemacandra (q.v.)
Devagaṇi	
Devamūrti	15th centuryA.D.
Devānanda	
Devanandin (See Pūjyapāda)	
Devanātha	
Devaprabha	12th-13th cent. A.D.
Devasena	Born 894 A.D.
Devavijaya	16th-17th cent. A.D.
Devavimala	
Devendrakīrti	
Dhanañjaya	
Dhanapāla	10th cent. A.D.
Dharmacandra	
Dharmakumāra	13th cent. A.D.
Dharmasiṃha	
Dharmavimala	
Dīpacandra	
Dodayya	
Durvinīta	
Gajadharlāl	
Gaṅgādhara	
Guṇabhadra	Earlier than Śubhacandra (q.v.)
Guṇacandra	11th cent. A.D.

Guṇākara	
Guṇa-samudra	
Guṇavinaya	
Haṃsagaṇi	
Hari	
Haribhadra	c. 705-775 A.D.
Haricandra (Hariścandra?)	
Harigovinda	
Hariprabha	
Hariṣeṇa	
Harṣakuñjara	
Harṣanandana	
Hemacandra	1089-1172 A.D.
Hemācārya (Same as Hemacandra)	
Hemavijaya	16th-17th cent. A.D.
Hīrālāla	
Hitaruci	
Indrahaṃsa	
Indravāmadeva	
Jambūnāga or Jambūkavi	
Jaṭācārya	
Jaṭāsiṃhanandin	
Jaṭila	
Jayānanda	
Jayasāgara	
Jayaśekhara	
Jayasena	
Jayatilaka	
Jinadāsa	15th cent. A.D.
Jinaharṣa	
Jinakīrti	15th cent. A.D.
Jinanandana	
Jinaprabha	13th cent. A.D.
Jinaratna	
Jinasena	8th cent. A.D.
Jinasūra	
Jinasūri	
Jinendrabhūṣaṇa	
Jinendrabuddhi (Same as Pūjyapāda q.v.)	
Jineśvara	11th cent. A.D.
Jīvarāja	
Jñānasāgara	15th cent. A.D.
Kakkasūri	
Kalyāṇasāgara	
Kanakanandin	10th cent. A.D.
Kavirāyacandra	
Keśavasena	
Kirticandra	
Kīrtivijaya	
Kṣamākalyāṇa	
Kṣemakara	
Kulabhadra	
Labdhisāgara	
Lakṣmaṇa	
Lakṣmītilaka	
Māghasiṃha	
Mahāsena	
Maheśvara (Same as Mahesara Sūri, contemporary of Hemacandra?)	
Malayahaṃsa	
Mallavādin	
Malliṣeṇa	13th cent. A.D.
Mānatuṅga	Divergent traditions place him in various periods e.g. 3rd, 5th, 7th, 8th, or 9th century A.D.
Maṇḍanakavi	
Māṇikyacandra	13th cent. A.D.
Māṇikyanandin	
Māṇikyasundara	15th cent. A.D.
Māṇikyasūri	There were several authors of this name. One of them flourished in the 13th cent., another in 16th
Matinandana	
Meghavijaya	

Merutuṅga	13th-14th cent. A.D.M.
Munibhadra	
Muniratna	
Munisundara	
Nāgavarman	
Naracandra	
Narendrakīrti	
Nayacandra	
Nayakuñjara	
Nayaraṅga	
Nemicandra	10th-11th cent.
Nemidatta (See Brahma Nemidatta)	16th cent. A.D.
Nyāyavarman	
Nyāyavijaya	
Oḍayadeva	11th cent. A.D.
Padmanandin (also called Kundakunda)	1st cent. A.D.
Padmānanda	
Padmaprabha	
Padmasāgara	
Padmasundara	16th cent. A.D.
Padmavijaya	
Pārśvanāga	
Pārśvadeva	
Pāṭhaka	
Prabhācandra	8th cent. A.D. There appears to have been also a later author of this name.
Pradyumnasūri	13th cent. A.D.
Premanjaya	
Pūjyapāda (Devanandin)	Bet. the 5th and 6th centuries A.D.
Pūrṇabhadra	
Pūrṇamalla	
Rājaśekhara (Different from Rājasekhara, author of the *Kāvyamīmāṃsā*)	14th cent. A.D.
Rājavallabha	
Rāmacandra (Pupil of Hemacandra, q.v.)	
Rāmasena	
Ratnabhūṣaṇa	
Ratnamaṇḍana	
Ratnamandira	
Ratnaśekhara	
Ratnayogīndra	
Ravigupta	
Raviṣeṇa	7th century A.D.
Ṛddhicandra	
Sādhuratna	
Sādhusundara	
Sakalabhūṣaṇa	
Sakalakīrti	(Died c. 1464 A.D.)
Samantabhadra	8th cent. A.D.
Samayasundara	17th cent. A.D.
Śāntirājakavi	
Sarvasundara	
Sarvānanda	
Sarvavijaya	
Satyarāja	
Saubhāgya-sāgara	
Siddharṣi	9th-10th cent. A.D.
Siddhasena Divākara	According to some earlier than the 7th cent. A.D. Acc. to others, 7th cent. A.D.
Siddhicandra	
Śikhāmaṇi	
Siṃhasūri	
Śīladeva	
Sīlasiṃha	
Śivijilla	
Śivakoṭi	
Siḍḍhala	
Somacaritra	10th cent. A.D.
Somadeva	
Somakīrti	
Somanandana	
Somaprabha	12th cent. A.D.
Somasundara	

Somatilaka	14th cent. A.D.
Someśvara	
Śrīdhara	
Śubhacandra	16th cent. A.D.
Śubhaśīla	15th cent. A.D.
Śubhavardhana	
Sudhākalaśa	
Sumativardhana	
Sūrācārya	11th cent. A.D.
Tārānātha	
Tattvavallabha	
Tejasiṃha	
Udayacandra	
Udayadharma	15th cent. A.D.
Udayaprabha	
Umāsvāmin (Same as Umāsvāti. Earlier than Siddhisena Divākara c. 135-219 A.D. according to Digambara *Paṭṭāvalīs*).	
Umāsvāti (See Umāsvāmin)	
Umedacandra	
Vādicandra	
Vādideva	
Vādirāja	11th cent. A.D.
Vāgbhaṭa	11th cent.-12th cent. A.D.

Vāghaji	
Vāmadeva	
Vardhamāna	11th cent. A.D.
Vastupāla	
Vatsarāja	
Vibudhaprabha	
Vidyābhūṣaṇa	
Vidyānanda or Vidyānandin	15th cent. A.D. (?)
Vikrama	
Vikramasiṃha	
Vimaladāsa	
Vimala	
Vimalācārya	
Vinayacandra	
Vinayavijaya	17th cent. A.D.
Vīranandin	10th cent. A.D.
Vīravijaya	
Viśvaśambhu	
Vītarāga	
Yaśaḥkīrti	
Yaśodeva	12th cent. A.D.
Yaśodhara	
Yaśovijaya	1624-1688 A.D.
Yogīndra	Earlier than Hemacandra.

XI

A NOTE ON INDIAN PALAEOGRAPHY[1]

It is impossible, in the present state of our knowledge, to ascertain precisely when the art of writing originated in India. The correct and full decipherment of the Indus Valley script is still eagerly awaited in order to have an idea of the genesis of the art of writing in India

The Indian tradition about this matter, preserved in the Brāhmaṇical and Jaina works, may be relegated to the region of fancy. Hiuen Tsang speaks of the high antiquity of Indian writing while the Brahmi script is stated, in the Chinese encyclopaedia Fa-Wan-Shu-Lin, to be the best of the scripts. Alberuni appears to have believed that Indian alphabet originated with the beginning of Kali Age (3102 B.C.). While some Greeks mention the existence of writing material in India, Megasthenes (305 B.C.) mentions milestones, almanacs, horoscopes, etc.—facts which point to the prevalence of writing. The testimony of the Buddhist literature leaves little doubt about the fact that writing was in vogue in India in the period between the sixth century and the fourth century

---

1. For details, see

Bhattacharyya, S.: *The Evolution of Script in M.E. India from C.A.D. 400 to 1200 with special reference to Bengal.*

Bühler, G.: Indian Palaeography, first published in *IA*, 1904 (Appendix).

———: On the origin of the Indian Brahma Alphabet, *CSS*, 1963 (3rd ed.).

Burn ell, R.C.: *Elements of South Indian Palaeography.*

Dani, A.H.: *Indian Palaeography*, Oxford, 1963.

Lambert, H.M.: *Introduction to the Devanagari Script*, London, 1953.

Ojha, G.S.: *The Palaeography of India*, 1971.

Pandey, R.B.: *Indian Palaeography*, Part I, Benares, 1952.

Renou and Filliozat: *L'inde Classique*, Tome II (Chap. on Palaeography).

Shama (Haitry) R.: *Origin and Development of Devanāgarī Alphabet.*

Sircar, D.C.: *Indian Palaeography*, Delhi.

The Art of Writing, UNESCO, 1965 (Chap. 15).

As regards the Indus Valley Script, enough of materials in the shape of seals etc. have been discovered. But, the script still remains to be deciphered. Some scholars, notably Samkarananda, Heras, S.K. Roy and Mahendra Kavyatirtha, claim to have deciphered it. But, their claim has not yet been established to the satisfaction of the scholarly world. For a resume of the work done so far in this field, reference may be made to the *History and Culture of the Indian People*, Vol. I. The Vedic Age, Bhāratīya Vidyā Bhavan. Also see M.V.N.K. Rao, *Indus Script Deciphered*; Śaṃkarānanda, *Indus People Speak*, Calcutta, 1955.

B.C. as a legacy of earlier times; far from being a novelty it was a continuity and a continuity from time immemorial.

The time of origin of the Veda is not precisely known. It can, however, be presumed that the art of writing was certainly known when the Vedic texts, particularly the *Ṛgveda*, were compiled into *Saṃhitās*.

The *Rāmāyaṇa* and the *Mahābhārata*, which originated probably in a period earlier than the 4th century B.C., the *Arthaśāstra* (c. 4th cent. B.C.), the *Sūtra* literature (bet. the 8th and 2nd cent. B.C.), Yāska, the pre-Pāṇini writer, the *Aṣṭādhyāyī* (c. 5th cent. B.C.), the *Upaniṣads* and some other early Sanskrit works clearly testify to the prevalence of writing.

Evidence of a more positive nature is furnished by inscriptions. In the arid history of writing in India stand out three very prominent landmarks, viz. Pre-Mauryan Inscriptions, Mauryan Inscriptions and the Indus Valley Script. From the inscriptions of the first class the conclusion is warranted that writing prevailed in India at least in the fifth century B.C. The inscriptions of Aśoka (3rd cent. B.C.), distributed over a very wide area of the sub-continent, are written in two principal scripts, Brāhmī and Kharoṣṭhī, prevailing in the then India. The discovery of the Indus Valley Script has led scholars to believe that writing was in vogue in India as far back as the fourth millenary B.C.

Despite the high antiquity of the art of writing in India, the fact remains that no specimen of writing earlier than the fifth century B.C. exists. It is difficult to explain this circumstance. Might be that the earlier specimens, preserved in such materials as leaves and crude paper, fell victims to the ravages of time.

The Jaina works *Pannavaṇā-sūtra* and the *Samavāyāṅga-sūtra* contain the names of eighteen scripts (*lipi*) including Brāhmī and Kharoṣṭhī, as stated above. The Buddhist Sanskrit work *Lalitavistara* gives a formidable list of 64 scripts of which the first two are respectively Brāhmī and Kharoṣṭhī. The scripts, mentioned in the literary works, may be divided into several groups.[1] e.g. provincial, tribal, sectarian etc. Some foreign scripts were also known to Indians. For example, mention may be made of *Yavanānī* (script of the Greeks) referred to by Pāṇini (III. 2. 21.).

Of the different Indian scripts, the chief were the Brāhmī[2] and the Kharoṣṭhī.[3] The former, written from left to right, was the most prevalent form in

1. For details, see Pandey's work, *op. cit.*
2. Invented by god Brahmā or the script in which the Brahma or Veda is preserved and which was mainly employed by Brāhmaṇas.
3. Formed from *Khara* (ass) and *Oṣṭha* (lip). The following derivative meanings have been suggested:—
(a) The inventor of the script was called Kharoṣṭha.
(b) Used by barbarous peoples (*Kharoṣṭhas*), like Yavanas, Śakas, Tuṣāras etc., inhabiting the north-western boundaries of India.
(c) *Kharoṣṭha* is the Sanskrit form of Kashgar, a province of Central Asia, which was the latest centre of this script.
(d) *Kharoṣṭha* is the Indian adaptation of the Iranian word *Kharoṣṭa* or *Kharaposta* (ass-skin); probably this script originally used to be written on ass-skin.

the major part of India, while the latter written from right to left, was confined to the extreme north-west of India, that is, to that part which, in the preceding age, belonged to Persian territory. The alphabet is common to both, but the characters are different. Regarding the provenance of these scripts, opinions differ. Most scholars take Brāhmī to be of indigenous origin, while Kharoṣṭhī is almost universally regarded as an importation from Western Asia. It may be added here that regarding the place, where the Indus Valley Script originated, there are various theories. Some scholars take it to be of Dravidian origin while others believe that it was imported from Sumeria or Egypt.

The extinction of Kharoṣṭhī is historically explained by the fact that it was, for a long time, associated with foreign rulers who held sway over the north-western India. Thus, the people of the rest of India looked upon it with aversion, if not contempt. So, with the rise of the Guptas, under whom the country was sought to be unified, Kharoṣṭhī was eliminated with the extinction of foreign rule. The earliest preserved records in Brāhmī and in Kharoṣṭhī date back to the third cent. B.C. These are the Aśokan inscriptions.

The Brāhmī script, generally supposed to have originated about 500 B.C., passed through a long process of evolution before it developed into the later forms in the new Indo-Aryan scripts. Strange as it may seem, Sanskrit language has no script of its own. It is written in what is known as Devanāgarī[1] script. The history of this script is traced back to Brāhmī and, through it, according to some scholars, to the script of the Indus Valley civilisation. It was as late as the eighteenth century A.D. when this script came to be used for writing Sanskrit all over India. Before that the manuscripts of Sanskrit works used to be written in regional scripts.

The materials, generally used for writing in India, were Birch-bark (*bhūrja-patra*), palm-leaves (*tāla-patra*), paper,[2] cotton cloth, wooden board (*phalaka*), leather, stone, brick and metal. Manuscripts of books were generally written in the above leaves, paper and cotton cloth while for land-grants, certain charms, etc. metals were used. Wooden boards appear to have been used as slates in schools and for the purpose of writing plaints with chalk in law-courts. Documents in connexion with loans also used to be written on boards. Works appear to have been carved on wooden boards; some manuscripts, engraved on wooden boards, still eixst. From sources, both Brāhmaṇical and Buddhistic, leather also appears, however rarely, to have been used as a writing material. Royal edicts were engraved on rocks, pillars and caves. Agreements, donations, grants, etc. also were sometimes written on stone. Some literary, and religious

---

(e) *Kharoṣṭha* is the form assumed in Sanskrit from the Aramaic word *Kharoṭṭha* used for this script.

1. The origin of the name is obscure. In its shorter form it is Nāgarī. Some think that it was the script of the 'people of the city' (nāgara—nagara, city). According to others, the name is derived from the Nagar Brāhmaṇas of Gujarat.

2. According to Nearchos, who accompanied Alexander (327 B.C.), paper was manufactured in India out of cotton. The earliest paper-MSS written in the Gupta script of the 5th century A.D., were discovered at Kashgar and Kugier in Central Asia.